# TPC -A Results ( under 11k$/tps-A) as of 1 January 1993

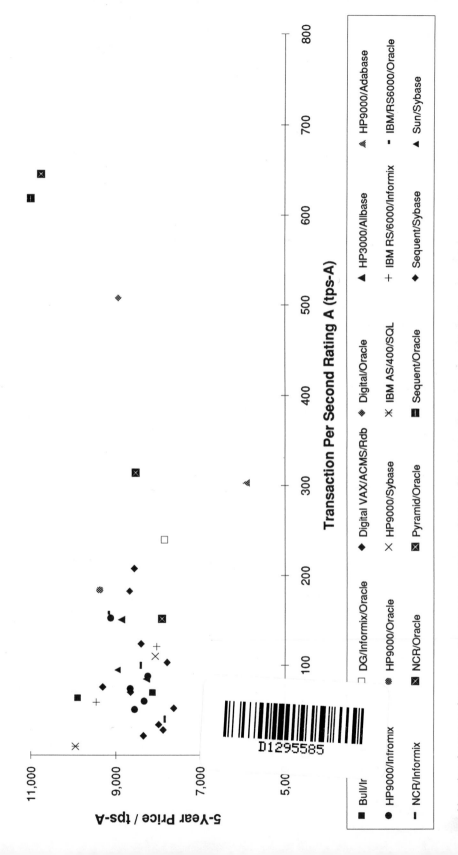

Note that the tps scale was not changed from 1991 to 1993, but the $/tps scale was reduced in both cases to ignore systems 40% more expensive than average. The average 1993 numbers are well below the best 1991 numbers. Also, notice the diseconomy of scale: the general trend line rises as TPS rises. Appendix B has the full list of TPC-A, TPC-B, and TPC-C results as of January, 1993.

# THE MORGAN KAUFMANN SERIES IN DATA MANAGEMENT SYSTEMS

**Series Editor, Jim Gray**

**The Benchmark Handbook for Database and Transaction Processing Systems, Second Edition**
Edited by Jim Gray (Digital Equipment Corporation)

**Understanding the New SQL: A Complete Guide**
Jim Melton (Digital Equipment Corporation) and Alan R. Simon

**Transaction Processing: Concepts and Techniques**
Jim Gray (Digital Equipment Corporation) and
Andreas Reuter (University of Stuttgart)

**Database Transaction Models for Advanced Applications**
Edited by Ahmed K. Elmagarmid (Purdue University)

**A Guide to Developing Client/Server SQL Applications**
Setrag Khoshafian (Portfolio Technologies, Inc.),
Arvola Chan (Versant Object Technology),
Anna Wong (CLaM Associates), and
Harry K.T. Wong (Nomadic Systems)

**Building an Object-Oriented Database System: The Story of $O_2$**
Edited by François Bancilhon ($O_2$ Technology),
Claude Delobel (Université de Paris-Sud), and
Paris Kanellakis (Brown University)

**Camelot and Avalon: A Distributed Transaction Facility**
Edited by Jeffrey L. Eppinger (Transarc Corporation),
Lily B. Mummert (Carnegie Mellon University), and
Alfred Z. Spector (Transarc Corporation)

**Database Modeling and Design: The Entity-Relationship Approach**
Toby J. Teorey (University of Michigan)

**Readings in Object-Oriented Database Systems**
Edited by Stanley B. Zdonik (Brown University) and
David Maier (Oregon Graduate Center)

**Readings in Database Systems**
Edited by Michael Stonebraker (University of California, Berkeley)

# The Benchmark Handbook

**FOR DATABASE AND TRANSACTION PROCESSING SYSTEMS**

SECOND EDITION.

# Table of Contents

# Acknowledgments

Tandem Computers, especially the San Francisco office, supported the editing of this book. Digital Equipment Corporation supported the final editing phase. This handbook represents the efforts of the authors, their colleagues, and students. The members of the Transaction Processing Performance Council each made significant contributions to the discipline by rigorously defining standard benchmarks. Their efforts are the centerpieces of this handbook. The handbook benefitted from careful reviews by Goetz Graefe and Bill Highleyman. Charles Levine provided machine-readable version of the TPC benchmark standard. Our editor/publisher Bruce Spatz of Morgan Kaufmann provided the encouragement and organizational skills needed to publish a book involving thirteen authors. Carol Leyba managed its production.

The handbook is dedicated to those who have lost nights, weeks, and months of their lives working on a benchmark.

Dina Bitton
dbstar
185 Berry Street, Suite 3511
San Francisco, CA 94107
(415) 512-0300

Rick Cattell
Sun Microsystems
M/S MTV21-121
2550 Garcia Ave.
Mt. View, CA 94043
rcattell@eng.sun.com

Samuel DeFazio
Digital Equipment Corp.
55 Northeastern Blvd.
Nashua, NH 03062
defazio@nova.enet.dec.com

David DeWitt
Dept. of Computer Science
University of Wisconsin
Madison, WI 53706
(608) 263-5489
dewitt@cs.wisc.edu

Kaivalya M. Dixit
IBM
11400 Burnet Rd., Zip 9443
Austin, TX 78758
(512) 838-2081
dixit@perfmap.austin.ibm.com

Jim Gray
Digital Equipment Corp.
455 Market Street, 7th floor
San Francisco, CA 94105
(415) 882-3955
gray@sfbay.enet.dec.com

Neal Nelson
Neal Nelson & Associates
330 North Wabash
Chicago, IL 60611
(312) 755-1000

Patrick O'Neil
7 Whittier Rd.
Lexington, MA 02173
(617) 863-1054
poneil@cs.umb.edu

Cyril Orji
University of Illinois
College of Engineering
Dept. of Electrical Engineering and Computer Science
Chicago, Ill 60680
(312) 996-0142

François Raab
Information Paradigm
115 N. Wahsatch Avenue, Suite 7
Colorado Springs, CO 80903
(719) 473-7555

Tom Sawyer
Performance Metrics, Inc.
15098 Elm Park
Monte Sereno, CA 95030
(408) 395-2243

Omri Serlin
ITOM International
P.O. Box 1450
Los Altos, CA 94023
(415) 948-4516
omris@cup.portal.com

Carolyn Turbyfill
Sun Microsystems
Bldg. 16
1501 Salado Drive
Mountain View, CA 94043
cturbyfill@eng.sun.com

# 1

# Introduction

Jim Gray

*Digital Equipment Corporation*

Benchmarks are becoming increasingly important because of an emerging consensus on what to measure and how to measure it. Benchmark results now appear in *Wall Street Journal* advertisements and in the trade press. Benchmarks have become important to everyone in the computer industry: Programmers use available benchmarks to choose among design alternatives; product developers benefit by comparing their work with their competitors' products; even computer managers and users with little interest in the technical aspects of benchmarks need to know of the range of performance they might experience with the different combinations of hardware and software they authorize for development or purchase.

This handbook is a compendium of popular computer system performance and price/performance metrics, with emphasis on metrics for database and transaction processing systems. Each benchmark tries to answer the question, What computer should I buy? Clearly, the answer is, The system that does the job with the lowest cost of ownership. Cost of ownership includes project risks, programming costs, operations costs, hardware costs, and software costs. It is difficult to quantify project risks, programming costs, and operations costs. In contrast, computer performance and cost *can* be quantified and compared.

This quantitative comparison starts with the definition of a *benchmark*, or *workload*. The benchmark is run on several different systems, and the performance and price of each system are measured and recorded. *Perfor-*

*mance* is typically a throughput metric (work/second), and *price* is typically a five-year cost-of-ownership metric. Together, they give a price/performance ratio.

For example, a transaction processing benchmark defines a standard transaction workload and a transaction per second (tps) metric. The benchmark can be run on various systems to produce a table like Table 1.1.

**Table 1.1**  Performance and price/performance of several systems on a hypothetical benchmark.

| System | Throughput | Price | Price/Performance |
|--------|-----------|-------|-------------------|
| A | 1 tps | 10 k$ | 10 k$/tps |
| B | 10 tps | 50 k$ | 5 k$/tps |
| C | 50 tps | 2 M$ | 40 k$/tps |
| D | 100 tps | 1 M$ | 10 k$/tps |

If the customer needs less than 1 tps, then system A is the most economic choice. If the customer needs between 1 and 10 tps, then system B is the most economic choice. If more than 10 tps are needed, then system D offers the best price and price/performance.

Generic benchmarks are often used as rough estimates of relative system performance because the cost of implementing and measuring specific applications on different systems is usually prohibitive. For example, measuring the data for Table 1.1 might cost several person-years and a million dollars—considerably more than the price of these systems.

Certain generic benchmarks are so widely recognized that vendors announce the performance of new products in terms of those benchmarks. For example, DEC, HP, and IBM state the relative performance and price/performance of new machines and system releases by stating their ratings on the Transaction Processing Performance Council's benchmark A (TPC-A) and on SPEC's CINT92 and CFP92 benchmarks.

Generic benchmarks give a sense of the relative performance and price/performance of a system. They are analogous to the energy ratings typically given for appliances and automobiles. All such performance ratings are somewhat crude. As the U.S. Environmental Protection Agency says of its gasoline mileage ratings for automobiles: "Your actual mileage may vary according to road conditions and driving habits. Use these numbers for comparison purposes only." Put another way, the performance numbers a salesperson quotes are really a guarantee that the product will *never exceed* the quoted performance. Despite these caveats, benchmarks and the concepts that underlie them are important tools in evaluating computer systems' performance and price/performance.

# 1.1   The Need for Domain-Specific Benchmarks

No single metric can measure the performance of computer systems on all applications. System performance varies enormously from one application domain to another. Each system is typically designed for a few problem domains and may be incapable of performing other tasks. For example, most supercomputers lack database and transaction processing software and so are inappropriate for most business applications.

The workstation community has developed benchmarks that measure system performance on numeric computations—the most popular among these is the SPEC suite described in Chapter 9. These scientific and time-sharing benchmarks do not give much guidance to someone evaluating a database system or a transaction processing system, because database system performance is dominated by the performance of software algorithms rather than by raw hardware speed. Even within the broad category of database systems, there is substantial diversity among the performance of systems on different problem domains. One system may be excellent at performing simple update-intensive transactions for an online database, but it may perform poorly on complex queries to that database. Conversely, a system that excels at decision-support queries may not even allow online transactional access to those same data. Several chapters in this book give examples of such systems.

*Domain-specific* benchmarks are a response to the diversity of computer system uses. Each such benchmark specifies a synthetic workload characterizing typical applications in that problem domain. The performance of this workload on various computer systems then gives a rough estimate of the relative performance of each system on that problem domain. This handbook contains eight domain-specific benchmarks covering database and transaction processing systems.

## 1.2    Standards Bodies Defining Benchmarks

Several consortia are defining standard domain-specific benchmarks, standard price metrics, and standard ways of measuring and reporting results. The most prominent are:

- **TPC (Transaction Processing Performance Council)**: A consortium of vendors defining benchmarks for transaction processing and database domains.

- **SPEC (Standard Performance Evaluation Corporation)**: A consortium of vendors defining benchmarks for the scientific and workstation domains, with an emphasis on UNIX™ systems. An overview of these benchmarks is given in Chapter 9.

- **BAPco (Business Application Performance Consortium)**: A consortium of personal computer hardware and software vendors defining benchmarks (SYSmarks and NETmarks) to measure the performance of personal computers used in typical client-server office and groupware applications. The benchmarks consist of application scripts invoking dBASE IV, Paradox, WordPerfect, WinWord, Excel, Lotus 1-2-3, QuatroPro, CCmail, Harvard Graphics, and Freelance software executing against a LAN file and application server. These benchmarks are still under development, but eventually they are likely to achieve the status of the TPC and SPEC benchmarks for their respective domains of PC and client-server benchmarks [BAPco].

This handbook presents the currently approved TPC benchmarks and other benchmarks widely used in the database area. The TPC benchmarks are especially interesting because they rigorously define how tests should be run, how a system's price should be measured, and how test results should be reported. The TPC began by formalizing the ad hoc DebitCredit and TP1 benchmarks. The resulting benchmarks are called TPC-A and TPC-B. Vendors now frequently quote the tps (transaction per second) ratings of their systems in terms of these TPC benchmarks. With the falling prices of hardware and increasing speeds of machines, TPC-A and TPC-B are too simple. Each transaction can be executed in less than 5 milliseconds, so they are becoming terminal-price and disc-price benchmarks. To better capture the real price/performance of database and transaction processing systems, the

TPC has defined a new and more demanding benchmark, TPC-C. Over the next few years, TPC-C will supplant the TPC-A and TPC-B benchmarks. The TPC is now defining benchmarks that capture complex query, batch, and operational aspects of transaction processing systems.

# 1.3 The Key Criteria for a Domain-Specific Benchmark

To be useful, a domain-specific benchmark must meet four important criteria:

1. **Relevance:** It must measure the peak performance and price/performance of systems when performing typical operations within that problem domain.

2. **Portability:** It should be easy to implement on many different systems and architectures.

3. **Scaleability:** It should be applicable to small and large computer systems. It should be possible to scale the benchmark up to larger systems and to parallel computer systems as computer performance and architecture evolve.

4. **Simplicity:** It must be understandable; otherwise, it will lack credibility.

As a case in point, consider the classic mips (millions of instructions per second) metric. It is certainly a simple benchmark. But mips is not a portable metric. For example, IBM/370 mips and DEC/VAX mips are not comparable. Mips is not a scaleable metric, since its application to multiprocessors is unclear: A multiprocessor consisting of 1000 one-mips processors is not equivalent to a single 1000-mips processor. The main criticism of the mips metric is irrelevance—it does not measure useful work. For example, different compilers on the same computer can give mips ratings that vary by factors of three. Consequently, software must be compared when comparing processors. Simple measures like mips and dollars/mips are *too* simple. They do not capture software performance and price/performance, and they miss the non-CPU component of hardware performance—the other 90 percent of the hardware [Patterson & Hennessy, 1990].

Scientific and workstation vendors developed specific benchmarks to replace mips as a measure of a processor's performance. They developed suites of programs typical of scientific computations. The Standard Performance Evaluation Corporation (SPEC) has been the most successful developer of such benchmark suites. Chapter 9 gives an overview of that family of benchmarks. Other examples of scientific benchmarks are the Perfect Club and SLALOM [Berry et al., 1988; Gustafson et al., 1990]. These benchmarks satisfy the basic requirements of relevance, portability, scaleability, and simplicity for measuring processor performance on numerical problems. SLALOM takes an interesting approach to scaleability: it measures how large a problem the system can solve in a minute. This is similar to the *equivalent database size* of the $AS^3AP$ benchmark, the largest database the system can handle in 12 hours (see Chapter 5, Section 5.2).

## 1.4 Domain-Specific Benchmarks for Database and Transaction Processing

Each benchmark in this handbook meets the criteria for domain-specific benchmarks: relevance to its domain, simplicity, scaleability, and portability—each has been ported to several computer systems. Performance measurements from several systems are included in most of the benchmark descriptions. A diskette containing some of these benchmarks is available from the publisher (see Appendix 1 at the end of this volume).

The DB and TP benchmarks in this handbook have the virtue of measuring an entire system: the processor, the I/O subsystem, the operating system, the compilers, and the database system. In addition, TPC-A and TPC-C measure network performance and price/performance. All the benchmarks adopt the pricing scheme that was pioneered by the Datamation benchmark and refined by the TPC. In that scheme, system price is the five-year price of hardware, software, and vendor maintenance with no special discounts [Anon. et al., 1985; *TPC Quarterly Review*]. Unfortunately, the metrics in this handbook do not measure ease of use, ease of programming, or ease of operations—they are purely performance and price/performance metrics.[1]

---

[1] *PC Week* conducts "shootouts" among vendors in which each implements a complete application within four days [*PC Week*, 1990]. This tests the functionality of the various systems, their ease of use, and the talents of the implementors. Such events point in the right direction, but the implementors should be typical customers rather than typical gurus.

The benchmarks included herein were selected from a large field. First, benchmarks outside the database and transaction processing domain were excluded (with the exception of the widely recognized SPEC benchmarks). Next, proprietary benchmarks were excluded (e.g., IBM's RAMPC and ONEK, Stratus' TP1) since their definitions are not publicly available. Then, one-time benchmarks were excluded (e.g., the California Department of Motor Vehicles [1989]) because they are not portable or scaleable. This narrowed the field considerably. The remaining set was evaluated for relevance, portability, scaleability, and simplicity. The main criterion for final selection was whether each benchmark was widely accepted within its domain-specific community.

# 1.5    A Historical Perspective on DB and TP Benchmarks

Several ad hoc benchmarks for database and transaction processing systems evolved over the last 20 years, creating vague measures such as *transactions per second* and *query processing performance*. Each vendor has a suite of benchmarks inherited from competitive bids. In addition, each has implemented the standard ad hoc benchmarks so that they can measure their performance against the competition. For example, most SQL vendors have implemented the Wisconsin query set (see Chapter 4) and use it to test the performance of each new release and each new machine. Many customers have repeated this effort to evaluate and compare various relational products. Similar activity surrounded the Datamation query set (DebitCredit, Sort, Scan), especially the DebitCredit transaction, also known as ET1 and TP1 [Anon. et al., 1985].

Occasionally, vendors published or leaked ad hoc benchmark results to the press, but generally the results were treated as company confidential. Vendors had little incentive to publish their performance results because they were often embarrassing. When a vendor did publish numbers, they were generally treated with skepticism. When comparative numbers were published by third parties or competitors, the losers generally cried foul and tried to discredit the benchmark. Such events often caused *benchmark wars*. A benchmark war starts when someone loses an important or visible benchmark evaluation. The loser reruns it using regional specialists and gets new and winning numbers. Then the opponent reruns it using its regional specialists and of course gets even better numbers. The loser then reruns it using some one-star gurus. This progression can continue all the way to five-star gurus. At a certain point, a special version of the system is employed, with promises that the enhanced performance features will be included in the next regular release.

*Benchmarketing* is a variation of benchmark wars. For each system, there is a benchmark that rates that system the best. Typically, the vendor's marketing organization defines such a domain-specific benchmark, highlighting the strengths of the product and hiding its weaknesses. The marketing organization then promotes the benchmark as a standard, often without disclosing the details of the benchmark. Benchmarketing leads to a proliferation of benchmarks and creates confusion. Ultimately, benchmarketing leads to universal skepticism of all benchmark results.

The claims and counterclaims surrounding benchmarketing and benchmark wars caused enormous confusion in the database and transaction processing community. In response, a consortium now numbering some 45 software and hardware vendors, originally led by Omri Serlin, founded the Transaction Processing Performance Council (TPC) in August, 1988. The TPC's goal is to define domain-specific benchmarks for transaction processing and database systems. Incident to this goal, they also define a way to calculate system price and a way to report performance results. The TPC has been successful in both areas.

By 1990 the TPC had defined two benchmarks, TPC-A and TPC-B (see Chapter 2). Those two benchmarks have dramatically reduced benchmark wars. Customers routinely request TPC ratings from vendors as part of the bid process. The TPC metrics capture peak performance and price/performance of transaction processing and database systems running simple update-intensive transactions. In addition, the TPC reporting procedures, while not airtight, have a "full disclosure" mechanism that makes it difficult to stretch the truth too much. The benchmark must be run on standard hardware and released software. Any special tuning or parameter-setting must be disclosed. The TPC highly recommends that an independent organization audit the benchmark tests.

An interesting thing has happened with the TPC-A and TPC-B benchmarks between 1990 and 1993. As late as 1992, the proprietary transaction processing systems from Digital (VAX), IBM (AS/400), nCube, and Tandem were the performance and price/performance leaders. But in mid-1992 the commodity and open systems (Oracle, Informix, Sybase) running on UNIX or Novell platforms took the lead in this race. Not unrelated to this change, the price of terminals and terminal interconnect is now more than

50 percent of TPC-A's system price, while disks are now the major component of TPC-B's price.

Many believe the TPC-A and TPC-B transaction profiles are too simple to capture the way computers are used in the 1990s. They want a benchmark that has simple read transactions, some queued "batch" transactions, and a complex data entry transaction. They also want a benchmark with realistic input-output formatting and with some data entry errors so that some transactions abort. The TPC worked for two years on defining the TPC BM™-C benchmark to meet these requirements and approved that benchmark's definition in August, 1992. We expect TPC-C to supplant TPC-A and TPC-B over time.

# 1.6 An Overview of the Benchmarks in This Handbook

The problem domains represented in this handbook and their associated benchmarks are:

- *Online Transaction Processing, including a LAN or WAN network:* TPC-A

- *Online Transaction Processing with no network:* TPC-B

- *Online Business Transaction Processing:* TPC-C

- *Relational Queries:* Wisconsin benchmark

- *Mixed Workload of Transactions, Relational Queries, and Utility Functions*: $AS^3AP$

- *Complex Queries and Reporting*: Set Query benchmark

- *Engineering Workstation-Server*: Engineering Database benchmark (OO1)

- *Full Text Document Retrieval Benchmark:* Content-based Text Retrieval benchmark

- *SPEC Benchmarks:* Technical applications CPU and system benchmarks

- *Neal Nelson Business Benchmark*: Multiuser UNIX benchmark

Some commercial benchmarks are sold by consulting organizations. The two most prominent of these organizations are Neal Nelson Associates and AIM Technology [AIM]. Each has proprietary UNIX-based benchmarks that consultants tailor to a customer's needs. The companies provide customers and vendors with competitive and comparative performance evaluations. A brief description of Neal Nelson's Business benchmark is included in Chapter 10 as a representative of such benchmarks and services.

Each benchmark in this handbook is presented by someone intimately familiar with it. For example, Omri Serlin was the founder of the TPC consortium. He augments the two standards documents with a historical perspective on the TPC itself, an overview of the two benchmarks, and representative performance figures. These benchmarks are the standard definitions of transactions per second (tps) and $/tps. They are now widely used to evaluate the approximate performance and price/performance of computer systems for online transaction processing workloads. The two differ in that TPC-A also measures the performance and price of a computer network, its software, and its terminals.

François Raab, the editor of the TPC-C, provides an overview of that new benchmark and its design rationale. Fundamentally, the TPC-A and TPC-B benchmarks are too simple. In 1980, the largest systems could process only 100 tps, and the cost per tps was balanced between terminals, CPU, and disc. Today, because of advances in hardware and software technology, workstations can run several hundred tps. The $/tps of TPC-A is dominated by terminal prices, and the $/tps of TPC-B is dominated by disc prices. It is time to shift to a more modern conception of tps and $/tps. TPC-C provides the new definition. It defines a more complex database, a set of five transaction profiles ranging from a simple read-only query to a complex minibatch online update. Overall, TPC-C is about ten times "heavier" than TPC-A, so the performance metric is transactions per minute (tpm-C) to distinguish it from tps-A.

These TPC benchmarks are the main reason for this handbook. They reflect the field's maturity. The remaining benchmarks are included because they are widely used in their particular domains. Each has proved its usefulness in measuring performance, but none has the rigor or force of the TPC benchmarks. Over time, we expect that they will either be adopted and refined by the TPC or replaced by comparable benchmarks from the TPC. But that may be many years away—the TPC is defining new metrics at a rate of 0.75 benchmarks per year.

The benchmarks presented in Chapters 4 through 6 test query-processing performance. They consist of (1) a set of pure relational queries, (2) a mixed workload of queries, system administration tasks, and some simple update jobs, and (3) a suite of complex queries typical of decision-support applications. Interestingly, systems that perform well on one of these three benchmarks do not necessarily perform well on the other two.

The first of these query benchmarks is called the *Wisconsin benchmark.* It is widely used to test the performance of relational query systems. Dave DeWitt, who with Carolyn Turbyfill and Dina Bitton [1983] invented the benchmark at the University of Wisconsin, restates the benchmark and database generator in modern (SQL) terms. He explains how to port the benchmark, how it scales, and how it is used to measure the performance of parallel database machines. The Wisconsin benchmark is a litmus test for the performance of relational systems on simple relational operators.

Dina Bitton, Cyril Orji, and Carolyn Turbyfill then present the $AS^3AP$ benchmark they developed as a more complete test of relational database systems. The traditional Wisconsin benchmark does not test utility functions, does not mix batch and interactive queries, and does not emphasize multiuser tests. $AS^3AP$ provides a more complete metric by including such features. In addition, it adopts the novel approach of setting a time limit on the benchmark and then measuring the largest database that the system can process within this time limit.[2] This gives each database system an *equivalent database size* rating. $AS^3AP$ gives a more balanced and realistic evaluation of the overall performance of a relational system used for database queries.

The third query benchmark in this series presents a much more complex query set. The *Set Query benchmark* is used to evaluate the ability of systems to process complex queries typically found in decision-support applications and data-mining applications. The Wisconsin and $AS^3AP$ query sets map to simple relational queries. Pat O'Neil points out that decision-support applications involve complex queries requiring efficient set processing. The Wisconsin and $AS^3AP$ queries do not capture this requirement, and most commercial systems do not implement the necessary techniques (notable exceptions are Model 204 and Adabase). O'Neil presents a scaleable database and a Set Query benchmark that measures this capability. This query set is based on extensive experience with decision-support customers in areas ranging from information retrieval to telemarketing. O'Neil then contrasts the performance of Model 204 with IBM's DB2 on this benchmark.

---

[2] This fixed-time approach is also adopted by the SLALOM benchmark, which limits the run to 1 minute. $AS^3AP$ runs are limited to 12 hours.

The next benchmark is variously called *OO1*, the *Engineering Database benchmark*, or simply the *Cattell benchmark*. It represents an emerging use of database systems to store engineering or object-oriented databases accessed from high-performance workstations in a client-server role. Rick Cattell characterizes such databases as having relatively rich interrelationships, and the transactions as navigating from one record to its many relatives. The performance of such operations is absolutely critical. Engineers need to be able to access complex objects within a few seconds. Similar problems arise with hypertext database and image processing applications. Cattell argues that, at present, this performance requirement precludes the use of general purpose database systems because their underlying system architectures are not suited to a workstation-server design and because the performance penalty of moving data between the application and a classical database system is too high. He presents a scaleable database and the *Engineering Database benchmark (EDB, OO1)* that captures these demands. By example, he shows that database systems with appropriate architectures outperform conventional systems by a factor of ten.

There is considerable activity to extend OO1 to cover features like multiuser, nonuniform data access, and large record sizes. No consensus has emerged, but the *OO7 benchmark* from the University of Wisconsin appears to be gaining converts. Whereas OO1 focuses mainly on traversal speed for pointers, with some locality, OO7 evaluates various read-only traversals, traversals with different update characteristics, bulk updates, and associative queries. In addition, there is a multiuser version of OO7. Like the Wisconsin benchmark, OO7 produces a vector of numbers rather than a single number. Users can weight the numbers appropriately for their own application domain [Carey, DeWitt, & Naughton, 1992].

Sam DeFazio presents the *Full-Text Document Retrieval benchmark*, which models the use of database systems for document storage, content-based search, and then retrieval. The basic storage unit is a partition containing 200,000 documents, occupying one gigabyte of storage, and supporting 50 search transactions per minute (50 spm). Search transactions involve selecting all documents that satisfy a randomly generated search expression consisting of words and proximity conditions (e.g., within a phrase, sentence, or paragraph). Documents are selected from all partitions of the database. In addition, there is relatively minor document retrieval activity. The benchmark scales by adding one partition per 50 search transactions. Scaling the application in this way creates the so-called *N*-squared problem: a system with twice as many terminals and twice the database does four times as much work since each search examines all partitions. To account for the *N*-squared problem, throughput is measured as *partitions searched per minute.* A database running 100 searches per minute on two partitions is rated at 200 spm throughput. The benchmark is written in the TPC format, uses the TPC pricing model, and has been submitted to the TPC for consideration as a standard.

Kaivalya Dixit, editor of SPEC's CINT92 and CFP92 specifications, provides an overview of the current SPEC benchmarks in Chapter 9 and describes the evolution of the SPEC consortium that set out to replace the mips metric. The single SPECmark89 metric has evolved into the spectrum of 20 different metrics in the CINT92 and CFT92 suites. SPEC has learned that no single number can characterize a processor's performance. SPEC has also defined a UNIX System-Development Multitasking benchmark (SDM) that simulates UNIX users editing, searching, printing, compiling, and building software systems. SPEC is also developing the LADDIS file server benchmark for UNIX systems.

The *Business benchmark* is used by Neal Nelson Associates to evaluate UNIX-based computer systems for specific customers. Neal Nelson presents the design rationale for the benchmark, and in three case studies he describes how it is used. He makes the argument that customers need a vendor-independent "Underwriters Laboratory" to evaluate database systems. His company provides such a laboratory.

The closing chapter presents an auditor's view of running and reporting benchmarks. Tom Sawyer, who has audited many commercial benchmarks, comments on the tasks and pitfalls of benchmarking. That chapter is by far the wisest and most amusing chapter of this handbook.

## 1.7 How to Use This Handbook

This handbook has two purposes—it is a tutorial for the novice and a reference for the professional. For those unfamiliar with the various benchmarks, it presents a tutorial as well as a detailed specification of each. The tutorials explain the rationale behind each benchmark design and give some sense of the problem domains each is intended to measure. In addition, the tutorial sections give a sense of the performance and price/performance of current systems on the benchmarks. Overall, the handbook gives a sense of benchmark design methodology and of the state of the art of benchmarking transaction processing systems and database systems.

Readers may find the text of the TPC benchmarks especially useful. The careful definitions of performance metrics, pricing, and reporting provide a template for requests-for-proposal and for bids. Note that the TPC standards material is *not* copyrighted and so may be freely copied and used in bids and proposals.

For the performance professional, this handbook is the standard reference for benchmark definitions. It provides a convenient package of the TPC benchmarks, the query benchmarks, and the engineering database benchmark. The professional may find some interesting insights in the tutorials and in the chapter by Tom Sawyer on how to conduct, report, and audit a benchmark.

Most importantly, this handbook brings together the main fragments of the database and transaction processing performance field. Much of the information here has not appeared in book form. In preparing the handbook, each of us discovered many standard benchmarks that we had never heard of, primarily because they were outside the problem domains we usually encounter. In addition, several of the benchmarks presented here have been collected on a diskette containing data generators, workload and report generators, and sample programs for the benchmarks. The software is also easy to port. Michael Franklin describes this software in Appendix 1.

## 1.8   How to Use These Benchmarks

These benchmarks can be used in many ways, but their main uses fall into one of the following four categories:

- **To Compare Different Software and Hardware Systems**: The benchmarks can be used to evaluate the relative performance of different systems on different hardware running the same application (e.g., CICS-DB2 on an IBM 3090/200 versus ACMS-Rdb on a DEC/VAX 4000). This is the classic competitive situation between two hardware vendors.

| System | tpsA-Local | k$/tps |
|---|---|---|
| DEC VAX/4000–Rdb | 52 | 7.6 |
| IBM AS/400–SQL | 55 | 18.0 |
| IBM RS/600–Informix | 51 | 13.5 |
| HP 900–Informix | 51 | 8.7 |
| Unisys 2200–DMS | 57 | 39.8 |

- **To Compare Different Software Products on The Same Machine:** The benchmarks can be used to evaluate the relative performance of two different software products running on the same hardware. O'Neil gives the example of Model 204 and DB2 both running the Set Query benchmark on an IBM ES/9000 Model 150 processor with all other software held the same. He measures the system performance as queries per minute (qpm) and the price/performance as dollars per qpm. This is the classic competitive situation between two software vendors:

| System | qpm | $/qpm |
|--------|-----|-------|
| Model 204 | 2.7 | 215k$ |
| DB2 | 0.63 | 803k$ |

- **To Compare Different Machines in a Compatible Family:** The benchmarks can be used to rate the relative performance of computer systems within a computer family. For example, the current ratings within the HP family are:

| System | tpsA-Local | k$/tps |
|--------|-----------|--------|
| HP 9000/800 F10–Informix | 30 | 11.0 |
| HP 9000/800 F20–Informix | 51 | 8.7 |
| HP 9000/800 F30–Informix | 60 | 8.3 |
| HP 9000/800 G40–Informix | 75 | 8.7 |
| HP 9000/800 H50–Informix | 153 | 9.1 |

- **To Compare Different Releases of a Product on The Same Machine:** The benchmarks can also be used to evaluate the performance improvement of one software release over its predecessor. Ideally, the new software will be a little faster, but often new features slow down old features. Thus, these benchmarks provide performance regression tests for vendors and customers alike when doing performance assurance of a new release. For example, the DEC ratings for the four most recent releases of Rdb/ACMS on the VAX 4000-300 are as follows:

| Release | tpsA-Local | k$/tps |
|---------|-----------|--------|
| Rdb release 3.0 VAX 4000-300 | 21.7 | 31.9 |
| Rdb release 4.0 VAX 4000-300 | 21.6 | 32.1 |
| Rdb release 4.1 VAX 4000-300 | 53.6 | 9.5 |

Of course, in each of these cases, the benchmarks must be chosen to reflect the problem-specific domain of interest.

# 1.9   Further Reading

The field of computer performance evaluation is undergoing a transformation, partly due to improved understanding and sophistication, and partly due to the shift of performance issues from the hardware domain to the broader perspective of hardware and software systems architecture. The recent book *Computer Architecture, A Quantitative Approach* by Dave Patterson and John Hennessy contains an excellent treatment of hardware performance issues and sound advice on performance metrics [Patterson & Hennessy, 1990]. The concepts they develop have broad applicability to hardware and software systems.

Within the field of software performance evaluation there are many texts. The one most relevant to the topics discussed here is Bill Highleyman's *Performance Analysis of Transaction Processing Systems* [1989]. It discusses relevant analytical techniques as well as measurement tools and techniques. The classic text in this field is Domenico Ferrari's *Computer Systems Performance Evaluation* [1978]. Raj Jain's recent *The Art of Computer Systems Performance Analysis: Techniques for Experimental Design, Measurement, Simulation and Modeling* [1991] is a wonderful compendium of techniques essential to designing, measuring, analyzing, and explaining a benchmark.

In presenting many of the benchmarks in this handbook, we assume the reader is familiar with the basics of databases and transaction processing and has a reading knowledge of SQL and C. In addition, the benchmark definitions use terms such as "ACID transactions," "degrees of isolation," "prefetch," and "join." Fortunately, several textbooks explain and consolidate these concepts. Tamer Ozsu and Patrick Valduriez's book *Principles of Distributed Database Systems* [1990] gives an excellent treatment of the transaction and database concepts that underlie most of the benchmarks in this book. *Transaction Processing Systems, Concepts and Techniques* [Gray & Reuter, 1993] complements Ozsu-Valduriez by focusing on implementation issues of transaction processing systems.

For more timely information, Omri Serlin's monthly newsletter, *FT Systems*, "analyzes company and product developments in fault-tolerant computers and transaction systems," to quote from its masthead (see References). It includes regular and insightful reports on the activities of the TPC. It also provides regular reports of benchmarketing activities and reports on the latest benchmark wars involving transaction processing and database systems. Serlin also publishes the monthly *Serlin Report on Paral-*

*lel Processing* which tracks performance issues related to supercomputers and massively parallel systems.

The primary source of information on the TPC is the *TPC Quarterly Report* (see References), which carries articles, news summaries, and reports on recent tests and on discussions within the TPC on the rationale, meaning, and interpretation of the benchmark specifications.

# 1.10  Future Database and Performance Benchmarks

This is the second edition of a handbook that is evolving. As the TPC defines new benchmarks, we hope to incorporate them in this handbook. The field is now in its infancy. There is consensus that standard benchmarks will appear in the following areas:

*   **Complex Queries:** The Wisconsin query set, the $AS^3AP$ query set, and the Set Query benchmark all try to model complex queries against a relatively large and complex database. The TPC is currently considering a benchmark that characterizes these same issues. This is a likely next step in the efforts of the TPC.

*   **Utility Operations:** As terabyte databases become common, the cost of managing them becomes a central issue. Dumping them at a rate of a megabyte per second will require over 12 days (and 8,000 magnetic tape pairs, using reel technology). Building an index on such a 10-billion–record file will break many sort programs, not to mention the elapsed time such sorts would require. A benchmark is needed to characterize the key utility operations on such large databases. Transaction processing systems have similar online utility needs, such as adding new transaction programs while the systems are operating. The TPC has a standing *mainframe* group defining the TPC-M benchmark to cover these issues.

*   **Mixed Workloads:** Most benchmarks measure an isolated aspect of a system. $AS^3AP$ and the Neal Nelson Business benchmark are exceptions. They measure systems performing a mixed workload of simple transactions, queries, reports, and utilities (such as database load and index creation). $AS^3AP$ is the only publicly specified benchmark that includes utility operations. The ability to support online operations and

mixed workloads against a single shared database is widely viewed as a critical performance issue.

- **New Applications:** The Engineering Database benchmark (OO1), the Set Query benchmark, and the Document Retrieval benchmark have their roots in problem-specific domains. They are just the first in a series of problem-specific domains needing special benchmarks. Domains such as image processing, geographic databases, and real-time transaction processing will likely foster new benchmarks.

Transaction and database-system performance measurement is a dynamic field. It is a key component of a multibillion dollar industry—the procurement of database and transaction processing systems. For many years the benchmark wars, claims, and counterclaims created chaos. But gradually standard terminology and metrics have emerged and are now endorsed by the major hardware and software vendors. There is every sign that this trend will continue and that each new industry will develop domain-specific benchmark standards that allow approximate performance and price/performance comparisons of products.

# References

*AIM Technology Procurement Guide.* AIM Technology, 4699 Old Ironsides Drive, Suite 150, Santa Clara, CA.

Anon. et al. (1985). A measure of transaction processing power. *Datamation*, 31 (7), April 1985, pp. 112–118.

Business Applications Performance Corporation. 2200 Mission College Blvd, Mail Stop RN-21, Santa Clara, CA 95052. Telephone: (408) 988-7654, fax: (408) 765-4920.

Berry, M.D., Chen, D., Koss, P., & Kuck, D. (1988). The perfect club benchmarks: Effective performance evaluation of supercomputers. CSRD Report No. 827. Center for Supercomputing Research and Development, University of Illinois at Urbana.

Bitton, D., DeWitt, D. J., & Turbyfill, C. (1983). Benchmarking database systems, a systematic approach. *Proceedings of the Ninth International Conference on Very Large Data Bases.*

California Department of Motor Vehicles (1989). *Database Redevelopment Project: DBMS Operational Assessment Final Report.* Volume 1: *Project Summary.* Volume 2: *Test Specification.* Volume 3: *Vendor Results.* Sacramento: State of California.

Carey, M. J., DeWitt, D. J., & Naughton, J. (1992). The OO7 Benchmark. University of Wisconsin Computer Science Technical Report TR-92.99.

Ferrari, D. (1978). *Computer systems performance evaluation.* Englewood Cliffs, NJ: Prentice Hall.

*FT Systems.* Monthly newsletter published by ITOM International, POB 1450, Los Altos, CA 94023.

Gray, J. N. & Reuter, A. (1993). *Transaction processing: Concepts and techniques.* San Mateo, CA: Morgan Kaufmann.

Gustafson, J., Rover, D., Elbert, S., & Carter, M. (1990). SLALOM, the first scaleable supercomputer benchmark. *Supercomputing Review,* 3 (11), Nov. 1990, pp. 56–61.

Highleyman, W. H. (1989). *Performance analysis of transaction processing systems.* Englewood Cliffs, NJ: Prentice Hall.

Jain, Raj (1991). *The art of computer systems performance analysis: Techniques for experimental design, measurement, simulation, and modeling.* New York: John Wiley.

Ozsu, T., & Valduriez, P. (1990). *Principles of distributed database systems.* Englewood Cliffs, NJ: Prentice Hall.

Patterson, D. A. & Hennessy, J. L. (1990). *Computer architecture: A quantitative approach.* San Mateo, CA: Morgan Kaufmann.

*PC Week* (1990). Database shootout: 17 database vendors go head-to-head to build a real-world computing solution. Aug. 27, pp. 70–78.

SPEC Benchmark Suite, Release 1.0 (1990). *Supercomputing Review,* 3 (9), Sept. 1990, pp. 48–57. Also available from SPEC, c/o Waterside Associates, 39510 Paseo Padre Parkway, Suite 350, Fremont, CA 94538.

*TPC Quarterly Report.* Shanley Public Relations, 777 N. First Street, Suite 600, San Jose, CA 95112-6311. Telephone: (408) 295-8894, fax: (408) 295-9768.

# 2

# The History of DebitCredit and the TPC

Omri Serlin

*ITOM International Co.*

This is a personal account of how the Transaction Processing Performance Council (TPC) came into being and how it created TPC benchmark™ A and B (commonly abbreviated TPC-A, TPC-B). I also describe how these tests differ from each other and from the DebitCredit and TP1 tests, their popular but nonstandardized predecessors. Finally, I offer an assessment of the value of the standards developed by the TPC and how they compare with standards developed by other recently formed performance measurement standards bodies, most notably, SPEC (System Performance Evaluation Cooperative).

## 2.1    Interest in OLTP Performance

In the early 1980s there was a renaissance of interest in characterizing the performance of on line transaction processing (OLTP) systems. This interest was driven by two seemingly contradictory trends. First, there were expectations of an increased demand for very high performance transaction systems. This demand was expected to arise from the increasing automation of common daily business transactions. The proliferation of automatic teller machines (ATMs) in the banking industry was often cited as a prime example of the trend. Indeed, some banks were developing large systems to handle the anticipated deluge of transactions arising from, for instance, gasoline stations converting their pumps to automatic operation, controlled by debit or credit cards. Interestingly, the deluge did not materialize, although card-operated fuel pumps have become rather popular in Europe.

In any event, the expectation of sharply increased transaction loads gave rise to intense debates among workers in the field about 1K tps systems [Good, 1985], i.e., those capable of sustaining 1000 transactions per second (tps). IBM publicized the results of an OLTP test known as the 1K test, which, as its name implied, was meant to prove specifically that an IBM mainframe could indeed perform 1000 tps [ONEKAY, 1987]. There was even a special conference launched to deal with this issue; dubbed HPTS, the International Workshop on High Performance Transaction Systems is a biannual conference that has been held three times since 1985.

At the other end of the spectrum, the success of Tandem Computers created a good deal of interest in medium-range OLTP systems. About a half-dozen would-be Tandem competitors entered the market in the early 1980s, expecting to derive their chief competitive edge from the use of high-performance microprocessor technology, compared with the minicomputer-style architecture and ad-hoc logic employed in the Tandem systems. With the notable exception of the highly successful Stratus computer, most of the "new wave" OLTP vendors soon fell by the wayside. Nevertheless, while they were actively making performance claims, the issue of OLTP performance characterization remained red-hot.

While there was general agreement that such metrics as mips and Dhrystones were wholly inadequate to characterize the performance of OLTP systems, there was no agreement on exactly how tps ratings were to be derived. Each vendor selected a test to suit that vendor's specific market orientation and system idiosyncracies. One such test was the so-called Wisconsin benchmark (see Chapter 3 in this book), a synthetic test for relational databases that gained some popularity but that did not take account of the on-line nature of transaction systems. Furthermore, in making their tps claims, the various vendors released few details regarding the test. Thus, while plenty of tps claims were being unleashed, it was not at all clear whether any of the published tps ratings were in any sense comparable [TP1/ET1, 1986].

## 2.2   Anon et al. Publishes a Paper

Against this background, in the summer of 1984 Jim Gray of Tandem Computers wrote an early version of what eventually became the celebrated "Anon et al." paper. This early version was distributed by Jim to a number of interested Tandem employees, as well as to nineteen other professional acquaintances in industry and academia for comments and suggestions. "Anon et. al." was used by Gray to indicate that the paper was the result of efforts by this entire group, as well as to avoid publication delays due to the need to obtain legal clearances from the relevant organizations. (Mail to Dr. E. A. Anon is still being received at Tandem.)

The paper recommended the adoption of three standard performance tests for OLTP systems: one on-line transaction processing test, dubbed *DebitCredit*, and two batch tests, a sort and a scan. The rationale for these three tests was that they would adequately characterize the key aspects of a system intended for commercial on-line transaction processing work.

For the on-line test, the paper proposed a highly stylized emulation of a teller support system in a large, multibranch bank. The key parameters of the emulated bank (e.g., number of customer accounts, number of branches, number of tellers per branch) roughly corresponded to the actual state of a well-known California bank (Bank of America) in the early 1970s. Indeed, this emulation was carried out by IBM, where Gray worked at that time, in order to analyze the performance bottlenecks and price-performance considerations that led the bank to select a minicomputer-based architecture for its initial teller support system, in preference to IBM mainframes. Gray's paper named this test *DebitCredit,* as a substitute for *ET1* and *TP1*, which were internal IBM code names. As it turned out, this profusion of terms led to very undesirable consequences later.

Although Gray's paper described the DebitCredit test (and the other two tests) in broad functional terms only, it did already contain several of the key ideas later codified in TPC-A and TPC-B. These could be summarized as simplicity, applicability to distributed systems, scaleability, comparability, and vendor neutrality.

## 2.3     Key Characteristics of DebitCredit

For simplicity, only a single transaction type was included (see Figure 2.1), representing a deposit by an account holder. The deposit activity was to be recorded in three randomly accessed indexed files: the account file, the branch file, and the teller file. In addition, the transaction details were to be recorded in a sequential history file. These four files are often abbreviated the ABTH files.

```
Read 100 bytes including Aid, Tid, Bid, Delta from terminal
    BEGIN TRANSACTION
        Update Account where Account_ID = Aid:
            Read Account_Balance from Account
            Set Account_Balance = Account_Balance + Delta
            Write Account_Balance to Account
        Write to History:
            Aid, Tid, Bid, Delta, Time_stamp
        Update Teller where Teller_ID = Tid:
            Set Teller_Balance = Teller_Balance + Delta
            Write Teller_Balance to Teller
        Update Branch where Branch_ID = Bid:
            Set Branch_Balance = Branch_Balance + Delta
            Write Branch_Balance to Branch
    COMMIT TRANSACTION
Write 200 bytes including Aid, Tid, Bid, Delta, Account_Balance to terminal
```

Aid (Account_ID), Tid (Teller_ID), and Bid (Branch_ID) are keys to the relevant records/rows.

**Figure 2.1**
The TPC-A Transaction Profile.

A measure of application realism was included by requiring that 15 percent of all incoming transactions involve account numbers residing at a different branch than the one at which the transaction was processed. This represented customers doing business at other than their "home" branches. More importantly, it was hoped that in systems employing multiple loosely coupled processors (such as those from Tandem and Stratus), this provision would force some inter-CPU communications and possibly invoke distributed transaction integrity mechanisms.

To assure scaleability, the rate at which each teller's terminal generated transactions was fixed (100 seconds per transaction in the Gray paper); and the size of the account, branch, teller, and history files was to be a function of the system's throughput; specifically, the Gray paper suggested a scaling of, for each input tps, 100,000 account records, 10 branches, and 100 tellers. In addition, the sequential history file was meant to hold a record for each transaction over a 90-day period, although the Gray paper did not specify whether the history data was to represent a 24-hour-a-day or an 8-hour-a-day operation.

The tps throughput of an OLTP system is closely dependent on the allowable response time constraints. When longer response times are permitted, higher tps ratings can generally be reported. In order to make tps ratings comparable, the paper proposed a constraint under which 95 percent of all transactions completed in 1 second or less.

Another important aspect of comparability is configuration control. The usual industry practice up to that time was to compare configurations that were in some sense equivalent (having the same amount of memory, disks, etc.) and report some CPU-only performance metric along with purchase costs of the systems being compared. The Gray paper introduced a novel idea in this respect. Instead of configuring equivalent systems, Gray suggested that the cost of the tested system be used as the rationalization factor. Thus vendors would be free to configure any system they deemed appropriate; but, in addition to the tps ratings, they would be required to publish the cost-per-tps for the tested system. In addition, Gray suggested that the costs in question should include not merely the initial purchase price but also the costs of software licenses and maintenance for a period of 60 months, the so-called five-year-cost-of-ownership.

The Gray proposal was vendor-neutral in two important respects. First, by stating the requirements of the test in a widely available trade publication, the test was, in effect, put in the public domain. Furthermore, by specifying the requirements at a high functional level, rather than as an executable program, the test became implementable on any hardware platform using any desired software components. No other OLTP test enjoyed these advantages.

## 2.4 Early Efforts to Garner Industry Consensus

When Gray distributed his original paper, this author was already engaged in a modest effort, through the *FT Systems* newsletter as well through personal contacts, to form an industry-consensus forum to establish performance measurement standards in the OLTP field. Dubbed the Working Group on Performance Measurement Standards (WG-PMS), this was a very loose association of (at its peak) some 50 individuals who in various forms had expressed interest in the subject.

In view of the relevance of the paper's suggestions, copies were sent to the WG-PMS, eliciting reactions or counterproposals. The lack of reaction indicated that a substantial effort would be required to make the organization into a going concern—an effort which at the time this author was not prepared to make. WG-PMS activity ceased altogether sometime in 1985.

Gray, however, continued work on his paper, which was published as Tandem Technical Report 85.2 in February, 1985. A slightly edited version of that report appeared under the title "A Measure of Transaction Processing Power" by Anon et al. in the April 1, 1985 issue of *Datamation* magazine. The actual names of the 23 members of the "et al." group were listed in TR 85.2 but not in the *Datamation* article.

The 1985 *Datamation* article proposed a rough guide for performance under the proposed benchmark or reasonable facsimiles thereof (Table 2.1). These results were derived or extrapolated from some actual tests, but the systems tested were not explicitly identified.

**Table 2.1**   "Typical" DebitCredit results from the *Datamation* article.

| Rating | K-Instructions | I/O | tps | $K/tps | Packets |
|---|---|---|---|---|---|
| Lean and Mean | 20 | 6 | 400 | 40 | 2 |
| Fast | 50 | 4 | 100 | 60 | 2 |
| Good | 100 | 10 | 50 | 80 | 2 |
| Common | 300 | 20 | 15 | 150 | 4 |
| Funny | 1000 | 20 | 1 | 400 | 8 |

K-Instructions is the number of instructions (in thousands) executed on behalf of the transaction. I/O is the number of actual disk I/Os per transactions. Tps is transactions per second, assuming the 95 percent under 1 second response. $K/tps is five-year cost of ownership divided by the tps rating. *Packets* refers to X.25 packets (the Gray proposal assumed an X.25 network linking the teller terminals to the central system).

The two proposed batch tests, sort and scan, were largely ignored, but the proposed on-line test quickly gained wide popularity following the *Datamation* article, with many vendors issuing a variety of ET1 and TP1 claims.

However, rather than decreasing the confusion, the publication of the article merely encouraged vendors to claim performance under the "industry standard benchmark." It soon became quite clear that the article was not sufficiently precise to allow unambiguous implementations [DebitCredit, 1986; Editor's Notebook, 1986]. Furthermore, even those aspects that were quite clearly stated were often violated. As an example, few of the published results used the proposed five-year cost of ownership formula, preferring instead to use initial hardware costs only.

## 2.5    TP1 Variation Muddies the Waters

The situation became even more critical around 1987, when suppliers of relational database systems began publishing so-called TP1 results with tps ratings that appeared to be abnormally high relative to the power and configuration of the hardware platforms employed in these tests. By early 1988, it became clear that, although these TP1 tests did use some variation of the DebitCredit transaction, they included a major simplification by ignoring entirely the user terminals and the X.25 connecting network [TP1 vs. DebitCredit, 1988].

Instead, TP1 as used by the database vendors relied on batch-type "transaction generator" processes that created transactions as fast as possible, without allowing for any "think time." In practical terms, this TP1 variation assumed that the transactions had already arrived at the memory of the system under test (SUT). This was essentially true, regardless of whether the transaction generators executed on the SUT itself or were placed on an external system connected to the SUT via a local area network (LAN).

In either case, the SUT was not burdened by the management of the connecting network and the large number of terminals that would have been required for the reported tps rate under a full DebitCredit implementation. The rationale for this simplification was that the database vendors were interested in characterizing the performance of their product while avoiding as much as possible the impact of extraneous factors, such as the efficiency of the operating system in handling terminal communications.

Although this simplification made good sense from the point of view of the database vendors, it introduced a significant new uncertainty regarding the comparability of results from the so-called industry standard OLTP test. In TP1 vs. DebitCredit [1988], which described the difference between the original DebitCredit and the new TP1 tests, the suggestion was made that vendors should report the former as "Class I" results and the latter as "Class II" results.

There was no industry response to this proposed classification scheme; stronger action was called for if further confusion regarding OLTP performance claims was to be avoided.

## 2.6   The Sawyer-Serlin Paper

By that time, the practice of hiring an auditor to certify the results of an OLTP test was beginning to take root. This trend began in March, 1987, when Tandem hired Codd & Date Consulting to certify the 208 tps result obtained under a version of DebitCredit on a 32-processor Tandem VLX system, using the NonStop SQL relational database system [Tandem Performs, 1987]. Tandem eventually published and made available to the public massive documentation supporting the performance and price performance claims and giving details of important parameters and configuration factors with potentially significant effects on the performance of the tested system [Tandem, 1987]. This document later became the model for what the TPC codified as the "full disclosure" report, a concept initially proposed as the "reporting checklist" in [DebitCredit, 1986].

Tom Sawyer of Codd & Date Consulting was the auditor on the Tandem NonStop SQL test; subsequently he officially witnessed a number of the database-only, TP1-type tests. Through this work, Sawyer became acutely aware of the ambiguities in the Anon et al. article and the confusion between the original DebitCredit and the newer TP1 tests. He was therefore very interested in establishing a more rigorous standard to help him in auditing both types of tests. Thus, when I approached him in June, 1988, regarding the possibility of generating a proposed standard document, he responded enthusiastically.

Sawyer and I spent a few evenings hammering out a proposed standard document for the DebitCredit and TP1 tests. The document, dated June 22, 1988, was titled "DebitCredit Benchmark—Minimum Requirements and Compliance List" and consisted of 13 pages, including several pages of comments and a reference list. The paper was included in its entirety in "Auditor's Report" [1988, 1989].

In this paper, we devised a scheme that we hoped would permit a rational combination of both the simplified TP1 test and the full-scale Debit-

Credit benchmark. The scheme consisted of a series of mandatory requirements, roughly corresponding to a TP1-type test. A test sponsor would earn 70 points for meeting the minimum requirements (essentially a TP1 test), 20 additional points for proper terminal network representation (essentially a DebitCredit test), and 10 additional points for protecting the transaction log from single failures (a higher measure of fault-tolerance). Our initial idea was that test sponsors would report the point rating in addition to the tps throughput and cost-per-tps figures.

Later, other schemes were proposed, such as reducing the attained tps throughput by multiplying it by the attained point percentage rating. All of these ideas were eventually rejected by the TPC, although in October, 1988, IBM actually managed to conduct a test on several 9370 and 4381 models using the proposed Sawyer-Serlin document as its authority [Auditor's Report, 1988, 1989].

It is worth noting that this test was awarded a score of 85 by the auditor, Tom Sawyer, meaning that it was a pretty complete DebitCredit test. Yet a similar DebitCredit test run by DEC on at least one virtually identical IBM model yielded substantially poorer results. This discrepancy provided additional fuel to the ongoing benchmarketing wars [IBM, DEC, 1988].

## 2.7    The TPC Gets Launched

Armed with the Sawyer-Serlin paper, this author then launched a new drive to form an industry-consensus body for creating and enforcing OLTP performance measurement standards. This time, the effort was successful. By the 10th of August, 1988, eight companies had agreed to join the newly formed Transaction Processing Performance Council (TPC), and an announcement to that effect was sent over the business wire on that day. The initial members were Control Data Corp., Digital Equipment Corp., ICL, Pyramid Technology, Stratus Computer, Sybase, Tandem Computers, and Wang Laboratories. By the end of 1988, there were 26 member companies. By late 1990, the membership list stood at 35, including all the major U.S. system and database vendors and a strong international contingent with both European and Far Eastern representation (the complete list is in Table 2.2).

**Table 2.2**   TPC membership as of August 1990.

| | |
|---|---|
| Arix | Oki Electric |
| AT&T | Olivetti |
| Bull | Oracle |
| Computer Associates | Prime Computer |
| Control Data Corp. | Pyramid Technology |
| Data General | Sequent Computer |
| Digital Equipment Corp. | Sequoia Systems |
| Fujitsu America | Siemens A.G. |
| Hewlett Packard | Software A.G. |
| Hitachi Ltd. | Stratus Computer |
| IBM | Sun Microsystems |
| ICL | Sybase |
| Informix | Tandem Computers |
| Ingres | Teradata |
| ITOM Int'l Co. | Unify |
| Mitsubishi Electric | Unisys |
| NCR | Wang Laboratories |
| NEC Corp. | |

Originally it was expected (somewhat naively) that the Council would achieve all of its work by means of audio teleconferences and written communications. However, it soon became quite clear that the bandwidth of audio teleconferences was too limited for the type of detailed discussions required, and written communications were too slow. Thus face-to-face meetings were indicated. Indeed, the TPC eventually required seven general meetings and 11 teleconferences to hammer out its first standard, TPC Benchmark™ A, a 42-page document published in November of 1989.

Early in its deliberations, the Council rejected the previously discussed idea of combining the DebitCredit and TP1 tests and opted instead for two separate standards. TPC-A is the Council's version of the DebitCredit test, and TPC-B, which was officially approved in August, 1990, represents the Council's version of the TP1 test. Accounts of the progress of the TPC were given in Serlin [1989, 1990].

TPC-A differs from DebitCredit in several important respects. These are summarized in Table 2.3.

By far the chief difficulty the TPC faced was that the DebitCredit test as originally formulated assumed a model in which a "glass-house" mainframe served relatively low-intelligence teller terminals over a wide area network. In contrast, the majority of TPC members were interested in smaller systems as well, especially ones that employed local area networks and/or the "client-server" model, with intelligent workstations taking the place of teller terminals. The diversity of system configurations considered in developing TPC-A can be seen in Figure 2.2. In an attempt to reach a

**Table 2.3** TPC-A compared with DebitCredit.

| Item | DebitCredit | TPC-A |
|---|---|---|
| Authority | None, published as a trade press article | Approved by TPC, the largest industry body dealing with computer performance standards |
| Transaction profile | Terminal I/O within transaction | Terminal I/O outside transaction; new account balance returned to terminal |
| System properties | Duplexed log | Strong ACID with tests specified |
| Response time | 95% under 1 second; measured at SUT | 90% under 2 seconds; measured at driver |
| File Scaling (per tps)<br>Branch records<br>Teller records<br>Account records<br>History records | <br>10<br>100<br>100,000<br>unclear | <br>1<br>10<br>100,000<br>2,592,000 |
| Transaction arrival distribution | Not specified | Random (negative exponential distribution) |
| Throughput calculation | Only one tps point required | Complete tps vs. RT graphs required |
| Number of terminals | 100 per tps | 10 per tps |
| Terminal type | 3270-type only | Intelligent "client" workstations as well as "dumb" terminals |
| History file | Unified | Horizontal partitioning permitted |
| Interconnect method | Wide-area X.25 network | WAN or LAN with any standard protocol |
| Required storage | 90 days of history data | 8 hours of actual SUT operation; plus 90 days history to be priced |
| Pricing | Only "computer room" equipment and software over 5 years | All hardware and software over 5 years except physical communications media |
| Full disclosure | No mention | Detailed report required; auditing recommended |
| Reporting metrics | tps and cost per tps | tpsA-Wide and/or tpsA-Local and cost per tps |

**LEGEND:**

ACID - atomicity, consistency, isolation, durability　　SUT - system under test
RT - response time　　WAN, LAN - wide (local) area network
tps - transactions per second.

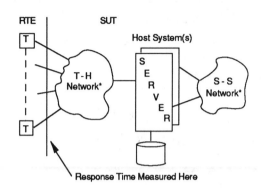

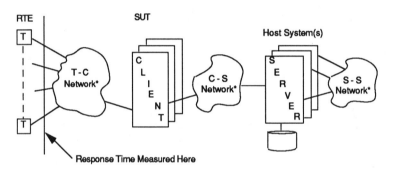

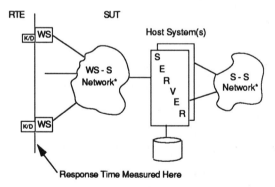

Legend: C=Client; H=Host; K/D=Keyboard/Display; RTE=Remote Terminal Emulator; S=Server; SUT=System Under Test; T=Terminal; WS=Workstation; *=Optional

**Figure 2.2**
Models of systems considered in TPC-A

compromise on these and other issues, the TPC clearly relaxed the "rules of the game" in a number of important areas in defining TPC-A.

For example, while the original benchmark demanded that 95 percent of all transactions must meet a 1-second response time criterion, TPC-A is satisfied with 90 percent of the transactions responding in 2 seconds. All else being equal, this means TPC-A results in substantially higher tps ratings.

Another significant easing of the requirements is in the area of transaction arrival time, or "think time." TPC-A can be satisfied with a 10-seconds average think time, meaning 10 terminals per tps; the original benchmark specified 100 seconds, meaning that 100 terminals must be emulated for each tps achieved. This meant that a 1K tps system would require that 100,000 terminals be emulated, an impractical and unduly severe requirement. Furthermore, this large number of terminals would have skewed the system cost to the point where the central system size would become irrelevant. The TPC grappled with this issue repeatedly; the relaxation to 10 terminals per tps was a compromise, which incidentally also leads to higher tps ratings for TPC-A relative to DebitCredit.

The removal of the requirement that there be only one history file in the system under test (SUT) removes the "hot spot" that is created as all transactions attempt to append a record at the end of that sequential file. This, too, improves tps throughput.

Finally, whereas DebitCredit visualized a configuration in which all terminals connected to the SUT over a wide-area, X.25 communications network, TPC-A also permits a local-area interconnect. Since it is generally believed that the LAN interconnect results in higher throughput, TPC-A demands that, in order to make clear which interconnect scheme was used, throughput must be stated as either tpsA-Wide or tpsA-Local, not merely tps.

The *A* appended to the term *tps* is meant to signify that the results are derived from TPC-A and not from some other OLTP test. Since OLTP tests by their very nature are highly nonlinear, the TPC standard specifically forbids test sponsors from making comparisons between TPC-A results and any other TPC or non-TPC benchmark.

It could be argued that the simplifications described above, and others, further weaken the ability of the test to represent a real-life application, but it is important to remember that the principal consideration in each case was the attainment of a consistent yardstick that could be applied to widely diverse systems. Application realism took second place wherever it conflicted with the common yardstick goal.

It is also important to note that TPC-A introduces more severe requirements in several important areas. For example, response time is to be measured at the driver system, where the terminals are emulated, rather than at the SUT. Thus the delays across the communications network are included in the RT, somewhat depressing the potential throughput. This turned out to be one of the happy instances where application realism (in this case, the measurement of RT as the terminal user would see it) also coincided with practical considerations (it is easier to measure RT at the driver).

Random rather than uniform transaction arrival rate is another example of a stiffened requirement. The Anon et al. paper did not specify this point; there is some theoretical and practical evidence that allowing uniform arrivals doubles the transaction rate.

Whereas DebitCredit only required the log file to be duplexed, allowing the system to maintain transaction integrity in the presence of a single failure, the TPC-A standard explicitly requires the SUT to meet fairly severe ACID (atomicity, consistency, isolation, and durability) properties; it even specifies tests to establish the presence of these properties.

By requiring a full disclosure report, TPC-A makes a critically important contribution to "truth in advertising." Those who wish to make claims under the TPC standard must submit to the TPC, as well as make available to the public at reasonable cost, a rather detailed report that gives many parameters and further specifies the test environment. Today, these parameters and environmental factors, which can be crucial to the full understanding of the test results, often go unreported.

## 2.8    TPC-A Official Results

By late 1990, several companies had reported results under TPC-A and TPC-B. Table 2.4 summarizes the published results. It is important to consult the relevant full disclosure reports for additional information and qualifications of these results.

Information on the full disclosure reports, as well as general TPC information and published standard specifications, may be obtained from the TPC Administrator at:

Shanley Public Relations
777 North First Street, Suite 600
San Jose, CA 95112-6311
Phone (408) 295-8894
FAX (408) 295-2613

Most of the test sponsors to date have chosen the local interconnect option and hence have reported tpsA-Local numbers. The cost per tps in both the local and wide-area variants is generally better than Gray's original "lean-and-mean" figure ($40K/tps; see Table 2.1) partly because of advances in hardware and software and partly because of the more relaxed TPC-A think-time and response-time constraints. In analyzing the cost-per-tps figures it is important to remember that the priced configuration may include one or more front-end processors in addition to the main system indicated in the table. The full disclosure reports provide detailed configuration data. When two disk figures are given, the first is for the tested system and the second (larger) figure for the priced configuration.

It is interesting to note that TPC-A results do not display the clear economies scale that the Anon et al. paper discovered (Table 2.1). There is, in fact, some evidence that, all else being equal, systems that deliver higher tps throughput sometimes do so at a poorer cost per tps than systems with more modest tps ratings. This can be seen in Table 2.4. This diseconomy of scale tends to match comparisons based on cost per mips, where, for example, it is quite clear than an IBM PC provides a much better price performance than an IBM 3090 mainframe.

## 2.9    TPC-B

TPC-B uses the same transaction profile, ACID requirements, and costing formula as TPC-A, but it permits the use of batch transaction generator processes, instead of terminal emulation, for creating incoming transactions. Because in this configuration the concept of a user does not really exist (there are no terminals with think time, only transaction generator processes), the term *response time* is not meaningful; it has been replaced by *residence time*, indicating essentially how long the transaction resided within the database server.

The two required performance curves, which in TPC-A are (a) number of transactions vs. response time and (b) 90 percent percentile response time vs. tps at 100 percent, 80 percent, and 50 percent of the reported tps rate, are replaced in TPC-B. The first curve is replaced by a plot of number of transactions versus residence time; the second is replaced by throughput in tps versus "level of concurrency." The level of concurrency is defined as the

**Table 2.4** Reported TPC results of 1993.

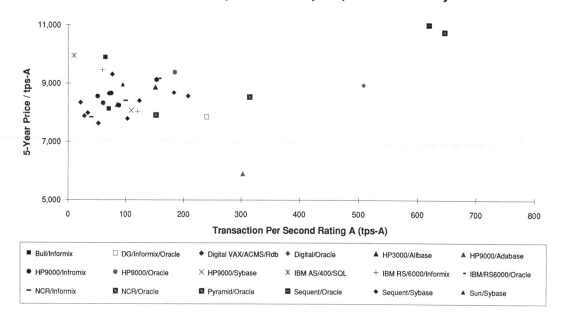

## TPC -A Results  ( under 11k$/tps-A) as of 1 January 1993

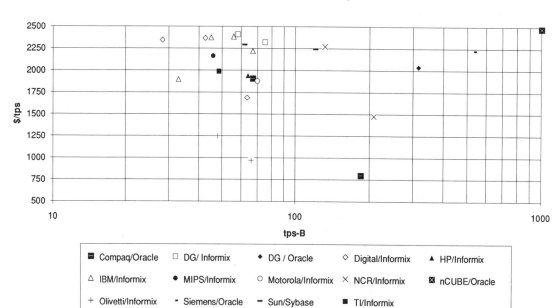

### TPC-B tps vs $/tps as of 1 January 1993
### for entries under 2.5K$/tps

product *TR*, where *T* is the reported tpsB rate, and *R* is the average residence time. The required points on this curve are at $C_L$ (low), $C_R$ (reported), and $C_H$ (high), subject to a formula that spreads these points so that any anomalies in the curve around the reported tps rate will be brought out.

## 2.10    Future Work

In August, 1992, the TPC approved a third benchmark, TPC-C, drawn from the inventory control and order entry milieu; Chapter 3 describes that benchmark in detail. In addition, the TPC is already at work on two other benchmark proposals. TPC-D uses complex query-only transactions to emulate a decision support environment; TPC-E is expected to address transaction processing in a mainframe-oriented environment.

## 2.11    Assessment

It is estimated that the TPC required nearly 1200 man-days of effort to define TPC-A. This figure excludes a much more extensive effort spent internally in each company on critiqueing and amending the intermediate drafts. When travel time and expenses are added, the resulting cost to the industry has been quite significant. It is fair to ask whether the results are worth all this effort.

The success of any standard has to be measured principally by the degree to which vendors and users adhere to that standard. In that respect, the TPC standards are an unqualified success. TPC results for some 180 system configurations from over 20 vendors are currently on the books, including 100 results for TPC-A-Local, 5 results for TPC-A-Wide, and even 4 results for the newest test, TPC-C. Several key vendors, including IBM, DEC, and HP, are regularly using TPC standard benchmarks to characterize the transaction performance of some or all of their new commercial systems. Many customers, especially in the public sector, now routinely require TPC results as part of their bidding and evaluation process.

Successful benchmarks inevitably encourage customizing in order to improve performance on the selected test. There is nothing wrong with this as long as the modifications are made accessible to all purchasers and are beneficial to other applications beyond the specific test. By this measure, too, TPC standard benchmarks have been successful. Vendors have quickly discovered some very effective yet legitimate artifices, including the liberal use of clients or front-end systems, which frequently leads to greatly improved TPC throughput with minimal or no adverse impact on price-performance. Another popular technique is to price very inexpensive user terminals from third parties, rather than the vendor's own, more expensive terminals. While there is no direct evidence of altering standard hardware or software to meet TPC specific exigencies, vendors are known to have conducted more TPC tests than those made public; the results of such private tests have been applied to removing some system bottlenecks, to the benefit of all applications.

The fears that TPC-B, because of its less stringent requirements, would overshadow TPC-A have not materialized. Indeed, there are significantly more TPC-A results (100) on the official list than TPC-B (71). It is also interesting to note that the operating systems used in TPC tests, originally heavily biased in favor of proprietary systems, are now led by Unix-based systems. For example, of the 100 TPC-A-Local results on the official list, 59 use Unix or a Unix-derived operating system.

The TPC initially refrained from adopting measures to judge the validity of tests performed under TPC standards; this was due to concerns over potential legal complications. These concerns were later resolved. The TPC now has in place a clear procedure that allows any member to challenge any perceived violation of TPC rules with any submitted test; members have a limited time (60 days since initial submission of the FD Report) to raise objections. If none are raised, the test is officially accepted by the TPC and results are placed on the official results list. A Technical Advisory Board (TAB) is responsible for studying any objections and for recommending to the Council whether to require the test sponsor to correct the defects before the report is officially accepted. While this mechanism is never friction-free, on the whole, it has worked remarkably well.

The TPC also has in place a mechanism for revising its standards documents to remove defects and ambiguities as they are discovered. For instance, TPC-A and TPC-B are now at their Revision 1.1 level; cut-off dates are imposed, beyond which tests performed under older revisions are no longer accepted by the Council. During the interim, test sponsors are required to state the revision level they used. Revisions to standards are, of course, kept to a minimum and are not issued any more frequently than once a year.

To allow new benchmarks to emerge, while limiting the proliferation of benchmark choices, the TPC is studying how to retire existing standards. No doubt, the mechanism will involve some grace period, after which the TPC will not accept tests conducted under decommissioned standards.

I believe that some of the key concepts introduced by the TPC will have lasting effects on future performance work. Among these is the full disclosure concept, namely, the idea that, to be credible, a test sponsor must furnish to the public sufficient backup data to allow independent observers or end-users to judge the validity of the associated performance claims.

Independent auditing, although not a mandatory requirement, is highly recommended in the TPC standards. Despite the high cost, this practice has been accepted, in OLTP performance measurement, as the rule rather than the exception.

The idea that a whole-system test should be specified at a high enough level to permit implementations on widely divergent hardware and software configurations is of fundamental importance and may well become the norm in future OLTP performance work.

## 2.12    Concluding Caveat

Users are always better off if they can get vendors to test proposed systems under benchmarks that represent the user's actual workloads. Users should also be aware that results obtained under TPC-A or TPC-B cannot be used to predict an OLTP system's performance under drastically different workloads. Nevertheless, as comparative tools, the TPC standardized benchmarks are more useful than nonstandard tests in the many cases where users do not wish to create and supervise custom benchmarks. Users who create custom benchmarks may also find the TPC standards useful as a model for stating the requirements for such benchmarks.

# References

Anon et al. (1985). A measure of transaction processing power. *Datamation*, p. 112. (Tandem Technical Report TR 85.2). April 1, 1985: Vol. 31, No. 7.

Auditor's report of IBM mid-range DebitCredit results announced October 11, 1988. *FT Systems*, *75*, p. 14, and *FT Systems*, *77*, p. 10.

DebitCredit: a standard? (1986). *FT Systems*, *47*, pp. 2-8.

Editor's Notebook. (1986). *FT Systems*, *47*, p. 1.

Good, B., Homan, P.W., Gawlick, D.E., & Sammer, H. (1985). One thousand transactions per second. *IEEE Compcon Proceedings*. San Francisco.

IBM, DEC disagree on DebitCredit results. (1988). *FT Systems*, *75*, pp. 1-5.

ONEKAY: IBM's 1K tps transaction benchmark. (1987). *FT Systems*, *63*, pp. 1-5.

Serlin, O. (1989). Toward an equitable benchmark. *Datamation*, p. 47. Feb. 1, 1989: Vol. 35, No. 3.

Serlin, O. (1990). Measuring OLTP with a better yardstick. *Datamation*, p. 62. July 15, 1990: Vol. 36, No. 14.

*Tandem NonStop SQL benchmark workbook*. (1987). (Tandem Publication No. 84160.)

Tandem Performs Massive DebitCredit Benchmark. (1987). *FT Systems*, *55*, pp. 4-8.

The TP1/ET1 fiasco. (1986). *FT Systems*, *47*, pp. 5-6.

TP1 vs. DebitCredit: what's in a name? (1988). *FT Systems*, *67*, pp. 1-7.

# TPC BENCHMARK™ A

Standard Specification
Revision 1.1


1 March 1992


Transaction Processing Performance Council (TPC)

Administered by
Shanley Public Relations
777 North First St., Suite 600
San Jose, CA 95112, USA
Phone: (408) 295-8894
FAX: (408) 295-2613
e-mail: shanley@cup.portal.com

A

# TPC MEMBERSHIP
## (August 1992)

| | | |
|---|---|---|
| Amdahl | Hitachi SW | Red Brick Systems |
| AT&T/NCR | IBM Corp. | Sequent Computer |
| Australian Dept. of Admin. | Informix Software | Sequoia Systems |
| Bull S.A. | Ingres Corp. | Siemens Nixdorf Information |
| Compaq Computers | Intel Corp. | Silicon Graphics |
| Computer Associates Int. | ITOM International | Solbourne Computers |
| Control Data Corp. | Mitsubishi Electric Corp. | Stratus Computer |
| Data General Corp. | NEC Systems Laboratory | Sun Microsystems |
| Digital Equipment Corp. | OKI Electric Industry | Sybase |
| EDS | Olivetti S.p.A | Tandem Computers |
| Encore Computer Corp. | Oracle Corp. | Texas Instruments |
| Fujitsu/ICL | Performance Metrics | Unify Corp. |
| Hewlett Packard | Pyramid Technology | |

Document History:

| Date | Version | Description |
|---|---|---|
| 10 November 1989 | First Edition | Standard specification released to public. |
| 1 March 1992 | Revision 1.1 | Revised standard specification. |

TPC Benchmark$^{TM}$ is a trademark of the Transaction Processing Performance Council.

# TPC BENCHMARK™ A: Standard Specification (1 March 1992)*

A

## TABLE OF CONTENTS

## CLAUSE 0: Preamble

TPC Benchmark A exercises the system components necessary to perform tasks associated with that class of on-line transaction processing (OLTP) environments emphasizing update-intensive database services. Such environments are characterized by:

- Multiple on-line terminal sessions

- Significant disk input/output

- Moderate system and application execution time

- Transaction integrity

This TPC Benchmark uses terminology and metrics which are similar to other past or future benchmarks, originated by the TPC or others. Such similarity in terminology does not in any way imply that results are comparable to benchmarks other than TPC Benchmark A.

The metrics used in TPC Benchmark A are throughput as measured in transactions per second (tps), subject to a response time constraint; and the associated price-per-tps. Comparison of price/performance results disclosed in one country may not be meaningful in another country because of pricing and product differences.

TPC Benchmark A can be run in a wide area or local area network configuration. The throughput metrics are "tpsA-Local" and "tpsA-Wide" respectively. The wide area and local area throughput and price-performance metrics are different and cannot be compared.

This benchmark uses a single, simple, update-intensive transaction to load the system under test (SUT). Thus the workload is intended to reflect an OLTP application, but does not reflect the entire range of OLTP requirements typically characterized by multiple transaction types of varying complexities. The single transaction type provides a simple, repeatable unit of work, and is designed to exercise the key components of an OLTP system.

The extent to which a customer can achieve the results reported by a vendor is highly dependent on how closely TPC Benchmark A approximates the customer application. Relative performance of systems derived from TPC Benchmark A do not necessarily hold for other workloads or environments. Extrapolations to unlike environments are not recommended.

A full disclosure report of the implementation details, as specified in Clause 10, must be made available along with the report results.

Benchmark results are highly dependent upon workload, specific application requirements, and system design and implementation. Relative system performance will vary as a result of these and other factors. Therefore TPC Benchmark A should not be used as a substitute for a specific customer application benchmarking when critical capacity planning and/or product evaluation decisions are contemplated.

> While separated from the main text for readability, "comments" are a part of the standard and must be enforced. The sample implementation included as Appendix A is provided only as an example and is specifically not part of the standard.

# CLAUSE 1: Transaction and Terminal Profiles

## 1.1    The Application Environment

**1.1.1**    This benchmark is stated in terms of a hypothetical bank.  The bank has one or more branches.  Each branch has multiple tellers.  The bank has many customers, each with an account.  The database represents the cash position of each entity (branch, teller, and account) and a history of recent transactions run by the bank.  The transaction represents the work done when a customer makes a deposit or a withdrawal against his account.  The transaction is performed by a teller at some branch.  These functions are enumerated in 1.2.

**1.1.2**    The database may be implemented using any commercially available database management system (DBMS), database server, file system, etc.  The terms "file/table", "record/row" and "field/column" are used in this document only as examples of physical and logical data structures.

If the application environment contains software that routes or organizes the execution of transactions (e.g., a transaction processing monitor), the software must be a generally available, commercial product that is fully supported as defined in Clause 9.

**Comment:** It is the intent that special purpose transaction processing monitors developed specifically for benchmarking or limited use not be utilized.

**1.1.3**    Implementors of this benchmark are permitted many possible system designs, insofar as they adhere to the standard model described and pictorially illustrated in Clause 8.

**1.1.4**    The word "terminal" as used in this standard refers to the teller interface device.  This may be an actual terminal or the keyboard/display portion of an intelligent processor such as a workstation (see 9.2.2.2).

A

## 1.2    The Transaction Profile

Read 100 bytes including Aid, Tid, Bid, Delta from terminal (see 1.3)

```
BEGIN TRANSACTION
    Update Account where Account_ID = Aid:
        Read Account_Balance from Account
        Set Account_Balance = Account_Balance + Delta
        Write Account_Balance to Account
    Write to History:
        Aid, Tid, Bid, Delta, Time_stamp
    Update Teller where Teller_ID = Tid:
        Set Teller_Balance = Teller_Balance + Delta
        Write Teller_Balance to Teller
    Update Branch where Branch_ID = Bid:
        Set Branch_Balance = Branch_Balance + Delta
        Write Branch_Balance to Branch
COMMIT TRANSACTION
Write 200 bytes including Aid, Tid, Bid, Delta, Account_Balance
to terminal (see 1.3)
```

Aid (Account_ID), Tid (Teller_ID), and Bid (Branch_ID) are keys to the relevant records/rows (see Clause 3.2).

## 1.3    Terminal Inputs and Outputs

**1.3.1**    For each transaction, the originating terminal shall send (see Clause 8) at least 100 user-level alphanumeric data bytes organized as at least four distinct fields, including Account_ID, Teller_ID, Branch_ID, and Delta.  Branch_ID in the input message is the identifier of the branch where the teller is located.

**1.3.2**    Each terminal shall receive from the SUT at least 200 user-level alphanumeric data bytes, organized as at least five distinct fields as follows: Account_ID, Teller_ id, Branch_ID, Delta, and Account_Balance resulting from successful commit of the transaction.

**Comment:** It is the intent of this Clause that the account balance in the database be returned to the application, i.e., that the application retrieve the account balance.

**1.3.3**    No compression shall be used on the user-level data in the message coming from or going to the terminal.

**1.3.4**    Any field(s) other than pure padding field(s) transmitted either way between the RTE (Remote Terminal Emulator, see Clause 8) and SUT (System Under Test, see Clause 8) in addition to the mandatory fields specified above must be disclosed, and the purpose of such field(s) explained.

**1.3.5**    The generation of input message fields is detailed in Clause 5.

## 1.4    Specific Non-Requirements

**1.4.1**    The order of the data manipulations within the transaction bounds is imma-terial, and is left to the latitude of the test sponsor, as long as the transaction profile is functionally equivalent to the one outlined in Clause 1.2.

**1.4.2**    The transaction profile does not require that the SUT (see Clause 8) return the teller and branch balances to the application program.

## CLAUSE 2: Transaction System Properties

## 2.1    The ACID Properties

**2.1.1**    The ACID (Atomicity, Consistency, Isolation, and Durability) properties of transaction processing systems must be supported by the system under test during the running of this benchmark.  It is the intent of this section to informally define the ACID properties and to specify a series of tests that must be performed to demon-strate that these properties are met.

**2.1.2**    No finite series of tests can prove that the ACID properties are fully sup-ported.  Passing the specified tests is a necessary, but not sufficient, condition for meeting the ACID requirements.

**2.1.3**    All mechanisms needed to insure full ACID properties must be enabled during both the measurement and test periods.  For example, if the system under test relies on undo logs, then logging must be enabled even though no transactions are aborted during the measurement period.  When this benchmark is implemented on a distributed system, tests must be performed to verify that home and remote transactions, including remote transactions that are processed on two nodes, satisfy the ACID properties. (See Clause 5 for the definition of home and remote transac-tions.)

## 2.2    Atomicity Requirements

**2.2.1**    *Atomicity Property Definition*
The system under test must guarantee that transactions are atomic; the system will either perform all individual operations on the data, or will assure that no partially-completed operations leave any effects on the data.

**2.2.2** *Atomicity Tests*

2.2.2.1    Perform the standard TPC Benchmark A™ transaction (see Clause 1.2) for a randomly selected account and verify that the appropriate records have been changed in the Account, Branch, Teller, and History files/tables.

2.2.2.2    Perform the standard TPC Benchmark A™ transaction for a randomly selected account, substituting an ABORT of the transaction for the COMMIT of the transaction. Verify that the appropriate records have not been changed in the Account, Branch, Teller, and History files/tables.

## 2.3    Consistency Requirements

**2.3.1** *Consistency Property Definition*

Consistency is the property of the application that requires any execution of a transaction to take the database from one consistent state to another.

**2.3.2** *Consistency Conditions*

A consistent state for the TPC Benchmark A™ database is defined to exist when:

a. the sum of the account balances is equal to the sum of the teller balances, which is equal to the sum of the branch balances;

b. for all branches, the sum of the teller balances within a branch is equal to the branch balance;

c. the history file has one logical record added for each committed transaction, none for any aborted transaction, and the sum of the deltas in the records added to the history file equals the sum of the deltas for all committed transactions.

If data is replicated, each copy must not violate these conditions.

**2.3.3** *Consistency Tests*

Due to the large size of the Account file/table, no test of its consistency is specified. To verify the consistency of the Branch, Teller, and History files, perform the following (2.3.3.1 through 2.3.3.3 are meant to be performed in sequence):

**2.3.3.1**    Verify that the Branch and Teller files are initially consistent by performing the following steps:

Step 1:    Determine the balance of each branch as reflected in the branch file.

Step 2:    For each branch, calculate the branch balance by summing the balances of the tellers associated with the branch.

Step 3:    Verify that the balance of each branch as obtained from Steps 1 and 2 is the same.

**2.3.3.2**    Verify that the Branch and Teller files are still consistent after applying transactions to the database by performing the following steps:

Step 1:    Compute the initial sum of the branch balances for later use.

Step 2:    Count the number of records in the History file and sum the deltas in the History file. (The file may be empty).

Step 3:    Using the standard driving mechanism, submit a number of standard TPC Benchmark A transactions equal to at least ten times the number of tellers and note the number of transactions that are reported as committed. For example, a 100 tps (1000 teller) system must submit at least 10,000 transactions. If the number of committed transactions is not equal to the number of submitted transactions, explain why.

Step 4:    Re-verify the consistency of the Branch and Teller files by repeating 2.3.3.1.

Step 5:    Compute the final sum of the branch balances for later use.

**2.3.3.3**    Verify that the History file is consistent by performing the following steps:

Step 1:    Count the number of records in the History file and sum the deltas.

Step 2:    Verify that the count equals the original count from 2.3.3.2, Step 2, plus the number of transactions reported as committed in 2.3.3.2, Step 3. (The History file should contain one record for each committed transaction and should not contain a record for any aborted transaction.)

Step 3:    Verify that the difference between the sum of the final and initial deltas in the History file is equal to the difference between the sum of the final and initial branch balances.

## 2.4    Isolation Requirements

### 2.4.1    *Isolation Property Definition*

Operations of concurrent transactions must yield results which are indistinguishable from the results which would be obtained by forcing each transaction to be serially executed to completion in some order.

This property is commonly called serializability. Sufficient conditions must be enabled at either the system or application level to ensure serializability of transactions under any mix of arbitrary transactions, not just TPC Benchmark A transactions. The system or application must have full serializability enabled, i.e., repeated reads of the same records within any committed transaction must have returned identical data when run concurrently with any mix of arbitrary transactions.

**2.4.2** *Isolation Tests*

For conventional locking schemes, isolation should be tested as described below, where transactions 1 and 2 are versions of the standard TPC Benchmark A transaction. Systems that implement other isolation schemes may require different validation techniques. It is the responsibility of the test sponsor to disclose those techniques and the tests for them.

**2.4.2.1** Isolation Test for Completed Transactions (conventional locking schemes):

> Start transaction 1.
> Stop transaction 1 immediately prior to COMMIT.
> Start transaction 2.
> Transaction 2 attempts to update the same account record as transaction 1.
> Verify that transaction 2 waits.
> Allow transaction 1 to complete. Transaction 2 should now complete.
> Verify that the account balance reflects the results of both updates.

**2.4.2.2** Isolation Test for Aborted Transactions (conventional locking schemes):

> Start transaction 1.
> Stop transaction 1 immediately prior to COMMIT.
> Start transaction 2.
> Transaction 2 attempts to update the same account record as transaction 1.
> Verify that transaction 2 waits.
> Abort transaction 1. Transaction 2 should now complete.
> Verify that the account balance reflects the results of transaction 2's update only.

**2.4.2.3** Repeat tests 2.4.2.1 and 2.4.2.2 for the branch and teller files.

## 2.5   Durability Requirements

The tested system must guarantee the ability to preserve the effects of committed transactions and insure database consistency after recovery from any one of the failures listed below in Clause 2.5.3.

**Comment:** No system provides complete durability, i.e., durability under all possible types of failures. The specific set of single failures addressed in 2.5.3 is deemed sufficiently significant to justify demonstration of durability across such failures.

**2.5.1.** *Durable Medium Definition*

A durable medium is a data storage medium that is either:

a. an inherently non-volatile medium, e.g., magnetic disk, magnetic tape, optical disk, etc., or

b. a volatile medium with its own self-contained power supply that will retain and permit the transfer of data, before any data is lost, to an inherently non-volatile medium after the failure of external power.

A configured and priced Uninterruptible Power Supply (UPS) is not considered external power.

**Comment:** A durable medium can fail; this is usually protected against by replication on a second durable medium (e.g., mirroring) or logging to another durable medium. Memory can be considered a durable medium if it can preserve data long enough to satisfy the requirement stated in (b) above—for example, if it is accompanied by an uninterruptible power supply, and the contents of memory can be transferred to an inherently non-volatile medium during the failure. Note that no distinction is made between main memory and memory performing similar permanent or temporary data storage in other parts of the system, e.g., disk controller caches.

### 2.5.2 Committed Property Definition

A transaction is considered committed when the transaction manager component of the system has written the commit record(s) associated with the transaction to a durable medium.

**Comment 1:** Transactions can be committed without the user subsequently receiving notification of that fact, since message integrity is not required for TPC Benchmark A.

**Comment 2:** Although the order of operations in the transaction profile (Clause 1.2) is immaterial, the actual transmission of the output message cannot begin until the commit operation has successfully completed.

### 2.5.3 List of single failures

**2.5.3.1** Permanent irrecoverable failure of any single durable medium containing database, ABTH files/tables, or recovery log data.

**Comment:** If main memory is used as a durable medium, then it must be considered as a potential single point of failure. Sample mechanisms to survive single durable medium failures are: i) database archiving in conjunction with a redo (after image) log, and ii) mirrored durable media. If memory is the durable medium and mirroring is the mechanism used to ensure durability, then the mirrored memories must be independently powered.

**2.5.3.2** Instantaneous interruption (system crash/system hang) in processing which requires system reboot to recover.

**Comment:** This implies abnormal system shutdown which requires loading of a fresh copy of the operating system from the boot device. It does not necessarily imply loss of volatile memory. When the recovery mechanism relies on the pre-failure contents of volatile memory, the means used to avoid the loss of volatile memory, e.g., uninterruptible power supply, must be included in the system cost calculation. A sample mechanism to survive an instantaneous interruption in processing is an undo/redo log.

**2.5.3.3** Failure of all or part of memory (loss of contents).

**Comment:** This implies that all or part of memory has failed. This may be caused by a loss of external power or the permanent failure of a memory board.

**2.5.4** The recovery mechanism cannot use the contents of the History file to support the durability property.

**2.5.5** Rollforward recovery from an archive database copy, e.g., a copy taken prior to the run, using redo log data is not acceptable as the recovery mechanism in the case of failures listed in 2.5.3.2 and 2.5.3.3. Note that "checkpoints", "control points", "consistency points", etc. of the database taken during a run are not considered to be archives.

**2.5.6** *Durability Tests*

The intent of these tests is to demonstrate that all transactions whose output messages have been received at the terminal or RTE have in fact been committed in spite of any single failure from the list in Clause 2.5.3.

It is not required to perform these tests under a full terminal load or with a fully scaled database. However, the test sponsor must state that to the best of their knowledge a fully loaded and fully scaled test would also pass the durability tests. It is required to use the same SUT configuration and database partitioning as was used in the measurement part of the test. Furthermore, at the time of the induced failures, it is required to have multiple home and remote transactions (see Clause 5) in progress and distributed systems must have distributed transactions in progress as well.

For each of the failure types defined in Clause 2.5.3, perform the following steps:

Step 1: Perform Step 1 of the History file Consistency Test in Clause 2.3.3.3.

Step 2: Start submitting TPC Benchmark A transactions. On the driver system, record committed transactions in a "success" file.

Step 3: Cause a failure selected from the list in Clause 2.5.3.

Step 4: Restart the system under test using normal recovery procedures.

Step 5: Compare the contents of the "success" file and the History file to verify that every record in the "success" file has a corresponding record in the History file. Also verify that the number of records in the History file is greater or equal to the original count, as obtained in Step 1, plus the number of records in the "success" file. If there is an inequality, the History file must contain additional records and the difference must be less than or equal to the number of terminals simulated. (**Comment:** This difference should be due only to transactions which were committed on the system under test, but for which the 200 byte output message was not transmitted back to the driver before the failure).

Step 6:  Perform the consistency test on the Branch and Teller files as specified in Clause 2.3.3.2.

**A**

## CLAUSE 3: Logical Database Design

## 3.1  Entities, Relationships, and Characteristics

**3.1.1**  The components of the database are defined to consist of four separate and individual files/tables: Account, Branch, Teller, and History. The relationships among these files/tables are defined in the following entity/relationship diagram and are subject to the business rules specified in 3.1.2. This diagram is a logical description and has no implication for physical implementation.

**Comment:**

•  The clustering of records within the database (as in hierarchical or CODASYL databases) is not excluded.

•  A view which represents the records/rows to avoid read/writes is excluded.

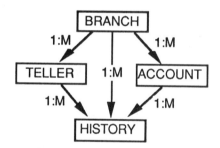

**3.1.2**  The entities in 3.1.1 are subject to the following business rules:

•  All branches must have the same number of tellers.

•  All branches must have the same number of accounts.

Other business rules specified elsewhere in this document also apply, e.g., consistency conditions in Clause 2.3.2.

**Comment:** There is no intent to model an environment in which accounts and tellers can be moved from branch to branch.

## 3.2 Record Layouts and Sizing

**3.2.1** In order for the transaction to represent a similar amount of work to all the systems, it is important that the records handled by the database servers, file systems, etc. be of the same size. Therefore, the records/rows must be stored in an uncompressed format. Where it is impossible to turn compression off, it is incumbent upon the test sponsor to store the records/rows using the minimum lengths specified in 3.2.2 through 3.2.5. Any space with unspecified values in the record/row descriptions in 3.2.2 through 3.2.5 may be used for additional user data; the storage for the access path (e.g., B-tree index structure) or any other data used by the database server may not be counted against the minimum record length specifications.

**3.2.2** Account records/rows must be at least 100 bytes in length and contain the following data in any order or representation:

| | |
|---|---|
| Account_ID | Must uniquely identify the record/row across the range of accounts. The Account_ID must be unique across the entire database. |
| Branch_ID | Branch where account is held. |
| Account_Balance | Must be capable of representing at least 10 significant decimal digits plus sign. |

**3.2.3** Branch records/rows must be at least 100 bytes in length and contain the following data in any order or representation:

| | |
|---|---|
| Branch_ID | Must uniquely identify the record/row across the range of branches. |
| Branch_Balance | Must be capable of representing at least 10 significant decimal digits plus sign. |

**3.2.4** Teller records/rows must be at least 100 bytes in length and contain the following data in any order or representation:

| | |
|---|---|
| Teller_ID | Must uniquely identify the record/row across the range of tellers. |
| Branch_ID | Branch where the teller is located. |
| Teller_Balance | Must be capable of representing at least 10 significant decimal digits plus sign. |

**3.2.5** History records/rows must be at least 50 bytes in length and contain the following data in any order or representation:

| | |
|---|---|
| Account_ID | Account updated by transaction. |
| Teller_ID | Teller involved in transaction. |
| Branch_ID | Branch associated with Teller. |

| Amount | Amount (delta) specified by transaction. Must be capable of representing at least 10 significant decimal digits plus sign. |
|---|---|
| Time_Stamp | A date and time taken between BEGIN TRANSACTION and COMMIT TRANSACTION. It must be capable of representing Date as YY:MM:DD and Time with a resolution of at least HH:MM:SS. |

**3.3**    The size of the identifier in each record/row must be sufficient for the size of the configured system (see Clause 4.2). Thus for a 100 tps test, the accounts file/table must include 10 million records/rows, and hence the account identifier, i.e., the Account_ID, must be able to represent at least 10 million unique values.

**3.4**    The record identifiers of the Account/Branch/Teller (ABT) files/tables must not directly represent the physical disk addresses of the records or any offsets thereof.  The application may not reference records using relative record numbers since they are simply offsets from the beginning of a file.  This does not preclude hashing schemes or other file organizations which have provisions for adding, deleting, and modifying records in the ordinary course of processing.  This Clause places no restrictions on the History file.

**Comment:** It is the intent of this Clause that the application executing the transaction not use physical identifiers, but logical identifiers for all accesses; i.e., it is not legitimate for the application to build a "translation table" of logical-to-physical addresses and use it for enhancing performance.

**3.5**    While inserts and deletes are not performed on the ABT files/tables, the SUT must not be configured to take special advantage of this fact.

# CLAUSE 4: Scaling Rules

**4.1**    The intent of the scaling rules is to maintain a fixed relationship between the transaction load presented to the system under test and the size of the files/tables accessed by the transactions.

**4.2**    For each nominal transaction-per-second (tps) configured, the test must use a minimum of (see Clause 4.4):

| | |
|---|---|
| Account records/rows | 100,000 |
| Teller records/rows | 10 |
| Branch records/rows | 1 |
| History record/rows | (See 4.3) |
| Terminals | 10 |

**4.2.1** All terminals should be active throughout the steady state period. The intent is that each terminal should contribute no more than 1/10th tps per terminal, i.e., the minimum mean inter-arrival time must be 10 seconds. The distribution of transactions with respect to time is specified in Clause 8.6.3.

**4.2.2** Should any value in 4.2 be exceeded, the others should be increased proportionately to maintain the same ratios among them as in 4.2. For example, if 200 terminals are used to generate 10 tps then there must be 20 branch records, 200 teller records, and 2,000,000 account records in the database and the price of the system must include 200 terminals (see Clause 9.1.2).

**4.3** The history file/table should be large enough to hold all history data generated during the steady state portion of the test. However, for the purpose of computing price per tpsA, storage must be maintained for the number of history records specified in Clause 9.2.3.1. This includes the overhead space required to manage and access the data as well as data space. The system under test must be physically configurable to support the amount of storage specified in Clause 9.2.3.1.

**4.4** Reported tpsA may not exceed the configured (nominal) rate represented by the file/table sizes in 4.2. While the reported tpsA may fall short of the maximum allowed by the configured system, the price per tpsA computation must report the price of the system as actually configured.

# CLAUSE 5: Distribution, Partitioning, & Message Generation

## 5.1 Types of Transactions and Nodes

**5.1.1** A transaction is **home** if the account is held at the same branch as the teller that is involved in the transaction (See Clause 3.1.1).

**5.1.2** A transaction is **remote** if the branch where the account is held is not the same as the branch associated with the teller involved in the transaction.

**5.1.3** A **remote** transaction may be processed entirely on a single-node or be distributed between two separate nodes. If the account branch and the teller branch exist on different nodes, the node containing the teller branch is referred to as the **native** node, and the node containing the account branch (the remote branch) is referred to as the **foreign** node.

## 5.2    Partitioning Rules

**5.2.1**    Horizontal partitioning of files/tables is allowed.  For example, groups of history records/rows may be assigned to different files, disks or areas.  If this partitioning is not transparent to the logic of the transaction program, details of the partitioning and transaction program logic must be disclosed.

**5.2.2**    Vertical partitioning of files/tables is not allowed.  For example, groups of fields/columns of one record/row may not be assigned to files, disks, or areas different from those storing the other fields/columns of that record/row.  The record must be processed as a series of contiguous fields.  Note: This restriction is included to normalize vendor benchmarks, since it is the intent of the standard that each TPC Benchmark A data operation accesses approximately 100 bytes, not some smaller, proper subset.

## 5.3    Input Message Generation

**5.3.1**    The input message fields (Account_ID, Branch_ID, Teller_ID, and Delta) must conform to the database fields definition of Clause 3.

**5.3.2**    The Branch_ID and Teller_ID are constant over the whole measurement period for any given terminal.

**5.3.3**    The Delta amount field is a random value within [-999999, +999999] selected independently for each transaction.

**5.3.4**    The Account_ID is generated as follows:

- A random number X is generated within [0,1]

- If  X<0.85 or branches = 1, a random Account_ID is selected over all <Branch_ID> accounts.

- If X>=0.85 and branches > 1, a random Account_ID is selected over all non-<Branch_ID> accounts.

**Comment 1:** This algorithm guarantees that, if there is more than one branch in the database, then an average of 15% of remote transactions is presented to the SUT. Due to statistical variations during a finite measurement period, the actual measured proportion of remote transactions may vary around 15%. Actual measured values must be within 14% to 16% for the set of transactions processed during the measurement interval (see Clauses 6.1 and 7.2).

**Comment 2:** In a distributed system, the 85-15 rule should be implemented so that the ratio of remote-branch transactions occurring on a foreign node is proportional to the actual distribution of accounts across the nodes.  For example, if 3000 branches are divided evenly between two nodes, approximately 7.5% (1500/2999 * 15%) of the transactions cause cross-node activities. With the same 3000 branches divided among three nodes, approximately 10% (2000/2999 * 15%) cause cross-node activities, etc. Note that 2999 is used since the home branch by definition does not qualify.

**5.3.5**   All transactions during steady state should be uniformly distributed over all Teller_IDs, within normal statistical variations.

## 5.4   Definition of Random

Within Clause 5, the term random means independently selected and uniformly distributed.

## CLAUSE 6: Response Time

## 6.1   Measurement Interval and Timing

**6.1.1**   In this Clause, the term "measurement interval" is the steady state period (see Clause 7.1) during the execution of the benchmark for which the test sponsor is reporting a tps number and response time data. The term "completed transaction" is a transaction which has been successfully committed at the SUT and whose output message has been recorded at the Remote Terminal Emulator (RTE; see Clause 8.4).

**6.1.2**   Each transaction submitted to the SUT must be individually timed.

## 6.2   Response Time Definition

Response times must be measured at the RTE. The response time (RT) of a transaction is defined by:

$$RT = T2 - T1$$

where T1 and T2 are measured at the RTE and defined as:

T1 - time stamp taken before the first byte of the input message is sent from the RTE to the SUT.

T2 - time stamp taken after the last byte of the output message from the SUT arrives at the RTE.

The resolution of the time stamps must be at least 0.1 seconds.

## 6.3     Response Time Constraint

90% of all transactions started and completed during the measurement interval must have a Response Time of less than 2 seconds.

**Comment:**  This response time criterion has been chosen to provide a single criterion for all configurations, and in particular systems with wide-area network (WAN) communications, and very-low throughput systems.

## 6.4     Computation of tps Rating

**6.4.1**     The reported tps is the total number of committed transactions which both started and completed at the RTE during the measurement interval, divided by the elapsed time of the interval.

**6.4.2**     For reporting the throughput of the SUT in units of transactions per second, the terminology should be "tpsA-Local" or "tpsA-Wide" for LAN and WAN configurations, respectively. These metrics are NOT comparable to other TPS metrics or to each other.

**6.4.3**     Reported tpsA must be expressed to a minimum precision of three significant digits, rounded down.

## 6.5     Interpolation, Extrapolation Prohibited

The reported tps rate must be measured rather than interpolated or extrapolated. For example, suppose 9.10 tps is measured on a 100 terminal test during which 90% of the transactions completed in less than 1.7 seconds and 9.7 tps is measured on a 110 terminal test during which 90% of the transactions completed in less than 2.3 seconds.  Then the reported tps is 9.1 rather than some interpolated value between 9.1 and 9.7.

## 6.6     Required Reporting

**6.6.1**     The frequency distribution of response times of transactions started and completed during the measurement interval must be reported.  The range of the X axis must be from 0 to 20 seconds response time. At least 20 different intervals, of equal one-second-or-less length, must be reported.  A sample graph is shown below. The maximum and average response times must also be reported.

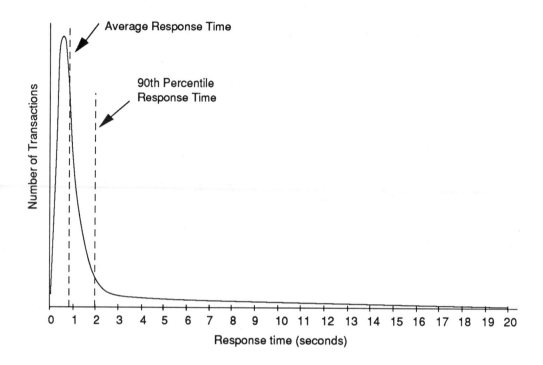

**6.6.2**    A complete curve of response times versus tpsA must be reported. The points on the curve must be of the form (x,y), where:

  x = measured tpsA

  y = corresponding 90th percentile of response times

A curve must be plotted at approximately 50%, 80%, and 100% of reported throughput points (additional points are optional).  The 50% and 80% points are to be measured on the same configuration as the 100% run, varying the think times.  Interpolation of the curve between these data points below the 100% level is permitted.  An example of such a curve is shown below.

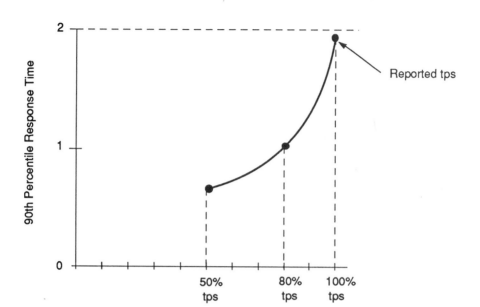

## CLAUSE 7: Duration of Test

### 7.1    Steady State

The test must be conducted in a "steady state" condition that represents the true "sustainable performance" of the system under test (SUT).

Although the measurement period as described below may be as short as 15 minutes, the system under test must be configured so that it is possible to run the test at the reported tps for a continuous period of at least eight hours. For example, the media used to store at least eight hours of log data must be configured, if required to recover from any single point of failure (see Clause 2.5.3.1).

**Comment:** An example of a configuration that would not comply is one where a log file is allocated such that better performance is achieved during the measured portion of the test than during the remaining portion of an eight hour test, perhaps because a dedicated device was used initially but space on a shared device is used later in the full eight-hour test.

## 7.2   Duration and Requirements

The measurement period must:

- Begin after the system reaches sustained "steady state";
- Be long enough to generate reproducible tps results;
- Extend uninterrupted for at least 15 minutes and no longer than 1 hour;
- For systems which defer database writes to durable media, recovery time from instantaneous interruptions (as defined in Clause 2.5.3.2) must not be appreciably longer at the end of the measurement period than at the beginning of the measurement period.

**Comment 1:** "Steady state" is easy to define, e.g., "sustained throughput," but difficult to prove. The test sponsor (and/or the auditor) is required to report the method used to verify steady state sustainable performance and the reproducibility of test results. The auditor is encouraged to use available monitoring tools to help determine steady state.

**Comment 2:** The intent of this Clause is to require that writes to disk or other durable media that would normally occur during a sustained test of at least eight hours duration (such as checkpointing, writing redo/undo log records to disk, etc.), are included in the measurement interval and are not deferred until after the measurement is complete.

**Note to Comment 2:** Some systems defer writes of changed pages/blocks to the durable-medium-resident database. Such systems can maintain buffers/caches in a volatile medium (e.g.,memory) for use by the DBMS, operating system, and disk control system, which are not synchronized with the durable-medium-resident database. Re-synchronizing these caches with the durable-medium-resident database is typically accomplished via "control points," "checkpoints," or "consistency points."

## CLAUSE 8: SUT, Driver, & Communications Definition

## 8.1    Models of the Target System

Models of the system which is the target (object) of this benchmark are shown pictorially below.  By way of illustration, the diagrams also depict the RTE/SUT boundary (see Clauses 8.3 and 8.4) where the response time is measured.

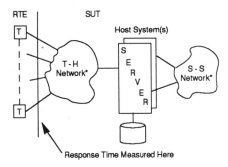

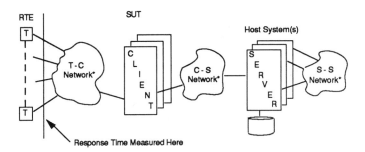

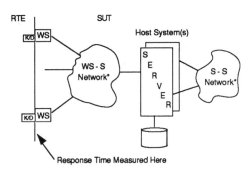

LEGEND: C - Client; H - Host; K/D - Keyboard/Display; RTE - Remote Terminal Emulator; S -Server; SUT - System Under Test; T - Terminal; WS - Workstation.  * - optional.

If any network other than the Server-Server network is a wide area network as defined in Clause 8.5.1, and at least one message of each transaction passes through the WAN, then the system is called a WAN-approach; otherwise, it is called a LAN-approach.

## 8.2 Test Configuration

The test configuration consists of the following elements:

- System Under Test (SUT)
- Driver System
- Driver/SUT Communications Interface

The tested configuration need not include the WAN long-haul communications lines.

## 8.3 System Under Test (SUT) Definition

The SUT consists of:

- One or more processing units (e.g., hosts, front-ends, workstations, etc.) which will run the transaction described in Clause 1, and whose aggregate performance will be described by the metric tpsA-Wide or tpsA-Local.

- Any front-end systems are considered to be part of the SUT. Examples of front-end systems are terminal demultiplexers, front-end data communications processors, cluster controllers, database clients (as in the 'client/server' model), and workstations.

- The hardware and software components of all networks required to connect and support the SUT components.

- Data storage media sufficient to satisfy both the scaling rules in Clause 4 and the ACID properties of Clause 2. The data storage media must hold all the data described in Clause 3 and be intimately attached to the processing units(s).

- The host system(s) including hardware and software supporting the database employed in the benchmark.

## 8.4 Driver Definition

**8.4.1** An external Driver System, which provides Remote Terminal Emulator (RTE) functionality, will be used to emulate the target terminal population during the benchmark run. The terminal population is scaled in accordance with Clause 4.

**8.4.2** The RTE:

- Generates and sends 100 byte transactional messages to the SUT;

- Receives 200 byte responses;

- Records message response times;

- Performs conversion and/or multiplexing into the communications protocol used by the communications interface between the driver and the SUT;

- Statistical accounting is also considered an RTE function.

The possibility of utilizing an actual real-terminal configuration as an RTE is not excluded.

**8.4.3** Normally, the Driver System is expected to perform RTE functions only. Work done on the Driver System in addition to the RTE as specified in 8.4.2 must be thoroughly justified as specified in Clause 8.6.4.

**8.4.4** The intent is that the Driver System must reflect the proposed terminal configuration and cannot add functionality or performance above the priced network components in the SUT. It must be demonstrated that performance results are not enhanced by using a Driver System. (See Clause 10.1.7.2).

**8.4.5** Any software or hardware which resides on the Driver which is not the RTE is to be considered as part of the SUT. For example, in a client-server model, the client software may be run or be simulated on the Driver system (see Clause 8.6.4).

## 8.5 Communications Interface Definitions

**8.5.1** *Wide Area Network (WAN) and Local Area Network (LAN) Definitions*

**8.5.1.1** A wide area network is defined as a communications interface capable of supporting remote sessions over a distance of at least 1500 kilometers, with a protocol supported by commercially available products.

**8.5.1.2** The upper limit on WAN communications bandwidth will be 64 kbps (Kbits/second) per communications line utilized, and the number of terminals simulated over a 64 kbps line is restrained only by the bandwidth of that line.

**Comment 1:** The communications line will operate at 64 kbps at both ends (Terminal and SUT), but may utilize higher bandwidth mechanisms in between. A maximum line speed of 64 kbps has been selected because of global availability, thus ensuring that country metrics can be published.

**Comment 2:** In order for a network to be considered a WAN:

- At least one message for each transaction must pass through a WAN.

- All components of the WAN (e.g., modems, multiplexers, etc.) must be capable of operating over a distance of at least 1500 kilometers. This implies that timeouts, turnaround delays, etc., must be accounted for.

**8.5.1.3** If a network is not a WAN, it is a Local Area Network (LAN).

**8.5.1.4** All protocols used must be commercially available.

**Comment:** It is the intention of this definition to exclude non-standard I/O channel connections. The following situations are examples of acceptable channel connections:

- Configurations or architectures where terminals or terminal controllers are normally and routinely connected to an I/O channel of a processor.

- Configurations where the processor(s) in the SUT is/are connected to the local communications network via a front-end processor which is channel connected. The front-end processor is priced as part of the SUT.

**8.5.2** *Driver/SUT Communications Interface*

**8.5.2.1** The communications interface between the Driver System and the SUT must be the mechanism by which the system would be connected with the end-user devices (terminals and/or workstations) in the proposed configuration.

## 8.6 Further Requirements on the SUT and Driver System

**8.6.1** *No Database on Driver System*

Copies of any part of the tested data base or file system or its data structures, indices, etc. may not be present on the Driver System during the test. Synchronization between RTE and SUT (e.g., through known initial values for ABT balances) is equally disallowed.

**8.6.2** *Individual Contexts for Emulated Terminals*

The SUT must contain context for each terminal emulated, and must maintain that context for the duration of that test. That context must be identical to the one which would support a real terminal. A terminal which sends a transaction cannot send another until the completion of that transaction.

**Comment:** The "context" referred to in 8.6.2 should consist of information such as terminal identification, network identification, and other information necessary for a real terminal to be known to (i.e., configured on) the SUT. The intention is to allow pseudo-conversational transactions.  The intent of 8.6.2 is simply to prevent a test sponsor from multiplexing messages from a very large number of emulated terminals into a few input lines and claiming or implying that the tested system supports that number of users regardless of whether the system actually supports that number of real terminals.

### 8.6.3   *Pacing of Transactions by Emulated Terminals*

Each emulated terminal, after sending a request to update the database to the SUT, must wait for a given "Think Time" after receiving that reply, before sending the next request.  By definition, the Response Time added to the Think Time gives the Cycle Time, which has to average at least 10 seconds (see diagram below).  The Think Time shall be approximated by a Delay, taken independently from the same truncated negative exponential distribution.  Computing overhead for Delay initiation and completion in the RTE has to be kept to a minimum so that difference between the Delay and the effective Think Time is minimized. The maximum value of the Delay distribution must be at least 10 times the mean.  The mean must be disclosed by the test sponsor.

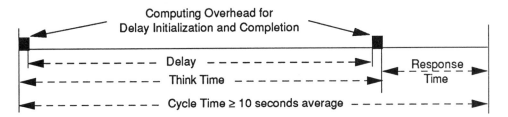

**8.6.3.1**   The frequency distribution of Think Times of transactions started and completed during the measurement interval must be reported.  The range of the X-axis must be from 0 to 20 seconds Think Times.  At least 40 different intervals, of equal 0.5 seconds or less length, must be reported.  A sample graph is shown below.  The maximum and average Think Times must also be reported.

**A**

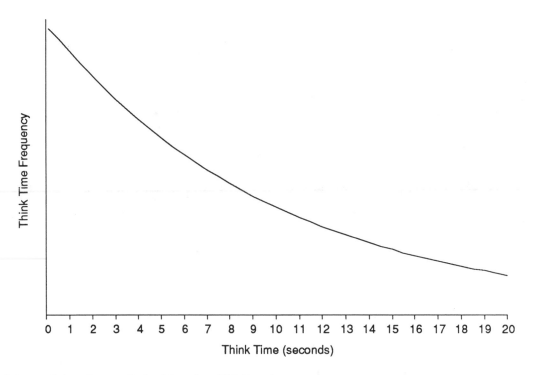

Think Time (seconds)

### 8.6.4   *Driver System Doing More than RTE Functions*

In the event that a Driver System must be used to emulate additional functionality other than that described in Clause 8.4, then this must be justified as follows:

**8.6.4.1**   It must be demonstrated that the architecture of the proposed solution makes it uneconomical to perform the benchmark without performing the work in question on the driver (e.g., in a client/server database implementation where the client software would run on a large number of workstations).

**8.6.4.2**   Clause 8.6.1 must NOT be violated.

**8.6.4.3**   It must be demonstrated that executables placed on the Driver System are functionally equivalent to those on the proposed (target) system.

**8.6.4.4**   It must be demonstrated that performance results are not enhanced by performing the work in question on the Driver System.  It is the intent that a test should be run to demonstrate that the functionality, performance and connectivity of the emulated solution is the same as that for the priced system.

**8.6.4.5**   Individual contexts must continue to be maintained from the RTE through to the SUT.

**8.6.4.6**   A complete functional diagram of both the benchmark configuration and the configuration of the proposed (target) system must be provided.  A detailed list of all software and hardware functionality being performed on the Driver System, and its interface to the SUT, must be provided.

**8.6.5**   *Disclosure of Network Configuration and Emulated Portions*

The test sponsor shall describe completely the network configurations of both the tested system and the proposed real (target) system which is being represented. A thorough explanation of exactly which parts of the proposed configuration are being replaced by the driver system must be given.

**8.6.6**   *Limits on Concentration*

The level of concentration of messages between the Driver System and the SUT in the benchmark configuration must not exceed that which would occur in the proposed (target) configuration. In particular, the number of communications packets which can be concentrated must not exceed the number of terminals which would be directly connected to that concentrator in the proposed configuration.

**Comment:** The intent is to allow only first level concentration on the RTE, but does not preclude additional levels of concentration on the SUT.

## 8.7   Reporting Metrics

A differentiation must be maintained between reporting of results in wide area and local attach methods of benchmarking. For reporting the throughput of the systems in units of transactions per second, the terminology should be "tpsA-Local" for the local attach method, and "tpsA-Wide" for the wide area approach. These two metrics are NOT comparable with each other.

## CLAUSE 9: Pricing

## 9.1   Pricing Methodology

**9.1.1**   The intent of this section is to define the methodology to be used in calculating the price/tps. The fundamental premise is that what is tested and/or emulated is priced and what is priced is tested and/or emulated.

**9.1.2**   The proposed system to be priced is the aggregation of the SUT, terminals and network components that would be offered to achieve the reported performance level. Calculation of the priced system consists of:

a.  Price of the SUT as tested and defined in Clause 8.3;

**A**

b. Price of the emulated terminals and network proposed components;

c. Price of on-line storage for 90 days of history records;

d. Price of additional products that are required for the operation, administration or maintenance of the priced system;

e. Price of additional products required for application development.

**9.1.3**   Pricing methodology assumptions:

- All hardware and software used in the calculations must be announced and generally orderable by customers, with a full disclosure of the committed delivery date for general availability of products not already generally released;

- Generally available discounts for the priced configuration are permissible;

- Generally available packaged pricing is acceptable;

- Local retail pricing and discount structure should be used in each country for which results are published.

- Price should be represented by the currency with which the customer would purchase the system.

For test sponsors who have only indirect sales channels, pricing must be actual generally available pricing from indirect channels which meet all other requirements of Clause 9.

**Comment 1:**   The intent of the pricing methodology is to allow packaging and pricing that is generally available to customers, and to explicitly exclude promotional and/or limited availability offerings.

**Comment 2:**   Revenue discounts based on total price are permissible. Any discount must be only for the configuration being priced and can not be based on past or future purchases; individually negotiated discounts are not permitted; special customer discounts (e.g. GSA schedule, educational schedule) are not permitted.

**Comment 3:**   The intent is to benchmark the actual system which the customer would purchase. However, it is realized that, typically, vendors will announce new products and disclose benchmark results before the products have actually shipped. This is allowed, but it specifically excludes any use of "one of a kind" hardware/software configurations which the vendor does not intend to ship in the future. Products must be generally available in the country where the SUT is priced.

**9.1.4**   For publishing in a country other than the country for which the results are originally published, it is permitted to substitute local components different from the original report, provided the substituted products are sold to the same product description or specification.

**Comment:** The intention is to encourage local country pricing by allowing substitution of equipment for country-specific reasons such as voltage, product numbering, industrial/safety, keyboard differences, etc., which do not affect performance.

## 9.2    Priced System

### 9.2.1    *SUT*

The entire price of the SUT as configured during the test must be used, including all hardware (new purchase price), software (license charges) and hardware/software maintenance charges over a period of 5 years (60 months). In the case where the driver system provides functionality in addition to the RTE described in Clause 8.4.2, then the prices of the emulated hardware/software described in Clause 9.2.2.1 are to be included.

**Comment 1:** The intent is to price the tested system at the full price a customer would pay. Specifically prohibited are the assumption of other purchases, other sites with similar systems, or any other assumption which relies on the principle that the customer has made any other purchase from the vendor. This is a one-time, stand-alone purchase.

**Comment 2:** Any usage pricing for TPC-A should be based on the number of emulated users.

### 9.2.2    *Terminals and Network Pricing*

**9.2.2.1**     The price of the driver system is not included in the calculation, although the prices of the devices the driver is emulating (controllers, multiplexors, systems used as concentrators, LAN components, front-end processors, workstations and terminals are some examples) are to be included.

**9.2.2.2**     The terminals must be commercially available products capable of entering via a keyboard all alphabetic and numeric characters and capable of displaying simultaneously the data and the fields described in Clause 1.3.2.

**9.2.2.3**     LAN Pricing—For the purposes of pricing, all components from the terminal to the SUT excluding LAN or direct connect cables must be priced.

**9.2.2.4**     WAN Pricing—For the purposes of pricing, the number of terminals to be connected to a single 64 kbps (or less) line must be no greater than that emulated per Clause 8.5.1.2. All hardware components which are required to connect to the 64 kbps line must be included in the pricing. The price of the 64 kbps line(s) is excluded.

**Comment:** The intent is that all components including PADS (packet assemblers-disassemblers), modems, concentrators, multiplexors, etc. required to attach to the 64 kbps line must be priced in addition to the price of the terminals/workstations.

### 9.2.3    *History Storage and Recovery Log Pricing*

**9.2.3.1**    Within the priced system, there must be sufficient on-line storage to support any expanding system files and durable history records/rows for 90 eight-hour days at the published tps rate (i.e., 90 x 8 x 60 x 60 = 2,592,000) records/rows per tpsA.

**Comment:** The 90-day history file is required so as to force configuration of a realistic amount of on-line storage.

**9.2.3.2**    For purposes of pricing storage for history records/rows, any unused on-line storage present in the SUT may count towards the history storage requirements. (However, note that unused storage may also be needed for expanding system files as required in Clauses 7.1 and 9.2.3.1.)

**9.2.3.3**    If it is necessary to price any additional storage devices to fulfill the ninety (90) day history storage requirement, such devices must be of the type(s) actually used in the SUT during the test, and must satisfy the normal system configuration rules.

**Comment:** The intent is to exclude unrealistic on-line storage devices or configurations from the pricing procedure.

**9.2.3.4**    The requirement to support 8 hours of recovery log data can be met with storage on any durable media (see 2.5.1) if all data required for recovery from failures listed in 2.5.3.2 and 2.5.3.3 are on-line.

### 9.2.4    *Additional Operational Components*

**9.2.4.1**    Additional products that might be included on a customer-installed configuration, such as operator consoles, magnetic tape drives and printers, are also to be included in the priced system if explicitly required for the operation, administration or maintenance of the priced system.

**9.2.4.2**    Copies of the software on appropriate media, and a software load device if required for initial load or maintenance updates, must be included.

**9.2.4.3**    The price of an Uninterruptible Power Supply specifically contributing to a durability solution must be included (see Clause 2.5.3.2).

### 9.2.5    *Additional Software*

**9.2.5.1**    The price must include the software licenses necessary to create, compile, link and execute this benchmark application; as well as all run-time licenses required to execute on host system(s) and connected workstations.

**9.2.5.2**    In the event the application code is developed on a system other than the SUT, the price of that system and any compilers and other software used must also be included as part of the priced system.

## 9.3    Maintenance

**9.3.1**        Hardware and software maintenance must be figured at a standard pricing which covers at least 5 days/week, 8 hours/day coverage, either on-site, or if available as standard offering, via a central support facility. Hardware maintenance maximum response time must not exceed 4 hours, on any part whose replacement is necessary for the resumption of operation.

**Comment:** Software maintenance means a standard offering which includes acknowledgement of new and existing problems within 4 hours and a commitment to fix defects within a reasonable time.

**9.3.2**        If central support is claimed, then the appropriate connection device, such as auto-dial modem, must be included in the hardware price. Also any software required to run the connection to the central support, as well as any diagnostic software which the central support facility requires to be resident on the tested system, must not only be included in pricing, but must also be installed during the benchmark runs.

**9.3.3**        Software maintenance must include update distribution for both the software and documentation. If software maintenance updates are separately priced, then pricing must include at least 3 updates over the 5 year period.

**Exception:**  Maintenance and warranty terms for terminals and workstations must cover at a minimum a return for repair service.

# CLAUSE 10: Full Disclosure

## 10.1    Full Disclosure Report Requirements

A full disclosure report is required for results to be considered compliant with TPC Benchmark™ A specifications.

**Comment:** The intent of this disclosure is for a customer to be able to replicate the results of this benchmark given the appropriate documentation and products.

A full disclosure report must include the following:

**10.1.1**    *General Items*

**10.1.1.1**    A statement identifying the sponsor of the benchmark and any other companies who have participated.

**10.1.1.2**    Program listing of application code and definition language statements for files/tables.

**10.1.1.3**    Settings for all customer-tunable parameters and options which have been changed from the defaults found in actual products, including but not limited to:

- Database options;
- Recovery/commit options;
- Consistency/locking options;
- System parameters, application parameters, and configuration parameters.

Test sponsors may optionally provide a full list of all parameters and options.

**10.1.1.4**    Configuration diagrams of both benchmark configuration and the priced system, and a description of the differences.

### 10.1.2    Clause 2 Related Items

**10.1.2.1**    Results of the ACIDity test (specified in Clause 2) must describe how the requirements were met. If a database different from that which is measured is used for durability tests, the sponsor must include a statement that durability works on the fully loaded and fully scaled database.

### 10.1.3    *Clause 3 Related Items*

**10.1.3.1**    The distribution across storage media of ABTH (Accounts, Branch, Teller, and History) files/tables and all logs must be explicitly depicted.

Provide two functional diagrams which show CPUs, storage devices, communication lines, terminals, and the interconnections between these components. The first diagram must correspond to the benchmark configuration and the second diagram must correspond to the 90-day priced configuration. A separate pair of diagrams must be provided for each reported result. (The diagrams used for clause 10.1.1.4 may already contain this information. In this case, the additional data required below may optionally be shown in tabular form with references to these diagrams.)

As part of each diagram, show the percentage of the total physical database which resides on each storage device for each of the ABTH files and logs. For the benchmark configuration, show database allocation during 8-hour steady state. For the 90-day priced configuration, show database allocation including storage of 90 days of history records. Data which are duplicated (e.g., mirrored) on more than one device must be clearly labeled to show what is duplicated and on which devices.

Two examples are shown below.

Example 1:

## Distribution of ABTH files and Logs in Benchmark Configuration

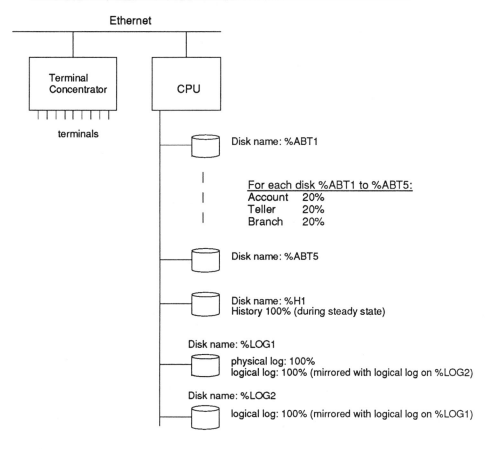

## Example 1 (cont.):

### Distribution of ABTH files and Logs in Priced Configuration

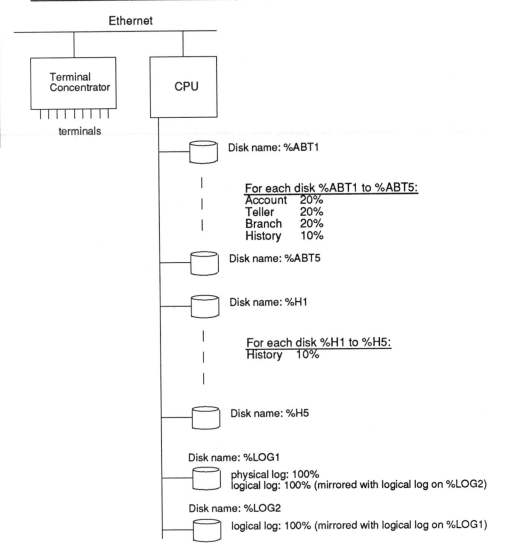

Ethernet

Terminal Concentrator

CPU

terminals

Disk name: %ABT1

For each disk %ABT1 to %ABT5:
Account   20%
Teller      20%
Branch   20%
History   10%

Disk name: %ABT5

Disk name: %H1

For each disk %H1 to %H5:
History   10%

Disk name: %H5

Disk name: %LOG1
physical log: 100%
logical log: 100% (mirrored with logical log on %LOG2)

Disk name: %LOG2
logical log: 100% (mirrored with logical log on %LOG1)

**Example 2:**

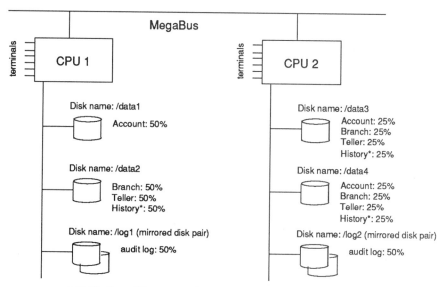

## Data Distribution in Benchmarked Configuration

* Distribution of History records represents 8-hour steady state.

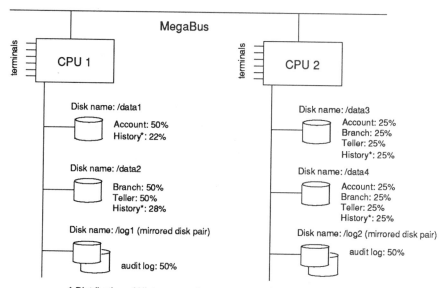

## Data Distribution in Priced Configuration

* Distribution of History records represents 90-day storage requirement.

**10.1.3.2**  A description of how the database was populated, along with sample contents of each ABTH file/table to meet the requirements described in Clause 3.

**10.1.3.3**  A statement of the type of database utilized, e.g., relational, Codasyl, flat file, etc.

**10.1.4**  *Clause 5 Related Items*

**10.1.4.1**  The method of verification of the random number generator should be described.

**10.1.4.2**  Vendors must clearly disclose if horizontal partitioning is used. Specifically, vendors must:

1. Describe textually the extent of transparency of the implementation.

2. Describe which tables/files were accessed using partitioning.

3. Describe how partitioned tables/files were accessed.

The intent of this clause is that details of non-transparent partitioning be disclosed in a manner understandable to non-programmer individuals (through use of flow charts, pseudo code, etc.).

**10.1.4.3**  The sponsor must disclose percentage of remote and home transactions, percentage of remote and foreign transactions, if applicable, and the actual distribution of accounts across the nodes, if applicable.

**10.1.5**  *Clause 6 Related Items*

**10.1.5.1**  Report all the data specified in Clause 6.6, including maximum and average response time, as well as performance curves for tpsA vs. response time and response time distribution (see Clauses 6.6.1 and 6.6.2).

**10.1.6**  *Clause 7 Related Items*

**10.1.6.1**  The method used to determine that the SUT had reached a steady state prior to commencing the measurement interval should be described.

**10.1.6.2**  A description of how the work normally performed during a sustained test (for example checkpointing, writing redo/undo log records, etc., as required by Clause 7.2), actually occurred during the measurement interval.

**10.1.6.3**  A description of the method used to determine the reproducibility of the measurement results.

**10.1.6.4**  A statement of the duration of the measurement period for the reported tpsA (it should be at least 15 minutes and no longer than 1 hour).

**10.1.7**   *Clause 8 Related Items*

**10.1.7.1**   If the RTE is commercially available, then its inputs should be specified. Otherwise, a description should be supplied of what inputs (e.g., scripts) to the RTE were used.

**10.1.7.2**   A proof that the functionality and performance of the components being emulated in the Driver System are equivalent to that of the priced system. The sponsor must list all hardware and software functionality of the driver and its interface to the SUT.

**10.1.7.3**   If the SUT contains a WAN or a LAN network, its bandwidth should be specified. The sponsor must describe the network configuration per clause 8.6.5.

**10.1.7.4**   The sponsor must disclose the mean and maximum think times and a graph of the distribution of think times.

**10.1.8**   *Clause 9 Related Items*

**10.1.8.1**   A detailed list of hardware and software used in the priced system. Each item must have vendor part number, description, and release/revision level, and either general availability status or committed delivery date. If package-pricing is used, contents of the package must be disclosed.

**10.1.8.2**   The total price of the entire configuration is required including: hardware, software and maintenance charges. Separate component pricing is recommended. The basis of all discounts used shall be disclosed.

**10.1.8.3**   A statement of the measured tpsA-Wide or tpsA-Local, and the calculated price/tpsA-Wide or price/tpsA-Local.

**10.1.8.4**   Additional Clause 9 related items may be included in the full disclosure report for each country specific priced configuration. Country-specific pricing is subject to Clause 9.1.4.

**10.1.9**   *Clause 11 Related Items*

**10.1.9.1**   If the benchmark has been independently audited, then the auditor's name, address, phone number, and a brief audit summary report indicating compliance must be included in the full disclosure report. A statement should be included, specifying when the complete audit report will become available and who to contact in order to obtain a copy.

# 10.2   Availability of the Full Disclosure Report

The full disclosure report is to be readily available to the public at a reasonable charge, similar to charges for similar documents by that test sponsor. The report is to be made available when results are made public. In order to use the phrase "TPC

Benchmark™ A", the full disclosure report must have been submitted to the TPC Administrator as well as written permission to distribute same.

## 10.3 Revisions to the Full Disclosure Report

Revisions to the full disclosure documentation shall be handled as follows:

**10.3.1** Fully documented price decreases can be reflected in a new published price/throughput. The benchmark need not be rerun to remain compliant. When cumulative price changes have resulted in an increase of 5% or more from the disclosed price/performance, the test sponsor must submit revised price/performance results to the TPC within 30 days of the effective date of the price changes to remain compliant. The benchmark need not be rerun to remain compliant.

**Comment:** The intent is that the published price/performance reflect actual current price/performance.

**10.3.2** Hardware or software product substitutions within the SUT require the benchmark to be rerun with the new components in order to re-establish compliance.

**10.3.3** The revised report should be submitted as defined in 10.2.

**10.3.4** A report may be revised to add or delete Clause 9 related items for country-specific priced configurations.

**Comment:** During the normal product life cycle problems will be uncovered which require changes, sometimes referred to as ECOs, FCOs, Patches, Updates, etc. If any of these changes causes the tps rating of the system to change by more than 5%, then the test sponsor will be required to re-validate the benchmark results.

## 10.4 Official Language

**10.4.1** The official full-disclosure report must be written in English but may be translated to additional languages.

## CLAUSE 11: Audit

**11.1** An independent audit of the benchmark results is highly recommended. An audit checklist is provided as part of this specification.

**11.2**     The audit report is to be made readily available to the public at a reasonable charge, similar to charges for similar documents.

**11.3**     Auditor's check list:

**11.3.1**   *Clause 1 Related Items*

**11.3.1.1**   Verify that the application program matches the transaction profile of Clause 1.2.

**11.3.1.2**   Verify that message sizes and content satisfy Clause 1.3 and that message compression is not used.

**11.3.2**   *Clause 2 Related Items*

**11.3.2.1** Verify that the requirements of each of the ACIDity tests were met.

**11.3.3**   *Clause 3 Related Items*

**11.3.3.1**   For each of the ABTH files verify that specified fields/columns and records/rows exist, and that they conform to the minimum lengths specified in Clause 3.2.

**11.3.3.2**   Verify that the ABT record/row identifiers are not disk or file offsets as specified in Clause 3.4.

**11.3.3.3**   Verify that the ABT files/tables support retrievals, inserts and deletes as specified in Clause 3.5.

**11.3.4**   *Clause 4 Related Items*

**11.3.4.1**   Verify that the ratios among the numbers of records/rows of each file/table are as specified in Clause 4.2.

**11.3.4.2**   Verify that the total number of tellers is at least 10 times the system's tpsA rating as specified in Clause 4.2.1.

**11.3.4.3**   Verify randomness of the Account_ID, Branch_ID, and Teller_ID sequences submitted to the SUT. Include verification that the values generated are uniform across the entire set of accounts necessary to support the claimed tps rating per Clause 4.4 (scaling).

**11.3.5**   *Clause 5 Related Items*

**11.3.5.1**   Verify that at least 15% of the transactions are remote, and that the distribution of Account_IDs of remote transactions is uniform across non-home branches.

**11.3.5.2**   If horizontal partitioning is used, establish whether or not it is transparent to the application program as defined in Clause 10.1.4.2.

**A**

**11.3.5.3**   Verify that vertical partitioning of the ABTH files is not used.

**11.3.6**   *Clause 6 Related Items*

**11.3.6.1**   Verify the method used to measure the response time at the RTE.

**11.3.6.2**   If part of the SUT is emulated, verify that the reported response time is no less than the response time that would be seen by a real terminal user.

**11.3.7**   *Clause 7 Related Items*

**11.3.7.1**   Verify the method used to determine that the SUT had reached a steady state prior to commencing the measurement interval.

**11.3.7.2**   Verify that all work normally done in a steady state environment actually occurred during the measurement interval, for example checkpointing, writing redo/undo log records to disk, etc., per Clause 7.2, Comment 2.

**11.3.7.3**   Verify the method used to determine the reproducibility of the measurement results.

**11.3.7.4**   Verify the duration of the measurement period for the reported tps (at least 15 minutes and no longer than 1 hour).

**11.3.7.5**   Verify that the response time and the tps were measured in the same time interval.

**11.3.8**   *Clause 8 Related Items*

**11.3.8.1**   Describe the method used to verify the accurate emulation of the tested terminal community by the driver system if one was used.

**11.3.9**   *Clause 9 Related Items*

**11.3.9.1**   Verify that all application development software is installed on the priced system and has been used to compile, link and execute the benchmark.

**11.3.9.2**   Verify that pricing includes all the hardware and software licenses as required in Clause 9.

**11.3.9.3**   Verify that the priced configuration includes sufficient storage for the database, history, and recovery logs as specified in 9.2.3, and can be configured in the priced system.

**11.3.9.4**   Assure that warranty coverage meets the requirements of Clause 9.3, or that additional costs for maintenance have been added to priced system.

**11.3.9.5**   Verify that all prices used, including discounts, are generally available.

# APPENDIX A: Sample Implementation

A

```
/*
 *   This is a sample implementation of the Transaction Processing Performance
 *   Council Benchmark A coded in ANSI C and ANSI SQL2.
 *   Any equivalent implementation is equally acceptable.
 *
 *   Exceptions:
 *       1. Since no standard syntax exists for networking, C standard IO is used.
 *          In an actual benchmark, this must be replaced with WAN or LAN
 *          message software.
 *       2. ANSI/ISO SQL have no explicit BEGIN WORK (begin transaction).
 *          To show that message handling is outside the transaction,
 *          explicit BEGIN WORK statements are included.
 *       3. The C language has only integer and float numerics - it does not
 *          support precision or scale.  So, in this implementation, money is
 *          represented as integer pennies (pence, pfennig, centimes,...)
 *       4. To clarify the schema, the following SQL2 features are used:
 *                  Primary Key
 *                  Foreign Key
 *                  DateTime datatype
 *                  Default values (to simplify handling of pad chars).
 *       5. For simplicity, the program does no error checking or handling.
 */

/* Global declarations                    */
exec sql BEGIN DECLARE SECTION;

/* tpc bm a scaling rules                 */
long tps        =          1;/* the tps scaling factor: here it is 1*/
long nbranches =           1;/* number of branches in 1 tps db*/
long ntellers  =          10;/* number of tellers in  1 tps db*/
long naccounts =      100000;/* number of accounts in 1 tps db*/
long nhistory  =     2592000;/* number of history recs in 1 tps db*/

/* working storage
*/
long i,sqlcode, Bid, Tid, Aid, delta, Abalance;

exec sql END DECLARE SECTION;
```

```
void CreateDatabase();
long DoOne();
#include <stdio.h>
/* main program,
 * Creates a 1-tps database, ie 1 branch, 10 tellers,...
 * runs one TPC BM A transaction
 */
main()
{
    CreateDatabase();
    DoOne();
}


/*
 *  CreateDatabase - Creates and Initializes a scaled database.
 */
void CreateDatabase()
{
exec sql BEGIN WORK;  /* start trans to cover DDL ops*/
exec sql CREATE TABLE branches (
        Bid                 NUMERIC(9),            PRIMARY KEY(Bid),
        Bbalance            NUMERIC(9),
        filler              CHAR(92) DEFAULT SYSTEM
                    );                          /* pad to 100 bytes*/
exec sql CREATE TABLE tellers (
        Tid                 NUMERIC(9),    PRIMARY KEY(Tid),
        Bid                 NUMERIC(9)     FOREIGN KEY REFERENCE TO branches,
        Tbalance            NUMERIC(9),
        filler      CHAR(88) DEFAULT SYSTEM
                    );                          /* pad to 100 bytes*/
exec sql CREATE TABLE accounts (
        Aid                 NUMERIC(9),    PRIMARY KEY(Aid),
        Bid                 NUMERIC(9)     FOREIGN KEY REFERENCE TO branches,
        Abalance            NUMERIC(9),
        filler      CHAR(88) DEFAULT SYSTEM
                    );                          /* pad to 100 bytes*/
exec sql CREATE TABLE history (
        Tid                 NUMERIC(9)     FOREIGN KEY REFERENCE TO tellers,
        Bid                 NUMERIC(9)     FOREIGN KEY REFERENCE TO branches,
        Aid                 NUMERIC(9)     FOREIGN KEY REFERENCE TO accounts,
        delta               NUMERIC(9),
        time                TIMESTAMP,
        filler              CHAR(26) DEFAULT SYSTEM
                    );                          /* pad to 50 bytes*/
```

```
/* prime database using TPC BM A scaling rules.
 *   Note that for each branch and teller:
 *         branch_id = teller_id  / ntellers
 *         branch_id = account_id / naccounts
 */
for (i = 0; i < nbranches*tps; i++)
    exec sql INSERT INTO branches(Bid,Bbalance) VALUES (:i,0);
for (i = 0; i < ntellers*tps; i++)
    exec sql INSERT INTO tellers(Tid,Bid,Tbalance) VALUES (:i,:i/:ntellers,0);
for (i = 0; i < naccounts*tps; i++)
    exec sql INSERT INTO accounts(Aid,Bid,Abalance) VALUES (:i,:i/:naccounts,0);
exec sql COMMIT WORK;
}         /* end of CreateDatabase*/


/*  DoOne - Executes a single TPC BM A transaction.
 */
void DoOne()
{
scanf("%ld %ld %ld %ld", &Bid, &Tid, &Aid, &delta);/* note: must pad to 100 bytes*/
exec sql BEGIN WORK;

exec sql UPDATE accounts
    SET        Abalance = Abalance + :delta
    WHERE      Aid = :Aid;

exec sql SELECT Abalance INTO :Abalance
    FROM       accounts
    WHERE      Aid = :Aid;

exec sql UPDATE tellers
    SET        Tbalance = Tbalance + :delta
    WHERE      Tid = :Tid;

exec sql UPDATE branches
    SET        Bbalance = Bbalance + :delta
    WHERE      Bid = :Bid;

exec sql INSERT INTO history(Tid, Bid, Aid, delta, time)
    VALUES (:Tid, :Bid, :Aid, :delta, CURRENT);

exec sql COMMIT WORK;
printf("%ld, %ld, %ld, %ld\n", Bid, Tid, Aid, Abalance, delta);
                              /* note: must pad to 200 bytes*/
}         /* end of DoOne                        */
```

# TPC BENCHMARK™ B

Standard Specification
Revision 1.1

1 March 1992

Transaction Processing Performance Council (TPC)
© 1992 Transaction Processing Performance Council

B

Administered by
Shanley Public Relations
777 North First St., Suite 600
San Jose, CA 95112, USA
Phone: (408) 295-8894
FAX: (408) 295-2613
e-mail: shanley@cup.portal.com

# TPC MEMBERSHIP
## (August 1992)

Amdahl
AT&T/NCR
Australian Dept. of Admin.
Bull S.A.
Compaq Computers
Computer Associates Int.
Control Data Corp.
Data General Corp.
Digital Equipment Corp.
EDS
Encore Computer Corp.
Fujitsu/ICL
Hewlett Packard

Hitachi SW
IBM Corp.
Informix Software
Ingres Corp.
Intel Corp.
ITOM International
Mitsubishi Electric Corp.
NEC Systems Laboratory
OKI Electric Industry
Olivetti S.p.A
Oracle Corp.
Performance Metrics
Pyramid Technology

Red Brick Systems
Sequent Computer
Sequoia Systems
Siemens Nixdorf Information
Silicon Graphics
Solbourne Computers
Stratus Computer
Sun Microsystems
Sybase
Tandem Computers
Texas Instruments
Unify Corp.

**B**

Document History:

| Date | Version | Description |
|------|---------|-------------|
| 23 August 1990 | First Edition | Standard specification released to public. |
| 1 March 1992 | Revision 1.1 | Revised standard specification. |

# TPC BENCHMARK™ B: Standard Specification (1 March 1992)*

## TABLE OF CONTENTS

B

*©1992 Transaction Processing Performance Council (TPC)

B

# CLAUSE 0: Preamble

TPC Benchmark™ B exercises the database components necessary to perform tasks associated with that class of transaction processing environments emphasizing update-intensive database services. Such environments are characterized by:

- Significant disk input/output
- Moderate system and application execution time
- Transaction integrity

This benchmark is not OLTP in that it does not require any terminals, networking, or think time. This benchmark uses terminology and metrics which are similar to other benchmarks, originated by the TPC and others. The only benchmark results comparable to TPC Benchmark™ B are other TPC Benchmark™ B results. In spite of similarities to TPC-A, TPC-B contains substantial differences which make TPC-B results not comparable to TPC-A.

The metrics used in TPC Benchmark™ B are throughput as measured in transactions per second (TPS), subject to a residence time constraint; and the associated price-per-TPS. The metric for this benchmark is "tpsB". All references to tpsB results must include both the tpsB rate and the price-per-tpsB to be compliant with the TPC Benchmark™ B standard. Comparison of price/performance results disclosed in one country many not be meaningful in another country because of pricing and product differences.

This benchmark uses a single, simple, update-intensive transaction to load the system under test (SUT). Thus the workload is intended to reflect the database aspects of an application, but does not reflect the entire range of OLTP requirements typically characterized by terminal and network input/output, and by multiple transaction types of varying complexities. The single transaction type provides a simple, repeatable unit of work, and is designed to exercise the basic components of a database system.

The extent to which a customer can achieve the results reported by a vendor is highly dependent on how closely TPC Benchmark™ B approximates the customer application. Relative performance of systems derived from TPC Benchmark™ B do not necessarily hold for other workloads or environments. Extrapolations to unlike environments are not recommended.

A full disclosure report of the implementation details, as specified in Clause 10, must be made available along with the reported results.

Benchmark results are highly dependent upon workload, specific application requirements, and systems design and implementation. Relative system performance will vary as a result of these and other factors. Therefore TPC Benchmark™ B should not be used as a substitute for a specific customer application benchmarking when critical capacity planning and/or product evaluation decisions are contemplated.

---

While separated from the main text for readability, "comments" are a part of the standard and must be enforced. The sample implementation included as Appendix A is provided only as an example and is specifically not part of the standard.

---

## CLAUSE 1: Transaction Profile

## 1.1   The Application Environment

**1.1.1**   This benchmark is stated in terms of a hypothetical bank. The bank has one or more branches. Each branch has multiple tellers. The bank has many customers, each with an account. The database represents the cash position of each entity (branch, teller, and account) and a history of recent transactions run by the bank. The transaction represents the work done when a customer makes a deposit or a withdrawal against his account. The transaction is performed by a teller at some branch. These functions are enumerated in Clause 1.2.

**1.1.2**   The database may be implemented using any commercially available database management system (DBMS), database server, file system, etc. The terms "file/table", "record/row" and "field/column" are used in this document only as examples of physical and logical data structures.

If the application environment contains software that routes or organizes the execution of transactions (e.g., a transaction processing monitor), the software must be a generally available, commercial product that is fully supported as defined in Clause 9.

**Comment:** It is the intent that special purpose transaction processing monitors developed specifically for benchmarking or limited use not be utilized.

**1.1.3**   Implementors of this benchmark are permitted many possible system designs, insofar as they adhere to the standard model described and illustrated in Clause 8.

## 1.2    The Transaction Profile

Given Aid, Tid, Bid, Delta by driver (see Clause 1.3 and 8):

```
BEGIN TRANSACTION
    Update Account where Account_ID = Aid:
        Read Account_Balance from Account
        Set Account_Balance = Account_Balance + Delta
        Write Account_Balance to Account
    Write to History:
        Aid, Tid, Bid, Delta, Time_stamp
    Update Teller where Teller_ID = Tid:
        Set Teller_Balance = Teller_Balance + Delta
        Write Teller_Balance to Teller
    Update Branch where Branch_ID = Bid:
        Set Branch_Balance = Branch_Balance + Delta
        Write Branch_Balance to Branch
COMMIT TRANSACTION
Return Account_Balance to driver
```

Aid (Account_ID), Tid (Teller_ID), and Bid (Branch_ID) are keys to the relevant records/rows (see Clause 3.2).

## 1.3    Transaction Inputs and Outputs

**1.3.1**    For each transaction, the driver shall present to the SUT (see Clause 8) at least four distinct fields including Account_ID, Teller_ID, Branch_ID, and Delta. Branch_ID in the input is the identifier of the branch where the teller is located.

**1.3.2**    Each transaction shall return to the driver the Account_Balance resulting from successful commit of the transaction.

**Comment:**  It is the intent of this clause that the account balance in the database be returned to the driver, i.e., that the application retrieve the account balance.

**1.3.3**    The generation of input fields is detailed in Clause 5.

## 1.4    Specific Non-Requirements

**1.4.1**    The order of the data manipulations within the transaction is immaterial, and is left to the latitude of the test sponsor, as long as the transaction profile is functionally equivalent to the one outlined in Clause 1.2.

**1.4.2**    The transaction profile does not require that the SUT (see Clause 8) return the teller and branch balances to the driver.

## CLAUSE 2: Transaction System Properties

## 2.1 The ACID Properties

**2.1.1** The ACID (Atomicity, Consistency, Isolation, and Durability) properties of transaction processing systems must be supported by the system under test during the running of this benchmark. It is the intent of this section to informally define the ACID properties and to specify a series of tests that must be performed to demonstrate that these properties are met.

**2.1.2** No finite series of tests can prove that the ACID properties are fully supported. Passing the specified tests is a necessary, but not sufficient, condition for meeting the ACID requirements.

**2.1.3** All mechanisms needed to insure full ACID properties must be enabled during both the measurement and test periods. For example, if the system under test relies on undo logs, then logging must be enabled even though no transactions are aborted during the measurement period. When this benchmark is implemented on a distributed system, tests must be performed to verify that home and remote transactions, including remote transactions that are processed on two nodes, satisfy the ACID properties. (See Clause 5 for the definition of home and remote transactions.)

## 2.2 Atomicity Requirements

**2.2.1** *Atomicity Property Definition*

The system under test must guarantee that transactions are atomic; the system will either perform all individual operations on the data, or will assure that no partially-completed operations leave any effects on the data.

**2.2.2** *Atomicity Tests*

**2.2.2.1** Perform the standard TPC Benchmark™ B transaction (see Clause 1.2) for a randomly selected account and verify that the appropriate records have been changed in the Account, Branch, Teller, and History files/tables.

**2.2.2.2** Perform the standard TPC Benchmark™ B transaction for a randomly selected account, substituting an ABORT of the transaction for the COMMIT of the transaction. Verify that the appropriate records have not been changed in the Account, Branch, Teller, and History files/tables.

## 2.3    Consistency Requirements

**2.3.1**    *Consistency Property Definition*

Consistency is the property of the application that requires any execution of the transaction to take the database from one consistent state to another.

**2.3.2**    *Consistency Conditions*

A consistent state for the TPC Benchmark™ B database is defined to exist when:

a.  the sum of the account balances is equal to the sum of the teller balances, which is equal to the sum of the branch balances;

b.  for all branches, the sum of the teller balances within a branch is equal to the branch balance;

c.  the history file has one logical record added for each committed transaction, none for any aborted transaction, and the sum of the deltas in the records added to the history file equals the sum of the deltas for all committed transactions.

If data is replicated, each copy must not violate these conditions.

**2.3.3**    *Consistency Tests*

Due to the large size of the Account file/table, no test of its consistency is specified. To verify the consistency of the Branch, Teller, and History files, perform the following (Clauses 2.3.3.1 through 2.3.3.3 are meant to be performed in sequence):

**2.3.3.1**    Verify that the Branch and Teller files are initially consistent by performing the following steps:

Step 1:    Determine the balance of each branch as reflected in the branch file.

Step 2:    For each branch, calculate the branch balance by summing the balances of the tellers associated with the branch.

Step 3:    Verify that the balance of each branch as obtained from Steps 1 and 2 is the same.

**2.3.3.2**    Verify that the Branch and Teller files are still consistent after applying transactions to the database by performing the following steps:

Step 1:    Compute the initial sum of the branch balances for later use.

Step 2:    Count the number of records in the History file and sum the deltas in the History file. (The file may be empty).

Step 3:     Using the standard driving mechanism, submit a number of standard TPC Benchmark™ B transactions equal to at least ten times the number of tellers and note the number of transactions that are reported as committed. For example, a 100 tpsB (1000 teller) system must submit at least 10,000 transactions. If the number of committed transactions is not equal to the number of submitted transactions, explain why.

Step 4:     Re-verify the consistency of the Branch and Teller files by repeating Clause 2.3.3.1.

Step 5:     Compute the final sum of the branch balances for later use.

**2.3.3.3**     Verify that the History file is consistent by performing the following steps:

Step 1:     Count the number of records in the History file and sum the deltas.

Step 2:     Verify that the count equals the original count from Clause 2.3.3.2, Step 2, plus the number of transactions reported as committed in Clause 2.3.3.2, Step 3. (The History file should contain one record for each committed transaction and should not contain a record for any aborted transaction.)

Step 3:     Verify that the difference between the sum of the final and initial deltas in the History file is equal to the difference between the sum of the final and initial branch balances.

## 2.4     Isolation Requirements

### 2.4.1     *Isolation Property Definition*

Operations of concurrent transactions must yield results which are indistinguishable from the results which would be obtained by forcing each transaction to be serially executed to completion in some order.

This property is commonly called serializability. Sufficient conditions must be enabled at either the system or application level to ensure serializability of transactions under any mix of arbitrary transactions, not just TPC Benchmark™ B transactions. The system or application must have full serializability enabled, i.e., repeated reads of the same records within any committed transaction must have returned identical data when run concurrently with any mix of arbitrary transactions.

### 2.4.2     *Isolation Tests*

For conventional locking schemes, isolation should be tested as described below, where transactions 1 and 2 are versions of the standard TPC Benchmark™ B transaction. Systems that implement other isolation schemes may require different validation techniques. It is the responsibility of the test sponsor to disclose those techniques and the tests for them.

**2.4.2.1**    Isolation Test for Completed Transactions (conventional locking schemes):

Start transaction 1.
Stop transaction 1 immediately prior to COMMIT.
Start transaction 2.
Transaction 2 attempts to update the same account record as transaction 1.
Verify that transaction 2 waits.
Allow transaction 1 to complete.  Transaction 2 should now complete.
Verify that the account balance reflects the results of both updates.

**2.4.2.2**    Isolation Test for Aborted Transactions (conventional locking schemes):

Start transaction 1.
Stop transaction 1 immediately prior to COMMIT.
Start transaction 2.
Transaction 2 attempts to update the same account record as transaction 1.
Verify that transaction 2 waits.
Abort transaction 1.  Transaction 2 should now complete.
Verify that the account balance reflects the results of transaction 2's update only.

**2.4.2.3**    Repeat Clauses 2.4.2.1 and 2.4.2.2 for the branch and teller files.

## 2.5    Durability Requirements

The tested system must guarantee the ability to preserve the effects of committed transactions and insure database consistency after recovery from any one of the failures listed below in Clause 2.5.3.

**Comment:**  No system provides complete durability, i.e., durability under all possible types of failures.  The specific set of single failures addressed in Clause 2.5.3 is deemed sufficiently significant to justify demonstration of durability across such failures.

### 2.5.1    *Durable Medium Definition*

A durable medium is a data storage medium that is either:

a.  an inherently non-volatile medium, e.g., magnetic disk, magnetic tape, optical disk, etc., or

b.  a volatile medium with its own self-contained power supply that will retain and permit the transfer of data, before any data is lost, to an inherently non-volatile medium after the failure of external power.

A configured and priced Uninterruptible Power Supply (UPS) is not considered external power.

**Comment:**  A durable medium can fail; this is usually protected against by replication on a second durable medium (e.g., mirroring) or logging to another durable medium.  Memory can be considered a durable medium if it can preserve data long enough to satisfy the requirement stated in (b) above. For example, memory can be considered a durable medium if it is accompanied by an uninterruptible power supply and the contents can be transferred to an inherently non-volatile medium during the failure. Note that no distinction is made between main memory and memory performing similar permanent or temporary data storage in other parts of the system, e.g., disk controller caches.

### 2.5.2   *Committed Property Definition*

A transaction is considered committed when the transaction manager component of the system has written the commit record(s) associated with the transaction to a durable medium.

**Comment 1:**   Transactions can be committed without the driver subsequently receiving notification of that fact, since a failure may occur after the transaction commits but before the driver records the transaction.

**Comment 2:** Although the order of operations in the transaction profile (see Clause 1.2) is immaterial, the return of the Account_Balance to the driver cannot begin until the commit operation has successfully completed.

### 2.5.3   *List of single failures*

**2.5.3.1**   Permanent irrecoverable failure of any single durable medium containing database, ABTH files/tables, or recovery log data.

**Comment:** If main memory is used as a durable medium, then it must be considered as a potential single point of failure. Sample mechanisms to survive single durable medium failures are: i) database archiving in conjunction with a redo (after image) log, and ii) mirrored durable media. If memory is the durable medium and mirroring is the mechanism used to ensure durability, then the mirrored memories must be independently powered.

**2.5.3.2** Instantaneous interruption (system crash/system hang) in processing which requires system reboot to recover.

**Comment:** This implies abnormal system shutdown which requires loading of a fresh copy of the operating system from the boot device. It does not necessarily imply loss of volatile memory. When the recovery mechanism relies on the pre-failure contents of volatile memory, the means used to avoid the loss of volatile memory, e.g., uninterruptible power supply, must be included in the system cost calculation. A sample mechanism to survive an instantaneous interruption in processing is an undo/redo log.

**2.5.3.3** Failure of all or part of memory (loss of contents).

**Comment:** This implies that all or part of memory has failed. This may be caused by a loss of external power or the permanent failure of a memory board.

**2.5.4**    The recovery mechanism cannot use the contents of the History file to support the durability property.

**2.5.5**    Rollforward recovery from an archive database copy, e.g., a copy taken prior to the run, using redo log data is not acceptable as the recovery mechanism in the case of failures listed in Clauses 2.5.3.2 and 2.5.3.3. Note that "checkpoints", "control points", "consistency points", etc., of the database taken during a run are not considered to be archives.

**2.5.6**    *Durability Tests*

The intent of these tests is to demonstrate that all transactions which have returned to the driver have in fact been committed in spite of any single failure from the list in Clause 2.5.3.

It is not required to perform these tests under a full driver load or with a fully scaled database. However, the test sponsor must state that to the best of their knowledge a fully loaded and fully scaled test would also pass the durability tests. It is required to use the same SUT configuration and database partitioning as was used in the measurement part of the test. Furthermore, at the time of the induced failures, it is required to have multiple home and remote transactions (see Clause 5) in progress and distributed systems must have distributed transactions in progress as well.

For each of the failure types defined in Clause 2.5.3, perform the following steps:

Step 1:    Perform Step 1 of the History file Consistency Test in Clause 2.3.3.3.

Step 2:    Start submitting TPC Benchmark™ B transactions. On the driver system, record committed transactions in a "success" file.

Step 3:    Cause a failure selected from the list in Clause 2.5.3.

Step 4:    Restart the system under test using normal recovery procedures.

Step 5:    Compare the contents of the "success" file and the History file to verify that every record in the "success" file has a corresponding record in the History file. Also verify that the number of records in the History file is greater or equal to the original count, as obtained in Step 1, plus the number of records in the "success" file. If there is an inequality, the History file must contain additional records. (Comment: This difference should be due only to transactions which were committed on the system under test, but which were not recorded by the driver before the failure.)

Step 6:    Perform the consistency test on the Branch and Teller files as specified in Clause 2.3.3.2.

**Comment:**  If the driver and "success" file are on the SUT, the sponsor must document the method used to make the "success" file an accurate representation of the completed transactions.

## CLAUSE 3: Logical Database Design

### 3.1 Entities, Relationships, and Characteristics

**3.1.1** The components of the database are defined to consist of four separate and individual files/tables, Account, Branch, Teller, and History. The relationships among these files/tables are defined in the following entity/relationship diagram and are subject to the business rules specified in Clause 3.1.2. This diagram is a logical description and has no implication for physical implementation.

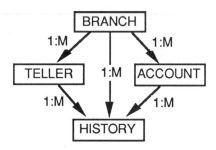

**Comment:** The clustering of records within the database (as in hierarchic or CODASYL databases) is not excluded. A view which represents the records/rows to avoid read/writes is excluded.

**3.1.2** The entities in Clause 3.1.1 are subject to the following business rules:

- All branches must have the same number of tellers.
- All branches must have the same number of accounts.

Other business rules specified elsewhere in this document also apply, e.g., consistency conditions in Clause 2.3.2.

**Comment:** There is no intent to model an environment in which accounts and tellers can be moved from branch to branch.

### 3.2 Record Layouts and Sizing

**3.2.1** In order for the transaction to represent a similar amount of work to all the systems, it is important that the records handled by the database servers, file systems, etc. be of the same size. Therefore, the records/rows must be stored in an uncompressed format. Where it is impossible to turn compression off, it is incumbent upon the test sponsor to store the records/rows using the minimum lengths specified in Clauses 3.2.2 through 3.2.5. Any space with unspecified values in the record/row descriptions in Clauses 3.2.2 through 3.2.5 may be used for additional user data; the storage for the access path (e.g., B-tree index structure) or any other data used by the database server may not be counted against the minimum record length specifications.

**3.2.2**   Account records/rows must be at least 100 bytes in length and contain the following data in any order or representation:

| | |
|---|---|
| Account_ID | Must uniquely identify the record/row across the range of accounts. The Account_ID must be unique across the entire database. |
| Branch_ID | Branch where account is held. |
| Account_Balance | Must be capable of representing at least 10 significant decimal digits plus sign. |

**3.2.3**   Branch records/rows must be at least 100 bytes in length and contain the following data in any order or representation:

| | |
|---|---|
| Branch_ID | Must uniquely identify the record/row across the range of branches. |
| Branch_Balance | Must be capable of representing at least 10 significant decimal digits plus sign. |

**3.2.4**   Teller records/rows must be at least 100 bytes in length and contain the following data in any order or representation:

| | |
|---|---|
| Teller_ID | Must uniquely identify the record/row across the range of tellers. |
| Branch_ID | Branch where the teller is located. |
| Teller_Balance | Must be capable of representing at least 10 significant decimal digits plus sign. |

**3.2.5**   History records/rows must be at least 50 bytes in length and contain the following data in any order or representation:

| | |
|---|---|
| Account_ID | Account updated by transaction. |
| Teller_ID | Teller involved in transaction. |
| Branch_ID | Branch associated with Teller. |
| Amount | Amount (delta) specified by transaction. Must be capable of representing at least 10 significant decimal digits plus sign. |
| Time_Stamp | A date and time taken between BEGIN TRANSACTION and COMMIT TRANSACTION. It must be capable of representing Date as YY:MM:DD and Time with a resolution of at least HH:MM:SS. |

B

**3.3** The size of the identifier in each record/row must be sufficient for the size of the configured system (see Clause 4.2). Thus for a 100 tpsB test, the accounts file/table must include 10 million records/rows, and hence the account identifier, i.e., the Account_ID, must be able to represent at least 10 million unique values.

**3.4** The record identifiers of the Account/Branch/Teller (ABT) files/tables must not directly represent the physical disk addresses of the records or any offsets thereof. The application may not reference records using relative record numbers since they are simply offsets from the beginning of a file. This does not preclude hashing schemes or other file organizations which have provisions for adding, deleting, and modifying records in the ordinary course of processing. This clause places no restrictions on the History file.

**Comment:** It is the intent of this clause that the application executing the transaction not use physical identifiers, but logical identifiers for all accesses; i.e., it is not legitimate for the application to build a "translation table" of logical-to-physical addresses and use it for enhancing performance.

**3.5** While inserts and deletes are not performed on the ABT files/tables, the SUT must not be configured to take special advantage of this fact.

**B**

# CLAUSE 4: Scaling Rules

**4.1** The intent of the scaling rules is to maintain a fixed relationship between the transaction load presented to the system under test and the size of the files/tables accessed by the transactions.

**4.2** For each nominal transaction-per-second configured, the test must use a minimum of (see Clause 4.4):

| | |
|---|---|
| Account records/rows | 100,000 |
| Teller records/rows | 10 |
| Branch records/rows | 1 |
| History record/rows | (See Clause 4.3) |

**4.2.1** The ratio of the values in Clause 4.2 must be maintained. Should any value be exceeded, the others must be increased proportionately.

**4.3** The history file/table should be large enough to hold all history data generated during the steady state portion of the test. However, for the purpose of computing price per tpsB, storage must be maintained for the number of history records specified in Clause 9.2.4.1. This includes the overhead space required to manage and access the data as well as data space. The system under test must be physically configurable to support the amount of storage specified in Clause 9.2.4.1.

**4.4** Reported tpsB may not exceed the configured (nominal) rate represented by the file/table sizes in Clause 4.2. While the reported tpsB may fall short of the maximum allowed by the configured system, the price per tpsB computation must report the price of the system as actually configured.

# CLAUSE 5: Distribution, Partitioning, and Transaction Generation

## 5.1 Types of Transactions and Nodes

**5.1.1** A transaction is **home** if the account is held at the same branch as the teller of the transaction (see Clause 3.1.1).

**5.1.2** A transaction is **remote** if the branch where the account is held is not the same as the branch of the transaction's teller.

**5.1.3** A **remote** transaction may be processed entirely on a single-node or be distributed between two separate nodes. If the account branch and the teller branch exist on different nodes, the node containing the teller branch is referred to as the **native** node, and the node containing the account branch (the remote branch) is referred to as the **foreign** node.

## 5.2 Partitioning Rules

**5.2.1** Horizontal partitioning of files/tables is allowed. For example, groups of history records/rows may be assigned to different files, disks or areas. If this partitioning is not transparent to the logic of the transaction program, details of the partitioning and transaction program logic must be disclosed

**5.2.2** Vertical partitioning of files/tables is not allowed. For example, groups of fields/columns of one record/row may not be assigned to files, disks, or areas different from those storing the other fields/columns of that record/row. The record must be processed as a series of contiguous fields. Note: This restriction is included to normalize vendor benchmarks, since it is the intent of the standard that each TPC Benchmark™ B data operation accesses approximately 100 bytes, not some smaller, proper subset.

## 5.3    Transaction Input Generation

**5.3.1**    The transaction input fields (Account_ID, Branch_ID, Teller_ID, and Delta) must conform to the database fields definition of Clause 3.

**5.3.2**    Multiple driver processes (see Clause 8) must produce independent random ID sequences to avoid a pseudo-random sequence within one driver process being replicated in any other driver process.

**5.3.3**    *Teller_ID Generation*

For each transaction the driver (or drivers) must choose a teller at random from some range of the Teller_ID values without regard for any concurrently pending transactions. For single node systems, the teller must be randomly chosen from the entire range of tellers. In the case of a multinode system in which the database is partitioned among nodes of a cluster or network, the teller may be randomly chosen from a subset of the total range of tellers corresponding to all the tellers on a single node, but no fewer.

**5.3.4**    *Branch_ID Generation*

Given the randomly chosen teller from Clause 5.3.3, the corresponding branch is determined (i.e., each teller resides at a known branch).

**5.3.5**    *Account_ID Generation*

The Account_ID is generated as follows:

- A random number X is generated within [0,1]

- If X<0.85 or branches = 1, a random Account_ID is selected over all <Branch_ID> accounts.

- If X>=0.85 and branches > 1, a random Account_ID is selected over all non-<Branch_ID> accounts.

**Comment 1:** This algorithm guarantees that, if there is more than one branch in the database, then an average of 15% of remote transactions is presented to the SUT. Due to statistical variations during a finite measurement period, the actual measured proportion of remote transactions may vary around 15%. Actual measured values must be within 14% to 16% for the set of transactions processed during the measurement interval (see Clauses 6.1 and 7.2).

**Comment 2:** In a distributed system, the 85-15 rule should be implemented so that the ratio of remote-branch transactions occurring on a foreign node is proportional to the actual distribution of accounts across the nodes. For example, if 3000 branches are divided evenly between two nodes, approximately 7.5% (1500/2999 * 15%) of the transactions cause cross-node activities. With the same 3000 branches divided among three nodes, approximately 10% (2000/2999 * 15%) cause cross-node activities, etc. Note that 2999 is used since the home branch by definition does not qualify.

**5.3.6**    *Delta Amount*

The Delta amount field is a random value within [-999999, +999999] selected independently for each transaction.

**5.3.7**    *Random Distribution*

All transactions during steady state should be uniformly distributed over all Teller_IDs, within normal statistical variations.

## 5.4    Definition of "Random"

Within Clause 5, the term random means independently selected and uniformly distributed.

## CLAUSE 6: Residence Time

## 6.1    Measurement Interval and Timing

**6.1.1**    In this clause, the term "measurement interval" is the steady state period (see Clause 7.1) during the execution of the benchmark for which the test sponsor is reporting a tpsB number and residence time data. The term "completed transaction" is a transaction which has been successfully committed at the SUT and whose output has been recorded at the driver (see Clause 8.4).

**6.1.2**    Each transaction must be individually timed.

## 6.2    Residence Time Definition

Residence time of a transaction is defined by:

$$RT = T2 - T1$$

where T1 and T2 are defined as:

T1 = time stamp taken by the driver before supplying transactional inputs to the SUT

T2 = time stamp taken by the driver after receiving corresponding response

The resolution of the time stamps must be at least 0.1 seconds.

**Comment:** Since the driver program does not represent a user terminal, residence times achieved in this benchmark do not represent response times at the stated throughput levels in an OLTP environment.

## 6.3    Residence Time Constraint

90% of all transactions started and completed during the measurement interval must have a Residence Time of less than 2 seconds.

**Comment:** This residence time criterion has been chosen to provide a single criterion for all configurations, and in particular for very-low throughput systems.

## 6.4    Computation of tpsB Rating

**6.4.1**    The reported tpsB is the total number of committed transactions which both started and completed during the measurement interval, divided by the elapsed time of the interval.

**6.4.2**    For reporting the throughput of the SUT in units of transactions per second, the terminology should be "tpsB". This metric is NOT comparable to other TPS metrics except "tpsB".

**6.4.3**    Reported tpsB numbers must be expressed to a minimum precision of three significant digits, rounded down.

## 6.5    Interpolation and Extrapolation Prohibited

The reported tpsB rate must be measured rather than interpolated or extrapolated. For example, suppose 9.13 tpsB is measured during which 90% of the transactions completed in less than 1.7 seconds and 9.77 tpsB is measured during which 90% of the transactions completed in less than 2.3 seconds. Then the reported tpsB is 9.13 rather than some interpolated value between 9.13 and 9.77.

## 6.6    Required Reporting

**6.6.1**    The frequency distribution of residence times of transactions started and completed during the measurement interval must be reported. The range of the X axis must be from 0 to 5 seconds residence time. At least 20 equal non-overlapping intervals must be reported. A sample is shown in Graph 1. The maximum and average residence times must also be reported.

Graph 1: Residence Time Distribution

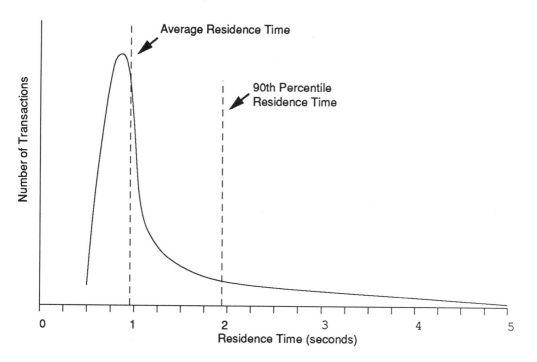

6.6.2    The percentage of **home** transactions must be between 84% and 86% and the percentage of **remote** transactions must be between 14% and 16% of the total completed transactions in the measurement interval. (See Clauses 5.1 and 5.3.5.) Report the percentage of transactions that started and completed in the measurement interval that are home and remote transactions.

6.6.3    The percentage of transactions that started but did not complete during the measurement interval must be less than 1% of the total that started. This number must be reported.

6.6.4    For systems that process remote transactions on two nodes (see Clause 5.1.3), report the percentage of **remote** transactions that started and completed during the measurement interval and involved a **foreign** node. Also, report the frequency distribution, maximum, and average residence times of these transactions.

B

### 6.6.5  TPS Stability Test

It must be demonstrated that the configuration, when tested at the reported tpsB rate, has the property of stable throughput despite small changes in the number of concurrently active transactions. This is to detect atypical throughput characteristics of the reported configuration.

**Comment:** In well-behaved systems, increases in the number of concurrently active transactions at the throughput limit result in increases in residence time while throughput (i.e., TPS) remains approximately constant.

For the reported tpsB rate T and residence time R, the average number of concurrently active transactions, C, can be calculated as:

$$C = T \cdot R$$

where:

$C$ = average number of concurrently active transactions

$T$ = reported tpsB rate

$R$ = average residency time for transactions in the measured interval

If $T_R$ is the reported tpsB rate and $R_R$ is the reported average residence time, then the corresponding $C_R$ must be reported. Also, two additional values of C must be reported and shown graphically as in the example below. These are $C_L$ and $C_H$, and must be in the following range:

$$.7\, C_R \le C_L \le .8\, C_R$$
$$C_H \ge 1.2\, C_R$$

Examples of how these two values are obtained include varying the number of transaction generators and changing the number of configured threads in a TP monitor.

**Comment:** $C_H$ must be measured on the same configuration as $C_R$, but the corresponding $T_H$ is not required to meet the residence time constraint.

An example of these results is illustrated in Graph 2.

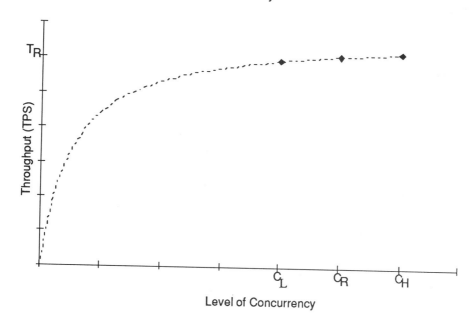

Graph 2: TPS vs. Concurrency

# CLAUSE 7: Duration of Test

## 7.1    Steady State

The test must be conducted in a "steady state" condition that represents the true "sustainable performance" of the system under test (SUT).

Although the measurement period as described below may be as short as 15 minutes, the system under test must be configured so that it is possible to run the test at the reported tpsB for a continuous period of at least eight hours. For example, the media used to store at least eight hours of log data must be configured, if required to recover from any single point of failure (see Clause 2.5.3.1).

**Comment:** An example of a configuration that would not comply is one where a log file is allocated such that better performance is achieved during the measured portion of the test than during the remaining portion of an eight-hour test, perhaps because a dedicated device was used initially but space on a shared device is used later in the full eight-hour test.

## 7.2    Duration and Requirements

The measurement period must:

- Begin after the system reaches sustained "steady state";
- Be long enough to generate reproducible tpsB results;
- Extend uninterrupted for at least 15 minutes and no longer than 1 hour;
- For systems which defer database writes to durable media, recovery time from instantaneous interruptions (as defined in Clause 2.5.3.2) must not be appreciably longer at the end of the measurement period than at the beginning of the measurement period.

**Comment 1:** "Steady state" is easy to define, e.g., "sustained throughput," but difficult to prove. The test sponsor (and/or the auditor) is required to report the method used to verify steady state sustainable performance and the reproducibility of test results. The auditor is encouraged to use available monitoring tools to help determine steady state.

**Comment 2:** The intent of this clause is to require that writes to disk or other durable media that would normally occur during a sustained test of at least eight hours duration (such as checkpointing, writing redo/undo log records to disk, etc.), are included in the measurement interval and are not deferred until after the measurement is complete.

**Note to Comment 2:** Some systems defer writes of changed pages/blocks to the durable-medium-resident database. Such systems can maintain buffers/caches in a volatile medium (e.g.,memory) for use by the DBMS, operating system, and disk control system, which are not synchronized with the durable-medium-resident database. Re-synchronizing these caches with the durable-medium-resident database is typically accomplished via "control points," "checkpoints," or "consistency points."

# CLAUSE 8: SUT Driver Definition

## 8.1    Models of the Target System

The driver presents transactions to the system under test (SUT). The SUT executes these transactions and replies to the driver. There are two forms of drivers: an **internal driver** resides on the SUT hardware and software. An **external driver** resides on a separate hardware and software complex, and typically communicates with the SUT via a communications network using a client/server remote procedure call mechanism. The following diagrams illustrate these two options. The driver is the shaded area and the SUT is the unshaded area. The diagram also depicts the driver/SUT boundary (see Clauses 8.3 and 8.4) where residence time is measured:

Items marked by an "*" are optional.

Two internal driver/SUT systems (a "mainframe" and a client/server configuration):

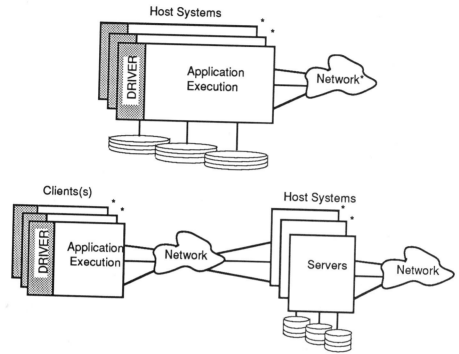

An external driver/SUT system:

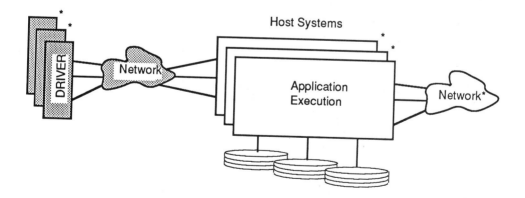

B

## 8.2 Test Configuration

The test configuration consists of the following elements:

- System Under Test (SUT)
- Driver System

## 8.3 System Under Test (SUT) Definition

The SUT consists of:

- One or more processing units (e.g., hosts, front-ends, workstations, etc.) which will run the application described in Clause 1, and whose aggregate performance will be described by the metric tpsB.
- Any front-end systems needed to communicate with an external driver system.
- The host system(s) including hardware and software supporting the database employed in the benchmark.
- The hardware and software components of all networks required to connect and support the SUT components.
- Data storage media sufficient to satisfy both the scaling rules in Clause 4 and the ACID properties of Clause 2. The data storage media must hold all the data described in Clause 3 and be intimately attached to the processing units(s).

## 8.4 Driver Definition

**8.4.1** As stated in Clause 8.1, an internal or external driver presents a transaction load to the SUT.

**8.4.2** The driver is a logical entity that can be implemented using one or more physical programs, processes, or systems and performs the following functions:

- Supplies the following transactional inputs to the SUT: Account_ID, Teller_ID, Branch_ID, and delta, and no other information;
- Receives transaction responses (new Account_Balance) from the SUT;
- Takes timestamps (T1 and T2) and records either T1 and T2 or RT as defined in Clause 6.2;
- May do statistical accounting of transaction residence times.

**8.4.3**   The driver, whether internal or external, is expected to do only the functions specified in Clause 8.4.2. Any other function performed by the driver must be: (1) justified as to why it is included (e.g., it is an integral part of a commercial driver product); (2) demonstrated to not improve performance. In addition, the code for any functionality not specified in Clause 8.4.2 must be disclosed unless it can be demonstrated to be a proprietary part of a commercially available and supported product. The intent is to prevent the use of special purpose driver code to enhance performance.

**8.4.4**   Any software or hardware used exclusively by the external driver (i.e., not used by the SUT) is not considered as part of the SUT.

**Comment:** The intent is that external drivers not priced with the SUT are allowed to perform only the functions outlined in Clause 8.4.2. For example, inclusion of procedure names or data locations by the external driver is prohibited.

## 8.5   Further Requirements on the SUT and Driver System

**8.5.1**   *No Database on External Driver System*

Copies of any part of the tested data base or file system or its data structures, indices, etc., may not be present on the external driver during the test. Synchronization between driver and SUT (e.g., through known initial values for ABT balances) is equally disallowed.

**8.6**   Any TPC-B results are comparable to other TPC-B results regardless of the form of driver (internal or external).

## CLAUSE 9: Pricing

## 9.1   Pricing Methodology

**9.1.1**   The intent of this section is to define the methodology to be used in calculating the price/tpsB. The fundamental premise is that what is tested and/or emulated is priced and what is priced is tested and/or emulated.

**9.1.2**   The proposed system to be priced is the aggregation of the SUT components that would be offered to achieve the reported performance level. Calculation of the priced system consists of:

a.  Price of the SUT as tested and defined in Clause 8.3;

b.  Price of on-line storage for 30 days of history records;

c. Price of additional products that are required for the operation, administration or maintenance of the priced system;

d. Price of additional products required for application development.

**9.1.3**   Pricing methodology assumptions:

- All hardware and software used in the calculations must be announced and generally orderable by customers, with a full disclosure of the committed delivery date for general availability of products not already generally released;

- Generally available discounts for the priced configuration are permissible;

- Generally available packaged pricing is acceptable;

- Local retail pricing and discount structure should be used in each country for which results are published.

- Price should be represented by the currency with which the customer would purchase the system.

For test sponsors who have only indirect sales channels, pricing must be actual generally available pricing from indirect channels which meet all other requirements of Clause 9.

**Comment 1:** The intent of the pricing methodology is to allow packaging and pricing that is generally available to customers, and to explicitly exclude promotional and/or limited availability offerings.

**Comment 2:** Revenue discounts based on total price are permissible. Any discount must be only for the configuration being priced and cannot be based on past or future purchases; individually negotiated discounts are not permitted; special customer discounts (e.g., GSA schedule, educational schedule) are not permitted.

**Comment 3:** The intent is to benchmark the actual system which the customer would purchase. However, it is realized that, typically, vendors will announce new products and disclose benchmark results before the products have actually shipped. This is allowed, but it specifically excludes any use of "one of a kind" hardware/software configurations which the vendor does not intend to ship in the future. Products must be generally available in the country where the SUT is priced.

**9.1.4**   For publishing in a country other than the country for which the results are originally published, it is permitted to substitute local components different from the original report, provided the substituted products are sold to the same product description or specification.

**Comment:** The intention is to encourage local country pricing by allowing substitution of equipment for country-specific reasons such as voltage, product numbering, industrial/safety, keyboard differences, etc., which do not affect performance.

## 9.2    Priced System

### 9.2.1    *SUT*

The entire price of the SUT as configured during the test must be used, including all hardware (new purchase price), software (license charges) and hardware/software maintenance charges over a period of 5 years (60 months).

**Comment 1:**  The intent is to price the tested system at the full price a customer would pay.  Specifically prohibited are the assumption of other purchases, other sites with similar systems, or any other assumption which relies on the principle that the customer has made any other purchase from the vendor.  This is a one-time, stand-alone purchase.

**Comment 2:** Any usage pricing for TPC-B should be that the number of users is at least the level of concurrency ($C_R$), rounded up to the next integer.  (See Clause 6.6.5.)

**9.2.2**    The price of hardware and software used *exclusively* by the driver is not included in the price calculation.

### 9.2.3    *Network Pricing*

In a distributed system and in a client/server system, the cost of all communications components within the SUT excluding LAN or WAN direct connect cables must be priced.

**Comment:**  The intent is that all components including PADS (packet assemblers-disassemblers), modems, concentrators, multiplexors, etc., required to attach clients and servers or to attach network nodes should be priced.

### 9.2.4    *History Storage and Recovery Log Pricing*

**9.2.4.1**    Within the priced system, there must be sufficient on-line storage to support any expanding system files and durable history records/rows for 30 eight-hour days at the published tpsB rate (i.e., 30 x 8 x 60 x 60 = 864,000 records/rows per tpsB).

**Comment:**  On-line storage includes magnetic discs, magnetic tapes, optical discs, and any combination of these.  Storage is considered on-line if any record can be accessed randomly within one second.

**9.2.4.2**    For purposes of pricing storage for history records/rows, any unused on-line storage present in the SUT may count towards the history storage requirements. (However, note that unused storage may also be needed for expanding system files as required in Clauses 7.1 and 9.2.4.1.)

B

**9.2.4.3**   If it is necessary to price any additional storage devices to fulfill the thirty (30) day history storage requirement, such devices must be of the type(s) actually used in the SUT during the test, and must satisfy the normal system configuration rules.

**Comment:** The intent is to exclude unrealistic on-line storage devices or configurations from the pricing procedure.

**9.2.4.4**   The requirement to support 8 hours of recovery log data can be met with storage on any durable media (see Clause 2.5.1) if all data required for recovery from failures listed in Clauses 2.5.3.2 and 2.5.3.3 are on-line.

**9.2.5**   *Additional Operational Components*

**9.2.5.1**   Additional products that might be included on a customer-installed configuration, such as operator consoles, magnetic tape drives and printers, are also to be included in the priced system if explicitly required for the operation, administration, or maintenance of the priced system.

**9.2.5.2**   Copies of the software on appropriate media, and a software load device if required for initial load or maintenance updates, must be included.

**9.2.5.3**   The price of an Uninterruptible Power Supply specifically contributing to a durability solution must be included (see Clause 2.5.3.2).

**9.2.6**   *Additional Software*

**9.2.6.1**   The price must include the software licenses necessary to create, compile, link, and execute this benchmark application, as well as all run-time licenses required to execute on host system(s) and connected workstations.

**9.2.6.2**   In the event the application code is developed on a system other than the SUT, the price of that system and any compilers and other software used must also be included as part of the priced system.

# 9.3   Maintenance

**9.3.1**   Hardware and software maintenance must be figured at a standard pricing which covers at least 5 days/week, 8 hours/day coverage, either on-site, or if available as standard offering, via a central support facility.  Hardware maintenance maximum response time must not exceed 4 hours on any part whose replacement is necessary for the resumption of operation.

**Comment:** Software maintenance means a standard offering which includes acknowledgement of new and existing problems within 4 hours and a commitment to fix defects within a reasonable time.

**9.3.2**    If central support is claimed, then the appropriate connection device, such as auto-dial modem, must be included in the hardware price.  Also any software required to run the connection to the central support, as well as any diagnostic software which the central support facility requires to be resident on the tested system, must not only be included in pricing, but must also be installed during the benchmark runs.

**9.3.3**    Software maintenance must include update distribution for both the software and documentation.  If software maintenance updates are separately priced, then pricing must include at least 3 updates over the 5 year period.

**Exception:**  In client/server designs based on workstations, maintenance and warranty terms for workstations must cover at a minimum a return for repair service.


# CLAUSE 10: Full Disclosure

## 10.1    Full Disclosure Report Requirements

A full disclosure report is required for results to be considered compliant with TPC Benchmark™ B specifications.

**Comment:**  The intent of this disclosure is for a customer to be able to replicate the results of this benchmark given the appropriate documentation and products.

A full disclosure report must include the following:

**10.1.1**    *General Items*

**10.1.1.1** A statement identifying the sponsor of the benchmark and any other companies who have participated.

**10.1.1.2** Program listing of application code and definition language statements for files/tables.

**10.1.1.3** Settings for all customer-tunable parameters and options which have been changed from the defaults found in actual products; including but not limited to:

• Database options;

• Recovery/commit options;

- Consistency/locking options;

- System parameters, application parameters, and configuration parameters.

Test sponsors may optionally provide a full list of all parameters and options.

**10.1.1.4** Configuration diagrams of both the benchmark configuration and the priced system, and a description of the differences.

### 10.1.2   *Clause 2 Related Items*

**10.1.2.1** Results of the ACIDity tests (specified in Clause 2) must describe how the requirements were met. If a database different from that which is measured is used for durability tests, the sponsor must include a statement that durability works on the fully loaded and fully scaled database.

### 10.1.3   *Clause 3 Related Items*

**10.1.3.1** The distribution across storage media of ABTH (Accounts, Branch, Teller, and History) files/tables and all logs must be explicitly depicted.

Provide two functional diagrams which show CPUs, storage devices, and the interconnections between these components. The first diagram must correspond to the benchmark configuration and the second diagram must correspond to the 30-day priced configuration. A separate pair of diagrams must be provided for each reported result. (The diagrams used for clause 10.1.1.4 may already contain this information. In this case, the additional data required below may optionally be shown in tabular form with references to these diagrams.)

As part of each diagram, show the percentage of the total physical database which resides on each storage device for each of the ABTH files and logs. For the benchmark configuration, show database allocation during 8-hour steady state. For the 30-day priced configuration, show database allocation including storage of 30 days of history records. Data which are duplicated (e.g., mirrored) on more than one device must be clearly labeled to show what is duplicated and on which devices.

Two examples are shown below.

**10.1.3.2** A description of how the database was populated, along with sample contents of each ABTH file/table to meet the requirements described in Clause 3.

**10.1.3.3** A statement of the type of database utilized, e.g., relational, Codasyl, flat file, etc.

### 10.1.4   *Clause 5 Related Items*

**10.1.4.1** The method of verification of the random number generator should be described.

# Example 1:

## Distribution of ABTH files and Logs in Benchmark Configuration

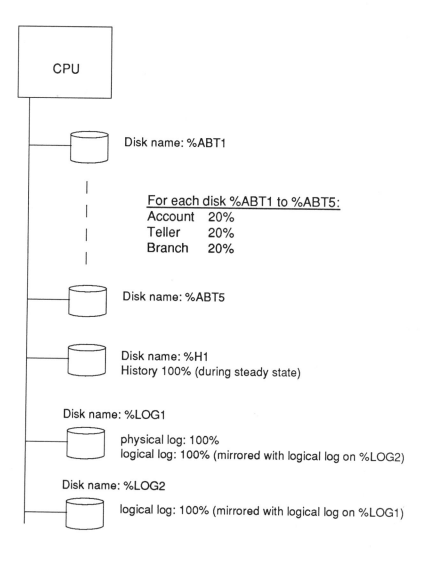

CPU

Disk name: %ABT1

For each disk %ABT1 to %ABT5:
Account    20%
Teller      20%
Branch     20%

Disk name: %ABT5

Disk name: %H1
History 100% (during steady state)

Disk name: %LOG1

physical log: 100%
logical log: 100% (mirrored with logical log on %LOG2)

Disk name: %LOG2

logical log: 100% (mirrored with logical log on %LOG1)

B

## Example 1 (cont.):

## Distribution of ABTH files and Logs in Priced Configuration

CPU

Disk name: %ABT1

For each disk %ABT1 to %ABT5:
Account  20%
Teller   20%
Branch   20%
History  10%

Disk name: %ABT5

Disk name: %H1

For each disk %H1 to %H5:
History   10%

Disk name: %H5

Disk name: %LOG1
physical log: 100%
logical log: 100% (mirrored with logical log on %LOG2)

Disk name: %LOG2
logical log: 100% (mirrored with logical log on %LOG1)

Example 2:

## Data Distribution in Benchmarked Configuration

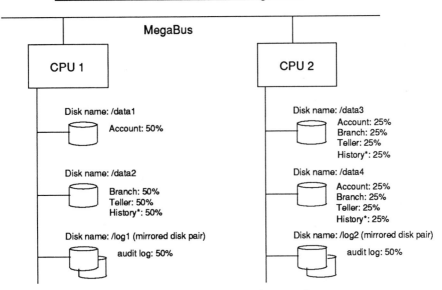

* Distribution of History records represents 8-hour steady state.

## Data Distribution in Priced Configuration

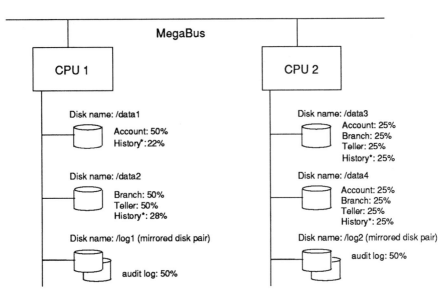

* Distribution of History records represents 90-day storage requirement.

B

**10.1.4.2** Vendors must clearly disclose if horizontal partitioning is used. Specifically, vendors must:

1. Describe textually the extent of transparency of the implementation.

2. Describe which tables/files were accessed using partitioning.

3. Describe how partitioned tables/files were accessed.

The intent of this clause is that details of non-transparent partitioning be disclosed in a manner understandable to non-programmer individuals (through use of flow charts, pseudo code, etc.).

**10.1.5**   *Clause 6 Related Items*

**10.1.5.1** Report all the data specified in Clause 6.6, including maximum and average residence time, as well as performance curves for number of transactions vs. residence time (see Clause 6.6.1) and throughput vs. level of concurrency for three data points (see Clause 6.6.5). Also, the sponsor must include the percentage of home and remote transactions, the number and percentage of in-process transactions, and the percentage of remote and foreign transactions, if applicable.

**10.1.6**   *Clause 7 Related Items*

**10.1.6.1** The method used to determine that the SUT had reached a steady state prior to commencing the measurement interval should be described.

**10.1.6.2** A description of how the work normally performed during a sustained test (for example checkpointing, writing redo/undo log records, etc., as required by Clause 7.2), actually occurred during the measurement interval.

**10.1.6.3** A description of the method used to determine the reproducibility of the measurement results.

**10.1.6.4** A statement of the duration of the measurement period for the reported tpsB (it should be at least 15 minutes and no longer than 1 hour).

**10.1.7**   *Clause 8 Related Items*

**10.1.7.1** If the driver is commercially available, then its inputs should be specified. Otherwise, a description of the driver should be supplied.

**10.1.7.2** A complete functional diagram of the hardware and software of the benchmark configuration including the driver must be provided. The sponsor must list all hardware and software functionality of the driver and its interface to the SUT.

**10.1.8**    *Clause 9 Related Items*

**10.1.8.1** A detailed list of hardware and software used in the priced system. Each item must have vendor part number, description, and release/revision level, and either general availability status or committed delivery date. If package-pricing is used, contents of the package must be disclosed.

**10.1.8.2** The total price of the entire configuration is required including: hardware, software, and maintenance charges. Separate component pricing is recommended. The basis of all discounts used shall be disclosed.

**10.1.8.3** A statement of the measured tpsB, and the calculated price/tpsB.

**10.1.8.4** Additional Clause 9 related items may be included in the full disclosure report for each country specific priced configuration. Country-specific pricing is subject to Clause 9.1.4.

**10.1.9**    *Clause 11 Related Items*

**10.1.9.1** If the benchmark has been independently audited, then the auditor's name, address, phone number, and a brief audit summary report indicating compliance must be included in the full disclosure report. A statement should be included, specifying when the complete audit report will become available and whom to contact in order to obtain a copy.

## 10.2    Availability of the Full Disclosure Report

The full disclosure report is to be readily available to the public at a reasonable charge, similar to charges for similar documents by that test sponsor. The report is to be made available when results are made public. In order to use the phrase "TPC Benchmark™ B", the full disclosure report must have been submitted to the TPC administrator as well as written permission to distribute same.

## 10.3    Revisions to the Full Disclosure Report

Revisions to the full disclosure documentation shall be handled as follows:

**10.3.1**    Fully documented price decreases can be reflected in a new published price/throughput. When cumulative price changes have resulted in an increase of 5% or more from the disclosed price/performance, the test sponsor must submit revised price/performance results to the TPC within 30 days of the effective date of the price changes to remain compliant. The benchmark need not be rerun to remain compliant.

**Comment:** The intent is that the published price/performance reflect actual current price/performance.

**10.3.2** Hardware or software product substitutions within the SUT require the benchmark to be rerun with the new components in order to re-establish compliance.

**10.3.3**   The revised report should be submitted as defined in Clause 10.2.

**10.3.4**   A report may be revised to add or delete Clause 9 related items for country-specific priced configurations.

**Comment:** During the normal product life cycle problems will be uncovered which require changes, sometimes referred to as ECOs, FCOs, Patches, Updates, etc. If any of these changes causes the tpsB rating of the system to change by more than 5%, then the test sponsor will be required to re-validate the benchmark results.

## 10.4   Official Language

**10.4.1**   The official full-disclosure report must be written in English but may be translated to additional languages.

## CLAUSE 11: Audit

**11.1**     An independent audit of the benchmark results is highly recommended. An audit checklist is provided as part of this specification.

**11.2**     The audit report is to be made readily available to the public at a reasonable charge, similar to charges for similar documents.

**11.3**     Auditor's check list:

**11.3.1**   *Clause 1 Related Items*

**11.3.1.1** Verify that the application program matches the transaction profile of Clause 1.2.

**11.3.1.2** Verify that transaction inputs and outputs satisfy Clause 1.3.

**11.3.2**   *Clause 2 Related Items*

**11.3.2.1** Verify that the requirements of each of the ACIDity tests were met.

**11.3.3**   *Clause 3 Related Items*

**11.3.3.1** For each of the ABTH files verify that specified fields/columns and records/rows exist, and that they conform to the minimum lengths specified in Clause 3.2.

**11.3.3.2** Verify that the ABT record/row identifiers are not disk or file offsets as specified in Clause 3.4.

**11.3.3.3** Verify that the ABT files/tables support retrievals, inserts, and deletes as specified in Clause 3.5.

**11.3.4**   *Clause 4 Related Items*

**11.3.4.1** Verify that the ratios among the numbers of records/rows of each file/table are as specified in Clause 4.2.

**11.3.4.2** Verify randomness of the Account_ID, Branch_ID, and Teller_ID sequences submitted to the SUT. Include verification that the values generated are uniform across the entire set of accounts necessary to support the claimed tpsB rating per Clause 4.4 (scaling).

**11.3.5**   *Clause 5 Related Items*

**11.3.5.1** Verify that at least 15% of the transactions are remote, and that the distribution of Account_IDs of remote transactions is uniform across non-home branches.

**11.3.5.2** If horizontal partitioning is used, establish whether or not it is transparent to the application program as defined in Clause 10.1.4.2.

**11.3.5.3** Verify that vertical partitioning of the ABTH files is not used.

**11.3.6**   *Clause 6 Related Items*

**11.3.6.1** Verify the method used by the driver to measure the residence time.

**11.3.7**   *Clause 7 Related Items*

**11.3.7.1** Verify that the SUT had reached a steady state prior to commencing the measurement interval using the method required by Clause 10.1.6.1.

**11.3.7.2** Verify that all work normally done in a steady state environment actually occurred during the measurement interval, for example checkpointing, writing redo/undo log records to disk, etc., per Clause 7.2, Comment 2.

**11.3.7.3** Verify the reproducibility of the tpsB rating using the method required by Clause 10.1.6.3.

**11.3.7.4** Verify the duration of the measurement period for the reported tpsB rate (at least 15 minutes and no longer than 1 hour).

**11.3.7.5** Verify that the residence time and the tpsB rate were measured in the same time interval.

**11.3.8**   *Clause 8 Related Items*

**11.3.8.1** Verify that the SUT is what is claimed and that the driver performs only driver functions.

**11.3.9**   *Clause 9 Related Items*

**11.3.9.1** Verify that all application development software is installed on the priced system and has been used to compile, link and execute the benchmark.

**11.3.9.2** Verify that pricing includes all the hardware and software licenses as required in Clause 9.

**11.3.9.3** Verify that the priced configuration includes sufficient storage for the database, history, and recovery logs as specified in 9.2.4, and can be configured in the priced system.

**11.3.9.4** Assure that warranty coverage meets the requirements of Clause 9.3, or that additional costs for maintenance have been added to priced system.

**11.3.9.5** Verify that all prices used, including discounts, are generally available.

# APPENDIX A: Sample Implementation

```
/*   This is a sample implementation of the Transaction Processing Performance
 *   Council Benchmark B coded in ANSI C and ANSI SQL2.
 *   Any equivalent implementation is equally acceptable.
 *   Exceptions:
 *        1.     ANSI/ISO SQL has no explicit BEGIN WORK (begin transaction).
 *               To show that the driver is outside the transaction,
 *               explicit BEGIN WORK statements are included.
 *        2      The C language has only integer and float numerics - it does not
 *               support precision or scale.  So, in this implementation, money is
 *               represented as integer pennies (pence, pfennig, centimes,...)
 *        3.     To clarify the schema, the following SQL2 features are used:
 *                       Primary Key
 *                       Foreign Key
 *                       DateTime datatype
 *                       Default values (to simplify handling of pad chars).
 *        4.     For simplicity, the program does no error checking or handling.
 */


/* Global declarations      */
exec sql BEGIN DECLARE SECTION;

/* tpc bm b scaling rules                                            */
long tps =                  1;        /* the tps scaling factor: here it is 1 */
long nbranches=             1;        /* number of branches in 1 tps db */
long ntellers=             10;        /* number of tellers in  1 tps db */
long naccounts=        100000;        /* number of accounts in 1 tps db */
long nhistory=         864000;        /* number of history recs in 1 tps db */
/* working storage          */
long i,sqlcode, Bid, Tid, Aid, delta, Abalance;
exec sql END DECLARE SECTION;
void CreateDatabase();
long DoOne(long Bid, long Tid,  long  Aid, long delta);
#include <stdio.h>
/* main program, creates a 1-tps database:  i.e. 1 branch, 10 tellers,...
 *                    runs one TPC BM B transaction
 */
main()
{
    CreateDatabase();
    Abalance = DoOne(1,1,1,100);   /* add 100 to account 1 by teller 1 at */
}                                  /* branch 1, return new balance */
```

```
/*
 * CreateDatabase - Creates and Initializes a scaled database. */
void CreateDatabase()
{

exec sql BEGIN WORK;/* start trans to cover DDL ops*/
exec sql CREATE TABLE branches (
        Bid                     NUMERIC(9),  PRIMARY KEY(Bid),
        Bbalance                NUMERIC(10),
        filler                  CHAR(88) DEFAULT SYSTEM
                                );          /* pad to 100 bytes*/
exec sql CREATE TABLE tellers (
        Tid                     NUMERIC(9), PRIMARY KEY(Tid),
        Bid                     NUMERIC(9)  FOREIGN KEY REFERENCES branches,
        Tbalance                NUMERIC(10),
        filler                  CHAR(84) DEFAULT SYSTEM
                                );          /* pad to 100 bytes*/
exec sql CREATE TABLE accounts (
        Aid                     NUMERIC(9), PRIMARY KEY(Aid),
        Bid                     NUMERIC(9) FOREIGN KEY REFERENCES branches,
        Abalance                NUMERIC(10),
        filler                  CHAR(84) DEFAULT SYSTEM
                                );          /* pad to 100 bytes*/

exec sql CREATE TABLE history (
        Tid                     NUMERIC(9) FOREIGN KEY REFERENCES tellers,
        Bid                     NUMERIC(9) FOREIGN KEY REFERENCES branches,
        Aid                     NUMERIC(9) FOREIGN KEY REFERENCES accounts,
        delta                   NUMERIC(10),
        time                    TIMESTAMP,
        filler                  CHAR(22) DEFAULT SYSTEM
                                );          /* pad to 50 bytes*/

/* prime database using TPC BM B scaling rules.
 *  Note that for each branch and teller:
 *      branch_id = teller_id  / ntellers
 *      branch_id = account_id / naccounts
 */
for (i = 0; i < nbranches*tps; i++)
    exec sql INSERT INTO branches(Bid,Bbalance) VALUES (:i,0);
for (i = 0; i < ntellers*tps; i++)
    exec sql INSERT INTO tellers(Tid,Bid,Tbalance) VALUES (:i,:i/:ntellers,0);
for (i = 0; i < naccounts*tps; i++)
    exec sql INSERT INTO accounts(Aid,Bid,Abalance) VALUES (:i,:i/:naccounts,0);
exec sql COMMIT WORK;
}               /* end of CreateDatabase*/
```

```
/*
 *  DoOne - Executes a single TPC BM B transaction.
 */

long DoOne(long Bid, long Tid,  long  Aid, long delta)
{

exec sql BEGIN WORK;

exec sql UPDATE accounts
    SET        Abalance = Abalance + :delta
    WHERE      Aid = :Aid;

exec sql SELECT Abalance INTO :Abalance
    FROM       accounts
    WHERE      Aid = :Aid;

exec sql UPDATE tellers
    SET        Tbalance = Tbalance + :delta
    WHERE      Tid = :Tid;

exec sql UPDATE branches
    SET        Bbalance = Bbalance + :delta
    WHERE      Bid = :Bid;

exec sql INSERT INTO history(Tid, Bid, Aid, delta, time)
    VALUES (:Tid, :Bid, :Aid, :delta, CURRENT);

exec sql COMMIT WORK;

return ( Abalance);

}               /* end of DoOne      */
```

B

# 3

# Overview of the TPC Benchmark™ C: A Complex OLTP Benchmark

François Raab

*Information Paradigm*

On July 23, 1992, the Transaction Processing Performance Council (TPC) approved the third in its series of benchmarks which measure the performance and price/performance of transaction processing systems. Like TPC-A, the TPC's first benchmark, the new TPC Benchmark™ C, or TPC-C, is an on-line transaction processing (OLTP) benchmark. However, TPC-C is different from and more complex than TPC-A because of its multiple transaction types, more complex database, and overall execution structure. This overview highlights the components of the new benchmark and discusses the main differences between TPC-A and TPC-C.

## 3.1 The Benchmark Development Methodology

The goal of TPC benchmarks is to provide end-users with apples-to-apples comparisons between transaction processing (TP) systems regardless of hardware and software architectures or operating systems. In developing benchmarks, the TPC defines a set of functional requirements that can be implemented freely using "proprietary" or "open" system components. The test sponsor must then submit proof, in the form of a full disclosure report (FDR), that all requirements have been met. To help guarantee apples-to-apples comparisons, all TPC members can review the FDR and challenge its compliance with the requirements. This methodology differs greatly from the one used with most other benchmarks, in which test sponsors are limited to comparing machines that run on just one operating system and execute a fixed set of prewritten software programs.

TPC benchmarks also differ from other benchmarks in that they are modeled after actual production applications and environments rather than stand-alone computer tests which may not evaluate such key performance factors as user interface, communications, disk I/Os, data storage, and database recovery. The difficulty in designing TPC benchmarks lies in reducing the diversity of operations found in a production application, while retaining its essential performance characteristics, namely the level of system utilization and the complexity of its operations. A large number of functions have to be performed to manage a production system. Since many of these functions are proportionally small in terms of utilization of system resources or in terms of frequency of execution, they are not of primary interest for performance analysis. Although these functions are vital for a production system, they would merely create excessive diversity and expense within the context of a standard benchmark and are, therefore, omitted.

TPC benchmarks are not designed to be models of how to build production applications. They are composed of a set of basic operations designed to exercise system functionalities, in a manner representative of most implementations, within the range of applications targeted by the benchmark. The benchmark's specification document defines each basic operation at a functional level to allow maximum freedom in the implementation. For instance, it is specified that a given set of data records must be updated, but no mention is made of the number of I/Os required for the update. Once specified, the basic operations are given a lifelike context to help users relate intuitively to the components of the benchmarks. In this sense, TPC-A was given the lifelike context of a banking application, and TPC-C was given the context of an order-entry application.

## 3.2 The TPC-C Framework

As an on-line transaction processing (OLTP) system benchmark, TPC-C simulates an environment in which a population of terminal operators executes transactions against a database. Given that its context is centered on an order-entry environment, the benchmark includes the activities of entering and delivering orders, recording payments, checking the status of orders, and monitoring the level of stock at the warehouses. However, it should be stressed that TPC-C is not designed to specify how best to implement an order-entry system. The benchmark portrays the activity of a wholesale supplier, but is not limited to the activity of any particular business segment; rather, it is designed to represent any industry in which one must manage, sell, or distribute a product or service.

### 3.2.1 Business Model

In the TPC-C business model, a supplier of wholesale parts (also called *the company*) operates out of a number of warehouses supplying their respective sales districts. The benchmark is designed to scale just as the company expands and new warehouses are created. However, certain requirements must be maintained as the benchmark is scaled. Each warehouse in the TPC-C model (see Figure 3.1) supplies ten sales districts, and each district serves 3000 customers.

Each warehouse tries to maintain stock for the 100,000 items in the company's catalog and to fill orders from that stock. As in reality, however, a warehouse will probably not have all the parts required to fill every order. Therefore, TPC-C is based on the assumption that close to 10 percent of all orders must be supplied, in part, by another warehouse.

An operator in a sales district can select, at any time, one of the five operations or transactions offered by the company's order-entry system. Like the transactions themselves, the frequency of the individual transactions are chosen to be representative of the targeted range of applications. Each transaction executes part of the processing of an order, from its entry to its delivery.

The performance metric reported by TPC-C measures the number of orders that can be fully processed per minute and is expressed in tpmC.

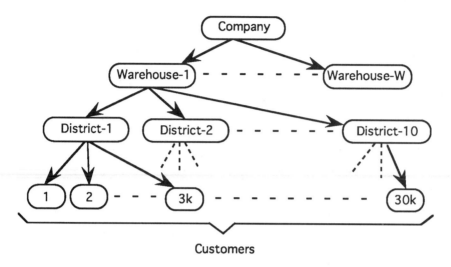

**Figure 3.1**
Context of the business environment portrayed by TPC-C.

## 3.2.2   The Five Transactions

The most frequent transaction consists of entering a new order which, on average, is composed of ten different items. Another frequent transaction is recording a payment received from a customer. Less frequently, operators will request the status of a previously placed order, process a batch of ten orders for delivery, or query the system for potential supply shortages by examining the level of stock at the local warehouse. A total of five types of business transactions, then, are used to model the processing of an order. Following is a more detailed description of the five business transactions:

- The **New-Order** transaction consists of entering a complete order through a single database transaction. It portrays a midweight, read-write transaction and has a high frequency of execution and a stringent response-time requirement to satisfy on-line users.

  This transaction is the backbone of the workload and is designed to have a variable size to reflect on-line database activity in a true production environment. In addition, failures are simulated by forcing the roll back of 1 percent of the New-Orders after most of the transaction has been processed.

- The **Payment** transaction updates the customer's balance, and the payment is reflected in the district's and warehouse's sales statistics, all within a single database transaction. It portrays a lightweight, read-write transaction and has a high frequency of execution and a stringent response-time requirement to satisfy on-line users.

  In addition, 10 percent of the Payment transactions display several lines of information retrieved from the database.

- The **Order-Status** transaction queries the status of a customer's most recent order within a single database transaction. It portrays a midweight, read-only transaction and has a low frequency of execution and a stringent response-time requirement to satisfy on-line users.

- The **Delivery** transaction processes ten new (not yet delivered) orders within one or more database transactions. It portrays a batch of midweight, read-write transactions being executed in the background without response to an on-line user and has a low frequency of execution and a relaxed execution-time requirement.

  This transaction is triggered by a user's request, but its actual execution is deferred through a queueing mechanism. The result of the deferred execution is recorded in a dedicated log file. In addition, the number of orders delivered within the same database transaction is implementation specific, but each order must be processed (delivered) in full within the scope of a single database transaction.

- The **Stock-Level** transaction determines the number of recently sold items that have a stock level below a specified threshold. It portrays a heavyweight, read-only database transaction and has a low frequency of execution and a relaxed response-time requirement.

  The consistency requirement is relaxed for this transaction, which can be implemented as one or more database transactions and is allowed to read data that are recent, but not necessarily the most current.

## 3.2.3    The Database

The entity/relationship diagram in Figure 3.2 illustrates the database used by TPC Benchmark™ C. The numbers in the entity ovals represent the cardinality (number of rows) in the tables. These numbers are multiples of $W$, the number of warehouses configured for the measured system. The number of warehouses is the basic unit of scaling in TPC-C ($k$ is used to represent 1,000).

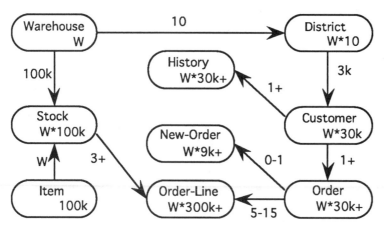

**Figure 3.2**
Entity relationship diagram of the TPC-C database.

The tables were defined to cover a wide range of cardinalities, from a few rows up to millions of rows. Similarly, the cardinality of relationships between tables ranges from one-to-one up to one-to-100k for the Warehouse-Stock relationship. In addition, some of the transaction's input data are chosen from a nonuniform distribution, resulting in skewed access to the database.

Initially, the database must be populated with a specific set of rows as defined in the specification document and summarized in Table 3.1. This initial population represents the data that would be generated over several days of activity. For each customer, an order and the record of a payment are created. Most orders, except for a randomly selected few, are marked as delivered. The stocks of all items are set to random values, creating low and high stocks in each warehouse.

**Table 3.1** Initial database population per warehouse.

| Table Name | Cardinality (in rows) | Row Length (in bytes) | Table Size (in 1,000 bytes) |
|---|---|---|---|
| WAREHOUSE | 1 | 89 | 0.089 |
| DISTRICT | 10 | 95 | 0.950 |
| CUSTOMER | 30k | 655 | 19,650 |
| HISTORY | 30k | 46 | 1,380 |
| ORDER | 30k | 24 | 720 |
| NEW-ORDER | 9k | 8 | 72 |
| ORDER-LINE | 300k | 54 | 16,200 |
| STOCK | 100k | 306 | 30,600 |
| ITEM | 100k | 82 | 8,200 |

## 3.2.4 Mixing and Pacing Transactions

The throughput of a TPC-C benchmark is driven by the activity of ten emulated terminals (or any other device with a display and a keyboard) connected to each warehouse. To increase the throughput requires that more warehouses and their ten associated terminals be configured. Each emulated terminal cycles through the seven steps illustrated in Figure 3.3.

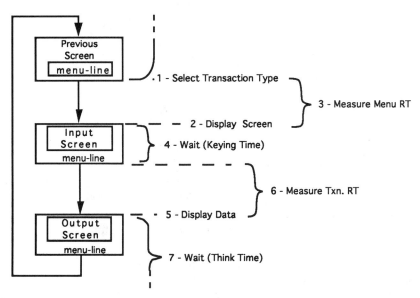

**Figure 3.3**
Pacing of transactions by emulated terminals.

The menu-line is used to select the type of transaction to be executed next (step 1). All five types of transactions are available at each terminal. Each type must be selected a minimum percentage of the time over the measurement interval. A remote terminal emulator (RTE) maintains the required mix of transaction types over the measurement interval via either of the following techniques:

- Randomly selecting a transaction type from a weighted distribution. The weights are chosen to achieve a minimum percentage of each type of transaction while meeting the requirements for the mix.

- Sequentially selecting a transaction type from a randomly shuffled deck of cards. Each card in the deck represents a type of transaction. The cards are dealt to meet the requirements for the mix.

The menu response time (step 3) represents the elapsed time between the selection of a transaction type from the menu-line and the display of the input screen for that transaction (step 2).

The keying time (step 4) represents the time spent entering data at the terminal. Minimum delays in keying time are specified for each transaction type and are proportional to the number of characters entered.

The transaction response time (step 6) is defined as the time needed to execute the transaction and display all of its resulting data on the output screen (step 5). It starts when the last character of the input screen has been entered. For each type, 90 percent of the transactions must be completed within a specified response-time constraint. These constraints are defined to give predominance to New-Order as the performance-limiting transaction. A somewhat generous response-time constraint of 5 seconds was chosen for this transaction to allow low-end systems to execute the benchmark. Yet, given that the constraint is placed on 90 percent of the transactions, the average response time of a transaction should be just above 2 seconds.

The think time (step 7) represents the time spent reading the result of the transaction at the terminal before another selection is made from the menu-line. Think times are taken from a negative exponential distribution with a fixed mean for each transaction type. The minimum value of the mean is specified to be proportional to the time needed to read the output data.

Table 3.2 summarizes the transaction mix, the minimum keying time and mean think-time delays, and the ninetieth percentile response-time requirements for each of the transaction types. The ninetieth percentile response-time constraint for the menu selection is set to 2 seconds.

**Table 3.2**   Transaction mix, delays, and response-time requirements.

| Transaction Type | Minimum % of Mix | Minimum Keying Time | 90th Percentile Response-Time Constraint | Minimum Mean of Think Time Distribution |
|---|---|---|---|---|
| New-Order | n/a | 18 sec. | 5 sec. | 12 sec. |
| Payment | 43 | 3 sec. | 5 sec. | 12 sec. |
| Order-Status | 4 | 2 sec. | 5 sec. | 10 sec. |
| Delivery[1] | 4 | 2 sec. | 5 sec. | 5 sec. |
| Stock-Level | 4 | 2 sec. | 20 sec. | 5 sec. |

[1]Shows the response time at the terminal (acknowledging that the transaction has been queued), not the execution of the transaction. At least 90 percent of the deferred executions must be completed within 80 seconds of their being queued.

Each terminal has an average transaction-cycle time of about 23 seconds, or an average submission rate of 2.6 transactions per minute. A warehouse, having ten terminals, will submit 26 transactions per minute. From these, only the New-Order transactions are reported. Since all other transactions must represent a minimum percentage of the mix, the number of New-Order transactions implicitly accounts for all the other transactions. The expected throughput of a single warehouse is, therefore, around 44 percent of 26 transactions per minute, or almost 11.5 tpmC.

# 3.3 TPC-C Versus TPC-A

With the addition of TPC Benchmark™ C, the TPC now has 2 OLTP benchmarks, TPC-A and TPC-C. The TPC continues to support and publish results on TPC-A, its first OLTP benchmark. TPC-A simulates all the major functions of a simple OLTP system and is now accepted by the industry as a valid means of comparing systems.

## 3.3.1 Sharing Basic OLTP Components

TPC-C was designed to carry over many of the characteristics of TPC-A, the TPC's standard version of DebitCredit. Therefore, TPC-C includes all the components of a basic OLTP benchmark. For the benchmark to be applicable to systems of varying computing powers, TPC-C implementations must scale both the number of terminals and the size of the database proportionally to the computing power of the measured system. To test whether the measured system is fully production-ready, including sufficient recovery capabilities, the database must provide what are defined as the ACID properties: atomicity, consistency, isolation, and durability.

To facilitate independent verification of the benchmark's results, the test sponsor must release, in a full disclosure report, all information necessary to reproduce the reported performance. This performance, which is a measure of the throughput of the system, must be reported, along with the total cost of the system.

The system's total cost is a close approximation of the true cost of the vendor-supplied portion of the system to the end-user. It includes the cost of all hardware and software components; maintenance costs over five years; and sufficient storage capacity to hold the data generated over a period of

180 eight-hour days of operation at the reported throughput, except for recovery log data, which can be archived off-line. Table 3.3 summarizes the storage capacity required to be priced.

**Table 3.3** Priced storage capacity for 180 days (in 1,000 bytes).

| Table Name | Initial Population | 8-hour Increment | Total Priced (for 180 days) |
|---|---|---|---|
| WAREHOUSE | 0.089 | 0 | 0.089 |
| DISTRICT | 0.950 | 0 | 0.950 |
| CUSTOMER | 19,650 | 0 | 19,650 |
| HISTORY | 1,380 | 253 | 45,540 |
| ORDER | 720 | 132.5 | 23,850 |
| NEW-ORDER | 72 | 0 | 72 |
| ORDER-LINE | 16,200 | 1,324.9 | 238,482 |
| STOCK | 30,600 | 0 | 30,600 |
| ITEM | 8,200 | 0 | 8,200 |

The basic characteristics shared by TPC-A and TPC-C can be summarized as follows:

- Multiuser benchmark that requires a remote terminal emulator (RTE) to emulate a population of terminals

- Database size that scales with the throughput of the system under test (SUT)

- Required support of the ACID properties of transactions

- Publication of a full-disclosure report

- Required reporting of both performance (transaction throughput) and price/performance (system price/throughput) metrics

## 3.3.2   More OLTP Features and Complexity

TPC-C provides the industry with an additional tool for measuring the performance of more complex OLTP systems. TPC-C involves a mix of five concurrent transactions of different types and complexity that are either executed on-line or queued for deferred execution.

Having multiple transactions of different natures compete for system resources stresses new components of the measured system and is one of the most significant extensions of the basic OLTP benchmarking model. Another significant extension is the increased complexity of the database's structure. The TPC-C database is composed of nine types of tables with a wide range of row sizes and cardinalities. As a result, there is greater diversity in the data that are manipulated by each of the five transactions and a higher level of database contention. The input data to the TPC-C transactions include some of the basic characteristics of real-life data input. For example, popular items are ordered more frequently than other items.

In moving toward modeling more realistic environments, TPC-C reduces the number of artificial limitations commonly found in other benchmarks. For example, to promote the use of fully functional terminals or workstations and screen management software, TPC-C requires all terminal inputs and displays to be usable by human operators. To that end, all screens must be formatted using labeled input and output fields, as specified, and must provide all the common screen manipulation features, including moving forward or backward through the input fields. Any physical database design technique that can be used to improve the performance of a real-life application, such as transparent partitioning or replication of data, is allowed in TPC-C. The use of database records by the transactions is carefully defined to preclude test sponsors from gaining unrealistic advantages from any of these techniques.

The major characteristics that take TPC-C beyond TPC-A can be summarized as follows:

- Multiple types of transactions of varying complexity

- On-line and deferred execution of transactions

- More complex database structure, resulting in

    — Greater diversity in the data that are manipulated

    — Higher levels of contention for data access and update

- Input data that include basic real-life characteristics, such as:

    — Nonuniform patterns of data access to simulate data hot spots

    — Data access by primary as well as secondary keys

- More realistic requirements, such as:

    — Terminal input/output with full-screen formatting

    — Required support for basic features of users' interface

    — Required application transparency for all database partitioning

- Transaction rollbacks

## 3.3.3 Comparative Processing Requirements

To further evaluate TPC-C, it is useful to compare its processing requirements with those of TPC-A. A simplistic approach consists of assuming that an average TPC-C transaction is ten times more complex than the average TPC-A transaction. Given that only the New-Order transactions are counted (i.e., 44 percent of all the TPC-C transactions), and that tpmC means transactions per minute rather than per second (i.e., must be factored by 60), a 100-tpsA system should be able to process 264 tpmC (calculated as 100/10 * 0.44 * 60).

A more detailed analysis can also be made. In both benchmarks the database scales with the throughput of the measured system, as discussed below.

For TPC-A the unit of scaling is the branch:

- One branch has 10 terminals.

- The average terminal cycle time is approximately 10 seconds, giving a per branch total of one transaction per second.

- Assuming the length of a typical instruction path to be 100 k instructions per transaction, the processing load consists of 100 k instructions per second per configured branch.

For TPC-C the unit of scaling is the warehouse:

- One warehouse has ten terminals.

- The average terminal cycle time can be given as ($Y*10$) seconds, where $Y$ denotes the ratio of the terminal cycle time of the average TPC-C transaction to that of the TPC-A transaction. From Table 3.2 we determine $Y$ to be approximately 2.36, giving a per-warehouse total of 0.42 transaction per second.[1]

- The length of the instruction path of the average TPC-C transaction is given by the weighted average of the instruction path lengths of individual TPC-C transactions, the weights being given by their percentage in the transaction mix. Assuming that the average instruction path length is ($X*100$ k) instructions per transaction, where $X$ denotes the ratio of the instruction path length of the average TPC-C transaction to that of

---

[1]We assume that 44 percent of the transactions in the mix are New-Order and 44 percent are Payment transactions, the keying times are minimums, and the average menu and transaction response times are half of their ninetieth percentile requirements.

the average TPC-A transaction, the processing load is approximately ($X$*42 k) instructions per second per configured warehouse.

Based on the relative processing requirements of the two workloads as described above, the scaling ratio between the number of TPC-C warehouses and the number of TPC-A branches that can be supported on a given system is thus approximately ($Y/X$). For example, given a terminal cycle time ratio of $Y$, a system that has a path length ratio $X$ and that can handle a TPC-A load of up to $B$ branches should be able to handle a TPC-C load of (($Y/X$)*$B$) warehouses.

During the design of the benchmark, the assumption was that an average TPC-C transaction would be ten times more complex than the TPC-A transaction. In other words, the path length ratio, $X$, was assumed to be around ten. As vendors are starting to publish results for both TPC-A and TPC-C, actual path length ratios can now be computed. Given that the number of transactions executed for TPC-C is equal to 2.27 times the reported tpmC, and given that the number of transactions executed per minute for TPC-A is equal to 60 times the reported tpsA, the path length ratio can be computed as $X = $ (tpsA *60)/(tpmC * 2.27). TPC-C results submitted to date by vendors have shown the path length ratios, $X$, to be between 4.87 and 9.53, as summarized in Table 3.4.

**Table 3.4**   Submitted TPC-C results as of February 93

| System Name | tpmC | tpsA | Path Length Ratio |
|---|---|---|---|
| HP 9000 Series 800 Model H40 | 406.65 | 74.93 | 4.87 |
| IBM AS/400 Model 9404 E10 | 33.81 | 9.92 | 7.76 |
| IBM AS/400 Model 9406 E35 | 54.14 | 14.00 | 6.83 |
| IBM AS/400 Model 9406 E70 | 268.76 | 54.90 | 5.40 |
| IBM RS/6000 Model 570 | 356.45 | 128.50 | 9.53 |

The wide range of path length ratio between TPC-A and TPC-C is a confirmation that the two benchmarks exercise different aspects of the systems under test. A given system might be very efficient at processing the short TPC-A transaction but comparatively less efficient at scheduling and processing the five different transactions of TPC-C. Conversely, systems that were never considered to be top performers with TPC-A might be well equipped to process TPC-C transactions.

# 3.4    A Measure of Business Throughput

The throughput of TPC-C is a direct result of the level of activity at the terminals. Each warehouse has ten terminals, and all five transactions are available at each terminal. The RTE maintains the required mix of transactions over the performance measurement interval. This mix represents the complete processing of an order as it is entered, paid for, checked, and delivered. More specifically, the required mix is defined to produce an equal number of New-Order and Payment transactions and to produce one Delivery transaction, one Order-Status transaction, and one Stock-Level transaction for every ten New-Order transactions.

The tpmC metric reported by TPC-C is the number of New-Order transactions executed per minute. Given the required mix and the wide range of complexity and types among the transactions, this metric more closely simulates a complete business activity, not just one or two transactions or computer operations. For this reason, the tpmC metric is considered to be *a measure of business throughput.*

## 3.4.1    A New Yardstick

Users of a benchmark's information and results, whether they be members of the press, market researchers, or commercial users, want to be assured that the results they see are valid measures of performance. To meet that demand, the TPC designs its benchmarks to simulate and test systems with all the necessary production-oriented features, including backup and recovery features. In addition, the TPC requires complete documentation of the benchmark's run (the full-disclosure report). These reports are available to any user and are subjected to the TPC's own internal review process. All these requirements help to ensure that users of TPC's benchmark results will receive valid, objective measures of performance.

TPC-C follows the TPC's benchmarking philosophy and methodology in all the above respects, but it also includes new elements and more complex requirements. TPC-C's performance measurement metric, tpmC, does not simply measure a few basic computer or database transactions; rather, it measures how many complete business operations can be processed per minute. This new benchmark should give users a more extensive, more complex yardstick for measuring the performance of OLTP systems.

*The views expressed in this chapter are those of the author and may differ from the official views of the TPC.*

# TPC BENCHMARK™ C

Standard Specification
Revision 1.0

13 August 1992

Transaction Processing Performance Council (TPC)
© 1992 Transaction Processing Performance Council

Administered by
Shanley Public Relations
777 N. First Street, Suite 600
San Jose, CA 95112-6311, USA
Phone (408) 295-8894
FAX (408) 295-2613
e-mail: shanley@cup.portal.com

C

# Acknowledgments

The TPC acknowledges the substantial contribution of François Raab, consultant to the TPC-C subcommittee and technical editor of the TPC-C benchmark standard. The TPC also acknowledges the work and contributions of the TPC-C subcommittee member companies: Amdahl, Bull, CDC, DEC, DG, Fujitsu/ICL, HP, IBM, Informix, Mips, Oracle, Sequent, Sun, Sybase, Tandem, and Unisys.

## TPC Membership
(as of August 1992)

Document History

| Date | Version | Description |
|---|---|---|
| 22 June 1992 | Draft 6.6 | Mail ballot version (proposed standard) |
| 13 August 1992 | Revision 1.0 | Standard specification released to the public |

# TPC BENCHMARK™ C: Standard Specification (13 August 1992)

## TABLE OF CONTENTS

C

C

# CLAUSE 0: Preamble

TPC Benchmark™ C (TPC-C) is an OLTP workload. It is a mixture of read-only and update intensive transactions that simulate the activities found in complex OLTP application environments. It does so by exercising a breadth of system components associated with such environments, which are characterized by:

- The simultaneous execution of multiple transaction types that span a breadth of complexity

- On-line and deferred transaction execution modes

- Multiple on-line terminal sessions

- Moderate system and application execution time

- Significant disk input/output

- Transaction integrity (ACID properties)

- Non-uniform distribution of data access through primary and secondary keys

- Databases consisting of many tables with a wide variety of sizes, attributes, and relationships

- Contention on data access and update

The performance metric reported by TPC-C is a "business throughput" measuring the number of orders processed per minute. Multiple transactions are used to simulate the business activity of processing an order, and each transaction is subject to a response time constraint. The performance metric for this benchmark is expressed in transactions-per-minute-C (tpmC). To be compliant with the TPC-C standard, all references to tpmC results must include the tpmC rate, the associated price-per-tpmC, and the availability date of the priced configuration.

Although these specifications express implementation in terms of a relational data model with conventional locking scheme, the database may be implemented using any commercially available database management system (DBMS), database server, file system, or other data repository that provides a functionally equivalent implementation. The terms "table", "row", and "column" are used in this document only as examples of logical data structures.

TPC-C uses terminology and metrics that are similar to other benchmarks, originated by the TPC or others. Such similarity in terminology does not in any way imply that TPC-C results are comparable to other benchmarks. The only benchmark results comparable to TPC-C are other TPC-C results conformant with the same revision.

Despite the fact that this benchmark offers a rich environment that emulates many OLTP applications, this benchmark does not reflect the entire range of OLTP requirements. In addition, the extent to which a customer can achieve the results reported by a vendor is highly dependent on how closely TPC-C approximates the customer application. The relative performance of systems derived from this benchmark does not necessarily hold for other workloads or environments. Extrapolations to any other environment are not recommended.

Benchmark results are highly dependent upon workload, specific application requirements, and systems design and implementation. Relative system performance will vary as a result of these and other factors. Therefore, TPC-C should not be used as a substitute for a specific customer application benchmarking when critical capacity planning and/or product evaluation decisions are contemplated.

Benchmark sponsors are permitted several possible system designs, insofar as they adhere to the model described and pictorially illustrated in Clause 6. A Full Disclosure Report of the implementation details, as specified in Clause 8, must be made available along with the reported results.

---

**Comment:** While separated from the main text for readability, comments are a part of the standard and must be enforced. However, the sample programs, included as Appendix A, the summary statements, included as Appendix B, and the numerical quantities summary, included as Appendix C, are provided only as examples and are specifically not part of this standard.

---

# CLAUSE 1: Logical Database Design

## 1.1    Business and Application Environment

TPC Benchmark™ C is composed of a set of basic operations designed to exercise system functionalities in a manner representative of complex OLTP application environments. These basic operations have been given a lifelike context, portraying the activity of a wholesale supplier, to help users relate intuitively to the components of the benchmark. The workload is centered around the activity of processing orders and provides a logical database design, which can be distributed without structural changes to transactions.

TPC-C does not represent the activity of any particular business segment, but rather any industry which must manage, sell, or distribute a product or service (e.g., car rental, food distribution, parts supplier, etc.). TPC-C does not attempt to be a model of how to build an actual application.

The purpose of a benchmark is to reduce the diversity of operations found in a production application, while retaining the application's essential performance characteristics, namely: the level of system utilization and the complexity of operations. A large number of functions have to be performed to manage a production order entry system. Many of these functions are not of primary interest for performance analysis, since they are proportionally small in terms of system resource utilization or in terms of frequency of execution. Although these functions are vital for a production system, they merely create excessive diversity in the context of a standard benchmark and have been omitted in TPC-C.

The Company portrayed by the benchmark is a wholesale supplier with a number of geographically distributed sales districts and associated warehouses. As the Company's business expands, new warehouses and associated sales districts are created. Each regional warehouse covers 10 districts. Each district serves 3000 customers. All warehouses maintain stocks for the 100,000 items sold by the Company. The following diagram illustrates the warehouse, district, and customer hierarchy of TPC-C's business environment.

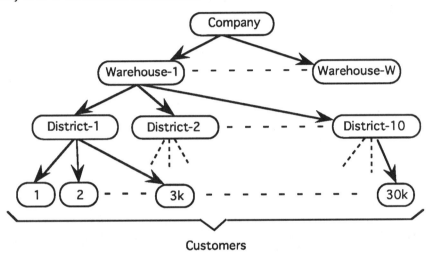

Customers

Customers call the Company to place a new order or request the status of an existing order. Orders are composed of an average of 10 order lines (i.e., line items). One percent of all order lines are for items not in stock at the regional warehouse and must be supplied by another warehouse.

The Company's system is also used to enter payments from customers, process orders for delivery, and examine stock levels to identify potential supply shortages.

## 1.2    Database Entities, Relationships, and Characteristics

**1.2.1**    The components of the TPC-C database are defined to consist of nine separate and individual tables. The relationships among these tables are defined in the entity-relationship diagram shown below and are subject to the rules specified in Clause 1.4.

**Legend:**

- All numbers shown illustrate the minimal database population requirements (see Clause 4.3).

- The numbers in the entity blocks represent the cardinality of the tables (number of rows). These numbers are factored by W, the number of Warehouses, to illustrate the database scaling. (See Clause 4.)

- The numbers next to the relationship arrows represent the cardinality of the relationships (average number of children per parent).

- The plus (+) symbol is used after the cardinality of a relationship or table to illustrate that this number is subject to small variations in the initial database population over the measurement interval (see Clause 5.5) as rows are added or deleted.

## 1.3   Table Layouts

**1.3.1**   The following list defines the minimal structure (list of attributes) of each table where:

- **N unique IDs** means that the attribute must be able to hold any one ID within a minimum set of N unique IDs, regardless of the physical representation (e.g., binary, packed decimal, alphabetic, etc.) of the attribute.

- **variable text, size N** means that the attribute must be able to hold any string of characters of a variable length with a maximum length of N. If the attribute is stored as a fixed length string and the string it holds is shorter than N characters, it must be padded with spaces.

- **fixed text, size N** means that the attribute must be able to hold any string of characters of a fixed length of N.

- **date and time** means that the attribute must be able to hold any date between 1st January 1900 and 31st December 2100 with a resolution of at least one second.

- **numeric, N digits** means that the attribute must be able to hold any N decimal digits value.

- **null** means out of the range of valid values for a given attribute and always the same value for that attribute.

**Comment 1:** For each table, the following list of attributes can be implemented in any order, using any physical representation available from the tested system.

**Comment 2:** Table and attribute names are used for illustration purposes only; different names may be used by the implementation.

### WAREHOUSE Table Layout

| Field Name | Field Definition | Comments |
|---|---|---|
| W_ID | 2*W unique IDs | *W Warehouses are populated* |
| W_NAME | variable text, size 10 | |
| W_STREET_1 | variable text, size 20 | |
| W_STREET_2 | variable text, size 20 | |
| W_CITY | variable text, size 20 | |
| W_STATE | fixed text, size 2 | |
| W_ZIP | fixed text, size 9 | |
| W_TAX | numeric, 4 digits | *Sales tax* |
| W_YTD | numeric, 12 digits | *Year-to-date balance* |

Primary Key: W_ID

### DISTRICT Table Layout

| Field Name | Field Definition | Comments |
|---|---|---|
| D_ID | 20 unique IDs | *10 are populated per warehouse* |
| D_W_ID | 2*W unique IDs | |
| D_NAME | variable text, size 10 | |
| D_STREET_1 | variable text, size 20 | |
| D_STREET_2 | variable text, size 20 | |
| D_CITY | variable text, size 20 | |
| D_STATE | fixed text, size 2 | |
| D_ZIP | fixed text, size 9 | |
| D_TAX | numeric, 4 digits | *Sales tax* |
| D_YTD | numeric, 12 digits | *Year-to-date balance* |
| D_NEXT_O_ID | 10,000,000 unique IDs | *Next available Order number* |

Primary Key: (D_W_ID, D_ID)
D_W_ID Foreign Key, references W_ID

C

## CUSTOMER Table Layout

| Field Name | Field Definition | Comments |
|---|---|---|
| C_ID | 6,000 unique IDs | *3,000 are populated per district* |
| C_D_ID | 20 unique IDs | |
| C_W_ID | 2*W unique IDs | |
| C_FIRST | variable text, size 16 | |
| C_MIDDLE | fixed text, size 2 | |
| C_LAST | variable text, size 16 | |
| C_STREET_1 | variable text, size 20 | |
| C_STREET_2 | variable text, size 20 | |
| C_CITY | variable text, size 20 | |
| C_STATE | fixed text, size 2 | |
| C_ZIP | fixed text, size 9 | |
| C_PHONE | fixed text, size 16 | |
| C_SINCE | date and time | |
| C_CREDIT | fixed text, size 2 | *"GC"=good, "BC"=bad* |
| C_CREDIT_LIM | numeric, 7 digits | |
| C_DISCOUNT | numeric, 4 digits | |
| C_BALANCE | signed numeric, 7 digits | |
| C_YTD_PAYMENT | numeric, 12 digits | |
| C_PAYMENT_CNT | numeric , 4 digits | |
| C_DELIVERY_CNT | numeric, 4 digits | |
| C_DATA | variable text, size 500 | *Miscellaneous information* |

Primary Key: (C_W_ID, C_D_ID, C_ID)
(C_W_ID, C_D_ID) Foreign Key, references (D_W_ID, D_ID)

## HISTORY Table Layout

| Field Name | Field Definition | Comments |
|---|---|---|
| H_C_ID | 6,000 unique IDs | |
| H_C_D_ID | 20 unique IDs | |
| H_C_W_ID | 2*W unique IDs | |
| H_D_ID | 20 unique IDs | |
| H_W_ID | 2*W unique IDs | |
| H_DATE | date and time | |
| H_AMOUNT | numeric, 6 digits | |
| H_DATA | variable text, size 24 | *Miscellaneous information* |

Primary Key: none
(H_C_W_ID, H_C_D_ID, H_C_ID) Foreign Key, references (C_W_ID, C_D_ID, C_ID)
(H_W_ID, H_D_ID) Foreign Key, references (D_W_ID, D_ID)

**Comment**: Rows in the History table do not have a primary key as, within the context of the benchmark, there is no need to uniquely identify a row within this table.

### NEW-ORDER Table Layout

| Field Name | Field Definition | Comments |
|---|---|---|
| NO_O_ID | 10,000,000 unique IDs | |
| NO_D_ID | 20 unique IDs | |
| NO_W_ID | 2*W unique IDs | |

Primary Key: (NO_W_ID, NO_D_ID, NO_O_ID)
(NO_W_ID, NO_D_ID, NO_O_ID) Foreign Key, references (O_W_ID, O_D_ID, O_ID)

### ORDER Table Layout

| Field Name | Field Definition | Comments |
|---|---|---|
| O_ID | 10,000,000 unique IDs | |
| O_D_ID | 20 unique IDs | |
| O_W_ID | 2*W unique IDs | |
| O_C_ID | 6,000 unique IDs | |
| O_ENTRY_D | date and time | |
| O_CARRIER_ID | 10 unique IDs, or null | |
| O_OL_CNT | from 5 to 15 | Count of Order-Lines |
| O_ALL_LOCAL | numeric, 1 digit | |

Primary Key: (O_W_ID, O_D_ID, O_ID)
(O_W_ID, O_D_ID, O_C_ID) Foreign Key, references (C_W_ID, C_D_ID, C_ID)

### ORDER-LINE Table Layout

| Field Name | Field Definition | Comments |
|---|---|---|
| OL_O_ID | 10,000,000 unique IDs | |
| OL_D_ID | 20 unique IDs | |
| OL_W_ID | 2*W unique IDs | |
| OL_NUMBER | 15 unique IDs | |
| OL_I_ID | 200,000 unique IDs | |
| OL_SUPPLY_W_ID | 2*W unique IDs | |
| OL_DELIVERY_D | date and time, or null | |
| OL_QUANTITY | numeric, 2 digits | |
| OL_AMOUNT | numeric, 6 digits | |
| OL_DIST_INFO | fixed text, size 24 | |

Primary Key: (OL_W_ID, OL_D_ID, OL_O_ID, OL_NUMBER)
(OL_W_ID, OL_D_ID, OL_O_ID) Foreign Key, references (O_W_ID, O_D_ID, O_ID)
(OL_SUPPLY_W_ID, OL_I_ID) Foreign Key, references (S_W_ID, S_I_ID)

C

### ITEM Table Layout

| Field Name | Field Definition | Comments |
|---|---|---|
| I_ID | 200,000 unique IDs | *100,000 items are populated* |
| I_NAME | variable text, size 24 | |
| I_PRICE | numeric, 5 digits | |
| I_DATA | variable text, size 50 | *Brand information* |

Primary Key: I_ID

### STOCK Table Layout

| Field Name | Field Definition | Comments |
|---|---|---|
| S_I_ID | 200,000 unique IDs | *100,000 populated per warehouse* |
| S_W_ID | 2*W unique IDs | |
| S_QUANTITY | numeric, 4 digits | |
| S_DIST_01 | fixed text, size 24 | |
| S_DIST_02 | fixed text, size 24 | |
| S_DIST_03 | fixed text, size 24 | |
| S_DIST_04 | fixed text, size 24 | |
| S_DIST_05 | fixed text, size 24 | |
| S_DIST_06 | fixed text, size 24 | |
| S_DIST_07 | fixed text, size 24 | |
| S_DIST_08 | fixed text, size 24 | |
| S_DIST_09 | fixed text, size 24 | |
| S_DIST_10 | fixed text, size 24 | |
| S_YTD | numeric, 8 digits | |
| S_ORDER_CNT | numeric, 4 digits | |
| S_REMOTE_CNT | numeric, 4 digits | |
| S_DATA | variable text, size 50 | *Make information* |

Primary Key: (S_W_ID, S_I_ID)
S_W_ID Foreign Key, references W_ID
S_I_ID Foreign Key, references I_ID

## 1.4    Implementation Rules

1.4.1    The physical clustering of records within the database is allowed.

1.4.2    A view which represents the rows to avoid logical read/writes is excluded.

**Comment:** The intent of this clause is to insure that the application implements the number of logical operations defined in the transaction profiles without combining several operations in one, via the use of a view.

1.4.3    All tables must have a minimum number of rows as defined by the minimal database population (see Clause 4.3).

**1.4.4**    Horizontal partitioning of tables is allowed. Groups of rows from a table may be assigned to different files, disks, or areas. If implemented, the details of such partitioning must be disclosed.

**1.4.5**    Vertical partitioning of tables is allowed. Groups of attributes (columns) of one table may be assigned to files, disks, or areas different from those storing the other attributes of that table. If implemented, the details of such partitioning must be disclosed (see Clause 1.4.9 for limitations).

**Comment:** In the two clauses above (1.4.4 and 1.4.5) assignment of data to different files, disks, or areas not based on knowledge of the logical structure of the data (e.g., knowledge of row or attribute boundaries) is not considered partitioning. For example, distribution or stripping over multiple disks of a physical file which stores one or more logical tables is not considered partitioning as long as this distribution is done by the hardware or the operating system without knowledge of the logical structure stored in the physical file.

**1.4.6**    Replication is allowed for all tables. All copies of tables which are replicated must meet all requirements for atomicity, consistency, and isolation as defined in Clause 3. If implemented, the details of such replication must be disclosed.

**Comment:** Only one copy of a replicated table needs to meet the durability requirements defined in Clause 3.

**1.4.7**    Attributes may be added and/or duplicated from one table to another as long as these changes do not improve performance.

**1.4.8**    Each attribute, as described in Clause 1.3.1, must be logically discrete and independently accessible by the data manager. For example, W_STREET_1 and W_STREET_2 cannot be implemented as two sub-parts of a discrete attribute W_STREET.

**1.4.9**    Each attribute, as described in Clause 1.3.1, must be accessible by the data manager as a single attribute. For example, S_DATA cannot be implemented as two discrete attributes S_DATA_1 and S_DATA_2. The following attributes are exceptions to this clause. No vertical partitioning can be defined between the two attributes used to implement these exceptions.

- All attributes holding a time-and-date value (i.e., C_SINCE, H_DATE, O_ENTRY_D, and OL_DELIVERY_D) can be implemented as a combination of two attributes: a date attribute and a time attribute.

- The attribute C_DATA can be implemented as two distinct attributes of equal size and using the same datatype.

**1.4.10**    The primary key of each table must not directly represent the physical disk addresses of the row or any offsets thereof. The application may not reference rows using relative addressing since they are simply offsets from the beginning of the storage space. This does not preclude hashing schemes or other file organizations which have provisions for adding, deleting, and modifying records in the ordi-

C

nary course of processing. Exception: The History table can use relative addressing but all other requirements apply.

**Comment:** It is the intent of this clause that the application program (see Clause 2.1.7) executing the transaction, or submitting the transaction request, not use physical identifiers, but logical identifiers for all accesses, and contain no user written code which translates or aids in the translation of a logical key to the location within the table of the associated row or rows. For example, it is not legitimate for the application to build a "translation table" of logical-to-physical addresses and use it to enhance performance.

**1.4.11**     While inserts and deletes are not performed on all tables, the system must not be configured to take special advantage of this fact during the test. Although inserts are inherently limited by the storage space available on the configured system, there must be no restriction on inserting in any of the tables a minimum number of rows equal to 5% of the table cardinality and with a key value of at least double the range of key values present in that table.

**1.4.12**     The minimum decimal precision for any computation performed as part of the application program must be the maximum decimal precision of all the individual items in that calculation.

**1.4.13**     Any other rules specified elsewhere in this document apply to the implementation (e.g., the consistency rules in Clause 3.3).

## 1.5     Integrity Rules

**1.5.1**     In any committed state, the primary key values must be unique within each table. For example, in the case of a horizontally partitioned table, primary key values of rows across all partitions must be unique.

**1.5.2**     In any committed state, no ill-formed rows may exist in the database. An ill-formed row occurs when the value of any attributes cannot be determined. For example, in the case of a vertically partitioned table, a row must exist in all the partitions.

## 1.6     Data Access Transparency Requirements

Data Access Transparency is the property of the system which removes from the application program any knowledge of the location and access mechanisms of partitioned data. An implementation which uses vertical and/or horizontal partitioning must meet the requirements for transparent data access described here.

No finite series of test can prove that the system supports complete data access transparency. The requirements below describe the minimum capabilities needed to establish that the system provides transparent data access.

**Comment**: The intent of this clause is to require that access to physically and/or logically partitioned data be provided directly and transparently by services implemented by commercially available layers below the application program such as the data/file manager (DBMS), the operating system, the hardware, or any combination of these.

**1.6.1**     Each of the nine tables described in Clause 1.3 must be identifiable by names which have no relationship to the partitioning of tables. All data manipulation operations in the application program (see Clause 2.1.7) must use only these names.

**1.6.2**     The system must prevent any data manipulation operation performed using the names described in Clause 1.6.1 which would result in a violation of the integrity rules (see Clause 1.5). For example: the system must prevent a non-TPC-C application from committing the insertion of a row in a vertically partitioned table unless all partitions of that row have been inserted.

**1.6.3**     Using the names which satisfy Clause 1.6.1, any arbitrary non-TPC-C application must be able to manipulate any set of rows or columns:

- Identifiable by any arbitrary condition supported by the underlying DBMS

- Using the names described in Clause 1.6.1 and using the same data manipulation semantics and syntax for all tables.

For example, the semantics and syntax used to update an arbitrary set of rows in any one table must also be usable when updating another arbitrary set of rows in any other table.

**Comment**: The intent is that the TPC-C application program uses general purpose mechanisms to manipulate data in the database.

# CLAUSE 2: Transaction and Terminal Profiles

## 2.1     Definition of Terms

**2.1.1**     The term **select** as used in this specification refers to the action of identifying (e.g., referencing, pointing to) a row (or rows) in the database without requiring retrieval of the actual content of the identified row(s).

**2.1.2**     The term **retrieve** as used in this specification refers to the action of accessing (i.e., fetching) the value of an attribute from the database and passing this value to the application program.

**Note**: Fields that correspond to database attributes are in uppercase. Other fields, such as fields used by the SUT, or the RTE, for computations, or communication with the terminal, but not stored in the database, are in *lowercase italics*.

C

**2.1.3** The term **database transaction** as used in this specification refers to a unit of work on the database with full ACID properties as described in Clause 3. A **business transaction** is composed of one or more database transactions. When used alone, the term transaction refers to a business transaction.

**2.1.4** The term *[x .. y]* represents a closed range of values starting with *x* and ending with *y*.

**2.1.5** The term **randomly selected within** *[x .. y]* means independently selected at random and uniformly distributed between *x* and *y*, inclusively, with a mean of *(x+y)/2*, and with the same number of digits of precision as shown. For example, [0.01 .. 100.00] has 10,000 unique values, whereas [1 ..100] has only 100 unique values.

**2.1.6** The term **non-uniform random**, used only for generating customer numbers, customer last names, and item numbers, means an independently selected and non-uniformly distributed random number over the specified range of values *[x .. y]*. This number must be generated by using the function **NURand** which produces positions within the range *[x .. y]*. The results of NURand might have to be converted to produce a name or a number valid for the implementation.

$$NURand(A, x, y) = (((random(0, A) \mid random(x, y)) + C) \% (y - x + 1)) + x$$

where:

exp-1 | exp-2 stands for the bitwise logical OR operation between exp-1 and exp-2

exp-1 % exp-2 stands for exp-1 modulo exp-2

random(x, y) stands for randomly selected within *[x .. y]*

A is a constant chosen according to the size of the range [x .. y]

for C_LAST, the range is [0 .. 999] and A = 255

for C_ID, the range is [1 .. 3000] and A = 1023

for OL_I_ID, the range is [1 .. 100000] and A = 8191

C is a run-time constant randomly chosen within [0 .. A] that can be varied without altering performance

**2.1.7** The term **application program** refers to code that is not part of the commercially available components of the system, but produced specifically to implement the transaction profiles (see Clauses 2.4.2, 2.5.2, 2.6.2, 2.7.4, and 2.8.2) of this benchmark. For example, stored procedures, triggers, and referential integrity constraints are considered part of the application program when used to implement any portion of the transaction profiles, but are not considered part of the application program when solely used to enforce integrity rules (see Clause 1.5) or transparency requirements (see Clause 1.6) independently of any transaction profile.

**2.1.8** The term **terminal** as used in this specification refers to the interface device capable of entering and displaying characters from and to a user with a minimum display of 24x80. This may be an actual terminal or the keyboard/display portion of an intelligent processor such as a workstation or PC.

## 2.2    General Requirements for Terminal I/O

### 2.2.1    *Input/Output Screen Definitions*

**2.2.1.1**    The layout (position on the screen and size of titles and fields) of the input/output screens, as defined in Clauses 2.4.3.1, 2.5.3.1, 2.6.3.1, 2.7.3.1, and 2.8.3.1, must be reproduced by the test sponsor as closely as possible given the features and limitations of the implemented system. Any deviation from the input/output screens must be explained.

**2.2.1.2**    Input/output screens may be altered to circumvent limitations of the implementation providing that no performance advantage is gained. However, the following rules apply:

1. Titles can be translated into any language.

2. The semantic content cannot be altered.

3. The number of individual fields cannot be altered.

4. The number of characters within the fields (i.e., field width) cannot be decreased.

5. Reordering or repositioning of fields is allowed.

6. A copy of the new screen specifications and layout must be included in the Full Disclosure Report.

**2.2.1.3**    The amount and price fields defined in Clause 2 are formatted for U.S. currency. These formats can be modified to satisfy different currency representation (e.g., use another currency sign, move the decimal point retaining at least one digit on its right).

**2.2.1.4**    For input/output screens with unused fields (or groups of fields), it is not required to enter or display these fields. For example, when an order has less than 15 items, the groups of fields corresponding to the remaining items on the input/output screen are unused and need not be entered or displayed after being cleared. Similarly, when selecting a customer using its last name, the customer number field is unused and need not be entered or displayed after being cleared.

**2.2.1.5**    All input and output fields that may change must be cleared at the beginning of each transaction even when the same transaction type is consecutively selected by a given terminal. Fields should be cleared by displaying them as spaces or zeros.

**Comment:** In Clauses 2.2.1.4 and 2.2.1.5, if the test sponsor does not promote using space or zero as a clear character for its implementation, other clear characters can be used as long as a given field always uses the same clear character.

C

**2.2.1.6** A **menu** is used to select the next transaction type. The menu, consisting of one or more lines, must be displayed at the very top or at the very bottom of the input/output screen. If an input field is needed to enter the menu selection, it must be located on the line(s) reserved for the menu.

**Comment:** The menu is in addition to the screen formats defined in the terminal I/O Clause for each transaction type.

**2.2.1.7** The menu must display explicit text (i.e., it must contain the full name of each transaction and the action to be taken by the user to select each transaction). A minimum of 60 characters (excluding spaces) must be displayed on the menu.

**2.2.1.8** Any input and output field(s), other than the mandatory fields specified in the input/output screens as defined in Clauses 2.4.3.1, 2.5.3.1, 2.6.3.1, 2.7.3.1, and 2.8.3.1, must be disclosed, and the purpose of such field(s) explained.

**2.2.2** *Entering and Displaying Fields*

**2.2.2.1** A field is said to be entered once all the significant characters that compose the input data for that field have been communicated to the SUT by the emulated terminal.

**2.2.2.2** A field is said to be displayed once all significant characters that compose the data for that field have been communicated by the SUT to the emulated terminal for display.

**2.2.2.3** Communicating input and output data does not require transferring any specific number of bytes. Methods for optimizing this communication, such as message compression and data caching, are allowed.

**2.2.2.4** The following features must be provided to the emulated user:

1. The input characters appear on the input/output screen (i.e., are echoed) as they are keyed in.

2. Input is allowed only in the positions of an input field (i.e., output-only fields, labels, and blank spaces on the input/output screen are protected from input).

3. Input-capable fields are designated by some method of clearly identifying them (e.g., highlighted areas, underscores, reverse video, column dividers, etc.).

4. It must be possible to key in only significant characters into fields. For alphanumeric fields, non-keyed positions must be translated to blanks or nulls. For numeric fields, keyed input of less than the maximum allowable digits must be presented right justified on the output screen.

5. All fields for which a value is necessary to allow the application to complete are required to contain input prior to the start of the measurement of the transaction RT, or the application must contain a set of error-handling routines to inform the user that required fields have not been entered.

6. Fields can be keyed and re-keyed in any order. Specifically:

  - The emulated user must be able to move the input cursor forward and backward directly to the input-capable fields.

  - The application cannot rely on fields being entered in any particular order.

  - The user can return to a field that has been keyed in and change its value prior to the start of the measurement of the transaction RT.

7. Numeric fields must be protected from non-numeric input. If one or more non-numeric characters is entered in a numeric field, a data entry error must be signaled to the user prior to, or at the time of, moving the cursor outside of the current numeric field.

**2.2.2.5**     All output fields that display values that are updated in the database by the current business transaction must display the "new" (i.e., committed) values for those fields.

## 2.3     General Requirements for Transaction Profiles

Each transaction must be implemented according to the specified transaction profiles. In addition:

**2.3.1**     The order of the data manipulations within the transaction bounds is immaterial (unless otherwise specified, see Clause 2.4.2.3), and is left to the latitude of the test sponsor, as long as the implemented transactions are functionally equivalent to those specified in the transaction profiles.

**2.3.2**     The transaction profiles specify minimal data retrieval and update requirements for the transactions. Additional navigational steps or data manipulation operations implemented within the database transactions must be disclosed, and the purpose of such addition(s) must be explained.

**2.3.3**     Each attribute must be obtained from the designated table in the transaction profiles.

**Comment**: The intent of this clause is to prevent reducing the number of logical database operations required to implement each transaction.

**2.3.4**     No data manipulation operation from the transaction profile can be performed before all input data have been communicated to the SUT, or after any output data have been communicated by the SUT to the emulated terminal.

**Comment**: The intent of this clause is to ensure that, for a given business transaction, no data manipulation operation from the transaction profile is performed prior to the timestamp taken at the beginning of the Transaction RT or after the timestamp taken at the end of the Transaction RT (see Clause 5.3). For example, in the New-Order transaction the SUT is not allowed to fetch the matching row from the CUS-

C

TOMER table until all input data have been communicated to the SUT, even if this row is fetched again later during the execution of that same transaction.

**2.3.5** If the application environment contains software that routes or organizes the execution of transactions (e.g., a transaction processing monitor), the software must be a generally available commercial product that is maintained as defined in Clause 7.3.3.

**Comment:** It is the intent that special purpose transaction processing monitors developed specifically for benchmarking, or limited use, not be utilized.

## 2.4 The New-Order Transaction

The New-Order business transaction consists of entering a complete order through a single database transaction. It represents a mid-weight, read-write transaction with a high frequency of execution and stringent response time requirements to satisfy on-line users. This transaction is the backbone of the workload. It is designed to place a variable load on the system to reflect on-line database activity as typically found in production environments.

### 2.4.1 *Input Data Generation*

**2.4.1.1** For any given terminal, the home warehouse number (W_ID) is constant over the whole measurement interval (see Clause 5.5).

**2.4.1.2** The district number (D_ID) is randomly selected within [1 .. 10] from the home warehouse (D_W_ID = W_ID). The non-uniform random customer number (C_ID) is selected using the `NURand(1023,1,3000)` function from the selected district number (C_D_ID = D_ID) and the home warehouse number (C_W_ID = W_ID).

**2.4.1.3** The number of items in the order (*ol_cnt*) is randomly selected within [5 .. 15] (an average of 10). This field is not entered. It is generated by the terminal emulator to determine the size of the order. O_OL_CNT is later displayed after being computed by the SUT.

**2.4.1.4** A fixed 1% of the New-Order transactions are chosen at random to simulate user data entry errors and exercise the performance of rolling back update transactions. This must be implemented by generating a random number *rbk* within [1 .. 100].

**Comment:** All New-Order transactions must have independently generated input data. The input data from a rolled back transaction cannot be used for a subsequent transaction.

**2.4.1.5** For each of the *ol_cnt* items on the order:

1. A non-uniform random item number (OL_I_ID) is selected using the `NURand(8191,1,100000)` function. If this is the last item on the order and *rbk* = 1 (see Clause 2.4.1.4), then the item number is set to an unused value.

**Comment**: An **unused** value for an item number is a value not found in the database such that its use will produce a "not-found" condition within the application program. This condition should result in rolling back the current database transaction.

2. A supplying warehouse number (OL_SUPPLY_W_ID) is selected as the home warehouse 99% of the time and as a remote warehouse 1% of the time. This can be implemented by generating a random number $x$ within [1 .. 100];

   - If $x > 1$, the item is supplied from the home warehouse (OL_SUPPLY_W_ID = W_ID).

   - If $x = 1$, the item is supplied from a remote warehouse (OL_SUPPLY_W_ID is randomly selected within the range of configured warehouses other than W_ID).

   **Comment 1**: With an average of 10 items per order, approximately 90% of all orders can be supplied in full by stocks from the home warehouse.

   **Comment 2**: If the system is configured for a single warehouse, then all items are supplied from that single home warehouse.

3. A quantity (OL_QUANTITY) is randomly selected within [1 .. 10].

**2.4.1.6** The order entry date (O_ENTRY_D) is generated within the SUT by using the current system date and time.

**2.4.1.7** An order-line is said to be **home** if it is supplied by the home warehouse (i.e., when OL_SUPPLY_W_ID equals O_W_ID).

**2.4.1.8** An order-line is said to be **remote** when it is supplied by a remote warehouse (i.e., when OL_SUPPLY_W_ID does not equal O_W_ID).

**2.4.2** *Transaction Profile*

**2.4.2.1** Entering a new order is done in a single database transaction with the following steps:

1. Create an order header, composed of:

   2 row selections with data retrieval,

   1 row selection with data retrieval and update,

   2 row insertions.

2. Order a variable number of items (average $ol\_cnt$ = 10), composed of:

   ($1 * ol\_cnt$) row selections with data retrieval,

   ($1 * ol\_cnt$) row selections with data retrieval and update,

   ($1 * ol\_cnt$) row insertions.

**Note**: The above summary is provided for information only. The actual requirement is defined by the detailed transaction profile below.

**2.4.2.2** For a given warehouse number (W_ID), district number (D_W_ID, D_ID), customer number (C_W_ID, C_D_ID, C_ ID), count of items (*ol_cnt*, not communicated to the SUT), and for a given set of items (OL_I_ID), supplying warehouses (OL_SUPPLY_W_ID), and quantities (OL_QUANTITY):

- The input data (see Clause 2.4.3.2) are communicated to the SUT.

- A database transaction is started.

- The row in the WAREHOUSE table with matching W_ID is selected and W_TAX, the warehouse tax rate, is retrieved.

- The row in the DISTRICT table with matching D_W_ID and D_ ID is selected, D_TAX, the district tax rate, is retrieved, and D_NEXT_O_ID, the next available order number for the district, is retrieved and incremented by one.

- The row in the CUSTOMER table with matching C_W_ID, C_D_ID, and C_ID is selected and C_DISCOUNT, the customer's discount rate, C_LAST, the customer's last name, and C_CREDIT, the customer's credit status, are retrieved.

- A new row is inserted into both the NEW-ORDER table and the ORDER table to reflect the creation of the new order. O_CARRIER_ID is set to a null value. If the order includes only home order-lines, then O_ALL_LOCAL is set to 1, otherwise O_ALL_LOCAL is set to 0.

- The number of items, O_OL_CNT, is computed to match *ol_cnt*.

- For each O_OL_CNT item on the order:

  — The row in the ITEM table with matching I_ID (equals OL_I_ID) is selected and I_PRICE, the price of the item, I_NAME, the name of the item, and I_DATA are retrieved. If I_ID has an unused value (see Clause 2.4.1.5), a "not-found" condition is signaled, resulting in a rollback of the database transaction (see Clause 2.4.2.3).

  — The row in the STOCK table with matching S_I_ID (equals OL_I_ID) and S_W_ID (equals OL_SUPPLY_W_ID) is selected. S_QUANTITY, the quantity in stock, S_DIST_xx, where xx represents the district number, and S_DATA are retrieved. If the retrieved value for S_QUANTITY exceeds OL_QUANTITY by 10 or more, then S_QUANTITY is decreased by OL_QUANTITY; otherwise S_QUANTITY is updated to (S_QUANTITY - OL_QUANTITY)+91. S_YTD is increased by OL_QUANTITY and S_ORDER_CNT is incremented by 1. If the order-line is remote, then S_REMOTE_CNT is incremented by 1.

  — The amount for the item in the order (OL_AMOUNT) is computed as:

  OL_QUANTITY * I_PRICE

  — The strings in I_DATA and S_DATA are examined. If they both include the string "ORIGINAL", the *brand-generic* field for that item is set to "B", otherwise, the *brand-generic* field is set to "G".

- — A new row is inserted into the ORDER-LINE table to reflect the item on the order. OL_DELIVERY_D is set to a null value, OL_NUMBER is set to a unique value within all the ORDER-LINE rows that have the same OL_O_ID value, and OL_DIST_INFO is set to the content of S_DIST_xx, where xx represents the district number (OL_D_ID)

- The *total-amount* for the complete order is computed as:

  sum(OL_AMOUNT) * (1 - C_DISCOUNT) * (1 + W_TAX + D_TAX)

- The database transaction is committed, unless it has been rolled back as a result of an *unused* value for the last item number (see Clause 2.4.1.5).

- The output data (see Clause 2.4.3.3) are communicated to the terminal.

**2.4.2.3**     For transactions that roll back as a result of an unused item number, the complete transaction profile must be executed with the exception that the following steps need not be done:

- Selecting and retrieving the row in the stock table with S_I_ID matching the unused item number.

- Examining the strings I_DATA and S_DATA for the unused item.

- Inserting a new row into the ORDER-LINE table for the unused item.

- Adding the amount for the unused item to the sum of all OL_AMOUNT.

The transaction is not committed. Instead, the transaction is rolled back.

**Comment 1**: The intent of this clause is to ensure that within the New-Order transaction all valid items are processed prior to processing the unused item. Knowledge that an item is unused, resulting in rolling back the transaction, can only be used to skip execution of the above steps. No other optimization can result from this knowledge (e.g., skipping other steps, changing the execution of other steps, using a different type of transaction, etc.).

**Comment 2**: This clause is an exception to Clause 2.3.1. The order of data manipulations prior to signaling a "not found" condition is immaterial.

**2.4.3**     *Terminal I/O*

**2.4.3.1**     For each transaction the originating terminal must display the following input/output screen with all input and output fields cleared (with either spaces or zeros) except for the Warehouse field which has not changed and must display the fixed W_ID value associated with that terminal.

C

```
                1           2           3           4           5           6           7           8
         1234567890123456789012345678901234567890123456789012345678901234567890123456789012345678901234567890
    1 ┌─────────────────────────────────────────────────────────────────────────────────┐
    2 │                                   New Order                                       │
    3 │ Warehouse: 9999     District: 99                  Date: DD-MM-YYYY hh:mm:ss        │
    4 │ Customer:  9999     Name: XXXXXXXXXXXXXXXX  Credit: XX   %Disc: 99.99              │
    5 │ Order Number: 99999999  Number of Lines: 99       W_tax: 99.99   D_tax: 99.99      │
    6 │                                                                                   │
    7 │ Supp_W   Item_Id   Item Name                    Qty   Stock  B/G  Price    Amount  │
    8 │  9999    999999    XXXXXXXXXXXXXXXXXXXXXXXX      99    999    X    $999.99  $9999.99│
    9 │  9999    999999    XXXXXXXXXXXXXXXXXXXXXXXX      99    999    X    $999.99  $9999.99│
   10 │  9999    999999    XXXXXXXXXXXXXXXXXXXXXXXX      99    999    X    $999.99  $9999.99│
   11 │  9999    999999    XXXXXXXXXXXXXXXXXXXXXXXX      99    999    X    $999.99  $9999.99│
   12 │  9999    999999    XXXXXXXXXXXXXXXXXXXXXXXX      99    999    X    $999.99  $9999.99│
   13 │  9999    999999    XXXXXXXXXXXXXXXXXXXXXXXX      99    999    X    $999.99  $9999.99│
   14 │  9999    999999    XXXXXXXXXXXXXXXXXXXXXXXX      99    999    X    $999.99  $9999.99│
   15 │  9999    999999    XXXXXXXXXXXXXXXXXXXXXXXX      99    999    X    $999.99  $9999.99│
   16 │  9999    999999    XXXXXXXXXXXXXXXXXXXXXXXX      99    999    X    $999.99  $9999.99│
   17 │  9999    999999    XXXXXXXXXXXXXXXXXXXXXXXX      99    999    X    $999.99  $9999.99│
   18 │  9999    999999    XXXXXXXXXXXXXXXXXXXXXXXX      99    999    X    $999.99  $9999.99│
   19 │  9999    999999    XXXXXXXXXXXXXXXXXXXXXXXX      99    999    X    $999.99  $9999.99│
   20 │  9999    999999    XXXXXXXXXXXXXXXXXXXXXXXX      99    999    X    $999.99  $9999.99│
   21 │  9999    999999    XXXXXXXXXXXXXXXXXXXXXXXX      99    999    X    $999.99  $9999.99│
   22 │ Execution Status: XXXXXXXXXXXXXXXXXXXXXXXX                      Total:   $99999.99 │
   23 │                                                                                   │
   24 └─────────────────────────────────────────────────────────────────────────────────┘
```

**2.4.3.2**    The emulated user must enter, in the appropriate fields of the input/output screen, the required input data which is divided in two groups and organized as follows:

- Two fields: D_ID and C_ID.

  **Comment:** The value for *ol_cnt* cannot be entered, but must be determined by the application upon processing of the input data.

- One repeating group of fields: OL_I_ID, OL_SUPPLY_W_ID and OL_QUAN-TITY. The group is repeated *ol_cnt* times (once per item in the order). The values of these fields are chosen as per Clause 2.4.1.5.

  **Comment:** In order to maintain a reasonable amount of keyed input, the supply warehouse fields must be filled in for each item, even when the supply warehouse is the home warehouse.

**2.4.3.3**    The emulated terminal must display, in the appropriate fields of the input/output screen, all input data and the output data resulting from the execution of the transaction. The display fields are divided in two groups as follows:

- One non-repeating group of fields: W_ID, D_ID, C_ID, O_ID, O_OL_CNT, C_LAST, C_CREDIT, C_DISCOUNT, W_TAX, D_TAX, O_ENTRY_D, *total_amount*, and an optional execution status message other than "Item number is not valid".

- One repeating group of fields: OL_SUPPLY_W_ID, OL_I_ID, I_NAME, OL_QUANTITY, S_QUANTITY, *brand_generic*, I_PRICE, and OL_AMOUNT. The group is repeated O_OL_CNT times (once per item in the order), equal to the computed value of *ol_cnt.*

**2.4.3.4**    For transactions that are rolled back as a result of an unused item number (1% of all New-Order transactions), the emulated terminal must display in the appropriate fields of the input/output screen the fields: W_id, d_id, C_ID, C_LAST, C_CREDIT, O_ID, and the execution status message "Item number is not valid". Note that no execution status message is required for successfully committed transactions. However, this field may not display "Item number is not valid" if the transaction is successful.

**Comment**: The number of the rolled back order, O_ID, must be displayed to verify that part of the transaction was processed.

**2.4.3.5**    The following table summarizes the terminal I/O requirements for the New-Order transaction:

| | Enter | Display | Display After rollback | Coordinates Row/Column |
|---|---|---|---|---|
| Non-repeating Group | | W_ID | W_ID | 2/12 |
| | D_ID | D_ID | D_ID | 2/29 |
| | C_ID | C_ID | C_ID | 3/12 |
| | | C_LAST | C_LAST | 3/25 |
| | | C_CREDIT | C_CREDIT | 3/52 |
| | | C_DISCOUNT | | 3/64 |
| | | W_TAX | | 4/51 |
| | | D_TAX | | 4/67 |
| | | O_OL_CNT | | 4/42 |
| | | O_ID | O_ID | 4/15 |
| | | O_ENTRY_D | | 2/61 |
| | | *total-amount* | | 22/71 |
| | | | "Item number is not valid" | 22/19 |
| Repeating Group | OL_SUPPLY_W_ID | OL_SUPPLY_W_ID | | 7-22/3 |
| | OL_I_ID | OL_I_ID | | 7-22/10 |
| | | I_NAME | | 7-22/20 |
| | OL_QUANTITY | OL_QUANTITY | | 7-22/45 |
| | | S_QUANTITY | | 7-22/51 |
| | | *brand-generic* | | 7-22/58 |
| | | I_PRICE | | 7-22/63 |
| | | OL_AMOUNT | | 7-22/72 |

**2.4.3.6**    For general terminal I/O requirements, see Clause 2.2.

C

## 2.5 The Payment Transaction

The Payment business transaction updates the customer's balance and reflects the payment on the district and warehouse sales statistics. It represents a light-weight, read-write transaction with a high frequency of execution and stringent response time requirements to satisfy on-line users. In addition, this transaction includes non-primary key access to the customer table.

### 2.5.1 *Input Data Generation*

**2.5.1.1** For any given terminal, the home warehouse number (W_ID) is constant over the whole measurement interval.

**2.5.1.2** The district number (D_ID) is randomly selected within [1 .. 10] from the home warehouse (D_W_ID) = W_ID). The customer is randomly selected 60% of the time by last name (C_W_ID, C_D_ID, C_LAST) and 40% of the time by number (C_W_ID , C_D_ID , C_ID). Independent of the mode of selection, the customer resident warehouse is the home warehouse 85% of the time and is a randomly selected remote warehouse 15% of the time. This can be implemented by generating two random numbers $x$ and $y$ within [1 .. 100];

- If $x <= 85$ a customer is selected from the selected district number (C_D_ID = D_ID) and the home warehouse number (C_W_ID = W_ID). The customer is paying through his/her own warehouse.

- If $x > 85$ a customer is selected from a random district number (C_D_ID is randomly selected within [1 .. 10]), and a random remote warehouse number (C_W_ID is randomly selected within the range of configured warehouses, and C_W_ID $\neq$ W_ID). The customer is paying through a warehouse and a district other than his/her own.

- If $y <= 60$ a customer last name (C_LAST) is generated according to Clause 4.3.2.3 from a non-uniform random value using the `NURand(255,0,999)` function. The customer is using his/her last name and is one of the possibly several customers with that last name.

  **Comment**: This case illustrates the situation when a customer does not use his/her unique customer number.

- If $y > 60$ a non-uniform random customer number (C_ID) is selected using the `NURand(1023,1,3000)` function. The customer is using his/her customer number.

**Comment**: If the system is configured for a single warehouse, then all customers are selected from that single home warehouse.

**2.5.1.3** The payment amount (H_AMOUNT) is randomly selected within [1.00 .. 5,000.00].

**2.5.1.4** The payment date (H_DATE) in generated within the SUT by using the current system date and time.

**2.5.1.5** A Payment transaction is said to be **home** if the customer belongs to the warehouse from which the payment is entered (when C_W_ID = W_ID).

**2.5.1.6** A Payment transaction is said to be **remote** if the warehouse from which the payment is entered is not the one to which the customer belongs (when C_W_ID does not equal W_ID).

**2.5.2** *Transaction Profile*

**2.5.2.1** The Payment transaction enters a customer's payment with a single database transaction and is composed of:

**Case 1**, the customer is selected based on customer number:

> 3 row selections with data retrieval and update,
>
> 1 row insertion.

**Case 2**, the customer is selected based on customer last name:

> 2 row selections (on average) with data retrieval,
>
> 3 row selections with data retrieval and update,
>
> 1 row insertion.

**Note**: The above summary is provided for information only. The actual requirement is defined by the detailed transaction profile below.

**2.5.2.2** For a given warehouse number (W_ID), district number (D_W_ID, D_ID), customer number (C_W_ID, C_D_ID, C_ ID) or customer last name (C_W_ID, C_D_ID, C_LAST), and payment amount (H_AMOUNT):

- The input data (see Clause 2.5.3.2) are communicated to the SUT.

- A database transaction is started.

- The row in the WAREHOUSE table with matching W_ID is selected. W_NAME, W_STREET_1, W_STREET_2, W_CITY, W_STATE, and W_ZIP are retrieved and W_YTD, the warehouse's year-to-date balance, is increased by H_ AMOUNT.

- The row in the DISTRICT table with matching D_W_ID and D_ID is selected. D_NAME, D_STREET_1, D_STREET_2, D_CITY, D_STATE, and D_ZIP are retrieved and D_YTD, the district's year-to-date balance, is increased by H_AMOUNT.

- **Case 1**, the customer is selected based on customer number: the row in the CUSTOMER table with matching C_W_ID, C_D_ID and C_ID is selected. C_FIRST, C_MIDDLE, C_LAST, C_STREET_1, C_STREET_2, C_CITY, C_STATE, C_ZIP, C_PHONE, C_SINCE, C_CREDIT, C_CREDIT_LIM, C_DISCOUNT, and C_BALANCE are retrieved. C_BALANCE is decreased by H_AMOUNT. C_YTD_PAYMENT is increased by H_AMOUNT. C_PAYMENT_CNT is incremented by 1.

C

**Case 2**, the customer is selected based on customer last name: all rows in the CUSTOMER table with matching C_W_ID, C_D_ID and C_LAST are selected sorted by C_FIRST in ascending order. Let $n$ be the number of rows selected. C_FIRST, C_MIDDLE, C_LAST, C_STREET_1, C_STREET_2, C_CITY, C_STATE, C_ZIP, C_PHONE, C_SINCE, C_CREDIT, C_CREDIT_LIM, C_DISCOUNT, and C_BALANCE are retrieved from the row at position ($n$/2 rounded up to the next integer) in the sorted set of selected rows from the CUSTOMER table. C_BALANCE is decreased by H_AMOUNT. C_YTD_PAYMENT is increased by H_AMOUNT. C_PAYMENT_CNT is incremented by 1.

- If the value of C_CREDIT is equal to "BC", then C_DATA is also retrieved from the selected customer and the following history information: C_ID, C_D_ID, C_W_ID, D_ID, W_ID, and H_AMOUNT are inserted at the left of the C_DATA field by shifting the existing content of C_DATA to the right by an equal number of bytes and by discarding the bytes that are shifted out of the right side of the C_DATA field. The content of the C_DATA field never exceeds 500 characters. The selected customer is updated with the new C_DATA field. If C_DATA is implemented as two fields (see Clause 1.4.9), they must be treated and operated on as one single field.

  **Comment**: The format used to store the history information must be such that its display on the input/output screen is in a readable format (e.g., the W_ID portion of C_DATA must use the same display format as the output field W_ID).

- H_DATA is built by concatenating W_NAME and D_NAME separated by 4 spaces.

- A new row is inserted into the HISTORY table with H_C_ID = C_ID, H_C_D_ID = C_D_ID, H_C_W_ID = C_W_ID, H_D_ID = D_ID, and H_W_ID = W_ID.

- The database transaction is committed.

- The output data (see Clause 2.5.3.3) are communicated to the terminal.

### 2.5.3 *Terminal I/O*

**2.5.3.1**    For each transaction the originating terminal must display the following input/output screen with all input and output fields cleared (with either spaces or zeros) except for the Warehouse field which has not changed and must display the fixed W_ID value associated with that terminal. In addition, all address fields (i.e., W_STREET_1, W_STREET_2, W_CITY, W_STATE, and W_ZIP) of the warehouse may display the fixed values for these fields if these values were already retrieved in a previous transaction.

C

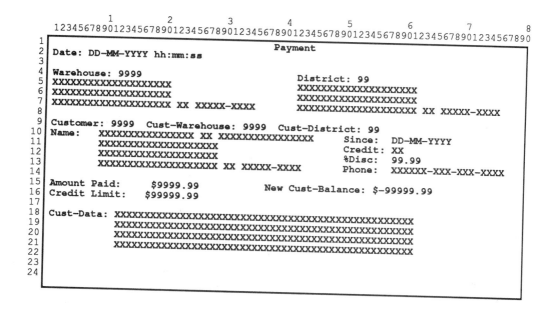

```
            1         2         3         4         5         6         7         8
   1234567890123456789012345678901234567890123456789012345678901234567890123456789012345670
 1 ┌─────────────────────────────────────────────────────────────────────┐
 2 │                                    Payment                            │
   │ Date: DD-MM-YYYY hh:mm:ss                                             │
 3 │                                                                       │
 4 │ Warehouse: 9999                              District: 99             │
 5 │ XXXXXXXXXXXXXXXXXXXXX                         XXXXXXXXXXXXXXXXXXXXX     │
 6 │ XXXXXXXXXXXXXXXXXXXXX                         XXXXXXXXXXXXXXXXXXXXX     │
 7 │ XXXXXXXXXXXXXXXXXXXXX XX XXXXX-XXXX           XXXXXXXXXXXXXXXXXXXXX XX XXXXX-XXXX │
 8 │                                                                       │
 9 │ Customer: 9999   Cust-Warehouse: 9999   Cust-District: 99             │
10 │ Name:    XXXXXXXXXXXXXXX XX XXXXXXXXXXXXXXXX    Since:  DD-MM-YYYY     │
11 │          XXXXXXXXXXXXXXXXXXXXX                  Credit: XX            │
12 │          XXXXXXXXXXXXXXXXXXXXX                  %Disc:  99.99         │
13 │          XXXXXXXXXXXXXXXXXXXXX XX XXXXX-XXXX    Phone:  XXXXXX-XXX-XXX-XXXX │
14 │                                                                       │
15 │ Amount Paid:       $9999.99        New Cust-Balance: $-99999.99       │
16 │ Credit Limit:      $99999.99                                          │
17 │                                                                       │
18 │ Cust-Data: XXXXXXXXXXXXXXXXXXXXXXXXXXXXXXXXXXXXXXXXXXXXXXXXXXXXXXXXX   │
19 │            XXXXXXXXXXXXXXXXXXXXXXXXXXXXXXXXXXXXXXXXXXXXXXXXXXXXXXXXX   │
20 │            XXXXXXXXXXXXXXXXXXXXXXXXXXXXXXXXXXXXXXXXXXXXXXXXXXXXXXXXX   │
21 │            XXXXXXXXXXXXXXXXXXXXXXXXXXXXXXXXXXXXXXXXXXXXXXXXXXXXXXXXX   │
22 │                                                                       │
23 │                                                                       │
24 └─────────────────────────────────────────────────────────────────────┘
```

**2.5.3.2**     The emulated user must enter, in the appropriate fields of the input/output screen, the required input data which is organized as the distinct fields: D_ID, C_ID or C_LAST, C_D_ID, C_W_ID, and H_AMOUNT.

**Comment:** In order to maintain a reasonable amount of keyed input, the customer warehouse field must be filled in even when it is the same as the home warehouse.

**2.5.3.3**     The emulated terminal must display, in the appropriate fields of the input/output screen, all input data and the output data resulting from the execution of the transaction. The following fields are displayed: W_ID, D_ID, C_ID, C_D_ID, C_W_ID, W_STREET_1, W_STREET_2, W_CITY, W_STATE, W_ZIP, D_STREET_1, D_STREET_2, D_CITY, D_STATE, D_ZIP, C_FIRST, C_MIDDLE, C_LAST, C_STREET_1, C_STREET_2, C_CITY, C_STATE, C_ZIP, C_PHONE, C_SINCE, C_CREDIT, C_CREDIT_LIM, C_DISCOUNT, C_BALANCE, the first 200 characters of C_DATA (only if C_CREDIT = "BC"), H_AMOUNT, and H_DATE.

C

**2.5.3.4** The following table summarizes the terminal I/O requirements for the Payment transaction:

| | Enter | Display | Coordinates Row/Column |
|---|---|---|---|
| Non-repeating Group | | W_ID | 4/12 |
| | D_ID | D_ID | 4/52 |
| | C_ID [1] | C_ID | 9/11 |
| | C_D_ID | C_D_ID | 9/54 |
| | C_W_ID | C_W_ID | 9/33 |
| | H_AMOUNT | H_AMOUNT | 15/19 |
| | | H_DATE | 2/7 |
| | | W_STREET_1 | 5/1 |
| | | W_STREET_2 | 6/1 |
| | | W_CITY | 7/1 |
| | | W_STATE | 7/22 |
| | | W_ZIP | 7/25 |
| | | D_STREET_1 | 5/42 |
| | | D_STREET_2 | 6/42 |
| | | D_CITY | 7/42 |
| | | D_STATE | 7/63 |
| | | D_ZIP | 7/66 |
| | | C_FIRST | 10/9 |
| | | C_MIDDLE | 10/26 |
| | C_LAST [2] | C_LAST | 10/29 |
| | | C_STREET_1 | 11/9 |
| | | C_STREET_2 | 12/9 |
| | | C_CITY | 13/9 |
| | | C_STATE | 13/30 |
| | | C_ZIP | 13/33 |
| | | C_PHONE | 13/58 |
| | | C_SINCE | 10/58 |
| | | C_CREDIT | 11/58 |
| | | C_CREDIT_LIM | 16/18 |
| | | C_DISCOUNT | 12/58 |
| | | C_BALANCE | 15/57 |
| | | C_DATA [3] | 18-21/12 |

[1] Enter only for payment by customer number.
[2] Enter only for payment by customer last name.
[3] Display the first 200 characters only if C_CREDIT = "BC".

**2.5.3.5** For general terminal I/O requirements, see Clause 2.2.

C

## 2.6   The Order-Status Transaction

The Order-Status business transaction queries the status of a customer's last order. It represents a mid-weight read-only database transaction with a low frequency of execution and response time requirement to satisfy on-line users. In addition, this table includes non-primary key access to the CUSTOMER table.

### 2.6.1   *Input Data Generation*

**2.6.1.1**   For any given terminal, the home warehouse number (W_ID) is constant over the whole measurement interval.

**2.6.1.2**   The district number (D_ID) is randomly selected within [1 .. 10] from the home warehouse. The customer is randomly selected 60% of the time by last name (C_W_ID, C_D_ID, C_LAST) and 40% of the time by number (C_W_ID, C_D_ID, C_ID) from the selected district (C_D_ID = D_ID) and the home warehouse number (C_W_ID = W_ID). This can be implemented by generating a random number $y$ within [1 .. 100];

- If $y <= 60$ a customer last name (C_LAST) is generated according to Clause 4.3.2.3 from a non-uniform random value using the `NURand(255,0,999)` function. The customer is using his/her last name and is one of the, possibly several, customers with that last name.

  **Comment:** This case illustrates the situation when a customer does not use his/her unique customer number.

- If $y > 60$ a non-uniform random customer number (C_ID) is selected using the `NURand(1023,1,3000)` function. The customer is using his/her customer number.

### 2.6.2   *Transaction Profile*

**2.6.2.1**   Querying for the status of an order is done in a single database transaction with the following steps:

1. Find the customer and his/her last order, composed of:

   **Case 1**, the customer is selected based on customer number:

     2 row selections with data retrieval.

   **Case 2**, the customer is selected based on customer last name:

     4 row selections (on average) with data retrieval.

2. Check status (delivery date) of each item on the order (average items-per-order = 10), composed of:

   (1 * items-per-order) row selections with data retrieval.

**Note:** The above summary is provided for information only. The actual requirement is defined by the detailed transaction profile below.

**2.6.2.2**   For a given customer number (C_W_ID , C_D_ID , C_ ID):

- The input data (see Clause 2.6.3.2) are communicated to the SUT.

C

- A database transaction is started.

- **Case 1**, the customer is selected based on customer number: the row in the CUSTOMER table with matching C_W_ID, C_D_ID, and C_ID is selected and C_BALANCE, C_FIRST, C_MIDDLE, and C_LAST are retrieved.

  **Case 2**, the customer is selected based on customer last name: all rows in the CUSTOMER table with matching C_W_ID, C_D_ID, and C_LAST are selected sorted by C_FIRST in ascending order. Let *n* be the number of rows selected. C_BALANCE, C_FIRST, C_MIDDLE, and C_LAST are retrieved from the row at position *n*/2 rounded up in the sorted set of selected rows from the CUSTOMER table.

- The row in the ORDER table with matching O_W_ID (equals C_W_ID), O_D_ID (equals C_D_ID), O_C_ID (equals C_ID), and with the largest existing O_ID, is selected. This is the most recent order placed by that customer. O_ID, O_ENTRY_D, and O_CARRIER_ID are retrieved.

- All rows in the ORDER-LINE table with matching OL_W_ID (equals O_W_ID), OL_D_ID (equals O_D_ID), and OL_O_ID (equals O_ID) are selected and the corresponding sets of OL_I_ID, OL_SUPPLY_W_ID, OL_QUANTITY, OL_AMOUNT, and OL_DELIVERY_D are retrieved.

- The database transaction is committed.

  **Comment**: a commit is not required as long as all ACID properties are satisfied (see Clause 3).

- The output data (see Clause 2.6.3.3) are communicated to the terminal.

## 2.6.3    *Terminal I/O*

**2.6.3.1**    For each transaction the originating terminal must display the following input/output screen with all input and output fields cleared (with either spaces or zeros) except for the Warehouse field which has not changed and must display the fixed W_ID value associated with that terminal.

C

```
            1         2         3         4         5         6         7         8
   12345678901234567890123456789012345678901234567890123456789012345678901234567890
                                    Order-Status
 1 Warehouse: 9999    District: 99
 2 Customer: 9999    Name: XXXXXXXXXXXXXXXX XX XXXXXXXXXXXXXXXX
 3 Cust-Balance: $-99999.99
 4
 5 Order-Number: 99999999    Entry-Date: DD-MM-YYYY hh:mm:ss    Carrier-Number: 99
 6 Supply-W      Item-Id    Qty     Amount     Delivery-Date
 7   9999        999999     99    $99999.99     DD-MM-YYYY
 8   9999        999999     99    $99999.99     DD-MM-YYYY
 9   9999        999999     99    $99999.99     DD-MM-YYYY
10   9999        999999     99    $99999.99     DD-MM-YYYY
11   9999        999999     99    $99999.99     DD-MM-YYYY
12   9999        999999     99    $99999.99     DD-MM-YYYY
13   9999        999999     99    $99999.99     DD-MM-YYYY
14   9999        999999     99    $99999.99     DD-MM-YYYY
15   9999        999999     99    $99999.99     DD-MM-YYYY
16   9999        999999     99    $99999.99     DD-MM-YYYY
17   9999        999999     99    $99999.99     DD-MM-YYYY
18   9999        999999     99    $99999.99     DD-MM-YYYY
19   9999        999999     99    $99999.99     DD-MM-YYYY
20   9999        999999     99    $99999.99     DD-MM-YYYY
21   9999        999999     99    $99999.99     DD-MM-YYYY
22
23
24
```

**2.6.3.2**    The emulated user must enter, in the appropriate field of the input/output screen, the required input data which is organized as the distinct fields: D_ID and either C_ID or C_LAST.

**2.6.3.3**    The emulated terminal must display, in the appropriate fields of the input/output screen, all input data and the output data resulting from the execution of the transaction. The display fields are divided in two groups as follows:

- One non-repeating group of fields: W_ID, D_ID, C_ID, C_FIRST, C_MIDDLE, C_LAST, C_BALANCE, O_ID, O_ENTRY_D, and O_CARRIER_ID;

- One repeating group of fields: OL_SUPPLY_W_ID, OL_I_ID, OL_QUANTITY, OL_AMOUNT, and OL_DELIVERY_D. The group is repeated O_OL_CNT times (once per item in the order).

**Comment 1**: The order of items shown on the Order-Status screen does not need to match the order in which the items were entered in its corresponding New-Order screen.

**Comment 2**: If OL_DELIVERY_D is null (i.e., the order has not been delivered), the terminal must display an implementation specific null date representation (e.g., blanks, 99-99-9999, etc.). The chosen null date representation must not change during the test.

C

**2.6.3.4** The following table summarizes the terminal I/O requirements for the Order-Status transaction:

| | Enter | Display | Coordinates Row/Column |
|---|---|---|---|
| Non-repeating Group | | W_ID | 2/12 |
| | D_ID | D_ID | 2/29 |
| | C_ID [1] | C_ID | 3/11 |
| | | C_FIRST | 3/24 |
| | | C_MIDDLE | 3/41 |
| | C_LAST [2] | C_LAST | 3/44 |
| | | C_BALANCE | 4/16 |
| | | O_ID | 6/15 |
| | | O_ENTRY_D | 6/38 |
| | | O_CARRIER_ID | 6/76 |
| Repeating Group | | OL_SUPPLY_W_ID | 8-22/3 |
| | | OL_I_ID | 8-22/14 |
| | | OL_QUANTITY | 8-22/25 |
| | | OL_AMOUNT | 8-22/33 |
| | | OL_DELIVERY_D | 8-22/47 |

[1] Enter only for query by customer number.
[2] Enter only for query by customer last name.

**2.6.3.5** For general terminal I/O requirements, see Clause 2.2.

## 2.7 The Delivery Transaction

The Delivery business transaction consists of processing a batch of 10 new (not yet delivered) orders. Each order is processed (delivered) in full within the scope of a read-write database transaction. The number of orders delivered as a group (or batched) within the same database transaction is implementation specific. The business transaction, composed of one or more (up to 10) database transactions, has a low frequency of execution and must complete within a relaxed response time requirement.

The Delivery transaction is intended to be executed in deferred mode through a queueing mechanism, rather than interactively, with terminal response indicating transaction completion. The result of the deferred execution is recorded into a result file.

### 2.7.1 *Input Data Generation*

**2.7.1.1** For any given terminal, the home warehouse number (W_ID) is constant over the whole measurement interval.

**2.7.1.2**    The carrier number (O_CARRIER_ID) is randomly selected within [1 .. 10].

**2.7.1.3**    The delivery date (OL_DELIVERY_D) is generated within the SUT by using the current system date and time.

**2.7.2**    *Deferred Execution*

**2.7.2.1**    Unlike the other transactions in this benchmark, the Delivery transaction must be executed in deferred mode. This mode of execution is primarily characterized by queueing the transaction for deferred execution, returning control to the originating terminal independently from the completion of the transaction, and recording execution information into a result file.

**2.7.2.2**    Deferred execution of the Delivery transaction must adhere to the following rules:

1.  The business transaction is queued for deferred execution as a result of entering the last input character.

2.  The deferred execution of the business transaction must follow the profile defined in Clause 2.7.4 with the input data defined in Clause 2.7.1 as entered through the input/output screen and communicated to the deferred execution queue.

3.  At least 90% of the business transactions must complete within 80 seconds of their being queued for execution.

4.  Upon completion of the business transaction, the following information must have been recorded into a result file:

    • The time at which the business transaction was queued.

    • The warehouse number (W_ID) and the carried number (O_CARRI-ER_ID) associated with the business transaction.

    • The district number (D_ID) and the order number (O_ID) of each order delivered by the business transaction.

    • The time at which the business transaction completed.

**2.7.2.3**    The **result file** associated with the deferred execution of the Delivery business transaction is only for the purpose of recording information about that transaction and is not relevant to the business function being performed. The result file must adhere to the following rules:

1.  All events must be completed before the related information is recorded (e.g., the recording of a district and order number must be done after the database transaction, within which this order was delivered, has been committed).

2.  No ACID property is required (e.g., the recording of a district and order number is not required to be atomic with the actual delivery of that order) as the result file is used for benchmarking purposes only.

C

3. During the measurement interval the result file must be located either on a durable medium (see clause 3.5.1) or in the internal memory of the SUT. In this last case, the result file must be transferred onto a durable medium after the last measurement interval of the test run (see Clause 5.5).

**2.7.3** *Terminal I/O*

**2.7.3.1** For each transaction the originating terminal must display the following input/output screen with all input and output fields cleared (with either spaces or zeros) except for the Warehouse field which has not changed and must display the fixed W_ID value associated with that terminal.

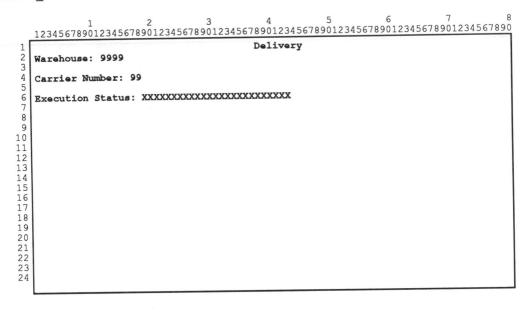

```
             1         2         3         4         5         6         7         8
    12345678901234567890123456789012345678901234567890123456789012345678901234567890
 1                                   Delivery
 2  Warehouse: 9999
 3
 4  Carrier Number: 99
 5
 6  Execution Status: XXXXXXXXXXXXXXXXXXXXXXXXXXX
 7
 8
 9
10
11
12
13
14
15
16
17
18
19
20
21
22
23
24
```

**2.7.3.2** The emulated user must enter, in the appropriate input field of the input/output screen, the required input data which is organized as one distinct field: O_CARRIER_ID.

**2.7.3.3** The emulated terminal must display, in the appropriate output field of the input/output screen, all input data and the output data which results from the queueing of the transaction. The following fields are displayed: W_ID, O_CARRIER_ID, and the status message "Delivery has been queued".

C

**2.7.3.4**    The following table summarizes the terminal I/O requirements for the Delivery transaction:

| | Enter | Display | Coordinates Row/Column |
|---|---|---|---|
| Non-repeating Group | | W_ID | 2/12 |
| | O_CARRIER_ID | O_CARRIER_ID | 4/17 |
| | | "Delivery has been queued" | 6/19 |

**2.7.3.5**    For general terminal I/O requirements, see Clause 2.2.

**2.7.4**    *Transaction Profile*

**2.7.4.1**    The deferred execution of the Delivery transaction delivers one outstanding order (average items-per-order = 10) for each one of the 10 districts of the selected warehouse using one or more (up to 10) database transactions. Delivering each order is done in the following steps:

1.    Process the order, composed of:

   1 row selection with data retrieval,

   (1 + items-per-order) row selections with data retrieval and update.

2.    Update the customer's balance, composed of:

   1 row selections with data update.

3.    Remove the order from the new-order list, composed of:

   1 row deletion.

**Comment:** This business transaction can be done within a single database transaction or broken down into up to 10 database transactions to allow the test sponsor the flexibility to implement the business transaction with the most efficient number of database transactions.

**Note:** The above summary is provided for information only. The actual requirement is defined by the detailed transaction profile below.

**2.7.4.2**    For a given warehouse number (W_ID), for each of the 10 districts (D_W_ID , D_ID) within that warehouse, and for a given carrier number (O_CARRIER_ID):

•    The input data (see Clause 2.7.3.2) are retrieved from the deferred execution queue.

•    A database transaction is started unless a database transaction is already active from being started as part of the delivery of a previous order (i.e., more than one order is delivered within the same database transaction).

•    The row in the NEW-ORDER table with matching NO_W_ID (equals W_ID) and NO_D_ID (equals D_ID) and with the lowest NO_O_ID value is selected. This is the oldest undelivered order of that district. NO_O_ID, the order number, is retrieved. If no matching row is found, then the delivery of an order for this district is skipped. The condition in which no outstanding order is present at a given district must be handled by skipping the delivery of an order for that district only and resuming the delivery of an order from all remaining districts of the selected warehouse. If this condition occurs in more than 1%, or in more than one, whichever is greater, of the business transactions, it must be reported. The result file must be organized in such a way that the percentage of skipped deliveries and skipped districts can be determined.

- The selected row in the NEW-ORDER table is deleted.

- The row in the ORDER table with matching O_W_ID (equals W_ ID), O_D_ID (equals D_ID), and O_ID (equals NO_O_ID) is selected, O_C_ID, the customer number, is retrieved, and O_CARRIER_ID is updated.

- All rows in the ORDER-LINE table with matching OL_W_ID (equals O_W_ID), OL_D_ID (equals O_D_ID), and OL_O_ID (equals O_ID) are selected. All OL_DELIVERY_D, the delivery dates, are updated to the current system time as returned by the operating system and the sum of all OL_AMOUNT is retrieved.

- The row in the CUSTOMER table with matching C_W_ID (equals W_ID), C_D_ID (equals D_ID), and C_ID (equals O_C_ID) is selected and C_BALANCE is increased by the sum of all order-line amounts (OL_AMOUNT) previously retrieved. C_DELIVERY_CNT is incremented by 1.

- The database transaction is committed unless more orders will be delivered within this database transaction.

- Information about the delivered order (see Clause 2.7.2.2) is recorded into the result file (see Clause 2.7.2.3).

## 2.8    The Stock-Level Transaction

The Stock-Level business transaction determines the number of recently sold items that have a stock level below a specified threshold. It represents a heavy read-only database transaction with a low frequency of execution, a relaxed response time requirement, and relaxed consistency requirements.

### 2.8.1    *Input Data Generation*

**2.8.1.1**    For any given terminal, the home warehouse number (W_ID) and the district number (D_ID) within the home warehouse (D_W_ID = W_ID) are constant over the whole measurement interval.

**2.8.1.2**    The threshold of minimum quantity in stock (threshold) is selected at random within [10 .. 20].

**2.8.2**     *Transaction Profile*

**2.8.2.1**     Examining the level of stock for items on the last 20 orders is done in one or more database transactions with the following steps:

1.  Examine the next available order number, composed of:

    1 row selection with data retrieval.

2.  Examine all items on the last 20 orders (average items-per-order = 10) for the district, composed of:

    (20 * items-per-order) row selections with data retrieval.

3.  Examine, for each distinct item selected, if the level of stock available at the home warehouse is below the threshold, composed of:

    At most (20 * items-per-order) row selections with data retrieval.

**Note:** The above summary is provided for information only. The actual requirement is defined by the detailed transaction profile below.

**2.8.2.2**     For a given warehouse number (W_ID), district number (D_W_ID, D_ID), and stock level threshold (*threshold*):

*   The input data (see Clause 2.8.3.2) are communicated to the SUT.

*   A database transaction is started.

*   The row in the DISTRICT table with matching D_W_ID and D_ID is selected and D_NEXT_O_ID is retrieved.

*   All rows in the ORDER-LINE table with matching OL_W_ID (equals W_ID), OL_D_ID (equals D_ID), and OL_O_ID (lower than D_NEXT_O_ID and greater than or equal to D_NEXT_O_ID minus 20) are selected. They are the items for 20 recent orders of the district. All OL_I_ID items in the order are retrieved.

*   All rows in the STOCK table with matching S_I_ID (equals OL_I_ID) and S_W_ID (equals W_ID) from the list of distinct item numbers and with S_QUANTITY lower than *threshold* are counted (giving *low_stock*).

    **Comment:** Stocks must be counted only for distinct items. Thus, items that have been ordered more than once in the 20 selected orders must be aggregated into a single summary count for that item.

*   The current database transaction is committed.

    **Comment:** A commit is not needed as long as all the required ACID properties are satisfied (see Clause 2.8.2.3).

*   The output data (see Clause 2.8.3.3) are communicated to the terminal.

**2.8.2.3**     Full serializability and repeatable reads are not required for the Stock-Level business transaction. All data read must be committed and no older than the most recently committed data prior to the time this business transaction was initiated. All other ACID properties must be maintained.

**Comment:** This clause allows the business transaction to be broken down into more than one database transaction.

### 2.8.3    Terminal I/O

**2.8.3.1**    For each transaction the originating terminal must display the following input/output screen with all input and output fields cleared (with either spaces or zeros) except for the Warehouse and District fields which have not changed and must display the fixed W_ID and D_ID values associated with that terminal.

```
          1         2         3         4         5         6         7         8
 12345678901234567890123456789012345678901234567890123456789012345678901234567890
 1                                  Stock-Level
 2 Warehouse: 9999    District: 99
 3
 4 Stock Level Threshold: 99
 5
 6 low stock: 999
 7
 8
 9
10
11
12
13
14
15
16
17
18
19
20
21
22
23
24
```

**2.8.3.2**    The emulated user must enter, in the appropriate field of the input/output screen, the required input data which is organized as the distinct field: *threshold*.

**2.8.3.3**    The emulated terminal must display, in the appropriate field of the input/output screen, all input data and the output data which results from the execution of the transaction. The following fields are displayed: W_ID, D_ID, *threshold*, and *low_stock*.

**2.8.3.4**    The following table summarizes the terminal I/O requirements for the Stock-Level transaction:

|  | Enter | Display | Coordinates Row/Column |
|---|---|---|---|
| Non-repeating Group |  | W_ID | 2/12 |
|  |  | D_ID | 2/29 |
|  | *threshold* | *threshold* | 4/24 |
|  |  | low_stock | 6/12 |

**2.8.3.5**    For general terminal I/O requirements, see Clause 2.2.

# Clause 3: TRANSACTION AND SYSTEM PROPERTIES

## 3.1    The ACID Properties

It is the intent of this section to informally define the ACID properties and to specify a series of tests that must be performed to demonstrate that these properties are met.

**3.1.1**    The ACID (Atomicity, Consistency, Isolation, and Durability) properties of transaction processing systems must be supported by the system under test during the running of this benchmark. The only exception to this rule is to allow non-repeatable reads for the Stock-Level transaction (see Clause 2.8.2.3).

**3.1.2**    No finite series of tests can prove that the ACID properties are fully supported. Passing the specified tests is a necessary, but not sufficient, condition for meeting the ACID requirements. However, for fairness of reporting, only the tests specified here are required and must appear in the Full Disclosure Report for this benchmark.

**Comment:** These tests are intended to demonstrate that the acid principles are supported by the SUT and enabled during the performance measurement interval. They are not intended to be an exhaustive quality assurance test.

**3.1.3**    All mechanisms needed to insure full ACID properties must be enabled during both the test period and the 8 hours of steady state. For example, if the system under test relies on undo logs, then logging must be enabled for all transactions including those which do not include rollback in the transaction profile. When this benchmark is implemented on a distributed system, tests must be performed to verify that home and remote transactions, including remote transactions that are processed on two or more nodes, satisfy the ACID properties (see Clauses 2.4.1.7, 2.4.1.8, 2.5.1.5, and 2.5.1.6 for the definition of home and remote transactions).

**3.1.4**    Although the ACID tests do not exercise all transaction types of TPC-C, the ACID properties must be satisfied for all the TPC-C transactions.

C

**3.1.5** Test sponsors reporting TPC results may perform ACID tests on any one system for which results have been disclosed, provided that they use the same software executables (e.g., operating system, data manager, transaction programs). For example, this clause would be applicable when results are reported for multiple systems in a product line. However, the durability tests described in Clauses 3.5.3.2 and 3.5.3.3 must be run on all the systems that are measured. All Full Disclosure Reports must identify the systems which were used to verify ACID requirements and full details of the ACID tests conducted and results obtained.

## 3.2 Atomicity Requirements

**3.2.1** *Atomicity Property Definition*

The system under test must guarantee that database transactions are atomic; the system will either perform all individual operations on the data, or will assure that no partially completed operations leave any effects on the data.

**3.2.2** *Atomicity Tests*

**3.2.2.1** Perform the Payment transaction for a randomly selected warehouse, district, and customer (by customer number as specified in Clause 2.5.1.2) and verify that the records in the CUSTOMER, DISTRICT, and WAREHOUSE tables have been changed appropriately.

**3.2.2.2** Perform the Payment transaction for a randomly selected warehouse, district, and customer (by customer number as specified in Clause 2.5.1.2) and substitute a ROLLBACK of the transaction for the COMMIT of the transaction. Verify that the records in the CUSTOMER, DISTRICT, and WAREHOUSE tables have NOT been changed.

## 3.3 Consistency Requirements

**3.3.1** *Consistency Property Definition*

Consistency is the property of the application that requires any execution of a database transaction to take the database from one consistent state to another, assuming that the database is initially in a consistent state.

**3.3.2** *Consistency Conditions*

Twelve consistency conditions are defined in the following clauses to specify the level of database consistency required across the mix of TPC-C transactions. A database, when populated as defined in Clause 4.3, must meet all of these conditions to be consistent. If data is replicated, each copy must meet these conditions. Of the twelve conditions, explicit demonstration that the conditions are satisfied is required for the first four only. Demonstration of the last eight consistency conditions is not required because of the lengthy tests which would be necessary.

**Comment**: The consistency conditions were chosen so that they would remain valid within the context of a larger order-entry application that includes the five TPC-C transactions (see Clause 1.1). They are designed to be independent of the length of time for which such an application would be executed. Thus, for example, a condition involving I_PRICE was not included here since it is conceivable that within a larger application I_PRICE is modified from time to time.

### 3.3.2.1    *Consistency Condition 1*

Entries in the WAREHOUSE and DISTRICT tables must satisfy the relationship:

$$W\_YTD = sum(D\_YTD)$$

for each warehouse defined by (W_ID = D_W_ID).

### 3.3.2.2    *Consistency Condition 2*

Entries in the DISTRICT, ORDER, and NEW-ORDER tables must satisfy the relationship:

$$D\_NEXT\_O\_ID - 1 = max(O\_ID) = max(NO\_O\_ID)$$

for each district defined by (D_W_ID = O_W_ID = NO_W_ID) and (D_ID = O_D_ID = NO_D_ID). This condition does not apply to the NEW-ORDER table for any districts which have no outstanding new orders (i.e., the number of rows is zero).

### 3.3.2.3    *Consistency Condition 3*

Entries in the NEW-ORDER table must satisfy the relationship:

$$max(NO\_O\_ID) - min(NO\_O\_ID) + 1 = [\text{number of rows in the NEW-ORDER table for this district}]$$

for each district defined by NO_W_ID and NO_D_ID. This condition does not apply to any districts which have no outstanding new orders (i.e., the number of rows is zero).

### 3.3.2.4    *Consistency Condition 4*

Entries in the ORDER and ORDER-LINE tables must satisfy the relationship:

$$sum(O\_OL\_CNT) = [\text{number of rows in the ORDER-LINE table for this district}]$$

for each district defined by (O_W_ID = OL_W_ID) and (O_D_ID = OL_D_ID).

### 3.3.2.5    *Consistency Condition 5*

For any row in the ORDER table, O_CARRIER_ID is set to a null value if and only if there is a corresponding row in the NEW-ORDER table defined by (O_W_ID, O_D_ID, O_ID) = (NO_W_ID, NO_D_ID, NO_O_ID).

C

**3.3.2.6** *Consistency Condition 6*

For any row in the ORDER table, O_OL_CNT must equal the number of rows in the ORDER-LINE table for the corresponding order defined by (O_W_ID, O_D_ID, O_ID) = (OL_W_ID, OL_D_ID, OL_O_ID).

**3.3.2.7** *Consistency Condition 7*

For any row in the ORDER-LINE table, OL_DELIVERY_D is set to a null date/time if and only if the corresponding row in the ORDER table defined by (O_W_ID, O_D_ID, O_ID) = (OL_W_ID, OL_D_ID, OL_O_ID) has O_CARRIER_ID set to a null value.

**3.3.2.8** *Consistency Condition 8*

Entries in the WAREHOUSE and HISTORY tables must satisfy the relationship:

$$W\_YTD = sum(H\_AMOUNT)$$

for each warehouse defined by (W_ID = H_W_ID).

**3.3.2.9** *Consistency Condition 9*

Entries in the DISTRICT and HISTORY tables must satisfy the relationship:

$$D\_YTD = sum(H\_AMOUNT)$$

for each district defined by (D_W_ID, D_ID) = (H_W_ID, H_D_ID).

**3.3.2.10** *Consistency Condition 10*

Entries in the CUSTOMER, HISTORY, ORDER, and ORDER-LINE tables must satisfy the relationship:

$$C\_BALANCE = sum(OL\_AMOUNT) - sum(H\_AMOUNT)$$

where:

H_AMOUNT is selected by (C_W_ID, C_D_ID, C_ID) = (H_C_W_ID, H_C_D_ID, H_C_ID)

and

OL_AMOUNT is selected by:

(OL_W_ID, OL_D_ID, OL_O_ID) = (O_W_ID, O_D_ID, O_ID) and

(O_W_ID, O_D_ID, O_C_ID) = (C_W_ID, C_D_ID, C_ID) and

(OL_DELIVERY_D is not a null value)

**3.3.2.11** *Consistency Condition 11*

Entries in the CUSTOMER, ORDER, and NEW-ORDER tables must satisfy the relationship:

(count(*) from ORDER) - (count(*) from NEW-ORDER) = sum(C_DELIVERY_CNT) for each district defined by (O_W_ID, O_D_ID) = (NO_W_ID, NO_D_ID) = (C_W_ID, C_D_ID).

**3.3.2.12**   *Consistency Condition 12*

Entries in the CUSTOMER and ORDER-LINE tables must satisfy the relationship:

$$C\_BALANCE + C\_YTD\_PAYMENT = sum(OL\_AMOUNT)$$

for any randomly selected customers and where OL_DELIVERY_D is not set to a null date/time.

**3.3.3**   *Consistency Tests*

**3.3.3.1**   Verify that the database is initially consistent by verifying that it meets the consistency conditions defined in Clauses 3.3.2.1 to 3.3.2.4. Describe the steps used to do this in sufficient detail so that the steps are independently repeatable.

**3.3.3.2**   Immediately after performing the verification process described in Clause 3.3.3.1, do the following:

1.  Use the standard driving mechanism to submit transactions to the SUT. The transaction rate must be within 10% of the reported tpmC rate and meet all other requirements of a reported measurement interval (see Clause 5.5), including the requirement that the interval contain at least one check-point (see Clause 5.5.2.2). The SUT must be run at this rate for at least 5 minutes.

2.  Stop submitting transactions to the SUT and then repeat the verification steps done for Clause 3.3.3.1. The database must still be consistent after applying transactions. Consistency Condition 4 need only be verified for rows added to the ORDER and ORDER-LINE tables since the previous verification.

# 3.4     Isolation Requirements

**3.4.1**   *Isolation Property Definition*

Operations of concurrent database transactions must yield results which are indistinguishable from the results which would be obtained by forcing each transaction to be serially executed (i.e., in isolation) to completion in some order.

This property is commonly called **serializability**. Sufficient conditions must be enabled at either the system or application level to ensure serializability of transactions under any arbitrary mix of TPC-C transactions, unless otherwise specified by the transaction profile (see Clause 2.8.2.3). The system or application must have full serializability enabled (i.e., repeated reads of the same rows within any committed transaction must return identical data when run concurrently with any arbitrary mix of TPC-C transactions), except in the case of the Stock-Level transaction. For the Stock-Level transaction, the isolation requirement is relaxed to simply require that the transaction see only committed data.

C

### 3.4.2    *Isolation Tests*

For conventional locking schemes, isolation should be tested as described below. Systems that implement other isolation schemes may require different validation techniques. It is the responsibility of the test sponsor to disclose those techniques and the tests for them. If isolation schemes other than conventional locking are used, it is permissible to implement these tests differently provided full details are disclosed. (Examples of different validation techniques are shown in Isolation Test 7, Clause 3.4.2.7.)

#### 3.4.2.1    *Isolation Test 1*

This test demonstrates isolation for read-write conflicts of Order-Status and New-Order transactions. Perform the following steps:

1.  Start a New-Order transaction T1.
2.  Stop transaction T1 immediately prior to COMMIT.
3.  Start an Order-Status transaction T2 for the same customer used in T1. Transaction T2 attempts to read the data for the order T1 has created.
4.  Verify that transaction T2 waits.
5.  Allow transaction T1 to complete. T2 should now complete.
6.  Verify that the results from T2 match the data entered in T1.

#### 3.4.2.2    *Isolation Test 2*

This test demonstrates isolation for read-write conflicts of Order-Status and New-Order transactions when the New-Order transaction is rolled back. Perform the following steps:

1.  Perform an Order-Status transaction T0 for some customer. Let T0 complete.
2.  Start a New-Order transaction T1 for the same customer used in T0.
3.  Stop transaction T1 immediately prior to COMMIT.
4.  Start an Order-Status transaction T2 for the same customer used in T0. Transaction T2 attempts to read the data for the order T1 has created.
5.  Verify that transaction T2 waits.
6.  Rollback transaction T1. T2 should now complete.
7.  Verify that the data returned from T2 match the data returned by T0.

#### 3.4.2.3    *Isolation Test 3*

This test demonstrates isolation for write-write conflicts of two New-Order transactions. Perform the following steps:

1.  Start a New-Order transaction T1.
2.  Stop transaction T1 immediately prior to COMMIT.
3.  Start another New-Order transaction T2 for the same customer as T1.

4.  Verify that transaction T2 waits.

5.  Allow transaction T1 to complete. T2 should now complete.

6.  Verify that the order number returned for T2 is one greater than the order number for T1. Verify that the value of D_NEXT_O_ID reflects the results of both T1 and T2, i.e., it has been incremented by two and is one greater than the order number for T2.

### 3.4.2.4    Isolation Test 4

This test demonstrates isolation for write-write conflicts of two New-Order transactions when one transaction is rolled back. Perform the following steps:

1.  Start a New-Order transaction T1 which contains an invalid item number.

2.  Stop transaction T1 immediately prior to rollback.

3.  Start another New-Order transaction T2 for the same customer as T1.

4.  Verify that transaction T2 waits.

5.  Allow transaction T1 to complete. T2 should now complete.

6.  Verify that the order number returned for T2 is one greater than the previous order number. Verify that the value of D_NEXT_O_ID reflects the result of only T2, i.e., it has been incremented by one and is one greater than the order number for T2.

### 3.4.2.5    Isolation Test 5

This test demonstrates isolation for write-write conflicts of Payment and Delivery transactions. Perform the following steps:

1.  Start a Delivery transaction T1.

2.  Stop transaction T1 immediately prior to COMMIT.

3.  Start a Payment transaction T2 for the same customer as one of the new orders being delivered by T1.

4.  Verify that transaction T2 waits.

5.  Allow transaction T1 to complete. T2 should now complete.

6.  Verify that C_BALANCE reflects the results of both T1 and T2.

**Comment:** If the Delivery business transaction is executed as multiple database transactions, then the transaction T1, in bullet 6 above, can be chosen to be one of these database transactions.

### 3.4.2.6    Isolation Test 6

This test demonstrates isolation for write-write conflicts of Payment and Delivery transactions when the Delivery transaction is rolled back. Perform the following steps:

1.  Start a Delivery transaction T1.

2.  Stop transaction T1 immediately prior to COMMIT.

3. Start a Payment transaction T2 for the same customer as one of the new orders being delivered by T1.

4. Verify that transaction T2 waits.

5. Roll back transaction T1. T2 should now complete.

6. Verify that C_BALANCE reflects the results of only transaction T2.

### 3.4.2.7    *Isolation Test 7*

This test demonstrates repeatable reads for the New-Order transaction while an interactive transaction updates the price of an item. Given two random item numbers x and y, perform the following steps:

1. Start a transaction T1. Query I_PRICE from items x and y. COMMIT transaction T1.

2. Start a New-Order transaction T2 for a group of items including item x twice and item y.

3. Stop transaction T2 after querying the price of item x a first time and immediately before querying the prices of item y and of item x a second time.

4. Start a transaction T3. Increase the price of items x and y by 10 percent.

**Case A**, if transaction T3 stalls:

5A. Continue transaction T2 and verify that the price of items x (the second time) and y match the values read by transaction T1. COMMIT transaction T2.

6A. Transaction T3 should now complete and be COMMITTED.

7A. Start a transaction T4. Query I_PRICE from items x and y. COMMIT transaction T4.

8A. Verify that the prices read by transaction T4 match the values set by transaction T3.

**Case B**, if transaction T3 does not stall and transaction T2 rolls back:

5B. Transaction T3 has completed and has been COMMITTED.

6B. Continue transaction T2 and verify that it is instructed to roll back by the data manager.

7B. Start a transaction T4. Query I_PRICE from items x and y. COMMIT transaction T4.

8B. Verify that the prices read by transaction T4 match the values set by transaction T3.

**Case C**, if transaction T3 rolls back:

5C. Verify that transaction T3 is instructed to roll back by the data manager.

6C. Continue transaction T2 and verify that the price of items x (the second time) and y match the values read by transaction T1. COMMIT transaction T2.

7C. Start a transaction T4. Query I_PRICE from items *x* and *y*. COMMIT transaction T4.

8C. Verify that the prices read by transaction T4 match the values read by transactions T1 and T2.

**Case D**, if transaction T3 does not stall and no transaction is rolled back:

5D. Transaction T3 has completed and has been COMMITTED.

6D. Continue transaction T2 and verify that the price of items *x* (the second time) and *y* match the values read by transaction T1. COMMIT transaction T2.

7D. Start a transaction T4. Query I_PRICE from items *x* and *y*. COMMIT transaction T4.

8D. Verify that the prices read by transaction T4 match the values set by transaction T3.

**Comment 1:** This test is successfully executed if either case A, B, C, or D of the above steps are followed. The test sponsor must disclose the case followed during the execution of this test.

**Comment 2:** If the implementation uses replication on the ITEM table and all transactions in Isolation Test 7 use the same copy of the ITEM table, updates to the ITEM table are not required to be propagated to other copies of the ITEM table. This relaxation of ACID properties on a replicated table is only valid under the above conditions and in the context of Isolation Test 7.

**Comment 3:** Transactions T1, T2, and T4 are not used to measure throughput and are only used in the context of Isolation Test 7.

## 3.5    Durability Requirements

The tested system must guarantee durability: the ability to preserve the effects of committed transactions and insure database consistency after recovery from any one of the failures listed in Clause 3.5.3.

**Comment:** No system provides complete durability (i.e., durability under all possible types of failures). The specific set of single failures addressed in Clause 3.5.3 is deemed sufficiently significant to justify demonstration of durability across such failures.

### 3.5.1    *Durable Medium Definition*

A durable medium is a data storage medium that is either:

1.  An inherently non-volatile medium (e.g., magnetic disk, magnetic tape, optical disk, etc.) or

2.  A volatile medium with its own self-contained power supply that will retain and permit the transfer of data, before any data is lost, to an inherently non-volatile medium after the failure of external power.

C

A configured and priced Uninterruptible Power Supply (UPS) is not considered external power.

**Comment**: A durable medium can fail; this is usually protected against by replication on a second durable medium (e.g., mirroring) or logging to another durable medium. Memory can be considered a durable medium if it can preserve data long enough to satisfy the requirement stated in item 2 above, for example, if it is accompanied by an Uninterruptible Power Supply, and the contents of memory can be transferred to an inherently non-volatile medium during the failure. Note that no distinction is made between main memory and memory performing similar permanent or temporary data storage in other parts of the system (e.g., disk controller caches).

### 3.5.2  *Committed Property Definition*

A transaction is considered committed when the transaction manager component of the system has either written the log or written the data for the committed updates associated with the transaction to a durable medium.

**Comment 1**: Transactions can be committed without the user subsequently receiving notification of that fact, since message integrity is not required for TPC-C.

**Comment 2**: Although the order of operations in the transaction profiles (Clause 2) is immaterial, the actual communication of the output data cannot begin until the commit operation has successfully completed.

### 3.5.3  *List of single failures*

**3.5.3.1**  Permanent irrecoverable failure of any single durable medium containing TPC-C database tables or recovery log data.

**Comment**: If main memory is used as a durable medium, then it must be considered as a potential single point of failure. Sample mechanisms to survive single durable medium failures are database archiving in conjunction with a redo (after image) log, and mirrored durable media. If memory is the durable medium and mirroring is the mechanism used to ensure durability, then the mirrored memories must be independently powered.

**3.5.3.2**  Instantaneous interruption (system crash/system hang) in processing which requires system re-boot to recover.

**Comment**: This implies abnormal system shutdown which requires loading of a fresh copy of the operating system from the boot device. It does not necessarily imply loss of volatile memory. When the recovery mechanism relies on the pre-failure contents of volatile memory, the means used to avoid the loss of volatile memory (e.g., an Uninterruptible Power Supply) must be included in the system cost calculation. A sample mechanism to survive an instantaneous interruption in processing is an undo/redo log.

**3.5.3.3**  Failure of all or part of memory (loss of contents).

**Comment**: This implies that all or part of memory has failed. This may be caused by a loss of external power or the permanent failure of a memory board.

### 3.5.4    *Durability Tests*

The intent of these tests is to demonstrate that all transactions whose output messages have been received at the terminal or RTE have in fact been committed in spite of any single failure from the list in Clause 3.5.3 and that all consistency conditions are still met after the database is recovered.

It is required that the system crash test(s) and the loss of memory test(s) described in Clauses 3.5.3.2 and 3.5.3.3 be performed under full terminal load and a fully scaled database. The durable media failure test(s) described in Clause 3.5.3.1 may be performed on a subset of the SUT configuration and database. For the SUT subset, all multiple hardware components, such as processors and disk/controllers in the full SUT configuration, must be represented by the greater of 10% of the configuration or two of each of the multiple hardware components. The database must be scaled to at least 10% of the fully scaled database, with a minimum of two warehouses. Furthermore, the standard driving mechanism must be used in this test. The test sponsor must state that to the best of their knowledge, a fully scaled test would also pass all durability tests.

For each of the failure types defined in Clause 3.5.3, perform the following steps:

1.  Compute the sum of D_NEXT_O_ID for all rows in the DISTRICT table to determine the current count of the total number of orders (count1).

2.  Start submitting TPC-C transactions. The transaction rate must be at least 10% of the reported tpmC rate and meet all other requirements of a reported measurement interval (see Clause 5.5), excluding the requirement that the interval contain at least one checkpoint (see Clause 5.5.2.2). The SUT must be run at this rate for at least 5 minutes. On the Driver System, record committed and rolled back New-Order transactions in a "success" file.

3.  Cause the failure selected from the list in Clause 3.5.3.

4.  Restart the system under test using normal recovery procedures.

5.  Compare the contents of the "success" file and the ORDER table to verify that every record in the "success" file for a committed New-Order transaction has a corresponding record in the ORDER table and that no entries exist for rolled back transactions.

    Repeat step 1 to determine the total number of orders (count2). Verify that count2-count1 is greater or equal to the number of records in the "success" file for committed New-Order transactions. If there is an inequality, the ORDER table must contain additional records and the difference must be less than or equal to the number of terminals simulated.

    **Comment**: This difference should be due only to transactions which were committed on the system under test, but for which the output data was not displayed on the input/output screen before the failure.

6.  Verify Consistency Condition 3 as specified in Clause 3.3.2.3.

### 3.5.5    *Additional Requirements*

**3.5.5.1**    The recovery mechanism cannot use the contents of the HISTORY table to support the durability property.

**3.5.5.2**    Rollforward recovery from an archive database copy (e.g., a copy taken prior to the run) using redo log data is not acceptable as the recovery mechanism in the case of failures listed in Clause 3.5.3.2 and 3.5.3.3. Note that "checkpoints", "control points", "consistency points", etc., of the database taken during a run are not considered to be archives.

# CLAUSE 4: Scaling and Database Population

## 4.1    General Scaling Rules

The throughput of the TPC-C benchmark is driven by the activity of the terminals connected to each warehouse. To increase the throughput, more warehouses and their associated terminals must be configured. Each warehouse requires a number of rows to populate the database along with some storage space to maintain the data generated during a defined period of activity called **180-day period**. These requirements define how storage space and database population scale with throughput.

**4.1.1**    The intent of the scaling requirements is to maintain the ratio between the transaction load presented to the system under test, the cardinality of the tables accessed by the transactions, the required space for storage, and the number of terminals generating the transaction load.

**4.1.2**    Should any scaling value in Clause 4.2 be exceeded, the others must be increased proportionally to maintain the same ratios among them as in Clause 4.2.

**4.1.3**    The reported throughput may not exceed the maximum allowed by the scaling requirements in Clause 4.2 and the pacing requirements in Clause 5.2. While the reported throughput may fall short of the maximum allowed by the configured system, the price/performance computation (see Clause 7.1) must report the price for the system as actually configured. To prevent over-scaling of systems, the reported throughput cannot fall short of 9 tpmC per configured warehouse.

**Comment:** The maximum throughput is achieved with infinitely fast transactions resulting in a null response time and minimum required wait times. The intent of this clause is to prevent reporting a throughput that exceeds this maximum, which is computed to be 12.7 tpmC per warehouse. The above 9 tpmC represents 70% of the computed maximum throughput.

## 4.2    Scaling Requirements

**4.2.1**    The WAREHOUSE table is used as the base unit of scaling. The cardinality of all other tables (except for ITEM) is a function of the number of configured warehouses (i.e., cardinality of the WAREHOUSE table). This number, in turn, determines the load applied to the system under test which results in a reported throughput (see Clause 5.4).

**Comment 1:** The cardinality of the HISTORY, NEW-ORDER, ORDER, and ORDER-LINE tables will naturally vary as a result of repeated test executions. The minimal database population and the transaction profiles are designed to minimize the impact of this variation on performance and maintain repeatability between subsequent test results.

**Comment 2:** The cardinality of the ITEM table is constant regardless of the number of configured warehouses, as all warehouses maintain stocks for the same catalog of items.

**4.2.2**    *Minimal Configuration*

The following scaling requirements represent the minimal configuration for the test described in Clause 5:

1.  For each configured warehouse in the database, the SUT must accept requests for transactions from a population of 10 terminals.

2.  For each table that composes the database, the cardinality of the minimal population per warehouse is specified as follows:

| Table Name | Cardinality (in rows) | Typical[1] Row Length (in bytes) | Typical[1] Table Size (in 1,000 bytes) |
|---|---|---|---|
| WAREHOUSE | 1 | 89 | 0.089 |
| DISTRICT | 10 | 95 | 0.950 |
| CUSTOMER | 30k | 655 | 19,650 |
| HISTORY[2] | 30k | 46 | 1,380 |
| ORDER[2] | 30k | 24 | 720 |
| NEW-ORDER[2] | 9k | 8 | 72 |
| ORDER-LINE[2] | 300k | 54 | 16,200 |
| STOCK | 100k | 306 | 30,600 |
| ITEM[3] | 100k | 82 | 8,200 |

[1] Typical lengths and sizes given here are examples, not requirements, of what could result from an implementation (sizes do not include storage/access overheads).

[2] Small variations: subject to test execution as rows may be inserted and deleted by transaction activity from test executions.

[3] Fixed cardinality: does not scale with number of warehouses.

**Note:** The symbol "k" used in the cardinality column means one thousand.

C

3. Storage must be priced for sufficient space to store and maintain the data generated during a period of 180 days of activity with an average of 8 hours per day at the reported throughput called the **180-day period**. This space must be computed according to Clause 4.2.3 and must be usable by the data manager to store and maintain the rows that would be added to the HISTORY, ORDER, and ORDER-LINE tables during the 180-day period.

4. The minimal increment (granularity) for scaling the database and the terminal population is one warehouse, composed of one WAREHOUSE row, 10 DISTRICT rows, their associated CUSTOMER, HISTORY, ORDER, NEW-ORDER, and ORDER-LINE rows, 100,000 STOCK rows, 10 terminals, and priced storage for the 180-day period.

### 4.2.3     *180-Day Space Computation*

The storage space required for the 180-day period must be determined as follows:

1. The test database must be built including the minimal database population (see Clause 4.3) and all indices present during the test.

2. The test database must be built to sustain the reported throughput during an eight-hour period. This excludes performing on the database any operation that does not occur during the measurement interval (see Clause 5.5).

3. The total storage space allocated for the test database must be decomposed into the following:

   - **Free-Space**: any space allocated to the test database and which is available for future use. It is composed of all database storage space not used to store a database entity (e.g., a row, an index, a metadatum) or not used as formatting overhead by the data manager.

   - **Dynamic-Space**: any space used to store existing rows from the dynamic tables (i.e., the HISTORY, ORDER, and ORDER-LINE tables). It is composed of all database storage space used to store rows and row storage overhead for the dynamic tables. It includes any data that is added to the database as a result of inserting a new row independently of all indices. It does not include index data or other overheads such as index overhead, page overhead, block overhead, and table overhead.

   - **Static-Space**: any space used to store static information and indices. It is composed of all space allocated to the test database and which does not qualify as either Free-Space or Dynamic-Space.

4. Given that the system must be configured to sustain the reported throughput during an eight hour period, the database must allow the dynamic tables to grow accordingly for at least eight hours without impacting performance. Free-Space used to allow growth of the dynamic tables for an eight-hour day at the reported throughput is called the **Daily-Growth**. Given W, the number of configured warehouses on the test system, the Daily-Growth must be computed as:

Daily-Growth = (Dynamic-Space / (W * 62.5)) * tpmC

**Note**: In the formula above, 62.5 is used as a normalizing factor since the minimum database population for each warehouse holds the Dynamic-Space required for an eight-hour day of activity at 62.5 tpmC.

5. Any Free-Space beyond 150% of the Daily-Growth is called **Daily-Spread**, and must be added to the Dynamic-Space when computing the storage requirement for the 180-day period. The Daily-Spread must be computed as:

   Daily-Spread = Free-Space - 1.5 * Daily-Growth

   If the computed Daily-Spread is negative, then a null value must be used for Daily-Spread.

6. The **180-Day-Space** must be computed as:

   180-Day-Space = Static-Space + 180 * (Daily-Growth + Daily-Spread)

7. The Dynamic-Space present in the test database is considered as part of the 180-Day-Space.

## 4.3   Minimal Database Population

**4.3.1**     The test described in Clause 5 requires that a minimal population be present in the test database. Each table must contain the minimum number of rows defined in Clause 4.2.2 prior to test execution (e.g., the New-Order table must contain a minimum of 2,000 rows per warehouse).

**4.3.2**     *Definition of Terms*

**4.3.2.1**     The term **random** means independently selected and uniformly distributed over the specified range of values.

**Comment**: For the purpose of populating the initial database only, random numbers can be generated by selecting entries in sequence from a set of at least 10,000 pre-generated random numbers. This technique cannot be used for the field O_OL_CNT.

**4.3.2.2**     The notation **random a-string [$x .. y$]** (respectively, **n-string [$x .. y$]**) represents a string of random alphanumeric (respectively, numeric) characters of a random length of minimum $x$, maximum $y$, and mean $(y+x)/2$.

**Comment 1**: The character set used must be able to represent a minimum of 128 different characters.

**Comment 2**: Generating such strings can be implemented by the concatenation of two strings selected at random from two separate arrays of strings, and where:

1. Both arrays contain a minimum of 10 different strings of characters.
2. The first array contains strings of $x$ characters.
3. The second array contains strings of lengths uniformly distributed between zero and ($y - x$) characters.

4. Both arrays may contains strings that are pertinent to the row and the attribute (e.g., use an actual first name for C_FIRST) instead of strings of random characters, as long as this does not bring any improvement to the reported metrics.

**4.3.2.3** The customer last name (**C_LAST**) must be generated by the concatenation of three variable length syllables selected from the following list:

| 0 | 1 | 2 | 3 | 4 | 5 | 6 | 7 | 8 | 9 |
|---|---|---|---|---|---|---|---|---|---|
| BAR | OUGHT | ABLE | PRI | PRES | ESE | ANTI | CALLY | ATION | EING |

Given a number between 0 and 999, each of the three syllables is determined by the corresponding digit in the three-digit representation of the number. For example, the number 371 generates the name PRICALLYOUGHT, and the number 40 generates the name BARPRESBAR.

**4.3.2.4** The notation **unique within [x]** represents any one value within a set of $x$ contiguous values, unique within the group of rows being populated. When several groups of rows of the same type are populated (e.g., there is one group of customer type rows for each district type row), each group must use the same set of $x$ contiguous values.

**4.3.2.5** The notation **random within [x .. y]** represents a random value independently selected and uniformly distributed between $x$ and $y$, inclusively, with a mean of $(x+y)/2$, and with the same number of digits of precision as shown. For example, [0.01 .. 100.00] has 10,000 unique values, whereas [1 .. 100] has only 100 unique values.

**4.3.2.6** The notation **random permutation of [x .. y]** represents a sequence of numbers from $x$ to $y$ arranged into a random order. This is commonly known as a permutation (or selection) without replacement.

**4.3.3** *Table Population Requirements*

**4.3.3.1** The minimal database population must be composed of:

- 100,000 rows in the ITEM table with:

   I_ID unique within [100,000]

   I_NAME random a-string [14 .. 24]

   I_PRICE random within [1.00 .. 100.00]

   I_DATA random a-string [26 .. 50]. For at least 10% of the rows, selected at random, the string "ORIGINAL" must be held by 8 consecutive characters starting at a random position within I_DATA

- 1 row in the WAREHOUSE table for each configured warehouse with:

  W_ID unique within [*number_of_configured_warehouses*]

  W_NAME random a-string [6 .. 10]

  W_STREET_1 random a-string [10 .. 20]

  W_STREET_2 random a-string [10 .. 20]

  W_CITY random a-string [10 .. 20]

  W_STATE random a-string of 2 letters

  W_ZIP random n-string of 9 numbers

  W_TAX random within [0.0000 .. 0.2000]

  W_YTD = 300,000.00

For each row in the WAREHOUSE table:

  — 100,000 rows in the STOCK table with:

  S_I_ID unique within [100,000]

  S_W_ID = W_ID

  S_QUANTITY random within [10 .. 100]

  S_DIST_01 random a-string of 24 letters

  S_DIST_02 random a-string of 24 letters

  S_DIST_03 random a-string of 24 letters

  S_DIST_04 random a-string of 24 letters

  S_DIST_05 random a-string of 24 letters

  S_DIST_06 random a-string of 24 letters

  S_DIST_07 random a-string of 24 letters

  S_DIST_08 random a-string of 24 letters

  S_DIST_09 random a-string of 24 letters

  S_DIST_10 random a-string of 24 letters

  S_YTD = 0

  S_ORDER_CNT = 0

  S_REMOTE_CNT = 0

  S_DATA random a-string [26 .. 50]. For at least 10% of the rows, selected at random, the string "ORIGINAL" must be held by 8 consecutive characters starting at a random position within S_DATA

— 10 rows in the DISTRICT table with:

> D_ID unique within [10]
>
> D_W_ID = W_ID
>
> D_NAME random a-string [6 .. 10]
>
> D_STREET_1 random a-string [10 .. 20]
>
> D_STREET_2 random a-string [10 .. 20]
>
> D_CITY random a-string [10 .. 20]
>
> D_STATE random a-string of 2 letters
>
> D_ZIP random n-string of 9 numbers
>
> D_TAX random within [0.0000 .. 0.2000]
>
> D_YTD = 30,000.00
>
> D_NEXT_O_ID = 3,001

For each row in the DISTRICT table:

— 3,000 rows in the CUSTOMER table with:

> C_ID unique within [3,000]
>
> C_D_ID = D_ID
>
> C_W_ID = D_W_ID
>
> C_LAST generated according to Clause 4.3.2.3, iterating through the range of [0 .. 999] for the first 1,000 customers, and generating a non-uniform random number using the function NURand(255,0,999) for each of the remaining 2,000 customers. The run-time constant C (see Clause 2.1.6) used for the database population must be randomly chosen independently from the test run(s).
>
> C_MIDDLE = "OE"
>
> C_FIRST random a-string [8 .. 16]
>
> C_STREET_1 random a-string [10 .. 20]
>
> C_STREET_2 random a-string [10 .. 20]
>
> C_CITY random a-string [10 .. 20]
>
> C_STATE random a-string of 2 letters
>
> C_ZIP random n-string of 9 numbers
>
> C_PHONE random n-string of 16 numbers

C_SINCE date/time given by the operating system when the CUS-TOMER table was populated.

C_CREDIT = "GC". For 10% of the rows, selected at random, C_CREDIT = "BC"

C_CREDIT_LIM = 50,000.00

C_DISCOUNT random within [0.0000 .. 0.5000]

C_BALANCE = -10.00

C_YTD_PAYMENT = 10.00

C_PAYMENT_CNT = 1

C_DELIVERY_CNT = 0

C_DATA random a-string [300 .. 500]

For each row in the CUSTOMER table:

— 1 row in the HISTORY table with:

H_C_ID = C_ID

H_C_D_ID = H_D_ID = D_ID

H_C_W_ID = H_W_ID = W_ID

H_DATE current date and time

H_AMOUNT = 10.00

H_DATA random a-string [12 .. 24]

— 3,000 rows in the ORDER table with:

O_ID unique within [3,000]

O_C_ID selected sequentially from a random permutation of [1 .. 3,000]

O_D_ID = D_ID

O_W_ID = W_ID

O_ENTRY_D current date/time given by the operating system

O_CARRIER_ID random within [1 .. 10] if O_ID < 2,101, null otherwise

O_OL_CNT random within [5 .. 15]

O_ALL_LOCAL = 1

C

For each row in the ORDER table:

— A number of rows in the ORDER-LINE table equal to O_OL_CNT, generated according to the rules for input data generation of the New-Order transaction (see Clause 2.4.1) with:

OL_O_ID = O_ID

OL_D_ID = D_ID

OL_W_ID = W_ID

OL_NUMBER unique within [O_OL_CNT]

OL_I_ID random within [1 .. 100,000]

OL_SUPPLY_W_ID = W_ID

OL_DELIVERY_D = O_ENTRY_D if OL_O_ID < 2,101, null otherwise

OL_QUANTITY = 5

OL_AMOUNT = 0.00 if OL_O_ID < 2,101, random within [0.01 .. 9,999.99] otherwise

OL_DIST_INFO random a-string of 24 letters

— 900 rows in the NEW-ORDER table corresponding to the last 900 rows in the ORDER table for that district (i.e., with NO_O_ID between 2,101 and 3,000), with:

NO_O_ID = O_ID

NO_D_ID = D_ID

NO_W_ID = W_ID

**4.3.3.2**    The implementation may not take advantage of the fact that some fields are initially populated with a fixed value. For example, storage space cannot be saved by defining a default value for the field C_CREDIT_LIM and storing this value only once in the database.

# CLAUSE 5: Performance Metrics and Response Time

## 5.1    Definition of Terms

**5.1.1**    The term **measurement interval** refers to a steady state period during the execution of the benchmark for which the test sponsor is reporting a throughput rating (see Clause 5.5 for detailed requirements).

**5.1.2**    The term **completed transactions** refers to any business transaction (see Clause 2.1.3) that has been successfully committed at the SUT and whose output data has been displayed by the Remote Terminal Emulator (in case of a New-Order, Payment, Order-Status, or Stock-Level transaction) or for which a complete entry has been written into a result file (in case of a Delivery transaction). New-Order transactions that are rolled back, as required by Clause 2.4.1.4, are considered as completed transactions.

## 5.2    Pacing of Transactions by Emulated Users

**5.2.1**    The figure below illustrates the cycle executed by each emulated user (see Clause 5.2.2). The active portion of the screen is represented with bold face text:

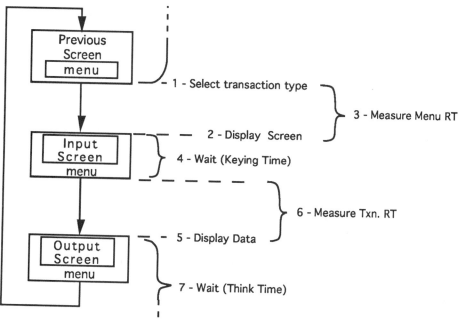

**5.2.2**    Each emulated user executes a cycle composed of screens, wait times, and response times (RTs) as follows:

1.  Selects a transaction type from the menu according to a weighted distribution (see Clause 5.2.3).

2.  Waits for the Input/Output Screen to be displayed.

3.  Measures the Menu RT (see Clause 5.3.3).

4.  Enters the required number of input fields (see Clause 2) over the defined minimum Keying Time (see Clause 5.2.5.2).

5. Waits for the required number of output fields (see Clause 2) to be displayed on the Input/Output Screen.

6. Measures the Transaction RT (see Clause 5.3.4).

7. Waits for the defined minimum Think Time (see Clause 5.2.5.4) while the Input/output screen remains displayed.

At the end of the Think Time (Step 7) the emulated user loops back to select a transaction type from the menu (Step 1).

**Comment**: No action is required on the part of the SUT to cycle from Step 7 back to Step 1.

**5.2.3** Each transaction type (i.e., business transaction) is available to each terminal through the Menu. Over the measurement interval, the terminal population must maintain a minimum percentage of mix for each transaction type as follows:

| Transaction Type | Minimum % of mix |
|---|---|
| New-Order[1] | n/a |
| Payment | 43.0 |
| Order-Status | 4.0 |
| Delivery | 4.0 |
| Stock-Level | 4.0 |

[1] There is no minimum for the New-Order transaction as its measured rate is the reported throughput.

**Comment 1**: The intent of the minimum percentage of mix for each transaction type is to execute approximately one Payment transaction for each New-Order transaction and approximately one Order-Status transaction, one Delivery transaction, and one Stock-Level transaction for every 10 New-Order transactions. This mix results in the complete business processing of each order.

**Comment 2**: The total number of transactions, from which the minimum percentages of mix are derived, includes all transactions that were selected from the Menu and completed (see Clause 5.1.2) within the measurement interval.

**5.2.4** *Regulation of Transaction Mix*

Transaction types must be selected uniformly at random while maintaining the required minimum percentage of mix for each transaction type over the measurement interval. This must be done using one of the techniques described in Clauses 5.2.4.1 and 5.2.4.2.

**5.2.4.1** A weight is associated to each transaction type on the menu. The required mix is achieved by selecting each new transaction uniformly at random from a weighted distribution. The following requirements must be satisfied when using this technique:

1. The actual weights are chosen by the test sponsor and must result in meeting the required minimum percentages of mix in Clause 5.2.3.

2. For the purpose of achieving the required transaction mix, the RTE can dynamically adjust the weight associated to each transaction type during the measurement interval. These adjustments must be limited so as to keep the weights within 5% on either side of their respective initial value.

**5.2.4.2**    One or more cards in a deck are associated to each transaction type on the Menu. The required mix is achieved by selecting each new transaction uniformly at random from a deck whose content guarantees the required transaction mix. The following requirements must be satisfied when using this technique:

1. Any number of terminals can share the same deck (including but not limited to one deck per terminal or one deck for all terminals).

2. A deck must be composed of one or more sets of 23 cards (i.e., 10 New-Order cards, 10 Payment cards, and one card each for Order-Status, Delivery, and Stock-level). The minimum size of a deck is one set per terminal sharing this deck. If more than one deck is used, then all decks must be of equal sizes.

   **Comment**: Generating the maximum percentage of New-Order transactions while achieving the required mix can be done for example by sharing a deck of 230 cards between 10 terminals.

3. Each pass through a deck must be made in a different uniformly random order. If a deck is accessed sequentially, it must be randomly shuffled each time it is exhausted. If a deck is accessed at random, cards that are selected cannot be placed back in the deck until it is exhausted.

**Comment**: All terminals must select transactions using the same technique. Gaining a performance or a price/performance advantage by driving one or more terminals differently than the rest of the terminal population is not allowed.

**5.2.5**    *Wait Times and Response Time Constraints*

**5.2.5.1**    The Menu step is transaction independent. At least 90% of all Menu selections must have a Menu RT (see Clause 5.3.3) of less than 2 seconds.

**5.2.5.2**    For each transaction type, the Keying Time is constant and must be a minimum of 18 seconds for New-Order, 3 seconds for Payment, and 2 seconds each for Order-Status, Delivery, and Stock-Level.

**5.2.5.3**    At least 90% of all transactions of each type must have a Transaction RT (see Clause 5.3.4) of less than 5 seconds each for New-Order, Payment, Order-Status, and Delivery, and 20 seconds for Stock-Level.

**Comment**: The total number of transactions, from which the Transaction RT of New-Order is computed, includes New-Order transactions that roll back as required by Clause 2.4.1.4.

**5.2.5.4**    For each transaction type, the Think Times must be taken independently from a negative exponential distribution with a minimum mean of 12 seconds each for New-Order and Payment, 10 seconds for Order-Status, and 5 seconds each for Delivery and Stock-Level. Each distribution may be truncated at 4 times its mean value.

**5.2.5.5**     The beginning of all wait times (Keying Times and Think Times) are to be taken after the last character of output has been displayed (see Clause 2.2.2) by the emulated terminal.

**5.2.5.6**     The 90th percentile response time for each transaction must be greater than or equal to the average response time of that transaction.

**5.2.5.7**     The following table summarizes the transaction mix, wait times, and response time constraints:

| Transaction Type | Minimum % of mix | Minimum Keying Time | 90th Percentile Response Time Constraint | Minimum Mean of Think Time Distribution |
|---|---|---|---|---|
| New-Order | n/a | 18 sec. | 5 sec. | 12 sec. |
| Payment | 43 | 3 sec. | 5 sec. | 12 sec. |
| Order-Status | 4 | 2 sec. | 5 sec. | 10 sec. |
| Delivery [1] | 4 | 2 sec. | 5 sec. | 5 sec. |
| Stock-Level | 4 | 2 sec. | 20 sec. | 5 sec. |

[1] The response time is for the terminal response (acknowledging that the transaction has been queued), not for the execution of the transaction itself. At least 90% of the transactions must complete within 80 seconds of their being queued (see Clause 2.7.2.2).

**Comment 1**: The response time constraints are set such that the throughput of the system is expected to be constrained by the response time requirement for the New-Order transaction. Response time constraints for other transactions are relaxed for that purpose.

**Comment 2**: The keying times for the transactions are chosen to be approximately proportional to the number of characters input, and the think times are chosen to be approximately proportional to the number of characters output.

**5.2.5.8**     For each transaction type, all configured terminals of the tested systems must use the same target Keying Time and the same target mean of Think Time. These times must comply with the requirements summarized in Clause 5.2.5.7.

## 5.3     Response Time Definition

**5.3.1**     Each completed transaction submitted to the SUT must be individually timed.

**5.3.2**     Response Times must be measured at the RTE. A **Response Time** (or **RT**) is defined by:

$$RT = T2 - T1$$

where:

T1 and T2 are measured at the RTE and defined as:

T1 = time stamp taken before the last character of input data is entered by the emulated user.

T2 = time stamp taken after the last character of output is received by the emulated terminal.

The resolution of the time stamps must be at least 0.1 seconds.

**Comment**: The intent of the benchmark is to measure response time as experienced by the emulated user.

**5.3.3**    The Menu Response Time (**Menu RT**) is the time between the time stamp taken before the last character of the Menu selection has been entered and the time stamp taken after the last character of the Input/Output Screen has been received (including clearing all input and output fields and displaying fixed fields; see Clause 2).

**Comment**: Systems that do not require SUT/RTE interaction for the Menu selection and the screen display can assume a null Menu RT.

**5.3.4**    The Transaction Response Time (**Transaction RT**) is the time between the timestamp taken before the last character of the required input data has been sent from the RTE (see Clause 2) and the timestamp taken after the last character of the required output data has been received by the RTE (see Clause 2) resulting from a transaction execution.

**Comment:** If the emulated terminal must process the data being entered or displayed, the time for this processing must be disclosed and taken into account when calculating the Transaction RT.

# 5.4    Computation of Throughput Rating

The TPC-C transaction mix represents a complete business cycle. It consists of multiple business transactions which enter new orders, query the status of existing orders, deliver outstanding orders, enter payments from customers, and monitor warehouse stock levels.

**5.4.1**    The metric used to report Maximum Qualified Throughput (**MQTh**) is a number of orders processed per minute. It is a measure of "business throughput" rather than a transaction execution rate. It implicitly takes into account all transactions in the mix as their individual throughput is controlled by the weighted Menu selection and the minimum percentages of mix defined in Clause 5.2.3.

**5.4.2**    The reported MQTh is the total number of completed New-Order transactions (see Clause 5.1.2), where the Transaction RT (see Clause 5.3.4) was completely measured at the RTE during the measurement interval, divided by the elapsed time of the interval. New-Order transactions that roll back, as required by

C

Clause 2.4.1.4, must be included in the reported MQTh. The reported MQTh can be no greater than the measured MQTh.

**5.4.3**       The name of the metric used to report the MQTh of the SUT is **tpmC**.

**5.4.4**       All reported MQTh must be measured, rather than interpolated or extrapolated, and expressed to exactly two decimal places, rounded to the hundreth place. For example, suppose 105.548 tpmC is measured on a 100 terminal test for which 90% of the New-Order transactions completed in less than 4.8 seconds and 117.572 tpmC is measured on a 110 terminal test for which 90% of the transactions completed in less than 5.2 seconds. Then the reported tpmC is 105.54 rather than some interpolated value between 105.548 and 117.572.

**5.5.1.6**       To be valid, the measurement interval must contain no more than 1% or no more than one (1), whichever is greater, of the Delivery transactions skipped because there were fewer than necessary orders present in the New-Order table.

## 5.5     Measurement Interval Requirements

**5.5.1**       *Steady State*

**5.5.1.1**       The test must be conducted in a **steady state** condition that represents the true sustainable throughput of the SUT.

**5.5.1.2**       Although the measurement interval may be as short as 20 minutes, the system under test must be configured so that it is possible to run the test at the reported tpmC for a continuous period of at least eight hours, maintaining full ACID properties. For example, the media used to store at least 8 hours of log data must be configured if required to recover from any single point of failure (see Clause 3.5.3.1).

**Comment 1**: An example of a configuration that would not comply is one where a log file is allocated such that better performance is achieved during the measured portion of the test than during the remaining portion of an eight-hour test, perhaps because a dedicated device was used initially but space on a shared device is used later in the full eight-hour test.

**Comment 2**: Steady state is easy to define (e.g., sustainable throughput) but difficult to prove. The test sponsor (and/or the auditor) is required to report the method used to verify steady state sustainable throughput and the reproducibility of test results. The auditor is encouraged to use available monitoring tools to help determine the steady state.

**5.5.1.3**       In the case where a ramp-up period is used to reach steady state, the minimal database population is required at the beginning of the ramp-up period. The transaction mix and the requirements summarized in Clause 5.2.5.7 must be followed during the ramp-up as well as steady state period.

**Comment**: The intent of this clause is to prevent significant alteration to the minimum database population during the ramp-up period.

**5.5.1.4**    To demonstrate the reproducibility of the steady state condition, a minimum of one additional measurement must be made and its tpmC must be disclosed and be within 2% of the reported tpmC.

**5.5.1.5**    While variability is allowed, the RTE cannot be artificially weighted to generate input data different from the requirements described in Clauses 2.4.1, 2.5.1, 2.6.1, 2.7.1, and 2.8.1. To be valid, the input data generated during a reported measurement interval must not exceed the following variability:

1.  At least 0.9% and at most 1.1% of the New-Order transactions must roll back as a result of an unused item number.

2.  The average number of order-lines per order must be in the range of 9.5 to 10.5 and the number of order-lines per order must be uniformly distributed from 5 to 15 for the New-Order transactions that are submitted to the SUT during the measurement interval.

3.  The number of remote order-lines must be at least 0.95% and at most 1.05% of the number of order-lines that are filled in by the New-Order transactions that are submitted to the SUT during the measurement interval.

4.  The number of remote Payment transactions must be at least 14% and at most 16% of the number of Payment transactions that are submitted to the SUT during the measurement interval.

5.  The number of customer selections by customer last name in the Payment transaction must be at least 57% and at most 63% of the number of Payment transactions that are submitted to the SUT during the measurement interval.

6.  The number of customer selections by customer last name in the Order-Status transaction must be at least 57% and at most 63% of the number of Order-Status transactions that are submitted to the SUT during the measurement interval.

**5.5.1.6**    To be valid, the measurement interval must contain no more than 1% or no more than one (1), whichever is greater, of the Delivery transactions skipped because there were fewer than necessary orders present in the New-Order table.

**5.5.2**    *Duration*

**5.5.2.1**    The measurement interval must:

1.  Begin after the system reaches steady state.

2.  Be long enough to generate reproducible throughput results which are representative of the performance which would be achieved during a sustained eight-hour period.

3.  Extend uninterrupted for a minimum of 20 minutes.

**5.5.2.2**    For systems which defer database writes to durable media, these writes must occur at least once within the measurement interval and at least every 30 minutes. In addition, if the number of times (C) that these writes occur during the measurement interval (MI) is three or fewer, then these writes must not occur during a **protected zone** (Z) centered around both ends of the measurement interval; where the length of Z is calculated as [MI * (2 / (C + 3))]. The figure below illustrates this requirement:

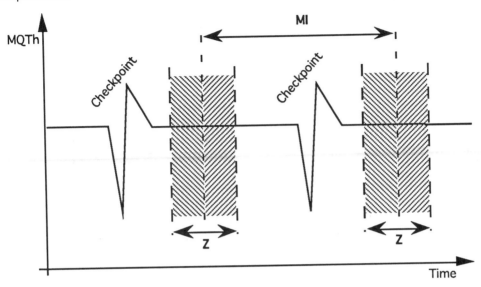

**Comment**: The intent of this clause is to require that writes to disk or other durable media that would normally occur during a sustained test of at least eight hours duration (such as checkpointing, writing redo/undo log records to disk, etc.), are included in the measurement interval, are not on the edges of that period, and are not deferred until after the measurement is complete.

**Note to Comment**: Some systems defer writes of changed pages/blocks to the durable-medium-resident database. Such systems can maintain buffers/caches in a volatile medium (e.g., memory) for use by the DBMS, operating system, and disk control system, which are not synchronized with the durable-medium-resident database. Re-synchronizing these caches with the durable-medium-resident database is typically accomplished via control points, checkpoints, or consistency points.

**5.5.2.3**     If more than one measurement interval is taken during a single test run (i.e., ramp-up followed by several measurement intervals followed by ramp-down), each measurement interval must be non-overlapping with any other measurement interval within the test run.

## 5.6    Required Reporting

**5.6.1**     The frequency distribution of response times of all transactions, started and completed during the measurement interval, must be reported independently for each of the five transaction types (i.e., New-Order, Payment, Order-Status, Delivery, and Stock-Level). The x-axis represents the transaction RT and must range from 0 to four times the measured 90th percentile RT (N) for that transaction. The y-axis represents the frequency of the transactions at a given RT. At least 20 different intervals, of equal length, must be reported. The maximum, average, and 90th percentile response times must also be reported. An example of such a graph is shown below.

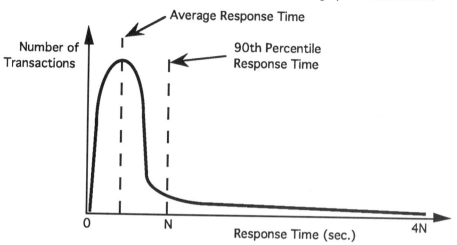

**5.6.2**   A graph of response times versus throughput for the New-Order transaction, run within the mix required in Clause 5.2.3, must be reported. The x-axis represents the measured New-Order throughput. The y-axis represents the corresponding 90th percentile of response times. A graph must be plotted at approximately 50%, 80%, and 100% of reported throughput rate (additional data points are optional). The 50% and 80% data points are to be measured on the same configuration as the 100% run, varying either the Think Time of one or more transaction types or the number of active terminals. Interpolation of the graph between these data points is permitted. Deviations from the required transaction mix are permitted for the 50% and 80% data points. An example of such a graph is shown below.

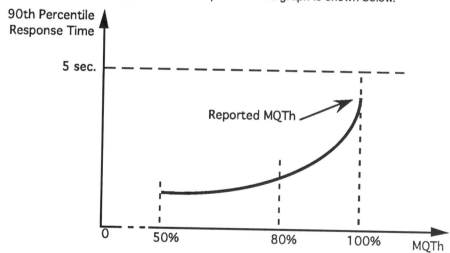

**5.6.3**     The frequency distribution of Think Times of all transactions, started and completed during the measurement interval, must be reported independently for each of the five transaction types (i.e., New-Order, Payment, Order-Status, Delivery, and Stock-Level). The *x*-axis represents the Think Time and must range from 0 to four times the actual mean of Think Time for that transaction. The *y*-axis represents the frequency of the transactions with a given Think Time. At least 20 different intervals, of equal length, must be reported. The mean Think Time must also be reported. An example of such a graph is shown below.

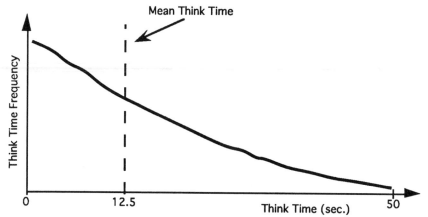

**5.6.4**     The frequency distribution of Keying Times of all transactions, started and completed during the measurement interval, must be reported independently for each of the five transaction types (i.e., New-Order, Payment, Order-Status, Delivery, and Stock-Level). The *x*-axis represents the Keying Time and must range from 0 to twice the actual average Keying Time for that transaction. The *y*-axis represents the frequency of the transactions with a given Keying Time. At least 10 different intervals, of equal length, must be reported. The average Keying Times must also be reported. An example of such a graph is shown below.

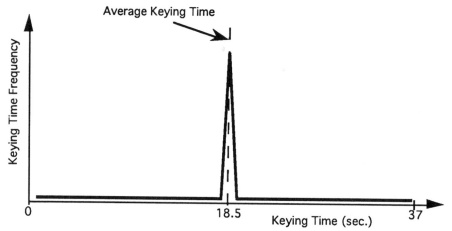

**5.6.5**     A graph of the throughput of the New-Order transaction versus elapsed time (i.e., wall clock) must be reported for both ramp-up time and measurement interval. The *x*-axis represents the elapsed time from the start of the run. The *y*-axis represents the throughput in tpmC. At least 20 different intervals should be used with a maximum interval size of 30 seconds. The opening and the closing of the measurement interval must also be reported. An example of such a graph is shown below.

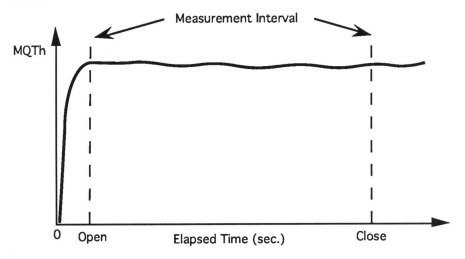

# CLAUSE 6: SUT, Driver, and Communications Definition

## 6.1     Models of the Target System

Some examples of a system which represents the target (object) of this benchmark are shown pictorially below. By way of illustration, the figures also depict the RTE/SUT boundary (see Clauses 6.3 and 6.4) where the response time is measured.

## 6.2     Test Configuration

The test configuration consists of the following elements:

- System Under Test (SUT)
- Driver System(s)
- Driver/SUT Communications Interface(s)

If one of the networks is a WAN, the tested configurations need not include the WAN long-haul communications lines.

C

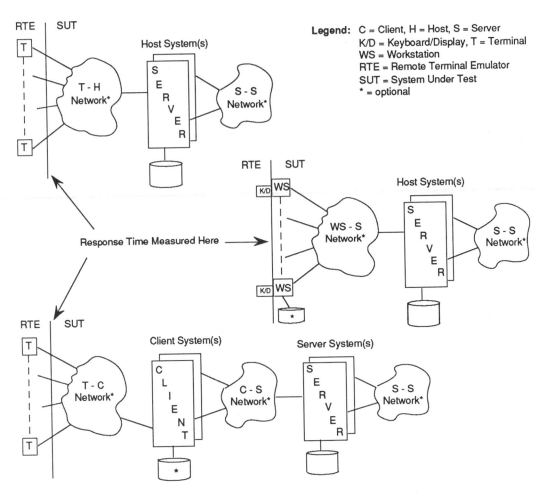

## 6.3 System Under Test (SUT) Definition

The SUT consists of:

- One or more processing units (e.g., host, front-ends, workstations, etc.) which will run the transaction mix described in Clause 5.2.3, and whose aggregate performance (total Maximum Qualified Throughput) will be described by the metric tpmC.

- Any front-end systems are considered to be part of the SUT. Examples of front-end systems are terminal demultiplexers, front-end data communication processors, cluster controllers, database clients (as in the client/server model), and workstations.

- The host system(s), including hardware and software, supporting the database employed in the benchmark.

- The hardware and software components of all networks required to connect and support the SUT components.

- Data storage media sufficient to satisfy both the scaling requirements in Clause 4.2 and the ACID properties of Clause 3.

## 6.4    Driver Definition

**6.4.1**    An external Driver System(s), which provides Remote Terminal Emulator (RTE) functionality, must be used to emulate the target terminal population and their emulated users during the benchmark run.

**6.4.2**    The RTE performs the following functions:

- Emulates a user entering input data on the input/output screen of an emulated terminal by generating and sending transactional messages to the SUT;

- Emulates a terminal displaying output messages on an input/output screen by receiving response messages from the SUT;

- Records response times;

- Performs conversion and/or multiplexing into the communications protocol used by the communications interface between the driver and the SUT;

- Performs statistical accounting (e.g., 90th percentile response time measurement, throughput calculation, etc.) is also considered an RTE function.

**6.4.3**    Normally, the Driver System is expected to perform RTE functions only. Work done on the Driver System in addition to the RTE as specified in Clause 6.4.2 must be thoroughly justified as specified in Clause 6.6.3.

**6.4.4**    The intent is that the Driver System must reflect the proposed terminal configuration and cannot add functionality or performance above the priced network components in the SUT. It must be demonstrated that performance results are not enhanced by using a Driver System.

**6.4.5**    Software or hardware which resides on the Driver which is not the RTE is to be considered as part of the SUT. For example, in a "client/server" model, the client software may be run or be simulated on the Driver System (see Clause 6.6.3).

C

# 6.5    Communications Interface Definitions

### 6.5.1    WAN and LAN Definitions

**6.5.1.1    A Wide Area Network** (WAN) is defined as a communications interface capable of supporting remote sessions over a distance of at least 1500 kilometers, with a protocol supported by commercially available products.

**6.5.1.2**    The upper limit on WAN communications bandwidth will be 64 kbps (k-bits/second) per communications line utilized, and the number of terminals simulated over a 64 kbps line is restrained only by the bandwidth of that line.

**Comment 1:** The communications line will operate at 64 kbps at both ends (Terminal and SUT), but may utilize higher bandwidth mechanisms in between. A maximum line speed of 64 kbps has been selected because of global availability, thus ensuring that country metrics can be published.

**Comment:** In order for a network to be considered a WAN:

- At least one message for each transaction must pass through a WAN.

- All components of the WAN (e.g., modems, multiplexers, etc.) must be capable of operating over a distance of at least 1500 kilometers. This implies that timeouts, turnaround delays, etc., must be accounted for.

**6.5.1.2**    If a network is not a WAN, it is a **Local Area Network** (LAN).

**6.5.1.3**    All protocols used must be commercially available.

**Comment:** It is the intention of this definition to exclude non-standard I/O channel connections. The following situations are examples of acceptable channel connections:

- Configurations or architectures where terminals or terminal controllers are normally and routinely connected to an I/O channel of a processor.

- Where the processor(s) in the SUT is/are connected to the local communications network via a front-end processor, which is channel connected. The front-end processor is priced as part of the SUT.

### 6.5.2    Driver/SUT Communications Interface

**6.5.2.1**    The communications interface between the Driver System(s) and the SUT must be the mechanism by which the system would be connected with the terminal (see Clause 2.1.8) in the proposed configuration.

## 6.6    Further Requirements on the SUT and Driver System

### 6.6.1    Restrictions on Driver System

Copies of any part of the tested database or file system or its data structures, indices, etc., may not be present on the Driver System during the test. Synchronization between RTE and SUT is also disallowed. This specifically prohibits database/transaction synchronization between the Driver and the SUT (e.g., queuing transactions on the Driver).

### 6.6.2    Individual Contexts for Emulated Terminals

The SUT must contain context for each terminal emulated, and must maintain that context for the duration of that test. That context must be identical to the one which would support a real terminal. A terminal which sends a transaction cannot send another until the completion of that transaction, with the exception of the deferred execution of the Delivery transaction.

**Comment**: The **context** referred to in this clause should consist of information such as terminal identification, network identification, and other information necessary for a real terminal to be known to (i.e., configured on) the SUT. The intention is to allow pseudo-conversational transactions. The intent of this clause is simply to prevent a test sponsor from multiplexing messages from a very large number of emulated terminals into a few input lines and claiming or implying that the tested system supports that number of users regardless of whether the system actually supports that number of real terminals.

### 6.6.3    Driver System Doing More Than RTE Function

In the event that a Driver System must be used to emulate additional functionality other than that described in Clause 6.4, then this must be justified as follows:

**6.6.3.1**    It must be demonstrated that the architecture of the proposed solution makes it uneconomical to perform the benchmark without performing the work in question on the driver (e.g., in a "client/server" database implementation, where the client software would run on a large number of workstations).

**6.6.3.2**    Rule 6.6.1 must not be violated.

**6.6.3.3**    It must be demonstrated that executables placed on the Driver System are functionally equivalent to those on the proposed (target) system.

**6.6.3.4**    It must be demonstrated that performance results are not enhanced by performing the work in question on the Driver System. The intent is that a test should be run to demonstrate that the functionality, performance, and connectivity of the emulated solution is the same as that for the priced system. These test data must be included in the Full Disclosure Report.

For example, if the Driver System emulates the function of a terminal concentrator, there must be test data to demonstrate that a real concentrator configured with the claimed number of attached devices would deliver the same (or better) response time as is measured with the Driver System. The terminal concentrator must be configured as it would be in the priced system and loaded to the maximum number of lines used in the priced configuration. The demonstration test must be run as part of the SUT configuration that is running a full load on a properly scaled database. The following diagram illustrates the configuration of a possible demonstration test:

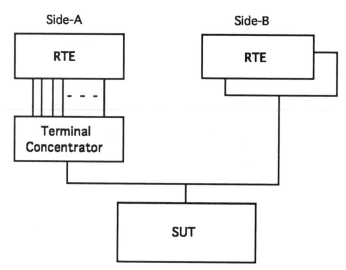

In the above example, the difference in the measured response time between Side-A and Side-B should be less than or equal to any adjustments to the response time reported in the Full Disclosure Report.

If the response time delay generated from a demonstration test is to be used in multiple benchmark tests, the demonstration must be performed on a SUT generating the highest tpmC rate on the terminal concentrator.

**6.6.3.5** Individual contexts must continue to be maintained from the RTE through to the SUT.

**6.6.3.6** A complete functional diagram of both the benchmark configuration and the configuration of the proposed (target) system must be disclosed. A detailed list of all software and hardware functionality being performed on the Driver System, and its interface to the SUT, must be disclosed.

**6.6.4** *Disclosure of Network Configuration and Emulated Portions*

The test sponsor shall describe completely the network configurations of both the tested services and the proposed real (target) services which are being represented. A thorough explanation of exactly which parts of the proposed configuration are being replaced by the Driver System must be given.

**6.6.5** *Limits on Concentration*

The level of concentration of messages between the Driver System(s) and the SUT in the benchmark configuration must not exceed that which would occur in the proposed (target) configuration. In particular, the number of communications packets which can be concentrated must not exceed the number of terminals which would be directly connected to that concentrator in the proposed configuration.

**Comment**: The intent is to allow only first level concentration on the RTE, but does not preclude additional levels of concentration on the SUT.

**6.6.6**    *Limits on Operator Intervention*

Systems which require operator intervention during normal operations to sustain the reported throughput for an eight-hour period are allowed provided that the following conditions are met:

- The need for operator intervention must be disclosed in the Full Disclosure Report. The report must describe the functions performed by the operator and the frequency of this activity.

- The mechanism by which the system indicates that operator intervention is needed must be described. This mechanism must be provided by commercially available hardware and software and be included in the SUT pricing.

- Any event (or combination of events) which requires operator intervention must allow at least 30 minutes for the operator to respond before the event could affect system performance.

**Comment**: The intent of this clause is to restrict the extent of operator intervention during normal operations of the system to a reasonable level. Because of the critical, on-line nature of the modeled application, a system which depends on rapid operator intervention to maintain throughput is not allowed.

# CLAUSE 7: Pricing

## 7.1    Pricing Methodology

**7.1.1**    The intent of this section is to define the methodology to be used in calculating the 5-year pricing and the price/performance (price/tpmC). The fundamental premise is that what is tested and/or emulated is priced and what is priced is tested and/or emulated. Exceptions to this premise are noted below.

**7.1.2**    The proposed system to be priced is the aggregation of the SUT, terminals and network components that would be offered to achieve the reported performance level. Calculation of the priced system consists of:

- Price of the SUT as tested and defined in Clause 6.
- Price of the emulated terminals and proposed network components.

- Price of on-line storage for the minimum database population, 8 hours of processing at the reported tpmC, data generated by an additional 180 8-hour days of processing at the reported tpmC, and the system software necessary to create, operate, administer, and maintain the application.

- Price of additional products that are required for the operation, administration or maintenance of the priced system.

- Price of additional products required for application development.

**7.1.3** The following pricing methodology must be used:

- All hardware and software used in the calculations must be announced and orderable by customers. For any product not already generally released, the Full Disclosure Report must include a committed general delivery date (see Clause 8.1.8). That date must not exceed 12 months beyond the Full Disclosure Report submittal date.

- Generally available discounts for the priced configuration are permissible.

- Generally available packaged pricing is acceptable.

- Local retail pricing and discount structure should be used in each country for which results are published.

- Price should be represented by the currency with which the customer would purchase the system.

- All hardware components used in the priced system must be new (i.e., not reconditioned or previously owned).

- For test sponsor(s) who have only indirect sales channels, pricing must be actual generally available pricing from indirect channels which meets all other requirements of Clause 7.

**Comment 1:** The intent of the pricing methodology is to allow packaging and pricing that is generally available to customers and to explicitly exclude promotional and/or limited availability offerings.

**Comment 2:** Revenue discounts based on total price are permissible. Any discount must be only for the configuration being priced and cannot be based on past or future purchases. Individually negotiated discounts are not permitted. Special customer discounts (e.g., GSA schedule, educational schedule) are not permitted.

**Comment 3:** The intent is to benchmark the actual system which the customer would purchase. However, it is realized that vendors may announce new products and disclose benchmark results before the products have actually shipped. This is allowed, but any use of one-of-a-kind hardware/software configurations, which the vendor does not intend to ship in the future, is specifically excluded. Products must be generally available in the country where the SUT is priced.

**7.1.4** The test sponsor(s) must disclose all pricing sources and effective date(s) of the prices.

**7.1.5**    The sponsor is required to state explicitly all the items and services which are not directly available through the sponsor. Each suppliers items and prices, including discounts, must be listed separately. Discounts may not be dependent on purchases from any other suppliers.

**7.1.6**    **Third-party pricing**: In the event that any hardware, software, or maintenance is provided by a third party not involved as a sponsor of the benchmark, the pricing must satisfy all requirements for general availability, standard volume discounts, and full disclosure. Furthermore, any pricing which is not directly offered by the test sponsor(s) and not derived from the third party vendor's generally available pricing and discounts must be guaranteed by the third party in a written price quotation for a period not less than 60 days from the date the results are submitted. This written quotation must be included in the Full Disclosure Report and state that the quoted prices are generally available, the time period for which the prices are valid, the basis of all discounts, and any terms and conditions which may apply to the quoted prices. The test sponsor must still comply with price changes as described in Clause 8.3.

**7.1.7**    Pricing shown in the Full Disclosure Report must reflect line item pricing from the vendor's price books.

**Comment**: The intent of this clause is that the pricing reflect the level of detail that an actual customer purchasing the priced equipment would see on an itemized billing, excluding taxes and shipping charges.

**7.1.8**    For publishing in another country other than the country for which the results are originally published, it is permitted to substitute local components from the original report providing the substituted products are sold to the same product description or specifications.

**Comment**: The intent of this clause is to encourage local country pricing by allowing substitution of equipment for country-specific reasons such as voltage, product numbering, industrial/safety, keyboard differences, etc., which do not affect performance.

## 7.2    Priced System

### 7.2.1    *SUT*

The entire price of the SUT as configured during the test must be used, including all hardware (new purchase price), software (license charges) and hardware/software maintenance charges over a period of 5 years (60 months). In the case where the Driver System provides functionality in addition to the RTE described in Clause 6, then the price of the emulated hardware/software described in Clause 7.2.2.1 is to be included.

**Comment 1**: The intent is to price the tested system at the full price a customer would pay. Specifically prohibited are the assumption of other purchases, other sites with similar systems, or any other assumption which relies on the principle that the customer has made any other purchase from the vendor. This is a one-time, stand-alone purchase.

**Comment 2**: Any usage pricing for TPC-C should be based on the number of emulated users.

**7.2.2** *Terminals and Network Pricing*

**7.2.2.1** The price of the Driver System is not included in the calculation, although the price of the devices the Driver System is emulating (e.g., controllers, multiplexers, systems used as concentrators, LAN components, front-end processors, workstations and terminals, etc.) are to be included.

**7.2.2.2** The terminals must be commercially available products capable of entering via a keyboard all alphabetic and numeric characters and capable of displaying simultaneously the data and the fields described in Clause 2.

**7.2.2.3** All components necessary to connect the terminals to the SUT must be priced, with the exception of network lines, LANs, drop cables, or direct connect tables. For WAN configurations, the number of terminals to be connected to a single line must be no greater than that emulated per Clause 6.

**Comment**: The intent is that all components, including PADS (packet assemblers-disassemblers), modems, concentrators, multiplexers, repeaters, tranceivers, bridges, etc., required to attach the terminals to the SUT must be priced in addition to the price of the terminals.

**7.2.3** *Database Storage and Recovery Log Pricing*

**7.2.3.1** Within the priced system, there must be sufficient on-line storage to support any expanding system files and the durable database population resulting from executing the TPC-C transaction mix for 180 eight-hour days at the reported tpmC (see Clause 4.2.3). Storage is considered on-line if any record can be accessed randomly and updated within 1 second. On-line storage may include magnetic disks, optical disks, or any combination of these, provided that the above mentioned access criteria is met.

**Comment 1**: The intent of this clause is to consider as on-line any storage device capable of providing an access time to data, for random read or update, of one second or less, even if this access time requires the creation of a logical access path not present in the tested database. For example, a disk-based sequential file might require the creation of an index to satisfy the access time requirement.

**Comment 2**: During the execution of the TPC-C transaction mix, the ORDER, NEW-ORDER, ORDER-LINE, and HISTORY tables grow beyond the minimum database population requirements of the benchmark as specified in Clause 4. Because these tables grow naturally, it is intended that 180 days of growth beyond the specified minimum database population also be taken into account when pricing the system.

**7.2.3.2** Recovery data must be maintained in such a way that the published tpmC transaction rate could be sustained for an 8-hour period. Roll-back recovery data must be either in memory or in on-line storage at least until transactions are committed. Roll-forward recovery data may be stored on an off-line device, providing the following:

- The process which stores the roll-forward data is active during the measurement interval.

- The roll-forward data which is stored off-line during the measurement interval (see Clause 5.5) must be at least as great as the roll-forward recovery data that is generated during the period (i.e., the data may be first created in on-line storage and then moved to off-line storage, but the creation and the movement of the data must be in steady state).

- All ACID properties must be retained.

**7.2.3.3**     It is permissible to not have the storage required for the 180-day space on the tested system. However, any additional storage device included in the priced system but not configured on the tested system must be of the type(s) actually used during the test and must satisfy normal system configuration rules.

**Comment**: Storage devices are considered to be of the same type if they are identical in all aspects of their product description and technical specifications.

**7.2.3.4**     The requirement to support eight hours of recovery log data can be met with storage on any durable media (see Clause 3.5.1) if all data required for recovery from failures listed in Clauses 3.5.3.2 and 3.5.3.3 are on-line.

**7.2.4**     *Additional Operational Components*

**7.2.4.1**     Additional products that might be included on a customer-installed configuration, such as operator consoles and magnetic tape drives, are also to be included in the priced system if explicitly required for the operation, administration, or maintenance of the priced system.

**7.2.4.2**     Copies of the software, on appropriate media, and a software load device, if required for initial load or maintenance updates, must be included.

**7.2.4.3**     The price of an Uninterruptible Power Supply, specifically contributing to a durability solution, must be included (see Clause 3.5.1).

**7.2.4.4**     The price of all cables used to connect components of the system (except as noted in Clause 7.2.2.3) must be included.

**7.2.5**     *Additional Software*

**7.2.5.1**     The price must include the software licenses necessary to create, compile, link, and execute this benchmark application as well as all run-time licenses required to execute on host system(s), client system(s) and connected workstation(s) if used.

**7.2.5.2**     In the event the application program is developed on a system other than the SUT, the price of that system and any compilers and other software used must also be included as part of the priced system.

C

## 7.3   Maintenance

**7.3.1**       Hardware and software maintenance must be figured at a standard pricing which covers at least 5 days/week, 8 hours/day coverage, either on-site or if available as standard offering, via a central support facility. Hardware maintenance maximum response time must not exceed 4 hours, on any part whose replacement is necessary for the resumption of operation.

**Comment**: Resumption of operation means the priced system must be returned to the same configuration that was present before the failure.

**7.3.2**       If central support is claimed, then the appropriate connection device, such as auto-dial modem, must be included in the hardware price. Also any software required to run the connection to the central support, as well as any diagnostic software which the central support facility requires to be resident on the tested system, must not only be included in pricing, but must also be installed during the benchmark runs.

**7.3.3**       Software maintenance must include maintenance update distribution for both the software and its documentation. If software maintenance updates are separately priced, then pricing must include at least 3 updates over the 5-year period.

**Comment**: Software maintenance, as defined above, means a standard offering which includes acknowledgment of new and existing problems within 4 hours and a commitment to fix defects within a reasonable time.

**7.3.4**       Exception: Maintenance and warranty terms for terminals must cover at a minimum a return for repair service.

## 7.4   Required Reporting

**7.4.1**       Two metrics will be reported with regard to pricing. The first is the total 5-year pricing as described in the previous clauses. The second is the total 5-year pricing divided by the reported Maximum Qualified Throughput (tpmC), as defined in Clause 5.4.

**7.4.2**       The 5-year pricing metric must be fully reported in the basic monetary unit of the local currency (see Clause 7.1.3) rounded up and the price/performance metric must be reported to a minimum precision of three significant digits rounded up. Neither metric may be interpolated or extrapolated. For example, if the total price is US$5,734,417.89 and the reported throughput is 105 tpmC, then the 5-year pricing is US$5,734,418 and the price/performance is US$54,700/tpmC (5,734,418/105).

C

# CLAUSE 8: Full Disclosure

## 8.1    Full Disclosure Report Requirements

A Full Disclosure Report is required in order for results to be considered compliant with the TPC-C benchmark specification.

**Comment**: The intent of this disclosure is for a customer to be able to replicate the results of this benchmark given the appropriate documentation and products.

This section includes a list of requirements for the Full Disclosure Report.

**8.1.1**    *General Items*

**8.1.1.1**    The order and titles of sections in the Test Sponsor's Full Disclosure Report must correspond with the order and titles of sections from the TPC-C standard specification (i.e., this document). The intent is to make it as easy as possible for readers to compare and contrast material in different Full Disclosure Reports.

**8.1.1.2**    The TPC Standard Summary Statement and Executive Summary Statement must be included near the beginning of the Full Disclosure Report. An example of the Summary Statements is presented in Appendix B.

**8.1.1.3**    The numerical quantities listed in the Full Disclosure Report must be summarized as shown in Appendix C.

**Comment**: The intent is for data to be conveniently and easily accessible in a familiar arrangement and style. It is not required to precisely mimic the layout shown in Appendix C.

**8.1.1.4**    The application program (as defined in Clause 2.1.7) must be disclosed. This includes, but is not limited to, the code implementing the five transactions and the terminal input and output functions.

**8.1.1.5**    A statement identifying the benchmark sponsor(s) and other participating companies must be provided.

**8.1.1.6**    Settings must be provided for all customer-tunable parameters and options which have been changed from the defaults found in actual products, including but not limited to:

- Database tuning options.
- Recovery/commit options.
- Consistency/locking options.
- Operating system and application configuration parameters.

**Comment**: This requirement can be satisfied by providing a full list of all parameters and options.

C

**8.1.1.7**   Explicit response to individual disclosure requirements specified in the body of earlier sections of this document must be provided.

**8.1.1.8**   Diagrams of both measured and priced configurations must be provided, accompanied by a description of the differences. This includes, but is not limited to:

- Number and type of processors.

- Size of allocated memory, and any specific mapping/partitioning of memory unique to the test.

- Number and type of disk units (and controllers, if applicable).

- Number of channels or bus connections to disk units, including their protocol type.

- Number of LAN (e.g, Ethernet) connections, including routers, workstations, terminals, etc., that were physically used in the test or are incorporated into the pricing structure (see Clause 8.1.8).

- Type and the run-time execution location of software components (e.g., DBMS, client processes, transaction monitors, software drivers, etc.).

**Comment:** Detailed diagrams for system configurations and architectures can widely vary, and it is impossible to provide exact guidelines suitable for all implementations. The intent here is to describe the system components and connections in sufficient detail to allow independent reconstruction of the measurement environment.

The following sample diagram illustrates a workstation/router/server benchmark (measured) configuration using Ethernet and a single processor. Note that this diagram does not depict or imply any optimal configuration for the TPC-C benchmark measurement.

**8.1.2**   *Clause 1 Logical Database Design-Related Items:*

**8.1.2.1**   Listings must be provided for all table definition statements and all other statements used to set up the database.

**8.1.2.2**   The physical organization of tables and indices, within the database, must be disclosed.

**Comment:** The concept of physical organization includes, but is not limited to: record clustering (i.e., rows from different logical tables are co-located on the same physical data page), index clustering (i.e., rows and leaf nodes of an index to these rows are co-located on the same physical data page), and partial fill-factors (i.e., physical data pages are left partially empty even though additional rows are available to fill them).

**8.1.2.3**   It must be ascertained that insert and/or delete operations to any of the tables can occur concurrently with the TPC-C transaction mix. Furthermore, any restriction in the SUT database implementation that precludes inserts beyond the limits defined in Clause 1.4.11 must be disclosed. This includes the maximum number of rows that can be inserted and the maximum key value for these new rows.

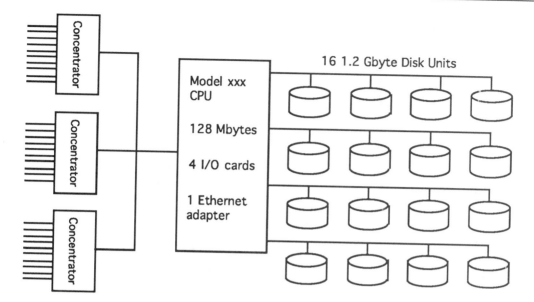

Concentrators:    System_WW with 10 diskless workstations each
LAN:              Ethernet using NET_XX routers
CPU:              Model_YY with 128 Mbytes of main memory, 4 I/O cards with
                  SCSI II protocol support
Disk:             Vendor_ZZ 1.2 Gbyte drives

**8.1.2.4**    While there are a few restrictions placed upon horizontal or vertical partitioning of tables and rows in the TPC-C benchmark (see Clause 1.6), any such partitioning must be disclosed. Using the CUSTOMER table as an example, such
partitioning could be denoted as:

C_part_1              C_ID
                      C_D_ID
                      C_W_ID
----------------------- vertical partition----------------
C_part_2              C_FIRST
                      C_MIDDLE
                      C_LAST
                      C_STREET-1
                      C_STREET-2
                      C_CITY
                      C_STATE
                      C_ZIP
                      C_PHONE
                      C_SINCE

```
----------------------- vertical partition----------------
C_part_3              C_CREDIT
                     C_CREDIT_LIM
                     C_DISCOUNT
                     C_BALANCE
                     C_YTD_PAYMENT
                     C_PAYMENT_CNT
                     C_DELIVERY_CNT
----------------------- vertical partition----------------
C_part_4              C_DATA
```

Once the partitioned database elements have been so identified, they can be referred to by, for example, their **T_part_N** notation when describing the physical allocation of database files (see Clause 8.1.5), where T indicates the table name and N indicates the partition segment number.

**8.1.3**    *Clause 2 Transaction and Terminal Profiles-Related Items*

**8.1.3.1**    The method of verification for the random number generation must be described.

**8.1.3.2**    The actual layouts of the terminal input/output screens must be disclosed.

**8.1.3.3**    The method used to verify that the priced terminals provide all the features described in Clause 2.2.2.4 must be explained.

**8.1.3.4**    Any usage of presentation managers or intelligent terminals must be explained.

**Comment 1**: The intent of this clause is to describe any special manipulations performed by a local terminal or workstation to off-load work from the SUT. This includes, but is not limited to: screen presentations, message bundling, and local storage of TPC-C rows.

**Comment 2**: This disclosure also requires that all data manipulation functions performed by the local terminal to provide navigational aids for transaction(s) must also be described. Within this disclosure, the purpose of such additional function(s) must be explained.

**8.1.3.5**    The percentage of home and remote order-lines in the New-Order transactions must be disclosed.

**8.1.3.6**    The percentage of New-Order transactions that were rolled back as a result of an unused item number must be disclosed.

**8.1.3.7**    The number of items per orders entered by New-Order transactions must be disclosed.

**8.1.3.8**    The percentage of home and remote Payment transactions must be disclosed.

**8.1.3.9**    The percentage of Payment and Order-Status transactions that used non-primary key (C_LAST) access to the database must be disclosed.

**8.1.3.10**    The percentage of Delivery transactions that were skipped as a result of an insufficient number of rows in the NEW-ORDER table must be disclosed.

**8.1.3.11**    The mix (i.e., percentages) of transaction types seen by the SUT must be disclosed.

**8.1.3.12**    The queuing mechanism used to defer the execution of the Delivery transaction must be disclosed.

**8.1.4**    *Clause 3 Transaction and System Properties-Related Items*

**8.1.4.1**    The results of the ACID tests must be disclosed along with a description of how the ACID requirements were met. This includes disclosing which case was followed for the execution of Isolation Test 7.

**8.1.5**    *Clause 4 Scaling and Database Population-Related Items*

**8.1.5.1**    The cardinality (e.g., the number of rows) of each table, as it existed at the start of the benchmark run (see Clause 4.2), must be disclosed.

**8.1.5.2**    The distribution of tables and logs across all media must be explicitly depicted for the tested and priced systems.

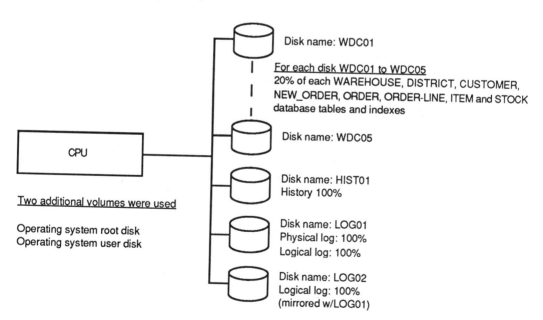

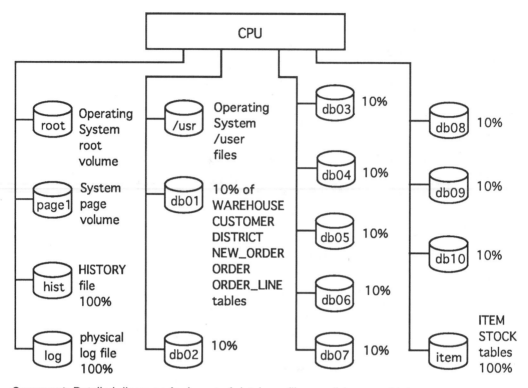

**Comment**: Detailed diagrams for layout of database files on disks can widely vary, and it is difficult to provide exact guidelines suitable for all implementations. The intent is to provide sufficient detail to allow independent reconstruction of the test database. The two figures below are examples of database layout descriptions and are not intended to depict or imply any optimal layout for the TPC-C database.

**8.1.5.3**    A statement must be provided that describes the database model implemented by the DBMS used (e.g., relational, CODASYL, flat file, etc.).

**8.1.5.4**    The mapping of database partitions/replications must be explicitly described.

**Comment**: The intent is to provide sufficient detail about partitioning and replication to allow independent reconstruction of the test database.

An description of a database partitioning scheme is presented below as an example. The nomenclature of this example was outlined using the CUSTOMER table (in Clause 8.1.2.1), and has been extended to use the ORDER and ORDER_LINE tables as well.

C

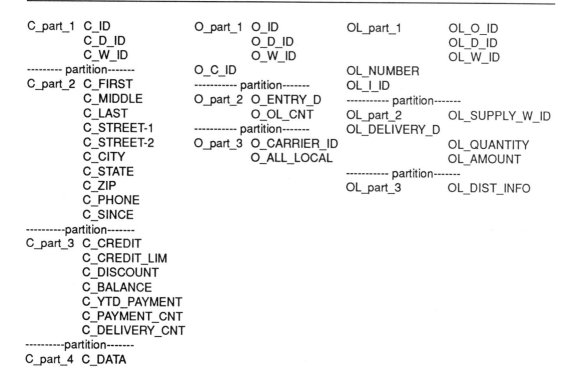

```
C_part_1  C_ID              O_part_1  O_ID           OL_part_1          OL_O_ID
          C_D_ID                      O_D_ID                            OL_D_ID
          C_W_ID                      O_W_ID                            OL_W_ID
--------- partition-------   O_C_ID                  OL_NUMBER
C_part_2  C_FIRST           ---------- partition-------  OL_I_ID
          C_MIDDLE          O_part_2  O_ENTRY_D      ---------- partition-------
          C_LAST                      O_OL_CNT       OL_part_2          OL_SUPPLY_W_ID
          C_STREET-1        ---------- partition-------  OL_DELIVERY_D
          C_STREET-2        O_part_3  O_CARRIER_ID                      OL_QUANTITY
          C_CITY                      O_ALL_LOCAL                       OL_AMOUNT
          C_STATE                                    ---------- partition-------
          C_ZIP                                      OL_part_3          OL_DIST_INFO
          C_PHONE
          C_SINCE
----------partition-------
C_part_3  C_CREDIT
          C_CREDIT_LIM
          C_DISCOUNT
          C_BALANCE
          C_YTD_PAYMENT
          C_PAYMENT_CNT
          C_DELIVERY_CNT
----------partition-------
C_part_4  C_DATA
```

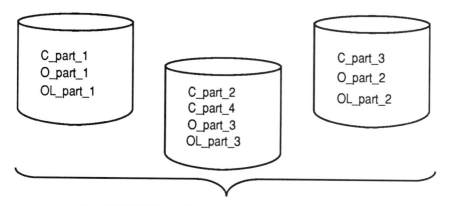

One WAREHOUSE Customer/Order/Order_line "cell"

**8.1.6** *Clause 5 Performance Metrics and Response Time-Related Items*

**8.1.6.1** All data specified in Clause 5, including measured and reported tpmC, must be reported.

**8.1..6.2** Ninetieth percentile, maximum and average response times must be reported for all transaction types as well as for the Menu response time.

**8.1.6.3** The minimum, the average, and the maximum keying and think times must be reported for each transaction type.

**8.1.6.4** Response Time frequency distribution curves (see Clause 5.6.1) must be reported for each transaction type.

**8.1.6.5** The performance curve for response times versus throughput (see Clause 5.6.2) must be reported for the New-Order transaction.

**8.1.6.6** Think Time frequency distribution curves (see Clause 5.6.3) must be reported for each transaction type.

**8.1.6.7** Keying Time frequency distribution curves (see Clause 5.6.4) must be reported for each transaction type.

**8.1.6.8** A graph of throughput versus elapsed time (see Clause 5.6.5) must be reported for the New-Order transaction.

**8.1.6.9** The method used to determine that the SUT had reached a steady state prior to commencing the measurement interval (see Clause 5.5) must be described.

**8.1.6.10** A description of how the work normally performed during a sustained test (for example checkpointing, writing redo/undo log records, etc.), actually occurred during the measurement interval must be reported.

**8.1.6.11** A description of the method used to determine the reproducibility of the measurement results must be reported.

**8.1.6.12** A statement of the duration of the measurement interval for the reported Maximum Qualified Throughput (tpmC) must be included.

**8.1.7** *Clause 6 SUT, Driver, and Communication Definition-Related Items*

**8.1.7.1** If the RTE is commercially available, then its inputs must be specified. Otherwise, a description must be supplied of what inputs (e.g., scripts) to the RTE had been used.

**8.1.7.2** It must be demonstrated that the functionality and performance of the components being emulated in the Driver System are equivalent to that of the priced system.

**8.1.7.3** The bandwidth of the network(s) used in the tested/priced configuration must be disclosed.

**8.1.7.4** If the configuration requires operator intervention (see Clause 6.6.6), the mechanism and the frequency of this intervention must be disclosed.

**8.1.8**    *Clause 7 Pricing Related Items*

**8.1.8.1**    A detailed list of hardware and software used in the priced system must be reported. Each item must have vendor part number, description, and release/revision level, and either general availability status or committed delivery date. If package-pricing is used, contents of the package must be disclosed. Pricing source(s) and effective date(s) of price(s) must also be reported.

**8.1.8.2**    The total 5-year price of the entire configuration must be reported, including: hardware, software, and maintenance charges. Separate component pricing is recommended. The basis of all discounts used must be disclosed.

**8.1.8.3**    The committed delivery date for general availability (availability date) of products used in the price calculations must be reported. When the priced system includes products with different availability dates, the reported availability date for the priced system must be the date at which all components are committed to be available.

**8.1.8.4**    A statement of the measured tpmC, as well as the respective calculations for 5-year pricing, price/performance (price/tpmC), and the availability date must be included.

**8.1.8.5**    Additional Clause 7 related items may be included in the Full Disclosure Report for each country-specific priced configuration. Country-specific pricing is subject to Clause 7.1.7.

**8.1.9**    *Clause 9 Audit Related Items*

**8.1.9.1**    If the benchmark has been independently audited, then the auditor's name, address, phone number, and a brief audit summary report indicating compliance must be included in the Full Disclosure Report. A statement should be included, specifying when the complete audit report will become available and who to contact in order to obtain a copy.

# 8.2    Availability of the Full Disclosure Report

The Full Disclosure Report must be readily available to the public at a reasonable charge, similar to charges for similar documents by that test sponsor. The report must be made available when results are made public. In order to use the phrase "TPC Benchmark™ C", the Full Disclosure Report must have been submitted to the TPC Administrator as well as written permission obtained to distribute same.

# 8.3    Revisions to the Full Disclosure Report

Revisions to the full disclosure documentation shall be handled as follows:

1.    Fully documented price changes can be reflected in a new published price/performance. The benchmark need not be rerun to remain compliant.

C

2. Hardware or software product substitutions within the SUT, with the exception of equipment emulated as allowed under Clause 6, require the benchmark to be re-run with the new components in order to re-establish compliance. For any substitution of equipment emulated during the benchmark, a new demonstration according to Clause 6.6.3.4 must be provided.

3. The revised report should be submitted as defined in Clause 8.2.

   **Comment:** During the normal product life cycle problems will be uncovered that require changes, sometimes referred to as ECOs, FCOs, Patches, Updates, etc. When the cumulative result of applied changes causes the tpmC rating of the system to decrease by more than 5% from the reported tpmC, then the test sponsor is required to re-validate the benchmark results.

4. Fully documented price decreases can be reflected in a new published price/performance. When cumulative price changes have resulted in an increase of 5% or more from the reported price/performance, the test sponsor must submit revised price/performance results to the TPC within 30 days of the effective date of the price change(s) to remain in conformance. The benchmark need not be rerun to remain in conformance.

   **Comment:** The intent of this clause is that published price/performance reflect actual current price/performance.

5. A change in the committed availability date for the priced system can be reflected in a new published availability date.

6. A report may be revised to add or delete Clause 7 related items for country-specific priced configurations.

7. Full Disclosure Report revisions may be required for other reasons according to TPC policies (see TPC Policy Document)

## 8.4   Official Language

The official Full Disclosure Report must be written and submitted in English, but can be translated to additional languages.

# CLAUSE 9: Audit

## 9.1   General Rules

9.1.1     An independent audit of the benchmark results is highly recommended. An audit checklist is provided as part of this specification.

**9.1.2**      If audited, the auditor's attestation letter must be made readily available to the public as part of the Full Disclosure Report, but a detailed report from the auditor is not required.

**9.1.3**      For the purpose of the audit, only transactions that are generated by the Driver System and the data associated with those transactions should be used for the audit tests, with the exception of the minimal database population verification.

**9.1.4**      In the case of audited TPC-C results which are used as a basis for new TPC-C results, the sponsor of the new benchmark can claim that the results were audited if, and only if:

1.   The auditor ensures that the hardware and software products are the same.

2.   The auditor reviews the Full Disclosure Report (FDR) of the new results and ensures that they match what is contained in the original sponsor's FDR.

3.   The auditor can attest to Clauses 9.2.8.2 and 9.2.8.4.

The auditor is not required to follow any of the remaining auditor's check list items from Clause 9.2.


## 9.2      Auditor's Checklist

**9.2.1**      *Clause 1 Logical Database Design-Related Items*

**9.2.1.1**      Verify that specified attributes (i.e., columns) and rows exist, and that they conform to the specifications.

**9.2.1.2**      Verify that the row identifiers are not disk or file offsets.

**9.2.1.3**      Verify that all tables support retrievals, inserts and deletes.

**9.2.1.4**      Verify the randomness of the input data to the system under test for all transactions. Include verification that the values generated are uniform across the entire set of rows in the configured database necessary to support the claimed tpmC rating per Clause 5.4.

**9.2.1.5**      Verify whether any horizontal and/or vertical partitioning has been used, and, if so, whether it was implemented in accordance with the TPC-C requirements.

**9.2.1.6**      Verify whether any replication of tables has been used, and, if so, whether it was implemented in accordance with the TPC-C requirements.

**9.2.1.7**      Verify that no more than 1%, or no more than one (1), whichever is greater, of the Delivery transactions skipped because there were fewer than necessary orders present in the New-Order table.

**9.2.2**      *Clause 2 Transaction and Terminal Profiles-Related Items*

**9.2.2.1**      Verify that the application programs match the respective transaction profiles.

C

**9.2.2.2**     Verify that the input data satisfy the requirements and that input/output screen layouts are preserved.

**9.2.2.3**     Verify that each New-Order transaction uses independently generated input data and not data from rolled back transactions.

**9.2.2.4**     Verify that the randomly generated input data satisfies the folllowing constraints:

1.  At least 0.9% and at most 1.1% of the New-Order transactions roll back as a result of an unused item number. For these transactions the required profile is executed, and the correct screen is displayed. Furthermore, verify that the application makes only permitted use of the fact that the input data contains an unused item number.

2.  The average number of order-lines per order is in the range of 9.5 to 10.5 and the number of order-lines is uniformly distributed from 5 to 15 for the New-Order transactions that are submitted to the SUT during the measurement interval.

3.  The number of remote order-lines is at least 0.95% and at most 1.05% of the number of order-lines that are filled in by the New-Order transactions that are submitted to the SUT during the measurement interval, and the remote warehouse numbers are uniformly distributed within the range of configured warehouses.

4.  The number of remote Payment transactions is at least 14% and at most 16% of the number of Payment transactions that are submitted to the SUT during the measurement interval, and the remote warehouse numbers are uniformly distributed within the range of configured warehouses.

5.  The number of customer selections by customer last name in the Payment transaction is at least 57% and at most 63% of the number of Payment transactions that are submitted to the SUT during the measurement interval.

6.  The number of customer selections by customer last name in the Order-Status transaction is at least 57% and at most 63% of the number of Order-Status transactions that are submitted to the SUT during the measurement interval.

**9.2.2.5**     Verify that results from executing the Delivery transaction in deferred mode are recorded into a result file. Verify that the result file is maintained on the proper type of durable medium. Furthermore, verify that no action is recorded into the result file until after the action has been completed.

**9.2.2.6**     Verify that data read by the Stock-Level transaction is not older than the most recently committed data prior to the time the transaction was initiated.

**9.2.2.7**     Verify that all input and output fields that may change on screens are cleared at the beginning of each transaction.

**9.2.2.8**     Using one of the priced terminals, verify that the input/output screen for each transaction type provides all the features described in Clause 2.2.2.4.

**9.2.2.9**    The auditor can further verify the compliance of the input data by querying the following attributes:

- O_ALL_LOCAL can be used to verify that approximately 10% of all orders contain at least one remote order-line.

- C_PAYMENT_CNT can be used to verify that within the Payment transaction customers were selected according to the required non-uniform random distribution.

- S_YTD can be used to verify that within the New-Order transaction the quantity ordered for each item was within the required range.

- S_ORDER_CNT can be used to verify that within the New-Order transaction items were selected according to the required non-uniform random distribution.

- S_REMOTE_CNT can be used to verify that within the New-Order transaction remote order-lines were selected according to the required uniform random distribution.

**9.2.3**    *Clause 3 Transactions and System Properties-Related Items*

**9.2.3.1**    Verify that the requirements of each of the ACID tests were met.

**9.2.4**    *Clause 4 Scaling and Database Population-Related Items*

**9.2.4.1**    Verify that the database is initially populated with the minimal required population.

**9.2.4.2**    Verify the correct cardinalities of the nine database tables, at the start of the benchmark run as well as at the end of it, and that the growth in the New-Order table, in particular, is consistent with the number and type of executed transactions.

**9.2.6**    *Clause 5 Performance Metrics and Response Time-Related Items*

**9.2.6.1**    Verify that the mix of transactions as seen by the SUT satisfies the required minimum percentage of mix.

**9.2.6.2**    Verify the validity of the method used to measure the response time at the RTE.

**9.2.6.3**    If part of the SUT is emulated, verify that the reported response time is no less than the response time that would be seen by a real terminal user.

**9.2.6.4**    Verify the method used to determine that the SUT had reached a steady state prior to commencing the measurement interval (see Clause 5.5).

**9.2.6.5**    Verify that all work normally done in a steady state environment actually occurred during the measurement interval, for example checkpointing, writing redo/undo log records to disk, etc.

**9.2.6.6**    Verify the method used to determine the reproducibility of the measurement results.

**9.2.6.7**    Verify the duration of the measurement interval for the reported tpmC.

C

**9.2.6.8**   Verify that the response times have been measured in the same time interval as the test.

**9.2.6.9**   Verify that the required Keying and Think Times for the emulated users occur in accordance with the requirements.

**9.2.6.10**   Verify that the 90th percentile response time for each transaction type is greater than or equal to the average response time of that transaction type.

**9.2.6.11**   If the RTE adjusts the weights associated to each transaction type, verify that these adjustments have been limited to keep the weights within 5% on either side of their respective initial value.

**9.2.6.12**   If the RTE uses card decks (see Clause 5.2.4.2) verify that they meet the requirements.

**9.2.6.13**   If periodic checkpoints are used, verify that they are properly scheduled and executed during the measurement interval.

**9.2.7**   *Clause 6 SUT, Driver, and Communications Definition-Related Items*

**9.2.7.1**   Describe the method used to verify the accurate emulation of the tested terminal population by the Driver System if one was used.

**9.2.7.2**   Verify that the restrictions on operator intervention are met.

**9.2.8**   *Clause 7 Pricing-Related Items*

**9.2.8.1**   Verify that all application development software is installed on the priced system and has been used to compile, link and execute the benchmark.

**9.2.8.2**   Verify that all prices used, including discounts, are generally available and that pricing includes all the hardware and software licenses as required.

**9.2.8.3**   Verify that the priced system (as defined in Clause 7.1.2) has sufficient disk storage for system software, database tables, and recovery logs.

**9.2.8.4**   Verify that warranty coverage meets the requirements, or that additional costs for maintenance have been added to the priced system.

# APPENDIX A: Sample Programs

The following are examples of the TPC-C transactions and database load program in SQL embedded in C. Only the basic functionality of the TPC-C transactions is supplied. All terminal I/O operations and miscellaneous functions have been left out of these examples. The code presented here is for demonstration purposes only, and is not meant to be an optimal implementation.

**Note:** The examples in this appendix, in some areas, may not follow all the requirements of the benchmark. In case of discrepancy between the specifications and the programming examples, the specifications prevail.

# A.1    The New-Order Transaction

```
int neword()
{
    EXEC SQL WHENEVER NOT FOUND GOTO sqlerr;
    EXEC SQL WHENEVER SQLERROR GOTO sqlerr;

    gettimestamp(datetime);

    EXEC SQL SELECT c_discount, c_last, c_credit, w_tax
             INTO :c_discount, :c_last, :c_credit, :w_tax
             FROM customer, warehouse
             WHERE w_id = :w_id AND c_w_id = w_id AND
                   c_d_id = :d_id AND c_id = :c_id;

    EXEC SQL SELECT d_next_o_id, d_tax INTO :d_next_o_id, :d_tax
             FROM district
             WHERE d_id = :d_id AND d_w_id = :w_id;

    EXEC SQL UPDATE district SET d_next_o_id = :d_next_o_id + 1
             WHERE d_id = :d_id AND d_w_id = :w_id;

    o_id=d_next_o_id;

    EXEC SQL INSERT INTO ORDERS (o_id, o_d_id, o_w_id, o_c_id,
                                 o_entry_d, o_ol_cnt, o_all_local)
             VALUES (:o_id, :d_id, :w_id, :c_id,
                     :datetime, :o_ol_cnt, :o_all_local);

    EXEC SQL INSERT INTO NEW_ORDER (no_o_id, no_d_id, no_w_id)
             VALUES (:o_id, :d_id, :w_id);

    for (ol_number=1; ol_number<=o_ol_cnt; ol_number++)
    {
      ol_supply_w_id=atol(supware[ol_number-1]);
      if (ol_supply_w_id != w_id) o_all_local=0;
      ol_i_id=atol(itemid[ol_number-1]);
      ol_quantity=atol(qty[ol_number-1]);

      EXEC SQL WHENEVER NOT FOUND GOTO invaliditem;

      EXEC SQL SELECT i_price, i_name , i_data
               INTO :i_price, :i_name, :i_data
               FROM item
               WHERE i_id = :ol_i_id;

      price[ol_number-1] = i_price;
      strncpy(iname[ol_number-1],i_name,24);

      EXEC SQL WHENEVER NOT FOUND GOTO sqlerr;
```

```
      EXEC SQL SELECT s_quantity, s_data,
                s_dist_01, s_dist_02, s_dist_03, s_dist_04, s_dist_05
                s_dist_06, s_dist_07, s_dist_08, s_dist_09, s_dist_10
              INTO :s_quantity, :s_data,
                :s_dist_01, :s_dist_02, :s_dist_03, :s_dist_04, :s_dist_05
                :s_dist_06, :s_dist_07, :s_dist_08, :s_dist_09, :s_dist_10
              FROM stock
              WHERE s_i_id = :ol_i_id AND s_w_id = :ol_supply_w_id;

      pick_dist_info(ol_dist_info, ol_w_id);  // pick correct s_dist_xx
      stock[ol_number-1] = s_quantity;

      if ( (strstr(i_data,"original") != NULL) &&
           (strstr(s_data,"original") != NULL) )
        bg[ol_number-1] = 'B';
      else
        bg[ol_number-1] = 'G';

  if (s_quantity > ol_quantity)
     s_quantity = s_quantity - ol_quantity;
  else
     s_quantity = s_quantity - ol_quantity + 91;

  EXEC SQL UPDATE stock SET s_quantity = :s_quantity
              WHERE s_i_id = :ol_i_id
              AND s_w_id = :ol_supply_w_id;

  ol_amount = ol_quantity * i_price * (1+w_tax+d_tax) * (1-c_discount);
  amt[ol_number-1]=ol_amount;
  total += ol_amount;

  EXEC SQL INSERT
              INTO order_line (ol_o_id, ol_d_id, ol_w_id, ol_number,
                              ol_i_id, ol_supply_w_id,
                              ol_quantity, ol_amount, ol_dist_info)
              VALUES (:o_id, :d_id, :w_id, :ol_number,
                      :ol_i_id, :ol_supply_w_id,
                      :ol_quantity, :ol_amount, :ol_dist_info);
   } /*End Order Lines*/

  EXEC SQL COMMIT WORK;
  return(0);

invaliditem:
  EXEC SQL ROLLBACK WORK;
  printf("Item number is not valid");
  return(0);

sqlerr:
  error();
}
```

## A.2  The Payment Transaction

```
int payment()
{
    EXEC SQL WHENEVER NOT FOUND GOTO sqlerr;
    EXEC SQL WHENEVER SQLERROR GOTO sqlerr;

    gettimestamp(datetime);

    EXEC SQL UPDATE warehouse SET w_ytd = w_ytd + :h_amount
            WHERE w_id=:w_id;

    EXEC SQL SELECT w_street_1, w_street_2, w_city, w_state, w_zip, w_name
            INTO :w_street_1, :w_street_2, :w_city, :w_state, :w_zip, :w_name
            FROM warehouse
            WHERE w_id=:w_id;

    EXEC SQL UPDATE district SET d_ytd = d_ytd + :h_amount
            WHERE d_w_id=:w_id AND d_id=:d_id;

    EXEC SQL SELECT d_street_1, d_street_2, d_city, d_state, d_zip, d_name
            INTO :d_street_1, :d_street_2, :d_city, :d_state, :d_zip, :d_name
            FROM district
            WHERE d_w_id=:w_id AND d_id=:d_id;

    if (byname)
    {
      EXEC SQL SELECT count(c_id) INTO :namecnt
            FROM customer
            WHERE c_last=:c_last AND c_d_id=:c_d_id AND c_w_id=:c_w_id;

      EXEC SQL DECLARE c_byname CURSOR FOR
            SELECT c_first, c_middle, c_id,
                c_street_1, c_street_2, c_city, c_state, c_zip,
                c_phone, c_credit, c_credit_lim,
                c_discount, c_balance, c_since
            FROM customer
            WHERE c_w_id=:c_w_id AND c_d_id=:c_d_id AND c_last=:c_last
            ORDER BY c_first;

      EXEC SQL OPEN c_byname;

      if (namecnt%2) namecnt++;    // Locate midpoint customer;
      for (n=0; n<namecnt/2; n++)
      {
        EXEC SQL FETCH c_byname
            INTO :c_first, :c_middle, :c_id,
                :c_street_1, :c_street_2, :c_city, :c_state, :c_zip,
                :c_phone, :c_credit, :c_credit_lim,
                :c_discount, :c_balance, :c_since;
      }
```

```
    EXEC SQL CLOSE c_byname;
  }
  else
  {
    EXEC SQL SELECT c_first, c_middle, c_last,
                    c_street_1, c_street_2, c_city, c_state, c_zip,
                    c_phone, c_credit, c_credit_lim,
                    c_discount, c_balance, c_since
              INTO :c_first, :c_middle, :c_last,
                    :c_street_1, :c_street_2, :c_city, :c_state, :c_zip,
                    :c_phone, :c_credit, :c_credit_lim,
                    :c_discount, :c_balance, :c_since
              FROM customer
              WHERE c_w_id=:c_w_id AND c_d_id=:c_d_id AND c_id=:c_id;
  }
  c_balance += h_amount;
  c_credit[2]='\0';
  if (strstr(c_credit, "BC") )
  {
    EXEC SQL SELECT c_data INTO :c_data
              FROM customer
              WHERE c_w_id=:c_w_id AND c_d_id=:c_d_id AND c_id=:c_id;

    sprintf(c_new_data,"| %4d %2d %4d %2d %4d $%7.2f %12c %24c",
                       c_id,c_d_id,c_w_id,d_id,w_id,h_amount
                       h_date, h_data);
    strncat(c_new_data,c_data,500-strlen(c_new_data));

    EXEC SQL UPDATE customer
              SET c_balance = :c_balance,  c_data = :c_new_data
              WHERE c_w_id = :c_w_id AND c_d_id = :c_d_id AND
                    c_id = :c_id;
  }
  else
  {
    EXEC SQL UPDATE customer SET c_balance = :c_balance
              WHERE c_w_id = :c_w_id AND c_d_id = :c_d_id AND
                    c_id = :c_id;
  }
  strncpy(h_data,w_name,10);
  h_data[10]='\0';
  strncat(h_data,d_name,10);
  h_data[20]=' ';
  h_data[21]=' ';
  h_data[22]=' ';
  h_data[23]=' ';

  EXEC SQL INSERT INTO history (h_c_d_id, h_c_w_id, h_c_id, h_d_id,
                               h_w_id, h_date, h_amount, h_data)
              VALUES (:c_d_id, :c_w_id, :c_id, :d_id,
                      :w_id, :datetime, :h_amount, :h_data);
```

```
    EXEC SQL COMMIT WORK;
    return(0);

sqlerr:
    error();
}
```

## A.3    The Order-Status Transaction

```
int ostat()
{
    EXEC SQL WHENEVER NOT FOUND GOTO sqlerr;
    EXEC SQL WHENEVER SQLERROR GOTO sqlerr;

    if (byname)
    {
      EXEC SQL SELECT count(c_id) INTO :namecnt
               FROM customer
               WHERE c_last=:c_last AND c_d_id=:d_id AND c_w_id=:w_id;

      EXEC SQL DECLARE c_name CURSOR FOR
               SELECT c_balance, c_first, c_middle, c_id
                 FROM customer
                 WHERE c_last=:c_last AND c_d_id=:d_id AND c_w_id=:w_id
                 ORDER BY c_first;
      EXEC SQL OPEN c_name;

      if (namecnt%2) namecnt++;    // Locate midpoint customer
      for (n=0; n<namecnt/2; n++)
      {
        EXEC SQL FETCH c_name
               INTO :c_balance, :c_first, :c_middle, :c_id;
      }

      EXEC SQL CLOSE c_name;
    }
    else {
      EXEC SQL SELECT c_balance, c_first, c_middle, c_last
               INTO :c_balance, :c_first, :c_middle, :c_last
               FROM customer
               WHERE c_id=:c_id AND c_d_id=:d_id AND c_w_id=:w_id;
    }
    EXEC SQL SELECT o_id, o_carrier_id, o_entry_d
             INTO :o_id, :o_carrier_id, :entdate
             FROM orders
             ORDER BY o_id DESC;
```

C

```
        EXEC SQL DECLARE c_line CURSOR FOR
                SELECT ol_i_id, ol_supply_w_id, ol_quantity,
                       ol_amount, ol_delivery_d
                  FROM order_line
                  WHERE ol_o_id=:o_id AND ol_d_id=:d_id AND ol_w_id=:w_id;

        EXEC SQL OPEN c_line;
        EXEC SQL WHENEVER NOT FOUND CONTINUE;

        i=0;
        while (sql_notfound(FALSE))
        {
          i++;
          EXEC SQL FETCH c_line
                  INTO :ol_i_id[i], :ol_supply_w_id[i], :ol_quantity[i],
                       :ol_amount[i], :ol_delivery_d[i];
        }

        EXEC SQL CLOSE c_line;
        EXEC SQL COMMIT WORK;
        return(0);

sqlerr:
    error();
}
```

## A.4    The Delivery Transaction

```
int delivery()
{
    EXEC SQL WHENEVER SQLERROR GOTO sqlerr;

    gettimestamp(datetime);

    /* For each district in warehouse */
    printf("W: %d\n", w_id);
    for (d_id=1; d_id<=DIST_PER_WARE; d_id++)
    {
        EXEC SQL WHENEVER NOT FOUND GOTO sqlerr;
        EXEC SQL DECLARE c_no CURSOR FOR
             SELECT no_o_id
               FROM new_order
               WHERE no_d_id = :d_id AND no_w_id = :w_id AND no_o_id
               ORDER BY no_o_id ASC;

        EXEC SQL OPEN c_no;

        EXEC SQL WHENEVER NOT FOUND continue;
        EXEC SQL FETCH c_no INTO :no_o_id;
```

```
    EXEC SQL DELETE FROM new_order WHERE CURRENT OF c_no;

    EXEC SQL CLOSE c_no;

    EXEC SQL SELECT o_c_id INTO :c_id FROM orders
            WHERE o_id = :no_o_id AND o_d_id = :d_id AND
                o_w_id = :w_id;

    EXEC SQL UPDATE orders SET o_carrier_id = :o_carrier_id
            WHERE o_id = :no_o_id AND o_d_id = :d_id AND
                o_w_id = :w_id;

    EXEC SQL UPDATE order_line SET ol_delivery_d = :datetime
            WHERE ol_o_id = :no_o_id AND ol_d_id = :d_id AND
                ol_w_id = :w_id;

    EXEC SQL SELECT SUM(ol_amount) INTO :ol_total
            FROM order_line
            WHERE ol_o_id = :no_o_id AND ol_d_id = :d_id
                AND ol_w_id = :w_id;

    EXEC SQL UPDATE customer SET c_balance = c_balance + :ol_total
            WHERE c_id = :c_id AND c_d_id = :d_id AND
                c_w_id = :w_id;

    EXEC SQL COMMIT WORK;
    printf("D: %d, O: %d, time: %d\n", d_id, o_id, tad);

    }
    EXEC SQL COMMIT WORK;
    return(0);

sqlerr:
    error();
}
```

## A.5    The Stock-Level Transaction

```
int slev()
{
    EXEC SQL WHENEVER NOT FOUND GOTO sqlerr;
    EXEC SQL WHENEVER SQLERROR GOTO sqlerr;

    EXEC SQL SELECT d_next_o_id INTO :o_id
            FROM district
            WHERE d_w_id=:w_id AND d_id=:d_id;
```

C

```
        EXEC SQL SELECT COUNT(DISTINCT (s_i_id)) INTO :stock_count
                 FROM order_line, stock
                 WHERE ol_w_id=:w_id AND
                       ol_d_id=:d_id AND ol_o_id<:o_id AND
                       ol_o_id>=:o_id-21 AND s_w_id=:w_id AND
                       s_i_id=ol_i_id AND s_quantity < :threshold;

        EXEC SQL COMMIT WORK;
        return(0);

sqlerr:
        error();
}
```

## A.6 Sample Load Program

```
/*==================================================================+
 | Load TPCC tables
 +==================================================================*/

#define MAXITEMS        100000
#define CUST_PER_DIST 3000
#define DIST_PER_WARE 10
#define ORD_PER_DIST  3000

extern long count_ware;

/* Functions */

long            NURand();
void            LoadItems();
void            LoadWare();
void            LoadCust();
void            LoadOrd();
void            LoadNewOrd();
void            Stock();
void            District();
void            Customer();
void            Orders();
void            New_Orders();
void            MakeAddress();
void            Error();
void            Lastname();

/* Global SQL Variables */
EXEC SQL BEGIN DECLARE SECTION;
    char        timestamp[20];
    long        count_ware;
EXEC SQL END DECLARE SECTION;
```

C

```
/* Global Variables */
    int         i;
    int         option_debug = 0;        /* 1 if generating debug output    */

/*===================================================================+
  |       main()
  | ARGUMENTS
  |       Warehouses n [Debug] [Help]
  +===================================================================*/
void main( argc, argv )
    int             argc;
    char *          argv[];
{
    char        arg[2];

EXEC SQL WHENEVER SQLERROR GOTO Error_SqlCall;

  count_ware=0;

  for (i=1; i<argc; i++)
  {
  strncpy(arg,argv[i],2);
  arg[0] = toupper(arg[0]);

  switch (arg[0]) {
   case 'W': /* Warehouses */
     if (count_ware)
     {
       printf("Error - Warehouses specified more than once.\n");
       exit(-1);
     }
     if (argc-1>i)
     {
       i++;
       count_ware=atoi(argv[i]);
       if (count_ware<=0)
       {
         printf("Invalid Warehouse Count.\n");
         exit(-1);
       }
     }
     else
     {
       printf("Error - Warehouse count must follow Warehouse keyword\n");
       exit(-1);
     }
     break;
```

C

```
/******* Generic Args *********************/
   case 'D': /* Debug Option */
     if (option_debug)
     {
       printf("Error - Debug option specified more than once\n");
       exit(-1);
     }
     option_debug=1;
     break;

   case 'H': /* List Args */
     printf("Usage - Warehouses n [Debug] [Help]\n");
     exit(0);
     break;

   default : printf("Error - Unknown Argument (%s)\n",arg);
     printf("Usage - Warehouses n [Debug] [Help]\n");
     exit(-1);
   }
}

   if (!(count_ware)) {
     printf("Not enough arguments.\n");
     printf("Usage - Warehouses n ");
     printf(" [Debug] [Help]\n");
     exit(-1);
   }

   SetSeed( time( 0 ) );
   /* Initialize timestamp (for date columns) */
   gettimestamp(timestamp);
   printf( "TPCC Data Load Started...\n" );
   LoadItems();
   LoadWare();
   LoadCust();
   LoadOrd();
   EXEC SQL COMMIT WORK RELEASE;
   printf( "\n...DATA LOADING COMPLETED SUCCESSFULLY.\n" );
   exit( 0 );
Error_SqlCall:
   Error();
}
```

C

```
/*===============================================================+
 | ROUTINE NAME
 |      LoadItems
 | DESCRIPTION
 |      Loads the Item table
 | ARGUMENTS
 |      none
 +===============================================================*/
void LoadItems()
{

    EXEC SQL BEGIN DECLARE SECTION;
        long    i_id;
        char    i_name[24];
        float   i_price;
        char    i_data[50];
    EXEC SQL END DECLARE SECTION;
        int     idatasiz;
        int     orig[MAXITEMS];
        long    pos;
        int     i;

    EXEC SQL WHENEVER SQLERROR GOTO sqlerr;

    printf("Loading Item \n");

    for (i=0; i<MAXITEMS/10; i++) orig[i]=0;
    for (i=0; i<MAXITEMS/10; i++)
    {
      do
      {
        pos = RandomNumber(0L,MAXITEMS);
      } while (orig[pos]);
      orig[pos] = 1;
    }
    for (i_id=1; i_id<=MAXITEMS; i_id++) {

      /* Generate Item Data */
      MakeAlphaString( 14, 24, i_name);
      i_price=((float) RandomNumber(100L,10000L))/100.0;
      idatasiz=MakeAlphaString(26,50,i_data);
      if (orig[i_id])
      {
        pos = RandomNumber(0L,idatasiz-8);
        i_data[pos]='o';
        i_data[pos+1]='r';
        i_data[pos+2]='i';
        i_data[pos+3]='g';
        i_data[pos+4]='i';
        i_data[pos+5]='n';
        i_data[pos+6]='a';
        i_data[pos+7]='l';
      }
```

C

```
        if ( option_debug )
            printf( "IID = %ld, Name= %16s, Price = %5.2f\n",
                    i_id, i_name, i_price );

        EXEC SQL INSERT INTO
            item (i_id, i_name, i_price, i_data)
            values (:i_id, :i_name, :i_price, :i_data);


        if ( !(i_id % 100) ) {
            printf(".");
            EXEC SQL COMMIT WORK;
            if ( !(i_id % 5000) ) printf(" %ld\n",i_id);
        }

    }

    EXEC SQL COMMIT WORK;
    printf("Item Done. \n");
    return;
sqlerr:
    Error();
}


/*===================================================================+
 | ROUTINE NAME
 |     LoadWare
 | DESCRIPTION
 |     Loads the Warehouse table
 |     Loads Stock, District as Warehouses are created
 | ARGUMENTS
 |     none
 +===================================================================*/
void LoadWare()
{

    EXEC SQL BEGIN DECLARE SECTION;
        long    w_id;
        char    w_name[10];
        char    w_street_1[20];
        char    w_street_2[20];
        char    w_city[20];
        char    w_state[2];
        char    w_zip[9];
        float   w_tax;
        float   w_ytd;
    EXEC SQL END DECLARE SECTION;

    EXEC SQL WHENEVER SQLERROR GOTO sqlerr;

    printf("Loading Warehouse \n");
    for (w_id=1L; w_id<=count_ware; w_id++) {
```

```
      /* Generate Warehouse Data */
      MakeAlphaString( 6, 10, w_name);
      MakeAddress( w_street_1, w_street_2, w_city, w_state, w_zip );
      w_tax=((float)RandomNumber(10L,20L))/100.0;
      w_ytd=3000000.00;

      if ( option_debug )
        printf( "WID = %ld, Name= %16s, Tax = %5.2f\n",
                w_id, w_name, w_tax );

      EXEC SQL INSERT INTO
        warehouse (w_id, w_name,
                    w_street_1, w_street_2, w_city, w_state, w_zip,
                    w_tax, w_ytd)
          values (:w_id, :w_name,
                    :w_street_1, :w_street_2, :w_city, :w_state,
                    :w_zip, :w_tax, :w_ytd);

      /** Make Rows associated with Warehouse **/
      Stock(w_id);
      District(w_id);

      EXEC SQL COMMIT WORK;
    }

    return;
sqlerr:
    Error();
}


/*===================================================================+
  | ROUTINE NAME
  |     LoadCust
  | DESCRIPTION
  |     Loads the Customer Table
  | ARGUMENTS
  |     none
  +===================================================================*/
void LoadCust()
{

   EXEC SQL BEGIN DECLARE SECTION;
   EXEC SQL END DECLARE SECTION;
   long    w_id;
   long    d_id;

   EXEC SQL WHENEVER SQLERROR GOTO sqlerr;

   for (w_id=1L; w_id<=count_ware; w_id++)
     for (d_id=1L; d_id<=DIST_PER_WARE; d_id++)
       Customer(d_id,w_id);
```

C

```
    EXEC SQL COMMIT WORK;   /* Just in case */

    return;
sqlerr:
    Error();
}

/*================================================================+
 | ROUTINE NAME
 |     LoadOrd
 | DESCRIPTION
 |     Loads the Orders and Order_Line Tables
 | ARGUMENTS
 |     none
 +================================================================*/
void LoadOrd()
{

    EXEC SQL BEGIN DECLARE SECTION;
      long  w_id;
      float w_tax;
      long  d_id;
      float d_tax;
    EXEC SQL END DECLARE SECTION;

    EXEC SQL WHENEVER SQLERROR GOTO sqlerr;

    for (w_id=1L; w_id<=count_ware; w_id++)
      for (d_id=1L; d_id<=DIST_PER_WARE; d_id++)
        Orders(d_id, w_id);

    EXEC SQL COMMIT WORK;   /* Just in case */

    return;
sqlerr:
    Error();
}
```

C

```
/*=================================================================+
 | ROUTINE NAME
 |      Stock
 | DESCRIPTION
 |      Loads the Stock table
 | ARGUMENTS
 |      w_id - warehouse id
 +=================================================================*/
void Stock(w_id)
    long w_id;
{

    EXEC SQL BEGIN DECLARE SECTION;
        long    s_i_id;
        long    s_w_id;
        long    s_quantity;
        char    s_dist_01[24];
        char    s_dist_02[24];
        char    s_dist_03[24];
        char    s_dist_04[24];
        char    s_dist_05[24];
        char    s_dist_06[24];
        char    s_dist_07[24];
        char    s_dist_08[24];
        char    s_dist_09[24];
        char    s_dist_10[24];
        char    s_data[50];
    EXEC SQL END DECLARE SECTION;
        int     sdatasiz;
        long    orig[MAXITEMS];
        long    pos;
        int     i;

    EXEC SQL WHENEVER SQLERROR GOTO sqlerr;
    printf("Loading Stock Wid=%ld\n",w_id);
    s_w_id=w_id;

    for (i=0; i<MAXITEMS/10; i++) orig[i]=0;
    for (i=0; i<MAXITEMS/10; i++)
    {
      do
      {
         pos=RandomNumber(0L,MAXITEMS);
      } while (orig[pos]);
      orig[pos] = 1;
    }

    for (s_i_id=1; s_i_id<=MAXITEMS; s_i_id++) {

      /* Generate Stock Data */
      s_quantity=RandomNumber(10L,100L);
      MakeAlphaString(24,24,s_dist_01);
```

```
        MakeAlphaString(24,24,s_dist_02);
        MakeAlphaString(24,24,s_dist_03);
        MakeAlphaString(24,24,s_dist_04);
        MakeAlphaString(24,24,s_dist_05);
        MakeAlphaString(24,24,s_dist_06);
        MakeAlphaString(24,24,s_dist_07);
        MakeAlphaString(24,24,s_dist_08);
        MakeAlphaString(24,24,s_dist_09);
        MakeAlphaString(24,24,s_dist_10);
        sdatasiz=MakeAlphaString(26,50,s_data);
        if (orig[s_i_id])
        {
          pos=RandomNumber(0L,sdatasiz-8);
          s_data[pos]='o';
          s_data[pos+1]='r';
          s_data[pos+2]='i';
          s_data[pos+3]='g';
          s_data[pos+4]='i';
          s_data[pos+5]='n';
          s_data[pos+6]='a';
          s_data[pos+7]='l';
        }

        EXEC SQL INSERT INTO
            stock (s_i_id, s_w_id, s_quantity,
                    s_dist_01, s_dist_02, s_dist_03, s_dist_04, s_dist_05,
                    s_dist_06, s_dist_07, s_dist_08, s_dist_09, s_dist_10,
                    s_data, s_ytd, s_cnt_order, s_cnt_remote)
            values (:s_i_id, :s_w_id, :s_quantity,
                    :s_dist_01, :s_dist_02, :s_dist_03, :s_dist_04, :s_dist_05,
                    :s_dist_06, :s_dist_07, :s_dist_08, :s_dist_09, :s_dist_10,
                    :s_data, 0, 0, 0);

        if ( option_debug )
            printf( "SID = %ld, WID = %ld, Quan = %ld\n",
                    s_i_id, s_w_id, s_quantity );

        if ( !(s_i_id % 100) ) {
            EXEC SQL COMMIT WORK;
            printf(".");
            if ( !(s_i_id % 5000) ) printf(" %ld\n",s_i_id);
        }

    }
    EXEC SQL COMMIT WORK;

    printf(" Stock Done.\n");
    return;
sqlerr:
    Error();
}
```

```
/*==================================================================+
 | ROUTINE NAME
 |      District
 | DESCRIPTION
 |      Loads the District table
 | ARGUMENTS
 |      w_id - warehouse id
 +==================================================================*/
void District(w_id)
    long w_id;
{

    EXEC SQL BEGIN DECLARE SECTION;
         long     d_id;
         long     d_w_id;
         char     d_name[10];
         char     d_street_1[20];
         char     d_street_2[20];
         char     d_city[20];
         char     d_state[2];
         char     d_zip[9];
         float    d_tax;
         float    d_ytd;
         long     d_next_o_id;
    EXEC SQL END DECLARE SECTION;

    EXEC SQL WHENEVER SQLERROR GOTO sqlerr;

    printf("Loading District\n");
    d_w_id=w_id;
    d_ytd=30000.0;
    d_next_o_id=3001L;
    for (d_id=1; d_id<=DIST_PER_WARE; d_id++) {

      /* Generate District Data */
      MakeAlphaString(6L,10L,d_name);
      MakeAddress( d_street_1, d_street_2, d_city, d_state, d_zip );
      d_tax=((float)RandomNumber(10L,20L))/100.0;

      EXEC SQL INSERT INTO
        district (d_id, d_w_id, d_name,
                  d_street_1, d_street_2, d_city, d_state, d_zip,
                  d_tax, d_ytd, d_next_o_id)
        values (:d_id, :d_w_id, :d_name,
                :d_street_1, :d_street_2, :d_city, :d_state, :d_zip,
                :d_tax, :d_ytd, :d_next_o_id);

      if ( option_debug )
        printf( "DID = %ld, WID = %ld, Name = %10s, Tax = %5.2f\n",
                d_id, d_w_id, d_name, d_tax );

    }
```

C

```
    EXEC SQL COMMIT WORK;

    return;
sqlerr:
    Error();
}


/*=======================================================================+
  | ROUTINE NAME
  |     Customer
  | DESCRIPTION
  |     Loads Customer Table
  |     Also inserts corresponding history record
  | ARGUMENTS
  |     id   - customer id
  |     d_id - district id
  |     w_id - warehouse id
  +=====================================================================*/
void Customer( d_id, w_id )
    long   d_id;
    long   w_id;
{
    EXEC SQL BEGIN DECLARE SECTION;
        long    c_id;
        long    c_d_id;
        long    c_w_id;
        char    c_first[16];
        char    c_middle[2];
        char    c_last[16];
        char    c_street_1[20];
        char    c_street_2[20];
        char    c_city[20];
        char    c_state[2];
        char    c_zip[9];
        char    c_phone[16];
        char    c_since[11];
        char    c_credit[2];
        long    c_credit_lim;
        float   c_discount;
        float   c_balance;
        char    c_data[500];
        float   h_amount;
        char    h_data[24];
    EXEC SQL END DECLARE SECTION;

    EXEC SQL WHENEVER SQLERROR GOTO sqlerr;

    printf("Loading Customer for DID=%ld, WID=%ld\n",d_id,w_id);

    for (c_id=1; c_id<=CUST_PER_DIST; c_id++) {

      /* Generate Customer Data */
```

```
      c_d_id=d_id;
      c_w_id=w_id;
      MakeAlphaString( 8, 16, c_first );
      c_middle[0]='O'; c_middle[1]='E';
      if (c_id <= 1000)
        Lastname(c_id-1,c_last);
      else
        Lastname(NURand(255,0,999),c_last);
      MakeAddress( c_street_1, c_street_2, c_city, c_state, c_zip );
      MakeNumberString( 16, 16, c_phone );
      if (RandomNumber(0L,1L))
        c_credit[0]='G';
      else
        c_credit[0]='B';
      c_credit[1]='C';
      c_credit_lim=50000;
      c_discount=((float)RandomNumber(0L,50L))/100.0;
      c_balance= -10.0;
      MakeAlphaString(300,500,c_data);

      EXEC SQL INSERT INTO
          customer (c_id, c_d_id, c_w_id,
                    c_first, c_middle, c_last,
                    c_street_1, c_street_2, c_city, c_state, c_zip,
                    c_phone, c_since, c_credit,
                    c_credit_lim, c_discount, c_balance, c_data,
                    c_ytd_payment, c_cnt_payment, c_cnt_delivery)
          values (:c_id, :c_d_id, :c_w_id,
                  :c_first, :c_middle, :c_last,
                  :c_street_1, :c_street_2, :c_city, :c_state, :c_zip,
                  :c_phone, :timestamp, :c_credit,
                  :c_credit_lim, :c_discount, :c_balance, :c_data,
                  10.0, 1, 0) ;

      h_amount=10.0;
      MakeAlphaString(12,24,h_data);
      EXEC SQL INSERT INTO
          history (h_c_id, h_c_d_id, h_c_w_id,
                   h_w_id, h_d_id, h_date, h_amount, h_data)
          values (:c_id, :c_d_id, :c_w_id,
                  :c_w_id, :c_d_id, :timestamp, :h_amount, :h_data);

      if ( option_debug )
          printf( "CID = %ld, LST = %s, P# = %s\n",
                  c_id, c_last, c_phone );
      if ( !(c_id % 100) ) {
          EXEC SQL COMMIT WORK;
          printf(".");
          if ( !(c_id % 1000) ) printf(" %ld\n",c_id);
      }
  }
  printf("Customer Done.\n");
```

C

```
    return;
sqlerr:
  Error();
}

/*==================================================================+
 | ROUTINE NAME
 |      Orders
 | DESCRIPTION
 |      Loads the Orders table
 |      Also loads the Order_Line table on the fly
 | ARGUMENTS
 |      w_id - warehouse id
 +==================================================================*/
void Orders(d_id, w_id)
   long d_id, w_id;
{

    EXEC SQL BEGIN DECLARE SECTION;
        long    o_id;
        long    o_c_id;
        long    o_d_id;
        long    o_w_id;
        long    o_carrier_id;
        long    o_ol_cnt;
        long    ol;
        long    ol_i_id;
        long    ol_supply_w_id;
        long    ol_quantity;
        long    ol_amount;
        char    ol_dist_info[24];
        float   i_price;
        float   c_discount;
    EXEC SQL END DECLARE SECTION;

    EXEC SQL WHENEVER SQLERROR GOTO sqlerr;

    printf("Loading Orders for D=%ld, W= %ld\n", d_id, w_id);
    o_d_id=d_id;
    o_w_id=w_id;
    InitPermutation();          /* initialize permutation of customer numbers */
    for (o_id=1; o_id<=ORD_PER_DIST; o_id++) {

      /* Generate Order Data */
      o_c_id=GetPermutation();
      o_carrier_id=RandomNumber(1L,10L);
      o_ol_cnt=RandomNumber(5L,15L);

      if (o_id > 2100)          /* the last 900 orders have not been delivered) */
      {
        EXEC SQL INSERT INTO
```

```
        orders (o_id, o_c_id, o_d_id, o_w_id,
                o_entry_d, o_carrier_id, o_ol_cnt, o_all_local)
        values (:o_id, :o_c_id, :o_d_id, :o_w_id,
                :timestamp, NULL, :o_ol_cnt, 1);
    EXEC SQL INSERT INTO
      new_order (no_o_id, no_d_id, no_w_id)
      values (:o_id, :o_d_id, :o_w_id);
}
else
  EXEC SQL INSERT INTO
    orders (o_id, o_c_id, o_d_id, o_w_id,
            o_entry_d, o_carrier_id, o_ol_cnt, o_all_local)
    values (:o_id, :o_c_id, :o_d_id, :o_w_id,
            :timestamp, :o_carrier_id, :o_ol_cnt, 1);



if ( option_debug )
  printf( "OID = %ld, CID = %ld, DID = %ld, WID = %ld\n",
          o_id, o_c_id, o_d_id, o_w_id);

for (ol=1; ol<=o_ol_cnt; ol++) {
/* Generate Order Line Data */
  ol_i_id=RandomNumber(1L,MAXITEMS);
  ol_supply_w_id=o_w_id;
  ol_quantity=5;
  ol_amount=0.0;

  MakeAlphaString(24,24,ol_dist_info);

  if (o_id > 2100)
    EXEC SQL INSERT INTO
      order_line (ol_o_id, ol_d_id, ol_w_id, ol_number,
                  ol_i_id, ol_supply_w_id, ol_quantity, ol_amount,
                  ol_dist_info, ol_delivery_d)
      values (:o_id, :o_d_id, :o_w_id, :ol,
              :ol_i_id, :ol_supply_w_id, :ol_quantity, :ol_amount,
              :ol_dist_info, NULL);
  else
    EXEC SQL INSERT INTO
      order_line (ol_o_id, ol_d_id, ol_w_id, ol_number,
                  ol_i_id, ol_supply_w_id, ol_quantity,
                  ((float)(RandomNumber(10L, 10000L))/100.0,
                  ol_dist_info, ol_delivery_d)
      values (:o_id, :o_d_id, :o_w_id, :ol,
              :ol_i_id, :ol_supply_w_id, :ol_quantity,
              :ol_amount,
              :ol_dist_info, datetime);

  if ( option_debug )
    printf( "OL = %ld, IID = %ld, QUAN = %ld, AMT = %8.2f\n",
            ol, ol_i_id, ol_quantity, ol_amount);
```

C

```
        }
        if ( !(o_id % 100) ) {
          printf(".");
          EXEC SQL COMMIT WORK;
          if ( !(o_id % 1000) ) printf(" %ld\n",o_id);
        }
    }
    EXEC SQL COMMIT WORK;

    printf("Orders Done.\n");
    return;
sqlerr:
    Error();
}


/*==================================================================+
 | ROUTINE NAME
 |      MakeAddress()
 | DESCRIPTION
 |      Build an Address
 | ARGUMENTS
 +==================================================================*/
void MakeAddress(str1,str2,city,state,zip)
     char *str1;
     char *str2;
     char *city;
     char *state;
     char *zip;
{
   MakeAlphaString(10,20,str1); /* Street 1*/
   MakeAlphaString(10,20,str2); /* Street 2*/
   MakeAlphaString(10,20,city); /* City */
   MakeAlphaString(2,2,state);  /* State */
   MakeNumberString(9,9,zip);   /* Zip */
}


/*==================================================================+
 | ROUTINE NAME
 |      Error()
 | DESCRIPTION
 |      Handles an error from a SQL call.
 | ARGUMENTS
 +==================================================================*/
void Error()
{
    printf( "SQL Error %d\n", sqlca.sqlcode);

    EXEC SQL WHENEVER SQLERROR CONTINUE;
    EXEC SQL ROLLBACK WORK RELEASE;

    exit( -1 );
}
```

```
/*=====================================================================+
  | ROUTINE NAME
  |      Lastname
  | DESCRIPTION
  |      TPC-C Lastname Function.
  | ARGUMENTS
  |      num  - non-uniform random number
  |      name - last name string
  +=====================================================================*/
void Lastname(num, name)
  int num;
  char *name;
{
  int i;
  static char *n[] =
    {"BAR", "OUGHT", "ABLE", "PRI", "PRES",
     "ESE", "ANTI", "CALLY", "ATION", "EING"};

  strcpy(name,n[num/100]);
  strcat(name,n[(num/10)%10]);
  strcat(name,n[num%10]);

 return;
}
```

C

## APPENDIX B: Summary Statements

### B.1   Standard Summary

The following table illustrates the format of the TPC Standard Summary Statement that must be used to report the summary benchmark results:

| Company Name | System Name | Database Software | Operating System Software |
|---|---|---|---|
| Company X | XJ 700 | InforBase 6.0 | XUX V5.3 |
| Availability Date:  16 December 1992 | | | |

| Total System Cost | TPC-C Throughput | Price/Performance |
|---|---|---|
| - Hardware<br>- Software<br>- 5 years maintenance | Sustained maximum throughput of system running TPC-C expressed in transactions per minute | Total system cost/tpm-C ($5,734,418/105) |
| $5,734,418 | 105 tpm-C | $54,700 per tpm-C |

### B.2   Executive Summary

The tables in the following two pages illustrate the format of the TPC Executive Summary Statement that must be used to report the summary benchmark results. The latest version of the required format is available upon request from the TPC administrator (see page 145).

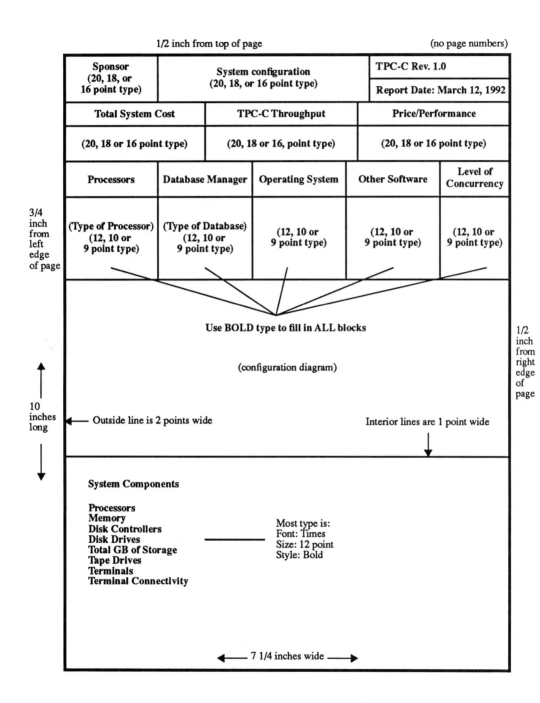

1/2 inch from top of page                                    (no page numbers)

| Sponsor<br>(20, 18, or<br>16 point type) | System configuration<br>(20, 18, or 16 point type) | TPC-C Rev. 1.0 |
| --- | --- | --- |
| | | Report Date: March 12, 1992 |

1/2
inch
from
left
edge
of
page

3/4
inch
from
right
edge
of page

Notes:

# APPENDIX C: Numerical Quantities Summary

The following table partially illustrates how to summarize all the numerical quantities required in the Full Disclosure Report:

| MQTh, computed Maximum Qualified Throughput | | | 105 tpmC |
|---|---|---|---|
| **Response Times** (in seconds) | | 90th percentile | Average |
| • New-Order | | 4.9 | 2.8 |
| • Payment | | 2.1 | 1.0 |
| • Order-Status | | 3.5 | 1.7 |
| • Delivery (interactive portion) | | 0.5 | 0.2 |
| • Delivery (deferred portion) | | 15.2 | 8.1 |
| • Stock-Level | | 17.8 | 9.5 |
| • Menu | | 0.2 | 0.1 |
| **Transaction Mix**, in percent of total transactions | | | |
| • New-Order | | | 44.5 % |
| • Payment | | | 43.1 % |
| • Order-Status | | | 4.1 % |
| • Delivery | | | 4.2 % |
| • Stock-Level | | | 4.1 % |
| **Keying/Think Times** (in seconds) | Min. | Average | Max. |
| • New-Order | 9.2/6.1 | 18.5/12.2 | 37.1/25.2 |
| • Payment | 1.6/6.1 | 3.1/12.2 | 6.2/24.7 |
| • Order-Status | 1.1/5.1 | 2.1/10.2 | 4.2/21.2 |
| • Delivery | 1.1/2.8 | 2.1/5.1 | 4.3/10.3 |
| • Stock-Level | 1.0/2.7 | 2.1/5.1 | 4.3/10.2 |
| **Test Duration** | | | |
| • Ramp-up time | | | 20 minutes |
| • Measurement interval | | | 40 minutes |
| • Transactions during measurement interval | | | 9,438 |
| • Ramp-down time | | | 5 minutes |
| **Checkpointing** | | | |
| • Number of checkpoints | | | 2 |
| • Checkpoint interval | | | 20 minutes |

(and all other numerical quantities required in the Full Disclosure Report)

C

# 4

# The Wisconsin Benchmark: Past, Present, and Future

David J. DeWitt

*University of Wisconsin*

## 4.1    Introduction

In 1981, as we were completing the implementation of the DIRECT database machine [Boral et al., 1982; DeWitt, 1979], attention turned to evaluating its performance. At that time, no standard database benchmark existed. There were only a few application-specific benchmarks. While application-specific benchmarks measure which database system is best for a particular application, it was very difficult to understand them. We were interested in a benchmark to measure DIRECT's speedup characteristics. Thus, we set out to develop a benchmark that could be used to evaluate DIRECT, both relative to itself and relative to the "university" version of Ingres.

The result of this effort was a benchmark for relational database systems and machines that has become known as the Wisconsin benchmark [Bitton, DeWitt, & Turbyfill, 1983]. The benchmark was designed with two objectives in mind. First, the queries in the benchmark should test the performance of the major components of a relational database system. Second, the semantics and statistics of the underlying relations should be well understood so that it is easy to add new queries and to understand their behavior.

We never expected this benchmark to become as popular as it did. In retrospect, the reasons for this popularity were only partially due to its technical quality. The primary reason for its success was that it was the first evaluation containing impartial measures of real products. By actually identifying the products by name, the benchmark triggered a series of "benchmark wars" between commercial database products. With each new release, each vendor would produce a new set of numbers claiming superiority. With some vendors releasing their numbers, other vendors were obliged to produce numbers for their own systems. So the benchmark quickly became a standard that customers knew about and wanted results for. In retrospect, had the products not been identified by name, there would have been no reason for the vendors to react the way they did, and the benchmark would most likely have simply been dismissed as an academic curiosity. We did not escape these wars completely unscarred. In particular, the CEO of one of the companies repeatedly contacted the chairman of the Wisconsin Computer Sciences Department complaining that we had not represented his product fairly.

The benchmark changed the database marketplace in several ways. First, by pointing out the performance warts of each system, vendors were forced to significantly improve their systems in order to remain competitive. Consequently, the significant performance differences among the various products observed in 1983 gradually disappeared. Although the vendors undoubtedly wasted some time fighting these wars, overall the customers clearly benefited from them.

The second major effect of developing the Wisconsin benchmark was to spur the development of the Datamation benchmark [Anon et al., 1988] by a large group led by Jim Gray. From their viewpoint [in 1984], the Wisconsin benchmark had little to do with "real" database applications— something the Datamation benchmark set out to rectify. Seven years later, the DebitCredit transaction of the Datamation benchmark has replaced the Wisconsin benchmark as the standard for relational products, despite the fact that it fails to test a number of the major components of a relational database system. For example, the Datamation benchmark does not detect whether a system even has a query optimizer, let alone determine whether nested loops is the only join method provided. Furthermore, most vendors have ignored the scan and sort components of the Datamation benchmark, implementing only the DebitCredit portion, diluting the value of the original benchmark significantly. Why then is the benchmark so popular? Ignoring its technical merits, one reason is that it reduces each system to one magic number, its tps rating (which, like a "sound bite," is attractive to the marketing types of the world), even though the benchmark says nothing about the performance of a system on applications that are not debit-credit.

Like the early relational products, the Wisconsin benchmark is not, however, without its flaws [Bitton & Turbyfill, 1988]. It is missing a number of easily added tests, such as bulk updates. Its most critical failing is that, being a single-user benchmark, it does not test critical features required for real-world applications. The most important features missing from the Wisconsin benchmark are tests of the concurrency control and recovery subsystems of a database system. Thus, the benchmark cannot distinguish a system that supports only relational-level locking from one that provides tuple-level locking. Although the benchmark has been widely criticized for its single-user nature, this criticism is not really justified. Immediately after completing the single-user benchmark we undertook the development of a multiuser version of the benchmark. As the result of technical disagreements, this produced two competing multiuser benchmarks [Boral & DeWitt, 1984; Bitton & Turbyfill, 1985], neither of which ever attracted widespread interest or use. In a number of ways, both of these benchmarks represent a much more scientific approach to designing a multiuser benchmark than did the debit-credit benchmark. Why is it that neither of these benchmarks gained the same popularity as the Wisconsin benchmark? There seem to be two possible explanations. The first is that, like the Wisconsin benchmark, neither reduced each system to a single number, making it more difficult to directly compare two systems (regardless of the superficiality of the comparison). Second, after our experiences with the Wisconsin benchmark, both benchmarks carefully avoided initiating a new benchmark war among the vendors. They considered the multiuser performance of only a single system. This enabled the vendors to simply ignore the results because nobody was provided with ammunition to keep the war going. In retrospect, being gun shy was a mistake. It is now clear that comparisons of actual systems are important if you want a benchmark to become popular.

The remainder of this chapter is organized as follows. Section 4.2 describes the Wisconsin benchmark, summarizing the key results obtained using the benchmark from Bitton, DeWitt, and Turbyfill, 1983. It also describes the weaknesses of the benchmark. Although the Wisconsin benchmark is no longer widely used to evaluate single-processor relational database systems, it is again finding applicability in evaluating the performance of ad-hoc queries on parallel database systems [DeWitt, Smith, & Boral,

1987; DeWitt, Ghandeharizadeh, & Schneider, 1988; DeWitt et al., 1990; Englert et al., 1989] and, hence, has come full circle to its original goal of evaluating highly parallel database machines. As demonstrated in Section 4.3, the benchmark is well suited for such applications. It is straightforward to use the benchmark to measure the speedup, scaleup, and sizeup characteristics of a parallel database system. This application of the benchmark is illustrated with results obtained for the Gamma database machine. Our conclusions are contained in Section 3.4.

# 4.2    An Overview of the Wisconsin Benchmark

This section begins with a description of the database that forms the basis of the Wisconsin benchmark, indicating how the relations that form the benchmark can be scaled to a wide range of sizes. Next, the benchmark queries are described, summarizing the results presented originally in Bitton, De–Witt, and Turbyfill, 1983. While the original numbers are no longer of any value, it is interesting to reflect on some of the technical limitations that the benchmark uncovered in the early relational products. Finally, we comment on what we did right and what we did wrong in designing the benchmark.

## 4.2.1    The Wisconsin Benchmark Relations

The development of the Wisconsin benchmark began with a database design flexible enough to allow straightforward specification of a wide range of retrieval and update queries. One of the early decisions was to use synthetically generated relations instead of empirical data from a real database. A problem with empirical databases is that they are difficult or impossible to scale. A second problem is that the values they contain are not flexible enough to permit the systematic benchmarking of a database system. For example, with empirical data it is very difficult to specify a selection query with a 10 percent or 50 percent selectivity factor or one that retrieves precisely 1000 tuples. For queries involving joins, it is even harder to model selectivity factors and build queries that produce results or intermediate relations of a certain size. An additional shortcoming of empirical data (versus "synthetic" data) is that one has to deal with very large amounts of data before it can be safely assumed that the data values are randomly distributed. By building a synthetic database, random number generators can be used to obtain uniformly distributed attribute values and yet keep the relation sizes tractable.

The database is designed so that one can quickly understand the structure of the relations and the distribution of each attribute value. Consequently, the results of the benchmark queries are easy to understand, and additional queries are simple to design. The attributes of each relation are designed to simplify the task of controlling selectivity factors in selections and joins, varying the number of duplicate tuples created by a projection, and controlling the number of partitions in aggregate function queries. It is also straightforward to build an index (primary or secondary) on some of the attributes and to reorganize a relation so that it is clustered with respect to an index.

## Overview of the Original Benchmark Relations

The original benchmark was composed of three relations, one with 1000 tuples (named `ONEKTUP`) and two others each with 10,000 tuples (named `TENKTUP1` and `TENKTUP2`). Each relation was composed of the thirteen integer attributes and three 52-byte string attributes. Two-byte integers were used in the original benchmark (because DIRECT was implemented using PDP 11 processors which did not support four-byte integers), but fairly early on most users of the benchmark switched to using four-byte integers. Thus, assuming no storage overhead, the length of each tuple is 208 bytes. The SQL statement to create the `TENKTUP1` relation is shown in Figure 4.1. The same basic schema is used to create other relations (e.g., a second 10,000 tuple relation or one containing a million tuples).

As discussed above, in designing the structure of the base relations for the benchmark, one goal was to make it easy to understand the semantics of each attribute so that a user could extend the benchmark by adding new queries. Table 4.1 summarizes the semantics of each attribute for the 10,000 tuple relation.

The values of the `unique1` and `unique2` attributes are uniformly distributed unique random numbers in the range 0 to MAXTUPLES-1, where MAXTUPLES is the cardinality of the relation. Thus, both `unique1` and `unique2` are candidate keys, but `unique2` is used whenever a declared key must be specified. When tests are conducted using indexes, `unique2` is used to build a clustered unique index, `unique1` is used to build a nonclustered unique index, and `hundred` is used to build a nonclustered, nonunique index.

```
CREATE TABLE TENKTUP1
(  unique1        integer NOT NULL,
   unique2        integer NOT NULL PRIMARY KEY,
   two            integer NOT NULL,
   four           integer NOT NULL,
   ten            integer NOT NULL,
   twenty         integer NOT NULL,
   hundred        integer NOT NULL,
   thousand       integer NOT NULL,
   twothous       integer NOT NULL,
   fivethous      integer NOT NULL,
   tenthous       integer NOT NULL,
   odd100         integer NOT NULL,
   even100        integer NOT NULL,
   stringu1       char(52) NOT NULL,
   stringu2       char(52) NOT NULL,
   string4        char(52) NOT NULL
)
```

**Figure 4.1**
SQL Create statement for the original 10,000 tuple relation.

**Table 4.1** Attribute specifications of original Wisconsin benchmark relations.

| Attribute Name | Range of Values | Order | Comment |
|---|---|---|---|
| unique1 | 0-9999 | random | candidate key |
| unique2 | 0-9999 | random | declared key |
| two | 0-1 | cyclic | 0,1,0,1,... |
| four | 0-3 | cyclic | 0,1,2,3,0,1,... |
| ten | 0-9 | cyclic | 0,1,...,9,0,1,... |
| twenty | 0-19 | cyclic | 0,1,...,19,0,1,... |
| hundred | 0-99 | cyclic | 0,1,...,99,0,1,... |
| thousand | 0-999 | cyclic | 0,1,...,999,0,1,... |
| twothous | 0-1999 | cyclic | 0,1,...,1999,0,1,... |
| fivethous | 0-4999 | cyclic | 0,1,...,4999,0,1,... |
| tenthous | 0-9999 | cyclic | 0,1,...,9999,0,1,... |
| odd100 | 1-99 | cyclic | 1,3,5,...,99,1,3,... |
| even100 | 2-100 | cyclic | 2,4,...,100,2,4,... |
| stringu1 | - | random | candidate key |
| stringu2 | - | cyclic | candidate key |
| string4 | - | cyclic | |

After the `unique1` and `unique2` attributes comes a set of integer-valued attributes that assume nonunique values. The main purpose of these attributes is to provide a systematic way to model a wide range of selectivity factors. Each attribute is named after the range of values the attribute assumes. For example, the `four` attribute assumes a range of values from 0 to 3. Thus, the selection predicate `x.four=2` will have a 25 percent selectivity, regardless of the size of the relation to which it is applied. As another example, the `hundred` attribute can be used to create 100 partitions in an aggregate query if a `group by hundred` clause is used.

Finally, each relation has three string attributes. Each string is 52 letters long, with three letters (the first, the middle, and the last) being varied, and two separating substrings that contain only the letter *x*. The three significant letters are chosen in the range (A,B,...,V), to allow up to 10,648 (22 * 22 * 22) unique string values. Thus all string attributes follow the pattern:

```
$xxxxxxxxxxxxxxxxxxxxxxxxx$xxxxxxxxxxxxxxxxxxxxxxxx$
  {25 x's}                    {24 x's}
```

where $ stands for one of the letters (A,B,...,V). Clearly, this basic pattern can be modified to provide a wider range of string values (by replacing some of the *x*'s by significant letters). On the other hand, by varying the position of the significant letters, the database designer can also control the CPU time required for string comparisons.

The first two string attributes are string versions of the `unique1` and `unique2` attributes. That is, `stringu1` and `stringu2` may be used as key attributes, and a primary index may be built on `stringu2`. For example, in the thousand tuple relation `ONEKTUP`, the `stringu2` attribute values are:

```
Axxxx ... xxxAxxx ... xxxA
Bxxxx ... xxxAxxx ... xxxA
Cxxxx ... xxxAxxx ... xxxA
        •••
Vxxxx ... xxxAxxx ... xxxA
Axxxx ... xxxBxxx ... xxxA
        •••
Vxxxx ... xxxBxxx ... xxxA
Axxxx ... xxxCxxx ... xxxA
        •••
Vxxxx ... xxxVxxx ... xxxA
Axxxx ... xxxAxxx ... xxxB
        •••
Ixxxx ... xxxBxxx ... xxxC
Jxxxx ... xxxBxxx ... xxxC
```

The following two queries illustrate how these string attributes can be utilized. Each query has a selectivity factor of 1 percent.

```
select * from TENKTUP1
where stringu2 < 'Axxx ... xxxExxx...xxxQ';

select * from TENKTUP1
where stringu2 between 'Bxxxx ... xxxGxxx ... xxxE'
                  and 'Bxxxx ... xxxLxxx ... xxxA'
```

The `stringu2` variables are initially loaded in the database in the same order in which they were generated, shown above, which is not in sort order. The attribute `stringu1` assumes exactly the same string values as `stringu2`, except that their position in the relation is randomly determined. A third string attribute, `string4`, assumes only four unique values:

```
Axxxx ... xxxAxxx ... xxxA
Hxxxx ... xxxHxxx ... xxxH
Oxxxx ... xxxOxxx ... xxxO
Vxxxx ... xxxVxxx ... xxxV
```

## Scaling the Benchmark Relations

Two criticisms of the benchmark relations were that the relations were difficult to scale (make larger) and that the structure of the string attributes were not realistic [Bitton & Turbyfill, 1988]. Although a two-megabyte relation was a reasonable choice in 1983, when most mid-range processors had main memories in the megabyte range, the 10,000 tuple relations have become much too small for current single-processor machines, let alone multiprocessor database machines. (However, one still finds people using them, even on machines with 16 or 32 megabytes of memory!)

While scaling most of the original attributes was straightforward, the meaning of certain attributes changed as the relations were scaled. To solve this problem, the specification of the benchmark relations was slightly modified as shown in Table 4.2.

The first six attributes (`unique1` through `twentyPercent`) remain basically the same, except for a couple of minor changes. First, while the values of `unique1` continue to be randomly distributed unique values between 0 and `MAXTUPLES-1`, the values of `unique2` are in sequential order from 0 to `MAXTUPLES-1`. Second, instead of the `two`, `four`, `ten`, and `twenty` attributes repeating in a cyclic pattern as before, these

**Table 4.2**   Attribute specification of "scaleable" Wisconsin benchmark relations.

| Attribute Name | Range of Values | Order | Comment |
|---|---|---|---|
| unique1 | 0-(MAXTUPLES-1) | random | unique, random order |
| unique2 | 0-(MAXTUPLES-1) | sequential | unique, sequential |
| two | 0-1 | random | (unique1 mod 2) |
| four | 0-3 | random | (unique1 mod 4) |
| ten | 0-9 | random | (unique1 mod 10) |
| twenty | 0-19 | random | (unique1 mod 20) |
| onePercent | 0-99 | random | (unique1 mod 100) |
| tenPercent | 0-9 | random | (unique1 mod 10) |
| twentyPercent | 0-4 | random | (unique1 mod 5) |
| fiftyPercent | 0-1 | random | (unique1 mod 2) |
| unique3 | 0-(MAXTUPLES-1) | random | unique1 |
| evenOnePercent | 0,2,4,...,198 | random | (onePercent * 2) |
| oddOnePercent | 1,3,5,...,199 | random | (onePercent * 2)+1 |
| stringu1 | - | random | candidate key |
| stringu2 | - | random | candidate key |
| string4 | - | cyclic | |

attributes are now randomly distributed, as they are generated by computing the appropriate mode of unique1. More significantly, the hundred through even100 attributes of the original relations have been replaced with a set of attributes that simplify the task of scaling selection queries with a certain selectivity factor. For example, the predicate twentyPercent = 3 will always return 20 percent of the tuples in a relation, regardless of the relation's cardinality.

The string attributes have also been completely redesigned to eliminate several of their earlier flaws. Their fixed-length nature was retained so that each disk page contains the same number of tuples. This simplifies the task of understanding the results of a benchmark. The string attributes, stringu1 and stringu2, are the string analogies of unique1 and unique2. Both are candidate keys and can be used in queries, just like unique1 and unique2. Both stringu1 and stringu2 consist of seven significant characters from the alphabet (A–Z) followed by 45 *x*'s. The seven significant characters of stringu1 (stringu2) are computed using the following procedure. This procedure converts a unique1 (unique2) value to its corresponding character string representation.

```
char   result[7];

char *convert(unique)
      int unique;
    {
      int i, rem;

      /* first set result string to "AAAAAAA" */
      for  ( i=0 ; i<7 ; i++)    result[i]='A';

      i = 6;
      /* convert unique value from right to left into an alphabetic string */
      /* in result*/
      while (unique > 0)
      {
            rem = unique % 26; /* '%' is the mod operator in C */
            result[i] = 'A' + rem;
            unique = unique / 26;
            i--;
      }
      return   (&result[0])
    }
```

The last string attribute, `string4`, assumes four values, AAAAxxx...,
HHHHxxx..., OOOOxxx..., and VVVVxxx... randomly:

```
    AAAAxxx...
    OOOOxxx...
    VVVVxxx...
    HHHHxxx...
    AAAAxxx...
    OOOOxxx...
    HHHHxxx...
    VVVVxxx...
```

In addition to the information contained in Table 4.2, in order to generate relations with a range of cardinalities, a mechanism is also needed for
generating `unique1` values. These values must be both unique and in random order. The C procedure in Figure 4.2, based on an algorithm developed
by Susan Englert and Jim Gray [1989], will efficiently produce such a
stream for relations with cardinalities up to 100 million tuples.

```
long    prime, generator;

main (argc, argv)
  int argc; char *argv[];
{
  int     tupCount; /* number of tuples in result relation */
  tupCount = atoi (argv[1]); /* get the desired table size */
  /* Choose prime and generator values for the desired table size */
  if      (tupCount <= 1000) { generator = 279; prime = 1009; }
  else if (tupCount <= 10000) { generator = 2969;prime = 10007; }
  else if (tupCount <= 100000) { generator = 21395;prime = 100003; }
  else if (tupCount <= 1000000) { generator = 2107;prime = 1000003; }
  else if (tupCount <= 10000000) { generator = 211; prime = 10000019; }
  else if (tupCount <= 100000000) { generator = 21; prime = 100000007;}
  else { printf("too many rows requested\n"); exit();}

  generate_relation(tupCount);
}


generate_relation (tupCount)
    int tupCount; /* number of tuples in relation */
{
    int unique1, i;
    long rand(),  seed;
    seed = generator;
    /* generate values */
    for (i=0;i<tupCount;i++)
    {  seed = rand(seed,(long)tupCount);
       unique1 = (int) seed - 1;
       unique2 = i;
       /* statements to generated other attribute values as per table 1 go here */
          insert into wisconsin_table values  (unique1, unique2, two, four,...);
    }
}


/* generate a unique random number between 1 and limit*/
long rand (seed, limit)
  long seed , limit;
  { do { seed = (generator * seed) % prime; } while (seed > limit);
    return (seed);
  }
```

**Figure 4.2**
Skeleton benchmark relation generator.

## 4.2.2   The Wisconsin Benchmark Query Suite

The suite of benchmark queries was designed to measure the performance of all the basic relational operations, including:

1. selection with different selectivity factors.

2. projections with different percentages of duplicate attributes.

3. single and multiple joins.

4. simple aggregates and aggregate functions.

5. append, delete, modify.

In addition, for most queries, the benchmark contains two variations: one that can take advantage of a primary, clustered index, and a second that can only use a secondary, nonclustered index. Typically, these two variations were obtained by using the `unique2` attribute in the first case, and the `unique1` attribute in the second. When no indexes have been created, the queries are the same. The benchmark contains a total of 32 queries. The SQL specification of each query is in the Appendix at the end of this chapter.

Several rules must be followed when running this benchmark in order to ensure that the results obtained accurately represent the system being tested. First, the size of the benchmark relations should be at least a factor of 5 larger than the total main memory buffer space available. Thus, if the buffer pool is 4 megabytes, the benchmark relations should each contain 100,000 tuples. If the tests are being performed on a shared-nothing multiprocessor, this sizing task should use the total aggregate buffer space available on all the processors. Second, for each of the 32 queries in the benchmark, the response time for a query must be measured by computing the average elapsed time of several "equivalent" queries. Typically, ten queries are used for the selection, update, and delete tests, and four queries are used for the join, aggregate, and projection tests. The queries in each set must alternate between two identical sets of base relations in order to minimize the impact of buffer pool hits on the actual execution times obtained [Bitton, DeWitt, & Turbyfill, 1983].

Elapsed time is used as the performance metric, as we have found that more detailed metrics (e.g., CPU time and/or the number of disk I/Os performed) vary unpredictably both among different operating systems and different database systems running on the same operating system due to inaccuracies in the accounting system of the various operating systems. The original Wisconsin benchmark did not incorporate the cost of the software and hardware being tested because the same hardware configuration was used for all the systems (except DIRECT). Scaling the average response time for each query with a price metric would, however, be possible [Anon et al., 1988]. Clearly such an adjustment is necessary if the systems being compared vary widely in price.

## Selection Queries

The speed at which a database system can process a selection operation depends on a number of factors, including:

1. the storage organization of the relation.

2. the selectivity factor of the predicate.

3. the hardware speed and the quality of the software.

4. the output mode of the query.

The selection queries in the Wisconsin benchmark explore the effect of each of these four factors. In addition, the effect of three different storage organizations is considered:

1. sequential (heap) organization.

2. primary clustered index on the `unique2` attribute (relation is sorted on `unique2` attribute).

3. secondary, dense, nonclustered indexes on the `unique1` and `one-Percent` attributes.

These three storage organizations were selected because they are representative of the access methods provided by most relational DBMSs.

The first six selection queries (Queries 1 to 6 in Appendix) explore the effects of two different selectivity factors (1 percent and 10 percent) and three different storage organizations. Our original experiments considered a wider range of selectivity factors, but the results indicated that selectivity factors of 1 percent and 10 percent produced representative results. These six queries insert their result tuples into a relation. Doing so can affect the response times in several ways. First, each time a page of output tuples must be written to disk, the disk heads must be moved from their current position over the source relation to the end of the result relation. Although the effect of this head movement is not that significant when the selectivity factor of the predicate is low, it can become significant. For example, with a 50 percent selectivity factor, for every two pages read, one will be written, causing two random seeks to occur for every 3 pages read at steady state (i.e., the buffer pool is full). Second, if the system being tested automatically eliminates duplicate tuples from a result relation, the cost of this duplicate elimination phase can become a significant fraction of the response time of the query.

Query 7 selects one tuple using a clustered index, returning the result tuple to the user. The response time for this very simple query provides a good measure of the path length of a system. Query 8 quantifies the cost of formatting and displaying tuples on a user's screen. Like Query 3, Query 8 has a selectivity factor of 1 percent and uses a clustered index to retrieve the qualifying tuples. Thus, the difference in the response time of the two queries provides a reasonable estimate of the time to format and display result tuples on a user's screen. Unfortunately, since most modern database systems employ a two-process structure, the response times for these two queries also include the cost of moving data to the user process from the database system process. Epstein [1987] estimates that the cost to format, transmit, and display each result tuple is about 15 ms.

Some of the most interesting results obtained using these queries in [Bitton, DeWitt, and Turbyfill, 1983] had to do with the relatively poor performance of DIRECT and ORACLE. The design of DIRECT suffered from two serious problems. First, it used message passing extensively to coordinate the processors working in parallel. Second, DIRECT's design attempted to substitute parallelism for indexes. As a consequence of these design flaws, DIRECT's performance was significantly worse than the other systems on both nonindexed and indexed queries. The relatively poor performance of ORACLE (in 1983) made it apparent that the system had some fairly serious problems that needed correction, for ORACLE was typically a factor of 5 slower than Ingres and the IDM 500 on most selection queries (it should now be obvious why Bitton, DeWitt, and Turbyfill (1983) set off a series of benchmark wars). One other interesting observation had to do with the execution of the 10 percent nonclustered index selection. Depending on the page size being used, in some cases it is faster to execute this query by scanning the relation sequentially rather than using the index. Some of the query optimizers in 1983 recognized this fact, but others did not. Even today, some optimizers fail to optimize this query correctly.

## Join Queries

The join queries in the benchmark were designed to study the effect of three different factors:

1. the complexity of a query on the relative performance of the different database systems.

2. the performance of the join algorithms used by the different systems.

3. the effectiveness of the query optimizers on complex queries.

Three basic join queries are used in the benchmark.

1. `JoinABprime` is a simple join of relations A and `Bprime`, where the cardinality of the `Bprime` relation is 10 percent of that of the A relation. Thus, if A contains 100,000 tuples, `Bprime` contains 10,000 tuples. The result relation has the same number of tuples as the `Bprime` relation.[1]

2. `JoinASelB` is composed of one join and one selection. A and B have the same number of tuples. The selection on B has a 10 percent selectivity factor, reducing B to the size of the `Bprime` relation in the `JoinABprime` query. The result relation for this query has the same number of tuples as the corresponding `JoinABprime` query. As shown in Query 9 in Appendix, the actual query was formulated with the join operation (`TENKTUP1.unique1` = `TENKTUP2.unique1`) preceding the selection operation (`TENKTUP1.unique2` < `1000`) in order to test whether the system has even a rudimentary query optimizer. Surprisingly, some of the early relational products did not and executed the join first.

3. `JoinCselASelB`, as shown in Figure 4.3, is composed of two selections and two joins. Relations A and B contain the same number of tuples. The selections on A and B each have a selectivity factor of 10 percent. Since each tuple joins with exactly one other tuple, the join of the restricted A and B relations yields an intermediate relation equal in size to its two input relations. This intermediate relation is then joined with relation C, which contains one-tenth of the number of tuples there are in A and B. For example, assume A and B contain 100,000 tuples. The relations resulting from selections on A and B will each contain 10,000 tuples. Their join results in an intermediate relation of 10,000 tuples. This relation will be joined with a C relation containing 10,000 tuples, and the result of the query will contain 10,000 tuples.

---

[1] For each join operation, the result relation contains all the fields of both input relations.

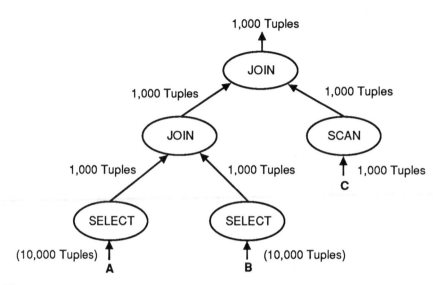

**Figure 4.3**
JoinCselAselB

There are three versions of each of these three queries, corresponding to either no index (Queries 9, 10, and 11), a clustered index (Queries, 12, 13, and 14), or a nonclustered index (Queries 15, 16, and 17) on the join attribute. The SQL specifications for these queries are contained in Queries 9 through 17 of the Appendix. Queries 11, 14, and 17, however, warrant additional explanation. In the original version of the benchmark, each of these queries specified selections on both the TENKTUP1 and TENKTUP2 relations. For example, the original "where" clause for Query 11 was:

```
WHERE (ONEKTUP.unique2 = TENKTUP1.unique2)
  AND (TENKTUP1.unique2 = TENKTUP2.unique2)
  AND (TENKTUP1.unique2 < 1000)
  AND (TENKTUP2.unique2 < 1000)
```

To further test the capabilities of the query optimizer, in the revised benchmark the selection TENKTUP2.unique2 < 1000 has been dropped for each of these three queries. The current generation of optimizers should be capable of recognizing that the remaining selection on TENKTUP1 can be propagated to TENKTUP2 since the selection and join predicates involve the same attribute.

The results in Bitton, DeWitt, and Turbyfill [1983] provided dramatic evidence of the relative performance of the different join algorithms. For example, in 1983, nested loops was the only join method supported by the IDM 500 and ORACLE. Each required over five hours to execute the `joinAse1B` query when no indexes were available. The commercial version of Ingres, on the other hand, included a sort-merge join method and could execute the same query in about two minutes! With indexes, all the systems performed similarly. DIRECT's use of parallelism was somewhat more successful than it had been with the selection tests, providing a speedup factor of about 2.58 with four processors. Its performance relative to the other systems was not all that impressive and led us to conclude that "limited parallelism" and a "dumb" algorithm (parallel nested loops) could not provide the same level of performance as a "smart" algorithm (sort merge) and "no parallelism."

**Projection Queries**

Implementation of the projection operation is normally done in two phases in the general case. First, a pass is made through the source relation to discard unwanted attributes. A second phase is necessary in order to eliminate any duplicate tuples that may have been introduced as a side effect of the first phase (i.e., elimination of an attribute that is the key or some part of the key). The first phase requires a complete scan of the relation. The second phase is normally performed in two steps. First, the relation is sorted to bring duplicate tuples together. Next, a sequential pass is made through the sorted relation, comparing neighboring tuples to see if they are identical (some sorts have an option to eliminate duplicates). Alternatively, hashing can be used to gather duplicate tuples together. Secondary storage structures such as indexes are not useful in performing this operation. In the special case where the projected fields contain a unique key, the duplicate elimination phase can be skipped. That case is not tested by the benchmark.

Initially, a wide variety of queries were considered, but we discovered that only two queries were needed to obtain indicative results on the relative performance of the different systems. The first query (Query 18, Appendix) has a projection factor of 1 percent, eliminating 99 percent of the relation as duplicates. For a 10,000 tuple relation, the result of this query contains 100 tuples. The second query (Query 19, Appendix) has a 100 percent projection factor. Although this query eliminates no duplicates, the result relation must still be sorted and then scanned for duplicates because the schema does not declare the projected fields to contain a unique key. This particular query provides an estimate of the cost of checking the result relation of an arbitrary query for duplicates.

## Aggregate Queries

The aggregate queries in the Wisconsin benchmark consider both scalar aggregate operations (e.g., the minimum value of an attribute) and complex aggregate functions. In an aggregate function, the tuples of a relation are first partitioned into nonoverlapping subsets using the SQL "group by" construct. After partitioning, an aggregate operation such as MIN is computed for each partition.

The benchmark contains three aggregate queries with two versions of each (without any indexes and with a secondary, nonclustered index):

1. MIN scalar aggregate queries (Queries 20 and 23).

2. MIN aggregate function queries (Queries 21 and 24).

3. SUM aggregate function queries (Queries 22 and 25).

The motivation for including an indexed version of each of these three queries was to determine whether any of the query optimizers would use an index to reduce the execution time of the queries. For the MIN scalar aggregate query, a very smart query optimizer could recognize that the query could be executed using the index alone. Although none of the query optimizers tested in Bitton, DeWitt, and Turbyfill [1983] performed this optimization, subsequent optimizers for the IDM 500 (and perhaps other systems as well) implemented this optimization to speed the execution of such operations.

For the two aggregate function queries, it had been anticipated that any attempt to use the secondary, nonclustered index on the partitioning attribute would actually slow the query down, as a scan of the complete relation through such an index will generally result in each data page being accessed several times. One alternative algorithm is to ignore the index, sort on the partitioning attribute, and then make a final pass collecting the results. Another algorithm that works very well if the number of partitions is not too large is to make a single pass through the relation hashing on the partitioning attribute.

## Update Queries

The update queries are probably the weakest aspect of the benchmark, as only the following four simple update queries are included:

1. Insert 1 tuple (Queries 26 and 29).

2. Update key attribute of 1 tuple (Queries 28 and 31).

3. Update non-key attribute of 1 tuple (Query 32).

4. Delete 1 tuple (Queries 27 and 30).

The principal objective of these queries was to examine the effect of clustered and nonclustered indexes on the cost of updating, appending, or deleting a tuple. In addition, the queries indicate the advantage of having an index to help locate the tuple to be modified. To accomplish this, two versions of each query were run: with and without indexes (one primary-clustered index on the `unique2` attribute, a unique, nonclustered index on the `unique1` attribute, and a nonunique, nonclustered index on the `onePercent` attribute). It should be noted, however, that not enough updates were performed to cause a significant reorganization of the index pages. A more realistic evaluation of update queries would require running these queries in a multiprogramming environment so that the effects of concurrency control and deadlocks were measured. In addition, bulk updates should have been included.

Even though these update queries are very (too) simple, they produced a number of interesting results in Bitton, DeWitt, and Turbyfill [1983]. First was the low cost of an append compared with the cost of a delete in the no-index case. The explanation for this discrepancy is that new tuples are generally inserted near the end of the file without checking if they are a duplicate of an existing tuple. Thus, appending a tuple only involves writing a new tuple. Deleting a tuple requires finding the tuple. Without an index, this requires that the entire relation be scanned. The performance of each system tested on the "modify nonkey" query (i.e., modify a tuple identified by a qualification on a nonkey, but indexed, attribute) demonstrated a very efficient use of a secondary index to locate the tuple. However, one could again argue that the right algorithm for this query would require verifying that the modified tuple not introduce a duplicate tuple.

Another interesting result occurs when the update query

```
UPDATE TENKTUP1
SET unique2=10002
WHERE unique2 = 1491        (Query 28, Appendix).
```

is executed in the presence of a clustered index on the `unique2` attribute.

This query is similar to one that causes a problem known as the Halloween problem [Tandem Database Group, 1987]. For example, if the query

```
UPDATE payroll
SET salary = salary*1.1
```

is executed using an index on the salary attribute, it will run forever if the updated tuples are inserted directly back into the index. As a simplistic solution to the problem, some systems (e.g., System R and early versions of SQL/DS) refused to use an index on any attribute if that attribute was one of the ones being updated, instead resorting, if necessary, to a sequential scan to process the query. Query 28 is not an instance of the Halloween problem, and it is incorrect for the optimizer to treat it as such.

## Evaluation

The Wisconsin benchmark, while certainly not perfect, did a good job of discovering performance anomalies in the early relational DBMS products. Although it no longer receives much public attention, a number of vendors and users still run it as part of their standard quality assurance and performance test suites. With scaled-up relations, it remains a fairly thorough single-user evaluation of the basic operations that a relational system must provide.

The benchmark has been criticized for a number of deficiencies [Bitton & Turbyfill, 1988; O'Neill, 1991; Turbyfill, 1987]. These criticisms are certainly valid: its single-user nature; the absence of bulk updates, database load and unload tests, and outer join tests; its use of uniformly distributed attribute values; its lack of tests involving host language variables; no "order by" clauses; overly simple aggregation tests; and the relative simplicity of the various complex join queries. The ASAP and Set Query benchmarks described elsewhere in this book correct most of these deficiencies.

It is not, however, so obvious that other criticisms, such as its weak collection of data types and the difficulty of scaling, are correct. For example, the design of the original string attributes and the lack of floating-point or decimal attributes have been widely criticized. The design of the original string fields was deficient, but the fact of the matter is that the benchmark was designed to study the relative performance of two database systems and not the relative string and integer performance of a single system. In particular, we assert that if system A is 20 percent faster than system B in processing selection predicates on integer attributes, then the relative performance of the two systems would vary only slightly if floating-point or string attributes were used instead (assuming, of course, a constant hardware platform). The only possible way that changing the attribute type could change the relative performance of two systems significantly is if the extra comparisons caused a system to change from being I/O bound to being CPU bound.

In our opinion, other than its single-user nature, the second most significant problem with the benchmark today is that the join queries it contains are too simple. The benchmark should be augmented to include much more complex join queries with a wider range of join selectivity factors. In addition, a cost component should have been included so that one could meaningfully compare the response times of systems with different costs. As suggested above, such an extension is straightforward.

## 4.3 Benchmarking Parallel Database Systems Using the Wisconsin Benchmark

Although the Wisconsin benchmark is no longer widely used to evaluate relational database systems on mono-processor configurations, it has been fairly extensively used to evaluate database systems running on parallel processors, including Teradata [DeWitt, Smith, & Boral, 1987], Gamma [DeWitt, Ghandeharizadeh, & Schneider, 1988; DeWitt et al., 1990], Tandem [Englert et al., 1989], and Volcano [Graefe, 1990]. This section describes how the Wisconsin benchmark can be used to measure the speedup and scaleup characteristics of such parallel systems. This discussion is illustrated with an evaluation of the Gamma database machine [DeWitt et al., 1990].

### 4.3.1 Speedup and Scaleup: Two Key Metrics for a Parallel Database System

As illustrated by Figure 4.4, speedup and scaleup are widely accepted as the two key metrics for evaluating the performance of a parallel database system (Englert et al., 1989; Smith et al., 1989). Speedup is an interesting metric because it indicates whether adding additional processors and disks to a system results in a corresponding decrease in the response time for a query. A system provides what is termed *linear speedup* if twice as much hardware can perform a given task in half the elapsed time. Figure 4.5a illustrates the ideal speedup curve. However, simply running a standard relational database system on a multiprocessor will not necessarily exhibit any degree of speedup unless the system decomposes each of the relational operators into subunits that can be executed independently and in parallel (Figure 4.5b). Although techniques to do this decomposition are now fairly well understood, our evaluation of DIRECT in Bitton, DeWitt, and Turbyfill (1983) demonstrated that this was not always the case.

Speedup                                    Batch Scaleup

**Figure 4.4**
The difference between a speedup design in which a one-minute job is done in 15 seconds, and a scaleup design in which a ten-times bigger job is done in the same time by a ten-times bigger system.

As illustrated by Figure 4.5c, the barriers to achieving linear speedup are startup, interference, and skew. Startup is the time needed to start a parallel computation. If thousands of processes must be started, this can easily dominate the actual computation time. This is especially true if the startup overhead for a query is a significant fraction of the total execution time of the query, as it can be for simple queries that retrieve and process only a few tuples. Interference is the slowdown each new process imposes on the others. Even if the interference is only 1 percent per process, with 50 processors and one process/processor, such a system will have a maximum speedup of 25. Finally, skew (variance) in the service times of the processes executing a job can begin to limit the obtainable speedup when an operation is divided into many very small pieces.

The second key metric for parallel database systems is scaleup. Basically, scaleup measures whether a constant response time can be maintained as the workload is increased by adding a proportional number of processors and disks. The motivation for evaluating the extent to which a database system scales is that certain, generally batch, jobs must be completed in a given window of time, regardless of whether the workload increases or not. The traditional solution has been to buy ever-faster mainframes. Parallel database systems that exhibit flat scaleup characteristics (such as those marketed by Teradata (1983, 1985) and Tandem (1987, 1988)) provide a way of

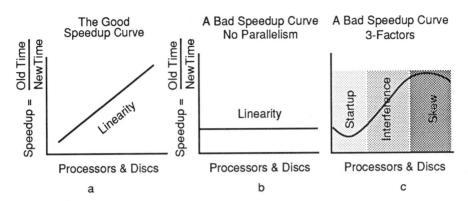

**Figure 4.5**
The standard speedup curves. The upper left curve is the ideal. The upper middle graph shows no speedup as hardware is added. The upper right curve shows the three threats to parallelism. Initial startup costs may dominate at first. As the number of processes increases, interference can increase. Ultimately, the job is divided so finely that the variance in service times (skew) causes a slowdown.

incrementally responding to increasing batch workloads. The ideal batch scaleup curve is shown in Figure 4.6a. A constant response time is maintained as the size of the problem and system grows incrementally. Figure 4.6b illustrates a bad scaleup curve for a system with the response time growing, even though resources proportional to increases in the workload are added.

Another metric related to scaleup is sizeup, in which the system configuration is kept constant while the workload is increased. A system is said to exhibit good sizeup characteristics if doubling the size of the data set being evaluated does not result in more than a twofold increase in the response time for a query. Sizeup can be considered to be a special case of the scaleup test in which the hardware configuration is kept constant. However, certain relational operations, such as sorting, the sort-merge join method, and B-tree searches, are logarithmic in nature. Since sorting is an $N\log N$ operation (where $N$ is the number of records to be sorted), one would expect to obtain only sublinear sizeup results. On the other hand, since the number of levels in a B-tree grows logarithmically, B-tree searches are likely to exhibit superlinear sizeup characteristics. For example, assume that a B-tree on the `unique2` attribute of a 100,000 tuple relation is two levels deep and that the corresponding index on a one million tuple relation is three levels deep. Assuming no buffer pool hits, a single tuple indexed selection of the 100,000 tuple relation will require three I/Os (two index I/Os plus one I/O

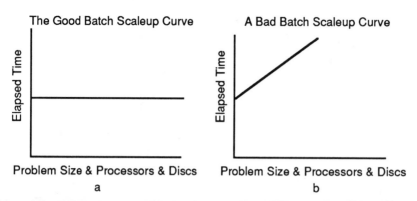

**Figure 4.6**
Batch scaleup curves: Figure 4.6a is a good batch scaleup curve showing constant processing time as proportionally more processing elements are applied to a proportionately larger problem. Figure 4.6b is a bad scaleup curve showing that, as the problem grows, the elapsed time grows, even though more processing and disk elements are applied to the problem.

to fetch the appropriate data page). The same query on the million tuple relation will require four, not 30, I/Os. Sizeup is an interesting metric in itself, but the real value of conducting sizeup measurements on a parallel database system is as an aid in understanding nonlinear scaleup results.

## 4.3.2   Using the Wisconsin Benchmark to Measure Speedup, Scaleup, and Sizeup

By definition, speedup tests are conducted by fixing the size of the relations in the database and the suite of queries while the number of processors and disks is varied. There are, however, several issues that must be carefully considered. First, the size of the benchmark relations must be chosen carefully. They must be large enough so that the number of levels in each index remains constant as the number of disks over which the relation has been declustered is increased, to avoid artificially producing superlinear speedup results. The actual size will depend on a number of factors, including the underlying page size that is used for the indexes and the maximum number of disks over which a relation is declustered. For example, when a 1 million tuple relation is stored on a single disk, the indexes on the `unique1` and `unique2` attributes will each contain 1 million entries and will be three levels deep (assuming that index entries consist of a 4-byte key field, a 4-byte count field, and an 8-byte `record_id` field). If the same relation is declustered over 100 disks, each disk will contain only 100,000 tuples, and the corresponding indexes will only be two levels deep. As discussed above, such changes tend to artificially produce superlinear speedup results and should be avoided if possible. On the other hand, the relation cannot be so large that it will not fit on a single disk drive if a single processor/disk pair is to be used as the base case. In some cases, it may be impossible to satisfy both of these constraints. In this case, the solution is to use more than a single processor/disk as the base case.

The second issue that must be considered when setting up a database for measuring the speedup of a system is interprocessor communication. If a single processor is used as the base case (assuming that the base relations fit), no interprocessor communications will occur. As the system is scaled from one to two processors, the interprocessor communications traffic may increase substantially, depending on the actual query being executed and the way in which the result relation is declustered. As a consequence, the observed speedups may very well be sublinear. This is reasonable if one is interested in determining the absolute speedup achievable by a system, but in some circumstances the objective is to predict what would happen if a currently operational system were scaled from 10 to 100 processors. Thus, for some applications, it may be valid to use more than a single processor as the base case.

Designing scaleup experiments is somewhat simpler. Again, the same query suite is used with each configuration tested. The basic decisions that must be made are to select a base relation size and a base hardware configuration that is scaled proportionally to increases in the sizes of the base relations. For example, assume that one million tuple benchmark relations are selected along with a base hardware configuration of five processors, each with one disk. If the benchmark relations are doubled in size, the hardware configuration is also doubled, expanding to ten processors with disks. As with the speedup tests, the selection of a base configuration size can significantly affect the results. Typically, a base configuration of between two and five processors is a reasonable compromise.

## 4.3.3 Sizeup, Speedup, and Scaleup Experiments on the Gamma Prototype

This section describes the results of conducting sizeup, speedup, and scaleup experiments on the Gamma prototype using a subset of the selection and join queries from the Wisconsin benchmark. It begins with an overview of the Gamma database machine. This is followed by a set of sizeup, speedup, and scaleup experiments on a subset of the selection and join queries from the Wisconsin benchmark. A more complete set of tests can be found in DeWitt et al. [1990]. A similar set of tests on Release 2 of Tandem's NonStop SQL system is described in Englert et al. [1989].

The tests began by constructing 100,000, 1 million, and 10 million tuple versions of the benchmark relations. Two copies of each relation were created and loaded. Except where noted otherwise, tuples were declustered by hash partitioning on the `unique1` attribute. In all cases, the results represent the average response time of a number of equivalent queries. Gamma was configured to use a disk page size of 8K bytes and a buffer pool of 2 megabytes per processor. The results of all queries were stored in the database. Returning data to the host was avoided in order to ensure that neither the speed of the communications link between the host and the database machine nor the speed of the host processor itself dominated the performance results obtained. By storing the result relations in the database, the effect of these factors was minimized—at the expense of incurring the cost of declustering and storing the result relations.

### Overview of the Gamma Database Machine

### Hardware

The design of the Gamma database machine is based on a shared-nothing architecture [Stonebraker, 1986], in which processors do not share disk drives or random access memory. They can communicate with one another only by sending messages through an interconnection network. Mass storage in such an architecture is distributed among the processors by connecting one or more disk drives to each processor, as shown in Figure 4.7. This architecture characterizes the database systems being used by Teradata [1985], Gamma [DeWitt et al., 1986; 1990], Tandem [1988], Bubba [Alexander et al., 1988; Copeland et al., 1988], and Arbre [Lorie et al., 1989].

The hardware platform currently used by Gamma is a 32 processor Intel iPSC/2 hypercube. Each processor is configured with an Intel 386 CPU, 8 megabytes of memory, and a 330-megabyte MAXTOR 4380 (5 1/4") disk drive. Each disk drive has an embedded SCSI controller, which provides a 45-Kbyte RAM buffer that acts as a disk cache for sequential read operations. The nodes in the hypercube are interconnected to form a hypercube using custom VLSI routing modules. Each module supports eight[2] full-

---

[2] On configurations with a mix of compute and I/O nodes, one of the 8 channels is dedicated for communication to the I/O subsystem.

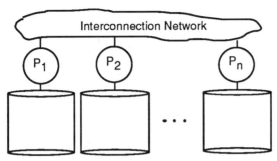

**Figure 4.7**
The basic shared-nothing design. Each processor has a private memory and one or
more disk drives. Processors communicate via a high-speed interconnect network.

duplex, serial, reliable communication channels, each operating at 2.8
megabytes/second. Small messages ($\leq$ 100 bytes) are sent as datagrams and
take less than a millisecond. For large messages, the hardware builds a communication circuit between the two nodes, over which the entire message is
transmitted without software overhead or copying. After the message has
been completely transmitted, the circuit is released. As an example of the
performance obtainable when sending page-sized messages, an 8-Kbyte
message takes about 4.5 milliseconds.

**Physical Database Organization**

Relations in Gamma are declustered[3] [Livny, Khoshafian, & Boral, 1987]
(see Figure 4.8) across all disk drives in the system. Declustering a relation
involves distributing the tuples of a relation among two or more disk drives
according to some distribution criteria, such as applying a hash function to
the key attribute of each tuple. One of the key reasons for using declustering
in a parallel database system is to enable the DBMS software to exploit the
I/O bandwidth by reading and writing multiple disks in parallel. By declustering the tuples of a relation, the task of parallelizing a scan operator
becomes trivial. All that is required is to start a copy of the operator on each
processor or disk containing relevant tuples and to merge their outputs at
the destination.

Gamma currently provides the user with three alternative declustering
strategies: round robin, hashed, and range partitioned. With the first strat-

---

[3] Declustering has its origins in the concept of horizontal partitioning initially developed as a distribution mechanism for distributed DBMS [RIES78].

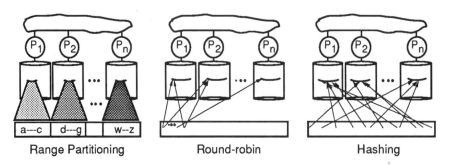

**Figure 4.8**
The three basic declustering schemes: range declustering maps contiguous fragments of a table to various disks. Round-robin declustering maps the *i*th record to disk *i* mod *n*. Hashed declustering, maps each record to a disk location based on some hash function. Each of these schemes spreads data among a collection of disks, allowing parallel disk access and parallel processing.

egy, tuples are distributed in a round-robin fashion among the disk drives. This is the default strategy and is used for all relations created as the result of a query. If the hashed partitioning strategy is selected, a randomizing function is applied to the key attribute of each tuple to select a storage unit. In the third strategy, the user specifies a range of key values for each node. The partitioning information for each relation is stored in the database catalog. Once a relation has been partitioned, Gamma provides the normal collection of access methods, including both clustered and nonclustered indexes. When the user requests that an index be created on a relation, the system automatically creates an index on each fragment of the relation. Gamma does not require that the clustered index for a relation be constructed on the partitioning attribute.

As a query is being optimized, the partitioning information for each source relation in the query is incorporated into the query plan produced by the query optimizer. In the case of hash and range-partitioned relations, this partitioning information is used by the query scheduler (discussed below) to restrict the number of processors involved in the execution of selection queries on the partitioning attribute. For example, if relation X is hash partitioned on attribute y, it is possible to direct selection operations with predicates of the form X.y = Constant to a single node, avoiding the use of any other nodes in the execution of the query. In the case of range-partitioned relations, the query scheduler can restrict the execution of the query to only those processors whose ranges overlap the range of the selection predicate (which may be either an equality or range predicate).

**Software Architecture**

Gamma is built on top of the NOSE operating system, which was designed specifically for supporting database management systems. NOSE provides multiple lightweight processes with shared memory. A nonpreemptive scheduling policy is used to help prevent convoys (Blasgen et al., 1979) from occurring. NOSE provides communications between processes using the reliable message-passing hardware of the Intel iPSC/2 hypercube. File services in NOSE are based on the Wisconsin Storage System (WiSS) [Chou et al., 1985].

The algorithms for all the relational operators are written as if they were to be run on a single processor. As shown in Figure 4.9, the input to an operator process is a stream of tuples, and the output is a stream of tuples that is demultiplexed through a structure termed a *split table*. Once the process begins execution, it continuously reads tuples from its input stream (which may be the output of another process or a table), operates on each tuple, and uses a split table to route the resulting tuple to the process indicated in the split table.

As an example, consider the query shown in Figure 4.10 in conjunction with the split tables in Figure 4.11. Assume that three processes are used to execute the join operator, and that five other processes execute the two scan operators—three processes are used to scan the three partitions of Table A, and two processes are used to scan the two partitions of Table B. Each of the three Table A scan nodes will have the same split table, sending all tuples with join attributes values between A and H to port 1 of join process 0, all between I and Q to port 1 of join process 1, and all between R and Z to

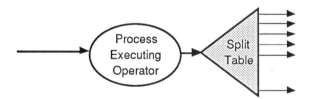

**Figure 4.9**
A relational dataflow graph showing a relational operator's output being decomposed by a split table into several independent streams. Each stream may be a duplicate of the input stream or a partitioning of the input stream into many disjoint streams. Using a combination of split tables and merge operators (which are provided implicitly in Gamma by the communications mechanisms of NOSE), a web of simple sequential dataflow nodes can be connected to form a parallel execution plan.

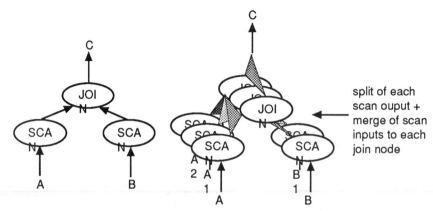

**Figure 4.10**
A simple relational dataflow graph showing two relational scans (project and select) consuming two input tables, A and B, and feeding their outputs to a join operator, which in turn produces a data stream C.

| Table A Scan Split Table | | Table B Scan Split Table | |
|---|---|---|---|
| **Predicate** | **Destination Process** | **Predicate** | **Destination Process** |
| A-H | (CPU 5, Process 3, Port 0) | A-H | (CPU 5, Process 3, Port 1) |
| I-Q | (CPU 7, Process 8, Port 0) | I-Q | (CPU 7, Process 8, Port 1) |
| R-Z | (CPU 2, Process 2, Port 0) | R-Z | (CPU 2, Process 2, Port 1) |

**Figure 4.11**
Sample split tables, which map tuples to different output streams (ports of other processes), depending on the range value of some attribute of the input tuple. The split table on the left is for the Table A scan in Figure 4.7, and the table on the right is for the Table B scan.

port 1 of join process 2. Similarly, the two Table B scan nodes have the same split table, except that their outputs are merged by port 1 (not port 0) of each join process. Each join process sees a sequential input stream of A tuples from the port 0 merge (the left scan nodes) and another sequential stream of B tuples from the port 1 merge (the right scan nodes). Four join methods are available to the query optimizer to choose from [DeWitt et al., 1984; Schneider & DeWitt, 1989]: simple hash, grace hash, hybrid hash, and sort-merge. Additional details on how queries are processed by Gamma can be found in DeWitt et al. [1990].

## Sizeup Experiments

### Selection Queries

The first set of selection tests was designed to determine how Gamma would respond as the size of the source relations was increased while the machine configuration was kept at 30 processors with disks. Ideally, the response time of a query should grow as a linear function of the size of input and result relations. For these tests, six different selection queries (Queries 1 to 5 and 7 from Appendix) were run on three sets of relations containing, respectively, 0.1 million, 1 million, and 10 million tuples. Query 6, a 10 percent selection through a nonclustered index query, was not included, as the Gamma query optimizer chooses to use a sequential scan for this query. Except for Query 7, the predicate of each query specifies a range of values and, thus, since the input relations were declustered by hashing, the query must be sent to all the nodes.

The results from these tests are tabulated in Table 4.3. For the most part, the execution time for each query scales as a fairly linear function of the size of the input and output relations. There are, however, several cases where the scaling is not perfectly linear. Consider, for example, the 10 percent selection using a clustered index. This query takes 5.02 seconds on the 1 million tuple relation and 61.86 seconds on the 10 million tuple relation. To understand why this happens, one must consider the effect of seek time on the execution time of the query. Since two copies of each relation were loaded, when two 1 million tuple relations are declustered over 30 disk drives, the fragments occupy approximately 53 cylinders (out of 1224) on

**Table 4.3** Selection queries, 30 processors with disks (all. execution times in seconds).

| Relation Query Description | Number of Tuples in Source | | |
|---|---|---|---|
| | 100,000 | 1,000,000 | 10,000,000 |
| 1% nonindexed selection (Query 1) | 0.45 | 8.16 | 81.15 |
| 10% nonindexed selection (Query 2) | 0.82 | 10.82 | 135.61 |
| 1% selection using clustered index (Query 3) | 0.35 | 0.82 | 5.12 |
| 10% selection using clustered index (Query 4) | 0.77 | 5.02 | 61.86 |
| 1% selection using nonclustered index (Query 5) | 0.60 | 8.77 | 113.37 |
| single tuple select using clustered index (Query 7) | 0.08 | 0.08 | 0.14 |

each disk drive. Two 10 million tuple relations fill about 530 cylinders on each drive. As each page of the result relation is written to disk, the disk heads must be moved from their current position over the input relation to a free block on the disk. Thus, with the 10 million tuple relation, the cost of writing each output page is much higher.

As expected, the use of a clustered B-tree index always provides a significant improvement in performance. One observation to be made from Table 4.3 is the relative consistency of the execution time of the selection queries through a clustered index. Notice that the execution time for a 10 percent selection on the 1 million tuple relation is almost identical to the execution time of the 1 percent selection on the 10 million tuple relation. In both cases, 100,000 tuples are retrieved and stored, resulting in identical I/O and CPU costs.

The final row of Table 4.3 presents the time required to select a single tuple using a clustered index and return it to the host. Since the selection predicate is on the partitioning attribute, the query is directed to a single node, avoiding the overhead of starting the query on all 30 processors. The response for this query increases significantly as the relation size is increased from 1 million to 10 million tuples because the height of the B-tree increases from two to three levels. It is interesting to note how the response time increases as the size of the relation increases. Although the B-tree for all three relations is only two levels deep (at each node), the number of entries in the root node increases from 4 to 330 as the relation size is increased from 100,000 to 10 million tuples. Consequently, significantly more time is required to do a binary search of the root node to locate the correct leaf page.

### Join Queries

Two join queries were used for the join scaleup tests: joinABprime and joinAselB. The A and B relations contain either 100,000, 1 million, or 10 million tuples. The Bprime relation contains, respectively, 10,000, 100,000, or 1 million tuples.

The first variation of the join queries tested involved no indexes and used a nonpartitioning attribute for both the join and selection attributes. Thus, before the join can be performed, the two input relations must be redistributed by hashing on the join attribute value of each tuple. The results from these tests are contained in the first two rows of Table 4.4. The second variation of the join queries also did not employ any indexes, but, in this case, the relations were hash partitioned on the joining attribute, enabling

**Table 4.4**   Join queries, 30 processors with disks (all execution times in seconds).

| A Query Description | Number of Tuples in Relation | | |
|---|---|---|---|
| | 100,000 | 1,000,000 | 10,000,000 |
| JoinABprime with nonpartitioning attributes (Query 10) of A and B used as join attributes | 3.52 | 28.69 | 438.90 |
| JoinAselB with nonpartitioning attributes (Query 9) of A and B used as join attributes | 2.69 | 25.13 | 373.98 |
| JoinABprime with partitioning attributes (Query 10) of A and B used as join attributes | 3.34 | 25.95 | 426.25 |
| JoinAselB with partitioning attributes (Query 9) of A and B used as join attributes | 2.74 | 23.77 | 362.89 |

the redistribution phase of the join to be skipped. The results for these tests are contained in the last two rows of Table 4.4.

The results in Table 4.4 indicate that the execution time of each join query increases in a fairly linear fashion as the size of the input relations are increased. Gamma does not exhibit linearity for the 10 million tuple queries because the size of the inner relation (208 megabytes) is twice as large as the total available space for hash tables. Hence, the Hybrid join algorithm (Schneider & DeWitt, 1989) needs two buckets to process these queries. While the tuples in the first bucket can be placed directly into memory-resident hash tables, the second bucket must be written to disk.

As expected, the version of each query in which the partitioning attribute was used as the join attribute ran faster. From these results, one can estimate a lower bound on the aggregate rate at which data can be redistributed by the Intel iPSC/2 hypercube. Consider the version of the joinABprime query in which a 1 million tuple relation is joined with a 100,000 tuple relation. This query requires 28.69 seconds when the join is not on the partitioning attribute. During the execution of this query, 1.1 million 208-byte tuples must be redistributed by hashing on the join attribute, yielding an aggregate total transfer rate of 7.9 megabytes/second during the processing of this query. This should not be construed, however, as an accurate estimate of the maximum obtainable interprocessor communications bandwidth, as the CPUs may be the limiting factor, (the disks are not likely to be the limiting factor, as from Table 4.3 one can estimate the aggregate bandwidth of the 30 disks to be about 25 megabytes/second).

## Speedup Experiments

### Selection Queries

This section examines how the response times for both the nonindexed and indexed selection queries on the 1 million tuple relation are affected by the number of processors used to execute the query[4]. Ideally, one would like to see a linear improvement in performance as the number of processors is increased from 1 to 30. Increasing the number of processors increases both the aggregate CPU power and I/O bandwidth available while reducing the number of tuples that must be processed by each processor.

Figure 4.12 presents the average response times for the nonindexed 1 percent and 10 percent selection queries (Queries 1 and 2) on the 1 million tuple relation. As expected, the response time for each query decreases as the number of processors and disks is increased. The response time is higher for the 10 percent selection due to the cost of declustering and storing the result relation. Although one could always store result tuples locally, by partitioning all result relations in a round-robin (or hashed) fashion, one can ensure that the fragments of every result relation each contain approximately the same number of tuples.

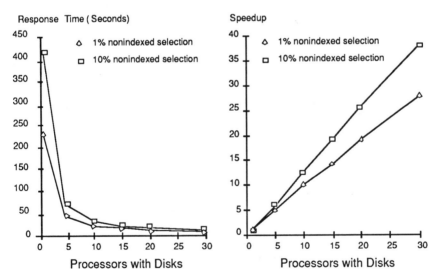

**Figure 4.12**
Response times and speedup of nonindexed selection queries.

---

[4] The 1 million tuple relation was used for these experiments because the 10 million tuple relation would not fit on one disk drive.

Figure 4.13 presents the average response time and speedup as a function of the number of processors for the following three queries: a 1 percent selection through a clustered index (Query 3), a 10 percent selection through a clustered index (Query 4), and a 1 percent selection through a nonclustered index (Query 5), all accessing the 1 million tuple relation.

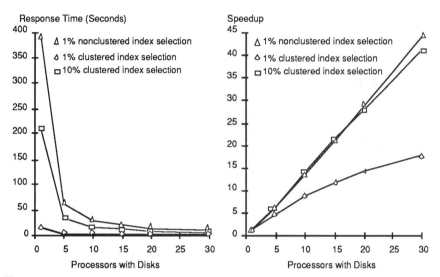

**Figure 4.13**
Response times and speedup of indexed selection queries.

Three queries in Figures 3.12 and 3.13 have superlinear speedup, one is slightly sublinear, and one is significantly sublinear. Consider first the 10 percent selection via a relation scan, the 1 percent selection through a non-clustered index, and the 10 percent selection through a clustered index. As discussed above, the source of the superlinear speedups exhibited by these queries is due to significant differences in the time the various configurations spend seeking. With one processor, the 1 million tuple relation occupies approximately 66 percent of the disk. When the same relation is declustered over 30 disk drives, it occupies about 2 percent of each disk. In the case of the 1 percent nonclustered index selection, each tuple selected requires a random seek. With one processor, the range of each random seek is approximately 800 cylinders; with 30 processors, the range of the seek is limited to about 27 cylinders. Since the seek time is proportional to the square root of the distance traveled by the disk head [Patterson & Hennessy, 1989], reducing the size of the relation fragment on each disk significantly reduces the amount of time that the query spends seeking.

A similar effect occurs with the 10 percent clustered index selection. In this case, once the index has been used to locate the tuples satisfying the query, each input page will produce one output page, and at some point the buffer pool will be filled with dirty output pages. In order to write an output page, the disk head must be moved from its position over the input relation to the position on the disk where the output pages are to be placed. The relative cost of this seek decreases proportionally as the number of processors increases, resulting in a superlinear speedup for the query. The 10 percent nonindexed selection shown in Figure 4.13 is also superlinear for similar reasons. The reason this query is not affected to the same degree is that, without an index, the seek time is a smaller fraction of the overall execution time of the query.

The 1 percent selection through a clustered index exhibits sublinear speedups because the cost of initiating a select and store operator on each processor (a total of 0.24 seconds for 30 processors) becomes a significant fraction of the total execution as the number of processors is increased.

### Join Queries

For the join speedup experiments, the `joinABprime` query is used with a 1 million tuple A relation and a 100,000 tuple `Bprime` relation. Two different cases were considered. In the first case, the input relations were declustered by hashing on the join attribute. In the second case, the input relations were declustered using a different attribute. The hybrid hash-join algorithm was used for all queries. The number of processors was varied from five to thirty. Since with fewer than five processors two or more hash join buckets are needed, including the execution time for one processor (which needs five buckets) would have made the response times for five or more processors appear artificially fast, resulting in superlinear speedup curves.

The resulting response times and speedups are plotted in Figure 4.14. From the shape of these graphs, it is obvious that the execution time for the query is significantly improved as additional processors are employed. Several factors prevent the system from achieving perfectly linear speedups. First, the cost of starting four operator processes (two scans, one join, and one store) on each processor increases as a function of the number of processors used. Second, the effect of short-circuiting local messages diminishes as the number of processors is increased. For example, consider a five-processor configuration and the nonpartitioning attribute version of the `JoinA prime` query. As each processor repartitions tuples by hashing on the join attribute, one fifth of the input tuples it processes are destined for

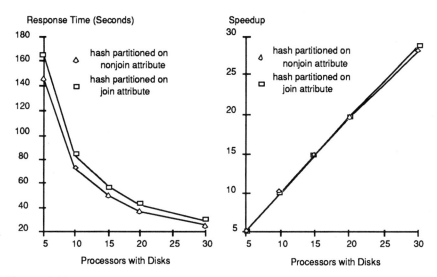

**Figure 4.14**
Response times and speedup of join queries.

itself and will be short-circuited by the communications software. In addition, as the query produces tuples of the result relation (which is partitioned in a round-robin manner), they too will be short circuited. As the number of processors is increased, the number of short-circuited packets decreases to the point where, with 30 processors, only 1/30th of the packets will be short-circuited. Because these intranode packets are less expensive than their corresponding internode packets, smaller configurations will benefit more from short-circuiting. In the case of partitioning-attribute joins, all input tuples will short-circuit the network along with a fraction of the output tuples.

**Scaleup Experiments**

**Selection Queries**

In the final set of selection experiments, the number of processors was varied from 5 to 30 while the size of the input relations was increased from 1 million to 6 million tuples, respectively. As shown in Figure 4.15, the response time for each of the five selection queries remains almost constant. The slight increase in response time is due to the overhead of initiating a selection and store operator at each node. Since a single process is used to initiate the execution of a query, as the number of processors employed is

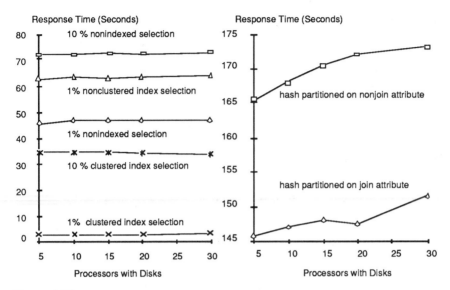

**Figure 4.15**
Scaleup response times of various queries.

increased, the load on this process is increased proportionally. Switching to a tree-based query initiation scheme [Gerber & DeWitt, 1987] would distribute this overhead among all the processors.

## Join Queries

The `JoinABprime` query was used for the join scaleup experiments. For these tests, the number of processors was varied from 5 to 30 while the size of the A relation was varied from 1 million to 6 million tuples in increments of 1 million tuples, and the size of `Bprime` relation was varied from 100,000 to 600,000 tuples in increments of 100,000. Two different cases were considered. In the first case, the input relations were declustered by hashing on the join attribute. In the second case, the input relations were declustered using a different attribute. For each configuration, only one join bucket was needed. The results of these tests are presented in Figure 4.15. Three factors contribute to the slight increase in response times. First, the task of initiating 4 processes at each node is performed by a single processor. Second, as the number of processors increases, the effects of short-circuiting messages during the execution of these queries diminishes, especially in the case when the join attribute is not the partitioning attribute. Finally, the response time may be limited by the speed of the communications network.

# 4.4    Conclusions

The original intent of the Wisconsin benchmark was to develop a relatively simple but fairly scientific benchmark that could be used to evaluate the performance of relational database systems and machines. We never envisioned that the benchmark would become widely used or cause the controversies that it did. In retrospect, had we realized what was to come, we would have tried to do a better job in a number of areas, including more complex queries and a better suite of update queries. In the conclusions of Bitton, DeWitt, and Turbyfill [1983], we ourselves admitted that the benchmark was "neither an exhaustive comparison of the different systems, nor a realistic approximation of what measurements in a multiuser environment would be like." However, starting with a single-user benchmark provided us with insights that would have been impossible to achieve had we begun instead with multiuser experiments.

The Wisconsin benchmark did a very good job of uncovering performance and implementation flaws in the original relational products. Since then, however, these flaws have been fixed, and the single-user performance differences among the various products have narrowed significantly. For the most part, the Wisconsin benchmark has been supplanted by the DebitCredit benchmark and its successor, the TPC BM A benchmark, regardless of the many deficiencies of this benchmark.

During the past few years, parallel database systems have evolved from research curiosities to highly successful products. For example, both Teradata and Tandem have shipped systems with over two hundred processors. Mainframe vendors have found it increasingly difficult to build machines powerful enough to meet the CPU and I/O demands of relational DBMSs serving large numbers of simultaneous users or searching terabytes of data, but parallel database systems based on a shared-nothing architecture [STON86] can be expanded incrementally and can be scaled to configurations containing certainly hundreds and probably thousands of processors and disks. The DebitCredit benchmark is used as one metric for such systems. Many customers of such systems use them for processing complex relational queries. As illustrated by the previous section, the Wisconsin benchmark provides a mechanism by which both the absolute performance and the speedup and scaleup characteristics of such systems can be measured.

**Acknowledgments**

Dina Bitton and Carolyn Turbyfill were instrumental in the development of the Wisconsin benchmark and in conducting the early tests. All too often the Wisconsin benchmark is cited as the "DeWitt" benchmark. Doing so slights the important contributions that Dina and Carolyn made in its development. Shahram Ghandeharizadeh and Donovan Schneider deserve all the credit for gathering the results on Gamma that were presented in Section 4.3, and for their major contributions implementing Gamma itself. Finally, I would like to acknowledge Susan Englert and Jim Gray for the benchmark generator described in Section 4.2.

This research was partially supported by the Defense Advanced Research Projects Agency under contract N00039-86-C-0578, by the National Science Foundation under grant DCR-8512862, by a DARPA/NASA sponsored Graduate Research Assistantship in Parallel Processing, and by research grants from Intel Scientific Computers, Tandem Computers, and Digital Equipment Corporation.

# References

Alexander, W., et al. (1988). Process and dataflow control in distributed data-intensive systems. *Proceedings of the ACM SIGMOD Conference*. Chicago, IL.

Anon et al. (1988). A measure of transaction processing power. In M. Stonebraker (Ed.), *Readings in Database Systems*, San Mateo, CA: Morgan Kaufmann.

Blasgen, M. W., Gray, J., Mitoma, M., & Price, T. (1979). The convoy phenomenon. *Operating System Review, 13*(2).

Bitton, D., DeWitt, D. J., & Turbyfill, C. (1983). Benchmarking database systems: A systematic approach. *Proceedings of the 1983 Very Large Database Conference.*

Bitton, D., & Turbyfill, C. (1985). Design and analysis of multiuser benchmarks for database systems. *Proceedings of the HICSS-18 Conference.*

Bitton, D., & Turbyfill, C. (1988). A retrospective on the Wisconsin benchmark. In M. Stonebraker (Ed.), *Readings in Database Systems*. San Mateo, CA: Morgan Kaufmann.

Boral, H., DeWitt, D.J., Friedland, D., Jarrell, N., & Wilkinson, W. K. (1982). Implementation of the database machine DIRECT. *IEEE Transactions on Software Engineering.*

Boral, H., & DeWitt, D.J. (1983). Database machines: An idea whose time has passed? A critique of the future of database machines. *Proceedings of the Third International Workshop on Database Machines*, Munich, Germany.

Boral, H., & DeWitt, D.J. (1984). A methodology for database system performance evaluation. *Proceedings of the 1984 SIGMOD Conference*, Boston, MA.

Chou, H.T., DeWitt, D.J., Katz, R., & Klug, T. (1985). Design and implementation of the Wisconsin Storage System (WiSS). *Software Practices and Experience, 15*(10).

Copeland, G., Alexander, W., Boughter, E., & Keller, T. (1988). Data placement in Bubba. *Proceedings of the ACM-SIGMOD. International Conference on Management of Data.* Chicago.

DeWitt, D.J. (1979). DIRECT—A multiprocessor organization for supporting relational database management systems. *IEEE Transactions on Computers.*

DeWitt, D.J., Katz, R., Olken, F., Shapiro, D., Stonebraker, M., & Wood, D. (1984). Implementation techniques for main memory database systems. *Proceedings of the 1984 SIGMOD Conference.* Boston, MA.

DeWitt, D., et al. (1986). GAMMA—A high performance dataflow database machine. *Proceedings of the 1986 VLDB Conference.* Japan.

DeWitt, D., Smith, M., & Boral, H. (1987). *A Single-User Performance Evaluation of the Teradata Database Machine.* (MCC Technical Report No. DB-081-87).

DeWitt, D., Ghandeharizadeh, S., & Schneider, D. (1988). A performance analysis of the gamma database machine. *Proceedings of the ACM-SIGMOD International Conference on Management of Data.* Chicago.

DeWitt, D., et al. (1990). The gamma database machine project. *IEEE Knowledge and Data Engineering,* 2(1).

Englert, S., Gray, J., Kocher, T. & Shah, P. (1989). *A Benchmark of NonStop SQL Release 2 Demonstrating Near-Linear Speedup and Scaleup on Large Databases.* (Tandem Computers, Technical Report 89.4. Tandem Part No. 27469).

Englert, S. & Gray, J. (1989). Generating Dense-Unique Random Numbers for Synthetic Database Loading, Tandem Computers.

Epstein, R. (1987). Today's technology is producing high-performance relational database systems. *Sybase Newsletter.*

Gerber, R. & DeWitt, D. (1987). *The Impact of Hardware and Software Alternatives on the Performance of the Gamma Database Machine.* (Computer Sciences Technical Report #708). Madison: University of Wisconsin.

Graefe, G. (1990). Encapsulation of parallelism in the volcano query processing system. *Proceedings of the 1990 ACM-SIGMOD International Conference on Management of Data.*

Graefe, G., & Ward, K. (1989). Dynamic query evaluation plans. *Proceedings of the 1989 SIGMOD Conference.* Portland, OR.

Gray, J., Sammer, H., & Whitford, S. (1988). *Shortest Seek vs. Shortest Service Time Scheduling of Mirrored Disks.* Tandem Computers.

Livny, M., Khoshafian, S., & Boral, H. (1987). Multi-disk management algorithms. *Proceedings of the 1987 SIGMETRICS Conference.* Banff, Alberta, Canada.

Lorie, R., Daudenarde, J., Hallmark, G., Stamos, J., & Young, H. (1989). Adding intra-transaction parallelism to an existing DBMS: Early experience. *IEEE Data Engineering Newsletter,* 12(1).

O'Neil, P.E. (1991). The Set Query Benchmark. In J. Gray (Ed.), *Database and Transaction Processing Performance Handbook.* San Mateo, CA: Morgan Kaufmann.

Patterson, D.A., & Hennessy, J.L. (1990). *Computer architecture, a quantitative approach.* San Mateo, CA: Morgan Kaufmann.

Schneider, D. & DeWitt, D. (1989). A performance evaluation of four parallel join algorithms in a shared-nothing multiprocessor environment. *Proceedings of the 1989 SIGMOD Conference.* Portland, OR.

Schneider, D. & DeWitt, D. (1990). Tradeoffs in processing complex join queries via hashing in multiprocessor database machines. *Proceedings of the Sixteenth International Conference on Very Large Data Bases.* Melbourne, Australia.

Smith, M., et al. (1989). An experiment in response time scalability. *Proceedings of the Sixth International Workshop on Database Machines.*

Stonebraker, M. (1986). The case for shared nothing. *Database Engineering, 9*(1).

Tandem Database Group. (1989). Nonstop SQL, A distributed, high-performance, high-reliability implementation of SQL. In *High Performance Transaction Systems.* (Springer-Verlag Lecture Notes in Computer Science, 359). New York: Springer-Verlag.

Tandem Performance Group. (1988). A benchmark of non-stop SQL on the Debit Credit Transaction. *Proceedings of the 1988 SIGMOD Conference.* Chicago, IL.

Teradata. (1983). *DBC/1012 data base computer concepts & facilities* (Teradata Corp., Document No. C02-0001-00).

Teradata. (1985). *DBC/1012 database computer system manual release 2.0* (Teradata Corp., Document No. C10-0001-02).

Turbyfill, C. (1987). *Comparative benchmarking of relational database systems.* Unpublished doctoral dissertation, Cornell University.

# Appendix. Wisconsin Benchmark Queries for 10,000 Tuple Relations

## Comments

1. For the selection, insert, update, and delete queries, ten variants of each query are used. For the join, aggregate, and projection queries four variants of each query are used. Queries alternate between two identical copies of each relation. For example, the selection predicates of the first four variants of Query 1 are:

```
... WHERE TENKTUP1.unique2 BETWEEN 0 AND 99
... WHERE TENKTUP2.unique2 BETWEEN 9900 AND 9999
... WHERE TENKTUP1.unique2 BETWEEN 302 AND 401
... WHERE TENKTUP2.unique2 BETWEEN 676 AND 775
```

Only one variant of each query is shown below.

2. For the indexed runs, a clustered index is constructed on the `unique2` attribute, and nonclustered indexes are constructed on the `unique1` and the `hundred` attribute.

3. *TMP* is used as a generic name for the result relation for those queries whose result tuples are stored in the database.

### Query 1 (No Index) and Query 3 (Clustered Index)—1 Percent Selection

```
INSERT INTO TMP
SELECT * FROM TENKTUP1
WHERE unique2 BETWEEN 0 AND 99
```

### Query 2 (No Index) and Query 4 (Clustered Index)—10 Percent Selection

```
INSERT INTO TMP
SELECT * FROM TENKTUP1
WHERE unique2 BETWEEN 792 AND 1791
```

### Query 5—1 Percent Selection via a Nonclustered Index

```
INSERT INTO TMP
SELECT * FROM TENKTUP1
WHERE unique1 BETWEEN 0 AND 99
```

### Query 6—10 Percent Selection via Nonclustered Index

```
INSERT INTO TMP
SELECT * FROM TENKTUP1
WHERE unique1 BETWEEN 792 AND 1791
```

### Query 7—Single Tuple Selection via Clustered Index to Screen

```
SELECT * FROM TENKTUP1
WHERE unique2 = 2001
```

### Query 8—1 Percent Selection via Clustered Index to Screen

```
SELECT * FROM TENKTUP1
WHERE unique2 BETWEEN 0 AND 99
```

### Query 9 (No Index) and Query 12 (Clustered Index)—JoinAselB

```
INSERT INTO TMP
SELECT * FROM TENKTUP1, TENKTUP2
WHERE (TENKTUP1.unique2 = TENKTUP2.unique2)
 AND (TENKTUP2.unique2 < 1000)
```

### Query to Make Bprime Relation

```
INSERT INTO BPRIME
SELECT * FROM TENKTUP2
WHERE TENKTUP2.unique2 < 1000
```

### Query 10 (No Index) and Query 13 (Clustered Index)—JoinABprime

```
INSERT INTO TMP
SELECT * FROM TENKTUP1, BPRIME
WHERE (TENKTUP1.unique2 = BPRIME.unique2)
```

### Query 11 (No Index) and Query 14 (Clustered Index)—JoinCselAselB

```
INSERT INTO TMP
SELECT * FROM ONEKTUP, TENKTUP1, TENKTUP2
WHERE (ONEKTUP.unique2 = TENKTUP1.unique2)
 AND (TENKTUP1.unique2 = TENKTUP2.unique2)
 AND (TENKTUP1.unique2 < 1000)
```

## Query 15 (Nonclustered Index)—`JoinAselB`

```
INSERT INTO TMP
SELECT * FROM TENKTUP1, TENKTUP2
WHERE (TENKTUP1.unique1 = TENKTUP2.unique1)
 AND (TENKTUP1.unique1 < 1000)
```

## Query 16 (Nonclustered Index)—`JoinABprime`

```
INSERT INTO TMP
SELECT * FROM TENKTUP1, BPRIME
WHERE (TENKTUP1.unique1 = BPRIME.unique1)
```

## Query 17 (Nonclustered Index)—`JoinCselAselB`

```
INSERT INTO TMP
SELECT * FROM ONEKTUP, TENKTUP1, TENKTUP2
WHERE (ONEKTUP.unique1 = TENKTUP1.unique1)
 AND (TENKTUP1.unique1 = TENKTUP2.unique1)
 AND (TENKTUP1.unique1 < 1000)
```

## Query 18—Projection with 1 Percent Projection

```
INSERT INTO TMP
SELECT DISTINCT two, four, ten, twenty, onePercent, string4
FROM TENKTUP1
```

## Query 19—Projection with 100 Percent Projection

```
INSERT INTO TMP
SELECT DISTINCT two, four, ten, twenty, onePercent, tenPercent,
twentyPercent, fiftyPercent, unique3, evenOnePercent,
oddOnePercent, stringu1, stringu2, string4
FROM TENKTUP1
```

## Query 20 (No Index) and Query 23 (with Clustered Index), minimum aggregate function

```
INSERT INTO TMP
SELECT MIN (TENKTUP1.unique2) FROM TENKTUP1
```

## Query 21 (No Index) and Query 24 (with Clustered Index), minimum aggregate function with 100 partitions

```
INSERT INTO TMP
SELECT MIN (TENKTUP1.unique3) FROM TENKTUP1
GROUP BY TENKTUP1.onePercent
```

## Query 22 (No Index) and Query 25 (with Clustered Index), sum aggregate function with 100 partitions

```
INSERT INTO TMP
SELECT SUM (TENKTUP1.unique3) FROM TENKTUP1
GROUP BY TENKTUP1.onePercent
```

## Query 26 (No Indexes) and Query 29 (with Indexes)—Insert 1 Tuple

```
INSERT INTO TENKTUP1 VALUES(10001,74,0, 2,0,10,50,688,
1950,4950,9950,1,100,
'MxxxxxxxxxxxxxxxxxxxxxxxxGxxxxxxxxxxxxxxxxxxxxxxxxC'
'GxxxxxxxxxxxxxxxxxxxxxxxxCxxxxxxxxxxxxxxxxxxxxxxxxA',
'OxxxxxxxxxxxxxxxxxxxxxxxxOxxxxxxxxxxxxxxxxxxxxxxxxO')
```

## Query 27 (No Index) and Query 30 (with Indexes)—Delete 1 Tuple

```
DELETE FROM TENKTUP1 WHERE unique1=10001
```

## Query 28 (No Indexes) and Query 31 (with Indexes)—Update Key Attribute

```
UPDATE TENKTUP1
SET unique2 = 10001 WHERE unique2 = 1491
```

## Query 32 (with Indexes)—Update Indexed Nonkey Attribute

```
UPDATE TENKTUP1
SET unique1 = 10001 WHERE unique1 = 1491
```

# 5

# AS³AP:
# An ANSI SQL Standard Scaleable and Portable Benchmark for Relational Database Systems

Carolyn Turbyfill
Cyril Orji
Dina Bitton[1]

*Sun Microsystems*
*University of Illinois, Chicago*
*Cadre Technologies*

## 5.1    Historical Perspective

In 1983, the first commercially available database machines were becoming available, and new prototypes, such as the GRACE database machine [Kitsuregawa, Tanaka, and Moto-Oka, 1983], had been proposed. The Wisconsin benchmark [Bitton, DeWitt, and Turbyfill, 1983] was created in an attempt to compare backend database machine architectures with software relational database systems running on a general purpose computer. Specifically, the database machines tested were the Britton-Lee IDM 500 and

---

[1] The initial version of this paper was written at the University of Illinois at Chicago.

DIRECT [DeWitt, 1979], and the software database systems were University Ingres on Berkeley UNIX and commercial Ingres on the VMS operating system [Stonebraker, 1986]. In attempting to compare these systems, we soon realized that an appropriate benchmarking methodology for comparing database system architectures was, in and of itself, a topic of research. Hence, the Wisconsin benchmark was born as an experiment in comparative benchmarking methodology.

The Wisconsin benchmark is a single-factor, controlled experiment using a synthetic database and a controlled workload. Every set of queries in the benchmark varied one factor while the other factors that could have affected performance were kept constant. For instance, the number of users (one), the size of the database (5 megabytes), and the number of tuples output by a query were all held constant across the tests. We expected, in the course of developing the benchmark, to encounter confounding variables that would require revision of our methodology. In order to develop a methodology for both benchmarking and analysis of results, we simplified the initial experiments, intentionally ignoring factors that we knew to be important, such as attribute type, data distribution, database size, and number of users. We used only two data types: fixed length strings and two-byte integers. All data were uniformly distributed. The database was 5 megabytes in size, and the queries were not designed to scale with different-sized databases. The initial tests were performed with only one user on the entire system (single-user and standalone). The benchmark was also not designed to be extensible, although some extensions were possible [Bitton and Turbyfill, 1985; Boral and DeWitt, 1984; Bitton, Hanrahan, and Turbyfill, 1987]. While our preliminary work on the Wisconsin benchmark and variants of the benchmark did provide valuable insight into benchmarking methodology, the database and queries as instantiated did not and were not intended to provide an adequate framework for comparative benchmarking.

Shortly after it was first published, the Wisconsin benchmark became a de facto industry standard. With numerous relational database systems becoming commercially available, the need for an evaluation and comparison tool emerged. The simplicity of the Wisconsin benchmark design was a major contributing factor to its widespread use as it was fairly easy to understand and implement. Another factor in its success was the widespread availability of the Wisconsin benchmark's measurements for different systems, which provided a common point of comparison for a wide variety of architectures and implementations [Bitton and Turbyfill, 1988]. Even though some of the test queries had confounding variables, such as predicate independence, which obscured the interpretation of the results

[Turbyfill, 1987], and the test suite was not comprehensive, the Wisconsin benchmark was a very useful tool at the time it became available.

Currently, there is a need for a general benchmark that can be used to compare relational database systems with vastly different architectures and capabilities over a variety of workloads. To achieve this goal in a cohesive and tractable benchmark, it is important that these criteria be central to the design of the benchmark, as opposed to being added as an afterthought to an existing benchmark. This was the motivation for the design of the $AS^3AP$ benchmark [Turbyfill, 1987; Turbyfill, Orji, and Bitton, 1989].

## 5.2    A Scaleable Benchmark

The benchmark described in this chapter is an ANSI SQL Standard Scaleable and Portable ($AS^3AP$) benchmark for relational database systems. It is designed to:

- provide a comprehensive but tractable set of tests for database processing power.

- have built-in scaleability and portability so that it can be used to test a broad range of systems.

- minimize human effort in implementing and running the benchmark tests.

- provide a uniform metric, the *equivalent database ratio*, for a straightforward and nonambiguous interpretation of the benchmark results.

For a particular DBMS, the $AS^3AP$ benchmark determines an *equivalent database size*, which is *the maximum size of the $AS^3AP$ database* for which the system is able to perform the designated $AS^3AP$ set of single and multiuser tests *in under 12 hours*. The equivalent database size is an absolute performance metric by itself. It can also provide a basis for comparing cost and performance of systems, as follows: the *cost per megabyte* of a DBMS is the *total price* of the DBMS divided by the equivalent database size (total price could be computed according to the TPC-B specifications: 5 year cost of hardware, software, and maintenance, and scaled to a 12-hour price by dividing by 3652). The *equivalent database ratio* for two systems is the ratio of their equivalent database sizes. Both the cost per megabyte and the equivalent database ratio provide global comparison metrics.

Current relational database systems vary widely in their capabilities, performance, and cost. Thus the task of defining meaningful measures of database processing power is complex, and the need for a scaleable and portable benchmark is critical. There have been a number of previous attempts at formalizing and standardizing a benchmarking methodology for database systems [Bitton, DeWitt, and Turbyfill, 1983; Anon et al., 1985; Bitton and Turbyfill, 1985; Bitton, Hanrahan, and Turbyfill, 1987; Rubenstein, Kubicar, and Cattell, 1987; Yao, Hevner, and Myers, 1987]. However, previously proposed benchmarks fail to provide a comprehensive and uniform measure of performance. For instance, one provides a measure of transaction power for short on-line transactions [Anon et al., 1985], while the other only tests features of the query optimizer [Bitton, DeWitt, and Turbyfill, 1983; Bitton and Turbyfill, 1988], and none of them tests important utilities such as the database load and restore.

Benchmarks often require too much human effort to be implemented, ported, or realistically scaled to evaluate a particular system. Finally, few benchmarks are designed to facilitate the interpretation of their results, and most fail to provide useful guidelines for fixing or improving the system under test. We have addressed these problems in the design of AS$^3$AP, by emphasizing scaleability, portability, and ease of use and interpretation.

## 5.3  Benchmark Scope

The AS$^3$AP tests are divided into two modules:

- Single-user tests, including:

  (a) utilities for loading and structuring the database.

  (b) queries designed to test access methods and basic query optimization—selections, simple joins, projections, aggregates, one-tuple updates, and bulk updates.

- Multiuser tests modeling different types of database workloads:

  (a) on-line transaction processing (OLTP) workloads.

  (b) information retrieval (IR) workloads.

(c) mixed workloads, including a balance of short transactions, report queries, relation scan, and long transactions.

The set of single-user tests is designed as a cross-section of the basic functions that a relational DBMS must support, as defined by the ANSI SQL 2 Standard [Melton, 1990]. The multiuser tests establish the maximum throughput for OLTP, measure degradation in response time as a function of the system load, and provide measures of DBMS performance as a function of the workload profile. In the multiuser tests, the mixed workload tests have been specifically designed to press the state of the art in OLTP [Turbyfill, 1988]. In combination with the equivalent database size metric, some of the single-user and multiuser tests are specifically designed to press the state of software maturity in parallel and distributed systems (see Section 5.6).

A basic trade-off we confronted in the design of this benchmark was tractability versus completeness. The benchmark is not a test of SQL completeness and is not intended to model a specific workload or query mix. We have achieved tractability by setting the time limit for the benchmark at 12 hours. With respect to completeness, we prioritized the tests so that the most fundamental and important queries and workloads will be included in the 12 hour limit, as opposed to more specialized queries and workloads[2].

The $AS^3AP$ database is designed so that special queries can be created to test: (1) correct optimization in the presence of nonuniform distributions, correlated attributes, and program variables; and (2) complex queries such as relational division, join-aggregates, and recursive queries.

## 5.4    Systems Under Test

Systems tested with the $AS^3AP$ benchmark are assumed to support common data types and to provide a complete relational interface with basic integrity, consistency, and recovery mechanisms. Otherwise, they may range

---

[2] In previous work we have found that queries that take a few minutes when properly optimized, can take hours when improperly optimized [Turbyfill, 1987]. Hence, for queries to be included in the 12 hour limit, we have endeavored to design queries that detect query optimization problems without completely dominating the benchmark if something goes wrong. For the same reason, aspects of query optimization, such as prediction of selectivities in precompiled queries with program variables, are tested only once and not in every possible query.

anywhere from a single-user microcomputer DBMS to a high-performance parallel or distributed DBMS.

The only hardware normalization required is that the logical size of the AS³AP database used for the benchmark be at least equal to the logical size of physical memory on the host(s). The logical size of the AS³AP database is defined as the flat files storage requirements of the tables (see Section 5.5 below):

(number of tuples per relation) × (100 bytes/tuple) × (4 relations in database)

This condition avoids biasing the computation of the equivalent database ratio in favor of systems that incur a high storage overhead for storing a database. It also makes testing main memory database systems [Bitton and Turbyfill, 1986; Bitton, Hanrahan, and Turbyfill, 1987] with the AS³AP benchmark meaningful since the test database can be as large as physical memory.

All systems, including micro DBMSs, should be tested with the first module, the single-user tests. All multiuser DBMSs should be tested with both modules, single-user and multiuser tests. For micro DBMSs, the equivalent database ratio is computed based on the single-user tests only. For other systems, it is computed based on the single-user and multiuser tests.

## 5.5    Measurements

The only measurement required by the AS³AP benchmark is query elapsed time, within the 12 hour window limit. Other performance data on CPU and I/O utilization must be collected for in-depth analysis of a DBMS performance. However, these additional measurements are not part of the AS³AP metrics. All the AS³AP queries composing a run are embedded in a host program, along with the required timing commands. All queries are precompiled, except for the multiuser cross-section queries listed in Table 5.11 and Appendix D. For the multiuser tests, a number of programs (processes) are forked concurrently, each running a simple script. The benchmark does not use a terminal emulator and does not generate streams of job arrivals. There are no think time or presentation services included in the measurements. Preliminary queries in the single-user tests isolate the cost of different output modes. For all the other queries, the results are discarded (e.g., redirected to /dev/null in UNIX).

Because of these simplifications, the benchmark can be set up to run very easily. The tests are grouped into a number of modules, according to the component of the DBMS that they are testing. It is a strict requirement that all the basic tests (single and multiuser) run in a total time of less than 12 hours. The benchmark can be run as one large program or as a set of independent modules if the host system is not available in standalone mode for a 12-hour interval of testing.

The database is not corrupted by the test suite as long as the user runs the complete suite in the specified order. This is achieved by interleaving special queries that save deleted tuples, reinsert the deleted tuples, and restore updated tuples to their original values

# 5.6    Test Database

## 5.6.1    Database Generator

The test database is generated using DBGEN [Bitton, Millman, and Orji, 1988], a parameterized C program, that provides random generators of numbers and character strings, with a number of common distributions (uniform, normal, exponential, zipfian[3]). It is parameterized so that the range, number of unique values, mean, standard deviation, and correlation factors can be specified.

Four flat character files are generated for AS[3]AP. After these files are generated, they should be loaded into four relations in the DBMS under test. The first AS[3]AP test consists of timing this load operation. The load utility varies widely from one system to the other. Some systems provide a simple file copy utility, and others include the cost of clustering the file and building indexes.

---

[3]Zipfian distributions are a family of nonuniform distributions that have been shown to accurately model text data. In the Zipf distribution, for each value, the product of rank and frequency is a constant [Knuth, 1973]. Rank is an ordering according to frequency of occurrence. In a zipfian (or Zipflike distribution), the product of a power of the rank and frequency is a constant. The power is called the decay factor. A decay factor of zero corresponds to the uniform distribution. The distribution becomes more skewed as the decay factor increases.

All four relations have the same average tuple width and the same number of tuples. The tuple length is 100 bytes on the average. However, actual tuple lengths vary due to the variable length string attribute *address*, which has a minimum length of two bytes and a maximum length of 80 bytes (Table 5.3).

The size of the four relations can be scaled from 1 megabyte to 100 gigabytes by varying the number of tuples from 10,000 to one billion. Table 5.1 summarizes the range of logical sizes for one relation and for the database. The physical storage required to store the database in the DBMS under test may be higher due to nonstandard implementation of data types and DBMS overhead.

**Table 5.1** Scaling the AS³AP database.

| Relation Size (tuples) | Relation Size (bytes) | Logical Database Size (bytes) |
|---|---|---|
| 10,000 | 1 megabyte | 4 megabytes |
| 100,000 | 10 megabytes | 40 megabytes |
| 1,000,000 | 100 megabytes | 400 megabytes |
| 10,000,000 | 1 gigabyte | 4 gigabytes |
| 100,000,000 | 10 gigabytes | 40 gigabytes |
| 1,000,000,000 | 100 gigabytes | 400 gigabytes |

As defaults for the test database, we provide a one-megabyte base relation (for micros) and a ten-megabyte base relation (for other systems). However, in order to get optimal rating of their DBMS on the benchmark, implementors must estimate the maximum size of the test database that will enable them to meet the 12 hour requirement.

This limit on the benchmark run time determines the *equivalent database size* for the DBMS under test. When choosing the size of their test database, implementors must balance two conflicting factors: the database size and the total time required to run the benchmark. In order to obtain shorter elapsed times for the test queries, they will want to have a smaller database. However, in order to compare favorably with other systems, implementors will want to run the benchmark with the largest possible database since the AS³AP comparison metric is the *equivalent database ratio*.

## 5.6.2    Structure of the Database

The AS³AP database contains five relations. One, the *tiny* relation, is a one tuple, one column relation, used only to measure overhead. The other are the four relations generated by the database generator, with the appropriate scaling. These relations are named as follows:

1. *uniques*: a relation where all attributes have unique values.

2. *hundred*: a relation where most of the attributes have exactly 100 unique values and are correlated. This relation provides absolute selectivities of 100 and projections producing exactly 100 multi-attribute tuples.[4]

3. *tenpct*: a relation where most of the attributes have 10 percent unique values. This relation provides relative selectivities of 10 percent.

4. *updates*: a relation customized for updates. Different distributions are used, and three types of indexes are built on this relation.

The four relations have the same ten attributes (columns) with the same names and types, and if needed to comply with tuple width specification, a *fill* attribute. The attributes (Table 5.2) cover the range of commonly used data types: signed and unsigned integer, floating point, exact decimal, alphanumeric, fixed and variable length strings, and an eight-character data type. The precision of floating point numbers is within the limits of the IEEE Standard floating point number. Furthermore, only range predicates (i.e., float between 998 and 1000) are used with floating point numbers as precision differences make equality predicates (such as float = 999) less portable.

The attribute lengths sum up to 100 bytes if the DBMS supports all the required data types with a standard length (i.e., 4 byte integers, 8 byte floating points, etc.) An additional attribute, *fill*, is provided to comply with the 100 byte tuple width requirement, when the DBMS does not support one or several of the data types as specified in Table 5.2. For systems that do not support the needed data types or do not store them efficiently, portability of the test database is enforced by providing precise substitution rules. For instance, if variable length character strings are not supported, the tenth attribute, *address*, should be a fixed length character string of 80 bytes, and the tuple width will be 160 bytes. Thus a DBMS that does not support variable length strings is penalized by higher storage requirements for the test database. If another data type, say exact decimal, is not supported and the

---

[4] To support projections producing 100 single attribute tuples, it is sufficient to have an attribute with 100 unique values. In order to obtain 100 tuples by projecting on more than one attribute, we generated correlated attribute values so that projecting any subset of nonunique values also produces exactly 100 unique values.

**Table 5.2** Attribute names, types, and length (in bytes).

| Attribute Number and Name[1] | | Type | Length |
|---|---|---|---|
| 1. | key | integer | 4 |
| 2. | int | unsigned integer | 4 |
| 3. | signed | signed integer | 4 |
| 4. | float | floating point | 4 |
| 5. | double | double precision | 8 |
| 6. | decimal | exact decimal | 18.2 |
| 7. | date | datetime | 8 |
| 8. | code | alphanumeric | 10 |
| 9. | name | character string | 20 (fixed) |
| 10. | address | variable length string | 2 to 80 (20 avg) |
| 11. | fill | char string | as needed |
| | | | total = 100 (avg) |

[1]Certain DBMSs do not allow using the same attribute name in two relations. In that case, we suggest prefixing the attribute names with their relation name.

implementor substitutes a shorter type for it, then the *fill* attribute should make up for the difference in storage requirement between the required type, exact decimal, and the substitute. Only integer values are generated by the test database generator so that all predicates on a numeric value will select the same values when a 4 byte integer is substituted for any numeric type.

The SQL schema for the test database is provided in Appendix A, where the data types are as specified in Table 5.2 and the tuple width is 100 bytes. An example is also provided where substitution rules require a *fill* attribute with 6 characters.

In the test database, the values of every attribute are randomly generated, with a uniform or a nonuniform distribution. Table 5.3 contains a detailed description of the attributes, including their type, the range and distribution of their values, whether they constitute a key or a foreign key, the type of index built on the attribute, if any, and how many unique values they have. We describe indexes as: clustered or nonclustered, primary or secondary, B-tree or hashed. Indexes are specified on subsets of attributes, here called the *index key*, not to be confused with the primary key of a relation. In a *clustered index*, the index determines the physical placement of the data. For instance, in a *clustered B-tree index*, the data are sorted on the index key. In a *clustered hashed index*, the page or bucket a row is placed in is determined by a hash function on the index key. In a *nonclustered index*, the data are not sorted on the index key. The index is used to locate a pointer to a row or rows containing the index key value. In a *nonclustered B-tree index*, the leaves of the tree usually contain one instance of each unique index key paired with pointers to each row containing attributes corresponding to the index key value. In a *nonclustered hashed index*, a hash function on the indexed key is used to locate pointers to the desired row(s). A *primary index* is an index on the relation primary key. A primary index is usually a clustered index. A *secondary index* is an index on attributes other than the primary key. A secondary index is usually nonclustered.

We assume that three types of indexes are supported by the DBMS under test:

1. A *B-tree clustered* index (abbreviated *cl. btree* in Table 5.3), which, for all the relations, is built as the primary index on the *key* field.

2. A *B-tree secondary nonclustered index* (abbreviated *sec. btree* in Table 5.3).

3. A *hashed secondary nonclustered index* (abbreviated *sec. hash* in Table 5.3).

We have one composite primary clustered index on the key and code attributes of the tenpcnt relation. Multiple secondary indexes are built on the relations, as indicated in Table 5.3. A secondary hash index is built on the alphanumeric field *code* for all four relations.

With respect to physical database design, the following substitution rules apply:

1. Any desired index can be substituted for a clustered B-tree index specified in Table 5.3. If available, a clustered index must be substituted instead of a nonclustered index.

2. Any desired nonclustered index can be substituted for a nonclustered B-tree index specified in Table 5.3.

3. Any desired nonclustered index can be substituted for the nonclustered hashed index specified in Table 5.3. If available, it must be different from the nonclustered B-tree index or the index substituted for the nonclustered B-tree.

Of course, systems that automatically invert or otherwise encode all attributes or tuples are allowed to do so.

**Table 5.3**   Description of the attributes of the four test relations.

| Attribute Name | Attribute Type | Uniques | Hundred | Tenpct | Updates |
|---|---|---|---|---|---|
| 1. key *prim. key* | integer(4) | $0-10^9$ 1 missing sparse uniform *cl. btree* | 0–#tuples 1 missing dense uniform *cl. btree* | $0-10^9$ 1 missing sparse uniform *cl. btree* | 0–#tuples 1 missing dense uniform *cl. btree* |
| 2. int | integer(4) unsigned | $0-10^9$ 1 missing sparse uniform | $0-10^9$ 1 missing sparse uniform | $0-10^9$ 1 missing sparse uniform *sec. btree* | 0–#tuples 1 missing dense uniform *sec. btree* |
| 3. signed | integer(4) nullable | $\pm 5\cdot10^8$ sparse uniform | 100–199 dense uniform *foreign key for updates* | $\pm 5\cdot10^8$ sparse uniform *sec. btree* | $\pm 5\cdot 10^8$ sparse uniform |
| 4. float | real(4) | $\pm 5\cdot10^8$ zipf | $\pm 5\cdot10^8$ uniform 100 uniques | $\pm 5\cdot10^8$ uniform 10% uniques *sec. btree* | $\pm 5\cdot 10^8$ zipf 10 uniques |
| 5. double | double(8) | $\pm 10^9$ normal distn | $\pm 10^9$ uniform 100 uniques | $\pm 10^9$ uniform 10% uniques *sec. btree* | $\pm 10^9$ normal distn all unique *sec. btree* |
| 6. decim | numeric(18,2) | $\pm 10^9$ | $\pm 10^9$ 100 uniques | $\pm 10^9$ 10% uniques *sec. btree* | $\pm 10^9$ all unique *sec. btree* |
| 7. date | datetime 8 bytes | 1/1/1900– 12/1/2000 uniform | 1/1/1900– 12/1/2000 uniform | 1/1/1900– 12/1/2000 uniform | 1/1/1900– 12/1/2000 uniform |
| 8. code *cand. key* | char(10) | alphanumeric *sec. hash* | alphanumeric *sec. hash* | alphanumeric *cl. btree sec. hash* | alphanumeric *sec. hash* |
| 9. name | char(20) | alphanumeric | alphanumeric 100 uniques | alphanumeric 10 uniques *sec. hash* | alphanumeric all unique |
| 10. address | var char(80) | alphanumeric | alphanumeric 100 uniques | alphanumeric 10% uniques | alphanumeric all unique |
| 11. fill | char(?) | alphanumeric | alphanumeric | alphanumeric | alphanumeric |

The range of values for an attribute is determined by its type and by the size of the relation. For some numeric types, two types of ranges are included, *dense* and *sparse*. In a dense range, every integer value in the range is represented in the table. For instance, the *key* in the *updates* has the range of 0 to (number of tuples) in the *updates* table. In the 4 megabyte database, the *key* in the *updates* table has a range from 0 to 10,000. In the 400 gigabyte database, its range is from 0 to 1 billion. With all dense ranges, the value 1 is omitted to allow "not-found-scans" for a value within the range of attribute. These scans measure the rate at which data can be read and tested.

Controlling query selectivity requires scaling in two ways. *Fixed selectivity* queries should always select the same number of tuples, independent of database. *Relative selectivity* queries select a number of tuples proportional to the database size. Dense ranges are used to phrase queries with *fixed selectivities* independent of the database size, such as the query **o_mode_100k**:

```
select * from updates where key <=100
```

which always selects 100 tuples. In a sparse range, the range is independent of the database size. For instance, the *key* attribute in the *uniques* relation is an integer with values in the range 0 to $10^9$, to allow for up to $10^9$ distinct values. When the number of tuples needed is smaller than $10^9$, the range is *sparse* (see Table 5.3). Sparse ranges are used to phrase queries with *relative selectivities* that are a function of the database size, such as the query **sel_10pct_cl** :

```
select key,int,signed,code,double,name
from uniques
where key <= 100000000
```

which always selects 10 percent of the tuples in the *uniques* relation.

The range and distribution of attributes with the same name may be different in the different relations, in order to provide the functionality required by the queries. For instance, the range of the *key* attribute in *uniques* is 0 to $10^9$ and it is sparse. In the *hundred* relation, the range for the same attribute is 0 to number of tuples and it is dense (except for the value 1, which is missing); And the *double* attribute has a normal distribution in the *uniques* relation but a uniform distribution in the *hundred* relation.

Ranges are defined for all ten attributes so that scaling of the database is straightforward, and the queries are not changed when the database is scaled. Once the number of tuples in the database relations is specified ($10^4$ to $10^9$), the generator program will generate the appropriate attribute values. *The queries are designed to automatically scale with the database.* In particular, the attribute ranges are specified so that the query selectivities remain unchanged and all the required constant values used in the predicates remain unchanged when the relation size is scaled.

# 5.7    Single-User Tests

Single-user tests are logically divided into operational issues and user queries. Operational issues include load, backup, building indexes, and a check of referential integrity. Queries include retrievals, single-tuple updates, and bulk updates. All are run in standalone mode, and the elapsed time for each test or query is measured. In our single-user tests, as the database gets larger, systems will be penalized if they do not use parallel and distributed algorithms in the execution of utilities or large retrievals. However, some of the simple queries, that access only a few database pages, will be fairly insensitive to database size as long as relevant indexes remain in memory. Our purpose is to identify systems that are truly capable of supporting large databases and processing large quantities of data. This is in contrast to the DebitCredit benchmark, where systems that do not employ parallel or distributed algorithms in the execution of a single query can perform quite well, both in elapsed time and in cost/performance metrics. What the DebitCredit benchmark does not show the user is the time required to load, backup, or restore the database or how any query that required processing large amounts of data, such as a batch or report query, would perform. A system could perform the random accesses required to perform the Debit-Credit benchmark superbly and still be completely inadequate when performing other functions expected of a relational database system.

Table 5.4 shows an estimate of the time that might be required to access data (sequential or random). By way of illustration, assume a relatively rapid time of 20 milliseconds for each random access to 8 Kbytes, and assume sequential accesses proceed at the rate of 3 million bytes per second. These are optimistic numbers for serial access to data at the application level. At 20 milliseconds per 8K of data, it would take 2.44 seconds to

**Table 5.4** Time to access large amounts of data by access type.

| Table Size (in bytes) | Random Access (at 8KB / 20 msec) | Sequential Access (at 3 MB/sec) |
|---|---|---|
| 1 megabyte | 2.44 seconds | 0.33 seconds |
| 1 gigabyte | 40.69 minutes | 5.56 minutes |
| 1 terabyte | 28.26 days | 3.86 days |

process a megabyte of data and 28.26 days to process a terabyte of data. With a sequential access rate of 3 megabytes per second, it would take 0.33 seconds to access one megabyte of data and 3.86 days to access a terabyte of data. Table 5.5 illustrates the fact that queries that process large amounts of data cannot be efficiently executed without the use of distributed and parallel algorithms for the execution of a single query. This is referred to as intra-query parallelism, as opposed to inter-query parallelism where several queries are executed in parallel. In practice, when new parallel and distributed architectures are implemented, the first software ported to the distributed or parallel hardware supports inter-query parallelism by dedicating a different CPU to each query. Systems capable of intra-query parallelism represent the current state-of-the-art in software maturity.

Below, the operational tests are described first. Then the queries, organized according to function, are described. The tests and queries expressed in SQL are listed in Appendix B. The order in which Section 5.7 and Appendix B list the queries is not the order in which they are run in the benchmark. AS$^3$AP uses a particular ordering of the queries to prevent the data of one query to be memory resident as a consequence of the previous query. It addition, the query order is designed to facilitate memory residence of relevant indexes when this is appropriate. A run-time sequence has been determined that differs from the logical organization presented below. The actual AS$^3$AP run sequence is shown in Appendix C.

Queries and operational tests are interleaved so that each query will access a relation different from the one(s) accessed by the previous query. This avoids lengthy operations that would otherwise be needed to flush the buffers. The probability of cache hits in main memory is also reduced as the database gets larger.

## 5.7.1    Operational Issues

After the AS$^3$AP database is created and the schema specified, the first measurement performed is the time to load the four data files generated by the generator program into four DBMS relations. The data files may be loaded from disk or tape. The load time should include any time to create catalogs, build the clustered index, and update table statistics from the loaded data. Then, one of the relations, the *updates* relation, is backed up to tape or other archive device, and the backup time is measured. A recovery of the *updates* relation is included in the multiuser tests.

We measure the time to build indexes. Usually, the load utility will cluster the file with respect to the declared primary key and build the appropriate primary index. In the event that the load does not include this function, the time for building a clustered index should be measured and added to the load time. Building the required indexes (clustered indexes if not handled by the load, and secondary indexes as needed by the test queries) is interleaved with the queries. In the *uniques, hundred,* and *updates* relations, the clustered index is on the *key* attribute. The *tenpct* relation has a composites primary clustered index on the *key* and *code* attributes. We measure the time for building two types of secondary indexes. For example, we build a secondary B-tree index on the integer attribute *int* of the *tenpct* relation; we build a secondary hashed index on the *code* attribute of each relation: *uniques, hundred, updates,* and *tenpct.*

A table scan is included to test sequential I/O performance (**table_ scan**):

```
select * from uniques where int=1
```

Since the value 1 is not present and no index is built on the *int* column, this query scans the entire table but retrieves no tuple. Partial table scans that retrieve 100 and 1000 sequential tuples to the screen or to a file are also included in the tests of output mode (see Output Mode Queries below).

## 5.7.2   Test Queries

### Output Mode Queries

The first set of tests exercises the three different output modes that a query may use. Results of a query may be retrieved to the screen; stored in a file; or stored in a database relation. We measure the overhead associated with each of these three output modes, per query (selection on *tiny* relation) and as a function of the amount of data retrieved (1K, 10K, or 100K bytes).[5] The output mode queries are briefly described in Table 5.5. Measurements for these queries and a comparison with the table scans provide a precise estimate for the time required by the DBMS to format, display, and store the result of a query. After this first set of tests, the results of all queries are discarded, so that a query elapsed time measures the effectiveness of query optimization independently of the output mode. In order to further normalize the measurements of query elapsed time, the width of the result tuple is kept equal to 50 bytes for most test queries.

**Table 5.5**  Output mode queries, each query repeated with output to screen, file, and relation.

| Query Name | Description |
|---|---|
| **o_mode_tiny** | selection on tiny relation |
| **o_mode_1K** | selection of 10 tuples |
| **o_mode_10K** | selection of 100 tuples |
| **o_mode_100K** | selection of 1000 tuples |

## Selections

The speed at which a DBMS can process a selection query depends primarily on the storage organization of the relation and on the selectivity factor of the query. These two parameters are controlled in our tests for selections. There are seven selection queries, as listed in Table 5.6. A selection query selects one tuple, or a *range* of 100 tuples, or 10 percent of the tuples. For each of these three selectivities, the query comes in two versions: one version uses a clustered index, and the other uses a secondary B-tree index.

**Table 5.6**  Selection queries.

| Query Name | Description |
|---|---|
| **sel_1_cl** | select 1 tuple using clustered index |
| **sel_1_ncl** | select 1 tuple using secondary hashed index |
| **sel_100_cl** | select 100 tuples using clustered index |
| **sel_100_ncl** | select 100 tuples using B-tree secondary index |
| **sel_10p_cl** | select 10% tuples using clustered index |
| **sel_10p_ncl** | select 10% tuples using B-tree secondary index |
| **variable_select** | range select predicated on program variable |

---

[5]In this context, 1K=1,000 bytes exactly. 1K corresponds to ten average logical tuples. The actual data moved may vary with implementations.

Finally, one selection query, variable_select, is a range selection with a secondary B-tree index, where the range is defined by a program variable. This query tests the ability of the query optimizer to correctly choose between a scan or the use of an index at run time.[6] In Appendix C, which specifies the run sequence of queries, the variable_select query is executed twice in a row, first with a low selectivity, when a nonclustered index should be used to evaluate the selection predicate, and second with a high selectivity, when the relation should be scanned to evaluate the predicate. Putting the two queries right after each other detects whether program variables are properly handled without overweighing the benchmark with two unnecessary relation scans. If the first variable_select is improperly executed by scanning the entire relation, the second will be relatively fast because the table should be memory resident for the second scan.

## Joins

The join queries test how efficiently the system makes use of available indexes and how query complexity affects the relative performance of the DBMS. There are eight join queries, differing in the number of relations that they reference and in the availability and type of index available on the join attribute (see Table 5.7). Seven of the eight queries are 1:1 joins and produce one result tuple. One query, Join_1_1pct, is a 1 to many join of two relations on the key attribute, and it produces one percent result tuples,

**Table 5.7** Join queries.

| Query Name | Number of Tables | Index Available | Tuples Retrieved |
|---|---|---|---|
| join_2 | 2 | no index | 1 |
| join_2_cl | 2 | clustered index | 1 |
| join_2_ncl | 2 | non-clustered hashed index | 1 |
| join_3_cl | 3 | clustered index | 1 |
| join_3_ncl | 3 | non-clustered hashed index | 1 |
| join_4_cl | 4 | clustered index | 1 |
| join_4_ncl | 4 | non-clustered hashed index | 1 |
| join_1_1pct | 2 | clustered index | 1% tuples |

---

[6] Three queries with program variables are included: variable_select, and the background queries in the multiuser tests, ir_select and oltp_update (Section 5.8 and Appendix D). Other tests isolate other access methods or other aspects of query optimization. We do not wish to confound those tests with improper handling of program variables, should it occur.

e.g., 100 out of 10,000 typles in the one megabyte relation. (Join_2) constitutes a simple test of performance on ad-hoc queries. When no index is available, a query optimizer should never use a nested loops join algorithm because of its $n^2$ complexity. Instead, it should sort or hash the operand relations on the join attribute(s) and then merge-join them in one pass. Thus, if correctly optimized, this query measures the efficiency of a basic access method—sorting or hashing; otherwise, it will exhibit very poor performance.

Use of the available indexes in the join algorithm is tested with three types of indexes: the primary clustered index, a secondary hashed index, and a secondary B-tree index. In each case the appropriate type of index is available on the join attribute in all the operand relations.

Query complexity is modeled by increasing the number of tables referenced from two to four. Although most query optimizers will use the correct access plan on two-way joins with a clustered or a nonclustered index, often they will not correctly optimize three and four-way joins because of the higher complexity involved in evaluating all the possible access methods.

### Projections

Most of the processing time for a projection is incurred by the elimination of duplicate tuples introduced when projecting on nonkey attributes. This makes the cost of a projection much higher than the cost of a selection query with similar selectivity. Duplicate elimination is usually performed by sorting. Thus tests of projections also provide a test of the sort utility used by the DBMS.

There are two test queries for projections (Table 5.8). One query projects the *hundred* relation on two columns, corresponding to a signed integer and a variable length character attributes, and it produces 100 result tuples. Thus it provides a test of how efficiently the DBMS handles two data types in a complex operation such as sorting. The second query projects on one column, corresponding to a decimal attribute, and has a 10 percent selectivity.

**Table 5.8**   Projection queries.

| Query Name | Description | Selectivity |
|------------|-------------|-------------|
| **proj_100** | project on *address* and *signed* attr. | 100 tuples |
| **proj_10pct** | project on *decim* attr. | 10% tuples |

## Aggregates

Six tests of aggregates are provided (Table 5.9). The first is a simple scalar aggregate, computing the minimum of the *key* value. The correct query execution strategy for this aggregate consists of looking up the first value stored in the clustered index. Thus the elapsed time should be comparable to the one tuple selection with a clustered index (sel_1_cl). The second query is a function aggregate, which computes the minimum value of *key* partitioned into 100 partitions.

The other four queries are more complex. The info_retrieval query is designed to test whether systems can use bit or pointer intersection algorithms for indexes to avoid a relation scan to evaluate complex predicates. The simple_report query is a scalar aggregate on the result of a 1:1 join of the keys of updates and hundred relations, with a 10 percent selection on the updates relations. The subtotal_report and total_report queries use a view that is a 1:1 join of the key of the updates and hundred relation. The SQL standard does not support the combination of subtotals and totals in the same query. One would expect this ability in a report generator. Hence the selection/aggregate function portion of the report has been broken into two queries. Any system that has a more sophisticated report generator is allowed to rephrase and execute the two queries (subtotal_report and total_report) as a single query using the report generation facility.

## Updates

The update tests are designed to check both integrity and performance. To check integrity, one query attempts to append a tuple with a duplicate key value, and a second attempts to violate referential integrity by updating a field that is a foreign key. Both queries apply to the *updates* table.

**Table 5.9** Aggregate queries.

| Query Name | Description | Result |
|---|---|---|
| scal_ag | minimum key | min value (1) |
| func_agg | minimum key grouped by name | 100 min values |
| info_retrieval | select w/ complex predicate, then min(key) | 1 |
| simple_report | select avg(x) where x in (select 10%) | 1 |
| subtotal_report | 10% select on view, min(a),max(a),avg(a), count(b), group by code,int | 100 |
| total_report | 10% select on view,min(a),max(a),avg(a), count(b) | 1 |

**Table 5.10** Update tests.

| Test Name | Description | Tuples Updated |
|---|---|---|
| append_duplicate | insert duplicate key | append 1, delete 1 |
| refer_integrity | insert invalid foreign key | insert 1, delete 1, insert 1 |
| update_key | insert middle, last key values | insert 2, modify 2, delete 2 |
| update_btree | 1 tuple updates of B-tree index | insert 1, modify 1, delete 1 |
| update_alpha | 1 tuple update of index on alpha field | insert 1, modify 1, delete 1 |
| bulk_append | bulk insertion in mid key range | insert 1000 tuples |
| bulk_modify | bulk update in mid key range | modify 1000 tuples |
| bulk_delete | bulk delete in mid key range | delete 1000 tuples |

To evaluate performance, tests that measure the overhead involved in updating each type of index are provided. Single-tuple updates and bulk updates are also provided. The single-tuple updates are grouped into three tests. Each consists of building an index, appending a tuple, modifying it, and deleting it. First the updates are performed with the *updates* relation having only one index, the clustered index on the key. Then a B-tree secondary index is built on *updates.int*, and the same updates are repeated. Finally a hashed (or another available type of index) secondary index is built on *updates.code*, and the updates repeated. Each of the three tests isolates and measures the overhead involved in maintaining the corresponding type of index.

The bulk updates include an append, a modify, and a delete of 1,000 consecutive tuples, located in the middle of the *updates* relation. The update tests are sequenced so that the database is restored to its initial state when all the tests are completed. Table 5.10 describes the update tests.

## 5.8 Multiuser Tests

There are four multiuser tests, each modeling a different workload profile:

1. An OLTP test, where all users execute a single-row update, oltp_update, on the same relation. This update randomly selects a single row

using a clustered index and updates a nonindexed attribute. It is executed with repeatable access (Level 3 isolation).[7]

2. An information retrieval (IR) test, where all users execute a single-row selection query, ir_select, on the same relation. This query selects a single row using a clustered index.  It is executed with browse access (Level 0 isolation).

3. A mixed workload IR Test, where one user executes a cross section of ten update and retrieval queries, and all the others execute the same IR query as in the second test.

4. A mixed workload OLTP Test, where one user executes a cross section of ten update and retrieval queries, and all the others execute the same OLTP query as in the first test.

The first two tests can be used to measure the throughput as a function of the number of concurrent database users; the third measures the degradation of response time for a cross section of queries caused by system load. In order to make the benchmark tractable, and to make the results meaningful with respect to the benchmark time limit and the equivalent database size metric, we have decided on strict guidelines for the execution of the multiuser tests, including the specification of the number of users according to an unambiguous formula.[8] The number of users is always equal to:

$$\frac{\text{logical database size in bytes}}{4 \text{ megabytes}}$$

Hence, for the 4 megabyte database, the number of users is 1; for the 40 megabyte database, the number of users is 10. This rule for determining the multi-programming level ensures that the system will be tested in multiuser mode. The mixed workloads contain some queries that are relegated to offline batch processing in current systems due to performance problems.

---

[7]In the SQL standard, there are four isolation levels called 0, 1, 2, and 3. SQL 2 level 3 is the default and is known as repeatable reads in DB2 and other systems—it gives complete isolation from concurrent updates by other transactions. SQL 2 level 1 is called cursor stability in IBM's DB2 and avoids dirty reads but allows nonrepeatable reads. SQL 2 level 0 allows dirty reads and is called browse access in Tandem's NonStop SQL. If a lower degree of isolation is not supported, then the higher degree must be used.  For example, cursor stability would be used in lieu of browse mode isolation for a DB2 system.

[8]Originally, we wanted to allow any number of users that maximizes throughput. However, when no think times are used, maximum throughput on systems we tested was achieved with only a few users—sometimes just one user. So this formula was developed to prevent single-user versions of the multiuser tests. It is always instructive to plot throughputs and response times from multiuser tests as a function of the number of users.

Hence, given the current state of commercial software, even with a low number of users, the mixed workload tests already press the state of the art in OLTP.

In the cross section (Table 5.11), the retrieval queries range from simple selections of one row to a simple report query. We test the ability of the system to provide different isolation levels dynamically by executing the selection query with browse, stable, and repeatable access. All update queries in the cross section should be executed with repeatable access (Level 3 isolation). Levels of isolation required for each cross section query are shown in Table 5.11. Also included in the cross section are four large transactions that update 100 tuples. With one of these large transactions, we check for correctness in aborting a transaction.

At the end of the multiuser tests, correctness of the bulk sequential and random updates is checked by comparing the updated relation with the temporary tables created by queries 5 and 6 (Table 5.11) from the cross section. The execution order for the multiuser tests is:

1. Backup the updates relation, including indexes, to tape or other device. This is done early on. See Appendix C.

2. Run IR (Mix 1) test for 15 minutes.

3. Measure throughput in IR test for 5 minutes.

4. Replace one background IR script with the cross-section script. This is the mixed workload IR test (Mix 3). This step is variable length.

5. Run queries to check correctness of the sequential and random bulk updates.

**Table 5.11** Ten cross-section queries.

| Query Name | Description | Isolation Level |
|---|---|---|
| 1. **o_mode_tiny** | overhead query | 3 |
| 2. **o_mode_100k** | retrieves 1000 tuples (100K bytes) | 2 |
| 3. **select_1_ncl** | 1 tuple select, executed at 3 isolation levels | 0,1,3 |
| 4. **simple_report** | select-join-aggregate | 2 |
| 5. **sel_100_seq** | select 100 clustered tuples into temporary | 3 |
| 6. **sel_100_rand** | select 100 random tuples into temporary | 3 |
| 7. **mod_100_seq_abort** | update 100 sequential tuples, abort | 3 |
| 8. **mod_100_rand** | update 100 random | 3 |
| 9. **unmod_100_seq** | undo previous sequential update | 3 |
| 10. **unmod_100_rand** | undo previous random update | 3 |

6. Recover the updates relation from the backup tape (Step 1) and log (from Steps 2, 3, 4, and 5).

7. Perform correctness checks, checkmod_100_seq and checkmod _100_rand. Remove temporary tables: sel100seq and sel100rand.

8. Run OLTP test for 15 minutes.

9. Measure throughput in IR test for 5 minutes.

10. Replace one background OLTP script with the cross-section script. This is the mixed workload OLTP test (Mix 4). This step is variable length.

11. Perform correctness checks, checkmod_100_seq and checkmod _100_rand. Remove temporary tables: sel100seq and sel100rand.

The order is specified to give the system time to warm up before throughput is measured without allowing an arbitrary time interval for reaching steady state. The recovery test is performed after the mixed workload IR test in order to allow testing recovery without having too many queries in the log to rollforward.

# 5.9    Summary

In this chapter, we have described a scaleable and portable benchmark for use in comparing relational database systems across architectures and hardware capabilities. Portability is achieved by using industry standards where appropriate. The ANSI SQL standard data definition language and query language are used in the specification of the attributes and queries.

There are five relations in the test database. One is a very small relation used only to measure overhead. The other four are relations with ten attributes and a scaleable number of tuples. The test queries are designed so that they need not be changed when the size of the database is scaled. The benchmark consists of two modules: single-user tests and multiuser tests.

The main AS³AP metric is the *equivalent database size*, which is the maximum size of the test database for which the single-user and multiuser AS³AP tests can be completed in under 12 hours. The single-user tests include operational functions, such as a database load and building indexes, and a complete set of relational queries and updates. The multiuser tests model mixed database workloads, including on-line transaction processing, information retrieval, and long transactions. A number of DBMS vendors have requested a copy of the benchmark and have ported AS$^3$AP or some portion of it on their own. Many reported difficulties in running the multiuser tests. Further work would be required to make the database generator portable and to develop script models for the multiuser tests.

Gabrielle Gagnon from *PC Magazine* ported the AS$^3$AP benchmark to a DBMS on a Compaq 385 PC. Eighteen vendors used this benchmark on their respective DMBS and results were published May 28, 1991 by *PC Magazine.*

## 5.10   Acknowledgments

Many people have contributed to this work. First, Jim Gray deserves a special acknowledgement for following the development of AS$^3$AP from the very beginning and contributing many ideas, comments, and criticisms. The design of the test database and the mixed workloads greatly benefitted from discussions with Andrea Borr, Jim Gray, and Franco Putzolu at Tandem Computers. The Argonne National Laboratories provided partial funding for the development and implementation of the benchmark, as well as a test environment. Sohail Merchant implemented the benchmark at AT&T in Naperville, on Informix, and provided useful comments on an early version of this chapter.

## References

Anon et al. (1985). A Measure of Transaction Processing Power. *Readings in Database Systems*, edited by M. Stonebraker. San Mateo, CA: Morgan Kaufmann.

Bitton, D., DeWitt, D.J.,& Turbyfill, C. (1983). Benchmarking database systems, a systematic approach. *Proceedings of the Ninth International Conference on Very Large Data Bases.*

Bitton, D., Hanrahan, M., & Turbyfill, C. (1987). Performance of complex queries in main memory database systems. *Proceedings of the International Conference on Third Data Engineering,* Los Angeles.

Bitton, D., Millman, J., & Orji, C. (1988). *Program documentation for DBGEN, a test database generator*. Chicago: University of Illinois.

Bitton, D. & Turbyfill, C. (1985). Evaluation of a backend database machine. *Proceedings of HICSS-18*.

Bitton, D. & Turbyfill, C. (1986). Main memory database support for office systems: a performance study. *IFIP TC8 Conference on Methods and Tools for Office Systems*, Pisa, Italy.

Bitton, D. & Turbyfill, C. (1988). A retrospective on the Wisconsin benchmark. In M. Stonebraker (Ed.), *Readings in Database Systems*. San Mateo, CA: Morgan Kaufmann.

Boral, H. & DeWitt, D.J. (1984). A methodology for database system performance. *Proceedings of ACM Sigmod 1984*.

DeWitt, D.J. (1979). DIRECT—a multiprocessor organization for supporting relational database management systems. *IEEE Transactions on Computers, C-28*(6).

Kitsuregawa, M., Tanaka, H., & Moto-Oka, T. (1983). Architecture and performance of database machine GRACE. *Proceedings of the International Conference on Parallel Processing*. St. Charles, IL.

Knuth, D.E. (1973). *The art of computer programming*, Vol. 3. Reading, MA: Addison-Wesley.

Melton, J. (Ed.). (1990) Database language SQL 2 (ISO working draft. (ANSI X3H2-90-264). Washington, D.C.: American National Standards Institute.

Rubenstein, W.B., Kubicar, M.S., & Cattell, R.G. (1987). Benchmarking simple database operations. *Proceedings of ACM Sigmod 1987*.

Stonebraker, M. (1986). *The Ingres papers*. Reading, MA: Addison-Wesley.

Turbyfill, C. (1987). Comparative benchmarking of relational database systems. Unpublished doctoral dissertation, TR 87-871, Cornell University.

Turbyfill, C. (1988). Disk performance and access patterns for mixed database workloads. *Database Engineering, 11*(1).

Turbyfill, C., Orji, C., & Bitton, D. (1989). ASAP: A comparative relational database benchmark. *Proceedings Compcon 1989*.

Yao, S.B., Hevner, A.R., & Myers, H.Y. (1987). Analysis of database system architectures using benchmarks. *IEEE Transactions on Software Engineering, 13*(6) pp. 709–725.

# Appendix A. SQL Schema

```
CREATE TABLE    uniques(
        key     INTEGER (4)         NOT NULL,
        int     INTEGER (4)         NOT NULL,
        signed  INTEGER (4)                 ,
        float   REAL (4)            NOT NULL,
        double  DOUBLE (8)          NOT NULL,
        decim   NUMERIC(18,2)       NOT NULL,
        date    DATETIME (8)        NOT NULL,
        code    CHAR (10)           NOT NULL,
        name    CHAR(20)            NOT NULL,
        address VARCHAR(20)         NOT NULL,
        PRIMARY KEY (key)                   )

CREATE TABLE    hundred(
        key     INTEGER (4)         NOT NULL,
        int     INTEGER (4)         NOT NULL,
        signed  INTEGER (4)                 ,
        float   REAL (4)            NOT NULL,
        double  DOUBLE (8)          NOT NULL,
        decim   NUMERIC(18,2)       NOT NULL,
        date    DATETIME (8)        NOT NULL,
        code    CHAR (10)           NOT NULL,
        name    CHAR(20)            NOT NULL,
        address VARCHAR(20)         NOT NULL,
        PRIMARY KEY (key)                   ,
        FOREIGN KEY (signed) REFERENCES UPDATES)

CREATE TABLE    tenpct(
        key     INTEGER (4)         NOT NULL,
        int     INTEGER (4)         NOT NULL,
        signed  INTEGER (4)                 ,
        float   REAL (4)            NOT NULL,
        double  DOUBLE (8)          NOT NULL,
        decim   NUMERIC(18,2)       NOT NULL,
        date    DATETIME (8)        NOT NULL,
        code    CHAR (10)           NOT NULL,
        name    CHAR(20)            NOT NULL,
        address VARCHAR(20)         NOT NULL,
        PRIMARY KEY (key,code)      )
```

```
CREATE TABLE    updates(
        key     INTEGER (4)         NOT NULL,
        int     INTEGER (4)         NOT NULL,
        signed  INTEGER (4)                  ,
        float   REAL (4)            NOT NULL,
        double  DOUBLE (8)          NOT NULL,
        decim   NUMERIC(18,2)       NOT NULL,
        date    DATETIME (8)        NOT NULL,
        code    CHAR (10)           NOT NULL,
        name    CHAR(20)            NOT NULL,
        address VARCHAR(20)         NOT NULL,
        PRIMARY KEY (key)                   )

CREATE TABLE    tiny(
        key     INTEGER (4)         NOT NULL,
        PRIMARY KEY (key)                   )
```

## Comments

In addition to a clustered index on the primary key, a number of secondary indexes must be built (see Table 5.3). The run sequence in Appendix C interleaves the commands to build indexes with queries in the single-user tests, as a way to flush the buffers without incurring additional overhead. Schema declarations may have to be modified by using a longer *address* field and/or adding a fill field. Systems that do not support variable-length strings should be penalized by carrying the maximum length of the *address* field, 80 bytes, instead of the average 20 bytes. Some systems may also not support other data types in the form we have shown in the above schema representation.

The following example shows how the schema should be modified for a system that does not support variable-length strings and decimal and date types as specified. In this example, the 8 byte MONEY data type is substituted for the 18 byte NUMERIC data type, and the 12 byte DATE is substituted for the 8 byte DATETIME. The MONEY and DATE data types combined occupy 20 bytes, whereas the NUMERIC and DATETIME data types combined occupy 26 bytes. As the substituted data types occupy 6 fewer bytes than the standard data types, the *fill* attribute is set to 6 bytes.

```
CREATE TABLE    uniques(
        key     INTEGER4        NOT NULL,
        int     INTEGER4        NOT NULL,
        signed  INTEGER4               ,
        decim   MONEY           NOT NULL,
        date    DATE            NOT NULL,
        float   FLOAT4          NOT NULL,
        double  FLOAT8          NOT NULL,
        code    C10             NOT NULL,
        name    C20             NOT NULL,
        address TEXT(80)        NOT NULL,
        fill    C6                     )
```

# Appendix B. Single-User Tests

## Operational Issues

```
load:
    /* file names for flat files generated by db generator are asap */
    /* .uniques, etc.   */
    INSERT INTO  uniques select * from asap.uniques
    INSERT INTO  hundred select * from asap.hundred
    INSERT INTO  tenpct  select * from asap.tenpct
    INSERT INTO  updates select * from asap.updates
    INSERT INTO  tiny    select * from asap.tiny
```

```
if load operation does not build clustered index on key, then build clustered index
on key attribute of uniques relation:
    CREATE UNIQUE INDEX uniques_idx ON  uniques (key) CLUSTER
```

```
build secondary B-tree index:
    CREATE  INDEX tenpct_int_bt ON tenpct (int)   BTREE
```

```
build secondary hashed index:
    CREATE  INDEX tenpct_code_h ON tenpct (code)   HASH
```

```
similar indexes are built on other relations (See Table 5.3 and Appendix C).
```

```
table_scan:
    select * from uniques where int = 1
```

## Queries Testing Output Modes (Table 5.5)

### Each Query Repeated three times: output to screen, file, and relation

```
    o_mode_tiny:
        select * from tiny
    o_mode_1k:
        select * from updates where key <= 10
    o_mode_10k:
        select * from hundred where key <= 100
    o_mode_100k:
        select * from hundred where key <= 1000
```

## Selections (Table 5.6)

```
sel_1_cl:
    select key, int, signed, code, double, name
    from updates
    where key = 1000
sel_1_ncl:
    select key, int, signed, code, double, name
    from updates
    where code = 'BENCHMARKS'
sel_10pct_cl:
    select key, int, signed, code, double, name
    from uniques
    where key <= 100000000
sel_100_cl:
    select key, int, signed, code, double, name
    from updates
    where key <= 100
sel_100_ncl:
    select key, int, signed, code, double, name
    from updates
    where int <= 100
sel_10pct_ncl:
    select key, int, signed, code, double, name
    from tenpct
    where name = 'THE+ASAP+BENCHMARKS+'
variable_select:
    select key, int, signed, code, double, name
    from tenpct
    where signed < :prog_var
    variable_select: with low selectivity, index should be used:
    Set :prog_var = -500,000,000.
    variable_select: with high selectivity, index should not be used:
    Set :prog_var = -250,000,000.
```

# Joins (Table 5.7)

```
join_2_cl:
    select uniques.signed, uniques.name,
           hundred.signed, hundred.name
    from uniques, hundred
    where uniques.key = hundred.key
      and uniques.key = 1000
join_2_n_cl:
    select uniques.signed, uniques.name,
           hundred.signed, hundred.name
    from uniques, hundred
    where uniques.code = hundred.code
      and uniques.code = 'BENCHMARKS'
join_2:
    select distinct uniques.signed, uniques.name,
           hundred.signed, hundred.name
    from uniques, hundred
    where uniques.address = hundred.address
      and uniques.address = 'SILICON VALLEY'
join_3_cl:
    select uniques.signed, uniques.date,
           hundred.signed, hundred.date,
           tenpct.signed, tenpct.date
    from uniques, hundred, tenpct
    where uniques.key = hundred.key
      and uniques.key = tenpct.key
      and uniques.key = 1000
join_3_ncl:
    select uniques.signed, uniques.date,
           hundred.signed, hundred.date,
           tenpct.signed, tenpct.date
    from uniques, hundred, tenpct
    where uniques.code = hundred.code
      and uniques.code = tenpct.code
      and uniques.code = 'BENCHMARKS'
join_4_cl:
    select uniques.date, hundred.date,
           tenpct.date, updates.date
    from uniques, hundred, tenpct, updates
    where uniques.key = hundred.key
      and uniques.key = tenpct.key
      and uniques.key = updates.key
      and uniques.key = 1000
```

```
join_4_ncl:
    select uniques.date, hundred.date,
           tenpct.date,  updates.date
    from uniques, hundred, tenpct, updates
    where uniques.code = hundred.code
      and uniques.code = tenpct.code
      and uniques.code = updates.code
      and uniques.code = 'BENCHMARKS'
join_1_1pct:
    select uniques.key, uniques.name,
           tenpct.key, tenpct.signed
    from uniques, tenpct
    where uniques.key >= 1,000,000,000
      and tenpct.key <= uniques.key
      and tenpct.key >= 990,000,000
```

## Projections (Table 5.8)

```
proj_100:
    select distinct address, signed from hundred
proj_10pct:
    select distinct decim from tenpct
```

## Aggregates (Table 5.9)

```
scal_agg:
    select min(key) from uniques
func_agg:
    select min(key)
    from hundred
    group by name
info_retrieval:
    select count(key)
    from tenpct
    where name = 'THE+ASAP+BENCHMARKS+'
      and int <= 100000000
      and signed between 1 and 99999999
      and not (float between -450000000 and 450000000)
      and double > 600000000
      and decim  < -600000000
```

```
simple_report:
    select avg(updates.decim)              .
    from updates
    where updates.key in
        (select updates.key
        from updates, hundred
        where hundred.key = updates.key
          and updates.decim > 980000000)
create_view
    create view
        reportview(key,signed,date,decim,name,code,int) as
            select updates.key,   updates.signed,
                    updates.date, updates.decim,
                    hundred.name, hundred.code, hundred.int
            from updates, hundred
            where updates.key = hundred.key
subtotal_report
    select avg(signed), min(signed), max(signed),
        max(date), min(date),
        count(distinct name), count(name),
        code, int
    from reportview
    where decim > 980000000
    group by code, int
total_report
    select avg(signed), min(signed), max(signed),
        max(date), min(date),
        count(distinct name), count(name),
        count(code), count(int)
    from reportview
    where decim > 980000000
```

## Updates (Table 5.10)

```
append_duplicate:
/* try to append duplicate key value */
    insert into updates values
        (6000, 0, 60000, 39997.90, 50005.00, 50005.00,
        '11/10/85', 'CONTROLLER', 'ALICE IN WONDERLAND',
        'UNIVERSITY OF ILLINOIS AT CHICAGO ')
remove_duplicate:
    delete updates where key = 6000 and int = 0
```

```
Test of referential integrity:
    /* make temp relation for restore */
    create table integrity_temp like hundred :
    insert into integrity_temp
        select *
        from hundred
        where int = 0
integrity_test:
    update hundred
    set signed =  -500000000
    where int = 0

integrity_restore:
/* restore hundred relation in case test failed */
    delete hundred where int = 0
    insert into hundred select * from integrity_temp
```

# One Tuple Updates, in Middle and End of Key Range

```
app_t_mid:
    insert into updates
     values  (5005, 5005, 50005, 50005.00, 50005.00,
            50005.00,'1/1/88',  'CONTROLLER',
            'ALICE IN WONDERLAND',
            'UNIVERSITY OF ILLINOIS AT CHICAGO ' )
mod_t_mid:
    update updates
    set key = -5000
    where key = 5005
del_t_mid:
    delete updates
    where key = -5000
app_t_end:
    insert into updates
    values  (1000000001, 50005, 50005, 50005.00, 50005.00,
            50005.00, '1/1/88', 'CONTROLLER',
            'ALICE IN WONDERLAND',
            'UNIVERSITY OF ILLINOIS AT CHICAGO ' )
mod_t_end:
    update updates
    set key = -1000
    where key = 1000000001
del_t_end:
    delete updates where key = -1000
```

```
/* test other indexes updates */
/* test b-tree secondary index */
app_t_mid (as above)
mod_t_int:
    update updates
    set int = 50015
    where key = 5005
del_t_mid (as above)
/* test hash index on alphanumeric field */
app_t_mid (as above)
mod_t_cod:
    update updates
    set code = 'SQL+GROUPS'
    where key = 5005
del_t_mid (as above)
```

## /* Bulk Updates */

```
bulk_save:
    insert into saveupdates
    select * from updates
    where key between 5000 and 5999
bulk_append:
    insert into updates
    select * from saveupdates
bulk_modify:
    update updates
    set key = key - 100000
    where key between 5000 and  5999
bulk_delete:
    delete updates
    where key < 0
```

# Appendix C. Run Sequence For Single-User Tests

This appendix lists the single-user tests in the order that they should be executed. This order is different from the logical order in which queries were listed in Appendix B because the operational tests and queries are interleaved in a way that prevents data from remaining in the buffer. The sequence below should be embedded in a host program, with one timing statement per test. The host program should be run in stand-alone mode. The embedded timing statements will provide stand-alone response time of precompiled queries.

Create and load database with clustered index on primary keys if provided by load utility.

Backup *updates* relation.

If index not built during load, build primary clustered index on key attribute of *updates.*

`o_mode_tiny` into a relation.

If index not built during load, build primary clustered composite index on key and code attributes of *tenpcnt* relation.

`o_mode_tiny` into a file.

`sel_1_cl`

If index not built during load, build primary clustered index on key attribute of *hundred* relation.

`o_mode_tiny` to the screen.

Build secondary nonclustered B-tree index on int attribute of *tenpcnt.*

`o_mode_100k` into a file.

If index not built during load, build primary clustered index on key of *uniques* relation.

`o_mode_1k` into a relation.

Build secondary nonclustered B-tree index on signed attribute in *tenpcnt.*

Build secondary nonclustered hashed index on code attribute of *uniques.*

`o_mode_1k` into a file.

Build secondary nonclustered B-tree index on double attribute of *tenpcnt* .

Build secondary nonclustered B-tree index on decim attribute of *updates.*

`o_mode_10k` into a file.

Build secondary nonclustered B-tree index on float attribute of *tenpcnt* .

Build secondary nonclustered B-tree index on int attribute of *updates*.

Build secondary nonclustered B-tree index on decim attribute of *ten-pcnt*.

Build secondary nonclustered hashed index on code attribute of *hundred*.

`o_mode_10k` into a relation.

Build secondary nonclustered hashed index on name attribute of *ten-pcnt*.

Build secondary nonclustered hashed index on code attribute of *updates*.

`o_mode_100k` into a relation.

Build secondary nonclustered hashed index on code attribute of *ten-pcnt*.

Build secondary nonclustered B-tree index on double attribute of *updates*.

```
o_mode_1k to the screen.
o_mode_10k to the screen.
o_mode_100k to the screen.
join_3_cl
sel_100_ncl
table_scan
func_agg
scal_agg
sel_100_cl
join_3_ncl
sel_10pct_ncl
simple_report
info_retrieval
create_view
subtotal_report
total_report
join_2_cl
join_2
variable_select — with low selectivity, should use index.
variable_select — with high selectivity, should not use index.
join_4_cl
proj_100
join_4_ncl
proj_10pct
sel_1_ncl
join_2_ncl
join_1_1pct
integrity_temp
integrity_test
integrity_restore
```

Remove all secondary indexes from *updates*.

```
bulk_save
bulk_modify
append_duplicate
remove_duplicate
app_t_mid
mod_t_mid
del_t_mid
app_t_end
mod_t_end
del_t_end
```

Build secondary nonclustered hashed index on code attribute of *updates*.

```
app_t_mid
mod_t_cod
del_t_mid
```

Build secondary nonclustered B-tree index on int attribute of *updates*.

```
app_t_mid
mod_t_int
del_t_mid
bulk_append
bulk_delete
```

# Appendix D. Multiuser Tests

As described in Section 5.8, there are four modules of multiuser tests: OLTP, IR, mixed OLTP, and mixed IR. We suggest that each module be set to run with one script; within one script, for each user, a concurrent program including queries and timing statements should be forked out. No think time or presentation services are included in the measurements. The queries required for the multiuser tests are listed below

```
/* 1 tuple update for OLTP and mixed OLTP tests */
    oltp_update:
        update updates
        set signed = signed + 1
        where key = :random_number
/* each user program starts with a different seed and generates a */
/* sequence of random numbers */

/* 1 tuple selection for IR and mixed IR test */
    ir_select:
        select key, code, date, signed, name
        from updates
        where key = :random_number
Cross section queries for mixed IR and mixed OLTP tests
    o_mode_tiny:
        select * from tiny
    o_mode_100k:
        select * from hundred where key<=1000

/* this selection query should be repeated 3 times with 3 isolation levels */
    sel_1_ncl:
        select key, int, signed, code, double, name
        from updates
        where code = 'BENCHMARKS'
    simple_report:
        select avg(updates.decim)
        from updates
        where updates.key in
            (select updates.key
            from updates, hundred
            where hundred.key = updates.key
              and updates.decim > 980000000)
```

**sel_100_seq:**
```
insert into sel100seq
    select * from updates
    where updates.key between 1001 and 1100
```
/* **build a temporary relation for random updates** */
**sel_100_rand:**
```
insert into sel100rand
    select * from updates
    where updates.int between 1001 and 1100
```
/* **abort update of sequential records** */
**mod_100_seq:**
```
begin work
update updates
    set double = double + 100000000
    where key between 1001 and 1100
rollback work
```
/* **updates some records randomly** */
**mod_100_rand:**
```
update updates
    set double = double + 100000000
    where int between 1001 and 1100
```
/* **restore (unmodify) the sequential records** */
**unmod_100_seq:**
```
update updates
    set double = double - 100000000
    where key between 1001 and 1100
```
/* **unmodify the random records** */
**unmod_100_rand**
```
update updates
    set double = double - 100000000
    where key between 1001 and 1100
```

At the end of the multiuser tests, the following two queries are run to check that the updates were performed correctly:

/* **check correctness of the sequential updates** */
**checkmod_100_seq:**
```
select count(*)
from updates, sel100seq
where updates.key = sel100seq.key
    and  not updates.double = sel100seq.double
```
/* **check correctness of the random updates** */
**checkmod_100_rand:**
```
select count(*) from updates, sel100rand
    where updates.int = sel100rand.int
        and not updates.double = sel100rand.double
```

# 6

# The Set Query Benchmark

Patrick E. O'Neil

*University of Massachusetts at Boston*

## 6.1    Introduction to the Benchmark

The Set Query benchmark is designed to measure the performance of a new class of systems that exploit the strategic value of operational data in commercial enterprises. A growing number of information managers are thinking in the following terms. "We have our operational data under control, the core of our business where we keep track of our orders. Now we want to set up a system to gain insight into the strategic value of the data. Who are our customers and how should we segment our markets? Which of our customers returns the most profit? What are product purchasing trends? Can we use our knowledge to gain competitive advantage, providing a market research service by advising our customers of their own needs so as to improve their sales of our products?" We refer to systems that support applications of this kind as strategic data access (SDA) systems, but a large number of other historical names exist, such as marketing information systems, decision support systems, management reporting, and direct marketing systems.

Database functions that support SDA applications generally use what we call *set queries*, queries that take into account data from numerous table rows at once in each question. Since the DebitCredit [Anon et al., 1988] and TPC [1991] benchmarks deal only with row-at-a-time updates, a very dif-

359

ferent type of processing, they fail to match these needs. However, experience has shown that information systems managers looking for hard performance numbers are likely to turn to DebitCredit results during product selection, simply because relatively up-to-date measurements are generally available. Wisconsin benchmark [Bitton, DeWitt, & Turbyfill, 1983] numbers are often not known for recent DBMS systems, and the $AS^3AP$ benchmark [Turbyfill, Orji, & Bitton, 1991] is quite new. The importance of set query functionality has not been properly articulated up to now, and even sophisticated users have not been sensitive to the distinction. But measurements from the Set Query benchmark show that computer resource usage by such queries can be extremely high, with surprising variations among different products, so that performance can be a critical issue. The Set Query benchmark presented here has been created to aid decision makers who require performance data relevant to strategic data applications.

```
SELECT NAME, ADDR FROM PROSPECTS
    WHERE SEX = 'F'
    AND FAMILYEARN > 40000
    AND ZIPCODE BETWEEN 02100 AND 12200
    AND EDUC = "COLLEGE"
    AND HOBBY IN ( "TENNIS", "RACQUETBALL");
```

**Figure 6.1**
An example of a Set Query used in a strategic data application. The query might be used to generate a mailing list for announcements of a new women's racquet sports magazine.

The Set Query benchmark differs from the Wisconsin and $AS^3AP$ benchmarks mainly in its focus on a set of queries as tools to perform the application tasks required. The Set Query benchmark chooses a list of basic set queries from a review of three major types of strategic data applications: document search, direct marketing, and decision support. Feedback was solicited from five system designers to ascertain that the queries chosen spanned the functions required by their systems. The Set Query benchmark also has a unique method to allow the price/performance rating for a measured DBMS to be customized for a particular site, by weighting the query performance measurements in proportion to their expected prevalence.

In the remainder of Section 6.1, the data and queries used in the Set Query benchmark are explained and motivated. In Section 6.2, benchmark results are presented for two leading database products used in large-scale operations: IBM's DB2 and Computer Corporation of America's (CCA's) MODEL 204. Surprisingly large performance differences, factors of ten or more for some queries, are observed with respect to I/O, CPU, and elapsed time; these differences emphasize the critical value of benchmarks in this area. In Section 6.3, a detailed explanation is given of how to generate the data and run the benchmark on an independent platform.

## 6.1.1   Features of the Set Query Benchmark

The Set Query benchmark has four key characteristics: portability, functional coverage, selectivity coverage, and scaleability.

1. *Portability.* The queries for the benchmark are specified in SQL, which is available on most systems, although different query language forms are permitted that give identical results. The data used is representative of real applications but is artificially generated using a portable random number algorithm, described in Section 6.3; this allows investigators to create the database on any system. Different platforms can then be compared on a price/performance basis.

2. *Functional coverage.* The benchmark queries are chosen to span the tasks performed by an important set of strategic data applications. Prospective users should be able to derive a rating for the particular weighted subset they expect to use most in the system being planned.

3. *Selectivity coverage.* Selectivity applies to a clause of a query and indicates the proportion of rows of the database selected. We say that SEX = 'M' where half the rows are returned, has very low selectivity, whereas SOCSECNO = '028343179' where a single row is returned has very high selectivity. The selectivity usually has a tremendous effect on the performance of a query, so the Set Query benchmark specifies measurements for a spectrum of selectivity values within each query type. Prospective users can then concentrate on measurements in the range of selectivity values they expect to encounter.

4. *Scaleability.* The database has a single table, known as the BENCH table, that contains an integer multiple of 1 million rows of 200 bytes each. The default size of 1 million rows is large enough to be realistic and to highlight a number of crucial performance issues. Set query performance differences are magnified on large databases, and this is significant as commercial databases grow rapidly with time. The ability to scale to a larger multimillion-row table size is also provided.

## Definition of the BENCH Table

To offer the desired variety of selectivity, the BENCH table has 13 indexed columns; in the default case of a 1 million row table, these columns are named KSEQ, K500K, K250K, K100K, K40K, K10K, K1K, K100, K25, K10, K5, K4, and K2. Twelve of these columns are unordered (randomly generated), and vary in cardinality (number of distinct values) from 2 to 500,000. Each such column has integer values ranging from 1 to its cardinality, which is reflected in the column name. Thus K2 has two values, 1 and 2; K4 has four values, 1, 2, 3, 4; K5 has five values . . .; up to K500K, which has 500,000 values. The remaining indexed column, KSEQ, is a clustered primary key, with values 1, 2, . . ., 1,000,000—the values occurring in the same order that the records are loaded. A pseudocode program for generating these column values is given in Figure 6.2 in Section 6.3.

**Table 6.1**    First ten rows of the BENCH database.

| KSEQ | K500K | K250K | K100K | K40K | K10K | K1K | K100 | K25 | K10 | K5 | K4 | K2 |
|------|-------|-------|-------|------|------|-----|------|-----|-----|----|----|----|
| 1 | 16808 | 225250 | 50074 | 23659 | 8931 | 273 | 45 | 4 | 4 | 5 | 1 | 2 |
| 2 | 484493 | 243043 | 7988 | 2504 | 2328 | 730 | 41 | 13 | 4 | 5 | 2 | 2 |
| 3 | 129561 | 70934 | 93100 | 279 | 1817 | 336 | 98 | 2 | 3 | 3 | 3 | 2 |
| 4 | 80980 | 129150 | 36580 | 38822 | 1968 | 673 | 94 | 12 | 6 | 1 | 1 | 2 |
| 5 | 140195 | 186358 | 35002 | 1154 | 6709 | 945 | 69 | 16 | 5 | 2 | 3 | 2 |
| 6 | 227723 | 204667 | 28550 | 38025 | 7802 | 854 | 78 | 9 | 9 | 4 | 3 | 2 |
| 7 | 28636 | 158014 | 23866 | 29815 | 9064 | 537 | 26 | 20 | 6 | 5 | 2 | 2 |
| 8 | 46518 | 184196 | 30106 | 10405 | 9452 | 299 | 89 | 24 | 6 | 3 | 1 | 1 |
| 9 | 436717 | 130338 | 54439 | 13145 | 1502 | 898 | 72 | 4 | 8 | 4 | 2 | 2 |
| 10 | 222295 | 227905 | 21610 | 26232 | 9746 | 176 | 36 | 24 | 3 | 5 | 1 | 1 |

In addition to these indexed columns, there are also a number of character columns, S1 (length 8), S2 through S8 (length 20 each), which fill out the row to a length of 200 bytes. These character strings can be generated with identical values, such as, "12345678900987654321," since they are never used in retrieval queries. Unindexed retrieval in large, low-update tables is extremely inadvisable. Note that certain database systems perform compression on the data stored—we do not want to choose values for s1 through s8 that result in compression to less than 200 bytes of data.

Where a BENCH table of more than 1 million rows is created, the column KSEQ is reinterpreted, and the two highest cardinality columns are renamed in a consistent way. For example, in a table with 10 million rows, the columns would be: KSEQ, K5M, K2500K, K100K, K40K, K10K, K1K, K100, K25, K10, K5, K4, and K2. The column KSEQ would then take on the values 1, 2, ..., 10,000,000, and the next two columns, formerly K500K and K250K, would be renamed to K5M and K2500K, so as to have ten times as many values as in the 1 million row case. The purpose is to achieve consistent scaling in the joins of Query Q6, explained below. The renamed columns would replace the default column names throughout the document, wherever they appear.

## 6.1.2 Achieving Functional Coverage

In determining the set of queries to include in this benchmark, the first aim was to reflect set query activity in common commercial use. Experience in the field suggested three general strategic data applications: document search, direct marketing, and decision support/management reporting. After describing the work done in these applications, a number of query types were chosen to support the activity, with a surprising amount of confirming overlap discovered at the lowest level of analysis. In preparation for publishing a Set Query article in *Datamation* (O'Neil, 1989), I contacted five companies with state-of-the-art strategic data applications. Each company was asked to list the queries from the Set Query benchmark that made up a large portion of their work and to identify any query type not on the list that they found to be important. As a result of this survey, one minor addition was made to the query set (to include a Boolean NOT on some equal match condition, Query Q2B). Otherwise, respondents generally felt that the query set chosen was quite representative of the use they experienced. We now describe the three strategic data applications studied and how these led to the selection of query types for our benchmark; a somewhat more detailed explanation of some queries, together with examples of the reporting form, is given in the results of Section 6.2.

## Document Search

In this application, the user begins by specifying one or more qualities desired in a set of retrieved rows; the application COUNTs the number of rows thus selected and returns this number to the user. Usually the user then adds new qualities to the ones specified and once again requests a count of rows so qualified. The ultimate object is to winnow down to a small number of documents (from 1 to a few hundred) that deserve closer scrutiny, at which point more detail from the record is printed out.

It is important to realize that the "documents" can represent any information. Well-known online database services, such as DIALOG and LEXIS, structure access to journal abstracts. For an application used in the field, we surveyed a company known as Petroleum Information, PI, of The Dun & Bradstreet Corporation, which provides a retrieval application and oil well data to most companies in the oil industry. There are two million oil wells involved, with 20 gigabytes of data on drilling permits, test data, drilling costs, production volumes, and so on. The method explained above of successive refinement of the set of qualities desired has become a standard for oil industry analysts, and the activity is predominant in PI applications.

The first thing we notice about this application is that it is much more common to COUNT than to actually retrieve data from a set of rows; a series of COUNT operations is performed to get to the point where a selected set of rows is printed out. This may be at variance with common perceptions of SQL, which emphasize queries such as SELECT *... rather than SELECT COUNT(*)..., but it is a pattern we see over and over. Aggregate functions, most significantly the COUNT function, provide an overview of the data which lets us grasp its significance.

Consideration of the document search application led us to specify three general query types, which are:

1. A COUNT of records with a single exact match condition, known as query Q1:

```
Q1:    SELECT COUNT(*) FROM BENCH
       WHERE  KN  =  2;
```

(Here and in later queries, KN stands for any member of a set of columns. Here, KN $\varepsilon$ {KSEQ, K100K,..., K4, K2}. The measurements are reported separately for each of these cases.)

2. A COUNT of records from a conjunction of two exact match conditions, query Q2A:

```
Q2A:   SELECT COUNT(*) FROM BENCH
       WHERE K2 = 2 AND KN = 3;
For each KN ε {KSEQ, K100K,..., K4, K2}
```

or an AND of an exact match with a negation of an exact match condition: query Q2B:

```
Q2B:    SELECT COUNT(*) FROM BENCH
        WHERE K2 = 2 AND NOT KN = 3;
For each KN ε {KSEQ, K100K,..., K4}
```

3. A retrieval of data (not counts) given constraints of three conditions, including range conditions, (Q4A), or constraints of five conditions, (Q4B).

```
Q4:     SELECT KSEQ, K500K FROM BENCH
        WHERE  constraint with (3 or 5) conditions ;
```

Details of the constraints are given in Section 6.2.2 under Q4: Multiple Condition Selection on page 378. Several of these query types recur in considerations of other applications, a good sign that they are fundamental queries. The outputs of these queries and all others are directed to an ASCII (or EBCDIC) file. This implies that the query engine must format the numeric answers in printable form.

## Direct Marketing

This is a class of applications whose general goal is to identify a list of households that are most likely to purchase a given product or service. The approach to selecting such a list usually breaks down into two parts: preliminary sizing and exploration of possible criteria for selection, and retrieving the data from the records for a mailing or other communication.

R.L. Polk, a respondent to our survey, is the largest direct marketing list compiler in North America, with demographic information on 80 million U.S. households. A typical query in the preliminary sizing phase might be to count the households from a set of ZIP codes, with income of $50,000 per year and up, that owns a car from a list of make/year categories. In most cases, the mailing to be performed is relatively explicit as to size, and a count above or below the target will mean that a new query must be specified, perhaps with a change in the set of ZIP codes or the income constraint. When the list of households in the list has been selected, the individual record data is retrieved in an offline batch run, together with other lists generated.

Saks Fifth Avenue has a very effective customer tracking application, with 3.8 million records and 30 million individual customer purchases for the prior 24 months, maintained as repeating fields. Analysts at Saks often create mailings out of several smaller subject profiles, such as this: a customer in the Chicago area, with total purchases of more than $1000.00 per year and purchases in the last six months in handbags. A different profile might require purchases six to twelve months ago in luggage. Each profile is chosen on the basis of a crosstabs report on cross purchasing, explained later. The counts desired in the mailing from each of the individual profiles are prechosen, and the intent is usually to choose the customers with largest total purchases per year within these constraints.

Consideration of the preliminary sizing phase of the direct marketing application reinforced our selection of the COUNT queries, Q2A and Q2B with two clauses, and the data retrieval phase reinforced queries Q4A and Q4B, which have three and five clauses, respectively. In addition, it led us to specify a pair of queries where a SUM of column K1K values is retrieved with two qualifying clauses restricting the selection, one an equal match condition and one a range query.

```
Q3A:    SELECT SUM(K1K) FROM BENCH
            WHERE KSEQ BETWEEN 400000 AND 500000 AND KN = 3;
For each KN ε { K100K,..., K4}
```

In addition, Query Q3B captures a slightly more realistic (but less intuitive) OR of several ranges corresponding to a restriction of ZIP codes:

```
Q3B:    SELECT SUM(K1K) FROM BENCH
            WHERE    ( KSEQ BETWEEN 400000 AND 410000
                  OR  KSEQ BETWEEN 420000 AND 430000
                  OR  KSEQ BETWEEN 440000 AND 450000
                  OR  KSEQ BETWEEN 460000 AND 470000
                  OR  KSEQ BETWEEN 480000 AND 500000)
            AND    KN = 3;
For each KN ε { K100K,..., K4}
```

The SUM aggregate in queries Q3A and Q3B requires actual retrieval of up to 25,000 records since it cannot be resolved in the indexes that are permitted; thus, a large data retrieval is assured.

### Decision Support and Management Reporting

This application area represents a wide class of applications, usually involving reports to aid operational decisions. One common example is a crosstabs report: a two-dimensional factor analysis table, where each two-coordinate cell is filled in with a count or sum of some field from the record set chosen. In this way, the effect of one factor on another can be analyzed.

The direct marketing subsidiary of the advertising firm of Young & Rubicam obtains initial mailing lists of perhaps two million records for clients and then subjects these lists to a great deal of further analysis to add value. A list is analyzed and segmented by the demographic and psycho-graphic data available; then a set of survey mailings with different promotional messages is sent to a statistical subset of each of the target segments. A large response of about 15 percent is obtained, and the response is analyzed—for example, to see if the message sent would tend to increase purchases. The results are often presented in crosstabs reports—for example, showing how hobbies (boating, hiking, etc.) might affect use of some product or how each of a set of promotional messages affects individual segments.

Saks Fifth Avenue has a large set of reports on buying habits of their customers. Reports that return numbers of customers with total sales by category serve to identify classes of customers who return the greatest profits to Saks; these customer classes can then be individually targeted. A two-dimensional array of cross-buying patterns by department supports decisions of what customer profiles should be used for mailings. For example, if we notice that customers with large luggage purchases often purchase new coats shortly after, we can include recent luggage buyers in a mailing for a coat sale.

The queries that arose out of this application area include various COUNT queries already mentioned as well as queries Q3A and Q3B, which return a SUM of a specified column from a set of selected records. The crosstabs application so common in this category is also modeled by Query Q5, a SQL GROUP BY query that returns counts of records that fall in cells of a two-dimensional array, determined by the specific values of each of two fields.

```
Q5:     SELECT  KN1, KN2, COUNT(*)  FROM BENCH
            GROUP BY KN1,KN2;
For each (KN1, KN2) ε { (K2,K100),(K10,K25), (K10,K25)}
```

This is as close as SQL comes in a nonprocedural statement to a crosstabs report.

Queries Q6A and Q6B exercise the join functionality that would be needed in the final two applications above, when data from two or more records in different tables must be combined.

```
Q6A:    SELECT COUNT(*) FROM BENCH B1,BENCH B2
            WHERE B1.KN = 49 AND B1.K250K = B2.K500K;
For each KN ε { K100K, K40K, K10K, K1K, K100}
```

```
Q6B:    SELECT B1.KSEQ, B2.KSEQ FROM BENCH B1,BENCH B2
        WHEREB1.KN = 99
        AND     B1.K250K = B2.K500K
        AND     B2.K25 = 19;
For each KN ε {K40K, K10K, K1K, K100}
```

Note that, although a COUNT is retrieved, such join queries cannot be resolved via the supported indexes without reference to a large number of table rows.

## 6.1.3    Running the Benchmark

In Section 6.2, we present an application of the Set Query benchmark to two different IBM System/370 commercial databases, DB2 and MODEL 204. The presentation should serve as a model for how the results are to be reported and as a good illustration of the kinds of performance considerations that arise; further details on how to run the benchmark and how to interpret the results will be covered in Section 6.3. But before diving into the welter of detail of a benchmark report of this kind, a few high-level observations are in order.

### Architectural Complexity

Measuring these two products exposes an enormous number of architectural features peculiar to each. Even the form of information reported is affected by this. The three modalities of resource utilization reported for each query are: elapsed time, CPU time, and I/O use. MODEL 204 uses standard (random) I/O, with a certain amount of optimization for sequential scans transparent to the user, but DB2 has two different types of I/O, random I/O (of a single page) and prefetch I/O (of a block of pages chained together for optimal access efficiency). Clearly we must report these two measures separately in the DB2 case. Similarly, MODEL 204 has a number of unique features, such as an Existence Bit Map, by which it is able to perform much more efficient negation queries (as illustrated in Table 6.6 in Section 6.2.2). A good familiarity with the architecture of any system is a necessary preliminary to a benchmark, if nothing else, to assure good tuning. But more than this, a perfect apples-to-apples comparison between two products in every feature is generally impossible. Some judgment must be applied with such features in order to achieve the best comparison possible among all products measured. For example, although in this example we generally tried to flush database buffers between queries, it turns out to be difficult to flush the pages of the Existence Bitmap of MODEL 204. On consideration, it seems appropriate to allow this small set of pages to remain in memory since it would be consistently present in buffer in any situation where queries involving the represented rows are at all frequent and therefore of concern from a performance standpoint.

## A Single Unifying Criterion

We are aided in our desire to compare different query engines with variant architectural features by the fact that our ultimate aim is to sum up our benchmark results with a single figure: dollar price per query per minute ($/QPM). This rating represents the five-year price of the system, hardware + software + maintenance, needed to support each query per minute, and it is analogous to the ratings of the DebitCredit and TPC benchmarks, which measure each platform in terms of dollar price per transactions per second ($/TPS). The time period of a minute (rather than a second) is used with set queries because of the much longer average response time as compared with TPC transactions. In looking through the many detailed query results of Section 6.2, the reader should keep in mind that this relatively simple criterion will guide judgments. Indeed, as explained in Section 6.4, the queries of this benchmark are meant to form a "spanning set" in terms of functionality and selectivity so that a site-specific set of applications can be compared between two platforms in terms of a weighted sum of the queries from the benchmark that are most representative. Thus, a single *custom* rating to compare $/QPM of two systems in a customized application environment can be constructed from a preexisting benchmark.

## Confidence in the Results

The results of Section 6.2 show occasional startling variations in performance between two products. Table 6.4 of Section 6.2.2, containing Q1 measurements, displays a maximum elapsed time of 39.69 seconds in one case and 0.31 seconds in the other. How can we have confidence that we have not made a measurement or tuning mistake when confronted with a variation of this kind? The answer lies in understanding the two system architectures. With sufficient understanding of the architectures involved, one can step back and confirm the measurements in terms of more detailed measures implicit in other queries. This is a form of "multiple entry bookkeeping," which helps validate the conclusions with "multiple strands" of evidence, rather than the "links of a chain" approach favored in certain areas, where failure of a single link invalidates the result. For example, the actual number of pages of I/O required by each architecture can be predicted in each of the queries of Section 6.2. This is why the benchmark has such a careful discussion following the various query tables: A consistency check must be performed whenever possible to increase confidence in the result. By analogy, if the period of recorded history is 4,000 years, then there is a record of the sun rising on 730,000 mornings. Yet we would probably be willing to offer 10,000,000 to 1 odds in a bet that the sun will rise tomorrow and think it a safe bet. Our understanding of the underlying scientific principles involved makes it inconceivable that we are in error on this point. Benchmark measurements on complex software systems of the kinds described here share many aspects of a scientific investigation.

### Output Formatting

The query results are directed to a user file, which represents the answers in printable form. About half the reports return very few records (only counts), and about half return a few thousand records.

## 6.2 An Application of the Benchmark

The Set Query benchmark was applied to two commercial databases for IBM System/370 machines, DB2 and MODEL 204. The results show variations of surprising magnitude in performance, much larger differences than are usually seen in DebitCredit measurements, for example; these differences are often due to fundamental variations in basic architecture, which the basic queries of the benchmark amply illustrate.

### 6.2.1 Hardware/Software Environment

We ran DB2, Version 2.2 with 1200 4 Kbyte memory buffers, and MODEL 204 Version 2.1 with 800 6K memory buffers, accessing the BENCH database loaded for each system on two 3380 disk drives. (These are the latest DBMS versions in commercial release as of December 1990.) All measurements were taken on a standalone 4381-3, a 4.5 mips dual processor. (Since this processor is no longer offered for sale by IBM, we derive price figures from the ES/9000 model 150, a recently released machine with the same mips rating.) Since all tests are single-user type, only one 2.25 mips CPU was ever utilized by the queries. Both database systems were running under the MVS XA 2.2 operating system. Interactive query interfaces were used in both cases: DB2 queries were run using the SPUFI interface on VTAM with the TSO attachment; MODEL 204 queries were also run on VTAM, with access through its own built-in interface.

The EXPLAIN command was used in DB2 to determine the access strategy employed by the system for each query. RUNSTATS was first run to update the various tables, such as SYSCOLUMNS and SYSINDEXES, on which the DB2 query optimizer bases its access strategy decisions. During the runs reported here, accounting trace Class 1 and Class 2 were turned on, resulting in CPU increase of about 10 percent. The SMF output was analyzed by DB2PM. Class 1 statistics reported here reflect time spent in interregion communication and time spent by the SPUFI application as well as DB2 time.

MODEL 204 statistics were put out to the interactive screen and the audit trail as each query was performed, using the TIME REQUEST command. This results in a CPU overhead of about 2 percent to 3 percent.

## 6.2.2   Statistics Gathered

To start with, we present the time required to load the BENCH table on the two systems in Table 6.2.

**Table 6.2**   Time to load BENCH database.

| | DB2 Elapsed | DB2 CPU | MODEL 204 Elapsed | MODEL 204 CPU |
|---|---|---|---|---|
| Table load | 124 m 19 s | 114 m 43 s | 108 m 34 s | 142 m 13 s |
| Runstats | 41 m 17 s | 33 m 47 s | 0 s | 0 s |
| Total | 165 m 36 s | 148 m 30 s | 108 m 34 s | 142 m 13 s |

For DB2, the RUNSTATS utility is viewed as an element of the load time since RUNSTATS is necessary in order to obtain the query performance measured in the benchmark. The RUNSTATS utility examines the data and accumulates statistics on value distributions, which are subsequently used by the DB2 query optimizer in picking query plans. MODEL 204 also performs some optimization on the basis of value distributions and the rest through programmer decision in the procedural query language; it gathers needed information for the optimization it performs as an integral part of loading, without employing a separate utility function. The MODEL 204 elapsed time is shorter than the CPU time recorded in Table 6.2 because the

MODEL 204 loader is able to overlap work on the dual processors of the 4381, the only multiprocessor use seen for either product in the current benchmark.

The disk space occupied by the BENCH database for the two products was: DB2, 313,660,000 bytes; MODEL 204, 265,780,000 bytes. The rows of the BENCH database were loaded in the DB2 and MODEL 204 database in identical fashion. All the indexed columns, KSEQ, K500K, ..., K2, were given a B-tree index. The indexes in both cases were loaded with leaf nodes 95 percent full. Since the lengths of the columns sum to 200 bytes, the rows in both databases were slightly in excess of 200 bytes in length as a result of required row storage overhead.

**Table 6.3**   DB2 index and data characteristics.

| | |
|---|---|
| Maximum number of index pages (K500K) | 2290 |
| Minimum number of index pages (K2-K100) | 1110 |
| Row length in bytes | 224 |
| Rows per tablespace page | 17 |
| Total tablespace pages | 58,824 |

The number of B-tree leaf pages is 1110 for many indexes, increasing to 2290 pages as the structure becomes more complex with a large number of values and a varying number of rows per value.

MODEL 204 databases deal with somewhat larger pages (6 Kbytes), and B-tree indexes have a complex indirect inversion structure. Basically, MODEL 204 B-tree entries need not contain lists of row IDs (RIDs) with duplicate values but may instead point indirectly to a list or "bitmap" of such RIDs, whichever MODEL 204 finds more efficient.

In MODEL 204, the native "User Language" was used to formulate these queries rather than SQL. User Language is a procedural 4GL recommended by CCA for its flexibility in application-building over the host language embedded approach. Query Q1, given below in SQL, would be written in user language as follows. The difference for most of the queries reported here is negligible, and only the SQL form is presented here.

```
BEGIN
    FIND AND PRINT COUNT  KN = 2
END
For each KN ε { KSEQ, K100K, ..., K4, K2}
```

**Q1: Count, Single Exact Match**

To restate Query Q1, mentioned above:

```
SELECT COUNT(*) FROM BENCH
    WHERE KN  =  2;
For each KN ε {KSEQ, K100K,..., K4, K2}
```

This is a typical early query in document retrieval search, to find the number of journal articles with some property (published in the *Journal of the Association of Computing Machinery*, containing the keyword *computer*, etc.).

**Table 6.4**  Q1 measurements (elapsed times in seconds).

| KN | DB2 Elapsed Time | MODEL 204 Elapsed Time | DB2 CPU Time | MODEL 204 CPU Time | DB2 Random I/Os | DB2 Prefetch I/Os | MODEL 204 Disk I/Os |
|------|------|------|------|------|------|------|------|
| KSEQ | 1.13 s | 0.05 s | 0.52 s | 0.01 s | 3 | | 2 |
| K100K | 1.11 s | 0.06 s | 0.53 s | 0.03 s | 3 | | 2 |
| K10K | 1.14 s | 0.12 s | 0.54 s | 0.07 s | 3 | | 2 |
| K1K | 1.21 s | 0.15 s | 0.58 s | 0.11 s | 4 | | 2 |
| K100 | 1.76 s | 0.22 s | 1.06 s | 0.16 s | 12 | | 5 |
| K25 | 5.02 s | 0.33 s | 3.56 s | 0.15 s | 3 | 6 | 22 |
| K10 | 9.63 s | 0.31 s | 8.14 s | 0.15 s | 3 | 10 | 23 |
| K5 | 17.65 s | 0.35 s | 15.77 s | 0.15 s | 3 | 12 | 22 |
| K4 | 20.36 s | 0.29 s | 19.48 s | 0.15 s | 2 | 13 | 22 |
| K2 | 39.69 s | 0.31 s | 38.42 s | 0.15 s | 1 | 19 | 22 |

As mentioned earlier, DB2 times come from DB2PM Class 1 statistics, which include time spent by the SPUFI application and cross-region communication. Class 2 statistics include only time spent within DB2 and compare with Class 1 in most of the queries reported by consistently subtracting almost exactly 0.8 seconds elapsed time and 0.3 seconds CPU time. This makes a large percentage difference for the smaller measures but is relatively insignificant for the larger ones.

Note that the I/O measures for DB2 are given in terms of the number of random single-page I/Os as well as the number of prefetch I/Os. With sequential prefetch reads, the disk head sweeps through a read of 32 blocks at once, performing the work of 32 random reads in about twice the time. The data to be accessed must lie on successive pages on disk for such reads to be of value, as here, where large numbers of successive equal match entries in a B-tree have been loaded in sort order. Note that, if we represent the total number of pages brought into memory by $N$, the prefetch reads by

$P$, and random reads by $R$, we see that: $N = R + 32 * P$. In the measured case where KN stands for K2 above, we find that $N = 1 + 32 * 19 = 609$, a bit more than half the number of pages in the 1110 pages of the K2 index B-tree, as we would expect.

We see in Table 6.4 a large disparity between DB2 and MODEL 204, with palpable slowdown in DB2 retrieval as the selectivity of the match column decreases. The EXPLAIN command gives the access plan of the DB2 SELECT statement, that it uses the index of the column in question and resolves COUNT(*) solely in the index, without access to the row data. This is perfectly appropriate. The entries in the B-tree that must be accessed are exactly that set of duplicate values in each index equal to 2. Note that, as mentioned above, all of the low selectivity column indexes have 1110 pages (Table 6.3), and the total number of pages read in each case is what we would expect, i.e., in the case of K2 = 2, approximately half the index pages.

The DB2 slowdown is not caused by the I/O, however; the CPU time is the culprit, as can be seen from the fact that CPU time is most of the elapsed time. Considering the K2 = 2 case shows a time of 38.42 seconds on a 2.25 mips CPU to count 500,000 B-tree entries. This means that DB2 uses about 173 instructions for each entry counted. This is an improvement from an earlier architecture, where successive entries in the B-tree were accessed by one software layer and counted by another, but it is still surprisingly CPU-consuming. In the MODEL 204 architecture, by contrast, in cases where a large number of records must be counted, MODEL 204 simply counts bits in several blocks of memory, an operation that can be highly optimized. This serves to explain the large difference seen.

### Q2: Count ANDing Two Clauses

This test query type performs a COUNT of records from an AND of two exact match conditions (query Q2A) or an AND of an exact match condition with a NOT of an exact match condition (query Q2B).

```
    SELECT COUNT(*) FROM BENCH
    WHERE K2 = 2 AND KN = 3;
For each KN ε {KSEQ, K100K,..., K4}
```

Query Q2A constrains two columns at once, one of low selectivity, the other varying. It is a typical query in the early stages of document retrieval search. It might also be used in direct marketing applications to get an early estimate of the number of prospects with a given set of qualities.

**Table 6.5**   Q2A measurements.

| KN | DB2 Elapsed Time | MODEL 204 Elapsed Time | DB2 CPU Time | MODEL 204 CPU Time | DB2 Random I/Os | DB2 Prefetch I/Os | MODEL204 Disk I/Os |
|------|------|------|------|------|------|------|------|
| KSEQ | 1.39 s | 0.10 s | 0.53 s | 0.01 s | 1 | | 3 |
| K100K | 1.43 s | 0.19 s | 0.54 s | 0.04 s | 1 | 1 | 9 |
| K10K | 2.34 s | 0.56 s | 0.58 s | 0.12 s | 1 | 4 | 23 |
| K1K | 12.41 s | 0.57 s | 1.00 s | 0.13 s | 2 | 31 | 24 |
| K100 | 74.50 s | 0.71 s | 5.41 s | 0.20 s | 15 | 287 | 26 |
| K25 | 119.77 s | 0.97 s | 19.16 s | 0.19 s | 16 | 929 | 43 |
| K10 | 143.80 s | 1.31 s | 38.32 s | 0.19 s | 4 | 1541 | 43 |
| K5 | 165.87 s | 0.98 s | 65.09 s | 0.19 s | 4 | 1811 | 43 |
| K4 | 138.17 s | 0.98 s | 65.92 s | 0.19 s | 3 | 1840 | 43 |

With the release of V2.2, DB2 was able to combine two or more indexes before accessing the tablespace by sorting the RIDs selected by individual match predicates and performing a merge-intersection. However, the EXPLAIN command reveals that DB2 avoids this here, using the index of higher selectivity of its ANDed conditions to cut down the number of rows to be searched, then accessing each of the rows in question to resolve the second condition (check if K2 = 2). In the last line of the query, where K2 = 2 AND K4 = 3, a tablespace scan would be used. The decision not to use index merge-intersect, even though it saves significantly in I/O cost, seems to reflect a costly CPU implementation of this feature.

In the heavy resource use of the last row of DB2 measures in Table 6.5, the I/O wait time accounts for the elapsed time. Each sequential prefetch of 32 pages requires over three full rotations of the disk for transfer alone, about 55 milliseconds; adding 10 ms for seek time and 8 ms for rotational latency, we arrive at an elapsed time for 1837 prefetch I/Os: 1837 * (0.055 + 0.010 + 0.008) = 134.10 seconds. Earlier rows of Table 6.5, such as the one for K100, demonstrate the new list prefetch feature of V2.2. With K100, it retrieves about 10,000 rows, on about 58,824 * (1 − exp(10,000/58824)) = 9,196 pages, scattered randomly through the tablespace. This is accomplished with 287 list prefetches (reported by DB2PM as sequential prefetches), where 32 pages at a time are retrieved through "chained" commands to the disk controller and channel—pages not sequentially placed but merely as clustered as possible! Note that the average time for each list prefetch in the K100 case is about 74.50/287 = 0.2596 second, more than three times as long as a sequential prefetch.

In the case of MODEL 204, all the information necessary for this query is resolved by combining the information of two indexes, which is basically a matter of ANDing the bitmaps of the two indexes.

Now consider the related Q2B query, which involves a NOT clause.

```
SELECT COUNT(*) FROM BENCH
WHERE K2 = 2 AND NOT KN = 3;
For each KN ε {KSEQ, K100K,..., K4}
```

**Table 6.6**   Q2B measurements.

| KN | DB2 Elapsed Time | MODEL 204 Elapsed Time | DB2 CPU Time | MODEL 204 CPU Time | DB2 Random I/Os | DB2 Prefetch I/Os | MODEL204 Disk I/Os |
|------|--------|--------|--------|--------|-----|------|-----|
| KSEQ | 137.68 s | 0.46 s | 84.76 s | 0.16 s | 13 | 1840 | 23 |
| K100K | 137.69 s | 0.45 s | 84.76 s | 0.16 s | 13 | 1840 | 22 |
| K10K | 137.93 s | 0.66 s | 84.82 s | 0.18 s | 13 | 1840 | 24 |
| K1K | 137.50 s | 0.66 s | 84.79 s | 0.19 s | 13 | 1840 | 24 |
| K100 | 137.99 s | 0.71 s | 84.57 s | 0.21 s | 13 | 1840 | 26 |
| K25 | 137.53 s | 0.96 s | 83.98 s | 0.20 s | 13 | 1840 | 43 |
| K10 | 137.83 s | 1.32 s | 82.59 s | 0.20 s | 13 | 1840 | 43 |
| K5 | 138.99 s | 0.98 s | 80.63 s | 0.20 s | 13 | 1840 | 43 |
| K4 | 137.72 s | 0.98 s | 79.30 s | 0.20 s | 13 | 1840 | 43 |

In all DB2 measures in Table 6.6, the EXPLAIN command tells us that a tablespace scan is being used. Clearly, the DB2 query optimizer sees no way to use clauses such as NOT KSEQ = 2 to reduce the work through the indexes. MODEL 204 repeats the work of Q2A in performing the queries of Q2B, except that the bitmap of records found in the KN = 3 clause is XORed with the Existence Bitmap, which represents a list of all records in the table, resulting in a bitmap of NOT KN = 3.

### Q3: Sum, Range, and Match Clause

This query type retrieves the sum of the values of an integer binary column, K1K, for a given set of rows. The first query set of this type, Q3A, is:

```
Q3A:    SELECT SUM(K1K) FROM BENCH
        WHERE KSEQ BETWEEN 400000 AND 500000
        AND KN = 3;
For each KN ε { K100K,..., K4}
```

This is an example of a query that MODEL 204 cannot resolve totally in the indexes—all the rows involved in the sum must actually be touched by both systems—and thus the work performed emulates a direct mailing application where name and address information is written out from each of about 25,000 rows. It is also representative of a class of management reporting application queries, such as finding average incomes of various selected classes of prospects.

**Table 6.7** Q3A measurements.

| KN | DB2 Elapsed Time | MODEL 204 Elapsed Time | DB2 CPU Time | MODEL 204 CPU Time | DB2 Random I/Os | DB2 Prefetch I/Os | MODEL204 Disk I/Os |
|---|---|---|---|---|---|---|---|
| K100K | 1.43 s | 0.27 s | 0.56 s | 0.06 s | 4 | 1 | 13 |
| K10K | 2.41 s | 1.84 s | 0.59 s | 0.30 s | 4 | 4 | 122 |
| K100 | 15.64 s | 27.99 s | 10.36 s | 16.65 s | 12 | 213 | 1148 |
| K25 | 15.61 s | 41.29 s | 10.82 s | 19.52 s | 10 | 211 | 2673 |
| K10 | 15.63 s | 46.07 s | 11.44 s | 23.00 s | 10 | 211 | 3583 |
| K5 | 15.63 s | 46.36 s | 11.89 s | 27.13 s | 9 | 209 | 3752 |
| K4 | 15.60 s | 45.82 s | 12.71 s | 29.00 s | 10 | 211 | 3753 |

Here DB2 performance is superior to MODEL 204 in the final five rows (Table 6.7). The EXPLAIN command says that the access strategy in these cases is to use the KSEQ BETWEEN clause to limit the search, then resolve the remaining condition, KN = 3, by access to the records themselves. Since the records are clustered by the KSEQ values, this limits us to accessing only one tenth of the tablespace records: the number of pages read is about $10 + 32 * 211 = 6762$, slightly more than one tenth of the tablespace (5,883 pages) + one tenth of the KSEQ index (220 pages). (See Table 6.3 for these statistics.) DB2's sequential prefetch provides a performance gain over MODEL 204, which must access the table pages using random I/O that is only partially optimized, leading to greater I/O wait time and CPU time to make more I/O calls.

Query set Q3A was meant to model a query ranging over ZIP-code values corresponding to a given geographical region. It turns out that such a query usually results in a set of ranges of ZIP codes that must be ORed together. This is captured by query Q3B:

```
SELECT SUM(K1K) FROM BENCH
    WHERE  (  KSEQ BETWEEN 400000 AND 410000
           OR KSEQ BETWEEN 420000 AND 430000
           OR KSEQ BETWEEN 440000 AND 450000
           OR KSEQ BETWEEN 460000 AND 470000
           OR KSEQ BETWEEN 480000 AND 500000)
    AND KN = 3;
For each KN ε { K100K,..., K4}
```

**Table 6.8**   Q3B measurements.

| KN | DB2 Elapsed Time | MODEL 204 Elapsed Time | DB2 CPU Time | MODEL 204 CPU Time | DB2 Random I/Os | DB2 Prefetch I/Os | MODEL204 Disk I/Os |
|---|---|---|---|---|---|---|---|
| K100K | 1.44 s | 0.38 s | 0.58 s | 0.08 s | 4 | 1 | 22 |
| K10K | 2.40 s | 1.83 s | 0.62 s | 0.43 s | 4 | 4 | 112 |
| K100 | 14.88 s | 17.15 s | 9.70 s | 10.19 s | 110 | 21 | 657 |
| K25 | 20.79 s | 25.77 s | 14.22 s | 12.14 s | 4 | 65 | 1642 |
| K10 | 31.44 s | 28.64 s | 23.67 s | 14.20 s | 111 | 104 | 2182 |
| K5 | 49.10 s | 28.83 s | 41.61 s | 16.60 s | 111 | 125 | 2290 |
| K4 | 57.35 s | 27.89 s | 50.36 s | 17.74 s | 111 | 128 | 2207 |

Starting at the row for K100, EXPLAIN tells us that DB2 combines the five KSEQ range clauses with merge-union, then performs a merge-intersect with the KN = 3 RIDs, and finally reads in each of the rows selected to accumulate a SUM. In the final row where K4 = 3, the total number of pages read is about (6/100) * (2290 (KSEQ index) + 58824 (data pages)) + (1/4) * (1110 (K4 index)) = 3940 (see Table 6.3 for these statistics), and this requires about 120 random reads and 120 prefetch reads of 32 pages to accomplish, close to the figures measured.

MODEL 204 accesses the same indexes and data as DB2. MODEL 204 is faster in elapsed time in the last three rows because of the CPU time expended, since the merge-union and merge-intersect operations of MODEL 204 are much less CPU-intensive.

## Q4: Multiple Condition Selection

The query type to be examined in this section retrieves data, rather than a count, from records satisfying multiple ANDed conditions:

```
SELECT KSEQ, K500K FROM BENCH
WHERE   constraint with (3 or 5) conditions ;
```

The output data is directed to a printable disk file. The constraints of these query sets are generated by ANDing 3, or 5, successive conditions chosen from the condition sequence below. In the three condition constraints, for example, we use conditions 1–3, then conditions 2–4, 3–5, etc. The total selectivity of each of the three conditions in sequence is such that the number of rows retrieved is between 785 and 10,294, whereas in the case of five conditions in sequence, the number of rows retrieved varies from 199 to 465. See Appendix for the count of rows retrieved in each case.

**Condition Sequence:**

(1)  K2 = 1;
(2)  K100 > 80;
(3)  K10K BETWEEN 2000 and 3000;
(4)  K5 = 3;
(5)  (K25 = 11 OR K25 = 19);
(6)  K4 = 3;
(7)  K100 < 41;
(8)  K1K BETWEEN 850 AND 950;
(9)  K10 = 7;
(10)  K25 BETWEEN 3 AND 4;

A conjoint query of this type is clearly a possible final query resulting from document retrieval search. It also might appear in the second phase of direct mail applications.

**Table 6.9**  Q4 constraint with three conditions.

| Condition Sequence Numbers | DB2 Elapsed Time | MODEL 204 Elapsed Time | DB2 CPU Time | MODEL 204 CPU Time | DB2 Random I/Os | DB2 Prefetch I/Os | MODEL204 Disk I/Os |
|---|---|---|---|---|---|---|---|
| 1-3 | 147.62 s | 114.03 s | 102.27 s | 20.95 s | 15 | 560 | 9006 |
| 2-4 | 120.38 s | 56.02 s | 100.41 s | 10.78 s | 19 | 157 | 4027 |
| 3-5 | 145.32 s | 27.99 s | 62.07 s | 6.03 s | 16 | 552 | 1854 |
| 4-6 | 195.21 s | 50.62 s | 108.97 s | 7.54 s | 16 | 1826 | 3959 |
| 5-7 | 174.53 s | 94.94 s | 110.47 s | 15.51 s | 13 | 1839 | 7408 |
| 6-8 | 163.08 s | 114.50 s | 114.58 s | 19.78 s | 16 | 674 | 9224 |
| 7-9 | 105.38 s | 54.13 s | 54.38 s | 9.30 s | 16 | 308 | 4056 |
| 8-10 | 54.10 s | 13.99 s | 46.76 s | 2.38 s | 19 | 54 | 930 |

EXPLAIN says that DB2 uses merge-intersects of RID sequences to AND pairs of clauses before accessing the data, except that clauses 1, 5, and 7 are never merged. Thus the sequence 5–7 only uses K4 = 3 to limit the search, whereas the sequence 4–6 merge-intersects K5 = 3 and K4 = 3. Sequences 2–4 and 8–10 merge all three indexes. The CPU times needed are generally quite large, a reflection of the DB2 cost of merging indexes, especially where B-tree scans are needed.

In the MODEL 204 case, the set of records satisfying the ANDed conditions is decided at the index level (all clauses are always ANDed); following this, the rows involved are accessed to form the SUM—thus, retrieving about 10,000 rows involves 9006 page I/Os in the first M204 row in Table 6.9, at about 13 ms elapsed for each of these random I/Os (a certain amount of optimization is built in, so random I/Os are faster than standard). The CPU utilized by MODEL 204 here is generally a small fraction of that used by DB2.

**Table 6.10** Q4 constraint with 5 conditions.

| Condition Sequence Numbers | DB2 Elapsed Time | MODEL 204 Elapsed Time | DB2 CPU Time | MODEL 204 CPU Time | DB2 Random I/Os | DB2 Prefetch I/Os | MODEL204 Disk I/Os |
|---|---|---|---|---|---|---|---|
| 1-5 | 119.64 s | 11.75 s | 81.99 s | 3.93 s | 19 | 157 | 486 |
| 2-6 | 119.47 s | 11.28 s | 81.56 s | 3.84 s | 19 | 157 | 411 |
| 3-7 | 133.65 s | 13.69 s | 89.29 s | 4.57 s | 20 | 187 | 533 |
| 4-8 | 137.56 s | 11.80 s | 92.77 s | 2.60 s | 19 | 191 | 541 |
| 5-9 | 99.42 s | 10.75 s | 72.98 s | 2.42 s | 19 | 113 | 448 |
| 6-10 | 54.37 s | 9.10 s | 43.73 s | 2.37 s | 19 | 54 | 404 |
| 7-1 | 54.11 s | 10.45 s | 43.87 s | 2.55 s | 19 | 54 | 480 |

Once again DB2 uses merge-intersects of RID sequences to AND pairs of clauses before accessing the data, except at most three clauses are ever used, and clauses 1, 5, and 7 are never merged (clause 6 is used only once).

MODEL 204 is much faster, both in elapsed time and CPU utilization, because it combines all index clauses very quickly, and at the end very few records actually need to be retrieved.

## Q5: Multiple Column GROUP BY

The query considered in this section is one where a count of rows is retrieved for a matrix of conditions based on two varying parameters.

```
Q5:     SELECT  KN1, KN2, COUNT(*)
        FROM BENCH
        GROUP BY KN1,KN2;
For each (KN1, KN2) ε { (K2,K100),(K4,K25),  (K10,K25)}
```

This is a reasonably common type of query used in management reporting and decision support to calculate the effect of one factor on another, as explained in Section 6.1.2 on page 363.

**Table 6.11** Q5 measurements.

| KN, KN2 | DB2 Elapsed Time | MODEL 204 Elapsed Time | DB2 CPU Time | MODEL 204 CPU Time | DB2 Random I/Os | DB2 Prefetch I/Os | MODEL204 Disk I/Os |
|---|---|---|---|---|---|---|---|
| K2,K100 | 535.38 s | 43.60 s | 526.13 s | 36.27 s | 3 | 1840 | 420 |
| K4,K25 | 508.25 s | 28.36 s | 500.99 s | 16.72 s | 3 | 1840 | 595 |
| K10,K25 | 540.96 s | 56.07 s | 533.58 s | 40.80 s | 3 | 1840 | 744 |

In this query, DB2 attempts to scan all rows in the tablespace and put out the KN1, KN2 values to a scratch file, then sort these value pairs and gather duplicates with a count. The sort involved is extremely resource-consuming. MODEL 204 is programmed to do the job by performing a double loop on the values involved (values in B-tree indexes can always be looped on in the procedural MODEL 204 user language) and counting the conjoint selection with each pair of values. This is a much more efficient approach than sorting in cases where the table for the end result fits in memory, as is usually the case in a GROUP BY query.

## Q6: Join Condition

The final query type considered involves a join of the BENCH table with itself. The join of the BENCH table with itself presents exactly the same problem to the query optimizer as the join of two separate (large) tables since the overlap between the outer join table and the inner join table is relatively insignificant. Overlap in buffering is therefore not a factor, and there exists no special-purpose strategy for a table self-join that is not comparable to joining two tables. We measure two different cases, Q6A and Q6B. In Query Set Q6A, there is an equality condition limiting the rows of the first table only, then a match across to the second table, and a COUNT is taken of the number of rows formed. We use a COUNT here, rather than retrieve up to 20,000 rows of data into the SPUFI buffer. The Query Q6B, however, retrieves data.

```
Q6A:    SELECT COUNT(*) FROM BENCH B1,BENCH B2
         WHERE B1.KN = 49 AND B1.K250K = B2.K500K;
For each KN ε { K100K, K40K, K10K, K1K, K100}
```

In Query Set Q6B, we retrieve data from a join of two tables, where equality conditions limit the rows on both tables of the join (see the query from Table 6.13). Queries such as Q6A and Q6B might arise in a direct

**Table 6.12** Q6A measurements.

| KN | DB2 Elapsed Time | MODEL 204 Elapsed Time | DB2 CPU Time | MODEL 204 CPU Time | DB2 Random I/Os | DB2 Prefetch I/Os | MODEL204 Disk I/Os |
|---|---|---|---|---|---|---|---|
| K100K | 1.83 s | 0.63 s | 0.73 s | 0.15 s | 30 | 1 | 33 |
| K40K | 2.11 s | 1.03 s | 0.78 s | 0.29 s | 33 | 1 | 53 |
| K10K | 3.41 s | 3.17 s | 1.14 s | 1.09 s | 99 | 4 | 209 |
| K1K | 15.52 s | 21.27 s | 4.95 s | 9.04 s | 644 | 31 | 1617 |
| K100 | 131.01 s | 196.36 s | 47.85 s | 87.58 s | 5608 | 292 | 14167 |

marketing mailing list application, where information for individual prospects are for some reason partitioned into separate tables.

The DB2 plan finds all rows for which B1.KN is equal to 49, then reads each of these rows (using list prefetch in later rows) to find its K250K value, and adds to a total count all rows whose K500K value is equal to this. MODEL 204 has a similar strategy. Both systems are forced to access all rows in the first table to determine the value of the join column, B1.K250K, and can then count the rows in the join by using the B-tree entries for B2.K500K. DB2 has an edge in the later times measured because of the list prefetch capability.

```
Q6B:    SELECT B1.KSEQ, B2.KSEQ
        FROM BENCH B1,BENCH B2
        WHERE B1.KN = 99
        AND B1.K250K = B2.K500K
        AND B2.K25 = 19;
For each KN ε {K40K, K10K, K1K, K100}
```

**Table 6.13** Q6B measurements.

| KN | DB2 Elapsed Time | MODEL 204 Elapsed Time | DB2 CPU Time | MODEL 204 CPU Time | DB2 Random I/Os | DB2 Prefetch I/Os | MODEL204 Disk I/Os |
|---|---|---|---|---|---|---|---|
| K40K | 3.01 s | 1.34 s | 0.87 s | 0.27 s | 23 | 41 | 69 |
| K10K | 9.62 s | 3.33 s | 1.58 s | 0.78 s | 169 | 98 | 232 |
| K1K | 75.31 s | 21.57 s | 9.46 s | 6.18 s | 1609 | 888 | 1710 |
| K100 | 697.34 s | 197.63 s | 89.74 s | 58.71 s | 16338 | 9006 | 15245 |

This query models name and address retrieval in a direct-marketing application. The access strategy in DB2 was to find all rows for which B1.KN is equal to 99, read each of these rows to find the B1.K250K value, then access all B2 rows whose B2.K500K value was equal to this and qualify them according to whether B2.25 = 19. Since there are an average of two B2 rows for each B1 row, Q6B accesses nearly three times as many rows as Q6A, and the elapsed time to perform the query is greater.

MODEL 204 uses the first strategy above but limits its accesses to table B2 by performing a COUNT of B2 rows with B2.K500K values equal to the B1.K250K value that *also* have the property that B2.K25 = 19. Since the count is resolved in the index, only about one row in 25 will have to be accessed in table B2. Thus, only a slight increase in resources over Q6A is required.

## 6.2.3 Rating DB2 and MODEL 204 in $/QPM

The ultimate rating of the Set Query benchmark for any platform measured is the five-year ownership price for each query per minute ($/QPM). As explained in Section 6.3.3, it is possible to weight the results of this benchmark and thus derive a customized measure for the work at a particular site. To report a single representative rating, we calculate the average query throughput under the assumption that all queries of the benchmark are of equal weight (certainly an unlikely real weighting since the queries requiring fewer resources will tend to be preferred).

In the 69 queries reported in Tables 6.4 through 6.13, the total elapsed time for DB2 was 6606.18 seconds, or 110.103 minutes. Thus DB2, on the hardware provided, supported 0.6267 queries per minute (QPM). MODEL 204 had a total elapsed time of 1535.27 seconds, or 25.588 minutes. Thus, MODEL 204 supported 2.697 QPM.

Since the 4381-3 is no longer sold by IBM, the price of an ES/9000 MODEL 150 with an equivalent mips rating was substituted; this machine was priced with 1 channel group, a rack enclosure, two 3990 mod 2 disk controllers, and a 3390 A18 disk with four actuators, to cost $474,235 plus $47,280 for maintenance through the end of a five-year period, for a total of $521,515. This hardware was used by both DB2 and MODEL 204 (actually, it was only half used since only one CPU and two disk arms were utilized, so in the calculation only one half of the total price will be charged).

The software charge for DB2 was calculated on the basis of 58 months (first two months free) of monthly charge for MVS-XA ($3,925), DB2 ($3,335), and DB2PM ($1,111), with a total five-year cost of $485,581. The total for hardware and software was $1,007,003, or $503,516 for half a machine. This half machine supported 0.6267 queries per minute, and so, dividing the cost of the half machine by 0.6267, we arrive at a rating of approximately $803,000/QPM for DB2.

The software charge for MODEL 204 was calculated by adding the five-year cost for MVS-XA, 58 months at $3,925, or $227,650, to the MODEL 204 price of $250,000 and five years of maintenance at a rate of $40,720 (first year free), for a grand total of $640,530. The total of hardware and software was $1,162,045, or $581,022 for half a machine. The half machine supported a rate of 2.345 QPM, and so, dividing the cost of the half machine by 2.697, we arrive at a rating of approximately $248,000/QPM for MODEL 204.

The results of these calculations are summarized in the following table.

**Table 6.14** QPM and $/QPM ratings.

| System | QPM | K$/QPM |
|--------|-----|--------|
| MODEL 204 | 2.697 | $215 |
| DB2 | 0.6267 | $803 |

# 6.3   How To Run the Set Query Benchmark

## 6.3.1   Generating the Data

The pseudocode procedure in Figure 6.2 gives the algorithm used to generate the 12 indexed random column values, K2 through K500K, for the BENCH table. The algorithm for this pseudo-random number generator is suggested by Ward Cheney and David Kincaid [1980], Section 9.1. This procedure is available on tape from Morgan Kaufmann, programmed in C.

```
PROCEDURE FIELDVGEN()              /* Procedure to generate indexed field values */
INTEGER I, J;                      /* Looping Variables */
DOUBLE SEED INIT (1.);             /* Seed For Random Number Generation */
INTEGER ARRAY COLVAL(1:12),        /* Array to hold one row of values */
    COLCARD(1:12)                  /* Array holding largest value in each field */
    INIT (500000,250000,100000,40000,10000,1000,100,25,10,5,4,2); /* Initialize */
FOR I FROM 1 TO 1000000;           /* One Million Rows */
    FOR J FROM 1 TO 12;            /* Twelve randomly generated column values */
        SEED = MOD(16807.0D * SEED, 2147483647.0D);
    /* I.E.: S_{i+1} = (7**5 * S_i ) MOD (2**31-1), where S_i is SEED, a random # */
        COLVAL(J) = MOD(SEED, COLCARD(J) )+1;   /* Generate next column value */
    END FOR J                      /* Row complete */
    PRINT COLVAL VALUES FOR THIS ROW TO OUTPUT;  /* Output row's values */
END FOR I                          /* We have generated One Million Rows */
END
```

**Figure 6.2**
Generator for indexed field data generation.

Note that the column values generated are whole integers, but the calculations are performed in double precision arithmetic. This is because the intermediate results in the calculation of successive random numbers can become as large as $(7^5) \times (2^{31}-2)$, too large for accurate representation as 32-

bit integers. Programmers lacking a MOD function, which applies to double precision whole numbers, should perform their own MOD calculation by performing the division and finding the remainder, being careful to choose the truncated whole number. The correct column values to generate for the first ten rows can be found in Table 6.1.

We see that the KSEQ values are not generated here (although they could be) since they are simply the successive values 1, 2, 3, . . ., the ordinal number of each row in order, which can often be created while the load is taking place. Recall, too, that in addition to these indexed columns, there are also a number of character columns, s1 (length 8), s2 through s8 (length 20 each) that fill out the row to a length of 200 bytes. These character strings are generated with identical values (not compressed by the database load) since they are never used in retrieval queries, a reflection of the fact that unindexed retrieval in large, low-update tables is extremely inadvisable.

## Loading the Data

Indexes for these 13 columns, KSEQ together with the columns K2 through K500K, are the only ones permitted for the BENCH table; to allow for range search and possible small corrections, the indexes should be of B-tree type (if available) and loaded 95 percent full. Although additional concatenated indexes may improve query performance in some products, there is difficulty in deciding which pairs or triples of columns should be concatenated; it is inappropriate to index all pairs, for example, since $(13 \times 12)/2$ indexes would be required, and this is extremely wasteful of space. Therefore, in the interests of comparing results between different systems, only these 13 indexes are allowed for the benchmark.

The Set Query benchmark permits the data to be loaded on as many disk devices as desired. However, only those systems that break down a single query into a number of parts for parallel execution and improved elapsed time performance can keep more than one disk arm busy at one time on behalf of a single user. Since all devices used must be included in the price of the system, two disks is usually sufficient on single-threaded systems, one disk for data and one for indexes. (Since the pattern of page references often alternates between data and index, using two disks for these purposes can often reduce seek time, with obvious improvement in performance.) The disks referred to above are rotating platter disks or equivalent devices, which contain the data when power is turned off. Semiconductor disks can also be configured on the system, but the time required to populate them at system startup must be reported.

## 6.3.2 Running the Queries: Buffer Flushing

With the advent of much cheaper memory on many systems, we must be extremely attentive to the question of how much of the data and indexes for the BENCH table we allow to be held in memory. There are a number of considerations to take into account.

First, assume that one platform provides much less expensive memory than another. Since our criterion of comparison between two systems is simply to compare the $/QPM ratings, we must prefer a platform that can make a larger portion of the BENCH table memory resident if this translates into a reduced value for this number. At the same time, we need to realize that the various commercial systems we are attempting to model with the Set Query benchmark might have different requirements of size. A 1 million row BENCH table can be completely loaded into a memory of about 300 million bytes. This implies that a 100 million row table will require 30 billion bytes of memory, which is not feasible on current machines. If we are trying to model a commercial system with size requirements comparable to the 1 million row table, the best strategy might be to start by loading all data and index into memory—naturally, this preparation time must be reported in the benchmark report. On the other hand, if we are modeling a 100 million row commercial system, we might wish to limit the memory size quite strictly since memory sizes that permit only a small fraction of data and index residence (10 percent, say), offer only a small advantage in performance, and this advantage may not be worth the additional memory price.

To support tuning decisions regarding memory purchase, the Set Query benchmark offers two approaches. First, it is possible to scale the BENCH table to any integer multiple of 1 million bytes, populating memory buffers in advance and thus modeling most closely the eventual size of the commercial system. As we will see in Section 6.3.3, a special scaling of the results is necessary to compare results of a 1 million row table with those of, say, a 10 million row table. The only problem with this approach is that no single benchmark provides appropriate results for all different sizes of databases modeled; in the worst case, a different proportion of data and index should be present in memory for each different size.

The default buffer strategy, under which a set of measurements should be included in all generic Set Query benchmark reports, normalizes the benchmark measurements by essentially flushing the buffers between successive queries so that the number of I/Os is maximum; this approach models an extremely large database, where a significant proportion of data and index residence in memory is out of the question. An advantage is that all different platforms and different-sized databases can be compared in terms of this measurement since it is possible to use the data of this default benchmark and by careful analysis project the performance where various proportions of the data and index are memory-resident. In general, the analyst will always know the access strategy and the index and data pages referenced; by estimating the proportion of the various entities that would be present in memory under different conditions, it is possible to project the number of resulting I/Os, reduce the CPU to reflect the overhead saved when I/O pages are found in buffer, and estimate the elapsed time, either CPU or I/O bound, that results.

In the default benchmark setup of Section 6.2, the amount of space used for memory buffering was strictly limited to 4.8 Mbytes (1200 4-Kbyte buffers), and an attempt was made to flush the buffers between queries in cases where a substantial amount of overlap of pages was evident. The reason that 1200 buffers were used was, first, that the DB2 query optimizer made a decision on the size of sequential and list prefetch based on the memory buffer size so that the best results were obtained with more than 1000 buffers, and, second, that by limiting the number of buffer pages we were able to flush the buffers in a shorter period of time. One method of flushing buffers used was to run Query Q6B in the K1K case; in this query, the number of (random) pages read was over 1600 for both products, most of them data pages distributed rather randomly over the BENCH table. Another possibility for flushing buffers is to bring down the database and bring it up again, but if this approach is used, the benchmark engineer should perform some short query at the beginning of each run to get database startup work out of the way. Note that flushing buffers is time consuming, and it is comforting that the entire sequence of queries in Table 6.4, for example, can be run without intervening flush actions (at least for the architecture of the two products measured here) since there is no overlap in the pages referenced. If in doubt whether two queries, A and B, have a large overlap in page access, the buffer-clearing technique can be followed by Query A and then Query B, in that order, then the buffer clearing again, followed by Query B and then Query A. If the measures for the two runs of

Query A or the two runs of Query B are significantly different, then it is clear that the queries have an effect on each other.

Recall from the discussion following Query Q1 in Section 2.2.1 that the 22 Existence Bitmap pages of MODEL 204 were allowed to remain in buffer from one query to another. The rationale for clearing buffers is that we do not wish to allow unfeasible buffer residence in the largest databases. A residence set of 22 pages per million rows was considered sufficiently small to be acceptable, and in practice these pages would be present at all times when queries against the table were common enough to make performance a major concern. Readers interested in an objective criterion for determining the economically feasible use of memory buffers should read the interesting article by Gray and Putzolu [1987].

The queries of the Set Query benchmark can be run using either an interactive ad-hoc interface or a programmatic embedded interface on a standalone machine. The type of interface used should be reported, along with approximate difference in resource use between the two interfaces, if known.

## 6.3.3    Interpreting the Results

A common demand of decision makers who require benchmark results is a single number, a measure rating the different platforms. It is all very well to make the case that there is so much diversity among the requirements of different Set Queries that boiling this diversity down to a single measure loses too much detail, but the simplistic demand for a single rating has an important point in its favor. The ultimate purpose of a benchmark is to form a basis for deciding on the acquisition of one platform over another, a simple ranking of the alternatives, which calls for a single measure. Viewed in this light, the only appropriate normative measure seems to be price per unit of throughput, which is the ultimate rating generated by the Set Query benchmark, just as it is for the TPC and the DebitCredit benchmarks. Naturally, requirements for a system may exist that are incomparable with price; a hard real-time requirement that a particular class of queries or transactions cannot take more than a specified length of time is the most obvious example. Requirements of this kind entail extra restrictions on the multiuser load and are outside the realm of current benchmarks.

The practice of reporting a spectrum of measurements along parameters of function and selectivity allows the system manager to generate a single rating on different platforms for the weighted subset of queries peculiar to his or her installation. We do not wish to lose this advantage by reporting a single number that fits no particular case. Fortunately, it is simple to specify a single price-related measure (with an equal weighting of all queries tested, which is probably quite unrealistic in most cases) and still require that the benchmark report on the details of the measurements so that customized ratings can still be created.

## Calculating the $/QPM Rating

The calculation of the $PRICE/QPM rating for the Set Query benchmark is quite straightforward, as we have already seen in Section 6.2.3. There are 69 queries in the benchmark, and if we say that the elapsed time to run all of them in series is $T$ minutes, then we are running $69/T$ queries per minute. The system on which the benchmark is run has a well-defined dollar price, $P$, for hardware + software + maintenance (where software cost and hardware maintenance charges are given as a rental fee, the common accounting technique is to add the costs over a five-year period and take this as the full price). Now the $/QPM rating is clearly given by $P \times T/69$.

This is the true $/QPM value for the benchmark measured. However, as the size of the BENCH table scales up, the resources needed for the average query also increase in a (slightly more than) linear fashion. To compare results from a 10 million row table with those from a 1 million row table, we normalize the value $/QPM in the 10 million row case by dividing by 10. Any benchmark results for a multimillion-row table should also report the default buffer flushed results and optimal price results for a 1 million row table so that analysts can compare with different platforms and see explicit scaleup factors on the platform measured.

To perform the above calculation for a custom system, we represent the set of queries performed during a time period $T$ as some weighted set of the queries, with nonnegative weights $W_i$. We can take this to mean that query $i$ is performed $W_i$ times during the time period (possibly a fractional number representing an average). Then if we assume that query $q_i$ takes $T_i$ minutes to complete, we can calculate the total time period $T$ with the formula $T = \Sigma_i W_i \times T_i$, where the total number of queries $K$ executed during this time period is $K = \Sigma_i W_i$. Then the custom rating for this weighting is given by $P \times T/K$. Again, a multimillion-row table should be scaled to a million-row table result by appropriate division.

## 6.4 Configuration and Reporting Requirements, a Checklist

The following is a checklist of steps, procedures, and tests that should be done in order to perform the Set Query benchmark.

- The data should be generated in the precise manner given in Figure 6.2; the first ten rows should have the values shown in Table 6.1; counts of queries specified in Appendix for the 1 million row BENCH table should be matched by the data.

- The BENCH table should be loaded on the appropriate number of stable devices (e.g., rotating media disks), and the resource utilization for the load, together with any preparatory utilities to improve performance (reorganization of table structure, index creation, statistics gathering for Query Optimizer, etc.) should be reported. The rows and 13 indexes should be loaded so that individual disk pages are 95 percent full. In general, when we refer to resource utilization in what follows, we are referring to elapsed time, CPU time, and disk I/Os (possibly, as with DB2, of more than one kind). For the load, we also require that the disk media space utilization be reported, together with the type of index utilization statistics reported here in Table 6.3.

- Naturally, care should be taken that the database system is properly tuned for nearly optimal access to the table; any deviation from this course should be explained.

- The exact hardware/software configuration used for the test should be reported (see first paragraph of Section 6.2.1), with vendor's mips rating, if known, the number of disks and channels, including the disk models used, OS Version, and Database System Version number. If multiple CPUs exist in the hardware, the exact number of CPUs utilized during the single-user benchmark queries should be reported.

- The access strategy for each Query reported should be explained in the report if this capability is offered by the database system.

- The benchmark should be run from either an interactive or an embedded program and the Page Buffer and Sort Buffer (if separate) space in Mbytes should be reported (e.g., 1200 4-Kbyte buffers, used for both buffering and sort). If a benchmark with memory resident data and index is being performed, a series of queries to populate the buffers should be performed in advance of any benchmark measurements, and the resource usage (elapsed time, CPU, and I/Os) required should be reported. If the default buffer-flush approach of Section 6.2 is being measured, it is necessary to assure that no large amount of useful information remains in buffers between one query and the next.

- All resource use should be reported for each of the queries, as reported here in Section 6.2.2. The overhead of taking statistics is difficult to measure, but any estimates by the vendor or software suppliers should be reported.

- The $/QPM should be calculated and reported as in Section 6.2.3, following the prescription given earlier in Section 6.3.3.

# 6.5   Concluding Remarks

Variation in resource use seen in Section 6.2 translates into large dollar price differences. The database industry is only beginning the cycle of design improvements in the area of Set Query performance. We can expect major new product releases in the next several years as better architectural approaches are consolidated. Standard benchmarks by which progress can be measured are therefore of the greatest importance.

Extensions to the Set Query benchmark have been suggested by a number of observers, and a multiuser Set Query benchmark is under development. Because of extremely long response time for the average query, a number of conceptual difficulties arise. It seems that the interactive model of the TPC benchmark is unrealistic for many queries on large tables, and so the response time cutoff by which transactional throughput is determined would be inappropriate. At the same time, the method used in the $AS^3AP$ benchmark to measure the total time expended has the implicit effect of imposing a specific weighting on each of the operations measured: We cannot separately weight the individual queries to arrive at a custom rating if we believe that the measures of the individual queries are sensitive to concurrent thread operations in an unpredictable way. The author has benchmarking experience to support a belief that multiuser throughput under varying workloads can be predicted from single-user measures of individual queries when the physical layout of the data is well balanced on secondary storage. Since purchasing extra disk drives should serve to make the CPU a more fully utilized resource with reasonably sophisticated systems, this implies that query CPU utilization will be the resource bottleneck for throughput under a multiuser workload. An observation such as this can have important implications in product comparisons where the elapsed time and CPU resources are not proportional. For example, the ratio of total elapsed time between the two products tested in Section 6.2 is DB2/M204 = 6606/1535, or about 4.3, and this ratio is reflected in the single-user QPM measures reported in Table 6.14; in the multiuser case, however, if throughput is more closely linked to total CPU time utilization, then the ratio increases to 4185/564, or about 7.4.

The most important implication of demonstrating predictability of multiuser throughput in terms of single-user results is that this will make it possible to generalize the customization approach of Section 6.3.3 to the multiuser case. The value of being able to customize results from a generic multiuser Set Query benchmark is obvious, and it is hoped that this capability will be present in the next Set Query benchmark version.

# Acknowledgments

It is appropriate to acknowledge here the debt that the current work owes to the Wisconsin benchmark [Bitton, DeWitt, & Turbyfill, 1983], in particular the importance of a "synthetic" database and a spectrum of selectivity factors. The author would also like to thank Richard Winter and the editor, Jim Gray, for many valuable suggestions and insights in bringing the Set Query benchmark to its current form.

# References

Anon et al. (1988). A measure of transaction processing power. In M. Stonebraker (Ed.), *Readings in Database Systems*, pp. 300–312. San Mateo, CA: Morgan Kaufmann.

Bitton, D., DeWitt, D. J., & Turbyfill, C. (1983). Benchmarking database systems: a systematic approach. *Proceedings of the Ninth International Conference on Very Large Databases*. Florence, Italy.

Cheney, W., & Kincaid, D. (1980). *Numerical mathematics and computing*. Monterey, CA: Brooks/Cole Publishing Company.

Gray, J., & Putzolu, F. (1987). The five minute rule for trading memory for disk accesses and the 10 byte rule for trading memory for CPU time. *Proceedings of the 1987 ACM SIG-MOD Conference*, pp. 395–398.

O'Neil, P. E. (1989). Revisiting DBMS benchmarks. *Datamation, 35*(18), pp. 47–52.

Transaction Processing Performance Council (TPC). (1991). TPC BENCHMARK A and TPC BENCHMARK B standard specifications. In *The Performance Handbook for Database and Transaction Processing Systems*. San Mateo, CA: Morgan Kaufmann.

Turbyfill, C., Orji, C., & Bitton, D. (1991). AS[3]AP: an ANSI SQL standard scaleable and portable benchmark for relational database systems. In *The Performance Handbook for Database and Transaction Processing Systems*. San Mateo, CA: Morgan Kaufmann.

# Appendix. Counts of Rows Retrieved by Queries

What follows is a listing of the number of rows selected in each of the queries measured, Q1 through Q6B. This is meant to serve as an aid to the researcher attempting to duplicate these results. In a few cases, other measures than number of rows selected are given.

| QUERY | CASE | ROW COUNT | |
|---|---|---|---|
| Q1 | KSEQ | 1 | |
| -- | K100K | 8 | |
| -- | K10K | 98 | |
| -- | K1K | 1,003 | |
| -- | K100 | 10,091 | |
| -- | K25 | 39,845 | |
| -- | K10 | 99,902 | |
| -- | K5 | 200,637 | |
| -- | K4 | 249,431 | |
| -- | K2 | 499,424 | |
| | | | |
| Q2A | KSEQ | 1 | |
| -- | K100K | 5 | |
| -- | K10K | 58 | |
| -- | K1K | 487 | |
| -- | K100 | 5,009 | |
| -- | K25 | 19,876 | |
| -- | K10 | 49,939 | |
| -- | K5 | 100,081 | |
| -- | K4 | 125,262 | |
| | | | |
| Q2B | KSEQ | 499,423 | |
| -- | K100K | 499,419 | |
| -- | K10K | 499,366 | |
| -- | K1K | 498,937 | |
| -- | K100 | 494,415 | |
| -- | K25 | 479,548 | |
| -- | K10 | 449,485 | |
| -- | K5 | 399,343 | |
| -- | K4 | 374,162 | |
| | | | **SUM** |
| Q3A | K100K | 1 | 434 |
| -- | K10K | 9 | 5,513 |
| -- | K100 | 991 | 496,684 |
| -- | K25 | 3,989 | 1,978,118 |
| -- | K10 | 9,920 | 4,950,698 |
| -- | K5 | 2011? | 10,027,345 |
| -- | K4 | 24,9?? | 12,499,521 |

| Q3B | K100K | 1 | 434 |
|-----|-------|---|-----|
| -- | K10K | 6 | 3,300 |
| -- | K100 | 597 | 299,039 |
| -- | K25 | 2,423 | 1,209,973 |
| -- | K10 | 5,959 | 2,967,225 |
| -- | K5 | 12,000 | 5,980,617 |
| -- | K4 | 15,031 | 7,496,733 |
| | | | |
| Q4A | 1-3 | 10,059 | |
| -- | 2-4 | 4,027 | |
| -- | 3-5 | 1,637 | |
| -- | 4-6 | 4,021 | |
| -- | 5-7 | 7,924 | |
| -- | 6-8 | 10,294 | |
| -- | 7-9 | 4,006 | |
| -- | 8-10 | 785 | |
| | | | |
| Q4B | 1-5 | 161 | |
| -- | 2-6 | 86 | |
| -- | 3-7 | 142 | |
| -- | 4-8 | 172 | |
| -- | 5-9 | 77 | |
| -- | 6-10 | 76 | |
| -- | 7-1 | 152 | |
| | | | |
| Q5 | K2=K100=1 | 4962 | |
| -- | K4=K25=1 | 9970 | |
| -- | K10=K25=1 | 4049 | |
| | | | |
| Q6A | K100K | 23 | |
| -- | K40K | 55 | |
| -- | K10K | 239 | |
| -- | K1K | 2,014 | |
| -- | K100 | 19,948 | |
| | | | |
| Q6B | K40K | 3 | |
| -- | K10K | 4 | |
| -- | K1K | 81 | |
| -- | K100 | 804 | |

# 7
# An Engineering Database Benchmark

R. G. G. Cattell

*Sun Microsystems*

## 7.1    Introduction

Performance is a major issue in the acceptance of object-oriented and extended relational database systems aimed at engineering applications such as computer-aided software engineering (CASE) and computer-aided design (CAD). Because traditional database system benchmarks such as those covered earlier in this book [Bitton, DeWitt, and Turbyfill, 1983; Anon et al., 1985; TPC, 1989] do not measure the performance of features essential to engineering applications, we designed a benchmark for operations on engineering database objects. The benchmark, named OO1 (Object Operations version 1), sometimes called the "Cattell Benchmark," has been run on a dozen database products and prototypes. This chapter describes the benchmark and the results obtained running it on a relational DBMS and on an object-oriented DBMS. This chapter derives from a paper by Cattell and Skeen [in press]. OO1 is a redesign of an earlier, more primitive benchmark described in Rubenstein, Kubicar, and Cattell [1987].

The OO1 benchmark is important because traditional DBMSs are a factor of ten times to one hundred times too slow for many engineering applications when compared with DBMSs specifically designed for engineering applications. Functionality of DBMSs aimed at engineering applications is not useful when the performance shortfall is large. Engineering applications are of particular interest to us, so we sought to bring focus on these performance issues. This chapter not only provides a careful specification and demonstration of the OO1 benchmark, it also shows that an order of magnitude difference in performance can result by reducing overhead in database calls, implementing new distributed database architectures, taking advantage of large main memories, and using link-based access methods.

Measuring engineering DBMS performance in a generic way is very difficult since every application has somewhat different requirements. However, most engineering applications are quite similar at the data-access level. The operations they perform on data are not easily expressed in the abstractions provided by SQL and other high-level query languages. Instead, engineering applications typically utilize a programming language interspersed with operations on individual persistent data objects. Although database access at this level is in some ways a step backward from modern query languages, it is a step forward from current ad hoc implementations and is the best solution available.

As an example, consider a CAD application. Components and their interconnections on a circuit board might be stored in a database, and an optimization algorithm might follow connections between components and rearrange them to reduce wire lengths. In a CASE application, program modules and their interdependencies might be stored in a database, and a system-build algorithm might traverse the dependency graph examining version numbers to construct a compilation plan. In both cases, hundreds or thousands of objects are accessed per second, perhaps executing the equivalent of a relational join for each object. Simply adding transitive closure to the query language is inadequate, as the steps performed at each junction can be arbitrarily complex. Either the DBMS must provide the full functionality of a programming language in the database query language, or it must be possible to efficiently mix the programming and query language statements.

## 7.2    Engineering Database Performance

The OO1 benchmark differs in a number of ways from the TPC-A and Wisconsin benchmarks described earlier in this book. TPC-A is designed to measure transaction throughput with large numbers of users, whereas OO1 focuses on an engineer with negligible contention with other users. Some of the Wisconsin measures are relevant to engineering performance, but they generally are too coarse and focus on the intelligence of the query optimizer on complex queries. Such set-oriented operations are rare in current engineering applications.

The most accurate measure of performance for engineering applications would be to run an actual application, representing data in the manner best suited to each potential DBMS. However, it is difficult or impossible to design an application whose performance would be representative of many different engineering applications, and we want a generic measure. Perhaps in the future someone will be successful at this more difficult task [Maier, 1987].

The generic benchmark measures in OO1 are operations expected to be most frequent in engineering applications, based on interviews with CASE and CAD engineers and feedback on the earlier Sun benchmark [Rubenstein, Kubicar, and Cattell, 1987]. OO1 substantially improves upon the earlier work, simplifying and focusing the measurement on these engineering database operations. An effort by Anderson et al. [1990] has also been made to improve on the earlier benchmark; however that work has gone in the direction of a more comprehensive set of measures rather than simpler ones. These benchmarks are contrasted in Section 7.5.

The OO1 measures include inserting objects, looking up objects, and following connections among objects. Engineering applications may also require more complex or ad hoc queries, so performance on OO1 alone does not make a system acceptable. However, current systems are orders of magnitude away from acceptable performance levels for engineering applications, so we aim to focus attention on the area where the highest performance is required, just as the TPC-A benchmark focuses on commercial online transaction processing.

The benchmark is designed to be applied to object-oriented, relational, network, or hierarchical database systems, even B-tree packages or custom application-specific database systems. It is designed to be scaleable, to be representative of small database working sets that can be cached in main memory and large ones that require efficient access methods. To make it portable, the benchmark is defined in terms of ANSI C and ANSI SQL. Any equivalent implementation is allowed (see Appendix A).

There is a tremendous gap between the performance provided by in-memory programming language data structures and that provided by disk-based structures in a conventional database management system. Existing database systems typically respond to random read queries in tenths of a second. In contrast, simple lookups using in-memory data structures can be performed in microseconds. This difference of 100,000:1 in response time is the result of many factors, not simply disk access. There is a place for a database system that fills the gap between these two systems, performing close to 1000 simple random read queries per second on typical engineering databases. This requirement comes from a desire to perform operations on complex objects with thousands of components in a few seconds.

How can much higher performance be achieved? Primarily, by exploiting characteristics of engineering applications, which are quite different from business applications. For example, an engineer may "check out" part of a design and work on it for hours, with no requirements for concurrent updates by other engineers, and the data can largely be cached in main memory on the engineer's workstation.

Large improvements in engineering database performance are probably not going to be accomplished through minor improvements in data model, physical representation, or query languages. The substantial improvements result from major changes in DBMS architecture: caching a large working set of data in main memory, minimizing overhead in transferring data between programming and query languages, implementing data access and concurrency on a network at a page level to reduce overhead, and providing new access methods with fixed rather than logarithmic access time. Differences in data models (e.g., relational and object-oriented) can be dwarfed by architectural differences, as long as the data model does not dictate implementation.

## 7.3   The Benchmark Database

The OO1 benchmark database is independent of the data model provided by the DBMS. The following should therefore be regarded as an abstract definition of the information to be stored, possibly as a single object type with list-valued fields, possibly as two or more record types in a relational system.

The database is defined as two logical records:

```
create table part ( id          integer      not null primary key,
                     type        char(10)     not null,
                     x           integer      not null,
                     y           integer      not null,
                     build       datetime     not null
                   );
create table connection (
                     from        integer      foreign key references (part.id),
                     to          integer      foreign key references (part.id),
                     length      integer      not null,
                     type        char(10)     not null,
                     primary key(from,to, length)
                   );
```

A database of $N$ parts will have dense unique part numbers (*part.id*) in the range [$1..N$]. Such a database will have $3N$ connections, with exactly three connections from each part to other (randomly selected) parts. The $x$, $y$, and *length* field values are randomly distributed in the range [$0..99999$], the *type* fields have values randomly selected from the strings {`"part-type0"` ... `"part-type9"`}, and the *build* date is randomly distributed in a ten-year range.

It is assumed that the database system allows data fields with the scalar types specified above, where `integer` is a 32-bit integer, `date` is some representation of a date and time, and `char(n)` is a variable-length string of maximum size n. The `from` and `to` fields of the connection relation are references to specific parts; they might be implemented by part-ID foreign keys in a relational DBMS or by unique identifiers in an object-oriented DBMS. Also, it is permissible to combine part and connection information in a single object, if the DBMS permits it. However, the information associated with connections (*type* and *length*) must be preserved. Also, it must be possible to traverse connections in either direction.

The random connections between parts are selected to produce some locality of reference. Specifically, 90 percent of the connections are randomly selected among the 1 percent of parts that are "closest," and the remaining connections are made to any randomly selected part. Closeness is defined using the parts with the numerically closest part-IDs. The following algorithm selects part connections, where rand[1..k] is a random integer in the range 1 to $k$, and $N$ is the number of parts in the database.

```
    halfPercent := N/200;
for part in [1..N]
    begin
    for connection in [1..3]
        begin
            if rand[1..10]>1 then      /* 90% of connection to closest 1% */
                begin
                cpart := part - halfPercent + rand[1 .. 2*halfPercent + 1];
                /* "double up" at the ends to stay in part-id range */
                if cpart < halfPercent then cpart := cpart + halfPercent;
                if cpart > N - halfPercent then cpart := cpart - halfPercent;
                end;
            else                /* 10% of time connect to any part [1..N] */
                cpart := rand[1..N];
        end;
            connect(part, cpart, length, type);        /* add connection */
    end;
```

Using part-IDs for locality is quite arbitrary; we justify why this is as good as any other criterion in Section 7.6.

A database of 20,000 parts comprises approximately two megabytes of attribute data, plus space overhead for access methods and record storage, which typically doubles this amount. As such, the typical database used in the experiments reported here is approximately four megabytes altogether and is a good representative of an engineering database working set that fits entirely in main memory—for example, the data associated with a CAD drawing shown on the screen, the data in one engineer's portion of a larger engineering design or software project, or a working set from a larger knowledge base used by an expert system.

A benchmark must also scale up to larger databases and working sets, exploiting access structures that use secondary memory efficiently. A *large* database is therefore included in the benchmark, identical to the smaller one except that all of the record counts are scaled up by a factor of ten. This database then requires approximately 40 megabytes of storage and overhead. Some database systems will not show a substantial performance difference on the larger database since they do not utilize large main memory caches and their access methods scale up well with database size. Other systems, e.g., a persistent programming language, may not even permit databases of this size.

Results for a *huge* 400-megabyte database are also examined to test performance on larger databases. However, the huge database is not part of the OO1 benchmark requirements since the results were found to differ less dramatically than the first two. Note that 400 megabytes might not be considered "huge" in other benchmarks covered by this book, and some engineering applications may have larger databases, but the most important characteristic of the database for our purposes will be whether it all fits in main memory. 400 megabytes is a huge *working set*, and 40 megabytes is large by these standards. In an engineering application, these working sets may be checked out of a larger database.

Unlike most other benchmarks, the OO1 specification requires that remote database access be implemented on a network. The results for both local and remote access to data must be reported, i.e., for a configuration in which the data are on disks attached to the same machine as the benchmark application or on another machine. Since most engineering applications run on a workstation with the data on a server, remote access is actually the more important configuration. The experimental results reported in Section 7.8 show that performance differs significantly from a benchmark with only local data: remote access is substantially affected by the caching and concurrency control architecture of the DBMS.

# 7.4   Benchmark Measures

The benchmark measures *response time* and is run by a single user.[1] This is consistent with the model of an engineer checking out a segment of data for exclusive use; indeed, adequate performance may not even be achievable with current technology if there is highly concurrent access by multiple users. However, it is important for the DBMS to *allow* multiuser access to the database. OO1 requires that the data used be locked or versioned in order to support multiple users.

The following three operations are the OO1 benchmark measures. Each measure is run ten times, measuring response time for each run to check consistency and caching behavior.

- *Lookup*. Generate 1000 random part IDs, and fetch the corresponding parts from the database. For each part, call a null procedure written in any host programming language, passing the $x,y$ position and type of the part.

- *Traversal*. Find all parts connected to a randomly selected part, or to a part connected to it, and so on, up to 7 hops (total of 3280 parts, with

---

[1]Response time is the real (wall clock) time elapsed from the point when a program calls the database system with a particular query, until the results of the query, if any, have been placed into the program's variables.

possible duplicates). For each part, call a null programming language procedure with the value of the $x$ and $y$ fields, and the part type. Perform the traversal depth-first. Also measure time for *reverse* traversal, swapping "from" and "to" directions, to compare the results obtained.

*Insert.* Enter 100 parts and three connections from each to other randomly selected parts. Time must be included to update indices or other access structures used in the execution of *lookup* and *traversal*. Call a programming language procedure to obtain the $x,y$ position for each insert. Commit the changes to the disk.

There is some value to a single overall performance time, as with the TPC-A benchmark. The OO1 benchmark is designed so that the three measures are executed approximately in proportion to their frequency of occurrence in representative applications (an order of magnitude more reads than writes, and several times more traversal operations than lookups, as a very rough estimate from interviews with CASE and CAD engineers), so that a single overall number can be computed by adding the three results. However, it is important not to abuse the overall number because the frequency of occurrence of these operations will differ widely between applications: the individual measures are important.

Note that the specification requires that the host programming language be called on each simple operation above or that each database operation be called from the host programming language, to simulate an engineering application where arbitrary programming operations must be mixed with database operations. For the three operations above, for example, the corresponding procedures might (1) display the part on the screen, (2) compute the total wire lengths, and (3) compute the $x,y$ position for placing the part in a diagram.

The requirement to call the host application programming language may be controversial, but it is an important feature of the OO1 benchmark. Using current relational DBMSs, frequent DBMS calls from an application program can only be reduced by copying all the desired data from the database in a single "batch" super-query or by embedding a portion of the application program (that cannot be expressed in the query language) as a procedure executed within the query on the database server.

Embedding application procedures in queries is not practical because the procedures cannot interact with the rest of the application program and must perform computation on the server instead of utilizing the distributed workstations. In a real application, a "traversal" would probably not traverse every node to a fixed depth; the application might perform arbitrary computation based on previous parts visited, global data structures, and perhaps even user input, to decide which nodes to traverse next.

Copying all the data at once is not practical for many engineering applications because of the limited expressiveness of the query language and the overhead of copying data between the environments. A *batch* version of OO1 has been proposed to represent applications that *can* perform a single database call, for example the 1000 *lookups*, without interaction with the application. However, only the *interactive* version results, as described here, have been reported to date.

The OO1 benchmark measures are designed to be representative of the data operations in common engineering applications. For example, in a CASE application, an operation very similar to the traversal must be performed to determine a compilation plan for a system configuration, an operation like the lookup is needed to find programs associated with a particular system or range of dates, and an operation like the insert is needed to enter new information after a new module is compiled. In an ECAD application, the traversal is needed to optimize a circuit layout, the lookup to find components with particular types, and the insertion to add new components to a circuit board.

The benchmark measures must be performed at least ten times, the first time with no data cached. These repetitions provide a consistency check on the variation on the results and also show the performance (on the second, third, and remaining iterations) as increasingly more data are in memory. Of course, there will be some cache hits even on the first iteration, depending on database system parameters such as page size, clustering, and caching strategy. As a result, the average cache hit rate for the first iteration can be as low as 10 percent or as large as 90 percent.

The results of the first iteration are called the *cold* start results, and the asymptotic best times (the tenth iteration, when the cache is fully initialized) are called the *warm* start results. In the systems we measured, the warm asymptote was achieved in only two or three iterations, with only small (under 10 percent) random variations after that.

A *different* set of random parts is fetched with each iteration of the measures. Thus, most or all of the database must be cached in order to obtain good performance: the small database constitutes a working set that can fit in memory; the large database constitutes a working set that does not fit in memory.

The benchmark implementor may cluster parts in the database so that the forward traversal in measure (2) may go faster than the reverse traversal. It is up to the user to decide whether the slower reverse traversal would be acceptable for their application. It is not acceptable to implement *no* access method for reverse traversal (e.g., do linear search to find parts connected to a part); this would take too long for almost any application. For example, in a CASE application it must be possible to find modules on which the current module depends as well as modules dependent upon the current module.

Note that the results for the reverse traversal may vary widely, as each part has three parts it is connected "to" but has a random number of parts it is connected "from" (three on average). However, the average should be similar to the forward traversal. It is convenient to count the number of nodes visited on the reverse traversal and then to normalize the result to obtain comparable figures. Since 3280 parts are visited in the forward traversal, the reverse traversal results can be normalized by multiplying the time by $3280/N$, where $N$ is the number of nodes actually visited.

It is not acceptable to take advantage of the fact that the benchmark part-IDs are numbered sequentially and compute disk address directly from part-ID—some sort of hash index, B-tree index, and/or record (object) ID-based link structure is necessary for a realistic implementation.

Engineering applications typically require some form of concurrency control, but there is currently much debate as to whether they require the atomic transactions of commercial DBMSs or whether some form of versions or locking plus logging of updates is better. The OO1 benchmark requires that (1) the DBMS provide serializability consistency under concurrent access, e.g., by locking data read and written, (2) the DBMS support some form of recovery for the insert measure, backing out updates if a failure occurs before all 100 parts and associated connections are inserted, and (3) these concurrency and recovery constraints be satisfied with multiple readers and writers on a network of machines. A transaction mechanism satisfies these constraints, but different implementations (e.g., based on new versions of data) are also acceptable. If the DBMS provides more than one choice, it is important to know the performance of each alternative .

The benchmark measures must be performed on both the small and large database, as described earlier. Both the space and time requirements must be reported.

The data must be located on a machine different from the user, on a remote database server on a network. Results may also be reported for a local database, as is done in Section 7.9; but, we believe the remote results are a more realistic model of new engineering and office applications.

## 7.5 Benchmark Justification

This section justifies many of the choices made in the design of OO1 and contrasts OO1 to our earlier benchmark and to the HyperModel benchmark.

### 7.5.1 Earlier Benchmark

The OO1 benchmark is both simpler and more realistic than that defined in Rubenstein, Cattell, and Kubicar [1987]. The database itself is similar, although OO1 incorporates locality of reference and uses a database of parts and connections instead of authors and documents (the database contents are a minor point, but it has been a source of confusion about intended applications).

OO1 drops two measures included in our original paper. The *range lookup* measure found the parts in a ten-day range of *part.build* dates. In our experience, the result of this measure is very similar to the OO1 *lookup* measure; in fact, they differed only when more than a few parts were found (in which case, the time was dominated by the copying time rather than by the index lookup). The *sequential scan* was also dropped; it enumerated all parts in the database to fetch the $x,y$ position for each.

The *reference* and *group* lookup measure in the original benchmark were replaced with the OO1 *traversal* measure. These measures involved following references (e.g., from a connection record to a part) or back-references (e.g., from a part to the connections that reference it). We had hoped to estimate the time to do complex operations, such as the *traversal* now in OO1, by composing individual *reference* and *group* lookup times. In practice, it was hard to specify these measurements in a way that different implementors got consistent numbers for their DBMS without including the set-up time, e.g., to fetch the record from which the reference emanated. So, they were replaced with the *traversal* measure.

We considered including *update* (in addition to *insert*) of part records but found the results for *update* and *insert* to be closely correlated. So only *insert* is present in OO1.

Thus, we chose the *lookup, traversal*, and *insert* operations as sufficient for a simple, focused benchmark. This eliminated *range lookup, sequential scan*, and *update* measures from the set. However, these additional measures may be important or significant for some applications or systems, so we recommend they be included in a complete application study (e.g.,

[Anderson et al., 1990]). In particular, it is essential that a DBMS include a B-tree or other access method that supports range lookup because these operations occur in many engineering applications.

## 7.5.2   HyperModel Benchmark

The HyperModel Benchmark [Anderson et al., 1990] extended the early benchmark and database defined in Rubenstein, Kubicar, and Cattell [1987] rather than simplifying it. These extensions resulted in 17 benchmark measures, four database entity types (tables like the OO1 part table), and four relationships (tables like the OO1 connection table). As of 1990, the HyperModel has not been widely implemented—it has only been used to measure the local-only behavior of two DBMSs. This is probably because HyperModel is more complex and harder to implement, and the specification is not as complete as OO1's. If work continues on the HyperModel benchmark, however, it could be a more thorough measure of engineering database performance than OO1.

The difference between OO1 and HyperModel might be likened to the difference between TPC-A [TPC, 1989] and the Wisconsin benchmarks [Bitton, DeWitt, and Turbyfill, 1983]—the intent of OO1 is to focus on overall performance for the few most important operations, whereas the HyperModel benchmark provides many different measures. As such, there is a place for both the HyperModel benchmark and OO1 in comparing systems. It is easy to port the OO1 benchmark to any DBMS for which the HyperModel benchmark has been implemented since the database and measures are more or less a subset of HyperModel (mapping "nodes" to "parts" and the "MtoN" relationship to "connections").

We will not enumerate all of the differences in the HyperModel benchmark, but note that:

1. The HyperModel database includes multiple relationships between objects, including a one-to-many subpart relationship, and a subtype relationship. It also includes a "blob" field that stores a multi-kilobyte value.

2. The HyperModel benchmark includes the six performance tests proposed by Rubenstein, Cattell, and Kubicar [1987], plus some new measures: a traversal measure similar to the OO1 *traversal*, and read/write operations on the "blob" field.

The extensions to the original benchmark provide additional information about a DBMS, and the choice of additions is good. However, we feel that these measures are of secondary importance to those included in OO1. The "blob" operations are not bottlenecks in the applications we are familiar with—blob operations are typically limited by disk speed. The additional relationships do seem to represent a more realistic database, but they appear to measure the same kinds of operations and access methods in the database; perhaps future experience with the HyperModel benchmark will show whether their traversal times are directly correlated.

Note that the HyperModel benchmark does not measure versions, distributed databases, operations on compound groups of objects, multi-engineer concurrency, or other substantially new DBMS functionality not already covered by OO1. If the HyperModel benchmark continues to evolve, such measures will be important additions to a comprehensive benchmark characterizing DBMS functionality and performance for engineering applications.

### 7.5.3 Summary of Engineering Database Benchmark Rationale

To summarize, OO1 was designed based on earlier benchmark experience and feedback. The HyperModel work provided a list of suggestions, as did vendors, referees, and benchmark users. The full list includes "blob" fields, aggregation and generalization relationships, versions, multi-user measures, and the "range" queries that we removed after our first paper. All these features belong in any more comprehensive benchmark; but they reduce the utility of a simple benchmark focused on basic performance. They make it harder to implement and reproduce. We have therefore resisted the temptation to expand the benchmark except where we felt it essential.

## 7.6 Running OO1 and Reporting Results

It is essential that a good benchmark be precisely reproducible. This section therefore specifies more detailed issues on the implementation of OO1.

In order to reproduce comparable results, it is necessary to run the benchmarks and DBMS on a similar configuration. Table 7.1 shows a number of pertinent particulars of the DBMS architecture and benchmark implementation that should be reported.

**Table 7.1**    Reportable benchmark information

| Area | Types of Reportable Information |
| --- | --- |
| Hardware | CPU type, amount of memory, controller, disk type/size/bandwidth |
| Software | OS version, size of cache |
| DBMS | Transaction properties (atomicity, degree of concurrency, degree of isolation, lock modes used, etc.); recovery and logging properties; size of database cache; process architecture (communication protocol, number of processes involved, etc.); security features (or lack thereof); network protocols; access methods used |
| Benchmark | Any discrepancies from the implementation described here; "wall clock" running time; CPU time and disk utilization time are also useful; size of database. Optionally: local performance. |

The benchmarks reported here used a database server machine consisting of a Sun 3/280 with 16 megabytes of memory (Motorola 68020, 25 MHz),[2] an SMD-4 disk controller (2.4 MB/sec transfer rate) connecting two Hitachi disks, 892 MB each, 15 ms avg seek time; one disk used for database, and one for system. The server ran the Sun UNIX O/S version 4.0.3 and was connected to the client via a standard 10 Mb/s Ethernet.

The client workstation, where the remote benchmark programs ran, was a Sun 3/260 with 8 MB of memory, SMD-4 disk controller, and two 892 MB disks (15 ms avg seek time). This system ran Sun UNIX O/S 4.0.3 Both the client and server machines were reserved exclusively for benchmarking during the runs. Swap space (virtual memory space) on both machines was generous, and paging activity was not an issue during the benchmark.

All the benchmark measures assume that the DBMS is initialized and that any object code or system information is already cached by a "database open." The database open call is permitted to swap in as much of the DBMS code as desired on the server and client machines, so that code swap time will not be counted in the actual benchmark measures. Closing the database is also not included in the measures; however, the time to commit

---

[2]The real-time clock on Sun machines "ticks" at a granularity of 1/60 of a second, which is accurate enough for the OO1 measurements.

updates (and open transactions) must be counted for inserts. It also is useful to measure the open and close times for applications where these are important.

Disk I/O overhead should be included in the OO1 benchmark response time measurements. However, many database systems *can* validly obtain better performance for engineering applications by caching data between the multiple lookups performed within one transaction or session. Repetitions in the measurements are specifically provided to allow reporting asymptotic warm results as well as the cold results on the first run. No data may be cached at the time the benchmark is started for the cold results. The database must be closed and reopened before each cold benchmark measure, to empty the cache. Since the operating system may cache file pages, it is necessary to run a program to clear all database file pages out of memory on both the client and server machines between each cold run. This is a subtle point that can make a major difference in the results; one solution is to run a program or system command that sequentially reads all the pages of a large file, at least 20 megabytes, to fill the system cache with other data.

Despite all of these precautions, the cold and warm measures can still be hard to define consistently. If the DBMS is capable of storing data on disk as an image of virtual memory, so that it can run faster when the database is mapped into the same memory space, we would consider this a "cool" start. If the DBMS can run much faster fetching exactly the same objects in each iteration of the benchmark rather than random ones, we would consider these "hot" results. Although such numbers may be interesting, for simplicity's sake they are not included here.

Thus, the general order of executing a specific benchmark of ten loops is:

- Clear the operating system cache
- Open the database
- Start timer

    — Perform cold run and report cold time for the first benchmark loop

    Include time for transaction checkpoint for "insert" measure

    — Continue execution for remaining 9 loops and report warm times for successive runs

    If stable asymptote emerges, report it as warm time; otherwise report average of the 9 runs

- Stop timer

- Restore the database to its original state (reverse all inserts)

- Close the database

For the small database, the entire database typically fits in main storage. The large and huge database are defined so that there is little advantage to a client cache larger than the small space required to hold root pages for indexes, system information, data schema, and similar information since 90 percent of the data will not fit in cache.

The client workstation is permitted to cache as much of the small database as it can. The large database should be at least ten times larger than the client cache and at least three times larger than the server cache.

For results reported here, 8 MB client machines had 5 MB for a cache split between the O/S or DBMS. This amount of memory is typical of what is available for cache use on 1990 workstations. It will no doubt increase as technology advances and manufacturing techniques improve, however.

Our benchmark could be scaled up for larger memories while retaining the important measures of a "small" database that fits in main memory and a "large" one that does not, by proportionately scaling the small and large databases with the formulas:

$$p = \frac{M - 3 \text{ megabytes}}{250 \text{ bytes}}$$

$$P = 10 \, p$$

where $M$ is the client machine memory size, $p$ is the number of parts in the small database, and $P$ is the number of parts in the large database. This formula allows three megabytes for software plus 250 bytes per part to fit the small database in memory. Note that benchmark results will not be strictly comparable to those in this chapter, however. Even if data structures are used (hash indexes, parent-child links) that require time constant with database size, the "small cold" results would be increased by the time needed to move the additional data over the network.

There are several issues with generation of the benchmark database:

1. *Generating IDs*: The small database is populated with 20,000 parts and 60,000 associated connections. These numbers are 200,000 and 600,000, respectively, for the large database. When the parts are loaded, successive records are given successive ID numbers; this allows the benchmark program to select a random part, which is guaranteed to

exist, by calculating a random integer. Indexes and other physical structures were chosen to achieve the best performance for each system. The physical structure may not be changed between benchmarks, i.e., the same index or link overhead must be included in the database size, update time, and read time.

2. *Connections*: There should be exactly three logical "connections" whose "from" field is set to each part, and the "to" fields for these connections should be randomly selected using the algorithm in Section 7.3. Multiple connections to the same "to" part, or a connection "to" the same part as "from," are acceptable, as long as they arise through normal random assignment. It is not acceptable to use a fixed-size array for the "from" references; the schema must work with any possible random database.

3. *Clustering*: Connections may be clustered in physical storage according to the part they connect. They may also be clustered with parts themselves, if this gives better performance. It is easy for the benchmark implementor to do this clustering because part connections are clustered on part-ID: the best way to group parts is sequentially by part-ID. In fact, when we designed the benchmark, it seemed that this was *too* easy, that it gave no advantage to a DBMS that could automatically cluster by connections. However, benchmark implementors could build the equivalent ordering from *any* underlying clustering statistics inherent in the benchmark database and group the parts accordingly. So, although using part-IDs for clustering may seem odd, it is not unrealistic or unfair as we see it.

As mentioned earlier, it is not permissible to exploit the consecutive part IDs in a way that would not work with a more sparse assignment of IDs—for example, using them to index into an array of addresses. However, it is permissible to use physical pointers instead of part IDs to represent the connections, as long as the benchmarks are faithfully reproduced (e.g., the parts are actually fetched in the *traversal* benchmark).

In the *insertion* benchmark, the new 100 parts and 300 connections are added to the original database, i.e., there will be a total of 20,100 parts in the database after the first execution of the benchmark. The three connections for each of these parts are selected using the same algorithm as the others, i.e., they are 90 percent likely to be to one of the parts with largest part-IDs, 10 percent likely to be to any existing part. The newly inserted parts and connections should actually be deleted in order to make the insert measure idempotent, i.e., so that are not 20,200 parts after two executions. However, it was found that the results were not noticeably larger with 21,000 parts, so ten iterations could probably be executed together.

Network load between the workstation and server machines should be minimized, though no measurable effect on the results was seen when this load was not controlled. This may be surprising but is consistent with experience at Sun—the Ethernet is rarely close to saturation even with 100 workstations on a single wire.

Be careful with random number generation; some operating systems provide randomizing utilities with nonrandom characteristics in the low-order bits. The OO1 benchmarks reported here used the random number generator suggested by Park and Miller [1988].

## 7.7    Porting OO1 to Three DBMSs

The OO1 benchmark has been implemented on a number of DBMSs. This section examines the results on three products that vary quite dramatically in their overall design, remote data access, concurrency control implementation, and traditional DBMS properties. They show some of the performance implications of different architectures.

### 7.7.1    OODBMS

The first system  is a prerelease ("beta") of a commercial object-oriented DBMS, which we call OODBMS. We believe this system to be representative of the current state of the industry: It supports objects, classes, inheritance, persistent storage, multi-user sharing of objects, transactions, and remote access. See Cattell [1991] for more information on work in this area. Since object-oriented products are new to the market, the numbers reported here should not be considered indicative of what will eventually be achieved with an object-oriented system.

The OO1 benchmark was implemented on the OODBMS with an object type *part* containing variable-size arrays with the connection information. Object references (and reverse references) are stored by the OODBMS as object identifiers that contain a logical page address in the upper-order bits, which can normally be mapped to the physical page and offset of the referenced object with no extra disk accesses. The particular implementation we chose did *not* allow OIDs to be automatically swizzled[3] into pointers by this OODBMS the first time an object is used. However, the mapping from OIDs to memory address is very fast when the object has been cached, requiring only table lookups.

The OODBMS's transaction mechanism supports transaction rollback and rollforward. The OODBMS works remotely over a network, fetching pages rather than objects, and caches pages on the workstation. Objects may be grouped in multi-page segments, with locking at a segment level. The benchmark design placed all of the parts and connections in one segment. Page-level locking is being implemented, and it will be informative to run the benchmark with these finer-grain locks. It will probably not be substantially slower because the implementation will use a page server in which lock requests can be "piggy-backed" on the page reads.

## 7.7.2 RDBMS

The second system, here named RDBMS, is a UNIX-based production release of a commercial relational DBMS. The benchmark measures were implemented in C with SQL calls for the lookup, *traversal*, and *insert* operations. Note that the DBMS calls are invoked many times for each measure since it mixes C and database operations. Queries were precompiled wherever possible, thus bypassing most of the usual query parsing and optimization costs, or at least incurring these costs only on the first execution.

Two tables were used, Part and Connection, indexed on *part.id* and *connection.from,* respectively. A single secondary index was also created, on the *connection.to* attribute; this permitted reasonable response times on the reverse traversal measure. B-trees were used as the storage structure for all three tables, with 100 percent fill factors on both index and leaf pages.

The RDBMS provides a relatively full set of DBMS features: atomic transactions, full concurrency support, network architecture (TCP/IP for our network benchmarks), and support for journalling and recovery. For the lookup and traversal benchmarks, we programmed the system to not place read locks, and we measured the system with the rollforward journalling features turned off. We believe these settings make sense for the model of engineering interaction we envision.

The RDBMS, like all current relational DBMS products, is implemented using a client-server architecture, i.e., every database call from the application must go over a network to the DBMS server where the data are

---

[3]*Swizzled* is a OODBism meaning in-place conversion of OIDs to pointers.

stored. This is very inefficient for an engineering application or benchmark such as ours—there is no way to cache data locally as in the OODBMS and INDEX. However, a stored procedure was also defined for each of the three benchmark measures, so the client/server interaction consisted of a single customized call per operation.

We considered implementing a cache ourselves, as a layer between the RDBMS and the application. However, doing so would effectively duplicate much of the functionality of the DBMS, as an "in-memory" DBMS: index lookups by part-ID, connection links between parts, and so on. In addition, the cache would not work properly with the RDBMS because the RDBMS transactions do not keep the data that are stored in the application cache locked. We feel our utilization of the RDBMS is representative of what an application implementor would expect of a DBMS.

## 7.7.3   INDEX

The third system is a B-tree package we had available at Sun. Throughout the balance of this chapter, this system is called INDEX. INDEX is included to show what can be done under ideal conditions, using a highly optimized access method with no high-level semantics.

The benchmark database was implemented as two files, one for parts and one for connections. A B-tree was created on the part-IDs in the parts file. This B-tree was used to perform the lookup operation.

In addition to B-trees, the INDEX package provides efficient lookup operations on record-IDs; record-IDs consist of a physical page number plus slot number on a page. For the traversal measures, the record-IDs for parent-child links as in System R [Astrahan et al., 1976] were used. Instead of storing part-IDs in the "from" and "to" fields of a connection record, we stored the record-IDs of these two parts for quick access. In the reverse direction, to quickly find the connections for a part, all of the "to" connection records for a part were linked together, with the record-ID of the head of the list stored in the part record, and all of the "from" connection records were maintained similarly. Thus, the connection records contained the type and length attributes, plus four record-ID attributes: two containing the record-IDs of the "from" and "to" parts it connects (its parent records), and two used to point to the next connection record for the "from" and "to" part lists (the child records). The part records contained the part-ID, type, $x$, $y$, and build attributes, plus two attributes containing the record-IDs for the first "from" and "to" connection records for the part.

Thus, our INDEX version of the benchmark database consisted of a parts file, a connection file interconnected to the parts file with record-IDs, and a B-tree file used for the lookup on parts.

To compare the performance of B-trees against parent-child links, the *traversal* measure was also performed using B-trees. Two more B-trees were created, one on the *connections.from* field and one on the *connections.to* field. Because the parent-child link implementation was faster than the B-tree approach, the results from this pure B-tree approach are not reported in the next section, they are deferred to Section 7.9. Note: The overall database creation time, marked with * in our tables, reflects the time for both the B-trees and links. The insert times reflect only the link access method used.

The INDEX package works over a network and is designed to be particularly fast when the data can be cached in workstation main memory, treating read-only data specially utilizing a novel network lock service to control access. The INDEX package caches one 8K contiguous chunk of records on each remote procedure call. The package provides update record and table level locks but no update logging for concurrency control and recovery. The measurements reported here used table granularity locks. Multi-statement atomic transactions are not supported, nor are native security features. Of course, there is no query optimizer; it is the duty of the applications programmer to design and program the fastest access paths, as just described. A single-process architecture is used (plus a remote lock-and-access server process in the networked case). The INDEX access libraries are linked directly into the benchmark program.

The INDEX system, although extremely powerful within its intended application domain, is not strictly comparable to full-function, transaction-oriented DBMSs. The present implementation does not satisfy our recovery requirement, and it performs file-level locks. However, these results are included for comparison because (1) gross-level concurrency and recovery such as this, with the addition of versions, might be adequate for many CASE and CAD applications, and (2) the INDEX results represent the best performance that might reasonably be obtained in the case where the cost of high-level semantics and transaction management can be made negligible.

# 7.8 OO1 Measurements on Three DBMSs

Table 7.2 shows the OO1 measurements for the most important scenario, the small remote database (i.e., 20,000 parts accessed over the network). As per our specifications, we performed the benchmark measures cold, after running a program to clear out any cached data in the operating system page cache as well as the DBMS. The data are graphically displayed in Figure 7.1 on page 427.

**Table 7.2** Small remote database (benchmark elapsed times in seconds)

| Measure | Cache | INDEX | OODBMS | RDBMS |
|---------|-------|-------|--------|-------|
| DB size | | 3.3 MB | 3.7 MB | 4.5 MB |
| Load Time (local) | | 1100.0* | 267.0 s | 370.0 s |
| Reverse traverse | cold | 23 | 22 | 95 |
| Lookup | cold | 7.6 | 20. | 29 |
| | warm | 2.4 | 1.0 | 19 |
| Traversal | cold | 17. | 17. | 94 |
| | warm | 8.4 | 1.2 | 84 |
| Insert | cold | 8.2 | 3.6 | 20 |
| | warm | 7.5 | 2.9 | 20 |
| Total | cold | 33. | 41. | 143 |
| | warm | 19. | 5. | 123 |

*As explained in the description of the INDEX database design, this time includes the time to create two indexes that are not actually used in the B-tree-plus-link design.

The table also shows the warm case, the asymptotic results we obtained after running the benchmark ten times as specified.[4] The relative weightings of the cold and warm results in choosing a database system are application-dependent. Most of the applications we encounter would have behavior between these two extremes.

---

[4]These asymptotic results were generally reached very quickly: with INDEX and OODBMS, where entire pages are added to the local cache with each data operation, nearly the entire small database was in the cache after the first iteration of the lookuip or traversal measure.

The INDEX and OODBMS results are clearly best. Though the results are close, INDEX wins on the cold results. The OODBMS wins by a substantial margin on the warm results.

The OODBMS results are surprisingly good, considering this is an early version of a product with little performance tuning. The OODBMS uses efficient access methods (links for traversal, B-trees for lookup), minimum concurrency overhead (table locking), no overhead for higher-level semantics, a local cache, and no interprocess communication to make database calls. We speculate that OODBMS does so well on the warm results because it uses an efficient representation to find objects in memory (different from the disk representation).

Note that the only measure on which the OODBMS does not beat INDEX on the cold results is lookup. In consulting with OODBMS implementors, we discovered that the OODBMS prerelease had a poor hash index implementation, now being reimplemented. This is probably the cause of the discrepancy.

Although the lack of more complex concurrency and higher-level semantics in INDEX makes it inapplicable to some applications, the results are interesting in demonstrating the kind of performance that can be obtained where access methods can be applied directly. The overall results are quite good. The load time is much higher than the other systems, but that time (marked with an *) included the overhead to redundantly create B-trees in addition to the parent-child links for the connection traversals. The INDEX access methods used are similar to the OODBMS, as is its ability to cache the database on the workstation.

The RDBMS times are worst, with an overall total of 143. The results reflect the overhead of accessing the DBMS for each operation in the benchmark application, approximately 5000 calls altogether. At 20 ms for a roundtrip network call, this overhead amounts for most of the time. As noted earlier, the RDBMS architecture is at least as important as the relational model in producing this poor performance.

A variety of other observations can be made of the results. Note that the database size does not differ substantially between the three systems. The *reverse traversal* results are only somewhat slower than *forward traversal* and are virtually identical for the relational system (*reverse traversal* is not added to the total at the bottom since it is included only for verification against *forward traversal*). Note also that the OODBMS shows the largest improvement between warm and cold results on the *lookup* and *traversal* operations, and the RDBMS shows the least improvement.

Which results are fast enough for engineering applications? Obviously that depends on the application. We can see that our rough goal of 1000 random read operations per second would require a result of approximately one second on the *lookup* measure; that result is achieved by the OODBMS on the warm results, and INDEX is close. Assuming applications that perform approximately three times as many *traversals* as *lookups*, and ten times as many *lookups* as *inserts*, the benchmark measures were designed to require performance in the 1–10 second range with a 90 percent cache hit rate[5] for most of the applications we examined. However, much higher performance is needed in some applications with higher hit rates, and much lower performance is tolerable for engineering data accessed directly by the user.

Table 7.3 shows the OO1 results for a large remote database. Now none of the products can take much advantage of a local cache. Again, this data is graphically displayed in Figure 7.2.

**Table 7.3**   Large remote database (benchmark elapsed times in seconds)

| Measure | Cache | INDEX | OODBMS | RDBMS |
|---|---|---|---|---|
| DB size | | 33.1 MB | 37.0 MB | 44.6 MB |
| Load Time (local) | | 16400.0 s* | 6000.0 s | 4500.0 s |
| Reverse traverse | cold | 100 | 84 | 212 |
| Lookup | cold | 47 | 49 | 49 |
| | warm | 18 | 43 | 24 |
| Traversal | cold | 56 | 68 | 135 |
| | warm | 41 | 59 | 107 |
| Insert | cold | 20 | 10 | 24 |
| | warm | 18 | 7.5 | 24 |
| Total | cold | 123 | 127 | 208 |
| | warm | 77 | 110 | 155 |

Note that there is much less difference between the three systems now, on either the cold or warm results. Nearly all of the results are within a factor of two. Furthermore, there is less speedup in the warm cases.

---

[5]The cold results would be at the high end of this range, and the warm results at the low end, since a 90 percent hit rate lies somewhere between.

We believe that most of the speed decrease in the larger database results are due to the larger *working set*, i.e., that the database no longer can be cached. The access methods seem to scale well with database size. Indeed, the link access method used for *traversal* in INDEX and OODBMS should require only one disk access regardless of database size, unlike the indexes used for the *lookup*.

The most significant differences between systems on the large remote case are that, on *traversal*, INDEX and OODBMS do better than the RDBMS. These differences do not surprise us because (1) the locality of reference inherent in *traversal* can provide benefits even when the database is not fully cached, and (2) INDEX and OODBMS use links instead of index lookups to traverse connections.

As an experiment, OO1 was run for the *huge* remote database. Because the create time to create for the database is so large, only the INDEX package was measured. The results are shown in Table 7.4.

**Table 7.4**  Huge remote database (benchmark elapsed times in seconds)

| Measure | Cache | INDEX | OODBMS | RDBMS |
|---|---|---|---|---|
| DB size | | 330.0 MB | -- | -- |
| Load (local) | | 78000.0+ s | -- | -- |
| Reverse traverse | cold | 109 | -- | -- |
| Lookup | cold | 109 | -- | -- |
| | warm | 106 | -- | -- |
| Traversal | cold | 143 | -- | -- |
| | warm | 142 | -- | -- |
| Insert | cold | 53 | -- | -- |
| | warm | 53 | -- | -- |
| Total | cold | 305 | -- | -- |
| | warm | 301 | -- | -- |

The totals are over twice as slow as the large database in the cold case, and over three times as slow in the warm case. Again, it appears that most of this result is due to inability to cache the larger working set. Note there is now essentially no difference between cold and warm times, a fact that supports this hypothesis.

With a 0 percent cache hit rate, 20–25 ms to read data off the disk, 15–20 ms to fetch a page over the network, one page access for the traversal operation, and two page accesses for the lookup (one for the index, one to fetch the data fields), the lookup measure would take 80 seconds, and the traversal about 120 seconds. Note this is very close the the results we actually obtained for the huge database. This suggests the results might not get much worse with a "very huge" database.

# 7.9   Variations

This section considers some variations of the benchmark configuration, beyond the results required by the benchmark definition, to better understand the differences among the DBMSs.

Table 7.5 shows the results for a local database, i.e., a database stored on disks attached directly to the user's machine. These results are important for some engineering applications, even though many will require remote data access.

**Table 7.5**   Cold local database (benchmark elapsed times in seconds)

| Measure | Size | INDEX | OODBMS | RDBMS |
|---------|------|-------|--------|-------|
| Lookup | small | 5.4 | 12.9 | 27 |
| | large | 24 | 32 | 44 |
| Traversal | small | 13 | 9.8 | 90 |
| | large | 32 | 37 | 124 |
| Insert | small | 7.4 | 1.5 | 22 |
| | large | 15 | 3.6 | 28 |
| Total | small | 26 | 24 | 139 |
| | large | 71 | 73 | 196 |

These results surprised us. We expected the results in the local case to be much better, especially for the RDBMS. The RDBMS results were essentially the same as the remote case. We expected them to be better because it is no longer necessary to make a remote call to the DBMS for every operation. However, the network call may not be the largest portion of the overhead in an application DBMS call. Even on one machine, this RDBMS, as with nearly all other RDBMS products, requires communication between an application process and DBMS process and copying data between the two. There is significant overhead in such an interprocess call. In addition, the benchmark application is competing for resources on the server machine in the local case.

It might seem that the INDEX and OODBMS results should be much better than for the remote database, but they are only 30–40 percent faster. Many people are surprised to hear that remote access to files is not much more expensive than local access. To quantify this, some rough measurements were performed running an application reading pages locally and remotely through NFS (Sun's Network File System). The measurements showed remote access to be only 30 percent slower. Of course, this rough measurement does not include time for locking or to flush altered pages back to the server. Note that OODBMS beats INDEX by a small margin in the small local case, though it lost in the small remote case; this switch is probably a result of minor differences in network access implementation.

As another experiment, consider the effect of the locality of reference that exists in the connections among parts. Table 7.6 shows these results.

**Table 7.6**    Small remote database without locality of reference (elapsed times in seconds)

| Measure | Cache | INDEX |
|---------|-------|-------|
| Lookup | cold | 7.9 |
| | warm | 2.4 |
| Traversal | cold | 24 |
| | warm | 7.9 |
| Insert | cold | 36 |
| | warm | 10 |
| Total | cold | 68 |
| | warm | 20 |

Note that the results for the cold *traversal* (24 seconds in Table 7.6 versus 17 seconds in Table 7.2) and *insert* (36 seconds versus 8 seconds) differ significantly without locality of reference in the small remote database. The *traversal* benefits from the likelihood that connected parts are frequently nearby, with the page-level caching provided by INDEX; the *insert* benefits because it also must fetch connected parts to create the parent-child links used for *traversal*. The performance differences caused by locality show that the addition of reference locality to OO1 is important.

Note there is little difference on the *lookup* numbers; this is as expected since the lookups are randomly distributed over all the parts. There is also little difference in the case of the warm numbers; this is not surprising since the entire database is cached in memory at this point, and locality is irrelevant.

On the large or huge database, one would expect there to be similar or larger differences without locality of reference, though these cases were not tested. Note that the large and huge database results are worse for at least two reasons: the database does not fit in memory, and in some cases access structures such as B-trees take longer to traverse. Only the former is substantially affected by locality.

We were curious about the effect of using B-trees instead of parent-child links to perform the traversal measure. Intuitively, one would expect the links to be faster since they can obtain the connection records and part records in a single disk access (or a few memory references, if cached), whereas the B-trees require at least one more page access and significantly more computation (to compare keys). Table 7.7 shows the measurements of OO1 when B-trees are created on the *connection.from* and *connection.to* fields and used for the traversal.

**Table 7.7**  Small remote database (3.9 MB) using B-trees instead of links (elapsed times in seconds)

| Measure | Cache | INDEX |
|---------|-------|-------|
| Lookup | cold | 7.9 |
|  | warm | 2.4 |
| Traversal | cold | 33 |
|  | warm | 21 |
| Insert | cold | 12 |
|  | warm | 9.1 |
| Total | cold | 53 |
|  | warm | 32 |

As expected (compared with Table 7.2), *traversal* is much slower: the parent-child links are about twice as fast as B-trees. The *insert* time does not differ substantially (the time for inserts into connection B-trees is comparable with the time to find connected parts and create links to them), and the lookup times are of course not affected.

This is a significant result, as it shows that the mainstay access method of relational DBMSs, B-trees, is substantially worse than links for applications represented by OO1. With a larger database, the difference will be even larger since links take a constant time to traverse but B-tree lookup time grows logarithmically with database size. Thus DBMSs for engineering applications should provide link-access methods or some other access method that is efficient for traversal. Extensible hash indexes might do well.

It should also be noted that B-trees, as used by the relational DBMS, do not preserve an ordering on the entries, as do the parent-child links. For the OODBMS, and parent-child link version of INDEX, the connections are traversed in exactly the same order they were created. If an application requires an ordering on the connections—for example, if the parts were portions of a document with a hierarchy of chapters, sections, and paragraphs—then the RDBMS versus OODBMS performance difference would be even greater, as the RDBMS would have to sort the connections during each query. It would be interesting, for further work, to measure this "ordered" version of the traversal.

## 7.10    Summary

The OO1 benchmark was originated to focus more emphasis on performance for engineering database applications. Its design is based on benchmarking experience and on the study of engineering applications. It consists of a scaleable database design with clustering and three simple operations representative of such applications (*lookup*, *traversal*, and *insert*). The operations are performed by a client accessing a remote database. The client and server are tested in two cases: a small database that can be cached and a large database that cannot be cached.

In addition to the results reported here, OO1 has been run on half a dozen object-oriented DBMSs and another relational DBMS at the time of this writing, with results consistent with those reported here (some of the OODBMSs had even faster warm results, essentially equal to hand-coded in-memory structures). OO1 operations are very similar to those in specialized CAD benchmarks [Barrett, 1990; Schwartz and Samco, 1990]; the results were correlated as high as .98 for the OODBMSs examined.

OO1 differs from other benchmarks in several important ways: (1) the database is remotely located, (2) the application logic must be intermixed with data operations at a fine grain, (3) conventional transactions may be replaced with versions or other concurrency control, and (4) the entire database working set can sometimes fit in main memory. These differences necessitate violations of conventional wisdom to obtain acceptable performance.

It should be emphasized that the results do *not* show that an object-oriented data model is better than a relational data model for engineering applications, although there may be some differences in data model performance for engineering applications as a results of expressibility (e.g., if lists must be represented by sorting relations on a cardinal attribute). The order of magnitude difference in the OODBMS and RDBMS results appear to result from a difference in the DBMS *architecture*.

All of the following changes to a conventional relational implementation should result in significant speedup on the OO1 benchmark:

1.  It is essential to integrate the DBMS with a persistent programming language or to otherwise reduce the overhead in accessing data from the application environment. Portals may afford some improvement [Stonebraker and Rowe, 1984], but they still require data to be translated between the DBMS representation and programming language representation on each database call.

2.  Caching data on a workstation is important because of the locality of reference present in the benchmark. The concurrency control architecture of the DBMS must support long-term checkout in order for this caching to work.

3.  Remote access, local caching, and concurrency control should be performed at a granularity of pages or through meta-queries that prefetch data that will be operated on by a series of application queries or operations.

4.  Parent-child links are useful for efficient traversal operations.

In theory, a relational DBMS could be built with these features; however, it would be a major reimplementation effort. Very little work has been done in this direction.

It should also be emphasized that this benchmark is intentionally simple to make it easy to port and perform. It is only a rough approximation of the requirements of engineering applications, based on experience and interviews with CASE and CAD engineers. The only truly accurate representation of performance is actually executing the application. Our goal is mainly to focus attention on broad issues—as shown in Section 7.9, there is an order of magnitude difference in performance among DBMS architectures.

To summarize the benchmark results, a prerelease of a commercial OODBMS performed well, as did a home-grown INDEX access method. These systems demonstrate that our goals for engineering DBMS performance are not impossibly high. A commercial RDBMS did poorly in comparison with these systems, but we believe that most of this difference is due to the architecture, not the data model, of the RDBMS. Figure 7.1 shows the results graphically (based on Table 7.2).

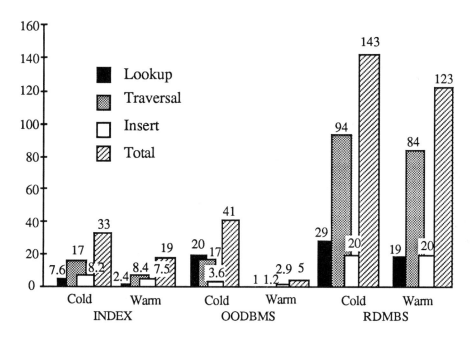

**Figure 7.1** Small remote database results with different DBMSs.

The benchmark was also executed under various configurations with an in-house system here called INDEX. Since INDEX had good overall results and we were familiar with its internal architecture, it was chosen for these comparisons. The results are shown graphically in Figures 7.2 and 7.3.

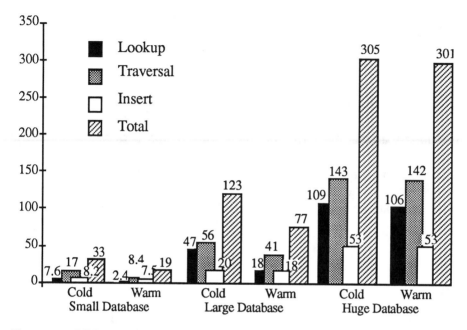

**Figure 7.2** INDEX results for remote access to small, large, and huge databases.

Figure 7.2 shows that the elapsed times grow with database size: each time the database grew by a factor of ten, the elapsed times rose by a factor of three or four. In addition, once the database grew past the cache size, there was little difference between the cold and warm results. This is especially clear for the huge database measurements in Figure 7.2. It is a consequence of less locality of reference and the increase in the number of disk accesses for index lookups and other operations.

As shown in Figure 7.3, when the database is local, the results are better for INDEX; this was also true with the OODBMS. These data support our contention that a local cache is important. However, it is also important to minimize the overhead per DBMS call in general; the RDBMS performed poorly even in the local case.

Without locality of reference, the results on the traversal measure are somewhat worse. This shows that it is important to include locality of refer-

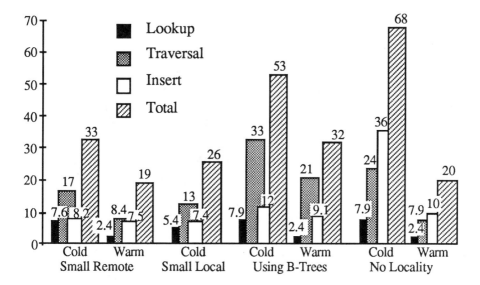

**Figure 7.3** INDEX results for the small database accessed locally, remotely, or via B-trees instead of links for connections, and without locality of reference in connections.

ence in a benchmark measure, assuming that the applications the benchmark is to represent exhibit such locality.

Finally, as shown by Figure 7.3, using B-trees instead of parent-child links for the benchmark produces significantly worse results than for traversal, with only minor effects on the other measures. This suggests that it is important to consider alternatives to B-trees for logical connections that are traversed in a "transitive-closure" type of operation.

In summary, database systems will not be used in many engineering applications unless they perform benchmark measures such as ours in 1–10 seconds with a 90 percent cache hit rate on commonly used workstations and servers. We have shown that such results are possible. We also have seen that products can fall short of these results, by as much as an order of magnitude. Good engineering database performance requires effective use and integration of the programming language data space, concurrency control allowing long-term check-out, and caching on a local workstation.

# References

Astrahan, M., et al. (1976). System R: Relational approach to database management. *ACM Transaction on Database Systems, 1*(1).

Anderson, T., Berre, A., Mallison, M., Porter, H., and Schneider, B. (1990). The HyperModel Benchmark. *Proceedings of Extended Database Technology '90* (Springer-Verlag Lecture Notes 416).

Anon et al. (1985). A measure of transaction processing power. *Datamation, 31*(7).

Barrett, M. (1990). C++ test driver for object-oriented databases, personal communication.

Bitton, D., DeWitt, D.J., and Turbyfill, C. (1983). Benchmarking database systems: A systematic approach. *Proceedings of VLDB Conference.* [Expanded and revised version available as Wisconsin Computer Science TR #526.]

Cattell, R.G.G. (1991). *Object Data Management.* Reading, MA: Addison-Wesley.

Cattell, R.G.G., and Skeen, J. (in press). Engineering database benchmark. *ACM Transactions on Databases Systems.*

Maier, D. (1987). *Making Database Systems Fast Enough for CAD Applications.* (Technical Report CS/E-87-016). Beaverton, OR: Oregon Graduate Center.

Park, S. and Miller, K. (1988). Random number generators: Good ones are hard to find. *CACM 31*(10).

Rubenstein, W.B., Kubicar, M.S., and Cattell, R.G.G. (1987). Benchmarking simple database operations. *Proceedings ACM SIGMOD 1987.*

Schwartz, J. and Samco, R. (1990). Object-oriented DBMS evaluation, personal communication.

Stonebraker, M. and Rowe, L.A. (1984). PORTALS: A new application program interface. *Proceedings of VLDB Conference.*

Transaction Processing Performance Council (TPC). (1989). *TPC Benchmark, a Standard.* Los Altos, CA: ITOM International Co.

# Appendix A. SQL Definitions

```
Database Definition
create table part ( id          integer      not null primary key,
                    type        char(10)     not null,
                    x           integer      not null,
                    y           integer      not null,
                    build       datetime     not null
                    );
create table connection (
                    from        integer      foreign key references (part.id),
                    to          integer      foreign key references (part.id),
                    length      integer      not null,
                    type        char(10)     not null,
                    primary key(from,to, length)
                    );

create index rconn on connection(to);

Example of C Code: Lookup
    /** obvious sql and c declares missing **/
    lp_start  = time100();
    for (i = 0; i < 1000; i++)
        {   starttime = time100();
            for (j = 0; j < nrepeats; j++)
                {           p_id = ((int) randf()* nparts) + 1;
                exec sql    select x, y, part_type
                                into :x, :y, :part_type
                                from part
                                where id = :p_id;
                    nullProc(x,y,type);
                }
            endtime = time100();
            printf (
            "\tTotal running time for loop %d is %10.2f seconds\n",
                            i+1,    (endtime - starttime) / 100);
            }
    endtime = time100();
    printf ("\n\nTotal running time %10.2f seconds\n\n",
                            (endtime - lp_start) / 100);
```

# Appendix B. More Recent Benchmark Results

The OO1 benchmark described in this chapter has now been run on Objectivity/DB, Object Design ObjectStore, Ontologic Ontos, and Versant (these names are trademarks of their respective companies). The results are shown here without identifying the respective companies, since the purpose of these numbers is to show the good performance of the new products relative to relational DBMSs, not for use as a basis for choosing a product. INDEX was an early version of the Sun NetISAM product. RDBMS1 was Sybase, and on an earlier version of the benchmark last year, we got results on Ingres that were within 10%–20% of Sybase. The results show compelling evidence for about 5 times speedup on "cold" results, and 30 times speedup on "warm" results, using current OODB rather than RDBMS products.

EDB Benchmark results in seconds: small remote database.

| Measure | OODB1 | OODB2 | OODB3 | OODB4 | RDBMS1 | INDEX |
|---|---|---|---|---|---|---|
| Lookup Cold | 18 | 13 | 22 | 20 | 29 | 7.6 |
| Traverse Cold | 27 | 13 | 18 | 17 | 94 | 17 |
| Insert Cold | 14 | 6.7 | 3.7 | 3.6 | 20 | 8.2 |
| R-Traverse Cold | 34 | 13 | 16 | 22 | 95 | 23 |
| L+T+I Cold | 63 | 33 | 44 | 41 | 143 | 33 |
| Lookup Warm | 0.1 | 0.03 | 1.1 | 1.0 | 19 | 2.4 |
| Traverse Warm | 0.7 | 0.1 | 1.2 | 1.2 | 84 | 8.4 |
| Insert Warm | 3.7 | 3.1 | 1.0 | 2.9 | 20 | 7.5 |
| L+T+I Warm | 4.5 | 3.2 | 3.3 | 5.1 | 123 | 18 |

EDB Benchmark results in seconds: small local database.

| Measure | OODB1 | OODB2 | OODB3 | OODB4 | RDBMS1 | INDEX |
|---|---|---|---|---|---|---|
| Database Size | 5.6MB | 3.4MB | 7.0MB | 3.7MB | 4.5MB | 3.3MB |
| Build Time | 133 | 50 | 47 | 267 | 370 | 1100 |
| Lookup Cold | 12 | 10 | 10 | 13 | 27 | 5.4 |
| Traverse Cold | 18 | 10 | 8.3 | 9.8 | 90 | 13 |
| Insert Cold | 9 | 5.3 | 1.9 | 1.5 | 22 | 7.4 |
| L+T+I Cold | 39 | 25 | 20 | 24 | 139 | 26 |

[Local warm results essentially same as remote warm.]

WARNING—These results should not be used to compare products or as an indicator of eventual product performance because: (1) They were obtained on versions of products that were available on Sun hardware in early 1990, and not all of the benchmarks were done in the same month. OODB4 was measured earliest, thus would show the most speedup. (2) In any particular application the relative frequency of cold and warm access, reads and writes, and a host of other requirements must be considered. The Warm and Cold totals are provided only to show that the OODBs are very close overall; they should not be used to choose an OODB. (3) The benchmark programs were written by the OODB vendors, not by Sun; we checked the programs for conformance to the benchmark specification, but accuracy is not guaranteed, and not all of the results were verified on Sun premises. (4) The OODB3 representation of the database was slightly too large to cache in 8MB of memory. Since this was not our intent for the small database, we allowed it the run using 16MB. (5) The OODB1 and OODB2 results were obtained using a 3/60 machine with slightly slower CPU, warm results may be off by as much as 20%.

# 8

# Overview of the Full-Text Document Retrieval Benchmark

Samuel DeFazio

*Digital Equipment Corporation*

## 8.1    Introduction

For most of recorded history, textual data have existed primarily in hard-copy format, and the related document retrieval process was essentially a manual task, possibly involving the assistance of cross-reference catalogs. By the mid-1960s, work was under way at the University of Pittsburgh to develop computer-assisted legal research systems [Harrington, 1984–85]. Also, during this period of time, computer-based document retrieval systems were beginning to emerge in commercial firms; for example, InfoBank at the *New York Times* [Harrington, 1984–85]. The most distinguishing characteristics of such systems include full-text Boolean search logic and support for proximity expressions (e.g., phrases). With this technology, termed full-text retrieval (FTR), documents are selected from a database in terms of *content*, rather than with predefined keywords or subject categories. For example, suppose that we were interested in locating articles about benchmarking full-text document retrieval systems. To formulate a search expression that would specify the desired content, we could select keywords (e.g., *benchmark, performance*) and phrases (e.g., *document retrieval, full-text retrieval, information retrieval*) which would likely be found within relevant documents. The reader should note that this simple example illustrates one important shortcoming of FTR systems: The inherent ambiguity of natural language makes FTR query formulation imprecise. Although FTR systems lack closed methods to formulate queries, this technology tends to be significantly less time-consuming than manual document retrieval, especially for large databases.

Since the early work on computer-based document retrieval systems, considerable progress has been made toward applying FTR technology to harness the information content of textual data. Progress is particularly evident within the information industries. For example, FTR software is the foundation for electronic information services such as Dialog, LEXIS/NEXIS, and BRS. During the 1980s, information service companies automated the literature search process for many important commercial areas of intellectual discourse. During the 1990s, deployment of FTR systems is likely to increase dramatically within industry, government, and academia. To support this growth, IDC expects shipments of FTR system software products to exceed two million copies per year by 1995 [IDC, 1991].

The primary advantage of the FTR scheme is that documents can be located according to content; however, providing this capability is costly in terms of computing resources. As document databases grow, the computing power needed to support content searches tends to increase at least linearly [DeFazio & Hull, 1991]. Thus, when the database grows by a factor of $N$, the computing power must increase correspondingly in order to maintain the same search response time. This property derives primarily from the underlying software technology. Rather than exhaustively searching the raw text, FTR systems normally employ surrogate file structures to improve response time [Faloutsos, 1985]. To effectively support proximity searching, these surrogate files usually contain an entry for each token (e.g., word, number, date, time) occurrence in the document database. Consequently, the surrogate files, search processing time, and answer sets generally grow in proportion to the document database size. As such, when both the number of searches and the database size grow by a factor of $N$, the demand for computing power to maintain response time tends to increase by a factor of $N^2$.

Although FTR technology has existed for some time, the computer industry lacks a widely accepted, standard benchmark that measures the performance and price/performance of full-text document retrieval systems. Assuming that a large number of FTR software products will be acquired during the 1990s [IDC, 1991], having a uniform method to compare the performance of such systems appears highly desirable. The full-text document retrieval benchmark presented below is designed to provide this capability.

Conceptually, this benchmark is similar to TPC-B in that the focus is performance of the "document retrieval engine" for some hardware configuration. Concentrating on the performance of this system component is justified since the related terminal workload for such applications tends to be much smaller and, therefore, less significant. That is, the FTR software for content searching typically generates most of the resource demands exhibited by full-text document retrieval systems. Thus, throughput for the benchmark is defined as partition searches completed per minute (SPM). Price/performance is computed as dollars per SPM, where dollars represents the total five-year ownership cost for the system.

To date, the benchmark has been validated at Sequent Computer Systems, Inc., with several commercially available FTR products. The initial validation tests indicated that the specification is complete and workable. Since those activities were not audited, we are only able to summarize the related results. Our preliminary findings indicate that operating on Sequent Symmetry 750 platforms, some FTR products can handle multiple gigabyte databases and sustain the maximum throughput rate as defined by the benchmark.

The following sections contain an overview of the benchmark's business, database, and system models, along with descriptions of the associated transactions, response time requirements, workload generation procedure, and performance measures.

## 8.2    Business Model

This benchmark models multiuser FTR systems that locate and retrieve documents in large (i.e., one or more gigabyte) collections of textual data. We refer to an application of this type as a **document retrieval service** (DRS). Users maintain accounts with the DRS and sign on for service from terminals, PCs, or workstations. The DRS provides read-only access to the document database. Customers can select documents from the database using FTR queries, display results, and transfer text to their terminals. The DRS does not support end-user operations that modify the database. The model assumes that all maintenance functions are handled by the database administrator.

This business model encompasses a large number of full-text document retrieval applications. Examples include commercial information retrieval services such as Dialog and BRS, competitive analysis systems, technical document libraries, customer support and problem-reporting systems, and litigation support applications. In effect, the DRS model accommodates almost any document-based, multiuser application that supports full-text search capabilities.

# 8.3 Database Model

Logically, the database is structured as a collection of document **partitions**. Each partition contains a set of documents that are stored as variable length records. A record includes the entire text of one document and is represented as an entry in the **text file**. As shown in the following figure, a partition may also have an associated structure called the **search file**. The search file, if present, contains an "index" that the FTR software uses to improve the response time for locating documents. In this context, an index is any surrogate file structure that the FTR software uses to avoid exhaustively scanning the textual data.

## Logical Document Partition

| Document $_1$ | Document $_2$ | . . . | Document $_n$ |
|---|---|---|---|

Text File

Text File Index

Search File

The benchmark specification requires that the test database contain only documents which were authored by people. As such, documents in the test database may not be machine generated. The basic reason for requiring a database population such as this is to help ensure uniformity in the generated workload. With respect to token usage patterns, large collections of naturally written text are statistically indistinguishable [Zipf, 1965]. Given this, when actual documents are used to build the test database, the generated workloads should be nearly identical for any body of text which conforms to the specification. Unfortunately, it is unclear whether this assertion can be made for a generated database. In the absence of such knowledge, the benchmark demands that "real" text be used to populate the test database.

# 8.4    System Model

The benchmark is based on the assumption that the DRS operates, logically, as a document server. In this model, users are represented by client processes that submit search and retrieval transactions to the DRS. Search transactions locate documents of interest, and each retrieval transaction fetches the text of one document. The DRS server handles search and retrieval transactions by performing read-only operations on the database. In the client process, each transaction is considered an atomic unit of work. The DRS server, however, may decompose transactions into smaller units of work.

# 8.5    Search Transactions

Search transactions are the means by which users locate documents, and they represent the major source of work for the benchmark. A transaction of this type contains a search expression that specifies the desired documents in terms of *content*. For this benchmark, a search expression is composed of terms and Boolean connectors (i.e., AND, OR, AND NOT). Each search term may be either a simple token (e.g., word) or a proximity operator (i.e., Phrase, WithinSentence, WithinParagraph). The output from a search transaction is an **answer set** that contains the unique identification, or *docid*, for each document which satisfies the related search expression.

The following example represents, with an SQL style syntax, the informal search expression described above for locating documents related to benchmarking full-text retrieval systems.

| | |
|---|---|
| SELECT | *docid* |
| FROM | *Document_Database* |
| WHERE | WithinParagraph("benchmark", "performance") |
| AND | Phrase("document retrieval") |
| OR | Phrase("full-text retrieval") |
| OR | Phrase("information retrieval") |

As illustrated, proximity operators provide scope for the associated tokens. For example, the search term Phrase("full-text retrieval") locates documents that contain the phrase "full-text retrieval." By contrast, a search expression containing the terms "full-text" AND "retrieval" finds documents in which the tokens "full-text" and "retrieval" appear anywhere in the related text.

The benchmark specifies that the input for search transactions be randomly generated. That is, terms and connectors are independently selected and uniformly distributed over the respective ranges. Search expressions may have from 1 to 50 tokens. Under this range of values, a search expression for the benchmark contains, on average, 25 tokens.

Tokens are selected for a search expression from the database vocabulary (i.e., the set of unique tokens in the database). Since token usage patterns in large collections of documents are known to follow a "Zipf" distribution [Zipf, 1965], random selection over the entire vocabulary would provide search expressions that differ from what one would expect to observe for FTR applications. To address this, the benchmark specification requires the vocabulary to be segmented into *high use, moderate use,* and *low use* tokens. This segmentation is performed on the **search vocabulary**, which is a subset of the database vocabulary with the numeric tokens and **noise words** (i.e., the 50 most frequently occurring tokens such as "or," "and," "of," "the," "a") removed. The *high use* segment contains that portion of the search vocabulary which generates 90 percent of the token occurrences. Zipf [1965] has shown that for large collections of text, the *high use* vocabulary (including noise words) is usually fewer than 10,000 tokens. The *low use* segment generates 5 percent of the token occurrences within the search vocabulary and corresponds to the least frequently used portion of the tokens. This segment contains most of the search vocabulary (typically about 90 percent of the tokens) and tends to be dominated by proper nouns, acronyms, misspelled words, and so on. The *moderate use* segment has those tokens that fall between the *low use* and *high use* vocabularies. The benchmark requires this segment to contain that portion of the search vocabulary which represents 5 percent of the token occurrences. Using these segments, tokens are selected for search expressions by first randomly choosing the segment, then randomly picking a token within that segment.

The search transaction is based on the notion of a traditional "Boolean query" augmented with proximity operators. Clearly, there are many other methods that can be used to specify the desired document content for a search transaction. It is not our intent to argue the merit of this approach; the commercial marketplace has already done so. That is, the overwhelming majority of commercially available products for document retrieval employ underlying Boolean search mechanisms which support, among other things, proximity operators. Thus, the benchmark as designed is applicable to a large number of existing products and, therefore, could benefit a significant portion of the customer base for document retrieval technology.

## 8.6 Retrieval Transactions

Retrieval transactions take a *docid* as input and return the full text of the related document. The acts of searching a database and retrieving documents from the associated answer set are not necessarily performed consecutively. As such, the benchmark does not attempt to relate search and retrieval transactions. The benchmark requires that the *docid* for a retrieval transaction be randomly selected over the range of possible values for the test database.

## 8.7 Response Time Requirements

The benchmark requires 90 percent of the search transactions to be completed within 20 seconds. Thus, the DRS application is forced to provide search transaction response times which are commensurate with the large amount of work that is required [DeFazio & Hull, 1991]. Relatively speaking, retrieval transactions are not very labor intensive. As such, the benchmark requires 90 percent of the retrieval transactions to be completed within 2 seconds. Consequently, the DRS application must ensure that users can obtain documents for display in a reasonable amount of time.

## 8.8    Workload Generation

The benchmark attempts to generate a realistic DRS workload by employing a process which is based on the following assumptions:

1. The complexity of search expressions, with respect to the number of tokens, must vary significantly.

2. The DRS workload must contain a relatively uniform mix of search and retrieval transactions.

3. The database size must scale with the number of search transactions.

These assumptions are cast into the benchmark specification by means of the following parameters:

1. **Search Expression Size.** The range of tokens for a search expression is from one to 50 tokens.

2. **Transaction Mix.** The ratio of retrieval transactions to search transactions in the workload is fixed at 10 to 1.

3. **Scaling.** The database increases in size by one partition for each 50 search transactions completed per minute. A partition contains 1 GB (i.e., $10^9$ bytes) of text and 200,000 documents.

To vary the complexity of search transactions, the benchmark specifies that the number of tokens be randomly selected over the stated range. According to Haskin [1982], the average number of tokens per search is approximately ten, but the variance tends to be high. Also, most DRS applications provide some form of query augmentation such as synonyms, stems, or wildcards. The net "logical" effect of all these features is to expand the number of tokens entered by the user. For example, given the wildcard "comput*", the search expression would be expanded to contain related tokens in the database vocabulary such as compute, computer, computing, and so on. Since such features are highly application specific, the benchmark does not include any such requirement for the generation of search expressions. The rationale is that by defining the range of tokens per search to be from one to 50, essentially the same behavior is obtained at significantly less complexity.

In practice, a DRS typically processes multiple retrieval transactions per search. Also, the average number of document retrievals executed by a DRS per search transaction tends to be relatively stable over time. The benchmark models this workload characteristic by requiring a fixed ratio of ten retrieval transactions for each search transaction.

Scaling for the benchmark is based on the search transaction rate. That is, the database grows by one partition (i.e., 1 GB of text) for each 50 search transactions completed per minute. The target for each search transaction is the entire database. To improve the performance of search transactions, the database may be physically partitioned. Thus, the related FTR system software may issue multiple database transactions for each search transaction as defined by the benchmark.

# 8.9    Performance Metrics

The benchmark includes throughput and price/performance metrics. Conceptually, the notion of throughput for the benchmark is multidimensional. One dimension of the throughput metric relates to search transactions completed per minute, and the other relates to database size. More formally, the benchmark defines throughput, denoted SPM, as partition searches completed per minute. The throughput value for a benchmark run is obtained by using the following computation:

throughput = [search transactions completed per minute] *
       [database size in partitions]

Using the search transaction rate as a throughput computation factor is rooted in the notion that performance is "linked" to finding documents. That is, the essence of this benchmark is the selection of documents from the database using FTR technology to process Boolean search expressions. The amount of work associated with each search transaction is proportional to the database size [DeFazio & Hull, 1991]. Since the benchmark scales in both database size and number of search transactions, the workload tends to grow quadratically. For example, 100 search transactions accessing a 2-GB database generate four times the amount of work associated with 50 search transactions that target a 1-GB database. The throughput metric reflects this property of FTR technology by including database size as a factor in the computation.

Notice that retrieval transactions are not used in the throughput computation. Conceptually, retrieval transactions are included as part of the workload only to ensure that while search processing is taking place, the system under test can deliver acceptable response times for requests to display, download, or print documents.

Price/performance for the benchmark is

dollars/throughput

where dollars is the five-year cost of ownership for the system and throughput is defined as above. Assuming both quadratically increasing resource demands and related hardware costs, different price/performance values can be compared directly, without needing intimate knowledge of the benchmark.

It should be recognized that the throughput metric defined above differs significantly from the standard benchmarks issued by the TPC. Given the nature of FTR technology, this difference appears necessary. Our formulation of throughput is certainly open for discussion, and possibly refinement over time based on experience gained from using the benchmark.

# 8.10 Benchmark Specification Style and Content

The full-text document retrieval benchmark specification has been submitted to the TPC for consideration. The format and content of the benchmark are consistent with other TPC standards. As with the TPC standard benchmarks, the specification is designed to minimize ambiguity at the expense of formality and to be complete. That is, one should be able to develop driver software and run the benchmark based strictly on the specification. Sample software to assist users in correctly interpreting the specification is presented in Appendix A and Appendix B of the benchmark. This software is not part of the benchmark specification.

# Acknowledgments

Early in 1991, work on the full-text document retrieval benchmark was initiated at Sequent Computer Systems, Inc. Since then, many knowledgeable individuals have reviewed and helped me refine the specification. I would like to take this opportunity to express my sincere gratitude to:

David Becker, Mead Data Central
Garth Boyd, Mead Data Central
Michael Cation, Verity
Peter Chellone, Oracle
Thomas Couvreur, Chemical Abstracts Service
Afsaneh Eshghi, Sequent Computer Systems
Aki Fleshler, Sequent Computer Systems
Hector Garcia-Molina, Stanford University
Jim Gray, Digital Equipment Corporation
Charles Greenwald, Mead Data Central
Clifford Reid, Verity
Michael Squires, Sequent Computer Systems
Anthony Tomasic, Stanford University

I hope that the contributions of these individuals will ultimately be rewarded by the emergence of a generally accepted standard benchmark, derived from this work, for measuring the performance of full-text document retrieval systems.

# References

DeFazio, S., & Hull, J. (1991). Toward servicing textual database transactions on symmetric shared memory multiprocessors. *Proceedings of the Fourth International Workshop on High Performance Transaction Processing Systems*. Asilomar Conference Center, September, 1991.

Faloutsos, C. (1985). Access methods for text. *ACM Computing Surveys, 17*(1), March, 1985, pp. 49–74.

Harrington, W. J. (1984–85). A brief history of computer-assisted legal research. *Law Library Journal, 77:453.* (1984–85), pp. 543–556.

Haskin, R. (1982). Hardware for searching very large databases. *Proceedings on Database Engineering.*

IDC (1991). *Workgroup application systems, full-text retrieval systems market review and forecast, 1989/90–1995.* Framingham, MA: International Data Corp., February, 1991.

Zipf, G. (1965). *The psycho-biology of language: An introduction to dynamic philology.* Boston: Houghton Mifflin, 1935; Cambridge, MA: MIT Press, 1965.

# Full-Text Document Retrieval Benchmark

Version 1.1
November, 1992

Samuel DeFazio
Sequent Computer Systems, Inc.
15450 SW Koll Parkway
Beaverton, OR 97006-6063

# TABLE OF CONTENTS

# CLAUSE 1: Database Design

## 1.1    Application Environment

This benchmark represents the workload generated by an electronic document retrieval service (DRS).  The DRS supplies a collection of documents that is accessed by many customers.  The workload generated by customers consists of those activities related to locating and retrieving documents of interest.  Customers have accounts with the DRS and access the service from PCs, terminals, or workstations.

The DRS workload specified in this benchmark does not represent any specific business entity but rather a class of applications that provide access to document repositories.  Examples of such applications include commercial firms which sell access to documents, electronic libraries supplied by government agencies, and document retrieval systems operating within industry, government, or educational environments.

## 1.2    Logical Database Model

Logically, the test database is viewed as a collection of document partitions.  A partition is the unit of storage for the database and contains 1 GB (i.e., $10^9$ bytes) of textual data.  Structurally, a partition is considered a file of variable length records, one per document.

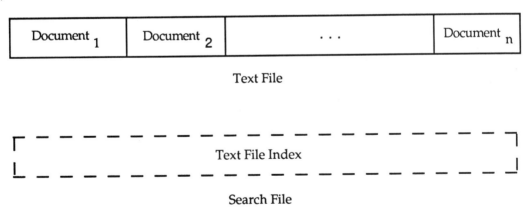

Figure 1. Logical database partition.

As depicted in Figure 1, database partitions may have a related search file which contains an "index" for the documents.  In this context, the term "index" means any surrogate data structure that is used to locate documents of interest, rather than exhaustively scanning the text file. If search files are employed to service the DRS workload, then the details of such constructs must be disclosed.

**Comment:** In practice, it is often the case that an index structure is assembled to make the process of locating relevant documents more efficient. The benchmark does not require nor preclude the use of such structures.

## 1.3    Record Layout

**1.3.1**    The documents in the test database should not be stored in a compressed format. Even when the system under test (SUT) can only operate with compressed documents, the average uncompressed record length specified in Clause 1.3.2 must be adhered to.

**1.3.2**    A document record is a variable length object which must satisfy the following size requirements:

| | |
|---|---|
| Maximum Size | 50000 |
| Minimum Size | 1000 |
| Average Size | 5000 |

All size values given here are in uncompressed bytes and do not include interword spaces. The standard deviation, $s$, for the average document size must be computed. The value of $s$ must not exceed 1000. This set of database size statistics and the standard deviation $s$ must be disclosed.

**Comment:** For the transactions to generate a similar amount of work across DRS applications, it is necessary for the document size to be relatively uniform within the test database. Assembling a collection of documents that fully satisfies this requirement may involve some filtering of the source data. That is, some of the larger or smaller documents from the source data may need to be excluded in order to construct a test database as specified.

**1.3.3**    The document record must contain at least the following fields:

DOC_ID    This field must uniquely identify the document in the database and be at least 4 bytes in size.

DOC_DATE    This field contains a date for the document which must be at least 4 bytes in size. It could be the publication date, creation date, or some other relevant date value for the document.

DOC_NAME    This field contains at least 50 bytes of descriptive text typically found in a document citation such as the author, publisher, and so on. The benchmark does not specify the content or format of this field.

DOC_TEXT    This field contains the data which makes up the document.

**Comment**: For purposes of this benchmark, the document text is considered to be unstructured. That is, although documents tend to have sections such as the abstract, introduction, and so on, there is no requirement to make this structure visible.

## 1.4    Physical Partitioning Rules

**1.4.1**    The document database can be horizontally partitioned into multiple physical units. That is, groups of documents may be assigned to different files, disks, or areas of storage. If implemented, the details of any such partitioning must be disclosed.

**1.4.2**    The document database may be vertically partitioned into multiple physical units. That is, groups of database fields may be assigned to files, disks, or storage areas. If implemented, the details of such partitioning must be disclosed.

**1.4.3**    When the implementation employs an index for the document database, this structure may be partitioned into physical units, each of which can be assigned to a different file, disk, or storage area. If implemented, the details of such physical partitioning must be disclosed.

**1.4.4**    The database along with any associated index structure may be replicated. That is, duplicate copies of the document database or index structure may be assigned to different files, disks, or storage areas. Note that replicated copies of the database are not included in the scaling values of Clause 4.2.1. If implemented, the details of such replication must be disclosed.

**1.4.5**    *Transparency of Partitioning*

The database must be physically partitioned in a transparent manner. The partitioning is said to be transparent when all of the following conditions are satisfied:

1.  The data processed by the priced system to select what physical partition(s) to use when servicing a transaction cannot be represented in a directly executable format (e.g., machine code), or indirectly executable (e.g., compiled code).

2.  The program logic that is used to select the physical partition(s) for a given transaction must be commercially available and executed by the priced system.

**Comment**: The purpose of this clause is to preclude the use of customized physical partitioning techniques which employ detailed knowledge of the test database or computing environment. That is, any physical partitioning scheme must be supported with generic code which processes a set of non-executable parameters.

## 1.5    Implementation

The document database for this benchmark may be implemented using any commercially available text retrieval system, database server, file system, and so on. The only requirement is that the implementation adheres to the standard model given in Clause 1.2.

# CLAUSE 2: Transactions and Profiles

## 2.1    Definition of Terms

**2.1.1**      The term **token** as used in this benchmark description refers to an atomic unit of text. By atomic unit we mean any contiguous string of characters terminated by a blank (e.g., ASCII SP) or punctuation mark (i.e., ' ". , ? : ; !). Special characters (e.g., < >{ } [ ] | ( ), and so on) may also be used as token terminators. Examples of textual tokens include words and numbers. Each instance of a token in the database is termed a **token occurrence**. The total number of occurrences for a token in the database is termed the **token occurrence count**.

**2.1.2**      As used in this benchmark specification, the distribution of token occurrence counts, where the tokens are ranked in highest to lowest order, is termed the **token occurrence distribution** for the database.

**2.1.3**      The term **noise word** as used in this benchmark specification refers to one of the 50 most frequently occurring tokens in the database.

**2.1.4**      The term **database vocabulary** as used in this benchmark specification refers to the collection of tokens which are found in the database.

**2.1.5**      The term **search vocabulary** as used in this benchmark specification refers to the subset of the database vocabulary where the 50 noise words and numeric tokens are excluded.

**2.1.6**      The term **sentence** as used in this benchmark specification refers to the conventional unit of connected writing which begins with a capital letter and ends with a terminating punctuation mark (i.e., period, question mark, exclamation point, or points of suspension).

**2.1.7**      The term **phrase** as used in this benchmark specification refers to an ordered, continuous sequence of words within a sentence.

**2.1.8**      The term **paragraph** as used in this benchmark specification refers to a distinct section or subsection of a document consisting of one or more continuous sentences.

**2.1.9**      The term **search** as used in this benchmark specification refers to the action of locating documents of interest within the database.

**2.1.10** The term **retrieve** as used in this benchmark specification refers to the action of requesting a specific document from the database.

**2.1.11** The term **transaction** as used in this benchmark specification refers to a single unit of work, as viewed by the DRS customer, related to either the action of searching for or retrieving documents from the database.

**2.1.12** The term **search expression** as used in this benchmark specification refers to an expression by which the desired document content is conveyed to the DRS application.

**2.1.13** The term **answer set** refers to a logical construct which represents the collection of documents located by a search transaction. Physically, an answer set only needs to contain identifying values for the documents such as the DOC_ID or DOC_NAME fields.

**2.1.14** The term **random** within this benchmark specification means independently selected and uniformly distributed over the specified range of values.

## 2.2 Search Transaction

To locate documents of interest, customers submit search transactions, each of which contains a search expression. The search transaction outputs an answer set. This transaction is the major part of the DRS workload. It is designed to have a range of search expressions which present a representative workload to the DRS application.

### 2.2.1 Input Data Generation

**2.2.1.1** The search transaction requires a search expression as input. The search expression for this transaction contains one or more tokens which are selected from distinct segments of the search vocabulary. These segments are formed in terms of cumulative token occurrence counts as defined within this clause.

Let V be the ordered list, ranked from highest to lowest by occurrence count, of the search vocabulary. Also, let $n$ be the number of tokens in V, and $c_i$ be the occurrence count for token i of V. Then,

$$T_c = \Sigma c_i, \ 1 \le i \le n$$

represents the total number of token occurrences, summed over the search vocabulary, for the test database. Using V, $T_c$, and $n$ we define the following token segments:

1. **High Use.** This segment contains the first $k$ tokens of V such that

$$0.9 * T_c = \Sigma c_i, \ 1 \le i \le k$$

The high use segment represents the $k$ tokens from the search vocabulary which occur most frequently in the database.

2. **Moderate Use**. This segment contains tokens $k+1$ through $l$ of V such that

$$0.05 * T_c = \Sigma c_i , \ k < i \leq l$$

This segment represents the set of tokens from the search vocabulary which occur a moderate number of times in the database.

3. **Low Use**. This segment contains tokens $l+1$ through $n$ of V. The low use segment represents those tokens in the search vocabulary which occur least frequently in the database.

Comment 1: The search vocabulary is segmented in order to compensate for token usage patterns in textual data. That is to say, most (about 90%) of the token occurrences in any large body of documents come from a relatively small (less than 10,000 tokens) portion of the associated vocabulary. However, most (about 90%) of the vocabulary occurs relatively infrequently in the data. As such, if tokens were selected uniformly, most of the search transactions would be directed at the low use portion of the vocabulary. The segments defined above are used to select search tokens in a manner more closely representing the DRS application.

Comment 2: The search vocabulary does not contain numeric tokens or the noise words. Since tokens are selected at random, excluding the noise words and numeric tokens improves the likelihood of building search expressions that yield reasonable answer sets.

**2.2.1.2** Tokens are selected for search expressions by first randomly choosing the segment, then randomly picking a token from that segment.

**2.2.1.3** Each search transaction contains a search expression which is assembled using:

1. Tokens from the search vocabulary.

2. Proximity operators with the following semantics:

   a. The Phrase($token_1$, $token_2$) operator locates all documents in the database where the two tokens appear as a phrase in the given order.

   b. The WithinSentence($token_1$, $token_2$) operator locates all documents in the database where the two tokens appear anywhere in a sentence.

   c. The WithinParagraph($token_1$, $token_2$) operator finds all documents in the database where the two tokens appear anywhere in a paragraph.

If the DRS application being tested does not support the WithinSentence or WithinParagraph operators, positional equivalents may be used. For this purpose, we define a sentence to be 10 tokens (or 100 bytes) in size, and a paragraph to be 50 tokens (or 500 bytes) in size.

3. Boolean connectors AND, OR, AND NOT. Notice that NOT is bound to AND and represents logical negation. In terms of precedence, AND NOT is equal to AND. The AND connector has higher precedence than OR, and all the connectors associate from left to right. For example, under these precedence and associativity rules, the following search expression

$$\text{token}_1 \text{ AND token}_2 \text{ OR token}_3 \text{ AND NOT token}_4$$

evaluates to

$$(\text{token}_1 \text{ AND token}_2) \text{ OR } (\text{token}_3 \text{ AND NOT token}_4)$$

Search expressions contain one or more terms, where each term is either a token or a proximity operator. Each search expression is formed as follows:

1. Randomly select the number of tokens for the search expression. The range of values for the search expression size is from 1 to 50 tokens.

2. Until the number of tokens for the search expression is exhausted, the following steps are performed:

   a. If the number of tokens remaining to be processed equals one, then add a single token to the search expression. Otherwise, randomly select the type of term (i.e., either a token or a proximity operator). When the outcome is a proximity term, randomly select the specific operator (i.e., Phrase, Within-Sentence, or WithinParagraph).

   b. Randomly select the token(s) for the term using the rules given in Clause 2.2.1.2.

   c. Join each pair of terms in the expression with a randomly selected Boolean connector.

**Comment:** It is often the case that search expressions, as entered by users, contain terms which are expanded by the DRS application. Examples of this include "wildcards", synonyms, and so on. These features are normally provided to help users form "better" search expressions. For all such features, the end result is, logically, an expression which contains more tokens than the original search request entered by the user. The search expression for the benchmark is specified with a relatively large range of tokens. Given this, using any of the common token expansion techniques is not necessary for our purposes. That is to say, we are primarily concerned with the work performed by the server to locate documents of interest, exclusive of query formulation. Furthermore, query formulation, including support for search term expansion features, is often handled by client processes.

**2.2.2** *Transaction Profile*

**2.2.2.1** The search transaction is assembled with an expression that is formulated using the rules given Clause 2.2.1. The search transaction is then submitted to the DRS application for processing and execution proceeds as follows:

1. The DRS system interrogates the database looking for all documents which satisfy the given search expression.

2. As documents are located, an answer set is assembled for the search transaction. The answer set entries must be sorted by the DRS software into a meaningful presentation sequence. By default, the answer set is to be ordered by the DOC_DATE field defined in Clause 1.3.3.

3. At the discretion of the DRS software, the answer set can be delivered to the driver (see Clause 7) incrementally, or in total when the transaction completes.

**2.2.2.2** A search transaction is not considered complete until the entire answer set is received by by the driver. The answer set may be limited to 10% of the number of documents in the test database. That is, the driver program may terminate a search transaction whenever this limit is exceeded. Note that in such cases, the answer set entries must still be sorted by the DRS into a meaningful presentation sequence as specified in Clause 2.2.2.1.

**2.2.2.3** The answer set for a search transaction must contain the DOC_ID. Optionally, the answer set may contain any of the other fields defined in Clause 1.3.3.

**2.2.2.4** After the driver obtains the entire answer set from the DRS system software, it may be discarded. That is, the driver is not required to retain the answer set generated for each search transaction.

**Comment:** For this benchmark, the driver is assumed to be "stateless." More specifically, the driver is not required to retain answer sets generated by search transactions.

# 2.3 Retrieval Transaction

Customers gain access to a document by submitting a retrieval transaction containing the related DOC_ID. A retrieval transaction returns the entire record corresponding to the given DOC_ID value.

**2.3.1** *Input Data Generation*

The retrieval transaction requires a DOC_ID value as input. The DOC_ID for a retrieval transaction is randomly selected over the range of DOC_ID values associated with the test database.

**Comment**: The act of searching a textual database and requesting a document need not necessarily occur in the same time frame. That is, searches may take place hours or even days before the user actually displays any of the documents located by a search transaction. Given this, the benchmark does not attempt to relate search and retrieval transactions.

### 2.3.2    *Transaction Profile*

**2.3.2.1**    Input for the retrieval transaction is formulated using the rules given in Clause 2.3.1. Once assembled, the retrieval transaction is submitted to the DRS system for processing and is serviced as follows:

1.  The DRS system locates the record which contains the requested document.

2.  The record is delivered unformatted to the driver (see Clause 7). A retrieval transaction is considered complete when the last byte for the related document is received by the driver.

**2.3.2.2**    This benchmark specification assumes that any formatting needed for document display is handled at the customer's terminal, PC, or workstation. The record returned by the retrieval transaction to the driver, however, must contain the data necessary to display the document at the user's terminal. Also, the content of the record delivered to the driver must be reported.

## CLAUSE 3:  Transaction Generation

## 3.1    Search Transaction Generation

**3.1.1**    The search transaction requires a search expression as input. Search expressions are constructed as defined in Clause 2.2.1.

**3.1.2**    Multiple driver processes (see Clause 7) must produce independent pseudo random search transaction sequences. The intent is to avoid a pseudo random sequence within one driver process being correlated with any other driver process.

## 3.2    Retrieval Transaction Generation

**3.2.1**    The retrieval transaction requires a DOC_ID value as input. The generation of DOC_ID values must follow the rules given in Clause 2.3.1.

**3.2.2**    Multiple driver processes (see Clause 7) must produce independent pseudo random sequences of retrieval transactions. As with generating search transactions, the intent is to avoid correlated sequences.

## 3.3 Workload Composition

**3.3.1** The generated workload must consist of 10 retrieval transactions per search transaction.

**3.3.2** The SUT reaches steady state (see Clause 6.1) when the workload being serviced by each driver process corresponds to the transaction ratio specified by Clause 3.3.1.

## CLAUSE 4: Scaling and Database Population

## 4.1 Database Scaling

The database scaling rules given in this benchmark specification are intended to maintain a fixed relationship between the transaction load presented to the SUT, and the amount of data accessed by the transactions.

## 4.2 General Scaling Rules

**4.2.1** For each 50 search transactions per minute (tpm-S) configured, the test must use a database with the following minimum size values:

| | |
|---|---|
| Database Size (in bytes) | 1,000,000,000 |
| Number of Documents | 200,000 |

**4.2.2** The ratio of the values given in Clause 4.2.1 must be maintained. Should any value be exceeded by more than 3%, the others must be increased proportionately.

**4.2.3** Given that documents by nature are of variable length, the actual values for the test database are permitted to differ slightly from those given above. The variation, however, must not exceed 3% of the values given in Clause 4.2.1.

**Comment:** There are clearly collections of textual data which, due to either small or large average document sizes, could not yield a database that satisfies the given scaling ratio. The intent of specifying such stringent scaling requirements is to achieve uniform results, knowing that doing so restricts the number of intellectual sources for test data.

**4.2.4** The reported tpm-S may not exceed the configured (nominal) rate represented by the database sizes specified in Clause 4.2.1. Although the reported tpm-S may be less than the maximum permitted by the configured system, the price/performance computation as given in Clause 8.1.4 must report the price of the system actually configured.

## 4.3    Database Population

**4.3.1**      The database can be populated with any collection of documents originally authored by people which satisfy the size requirements specified in Clause 1.3.2 and the scaling rules presented in Clause 4.2.1.

**4.3.2**      Documents may not be replicated in the test database. That is, for purposes of scaling the test database, each document must be unique. Note that replication is permitted to improve performance as specified in Clause 1.4.4.

**4.3.3**      The token occurrence distribution for the textual data used to populate the database must exhibit a curve which is similar to the one shown in Graph 1. In addition to a plot, the coordinate values must be disclosed for this distribution. A similar plot and related coordinate values must be disclosed for the search vocabulary.

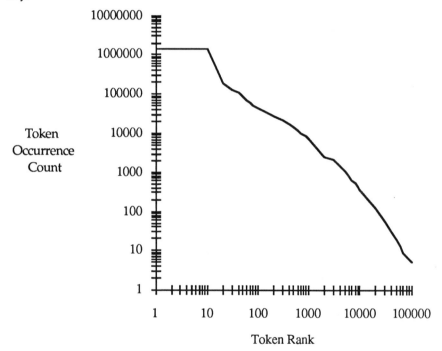

Graph 1.  Token Occurrence Distribution.

**Comment**: The plot in Graph 1 is often referred to as a "Zipf" curve. It has been shown by Zipf and others that the token occurrence distribution for any large body of textual data exhibits a line with approximately negative one slope when plotted as shown in Graph 1. As such, the corresponding plot for any test database must exhibit a "reasonably" similar curve.

## CLAUSE 5: Residence Time

## 5.1 Measurement Interval Definitions

**5.1.1** The term **measurement interval** as used in this benchmark definition refers to the steady state period (see Clause 6.1) during the execution of the benchmark for which the test sponsor is reporting a tpm number and residence time data.

**5.1.2** A **completed transaction** as used in this specification is one that has successfully completed and whose output has been delivered to the driver program (see Clause 7.4).

## 5.2 Timing

Each transaction must be individually timed.

## 5.3 Residence Time Definition

The residence time of a transaction is defined by:

$$RT = T2 - T1$$

where T1 and T2 are defined as:

T1 = time stamp taken by the driver before supplying the SUT transactional inputs, and

T2 = time stamp taken by the driver after receiving the complete response.

The resolution of the time stamps must be at least 0.1 seconds.

**Comment:** It should be noted that the driver program does not represent a user terminal. As such, the residence times do not directly correspond to response times of an OLTP environment.

## 5.4 Residence Time Constraints

**5.4.1** 90% of all search transactions started and completed during the measurement interval must have a residence time of less than 20 seconds.

**5.4.2** 90% of all retrieval transactions started and completed during the measurement interval must have a residence time of less than two seconds.

## 5.5    Computation of Throughput Rating

**5.5.1**    The tpm rating for each transaction type is the number of transactions which started and completed during the measurement interval, divided by the elapsed time.

**5.5.2**    Reported tpm numbers must be expressed to a minimum precision of three significant digits, rounded down.

**5.5.3**    Throughput for the benchmark is reported as partition searches completed per minute and denoted SPM.    This performance metric is computed as:

> [tpm-S] * [database size in partitions]

The database size used for this computation is determined as specified in Clause 4.2.

**5.5.4**    The number of retrieval transactions completed per minute (tpm-R) must be reported.   Note that this value must exceed the reported tpm-S for the benchmark by a factor of 10, but does not directly contribute to the throughput rating.

## 5.6    Interpolation and Extrapolation

The reported tpm rates must be measured rather than interpolated or extrapolated. For example, suppose that 30.15 tpm-S is measured during which 90% of the transactions completed in less than 19.5 seconds, and 30.75 tpm-S is measured during which 90% of the transactions completed in 21.5 seconds.   Then the reported tpm-S for the benchmark is 30.15 rather than some interpolated value between 30.15 and 30.75.

## 5.7    Required Reporting

**5.7.1**    The frequency distribution of residence times for all search transactions started and completed during the measurement interval must be reported.    An example is shown in Graph 2. The x axis values must range from 0 to 30 seconds of residence time. At least 20 non-overlapping intervals must be reported.

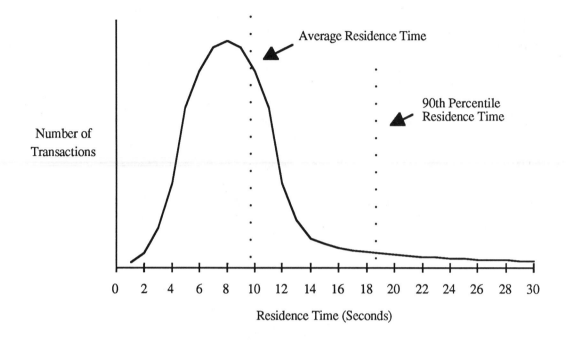

Graph 2.  Residence Time Distribution.

**5.7.2**      The residence time distribution defined in Clause 5.7.1 must also be reported for search transactions with search expression sizes, as specified in Clause 2.2.1, that fall within the intervals [1, 10], [11, 20], [21, 30], [31, 40], and [41, 50].

**5.7.3**      The frequency distribution of residence times for the retrieval transactions started and completed during the measurement interval must be reported. The range of the *x* axis must be from 0 to 5 seconds. At least 20 non-overlapping intervals must be reported. The required plot is analogous to the one shown in Graph 2.

**5.7.4**      The percentage of search transactions that started but did not complete during the measurement interval must be less than 1% of the total started. This percentage must be reported.

**5.7.5**      The percentage of retrieval transactions that started but did not complete during the measurement interval must be less than 1% of the total started. This percentage must be reported.

## 5.8   Test Stability

When operated at the reported tpm-S rate, the configured system must have the property of **stable throughput.** That is, in the context of relatively small changes to the number of concurrently active search transactions, the tpm-S rate must remain well behaved. This test is intended to detect atypical throughput properties of the reported configuration.

**Comment:** For well-behaved systems, increasing the number of concurrently active transactions at the throughput limit tends to yield increases in residence time while the TPM rate remains approximately constant.

For the reported tpm-S rate T and residence time R given in minutes, the average number of concurrently active transactions, C, can be calculated as:

$$C = T * R$$

where

C = average number of currently active transactions,

T = reported tpm rate, and

R = average residence time for transactions in the measured interval.

If $T_R$ is the reported tpm-S rate and $R_R$ is the reported average residence time, then the related $C_R$ must be reported. Also, two additional C values, $C_L$ and $C_H$, must be reported and shown graphically as illustrated in Graph 3.

The $C_L$ and $C_H$ values must be in the following range:

$$.7\ C_R <= C_L <= .8\ C_R,$$

and

$$C_H >= 1.2\ C_R$$

The $C_L$ and $C_R$ values can be obtained, for example, by varying the number of drivers (see Clause 7) and DRS system processes configured for servicing transactions.

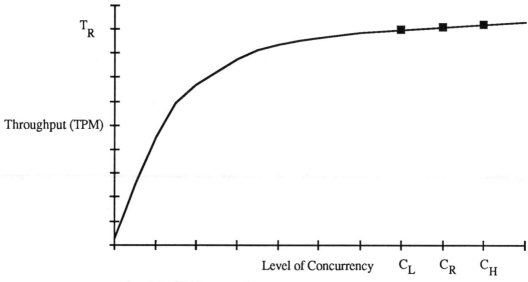

Graph 3.  TPM versus Concurrency.

## CLAUSE 6:  Duration of Test

## 6.1    Steady State

**6.1.1**       This benchmark must be conducted in a condition that represents the sustainable performance of the SUT.  For the SUT, we refer to this as the **steady state** condition.

**Comment:** Although steady state is easy to define in terms of "sustainable throughput", operating in this condition is difficult to prove.

**6.1.2**       The test sponsor (and/or the auditor) must report the method used for verifying steady state sustainable performance and reproducibility of the test results. The auditor should use monitoring tools provided by the hardware or operating system to help determine steady state.

**6.1.3**       The SUT must be configured so that it is possible to run the test at the reported tpm rates for a continuous period of at least eight hours.  Notice, however, that the measurement period as described below may be as short as one hour.

## 6.2　Duration Requirements

The measurement period must:

1. Begin after the SUT reaches steady state.

2. Be long enough to generate reproducible results.

3. Extend uninterrupted for at least 1 hour.

**Comment**: The intent of this clause is to help ensure that the SUT is operated long enough to process a statistically significant number of search expressions for each value in the required range of tokens.

# CLAUSE 7: SUT Driver Definition

## 7.1　Models of the Target System

The **driver** presents transactions to the SUT for processing. The SUT services these transactions and replies to the driver when each transaction completes. There are two types of drivers:

1. **Internal.** As depicted in Figure 2, this driver resides within the SUT hardware and software.

2. **External.** This driver, as illustrated in Figure 3, resides within a separate hardware and software complex and communicates with the SUT using a communications network. Typically, the SUT and external servers communicate using a client/server or remote procedure call protocol. Notice that for this type of driver, residence times include any associated network overhead.

In Figures 2 and 3, the driver area is shaded and the SUT is not shaded, and items marked with an "*" are optional.

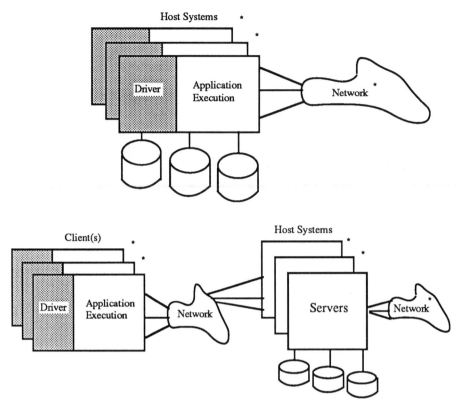

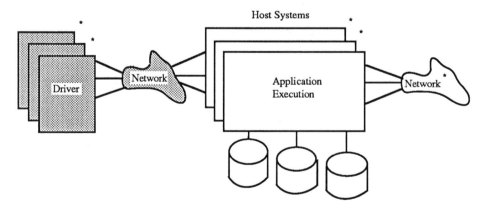

Figure 2. Internal Driver/SUT Models (Host-based and Client/Server).

Figure 3. External Driver/SUT Model.

Notice that Figures 2 and 3 show the driver/SUT boundary (see Clauses 7.3 and 7.4) where the residence time is measured.

## 7.2 Test Configuration

The test configuration consists of the SUT and the driver system.

## 7.3 SUT Definition

The SUT consists of:

1. One or more processing units (e.g., hosts, front-ends, workstations, and so on) which run the application described in Clause 1, and whose aggregate performance will be measured and reported as described in Clause 5.

2. Any front-end systems needed to communicate with an external driver system.

3. The host system(s) including hardware and software supporting the database employed in the benchmark.

4. The hardware and software components of all networks required to connect and support the SUT components.

5. Data storage media sufficient to satisfy the scaling rules in Clause 4. The data storage media must hold all the data described in Clause 1 and be directly attached to the processing unit(s).

## 7.4 Driver Definition

**7.4.1** As described in Clause 7.1, an internal or external driver presents a transaction load to the SUT.

**7.4.2** The driver is a logical entity that can be implemented using one or more programs, processes, or systems and performs the following functions:

1. Supplies a search expression as input for search transactions.

2. Receives search transaction responses (i.e., answer sets) from the SUT.

3. Supplies a DOC_ID value as input for retrieval transactions.

4. Receives retrieval transaction responses (i.e., documents) from the SUT.

5. May do statistical accounting of transaction residence times.

**7.4.3** An external driver must perform driver functions only as outlined in Clause 7.4.2. If any additional functions are performed, the driver must be included as part of the SUT.

**7.4.4** Any software or hardware used exclusively by the external driver (i.e., not used by the SUT) is not considered part of the system under test.

**Comment:** The intent is that external drivers not priced with the SUT are permitted only to perform the functions outlined in Clause 7.4.2. For example, an external driver would not be permitted to execute retrieval transactions.

## 7.5 Additional SUT and Driver Requirements

**7.5.1** No portion of the database may reside on an external driver system. Also, copies of any part of the database, or file system, or its data structures, indices and so on, may not be present on the external driver during the benchmark test.

**7.5.2** Any results of this benchmark must be comparable to other such results regardless of the driver type (internal or external) that is used.

# CLAUSE 8: Pricing

## 8.1 Pricing Methodology

**8.1.1** This section defines the methodology to be used for calculating 5-year pricing and price/performance for the SUT. The fundamental premise being employed is that what is tested and/or emulated must be priced, and what is priced must be tested and/or emulated.

**8.1.2** The system to be priced is the aggregation of the SUT components that are needed to achieve the reported performance level. Calculation of the priced system consists of:

1. Price of the SUT as tested and defined in Clause 7.3.

2. Price of additional products that are needed for the operation, administration, or maintenance of the priced system.

3. Price of additional application development products (e.g., compilers).

**8.1.3**    The pricing methodology is based on the following assumptions:

1. All hardware and software used in the calculations must be announced and generally orderable by customers, with full disclosure of the committed delivery date for general availability of products not already released.

2. Generally available discounts for the priced configuration are permissible.

3. Generally available packaged pricing is acceptable.

4. Local retail pricing and discount structure should be used in each country for which the results are published.

5. Prices should be represented by the currency with which the customer would purchase the system.

**8.1.4**    Price/performance for the benchmark is reported as

price / throughput

where price is the 5-year cost of ownership as given in Clause 8.2, and throughput is partition searches completed per minute, SPM, as defined in Clause 5.5.

**Comment 1:** The intent of the pricing methodology is to allow packaging and pricing that is generally available to customers, and to explicitly exclude promotional and/or limited availability offerings.

**Comment 2:** Revenue discounts based on total price are permissible. Any discount must be only for the configuration being priced and cannot be based on past or future purchases. Individually priced discounts are not permitted. Also, special customer discounts (e.g., GSA schedule, educational schedule) are not permitted.

**Comment 3:** The intent is to benchmark the actual system which the customer would purchase. It is recognized, however, that vendors will announce new products and disclose benchmark results before the products are actually shipped. This is allowed, but any "one of a kind" hardware/software configurations which the vendor does not intend to ship in the future are excluded. In addition, products must be generally available in the country where the SUT is priced.

**Comment 4:** The benchmark assumes that the demand for computing power exhibited by search transactions tends to increase linearly with database size. Working under this assumption, resource demand and throughput values will increase quadratically as the workload scales. Notice, however, that price/performance computation for the benchmark reflects this property of FTR technology.

## 8.2 Priced System

### 8.2.1 *SUT*

The entire price of the SUT as configured during the benchmark test must be used, including all hardware (new purchase price), software (license charges), along with hardware and/or software maintenance charges over a period of 5 years (60 months).

**Comment:** The intent is to price the tested system at the full price a customer would pay. Specifically prohibited are the assumption of other purchases, other sites with similar systems, or any other assumption which relies on the principle that the customer has made other purchases from the vendor. This is a one-time, stand-alone purchase.

### 8.2.2 *Driver*

The price of hardware and software used exclusively by the driver is not included in the price calculation.

### 8.2.3 *Network Pricing*

In a distributed system or client/server system, the cost of all communications components within the SUT excluding LAN or WAN direct connect cables must be priced.

**Comment:** The intent is that all components including PADs (packet assemblers-disassemblers), modems, concentrators, multiplexors, and so on, required to attach clients and servers or to attach network nodes should be priced.

### 8.2.4 *Additional Operational Components*

Additional products that may be included on a customer installed configuration, such as operator consoles, magnetic tape drives and printers, are also to be included in the priced system if explicitly required for the operation, administration, or maintenance of the priced system.

## 8.3 Maintenance

**8.3.1** Hardware and software maintenance must be figured at a standard pricing which covers at least 5 days/week, 8 hours/day coverage, either on-site or, if available as a standard offering via a central facility. The maximum service response time for hardware maintenance must not exceed 4 hours on any part whose replacement is necessary for resumption of the operation.

**8.3.2** If central support is claimed, then the appropriate connection device, such as an auto-dial modem, must be included in the hardware price. Also, any software required to run the central support connection, as well as diagnostic software required by the central support facility, must be included in the pricing. Also, it must be installed on the SUT during the benchmark testing.

**8.3.3**     Software maintenance must include update distribution of both the software and documentation.  If software maintenance updates are separately priced, then pricing must include at least three updates over the 5-year period.

**Exception:**  In client/server designs based on workstations, maintenance and warranty terms for workstations must cover at a minimum a return for repair service.

# CLAUSE 9: Full Disclosure

## 9.1     Full Disclosure Report

A full disclosure report is required when reporting results for this benchmark.

**Comment:** The intent of this report is to provide the information necessary to replicate the benchmark given the appropriate documentation and products.

The full disclosure report must include the following:

**9.1.1**     *General Items*

**9.1.1.1**     A statement identifying the sponsor of the benchmark and any other companies who have participated.

**9.1.1.2**     A program listing of the application code and definition statements used to build the test database.

**9.1.1.3**     Settings for all customer-tunable parameters and options which have been changed from the defaults found in the actual products; including but not limited to:

1.  Database definition options.

2.  System parameters, application parameters, and configuration parameters.

Test sponsors may optionally provide a full list of all parameters and options.

**9.1.1.4**     Configuration diagrams of both the benchmark configuration and the priced system, and a description of the differences.

**9.1.2**     *Clause 1 Related Items*

**9.1.2.1**     A complete description of the logical database model including the record layout, index structures, and the statistics described in Clause 1.3.2.

**9.1.2.2**     If employed by the DRS system, a diagram and description of the storage structures used for physical data partitioning.

**9.1.2.3**     A description of how the database was populated, the source of the textual data, and some sample documents.

**9.1.2.4** A description of the DRS software that was used.

**9.1.3** *Clause 2 Related Items*

**9.1.3.1** A definition of the proximity operators that were used to build search expressions.

**9.1.3.2** A description of the search answer set content in terms of the document record structure described by Clause 1.3.3.

**9.1.3.3** A description of the method used to determine that the SUT was generating valid answer sets as described in Clause 2.2.2.

**9.1.3.4** The random number generator used to select terms and connectors for search expressions, and DOC_ID values for retrieval transactions. Also, a description of the method used to verify the randomness of the function.

**9.1.4** *Clause 3 Related Items*

**9.1.4.1** The distribution for the number of tokens contained in the search expressions.

**9.1.4.2** A definition of the random number function used to generate the workload as described in Clause 3. Also, a description of the randomness verification method.

**9.1.5** *Clause 4 Related Items*

**9.1.5.1** The token occurrence distributions for the database vocabulary and search vocabulary.

**9.1.5.2** The actual database size and the related number of documents.

**9.1.6** *Clause 5 Related Items*

A report containing all the data specified in Clause 5.7.

**9.1.7** *Clause 6 Related Items*

**9.1.7.1** The method used to determine that the SUT had reached steady state prior to commencing the measurement interval.

**9.1.7.2** A description of the method used to determine the reproducibility of the measured results.

**9.1.7.3** A statement of the duration of the measurement period for the reported tpm rates.

**9.1.8** *Clause 7 Related Items*

**9.1.8.1** If the driver is commercially available, then a definition of its inputs must be described. Otherwise, a description of the driver must be provided.

**9.1.8.2** A complete functional diagram of the hardware and software of the benchmark configuration.

**9.1.9**    *Clause 8 Related Items*

**9.1.9.1**    A detailed list of the hardware and software used in pricing the system. Each item must have a vendor part number, description, and release/version level, and either general availability status or a committed delivery date. If package-pricing is used, the package contents must be disclosed.

**9.1.9.2**    The total price of the entire configuration is required including hardware, software, and maintenance charges. Separate component pricing is recommended. The basis of all discounts must be disclosed.

**9.1.9.3**    A statement of the measured tpm for the search and retrieval transactions, and the calculated price/performance.

**9.1.10**    *Clause 10 Related Items*

If the benchmark has been independently audited, then the auditor's name, address, phone number, and a brief audit summary report indicating compliance must be included in the full disclosure report. A statement should be included specifying when the complete audit report will become available and how to obtain a copy.

## 9.2    Availability of Full Disclosure Report

The full disclosure report is to be readily available to the public at a reasonable charge, that is, similar in cost to other generally available benchmark disclosure reports. The report is to be made available when the benchmark results are made public.

## 9.3    Revisions to Full Disclosure Report

Revisions to the full disclosure documentation must be handled as follows:

**9.3.1**    Fully documented price changes can be reflected in a new published price/performance value. The benchmark need not be rerun to remain compliant.

**9.3.2**    Hardware or software product substitutions within the SUT require the benchmark to be rerun with the new components in order to re-establish compliance.

## 9.4    Official Language

The official full disclosure report must be written in English but may be translated to other languages.

# CLAUSE 10: Audit

## 10.1 Benchmark Audit

An independent audit of the benchmark results is highly recommended. An audit checklist is provided as part of this specification.

## 10.2 Benchmark Audit Report

The audit report is to be made readily available to the public at a reasonable charge, that is, analogous to the charge for similar documents.

## 10.3 Auditor's Checklist

**10.3.1** *Clause 1 Related Items*

**10.3.1.1** Verify that the test database conforms to the model as specified in Clause 1.2 of the benchmark.

**10.3.1.2** Verify that the record layout of the test database conforms to the specification given in Clause 1.3.

**10.3.1.3** Verify that any physical partitioning of the test database conforms to the rules that are specified in Clause 1.4.

**10.3.2** *Clause 2 Related Items*

**10.3.2.1** Verify that the search transaction input data are generated in a random fashion as specified in Clause 2.2.1.

**10.3.2.2** Verify that the application program which executes search transactions produces valid answer sets and matches the profile given in Clause 2.2.2.

**10.3.2.3** Verify that the retrieval transaction input data are randomly generated as specified in Clause 2.3.1.

**10.3.2.4** Verify that the application program which services retrieval transactions outputs the complete text of documents and matches the profile specified in Clause 2.3.2.

**10.3.3** *Clause 3 Related Items*

**10.3.3.1** Verify that the search transactions are generated by the driver program as specified in Clause 3.1.

**10.3.3.2** Verify that the retrieval transactions are generated by the driver program as specified in Clause 3.2.

**10.3.3.3** Verify that the workload has the specified ratio of search and retrieval transactions.

**10.3.4**    *Clause 4 Related Items*

**10.3.4.1** Verify that the test database size (in bytes and number of documents) conforms to the scaling rules given in Clause 4.2.

**10.3.4.2** Verify that the test database is populated with a "reasonable" collection of documents as specified in Clause 4.3.

**10.3.5**    *Clause 5 Related Items*

**10.3.5.1** Verify the method used by the driver to measure residence time.

**10.3.5.2** Verify that the computation for determining the throughput rating conforms to the specification given in Clause 5.5.

**10.3.5.3** Verify that the reported tpm rates for the search and retrieval transactions are reproducible.

**10.3.5.4** Verify that the residence time and the tpm rate were measured in the same time interval.

**10.3.5.5** Verify that the SUT exhibited the stable throughput property as given in Clause 5.8.

**10.3.6**    *Clause 6 Related Items*

**10.3.6.1** Verify that the SUT reached a steady state before the measurement interval as specified in Clause 6.1.

**10.3.6.2** Verify the duration of the measurement period and that the benchmark was actually executed the required amount of time.

**10.3.7**    *Clause 7 Related Items*

**10.3.7.1** Verify that the SUT is what is claimed and that the driver performs only driver functions as specified in Clause 7.4.

**10.3.8**    *Clause 8 Related Items*

**10.3.8.1** Verify that all application development software is installed on the priced system and has been used to compile, link, and execute the benchmark.

**10.3.8.2** Verify that pricing includes all the hardware and software licenses as required by Clause 8.

**10.3.8.3** Verify that the priced configuration includes sufficient storage for the test database, and that this storage can be configured in the priced system.

**10.3.8.4** Verify that the warranty coverage meets the requirements of Clause 8.3, or that additional costs for maintenance have been added to the priced system.

**10.3.8.5** Verify that all prices used, including discounts, are generally available to customers as specified in Clause 8.1.

# Appendix A. Sample Driver Program

This appendix contains a sample driver program written in ANSI standard C. As indicated in the initial comment block, the driver program is only an example and is incomplete in several respects.

```
/*----------------------------------------------------------------*/
/* This sample program executes the Full-Text Document Retrieval  */
/* Benchmark. The program is not complete in the following respects: */
/*                                                                */
/*    1. It is assumed that the test database is built and contains */
/*       100,000 documents.                                       */
/*                                                                */
/*    2. A file of token segment records has been prepared for the */
/*       test database.  Also, the maximum token size is 20 bytes. */
/*                                                                */
/*    3. The functions for search and retrieval transactions are  */
/*       application specific and only skeleton code is provided.  */
/*                                                                */
/*    4. No statistics on transaction execution times are gathered or */
/*       reported.                                                */
/*----------------------------------------------------------------*/

#include <stdio.h>
#include <ctype.h>
#include <string.h>
#include <time.h>

/*----------------------------------------------------------------*/
/* Token Occurrence Segments                                      */
/*----------------------------------------------------------------*/
typedef struct _token              /* token string                */
{
    char text[21];                 /* 20 byte maximum token size  */
} Token;
Token *husetok;                    /* high use tokens             */
int hutokcnt = 0;                  /* number of high use tokens   */
Token *musetok;                    /* moderate use tokens         */
int mutokcnt = 0;                  /* number of moderate use tokens */
Token *lusetok;                    /* low use tokens              */
int lutokcnt = 0;                  /* number of low use tokens    */

/*----------------------------------------------------------------*/
/* Functions                                                      */
/*----------------------------------------------------------------*/
void InitTokSeg();                 /* initialize token segments   */
void SrchExp(char *);              /* build search expression     */
void AddToken(char *);             /* add token to expression     */
void AddProx(char *, int);         /* add proximity to expression */
void AddBool(char *);              /* add boolean to expression   */
int SelToken(int);                 /* select token for expression */
void RetvTran(int);                /* execute retrieval transaction */
void SrchTran(char *);             /* execute search transaction  */
double drand48();                  /* random number generator     */
void srand48(long);                /* set random number seed      */
```

```
/*------------------------------------------------------------*/
/* Main: present a benchmark workload to the DRS system software.  */
/*       The test executes for 60 minutes.                         */
/*------------------------------------------------------------*/
main(int argc, char *argv[])
{
    FILE *toksegfh;
    char srchexp[4096];
    time_t runtime = 3600;
    time_t stime, elaptime = 0;
    int docid;

    /* Initialize token segments and random number generator. */

    if ((toksegfh = fopen("tokseg", "r")) == NULL)
    {
        perror("Open of token occurrence segments file failed");
        exit(-1);
    }
    InitTokSeg(toksegfh);
    srand48((long)(stime = time(NULL)));

    /* Submit transactions until time expires */

    while (elaptime < runtime)
    {
        /* drand48 returns a real number in the interval [0,1} */

        if ((int)((drand48() * 11) + 1) > 1)
        {
            /* Generate docid and execute retrieval transaction. */

            docid = (int)((drand48() * 100000) + 1);
            RetvTran(docid);
        }
        else
        {
            /* Build search expression and execute transaction. */

            SrchExp(srchexp);
            SrchTran(srchexp);
        }

        elaptime = time(NULL) - stime;
    }
}
```

```c
/*--------------------------------------------------------------------*/
/* Function: initialize token occurrence segments.                    */
/*--------------------------------------------------------------------*/
void InitTokSeg(FILE *tokfh)
{
    char token[21];
    int hucnt, mucnt, lucnt, segment, nbytes = 0;

    /* Read segment sizes and allocate storage for segments. */

    if (fscanf(tokfh, "%d %d %d", &hucnt, &mucnt, &lucnt) <= 0)
    {
        perror("Read for token occurrence segments file failed");
        exit(-1);
    }
    husetok = (Token *)malloc(hucnt * sizeof(Token));
    musetok = (Token *)malloc(mucnt * sizeof(Token));
    lusetok = (Token *)malloc(lucnt * sizeof(Token));
    if ((husetok == NULL) || (musetok == NULL) || (lusetok == NULL))
    {
        perror("Memory allocation failed");
        exit(-1);
    }

    /* Build the token segments. */

    while (nbytes != EOF)
    {
        if ((nbytes = fscanf(tokfh, "%s %d", token, &segment)) <= 0)
        {
            if (nbytes != EOF)
            {
                perror("Read for token occurrence segment file failed");
                exit(-1);
            }
        }
        if ((strlen(token) < 20) && (nbytes > 0))
        {
            switch(segment)
            {
                case 1:
                    strcpy(husetok[hutokcnt++].text, token);
                    break;

                case 2:
                    strcpy(musetok[mutokcnt++].text, token);
                    break;

                case 3:
                    strcpy(lusetok[lutokcnt++].text, token);
                    break;
            }
        }
    }
}
```

```
/*-------------------------------------------------------------------*/
/* Function: build search expression.                                */
/*-------------------------------------------------------------------*/
void SrchExp(char *srchexp)
{
    int ntokens, termtype;
    int nptokens = 2;
    int tokencnt = 0;

    /* Randomly select number of tokens and build search expression. */

    ntokens = (int)((drand48() * 50) + 1);
    srchexp[0] = '\0';
    while (tokencnt < ntokens)
    {
        /* Randomly select type of term when 2 or more tokens remain. */

        if ((ntokens - tokencnt) > 1)
            termtype = (int)((drand48() * 2) + 1);
        else
            termtype = 1;

        /* Add term to search expression. */

        switch(termtype)
        {
            case 1:
                AddToken(srchexp);
                ++tokencnt;
                break;

            case 2:
                AddProx(srchexp, nptokens);
                tokencnt += nptokens;
                break;
        }

        /* Add boolean connector for all except the last term. */

        if (tokencnt < ntokens)
            AddBool(srchexp);
    }
}
```

```
/*-----------------------------------------------------------------*/
/* Function: add token to the search expression.                   */
/*-----------------------------------------------------------------*/
void AddToken(char *srchexp)
{
    int segment, token;

    /* Randomly select segment and token, then add to expression. */

    segment = (int)((drand48() * 3) + 1);
    token = SelToken(segment);
    switch(segment)
    {
        case 1:
            strcat(srchexp, husetok[token].text);
            break;

        case 2:
            strcat(srchexp, musetok[token].text);
            break;

        case 3:
            strcat(srchexp, lusetok[token].text);
            break;
    }
}


/*-----------------------------------------------------------------*/
/* Function: add boolean connector to the search expression.       */
/*-----------------------------------------------------------------*/
void AddBool(char *srchexp)
{
    int boolcon;

    /* Randomly select boolean connector and add to search expression. */

    boolcon = (int)((drand48() * 3) + 1);
    switch(boolcon)
    {
        case 1:
            strcat(srchexp, " AND ");
            break;

        case 2:
            strcat(srchexp, " OR ");
            break;

        case 3:
            strcat(srchexp, " AND NOT ");
            break;
    }
}
```

```
/*---------------------------------------------------------------*/
/* Function: add proximity operator to the search expression.    */
/*---------------------------------------------------------------*/
void AddProx(char *srchexp, int ntokens)
{
    int proxop, i;

    /* Randomly pick proximity operator and add to search expression. */

    proxop = (int)((drand48() * 3) + 1);
    switch(proxop)
    {
        case 1:
            strcat(srchexp, "Phrase(");
            break;

        case 2:
            strcat(srchexp, "WithinParagraph(");
            break;

        case 3:
            strcat(srchexp, "WithinSentence(");
            break;
    }

    /* Add tokens to proximity operator separated by a comma. */

    for (i = 1; i <= ntokens; i++)
    {
        AddToken(srchexp);
        if (i != ntokens)
            strcat(srchexp, ",");
    }
    strcat(srchexp, ")");
}
```

```c
/*----------------------------------------------------------------*/
/* Function: randomly select a token from the given segment.     */
/*----------------------------------------------------------------*/
int SelToken(int segment)
{
    int token;

    /* Randomly pick token from high, low, or moderate use segment. */

    switch(segment)
    {
        case 1:
            token = (int)(drand48() * hutokcnt);
            break;

        case 2:
            token = (int)(drand48() * mutokcnt);
            break;

        case 3:
            token = (int)(drand48() * lutokcnt);
            break;
    }

    return(token);
}


/*----------------------------------------------------------------*/
/* Function: skeleton code which must be provided for the specific */
/*           system under test to execute a retrieval transaction. */
/*----------------------------------------------------------------*/
void RetvTran(int docid)
{
    /* This code must retrieve the document text related to docid. */
}


/*----------------------------------------------------------------*/
/* Function: skeleton code which must be provided for the specific */
/*           system under test to execute a search transaction.   */
/*----------------------------------------------------------------*/
void SrchTran(char *srchexp)
{
    /* The code must locate the documents for the search expression. */
}
```

# Appendix B.  Sample Token Segment Building Program

This appendix contains a sample program written in ANSI standard C to construct the token segments file required by the benchmark driver code given in Appendix A. As indicated in the initial comment block, the program is only an example and is incomplete in several respects.

```
/*----------------------------------------------------------------------*/
/* This sample program prepares the search vocabulary segments as        */
/* required by the benchmark driver program.  The program is not         */
/* complete in the following respects:                                   */
/*                                                                       */
/*  1. The test database is assumed to be built.                         */
/*                                                                       */
/*  2. It is assumed that the DRS has a utility program which built      */
/*     a file with tuples of the form (token, count), where count       */
/*     is the number of occurrences for the token in the search         */
/*     vocabulary.                                                       */
/*                                                                       */
/*  3. The token occurrence file described above is assumed to be        */
/*     sorted in descending sequence by occurrence count.                */
/*----------------------------------------------------------------------*/

#include <stdio.h>
#include <ctype.h>
#include <string.h>
#include <time.h>

/*----------------------------------------------------------------------*/
/* Token Occurrence Counters                                             */
/*----------------------------------------------------------------------*/
int hutokcnt = 0;              /* number of high use tokens      */
int mutokcnt = 0;              /* number of moderate use tokens  */
int lutokcnt = 0;              /* number of low use tokens       */
int totocc = 0;                /* total token occurrences        */

/*----------------------------------------------------------------------*/
/* Functions                                                             */
/*----------------------------------------------------------------------*/
void CountOcc(FILE *);         /* count token occurrences        */
void SegSize(FILE *);          /* find token segment sizes       */
void SegOut(FILE *, FILE *);   /* build token segments file      */
```

```
/*------------------------------------------------------------------*/
/* Main: read the token occurrence file and generate the segments.  */
/*------------------------------------------------------------------*/
main(int argc, char *argv[])
{
    FILE *tokoccfh, *toksegfh;

    /* Find total token occurrence count. */

    if ((tokoccfh = fopen("tokocc", "r")) == NULL)
    {
        perror("Open of token occurrence file failed");
        exit(-1);
    }
    CountOcc(tokoccfh);

    /* Find token segment sizes. */

    rewind(tokoccfh);
    SegSize(tokoccfh);

    /* Build token segment output file. */

    if ((toksegfh = fopen("tokseg", "w")) == NULL)
    {
        perror("Open of token segment output file failed");
        exit(-1);
    }
    rewind(tokoccfh);
    SegOut(tokoccfh, toksegfh);
}
```

```
/*--------------------------------------------------------------------*/
/* Function: find total occurrence count for the search vocabulary.  */
/*--------------------------------------------------------------------*/
void CountOcc(FILE *tokfh)
{
   char token[80];
   int count, nbytes = 0;

   /* Read the search vocabulary and sum the occurrence counts. */

   while (nbytes != EOF)
   {
      if ((nbytes = fscanf(tokfh, "%s %d", token, &count)) <= 0)
      {
         if (nbytes != EOF)
         {
            perror("Read for token occurrence file failed");
            exit(-1);
         }
      }
      else
         totocc += count;
   }
}
```

```
/*---------------------------------------------------------------------*/
/* Function: find token segment sizes.                                 */
/*---------------------------------------------------------------------*/
void SegSize(FILE *tokfh)
{
    char token[80];
    int count, numocc = 0, nbytes = 0;

    /* Read the search vocabulary and find the segment sizes. */

    while (nbytes != EOF)
    {
        if ((nbytes = fscanf(tokfh, "%s %d", token, &count)) <= 0)
        {
            if (nbytes != EOF)
            {
                perror("Read for token occurrence file failed");
                exit(-1);
            }
        }
        else
        {
            if ((numocc + count) < ((int)(0.9 * totocc)))
                ++hutokcnt;
            else
            {
                if ((numocc + count) < ((int)(0.95 * totocc)))
                    ++mutokcnt;
                else
                    ++lutokcnt;
            }
            numocc += count;
        }
    }
}
```

```c
/*----------------------------------------------------------------------*/
/* Function: build and output token segments file.                     */
/*----------------------------------------------------------------------*/
void SegOut(FILE *tokfh, FILE *segfh)
{
    char outbuf[80], token[80];
    int count, outcnt = 0, nbytes = 0;

    /* Write header record for token segments file. */

    sprintf(outbuf, "%d %d %d \n", hutokcnt, mutokcnt, lutokcnt);
    if (fputs(outbuf, segfh) <= 0)
    {
        perror("Write for output segments file failed");
        exit(-1);
    }

    /* Write (token, segment) tuples to segments file. */

    while (nbytes != EOF)
    {
        if ((nbytes = fscanf(tokfh, "%s %d", token, &count)) <= 0)
        {
            if (nbytes != EOF)
            {
                perror("Read for token occurrence file failed");
                exit(-1);
            }
        }
        else
        {
            if (++outcnt <= hutokcnt)
                sprintf(outbuf, "%s %d \n", token, 1);
            else
            {
                if (outcnt <= (mutokcnt + hutokcnt))
                    sprintf(outbuf, "%s %d \n", token, 2);
                else
                    sprintf(outbuf, "%s %d \n", token, 3);
            }
            if (fputs(outbuf, segfh) <= 0)
            {
                perror("Write for output segments file failed");
                exit(-1);
            }
        }
    }
}
```

# Overview of the SPEC Benchmarks

Kaivalya M. Dixit

*IBM Corporation*

*"The reputation of current benchmarking claims regarding system performance is on par with the promises made by politicians during elections."*

Standard Performance Evaluation Corporation (SPEC) was founded in October, 1988, by Apollo, Hewlett-Packard,MIPS Computer Systems and SUN Microsystems in cooperation with *E. E. Times*. SPEC is a nonprofit consortium of 22 major computer vendors whose common goals are "to provide the industry with a realistic yardstick to measure the performance of advanced computer systems" and to educate consumers about the performance of vendors' products. SPEC creates, maintains, distributes, and endorses a standardized set of application-oriented programs to be used as benchmarks.

# 9.1   Historical Perspective

Traditional benchmarks have failed to characterize the system performance of modern computer systems. Some of those benchmarks measure component-level performance, and some of the measurements are routinely published as system performance. Historically, vendors have characterized the performances of their systems in a variety of confusing metrics. In part, the confusion is due to a lack of credible performance information, agreement, and leadership among competing vendors.

Many vendors characterize system performance in millions of instructions per second (MIPS) and millions of floating-point operations per second (MFLOPS). All instructions, however, are not equal. Since CISC machine instructions usually accomplish a lot more than those of RISC machines, comparing the instructions of a CISC machine and a RISC machine is similar to comparing Latin and Greek.

## 9.1.1   Simple CPU Benchmarks

Truth in benchmarking is an oxymoron because vendors use benchmarks for marketing purposes. There are three types of popular benchmarks: kernel, synthetic, and application.

*Kernel* benchmarks are based on analysis and the knowledge that in most cases 10 percent of the code uses 80 percent of the CPU resources. Performance analysts have extracted these code fragments and have used them as benchmarks. Examples of kernel benchmarks are Livermore Loops and Linpack benchmarks [Weicker, 1991]. The fundamental problems with kernel benchmarks are that they are usually small, fit in cache, are prone to attack by compilers, and measure only CPU performance.

*Synthetic* benchmarks are based on performance analysts' experience and knowledge of instruction mix. Examples of synthetic benchmarks are Dhrystone and Whetstone. New technologies and instruction set architectures make some older assumptions regarding instruction mix obsolete. Synthetic benchmarks offer problems similar to those of kernel benchmarks.

From a user's perspective, the best benchmark is the user's own application program. Examples of application benchmarks are Spice (circuit designers) and GNU compiler (software developers using GNU environments). Unfortunately, there are thousands of applications, and many of them are proprietary. A benchmark suite with a large number of applications is also impractical because of difficulties in porting and evaluation and long runtime.

## 9.1.2    Aging CPU Benchmarks

Popular benchmarks, such as Dhrystone, Linpack, and Whetstone, suffer from the following problems, which make their use in comparing machines difficult:

*   Small, fit in cache

*   Obsolete instruction mix

*   Uncontrolled source code

*   Prone to compiler tricks

*   Short runtimes on modern machines

*   Single-number performance characterization with a single benchmark

*   Difficult to reproduce results (short runtime and low-precision UNIX timer)

*Dhrystone* was developed by Reinhold Weicker in 1984. This synthetic benchmark spends significant time on string functions. It was designed to measure the integer performance of small machines with simple architectures. RISC machines generally beat CISC machines on this benchmark because of RISC machines' large number of registers and the localities of code and data. The performance metric is Dhrystones per second [Weicker, 1991].

*Linpack* is a collection of linear algebra subroutines authored by Jack Dongarra in 1976. It is used to characterize the floating-point performance of machines. This benchmark operates on a 100x100 matrix, which was considered to be a large matrix in 1976. The program fits comfortably in the caches of many machines. Its performance is characterized by millions of floating-point operations per second (MFLOPS). The performance metrics are single- and double-precision MFLOPS [Dongarra, 1983].

*Whetstone* is a popular synthetic floating-point benchmark originally written by H. J. Curnow and B. A. Wichman in 1976. It contains ten modules that perform a variety of numerical computations (e.g., arrays, trigonometric functions). The benchmark is small and sensitive to the ordering of library modules and size of caches. The performance metrics are single- and double-precision Whetstones per second [Curnow, 1976].

The above benchmarks have had long lives, considering the dynamics of technological advances in the computer industry, but it is time to gracefully retire them.

## 9.1.3 Evolution of SPEC Benchmark Suites

A computer system's performance cannot be characterized by a single number or a single benchmark. Characterization of a system's performance with a single benchmark is akin to the fabled blind man's description of an elephant. Many users (decision makers), however, are looking for a *single-number* performance characterization. The customer faces a plethora of confusing performance metrics and reluctance by the press to publish complete information on performance and configuration. There are no simple answers. Both the press and the customer, however, must be informed about the danger and the folly of relying on either a single performance number or a single benchmark [Dixit, 1991a].

Unfortunately, computer vendors have, until recently, been unable or unwilling to agree on a set of standard benchmarks, which has made it virtually impossible for customers to evaluate and compare competing systems. The lack of standards in benchmarking has also created problems for vendors and hardware, software, and system designers. There is no absolute objective truth in comparing benchmarking results.

SPEC started to address these issues by selecting and developing real application benchmarks that would exercise major system components. SPEC's members struggled with questions like, Do we need one benchmark or many benchmarks? What workload should be used to show a particular system in the best light? What is system performance and how can we compare different computer systems in an objective manner?

SPEC wanted to compare system performance across many different technologies, architectures, implementations, memory systems, I/O subsystems, operating systems, clock rates, bus protocols, compilers, libraries, and application software. Additional problems, such as scaling system performance with multiple processors and peripherals, had to be considered. And other factors, like graphics and networking, complicated matters.

The raw hardware performance depends on many components: CPUs, floating-point units (FPUs), I/Os, graphics and network accelerators, peripherals, and memory systems. However, system performance as seen by the user depends on the efficiency of the operating system, compiler, libraries, algorithms, and application software.

With so many variables, SPEC's major goal was that the same source code (machine independent) would run on all members' machines, which required that all benchmarks be ported to SPEC members' machines. This turned out to be a nontrivial task.

Portability conflicts are resolved by SPEC members at SPEC *bench-a-thons*. A bench-a-thon is an intense five-day workshop during which engineers from SPEC's member companies develop benchmarks and tools that are portable across operating systems and platforms.

SPEC chose a simple measure, elapsed time, to run the benchmark. A simple speed metric and machine-independent code were keys to providing a comprehensive and fair comparison between competing machines.

SPEC measures performance by determining the times required to run a suite of applications and then comparing the time for completion of each with the time of a reference machine (DEC VAX 780). The individual results are called the SPECratios for that particular machine. There is general consensus that the use of a single number is not the best way to represent the results of a suite of benchmarks. Unfortunately, pressures exist that force the development of just such a number. By definition, all SPEC metrics for DEC VAX 780 are one. (For definitions of SPEC metrics, see Appendix D. of this chapter).

The experts seem to be split between those who favor the use of the weighted arithmetic mean and others who believe the geometric mean of the numbers provides the best composite number [Hennessy and Patterson, 1990]. Following extensive debate, SPEC selected the geometric mean—a composite metric—for the following reasons:

- It provides for ease of publication.

- Each benchmark carries the same weight.

- SPECratio is dimensionless, so use of the harmonic mean did not make sense.

- It is not unduly influenced by long running programs.

- It is relatively immune to performance variation on individual benchmarks.

- It provides a consistent and fair metric.

The SPEC{mark89, int89, fp89, int92, fp92} metrics are an overall (geometric mean) statistical measure of performance on SPEC CPU benchmark suites. However, SPEC strongly recommends that all SPECratios be published and used to make informed comparisons.

# 9.2   History of SPEC Products

SPEC has developed a series of CPU benchmark suites: SPEC Release 1, CINT92, and CFP92. CINT92 and CFP92 replace the SPEC Release 1 CPU benchmark suite [Dixit, 1992]. The system development multitasking (SDM) suite was developed to measure the throughput capacity of machines [Dronamraju, Naseem, & Chelluri, 1990].

SPEC Release 1 was announced in October, 1989, and contains four C (integer computation) benchmarks and six FORTRAN (double-precision floating-point computation) benchmarks (SPEC Benchmark Suite Release 1.0, 1990). SPEC Release 1 characterized CPU performance with the speed performance metrics: *SPECint89, SPECfp89,* and a composite *SPEC-mark89.*

In May, 1991, SPEC announced its SDM Release 1, which contains two system-level benchmarks. The benchmarks in CPU suites (SPEC Release 1, CINT92, and CFP92) spend over 99 percent of their time in the "user mode" and do not stress either the operating system or I/O subsystem. SDM Release 1 characterizes the peak throughput performance of the system in *scripts per hour* [Dronamraju, Balan, & Morgan, 1991]. The SDM suite was developed to address the throughput capacity of machines and does not replace CPU suites. The prefix "S" in SDM Release 1 identifies it as a system-level benchmark suite.

In January, 1992, SPEC released two component-level CPU suites (CINT92 and CFP92) to replace the SPEC Release 1.2b suite. The prefix "C" in CINT92 and CFP92 identifies them as component benchmark suites.

CINT92 contains six integer benchmarks, and CFP92 contains 14 floating-point benchmarks. CINT92 measures the integer speed performance of the CPU with metric *SPECint92,* and CFP92 measures the floating-point speed performance of the CPU with metric *SPECfp92.*

SPEC defined a new methodology and developed two new capacity metrics in June of 1992: SPECrate_int92 and SPECrate_fp92 [Carlton, 1992].

# 9.3 SPEC Release 1

SPEC Release 1 provides CPU speed performance measurements that are analogous to a sports car's lap times (elapsed time) on ten different race tracks (ten benchmarks) [Mashey, 1990]. SPEC Release 1 is a CPU benchmarking suite of four integer benchmarks written in C and six double-precision floating-point benchmarks written in FORTRAN. SPEC Release 1 is now obsolete.

SPEC Release 1 characterized CPU performance with the speed performance metrics *SPECint89*, *SPECfp89*, and a composite *SPECmark89*. SPEC released a throughput version of SPEC Release 1 as SPEC Release 1.2b in March, 1990. SPEC Release 1.2b characterizes the multiprocessor (MP) systems with the capacity metrics *SPECintThruput*, *SPECfpThruput* and *SPECThruput* [Greenfield, Raynoha, & Bhandarkar, 1990]. Table 9.1 summarizes the SPEC Release 1 suite.

**Table 9.1** SPEC Release 1 benchmarks.

| Benchmarks | Type | Application Description |
|---|---|---|
| 001.gcc | INT[1] | GNU C compiler |
| 008.espresso | INT | PLA optimizing tool |
| 013.spice2g6 | FP[2] | Circuit simulation and analysis |
| 015.doduc | FP | Monte Carlo simulation |
| 020.nasa7 | FP | Seven floating-point kernels |
| 022.li | INT | LISP interpreter |
| 023.eqntott | INT | Conversions of equations to truth table |
| 030.matrix300 | FP | Matrix solutions |
| 0.42fpppp | FP | Quantum chemistry application |
| 047.tomcatv | FP | Mesh generation application |

Notes: 1. INT = Integer intensive benchmark.
2. FP = Double-precision floating-point benchmark.

Experience has shown that useful information is obscured by the monochromatic (SPECmark89—a single number) view of performance and that the complete spectrum—all ten SPECratios—should be used to make fair comparisons.

Over 150 SPEC Release 1 results on a variety of platforms ranging from personal computers to high-end servers have been reported in SPEC newsletters. Tables B.1 and B.2 (Appendix B, this chapter) provide SPEC Release 1 results and SPEC Thruput Method A results extracted from recent issues of the SPEC newsletter.

## 9.4    Reasons for New CPU Suites CINT92 and CFP92

CPU performance more than doubles every year. SPEC Release 1 appeared in 1989, and since then improvements in architecture, hardware, clock rates, and software have dramatically reduced the runtimes of SPEC Release 1 benchmarks (e.g., 030.matrix300, 042.fpppp, and 047.tomcatv), thereby increasing the potential for errors in measurement. SPECmark89 was significantly influenced by the floating-point bias (e.g., six of the ten benchmarks in FORTRAN) in the suite and especially the peak floating-point performance (achieved by using vector preprocessors) on 030.matrix300 and 020.nasa7—kernel benchmarks [Keatts, Balan, & Bodo, 1991].

To alleviate the above problems, SPEC announced two new benchmark suites—CINT92 and CFP92. These suites build on the real end-user benchmarks in SPEC Release 1. They contain several additional application benchmarks and enhancements that enable them to keep pace with faster hardware and smarter optimizing compilers.

In spite of the popularity of SPECmark89, SPEC's members voted not to combine the results of two fundamentally different workloads (integer and floating-point), and so SPEC has not defined SPECmark92. CINT92 and CFP92 provide CPU speed performance measurements that are analogous to a sports car's lap times (elapsed time) on 20 different race tracks (20 benchmarks).

SPEC strongly encourages users and vendors to publish the results they have obtained with the new CINT92 and CFP92 suites. CINT92 measures the integer speed performance of the CPU with metric *SPECint92,* and CFP92 measures the floating-point speed performance of the CPU with metric *SPECfp92.* In June of 1992, SPEC defined a new methodology and two new capacity metrics for both uniprocessors and multiprocessors: *SPECrate_int92* and *SPECrate_fp92.* For a detailed understanding of the SPECrate, the reader is directed to the article by Carlton [1992]. See Appendix D. (this chapter) for definitions of various metrics.

### 9.4.1    Integer Suite, CINT92

The new integer suite, CINT92, contains six CPU intensive integer benchmarks written in C [Dixit, 1991b]. CINT92 retains three benchmarks (008.espresso, 022.li, and 023.eqntott) from SPEC Release 1. Two new

benchmarks, 026.compress and 072.sc, are applications commonly available on UNIX systems. The longer running 085.gcc replaces 001.gcc from
SPEC Release 1. The CINT92 suite supersedes SPEC Release 1. Tables A.1
and A.2 (Appendix A, this chapter) show recently reported results on
CINT92. Table 9.2 summarizes applications in the CINT92 suite.

**Table 9.2** The CINT92 suite.

| Benchmarks | LOC[1] | Object[2] | Application Description |
|---|---|---|---|
| 008.espresso | 14,800 | 276 | Programmable logic array (PLA) optimizing tool |
| 022.li | 7,700 | 235 | LISP interpreter |
| 023.eqntott | 3,500 | 397 | Conversion of equations to truth table |
| 026.compress | 1,500 | 510 | Text compression algorithm |
| 072.sc | 8,500 | 343 | Spreadsheet application |
| 085.gcc | 87,800 | 884 | GNU compiler application |

Notes: 1. LOC = lines of source code.
2. Object = Static size (KB) of SPARC executable.

### 9.4.1.1 Descriptions of the CINT92 Benchmarks

*008.espresso* is a tool for the generation and optimization of programmable
logic arrays (PLAs). It characterizes work in the electronic design automation market and the logic-simulation and routing-algorithm areas [UC Berkeley, 1988]. The elapsed time to run a set of four different input models
characterizes 008.espresso's performance. The program manipulates arrays
in small loops, and its performance is sensitive to the storage allocation
algorithm (e.g., *malloc*) and cache size. This benchmark represents circuit
design applications.

*022.li* is a LISP interpreter that solves nine queens' problem. The backtracking algorithm is recursive [Betz, 1988]. This benchmark is based on
XLISP 1.6, which is a small implementation of LISP. The backtracking
algorithm poses a challenge for register window architectures. This benchmark represents object-oriented programming applications.

*023.eqntott* translates a logical representation of an equation to a truth
table. The primary computation is a sort operation [UC Berkeley, 1985].
The program fits comfortably in the instruction cache of most machines, but
the large data size may cause data cache misses on some machines. A small
loop with several conditional branches poses a challenge to minimize bub-
bles in the pipeline. This benchmark represents circuit design applications.

*026.compress* is a text compression and decompression utility that reduces the size of the named files using adaptive Lempel-Ziv coding. This benchmark compresses and decompresses a 1-MB file 20 times. The amount of compression that is obtained depends on the size of the input, the number of bits per code, and the distribution of common substrings. Two processes (compress and uncompress) communicate via *pipes,* which is unique to this benchmark in the benchmark suite. This benchmark represents data compression applications.

*072.sc* is a spreadsheet benchmark that calculates budgets, SPECmarks, and 15-year amortization schedules. It performs standard spreadsheet operations: cursor movement, data entry, data movement, file handling, row and column operations, operation on ranges, numeric expressions, and evaluations. All output is directed to a file to alleviate problems of window sizes and output validation. An efficient *curses* package should improve the performance on this benchmark. 072.sc performs a small (less than 1 percent) amount of floating-point computation. This benchmark represents spreadsheet applications.

*085.gcc* is a popular C compiler used as a benchmark [Stallman, 1989]. It is a CPU intensive C benchmark that spends about 10 percent of its runtime in I/O operations and executes code spread over many subroutines. Its performance is sensitive to cache size and the speed of the I/O device [Phillip, 1992]. The benchmark measures the time it takes for the GNU C compiler to convert 76 preprocessed source files into optimized SUN-3 assembly (.s files) language output. This benchmark characterizes work done in a workstation-based software development environment.

### 9.4.1.2 Instruction Profile of the CINT92 Suite

Instruction profiling is used to understand benchmark behavior and locate potential sources of bottlenecks in hardware and software. It is very important to remember that the number of instructions executed and the instruction mix are highly dependent on the architecture, implementation, instruction set, preprocessors (e.g., KAP, VAST), compiler efficiency, optimization level, and runtime libraries. The instruction profiles will be different for other platforms (e.g., HP, IBM, DEC, Intel, Motorola) [Austin & Sohi, 1992]. The following profiling information relates to the CINT92 benchmark suite compiled for SPARCstation 2 (SS-2) with the SUN C 1.1 compiler.

The benchmarks were analyzed with *SpixTools,* a set of SUN internal performance measurement tools. *SpixTools* assume infinite cache and trace instructions only in the user mode. The instruction mix shown in Table 9.3 does not include code executed in the operating system. Most of the benchmarks spend 95–99 percent of their time in the user mode, so instruction trace is fairly accurate. 085.gcc spends about 10 percent of its time in the kernel mode, and those instructions are not reflected in the instruction counts. The data represented in Table 9.3 were extracted from the output of *SpixTools*. The salient runtime behavior (e.g., memory references, branch operations, and instruction counts) is detailed in Table 9.3.

**Table 9.3** CINT92—SPARC instruction counts.

| Benchmarks | Memory % | Branch % | Other % | Millions of Instructions |
|---|---|---|---|---|
| 008.espresso | 28.1 | 20.4 | 51.5 | 2,931 |
| 022.li | **33.3** | 23.7 | *43.0* | **4,661** |
| 023.eqntott | *16.5* | **26.5** | 57.0 | 1,322 |
| 026.compress | 25.7 | *16.6* | **57.7** | 2,699 |
| 072.sc | 24.1 | 21.8 | 54.1 | *1,255* |
| 085.gcc | 26.6 | 20.2 | 53.2 | 4,624 |
| TOTAL | 27.3 | 23.3 | 49.4 | 17,692 |

Memory = loads + stores; Other = total − memory − branch.
Italics indicates the lowest number in the column.
Bold indicates the highest number in the column.

The programs executing high percentages of memory (load + store) and branch operations are more likely to cause cache misses and pipeline stalls. In the CINT92 suite, 022.li is the most memory intensive (33 percent) and 023.eqntott is the most branch intensive (27 percent) benchmark. The CINT92 suite exhibits an interesting range of instruction mix:

- Memory operations:  17–33 percent
- Branch operations:  17–27 percent
- Other operations:  43–58 percent

These numbers vary with different preprocessors' and compilers' options.

## 9.4.2 Floating-Point Suite, CFP92

The component-level CPU intensive floating-point benchmark suite contains 14 benchmarks that represent applications in circuit theory, nuclear simulation, quantum chemistry, electromagnetic particle-in-cell simulation, mesh generation, optical ray tracing, neural network, simulation of human ear, weather prediction, quantum physics, astrophysics, and several kernels used by NASA Ames.

CFP92 contains 12 floating-point benchmarks written in FORTRAN and two benchmarks written in C. CFP92 retains three benchmarks (013.spice2g6, 015.doduc, and 047.tomcatv) from SPEC Release 1. The new 093.nasa7 replaces 020.nasa7, and the longer running 094.fpppp replaces 042.fpppp. The suite contains two kernel benchmarks—015.doduc and 093.nasa7. Nine benchmarks represent double-precision applications, and five benchmarks represent single-precision applications. The CFP92 suite supersedes SPEC Release 1. See Appendix D. (this chapter) for definitions of CFP92 metrics (SPECfp92 and SPECrate_fp92). Tables A.1 and A.2 in Appendix A show recently reported results on CFP92. Table 9.4 summarizes applications in the CFP92 suite.

### 9.4.2.1 Descriptions of the CFP92 Benchmarks

*013.spice2g6* is an analog circuit simulation application that is heavily used in electronic design automation (EDA) markets. This application stresses the data cache (UC Berkeley, 1987). It is written mostly in FORTRAN, and the UNIX interface of the program is written in C. *013.spice2g6* runs five copies of the "grey code" circuit and spends about 4 percent of its runtime performing floating-point computations. The data accesses cause high data cache misses. More than 80 percent of assignments are memory-to-memory transfers. This benchmark represents circuit design applications.

*015.doduc* is a Monte Carlo simulation of the time evolution of a thermo-hydraulical model ("hydrocode") for a nuclear reactor's component. It includes little I/O, has an abundance of short branches and loops, and executes code spread over many subroutines. This benchmark is difficult to vectorize. 015.doduc is a large kernel benchmark that represents electronic computer-aided design (ECAD) and high-energy physics applications (Doduc, 1989).

*034.mdljdp2* solves equations of motion for a model of 500 atoms interacting through the idealized Lennard-Jones potential. This would be a typical system used to model the structure of liquid argon. At each time step in the calculation, the position and velocity of each particle in the model sys-

**Table 9.4** The CFP92 suite.

| CFP92 | LOC[1] | Object[2] | Application Description |
|---|---|---|---|
| 013.spice2g6 | 18,900 | 8,422 | Circuit design (FDP)[3] |
| 015.doduc | 5,300 | 408 | Nuclear simulation, Monte Carlo (FDP) |
| 034.mdljdp2 | 4,500 | 457 | Molecular dynamics—Chemistry (FDP) |
| 039.wave5 | 15,100 | 14,634 | Maxwell's equation (FSP)[4] |
| 047.tomcatv | 200 | 3,800 | Mesh generation—Airfoil (FDP) |
| 048.ora | 500 | 202 | Optical ray tracing (FDP) |
| 052.alvinn | 300 | 581 | Neural network—Robotics (CSP)[5] |
| 056.ear | 5,200 | 212 | Simulation of human ear (CSP) |
| 077.mdljsp2 | 3,900 | 418 | Molecular dynamics—Chemistry (FSP) |
| 078.swm256 | 500 | 3,826 | Shallow water model, weather prediction (FSP) |
| 089.su2cor | 2,500 | 4,367 | Quantum physics, Quark-Gluon theory (FDP) |
| 090.hydro2d | 4,500 | 555 | Astrophysics, Navier Stokes equations (FDP) |
| 093.nasa7 | 1,200 | 3,062 | Seven NASA Ames kernels (FDP) |
| 094.fpppp | 2,700 | 564 | Quantum chemistry (FDP) |

Notes: 1. LOC = Lines of source code.
2. Object = Static size (KB) of SPARC object code.
3. (FDP) = Double-precision floating-point benchmark in FORTRAN.
4. (FSP) = Single-precision floating-point benchmark in FORTRAN.
5. (CSP) = Single-precision floating-point benchmark in C.

tem are used to calculate the configurational energy and pressure through equations of statistical mechanics. The density and temperature for the model are supplied through an input file. This benchmark represents quantum chemistry applications.

*039.wave5* solves Maxwell's equations and particle equations of motion on a Cartesian mesh with a variety of field and particle boundary conditions. It is a two-dimensional, relativistic, electromagnetic particle-in-cell simulation code used to study various plasma phenomena. The benchmark problem involves 500,000 particles on 50,000 grid points for five time steps. This benchmark computes in single-precision and causes high data cache misses. This benchmark represents scientific and engineering applications.

*047.tomcatv* is a highly (90–98 percent) vectorizable program for the generation of two-dimensional coordinate systems around general geometric domains such as airfoils and cars. It uses two Poisson equations to produce a mesh that adapts to the physical region of interest. The transformed nonlinear equations are replaced by a finite difference approximation, and the resulting system is solved using successive line over-relaxation. It causes high data cache misses on several platforms. This benchmark represents computer-aided design (CAD) and other engineering applications.

*048.ora* traces rays through an optical system composed of spherical and plane surfaces. The design of high-quality lenses, such as those used in 35 mm reflex cameras, is a compute-intensive task. The many types of image evaluation that can be computed for optical systems, several of which include diffraction effects, are also based on ray tracing. Much of the computation time is consumed by ray tracing, that is, tracing the precise simulation of light passing through the optical system. 048.ora is the most floating-point intensive application in the suite and favors architectures that support "square-root" instruction in hardware. This benchmark represents optical ray tracing applications.

*052.alvinn* trains a neural network called ALVINN (autonomous land vehicle in a neural network) using backpropagation. It is a CPU intensive single-precision robotic application in C. 052.alvinn is designed to take as input sensory data from a video camera and a laser range finder and compute as output directions for a vehicle to travel in order to stay on the road. The 1220 input units comprise the two retinas, one from a video camera and one from a laser range finder. This benchmark represents neural network applications.

*056.ear* simulates the human ear. It is a CPU intensive single-precision floating-point benchmark written in C. 056.ear takes a sound file as input and produces a cochleagram—a representation that roughly corresponds to spectral energy as a function of time. It makes extensive use of complex fast Fourier transform (FFT) and other *math library* functions. The program creates a 1-MB output file. This benchmark represents engineering and scientific applications.

*077.mdljsp2* solves the equations of motion for a model of 500 atoms interacting through the idealized Lennard-Jones potential. This would be a typical system used to model the structure of liquid argon. At each time step in the calculation, the position and velocity of each particle in the model system are used to calculate the configurational energy and pressure through equations of statistical mechanics. The density and temperature for the model are supplied through an input file. 077.mdljsp2 is a single-precision version of 034.mdljdp2. This benchmark represents quantum chemistry applications.

*078.swm256* solves the system of shallow water equations using finite difference approximations on a 256x256 grid. It is a memory and floating-point intensive, single-precision FORTRAN benchmark. This benchmark represents weather prediction and other scientific and engineering applications.

*089.su2cor* solves for masses of elementary particles that are computed in the framework of the quark-gluon theory. The data are computed with a Monte Carlo method taken from statistical mechanics. The configuration is generated by the warm bath method. The benchmark is highly vectorizable (90–98 percent). This benchmark represents an area of quantum physics.

*090.hydro2d* solves hydrodynamical Navier Stokes equations to compute galactical jets. Almost all of the benchmark code is vectorizable (95–99 percent). This benchmark represents an area of astrophysics.

*093.nasa7* is a collection of seven kernels that calculate matrix multiplication, complex radix 2 FFT, Cholesky decomposition, block tridiagonal matrix, vortex solution, vortex creation, and inversion of three matrix pentadiagonals [Bailey & Barton, 1985]. This benchmark represents a variety of engineering and scientific applications commonly used by NASA Ames.

*094.fpppp* measures performance on one style of computation (two electron integral derivative) which occurs in the Gaussian series of programs. This benchmark has a very large basic block and is difficult to vectorize. The amount of computation is proportional to the fourth power of the number of atoms (the benchmark solves the problem for 16 atoms). It is a memory and floating-point intensive double-precision FORTRAN benchmark, and it represents an area of quantum chemistry.

### 9.4.2.2 Instruction Profile of the CFP92 Suite

The benchmarks were analyzed with *SpixTools*, a set of SUN internal performance measurement tools. The data shown below were extracted from the output of *SpixTools*. The salient runtime behavior (i.e., memory references, floating-point operations, branch operations, and instruction mix) is detailed in Table 9.5.

The programs that execute high percentages of memory (load + store), floating-point operations, and branch operations are more likely to cause cache misses and pipeline stalls. In the CFP92 suite, 052.alvinn is the most memory intensive (48 percent) benchmark, 048.ora is the most floating-point intensive (56 percent) benchmark, and 013.spice2g6 is the most branch intensive (14 percent) benchmark. It is obvious that 013.spice2g6 is not very floating-point intensive (4 percent) on the input circuit model used in the benchmark. The CFP92 suite exhibits an interesting range of instruction mix:

- Memory operations:        13–48 percent
- Floating-point operations:  4–56 percent

**Table 9.5** CFP92 - SPARC instruction counts.

| Benchmarks | Memory % | Fpop % | Branch % | Other % | Millions of Instructions |
|---|---|---|---|---|---|
| 013.spice2g6 | 25.0 | *4.2* | 13.6 | **57.2** | 22,878 |
| 015.doduc | 29.4 | 25.9 | 8.4 | 36.2 | *1,303* |
| 034.mdljdp2 | 26.7 | 47.7 | 2.0 | 23.7 | 3,217 |
| 039.wave5 | 33.7 | 21.9 | 7.4 | 37.0 | 4,432 |
| 047.tomcatv | 45.0 | 32.9 | 1.8 | 20.3 | 1,406 |
| 048.ora | *13.2* | **56.3** | 7.4 | 23.1 | 1,695 |
| 052.alvinn | **48.3** | 27.6 | 5.1 | 18.9 | 3,506 |
| 056.ear | 35.3 | 26.4 | 6.2 | 32.1 | 17,768 |
| 077.mdljsp2 | 21.4 | 52.8 | 2.4 | 23.5 | 3,017 |
| 078.swm256 | 43.2 | 46.6 | *0.6* | *9.5* | 10,810 |
| 089.su2cor | 33.3 | 31.8 | 4.3 | 30.6 | 4,915 |
| 090.hydro2d | 28.5 | 38.0 | 3.9 | 29.6 | 7,891 |
| 093.nasa7 | 38.9 | 28.0 | 5.0 | 28.1 | 5,917 |
| 094.fpppp | 47.2 | 34.7 | 3.0 | 15.1 | 5,076 |
| TOTAL | 33.2 | 27.2 | 6.5 | 33.1 | 93,741 |

Memory = loads + stores; Fpop = floating-point operations;
Other = total – memory – fpop – branch
Italics indicates the lowest value in the column; bold indicates the highest value.

- Branch operations:  1–14 percent
- Other operations:  10–57 percent

It is important to remember that floating-point benchmarks contain significant integer computational components as seen above. These numbers vary with different preprocessors' and compilers' options.

## 9.5 The System Development Multitasking (SDM) Suite

CPU suites (SPEC Release 1, CINT92, and CFP92) provide insights into the speeds (how fast) of machines; they do not provide adequate information about the throughput (how much) of machines. The benchmarks in the CPU suites are single-threaded, CPU (integer and floating-point) intensive programs. SPEC Release 1, CINT92, and CFP92 benchmarks spend over

99 percent of their time in the user mode and do not stress either the operating system or I/O subsystem.

The SPECthruput metric, also in SPEC Release 1, provided means to measure and report performance results of multiprocessors. This methodology did not stress additional system resources (e.g., system calls, I/O, and interprocessor communications), because it used a CPU intensive workload. However, the methodology still provided a level playing field for all existing vendors of multiprocessors, and many vendors have reported results.

The SDM suite was developed to address the throughput capacities of machines.

## 9.5.1    SDM Benchmarks

The SDM Release 1 benchmark suite contains two multitasking system-level benchmarks for UNIX systems: 057.sdet and 061.kenbus1. Both benchmarks stress a variety of system components (e.g., CPU, I/O, memory, operating system, and many UNIX utilities). These benchmarks enable system developers to compare different releases of hardware and software, including the UNIX operating system. They allow end-users to compare systems based on the behavior of each system's throughput as the load varies on the system.

This release addresses a simple question from a user's perspective: how much work can I get done on my system? Unfortunately, typical work is difficult to define because it varies with users' applications and environments.

As mentioned earlier, CPU suites CINT92 and CFP92 provide CPU performance measurements analogous to a sports car's lap times on 20 different race tracks. By contrast, the SDM suite provides (using two different loads) measurements of system capacity (e.g., acceleration, capacity) analogous to a loaded truck going up two different hills.

SDM Release 1 measures performance by systematically increasing the workload on the system. The gradual increase of the workload is achieved by increasing the number of concurrent copies (scripts) of the benchmark. A script under execution is commonly known as a *user process* in UNIX parlance. The terms *script*, *simulated user*, *user*, *user process* and *clone* are synonyms in this context.

As the system's workload increases, throughput typically increases to some maximum and then either stays constant or decreases. At a minimum, the workload on the system is increased until the system thrashes, the system's resources are exhausted (e.g., swap, proc table overflows, disk I/O bottleneck) and the system's performance degrades to 70 percent of the peak throughput value, or the system is subjected to twice the workload of the peak throughput value. SDM measures and reports this maximum throughput (peak value).

Obtaining the peak performance is an iterative process. System resources and tuning parameters are changed to obtain optimum (peak) system performance.

### 9.5.1.1 SPEC Metrics for SDM Benchmarks

SDET peak throughput is the maximum value of the throughput reached by monotonically increasing the number of concurrently executed SDET scripts while running the 057.sdet benchmark. It is measured in SDET scripts per hour.

KENBUS1 peak throughput is the maximum value of the throughput reached by monotonically increasing the number of concurrently executed KENBUS1 scripts while running the 061.kenbus1 benchmark. It is measured in KENBUS1 scripts per hour.

The performance metric is defined as the total amount of work done in a given time (scripts per hour). The scripts per hour metrics of two benchmarks cannot be compared, because their workloads are different and unrelated.

### 9.5.1.2 057.sdet

This benchmark is derived from an AT&T proprietary benchmark called Gaede. The workload is characterized as a software development in commercial UNIX environments. The benchmark is designed to find the throughput of a system when several processes are executed concurrently; each process executes a script from the scripts directory. Each script is a random collection of UNIX commands, and the frequency and number of UNIX commands are the same for all the scripts, as shown in Table 9.6. Each script runs this set of 141 UNIX commands in a random order.

### 9.5.1.3 061.kenbus1

This benchmark is derived from the Monash University suite for benchmarking the UNIX system (MUSBUS Ver 5.2), which was developed by Ken J. McDonell. The workload is characterized as software development in a research and development UNIX environment.

**Table 9.6** UNIX commands per workload: 057.sdet.

| Command | Frequency | Command | Frequency | Command | Frequency |
|---------|-----------|---------|-----------|---------|-----------|
| nroff/spell | 1/1 | echo | 23 | cat | 4 |
| ed | 12 | ls | 6 | ps | 1 |
| make/cc | 1/6 | cp | 1 | find | 7 |
| mkdir | 4 | mv | 1 | time | 1 |
| rm | 21 | pr | 4 | spell | 1 |
| rmdir | 1 | sh | 1 | touch | 2 |
| cd | 33 | diff | 1 | who | 1 |
| grep | 2 | wc | 2 | cpio | 3 |

In contrast to 057.sdet, this benchmark includes a concept of *think time.* The rate at which human users *peck* at keyboards is approximately three characters per second, based on a recent human-factors study by NCR. The frequency and the total number of UNIX commands are the same for all the scripts, as shown in Table 9.7. Each script runs this set of 18 UNIX commands in a random order.

**Table 9.7** UNIX commands per workload: 061.kenbus1.

| Command | Frequency | Command | Frequency | Command | Frequency |
|---------|-----------|---------|-----------|---------|-----------|
| rm | 5 | cc | 2 | chmod | 2 |
| cp | 2 | ed | 2 | cat | 1 |
| export | 1 | grep | 1 | ls | 1 |
| mkdir | 1 | | | | |

## 9.5.2 Reading SDM Results

SDM benchmarks stress system resources: CPU, memory, disk I/O, and UNIX software. At peak throughput workloads, one or more of these resources become a bottleneck, and the only way to improve performance is to remove the bottleneck. To obtain optimal results on these benchmarks requires tuning the operating system and the disk I/O subsystem. Unlike the CINT92 and CFP92 metrics, SDM performance is highly dependent on the system's configuration (number of CPUs, controllers, disks, and the operating system). Table C.1 (Appendix C) shows recently reported results on SDM benchmarks.

System performance is characterized by a throughput curve. The SDM performance characterization provides more insights to the strengths and weaknesses of the system. The shape of the curve is especially telling. For example, on an ideal machine (infinite resources), the system's performance should never degrade.

A machine with a flat curve following a high peak is the closest a machine can come to being an ideal machine. In practice, a trapezoidal shape is expected. Obviously, high scripts per hour indicates a system that has excellent multitasking capabilities.

A curve that quickly (on light load) becomes nonlinear may indicate a poorly tuned system. A slow-rising curve may indicate a poorly tuned disk subsystem (possibly poor overlapping disk performance). More disks and better load distribution may improve the performance.

A sharp peak may indicate two possible bottlenecks in the system, namely memory contention (paging or swapping) or less overlap (concurrency) in disk I/O operations. Additional memory and disks may improve both the peak value and the shape of the curve.

A steep drop in throughput after a peak may indicate that the system is unable to sustain heavier workloads due to thrashing or other bottlenecks. It may also indicate that disk contention might be very high and/or that the system is paging and swapping heavily.

The width of a flat curve after the peak throughput value indicates the system's resiliency to sustained overloads. Thus, the length of the plateau is an indicator of CPU power. If the peak does not improve with a change to a faster CPU, or larger memory or faster controllers and disks, then there might be a problem with the operating system.

The workloads of 057.sdet and 061.kenbus1 are different, and the results from the two benchmarks should not be compared. The most exciting attribute of the SDM suite is that it provides a convenient framework for handling many different workloads.

## 9.6 SPEC Organization

SPEC has grown since October, 1988. Today, members include AT&T/ NCR, Bull S.A., Compaq Computer Corporation, Control Data Corporation, Data General Corporation, Digital Equipment Corporation, Electronic Data Systems, Fujitsu Limited, HaL Computer Systems Inc., Hewlett-Packard Company, IBM Corporation, Intel Corporation, Intergraph Corporation, MIPS Computer Systems, Motorola Inc., NeXT Computer Inc., Olivetti,

Siemens Informationssysteme AG, Silicon Graphics Inc., Solbourne Computer, SUN Microsystems Inc., and Unisys Corporation.

SPEC's organization includes board members AT&T/NCR, HP, IBM, Intel, and SUN and an eight-member steering committee (AT&T/NCR, DG, DEC, HP, IBM, Intel, Siemens Nixdorf, and SUN). The steering committee's members are required to dedicate at least one full-time engineer to help develop SPEC benchmarks. The general membership votes for the board of directors, the steering committee's chair, and the final selection of the benchmarks in a suite.

Additionally, SPEC has a planning committee, an analysis committee, and release managers assigned to manage product development efforts. The planning committee works with the steering committee to determine product priorities and global issues for the future. The analysis committee examines the strengths and weaknesses of the benchmarks and makes recommendations to the steering committee. The product release managers work with the project leaders, the planning committee, the steering committee, and the publication organization to release quality SPEC products.

For additional information on SPEC products, please contact:

SPEC
c/o NCGA
2722 Merrilee Drive, Suite 200
Fairfax, VA 22031
Phone: (703) 698-9600, x318   FAX: (703) 560-2752

## 9.7    The Benchmark Development Process

Anyone with a sponsor can submit a benchmark to SPEC for its consideration (any steering committee member can be a sponsor). The sponsor works in cooperation with the submitter and assigns a project leader, who is responsible for solving porting problems and selling the merits of the benchmark initially to the steering committee and subsequently to the SPEC membership.

The steering committee members, along with the other SPEC members, develop, analyze, port, and test benchmarks on member platforms. Porting conflicts are resolved at bench-a-thons hosted by SPEC members. A bench-a-thon is an intense effort—five to six days and nights of working sessions during which engineering professionals from 10 to 15 member companies set aside their egos and resolve porting conflicts. When all porting problems are resolved, the steering committee votes on each benchmark. A two-thirds majority vote of the steering committee is necessary for a benchmark to be included in a suite. The suite is provided to the general membership for 30–60 days for further testing and evaluation. The general membership then votes on each benchmark for inclusion in the final product. All reasons for rejections are documented, and any rejected benchmark can be resubmitted for the next release.

## 9.8   Future Benchmarks

SPEC is working with the LADDIS (see below) group to release SPEC's version of the system file server (SFS) benchmark in 1993. A preliminary version of this benchmark was released in 1992 to obtain critical feedback from users. LADDIS was formed by representatives of Legato, Auspex, Data General, Interphase, and SUN Microsystems.

Written in C, the LADDIS benchmark is loosely based on Legato's 1989 *nhfsstone* benchmark. SFS minimizes NFS clients' platform sensitivity, offers improved accuracy of generated load, and normalizes such NFS implementation issues as file attribute and data caching across different vendors' platforms. The multiclient capability of SFS allows collections of NFS clients to be used to generate an aggregate load on an NFS server using one or more TCP/IP networks. This is important since a single client or a network may become saturated before a given server becomes saturated. Interoperability testing and porting efforts are in the final stages. At present, run and reporting rules for the SFS benchmarks are being debated, as are price/performance issues and models [Keith, 1992].

SPEC is also working on I/O intensive benchmarks, networking benchmarks, and new workloads to run under the SDM framework.

## 9.9   Concluding Remarks

The CINT92 and CFP92 suites provide a wider "SPECtrum" (20 colors) of performance characterization by adding new application benchmarks to both the integer and floating-point suites. SPEC strongly discourages a monochromatic view of performance characterization (e.g., SPECmark) and advocates reporting (full disclosure) of all 20 SPECratios and complete details of configuration (hardware, software, etc.). The benchmark results are reviewed by the steering committee for clarity, sanity, and rule compliance.

The measurement methodology of SDM Release 1 is not impacted by the number of CPU(s) and memory technologies. The unique feature of the SDM benchmarks is that their implementation provides a simple mechanism for introducing a variety of new workloads (e.g., network, database, and graphics applications).

Work with the SDM benchmarks showed that performance bottlenecks in the systems can be moved rather than removed. For example, adding CPUs will not help if disks are the bottlenecks, adding disks will not help if either the controller or CPU is the bottleneck, adding memory will not help if the operating system is the bottleneck, and nothing will help if the benchmark can't scale properly.

Even today, many people define performance as "hardware performance" (improvement in clock rate or cache organization). In fact, the user sees only the performance delivered by the system (combination of hardware, software—compilers, libraries, operating systems). Some performance *pundits* claim that performance improvement obtained by software is *cheating*. This is simply not true.

The fundamental difference between SPEC benchmark suites and other benchmarks is that vendors *tune* other benchmarks to show performance improvements, whereas with SPEC benchmark suites, vendors are challenged to improve compilers, preprocessors, and operating systems to improve performance. In fact, many performance improvements on SPEC are direct results of better optimizing compilers that benefit many other user applications.

Decision makers should not depend on a single benchmark or a single performance number in selecting systems. Their selection criteria should be based on the performance spectrum of speed, capacity, throughput, response time information on several standard benchmark suites, and performance on users' applications on a system configuration under consideration. A system's price, upgrade price, scalability, cost of support (hardware, software), interoperability, and future products are other important selection criteria.

SPEC's membership has debated for a long time whether it should implement a price/performance metric. The basic problem in doing so is that price is a transient marked by announcements and requires extensive investment in pricing models. Even a simple model (e.g., the list price of the reported configuration) requires much work and frequent updates. Dollars per SPECmetric is sometimes reported by vendors. For server configurations and system benchmarks (e.g., SFS), SPEC is formulating a simple price/performance metric.

SPEC is a very open and dynamic organization that listens to its critics and customers. It solicits new ideas and application benchmarks from critics of kernel and synthetic benchmarks and provides simple and inexpensive benchmark suites to users to validate performance claims and make informed comparisons.

# 9.10 Credits and Caveats

My sincere thanks to SPEC members who worked hard at developing these benchmark suites. I am grateful to Bob Cmelik (SUN) who developed Spix-Tools. I am indebted to release managers Dr. Sivram (Ram) Chelluri (AT&T/NCR) and Dr. Krishna Dronamraju (AT&T/NCR) for SDM, Jeff Reilly (Intel) for CINT92 and CFP92, Bruce Keith (DEC) for SFS/LADDIS, Bill Keatts (CDC) and John Freeman (CDC) for I/O suite.

I want to thank steering committee chairs Bob Novak (MIPS), Jack McClurg (HP), Bud Funk (Unisys), and Walter Bays (SUN) who focused on difficult issues and have helped solve many problems. I can't adequately thank bench-a-thon hosts for their very generous contributions: John Mashey (MIPS), John Laskowski (IBM), Jeff Garelick (IBM), Rod Skinner (Intel), Dr. Chelluri (AT&T/NCR) and John Dooley (Motorola), Frank Lee (Compaq), Larry Gray (HP), Doug Fears (NCR), Bhagyam Moses (DEC), Paula Smith (DEC), and Tom Morgan (DG). I also want to thank Dr. Reinhold Weicker (Siemens Nixdorf) who chaired the benchmark analysis committee. Most of SPEC's development work consisted of creating usable tools, and for that effort I extend thanks to Anne Skamrock (Solbourne), Vicki Scott (MIPS), Jeff Garelick (IBM), Todd Clayton (IBM), and Jeff Reilly (Intel).

Most of the data presented herein are from SPEC newsletters, and I want to thank the authors and the editors: Subra Balan (IBM), Walter Bays (SUN), and Alexander Carlton (HP). I am grateful to SUN Microsystems and IBM Corporation for supporting this effort.

A number of my colleagues and friends read drafts and helped improve readability. Thanks are due to Varun Mehta, Walter Bays, and Nhan Chu at SUN and to Mike Zarrillo, Sohel Saiyed, and Jeanette McWilliams at IBM. I want to thank Jim Gray (DEC), Bob Klingensmith (copyeditor), and Carol Leyba (Production Editor, Morgan Kaufmann) who translated this chapter from *Sanskrit* to *English*. Finally, I want to thank my wife Evelyn for enduring lonely evenings and weekends while I worked on this chapter.

**Performance numbers change frequently, so users should always obtain the latest available results from SPEC.** Appendix Tables A.1, A.2, B.1, B.2 and C.1 show recently reported results (December, 1991, March, 1992, June, 1992, September, 1992, and December, 1992). Appendix D contains definitions of various SPEC metrics.

The opinions expressed in this article are not necessarily endorsed by SPEC or its members.

# References

Austin, Todd M. & Sohi, Gurindar (1992). Dynamic Dependency Analysis Of Ordinary Programs, pages 342–347, 1992 ACM.

Bailey, D. H. & Barton, J. T. (1985). The NAS kernel benchmark program. NASA Tech. Memo. 86711, Aug. 1985.

Berry, M., Cybenko, G. & Larson, J. (1991). Scientific benchmark characterizations. *Parallel Computing*, 17:1173–1194 (December 1991).

Betz, David Michael (1988). 1.6, Revision 1.0, November 1988.

Carlton, Alexander (1992). CINT92 and CFP92 homogeneous capacity method offers fair measure of processing capacity. *SPEC Newsletter*, 4 (2), June 1992.

Curnow H. J. & Wichmann, B. A . (1976). A synthetic benchmark. *The Computer Journal*, 19 (1).

Dixit, Kaivalya M. (1991a). Truth in SPECmarking. *SunWorld*, 4 (9), September 1991.

Dixit, Kaivalya M. (1991b). CINT92 and CFP92 benchmark descriptions. *SPEC Newsletter*, 3 (4), December 1991.

Dixit, Kaivalya M. (1991c). The SPEC benchmarks. *Parallel Computing*, 17:1195–1205, December 1991.

Dixit, Kaivalya M. (1991d). Interpreting SPEC Release 1 benchmark results. *SPEC Newsletter*, 3 (4), December 1991.

Dixit, Kaivalya M. (1992). New CPU benchmark suites from SPEC. compcon92, Digest of papers, pages 305–310.

Dixit, Kaivalya M. & Novak, Robert (1990). SPEC refines reporting format to ensure level playing field. *SPEC Benchmark Results*, 2 (1), Winter 1990.

Dixit, Kaivalya M., & Reilly, Jeff (1991). SPEC developing new component benchmark suites. *SPEC Newsletter*, 3 (4), December 1991.

Doduc, Nhuan (1989). FORTRAN execution time benchmark. *Framentec*, V29, March 1989.

Dongarra, J. J. (1983), Performance of various computers. *Computer Architecture News*, 1983.

Dronamraju, S. Krishna, Balan, Subra, & Morgan, Tom (1991). System analysis and comparison using SPEC SDM 1. *SPEC Newsletter*, 3 (4), December 1991.

Dronamraju, S. Krishna, Naseem, Asif, & Chelluri, Sivram (Ram) (1990). System level benchmarking. *SPEC Newsletter*, 2 (4), Fall 1990.

Flemming, P. J. & Wallace, J. J. (1986). How not to lie with statistics: The correct way to summarize benchmark results. *Communications of the ACM* 29, 3 (Mar. 1986): 218–221.

Greenfield, Mike, Raynoha, Paul, & Bhandarkar, Dileep (1990). SPEC adopts new methodology for measuring system throughput. *SPEC Newsletter*, 2 (2), Spring 1990.

Hennessy, J. L. & Patterson, D. A. (1990). Computer Architecture, A Quantitative Approach. Morgan Kaufmann Publishers, Inc.

Jain, Raj (1991). The Art of Computer Systems Performance Analysis, pp. 186–192. John Wiley & Sons.

Keatts, Bill, Balan, Subra, & Parady, Bodo (1991). matrix300 Performance Concerns. *SPEC Newsletter*, 3 (4), December 1991.

Keith, Bruce (1992). LADDIS file server benchmark. *SPEC Newsletter*, 4 (1), March 1992.

Mashey, John (1990). SPEC results help normalize vendor Mips-ratings for sensible comparison. *SPEC Newsletter*, 2 (3), Summer 1990.

Novak, Robert E. (1991). SPEC defines two new measures of performance. *SPEC Newsletter*, 3 (1), Winter 1991.

Phillip, Michael J. (1992). Performance issues for the 88110 RISC microprocessor. compcon92, Digest of papers, pp. 163–168.

Savedra-Barrera & Rafael H. (1990). The SPEC and Perfect Club benchmarks: Promises and limitations. Hot Chips-2 Symposium, August 20, 1990.

Smith, J. E. (1988). Characterizing computer performance with a single number. *Communications of the ACM*, 10 Oct. 1988, pp. 1202–1206.

SPEC Benchmark Suite Release 1.0 (1990). Staff Report, *SPEC Newsletter*, 2 (2), Spring 1990.

Stallman, Richard M. (1989). GNU CC Compiler Version 1.35. Free Software Foundation, 675 Mass Ave., Cambridge, MA, April 1989.

Stephens, Chriss, Cogswell, Bryce, Heinlein, John, Palmer, Gregory, & Shen, John (1991). Instruction level profiling and evaluation of the IBM RS/6000. *Computer Architecture News*, 19 (3):180–189, May 1991.

U. C. Berkeley (1987). CAD/IC Group, EECS/ERL of U. C. Berkeley, SPICE2G.6, Release date March 1987.

U. C. Berkeley (1988). EECS Department of U. C. Berkeley, Espresso Version #2.3, Release date 01/31/88.

U. C. Berkeley (1985). The Industrial Liaison Program, Eqntott #V9, released 1985.

Weicker, Reinhold P. (1991). A detailed look at some popular benchmarks. *Parallel Computing*, 17:1153–1172, December 1991.

Weicker, Reinhold, & Bays, Walter (1992). Point: Why SPEC should burn (almost) all flags: Counterpoint: Defending the flag. *SPEC Newsletter*, 4 (2), June 1992.

# Trademark Information

SPEC{ratio, int89, fp89, mark89, Thruput89, intThruput89, fpThruput89} are trademarks of Standard Performance Evaluation Corporation (SPEC).

SPEC{int92, fp92} are trademarks of SPEC.

SPECrate_{int92, fp92} are trademarks of SPEC.

UNIX is a registered trademark of Unix System Laboratories (USL).

VAST is a registered trademark of Pacific Sierra Research Corporation.

KAP is a registered trademark of Kuck and Associates.

SPARC, SunOS, SPARCstation 2 are registered trademarks of SUN Microsystems.

AIX, RISC System 6000, POWER are registered trademarks of IBM Corporation.

PA-RISC and HP-UX are registered trademarks of Hewlett-Packard/ Apollo.

AViion and DG/UX are registered trademarks of Data General Corporation.

Sinix is a registered trademark of Siemens Nixdorf Information Systems.

DECsystem, VAX, VMS are registered trademarks of Digital Equipment Corporation.

Intel, i860 and i486 are registered trademarks of Intel Corporation.

DESKPRO 486/50L is a registered trademark of Compaq Corporation.

EPIX and InfoServer are registered trademarks of Control Data Corporation.

# Appendix A

**Table A.1** CINT92 and CFP92 results (Page 1 of 2).

| Model | MHz | Cache | MB | SPEC Int92 | SPEC fp92 |
|---|---|---|---|---|---|
| ALR Business 486 ASX | 20 | 8I+D+64(E) | 16 | 10.7 | 4.9 |
| Compaq Deskpro/66M | 33/66 | 8I+D+256(E) | 16 | 32.2 | 16.0 |
| Compaq Deskpro/50M | 25/50 | 8I+D+256(E) | 16 | 25.7 | 12.2 |
| Compaq 486/33L | 33 | 8I+D+128(E) | 16 | 18.2 | 8.3 |
| Compaq Deskpro/i | 25 | 8I+D+64(E) | 25 | 14.2 | 6.7 |
| Compaq 486s/16M | 16 | 8I+D | 16 | 9.3 | 4.3 |
| CDC 4680-312 | 80 | 64I+16D+2M(E) | 128 | - | 61.9 |
| CDC 4680-313 | 80 | 64I+16D+2M(E) | 256 | 61.9 | - |
| CDC 4330-300 | 33 | 32I+32D | 128 | 24.5 | 25.7 |
| CDC 4360-300 | 33 | 64I+64D | 256 | 24.9 | 26.7 |
| CDC 4680 | 60 | 64I+64D+512(E) | 256 | 40.6 | 45.1 |
| DG AV/4100 | 20 | 16I+16D | 64 | 13.1 | - |
| DG AV/4300 | 25 | 16I+16D | 128 | 17.4 | - |
| DG AV/4600 | 33.3 | 16I+16D | 128 | 22.6 | - |
| DG AV/4605 | 33 | 64I+32D | 128 | 26.1 | - |
| DG AV/5225 (#2) | 25 | 64I+64D | 256 | 20.3 | - |
| DG AV/6240 (#4) | 25 | 64I+64D | 320 | 20.1 | - |
| Decstation/20 | 20 | 64I+64D | 40 | 13.7 | 14.8 |
| Decstation/25 | 25 | 64I+64D | 16 | 15.8 | 17.5 |
| DECstation 5000/33 | 33 | 64I+128D | 24 | 20.9 | 23.4 |
| DECstation 5000/125 | 25 | 64I+64D | 32 | 16.0 | 17.5 |
| DECstation 5000/133 | 33 | 64I+128D | 64 | 20.1 | 23.5 |
| DECstation 5000/240 | 40 | 64I+64D | 64 | 27.3 | 29.9 |
| DECsystem 5900 | 40 | 64I+64D | 128 | 27.3 | 29.9 |
| DEC VAX 4000/60 | 18ns | 256I+D | 104 | - | 10.4 |
| DEC VAX 4000/90 | 71.43 | 2I+8D | 32 | - | 30.2 |
| DEC VAX 6000/410 | 28ns | 128I+D | 256 | - | 7.1 |
| DEC VAX 6000/510 | 16ns | 512I+D | 256 | - | 13.3 |
| DEC VAX 6000/610 | 12ns | 2M I+D | 256 | - | 39.2 |
| HP 9000/705 | 35 | 32I+64D | 16 | 21.9 | 33.0 |
| HP 9000/710 | 50 | 32I+64D | 16 | 31.6 | 47.6 |
| HP 9000/720 | 50 | 128I+256D | 16 | 36.4 | 58.2 |
| HP 9000/730 | 66 | 128I+256D | 64 | 52.4 | 86.8 |
| HP 9000/750 | 66 | 256I+256D | 32 | 48.1 | 75.0 |

**Table A.1**   CINT92 and CFP92 results (Page 2 of 2).

| Model | MHz | Cache | MB | SPEC int92 | SPEC fp92 |
|---|---|---|---|---|---|
| HP 9000/807 | 32 | 32I+64D | 16 | 20.2 | - |
| HP 9000/817 | 48 | 64I+64D | 32 | 31.4 | - |
| HP 9000/837 | 48 | 256I+256D | 64 | 34.9 | - |
| HP 9000/857 | 48 | 256I+256D | 64 | 34.8 | - |
| HP 9000/867 | 64 | 256I+256D | 64 | 45.6 | - |
| HP 9000/877 | 64 | 256I+256D | 64 | 45.8 | - |
| HP 9000/887 | 96 | 256I+256D | 192 | 78.2 | - |
| HP 9000/887S | 96 | 256I+256D | 192 | - | 141.6 |
| IBM 6000/220 | 33 | 8I+D | 32 | 15.9 | 22.9 |
| IBM 6000/320H | 25 | 8I+32D | 32 | 20.9 | 39.4 |
| IBM 6000/340 | 33 | 8I+32D | 32 | 27.7 | 51.9 |
| IBM 6000/350 | 41.67 | 8I+32D | 32 | 34.6 | 65.0 |
| IBM 6000/520H | 25 | 8I+32D | 32 | 20.9 | 39.6 |
| IBM 6000/530H | 33 | 8I+64D | 32 | 28.2 | 57.5 |
| IBM 6000/560 | 50 | 8I+64D | 64 | 42.1 | 85.5 |
| IBM 6000/970 | 50 | 32I+64D | 64 | 47.1 | 93.6 |
| IBM 6000/580 | 62.5 | 32I+64D | 64 | 59.1 | 124.8 |
| IBM 6000/980 | 62.5 | 32I+64D | 64 | 59.1 | 124.8 |
| XPRESS 486DX50 | 50 | 8I+D+256(E) | 56 | 30.1 | 14.0 |
| SGI Crimson | 50 | 8I+8D+1M (E) | 256 | 58.3 | 61.5 |
| SGI Indigo R4000 | 50 | 8I+8D+1M (E) | 64 | 57.6 | 60.3 |
| SGI IRIS Indigo | 33 | 32I+32D | 32 | 22.4 | 24.2 |
| SNI MX300-75 | 50 | 8I+D+256 (E) | 64 | 28.4 | - |
| Solbourne 5E/901 | 40.1 | 128I+D | 128 | 22.2 | 23.4 |
| Solbourne 6/901 | 33.33 | 20I+16D+1M(E) | 128 | 44.0 | 52.5 |
| SPARCstation 10/30 | 36 | 20I+16D | 64 | 44.1 | 49.4 |
| SPARCstation 10/30 | 36 | 20I+16D+256(E) | 64 | 45.2 | - |
| SPARCstation 10/41 | 40.33 | 20I+16D+1M (E) | 64 | 53.2 | 63.4 |
| SPARCstation IPX | 40 | 64I+D | 32 | 21.8 | 21.5 |
| SPARCstation LT | 25 | 64I+D | 16 | 15.3 | 13.7 |
| SPARCserver 490 | 33 | 128I+D | 32 | 21.7 | 19.5 |
| SPARCstation ELC | 33 | 64I+D | 24 | 18.2 | 17.9 |
| SPARCstation IPC | 25 | 64I+D | 24 | 13.8 | 11.1 |
| SPARCstation 2 | 40 | 64I+D | 32 | 21.8 | 22.7 |

Notes:   1.  Separate instruction and data cache values are reported in kilobytes, e.g., 32I + 64D.
2.  Combined instruction and data cache values are reported in kilobytes, e.g., 128I+D.
3.  External cache are reported in kilobytes, e.g., 256(E); or in megabytes 1 M(E).
4.  Memory is reported in megabytes (MB).

**Table A.2** CINT92 and CFP92 Capacity Results (SPECrates).

| Model | MHz | Cache | MB | SPECrate_ Int92 | SPECrate_ fp92 |
|---|---|---|---|---|---|
| CDC 4680 | 60 | 64I+64D+512(E) | 256 | - | 1130.4 |
| CDC 4680(#2) | 60 | 64I+64D+512(E) | 256 | - | 2231.7 |
| CDC 4680-312 (#2) | 80 | 64I+16D+2M(E) | 128 | 2674.0 | 2676.0 |
| CDC 4680-312 (#4) | 80 | 64I+16D+2M(E) | 128 | 5300.0 | 5523.0 |
| DG AV/4320 (#2) | 25 | 16I+16D | 128 | 732.6 | - |
| DG AV/4620 (#2) | 33 | 16I+16D | 128 | 933.4 | - |
| DG AV/4625(#2) | 33 | 64I+32D | 128 | 1097.9 | - |
| DG AV/5225(#2) | 25 | 64I+64D | 256 | 868.1 | - |
| DG AV/6240(#4) | 25 | 64I+64D | 384 | 1590.7 | - |
| DG AV/6280(#8) | 25 | 64I+64D | 384 | 3245.0 | - |
| HP 9000/807S | 32 | 32I+64D | 64 | 523.0 | 876.0 |
| HP 9000/817S/827S | 48 | 64I+64D | 64 | 816.0 | 1335.0 |
| HP 9000/837S/847S | 48 | 256I+256D | 64 | 890.0 | 1483.0 |
| HP 9000/867S/877S | 64 | 256I+256D | 64 | 1201.0 | 1937.0 |
| HP 9000/870/100 | 50 | 512I+512D | 64 | 835.4 | - |
| HP 9000/870/200(#2) | 50 | 512I+512D | 64 | 1514.9 | - |
| HP 9000/870/300(#3) | 50 | 512I+512D | 64 | 2051.3 | - |
| HP 9000/870/400(#4) | 50 | 512I+512D | 64 | 2478.8 | - |
| HP 9000/890 | 60 | 2M I+2M D | 256 | 1215.0 | 1180.0 |
| HP 9000/890 (#2) | 60 | 2M I+2M D | 256 | 2253.0 | 2360.0 |
| HP 9000/890 (#3) | 60 | 2M I+2M D | 256 | 3306.0 | 3529.0 |
| HP 9000/890 (#4) | 60 | 2M I+2M D | 256 | 4301.0 | 4685.0 |
| HP 9000/887S | 96 | 256I+256D | 192 | 1854.0 | 3490.0 |
| SNI MX500-90/2 (#4) | 50 | 8I+D+512(E) | 128 | 1919.0 | - |
| SNI MX500-90/2 (#8) | 50 | 8I+D+512(E) | 128 | 3474.0 | - |
| SNI MX500-90/2 (#12) | 50 | 8I+D+512(E) | 128 | 4870.0 | - |
| SNI RM600 15/25 (#4) | 37 | 256I+256D+4M(E) | 256 | 2298.0 | 2016.0 |
| SNI RM600 15/25 (#8) | 37 | 256I+256D+4M(E) | 256 | 4506.0 | 3952.0 |
| SNI RM600 15/25 (#12) | 37 | 256I+256D+4M(E) | 256 | 6527.0 | 5403.0 |
| Solbourne 6/901 | 33.33 | 20I+16D+1M(E) | 128 | 1028.0 | 1236.0 |
| Solbourne 6/908 (#8) | 33.33 | 20I+16D+1M(E) | 256 | 6664.0 | 8693.0 |
| SPARCstation 2 | 40 | 64I+D | 32 | 517.0 | 537.0 |
| SPARCstation 10/30 | 36 | 20I+16D | 64 | 1046.0 | 1253.0 |
| SPARCstation 10/41 | 40.33 | 20I+16D+1M (E) | 64 | 1263.0 | 1503.0 |
| SPARCserver600/120 (#2) | 40 | 64I+D | 128 | 1043.0 | 1066.0 |
| SPARCserver600/140 (#4) | 40 | 64I+D | 128 | 1847.0 | 1930.0 |

Note: (#N) = Number of CPUs; e.g., (#3) = three CPUs.

# Appendix B

**Table B.1** SPEC Release 1 results (Page 1 of 2).

| Vendor Model | MHz | Cache | SPEC mark89 | SPEC int89 | SPEC fp89 |
|---|---|---|---|---|---|
| Compaq 486/50L | 50 | 8I+D+256E | 19.3 | 27.6 | 15.2 |
| DEC DECst. 5000-133 | 33 | 64I+128D | 25.5 | 20.9 | 29.1 |
| DEC DECst. 5000-240 | 40 | 64I+64D | 32.4 | 27.9 | 35.8 |
| DEC DECstation 20 | 20 | 64I+64D | 16.3 | 13.5 | 18.4 |
| DEC DECstation 25 | 25 | 64I+64D | 19.1 | 15.7 | 21.7 |
| DEC DECstation 33 | 33 | 64I+128D | 26.5 | 23.3 | 29.0 |
| DEC DECsystem 5900 | 40 | 64I+64D | 32.8 | 28.4 | 36.2 |
| DEC VAX 4000-90 | 71.43 | 2I+8D | 32.7 | 26.7 | 37.4 |
| DEC VAX 4000-200 | 35ns | 64I+D | 5.6 | 5.4 | 5.8 |
| DEC VAX 4000-300 | 28ns | 128I+D | 9.2 | 8.4 | 9.8 |
| DEC VAX 4000-400 | 16ns | 128I+D | 22.3 | 17.2 | 26.6 |
| DEC VAX 4000-500 | 14ns | 128I+D | 30.7 | 24.9 | 35.4 |
| DEC VAX 4000-600 | 12ns | 512I+D | 41.1 | 31.8 | 48.7 |
| DEC VAX 6000-410 | 28ns | 128I+D | 8.5 | 7.8 | 9.0 |
| DEC VAX 6000-510 | 16ns | 512I+D | 15.6 | 14.7 | 16.3 |
| DEC VAX 6000-610 | 12ns | 2M I+D | 42.1 | 31.5 | 51.1 |
| DEC VAX 7000-610 | 11ns | 4M I+D | 46.6 | 34.0 | 57.6 |
| DG AV 530 | 33 | 16I+16D | 18.2 | 24.1 | 15.1 |
| HP 700-705 | 35 | 32I+64D | 34.6 | 24.6 | 43.4 |
| HP 700-710 | 50 | 32I+64D | 49.7 | 35.4 | 62.4 |
| HP 700-720 | 50 | 128I+256D | 66.5 | 42.2 | 89.9 |
| HP 700-750 | 66 | 256I+256D | 86.6 | 55.7 | 116.1 |
| IBM 6000/220 | 33 | 8I+D | 25.9 | 17.5 | 33.7 |
| IBM 6000/320H | 25 | 8I+32D | 43.4 | 21.8 | 68.8 |
| IBM 6000/340 | 33 | 8I+32D | 56.6 | 28.8 | 88.7 |
| IBM 6000/350 | 42 | 8I+32D | 71.4 | 36.2 | 112.3 |
| IBM 6000/520H | 25 | 8I+32D | 43.5 | 21.8 | 58.9 |
| IBM 6000/530H | 33 | 8I+64D | 59.9 | 29.2 | 96.7 |
| IBM 6000/550 | 42 | 8I+64D | 75.9 | 36.8 | 123.0 |
| IBM 6000/560 | 50 | 8I+64D | 89.3 | 43.8 | 143.6 |
| IBM 6000/970 | 50 | 32I+64D | 100.3 | 49.3 | 160.9 |
| IBM 6000/580 | 62.5 | 32I+64D | 126.4 | 61.3 | 204.8 |
| IBM 6000/980 | 62.5 | 32I+64D | 126.4 | 61.3 | 204.8 |
| Ingr InterServe 6605 | 40 | 128I+D | 40.0 | 23.1 | 57.7 |
| Intel AL860XP-50 | 50 | 16I+16D | 31.4 | 53.1 | 43.0 |
| SGI Crimson | 50 | 8I+D+1M (E) | 70.4 | 60.6 | 77.8 |
| SGI INDIGO R4000 | 50 | 8I+D+1M (E) | 70.2 | 61.1 | 77.0 |
| SNI MX300-60/5 | 50 | 8I+D +256(E) | 17.0 | 24.8 | 13.2 |
| SNI Targon/31-25 | 25 | 4I+4D | 8.8 | 14.3 | 6.4 |

**Table B.1** SPEC Release 1 results (Page 2 of 2).

| Vendor Model | MHz | Cache | SPEC mark89 | SPEC int89 | SPEC fp89 |
|---|---|---|---|---|---|
| SPARCserver 490 | 33 | 128I+D | 22.7 | 20.7 | 24.1 |
| SPARCstation 2 | 40 | 64I+D | 25.0 | 21.7 | 27.4 |
| SPARCstation ELC | 33 | 64I+D | 20.3 | 18.0 | 22.0 |
| SPARCstation IPC | 25 | 64I+D | 13.5 | 12.8 | 14.0 |
| SPARCstation LT | 25 | 64I+D | 16.7 | 14.9 | 18.1 |
| SPARCstation IPX | 40 | 64I+D | 24.4 | 21.7 | 26.5 |

**Table B.2** SPEC Thruput89 Method A* results.

| Vendor Model | MHz | Cache | SPEC thruput89 | SPECint thruput89 | SPECfp thruput89 |
|---|---|---|---|---|---|
| CDC  Infoserver 4375(#2) | 40 | 64I+64D+1M(E) | 2@28.8 | 2@24.3 | 2@32.2 |
| CDC  Infoserver 4375(#4) | 40 | 64I+64D+1M(E) | 4@28.2 | 4@24.0 | 4@31.4 |
| CDC  Infoserver 4375(#8) | 40 | 64I+64D+1M(E) | 8@23.1 | 8@20.7 | 8@24.0 |
| CDC  Infoserver 4680(#2) | 60 | 16I+64D+512(E) | 2@54.4 | 2@44.3 | 2@62.4 |
| CDC  Infoserver 4680(#3) | 60 | 16I+64D+512(E) | 3@53.6 | 3@44.1 | 3@61.1 |
| CDC  Infoserver 4680(#4) | 60 | 16I+64D+512(E) | 4@51.4 | 4@42.3 | 4@58.5 |
| DG    AV 4320(#2) | 25 | 64I+16D | 2@12.7 | 2@17.2 | 2@10.3 |
| DG    AV 4620(#2) | 33.3 | 16I+16D | 2@16.6 | 2@22.7 | 2@13.5 |
| DG    AV 4625(#2) | 25 | 64I+64D | 2@15.0 | 2@20.1 | 2@12.3 |
| DG    AV 6240(#4) | 25 | 64I+64D | 4@12.7 | 4@18.9 | 4@9.8 |
| DEC  VAX 6000-660(#6) | 12ns | 2M I+D | 6@32.8 | 6@24.0 | 6@40.4 |
| DEC  VAX 7000-620 (#2) | 11ns | 4M I+D | 2@42.0 | 2@30.7 | 2@51.7 |
| DEC  VAX 7000-640 (#4) | 11ns | 4M I+D | 4@39.4 | 4@28.1 | 4@49.2 |
| Solbourne 5/7021(#2) | 33.3 | 128 I+D | 2@18.0 | 2@18.2 | 2@17.9 |
| Solbourne 5/7041(#4) | 33.3 | 128 I+D | 4@17.4 | 4@17.4 | 4@17.3 |
| Solbourne 5E/903(#3) | 40.1 | 128 I+D | 3@20.4 | 3@21.0 | 3@20.1 |
| Solbourne 5E/908(#8) | 40.1 | 128 I+D | 8@17.3 | 8@18.8 | 8@16.4 |
| SPARCserver 600/120(#2) | 40 | 64 I+D | 2@25.4 | 2@21.4 | 2@28.5 |
| SPARCserver 600/140(#4) | 40 | 64 I+D | 4@22.8 | 4@19.4 | 4@25.4 |

Notes: 1. (#N) = Number of CPUs, e.g., (#6) = 6 CPUs.
2. * = Method A = Homogeneous Load.

# Appendix C

**Table C.1** SPEC SDM 1 results.

| Vendor Model | MHz | Cache | 057.sdet scripts/hr | 061.kenbus1 scripts/hr | #Contr.& #disks |
|---|---|---|---|---|---|
| AT&T/NCR Serv E 660 (#4) | 66 | 8I+D+512(E) | 770.1 | - | 4/13 |
| Compaq 486/50L | 50 | 8I+D+256(E) | 188.6 | - | 1/3 |
| CDC 4330-300 | 33 | 32I+32D | 222.4 | - | 1/3 |
| CDC 4350-300 | 33 | 64I+64D | 242.9 | - | 2/5 |
| CDC 4360-300 | 33 | 64I+64D | 246.2 | 1773.2 | 2/5 |
| CDC Infoserver 4680 | 60 | 64I+16D+512(E) | 397.4 | - | 2/8 |
| CDC Infoserver 4680(#2) | 60 | 64I+16D+512(E) | 686.3 | 3763.4 | 5/17 |
| CDC Infoserver 4680(#4) | 60 | 64I+16D+512(E) | 1042.9 | - | 4/13 |
| Dell 450-DE | 50 | 8I+D+128(E) | 206.2 | 1296.5 | 2/4 |
| DEC DECstation/20 | 20 | 64I+64D | - | 301.8 | 1/3 |
| DEC DECstation/25 | 25 | 64I+64D | 62.3 | 566.3 | 1/3 |
| DEC DECstation/133 | 33 | 64I+128D | 90.6 | 703.7 | 1/5 |
| DEC DECstation/240 | 40 | 64I+64D | 222.5 | 1212.3 | 1/5 |
| DEC DECsystem 5900 | 40 | 64I+64D | 233.4 | 1299.8 | 1/5 |
| DEC 433MP (#3) | 33 | 256 I+D | 298.3 | 1406.4 | 3/15 |
| DEC 433MP (#4) | 33 | 256 I+D | 374.0 | 1712.3 | 3/15 |
| HP 9000/867S | 64 | 256I+256D | - | 2244.0 | 5/16 |
| IBM 6000/320H | 25 | 8I+32D | 140.1 | - | 1/5 |
| IBM 6000/340 | 33 | 8I+32D | 184.6 | - | 1/5 |
| IBM 6000/350 | 41.67 | 8I+32D | 227.4 | 1479.7 | 1/5 |
| IBM 6000/520 | 25 | 8I+64D | 140.3 | - | 1/5 |
| IBM 6000/530H | 33 | 8I+64D | 188.9 | - | 1/5 |
| IBM 6000/550 | 41.67 | 8I+64D | 236.2 | - | 1/5 |
| IBM 6000/560 | 50 | 8I+64D | 271.3 | 1899.0 | 2/6 |
| IBM 6000/970 | 50 | 32I+64D | 326.0 | 2238.9 | 2/8 |
| Intel XPRESS 486DX50 | 50 | 8I+D+256(E) | 290.8 | - | 2/4 |
| Intel XPRESS 486DX50 | 50 | 8I+D+256(E) | 269.1 | - | 3/8 |
| SGI 4D/35 | 36 | 64I+64D | 236.5 | - | 1/8 |
| SGI Indigo R4000 | 50 | 8I+8D+1M(E) | 232.1 | - | 1/3 |
| SGI IRIS Indigo 4D/RPC | 33 | 32I+32D | 182.6 | - | 1/7 |
| Unisys U6000/65 | 33 | 8I+D+256(E) | - | 902.0 | 1/7 |
| Unisys U6000/65(#2) | 33 | 8I+D+256(E) | - | 1595.0 | 1/6 |

# Appendix D. Definition of SPEC Metrics

## SPEC Metrics for CINT92 and CFP92 Suites

By definition the SPECint92 and SPECfp92 for a VAX-780 are 1.

*SPEC Reference Time* is the time it takes a DEC VAX 780 to run each individual benchmark in the suites. The SPEC Reference Time for both suites is shown below:

| CINT92<br>Benchmark<br>Names | SPEC<br>Reference Time<br>Seconds |
|---|---|
| 008.espresso | 2,270 |
| 022.li | 6,210 |
| 023.eqntott | 1,100 |
| 026.compress | 2,770 |
| 072.sc | 4,530 |
| 085.gcc | 5,460 |

| CFP92<br>Benchmark<br>Names | SPEC<br>Reference Time<br>Seconds |
|---|---|
| 013.spice2g6 | 24,000 |
| 015.doduc | 1,860 |
| 034.mdljdp2 | 7,090 |
| 039.wave5 | 3,700 |
| 047.tomcatv | 2,650 |
| 048.ora | 7,420 |
| 052.alvinn | 7,690 |
| 056.ear | 25,500 |
| 077.mdljsp2 | 3,350 |
| 078.swm256 | 12,700 |
| 089.su2cor | 12,900 |
| 090.hydro2d | 13,700 |
| 093.nasa7 | 16,800 |
| 094.fpppp | 9,200 |

*SPECratio* for a benchmark is the quotient derived from dividing the SPEC Reference Time by a particular machine's elapsed time.

*Geometric Mean* (GM) of $n$ items is defined as the $n$th root of the product of $n$ items. For example, the GM of the following six SPECratios—24.8, 25.0, 24.4, 28.7, 26.2 and 27.6—is the sixth root of the product (24.8 * 25.0 * 24.4 * 28.7 * 26.2 * 27.6) = 26.1.

*SPECint92* is the GM of the six SPECratios (008.espresso, 022.li and 023.eqntott, 026.compress, 072.sc and 085.gcc) of the CINT92 suite.

*SPECfp92* is the GM of the 14 SPECratios (013.spice2g6, 015.doduc, 039.wave5, 042.fpppp, 047.tomcatv, 048.ora, 052.alvinn, 056.ear, 077.mdl-jsp2, 078.swm256, 089.su2cor, 093.nasa7 and 094.fpppp) of the CFP92 suite.

*SPECrate* is a capacity measure for an individual benchmark. It is a function of the number of copies run, a reference factor for normalization and the elapsed time. This provides a measure in jobs per second and is then scaled to jobs/week (which allows the reference machine DEC VAX 780 to have a measure somewhat greater than 1). The reference factor for a given benchmark is calculated by dividing the SPEC reference time into the longest SPEC reference time. 25,500 seconds (for benchmark 056.ear). The number of seconds in a week is 604,800.

Thus for a given benchmark, the SPECrate is calculated as:

SPECrate = {# of copies run *
(benchmark reference time / 25,500 seconds) *
(604,800 / elapsed time) }.

*SPECrate_int92* is the GM of the SPECrates from the six benchmarks in CINT92.

*SPECrate_fp92* is the GM of the SPECrates from the 14 benchmarks in CFP92.

## SPEC Metrics for SPEC SDM Release 1 Suite

SDET Peak Throughput is the maximum value of the throughput reached by monotonically increasing the number of concurrently executed SDET scripts, while running the 057.sdet benchmark. It is measured in SDET scripts/hour.

KENBUS1 Peak Throughput is the maximum value of the throughput reached by monotonically increasing the number of concurrently executed KENBUS1 scripts, while running the 061.kenbus1 benchmark. It is measured in KENBUS1 scripts/hour.

SDET scripts/hour and KENBUS1 scripts/hour are not comparable.

## SPEC Metrics for SPEC Release 1 Suite

By definition the SPECint89, SPECfp89, and SPECmark89 for a VAX 780 are 1.

*SPEC Reference Time* is the time it takes a DEC VAX 780 to run each individual benchmark in the suite. The SPEC Reference Time for SPEC Release 1 is shown below:

| SPEC Release 1 Benchmark Names | SPEC Reference Time Seconds |
|---|---|
| 001.gcc | 1,481.5 |
| 008.espresso | 2,266.0 |
| 013.spice2g6 | 23,951.4 |
| 015.doduc | 1,863.0 |
| 020.nasa7 | 20,093.1 |
| 022.li | 6,206.2 |
| 023.eqntott | 1,100.8 |
| 030.matrix300 | 4,525.1 |
| 042.fpppp | 3,038.4 |
| 047.tomcatv | 2,648.6 |

*SPECint89* is the GM of the four SPECratios (001.gcc, 008.espresso, 022.li and 023.eqntott) of the SPEC Release 1 suite.

*SPECfp89* is the GM of the six SPECratios (013.spice2g6, 015.doduc, 020.nasa7, 030.matrix300, 042.fpppp and 047.tomcatv) of the SPEC Release 1 suite.

*SPECmark89* is the GM of the ten SPECratios of the SPEC Release 1 suite.

*SPECintThruput89* is the GM of the four Thruput Ratios from the four integer benchmarks of the SPEC Release 1 suite.

*SPECfpThruput89* is the GM of the six Thruput Ratios from the six floating-point benchmarks of the SPEC Release 1 suite.

# 10

# The Neal Nelson Database Benchmark™: A Benchmark Based on the Realities of Business

Neal Nelson

*Neal Nelson & Associates*

Neal Nelson & Associates is an independent benchmarking firm based in Chicago. They create and market benchmarks as well as offer consulting services on computer performance. This chapter describes the Neal Nelson Database Benchmark™.

## 10.1    Introduction

Database management systems are commonly benchmarked by several different types of organizations. Each of these organizations has a different set of goals and faces different constraints when conducting a DBMS benchmark.

1. DBMS companies conduct benchmarks to demonstrate the strengths of their products (and persuade potential customers to buy). They will expend massive amounts of effort to tweak, tune, and optimize a test to wring the last ounce of performance from a particular configuration. They will try to hide any product limitations. They like to set up and perform preliminary testing in private, bring the customer in to witness the test, and then get the customer out quickly before anything can go wrong.

2. Computer equipment companies conduct DBMS benchmarks to show how well their machines perform. A DBMS benchmark is viewed as a necessary evil to accomplishing the real goal (sell the computer). Computer equipment companies are not interested in accurately profiling all the strengths and weaknesses of several database management systems, but rather they want to show the customer just enough to close the sale. Sometimes there are "strategic relationships" between computer equipment companies and certain DBMS vendors. In this case the computer equipment company may try to direct the customer to select one particular DBMS product. The computer company may tweak and tune to make one product look particulary good.

3. Magazines, newspapers, and other publications will sometimes sponsor benchmarks to be included in product reviews. The selection of products for measurement and the timetable for the reported results are all governed by the editorial calendar of the publication. If a customer is interested in some other product or needs to make a decision before the article is published, he's out of luck. The reported figures are usually brief because the publication will not have space to devote to a lengthy report of highly detailed information. The technical people conducting the test cannot investigate every significant issue because they have a deadline that must be met.

4. Universities and other academic institutions will sometimes report results from database benchmark tests. Occasionally, these tests are part of a research project linked to a particular hardware or software product. Sometimes the tests compare experimental or research versions of machines and/or DBMS products. These tests can be very detailed and specific in some areas and completely omit areas not relevant to the particular research topic. In any case, the products tested, platforms used, and timetable of the tests are controlled by the researchers.

5. Finally, customers conduct their own DBMS benchmarks to try to profile the strengths and weaknesses of a database management system. This is like "do it yourself bridge design." At first glance the process seems simple, but there are some subtle issues that can cause serious problems (and occasionally complete failure). A customer will typically involve one or more database vendors and a computer hardware vendor in this process. These organizations will not encourage the customer to conduct more thorough and detailed tests because such tests take longer and are more likely to uncover problems that might kill the sale. The customer will be encouraged to hurry the testing process and make the selection.

Some important areas of database benchmarking are not being met by any of these existing methods.

The market needs an experienced database benchmarking organization that is not tied to any hardware or software vendor. This organization could run tests on computers selected by the customer, with DBMS products chosen by the customer, according to time schedules specified by the customer. The independent organization's goal would not be to sell a computer or a database package but rather to learn and report the truth to the customer.

The organization should offer a benchmark that was written by a single group of programmers with essentially identical syntax for all popular DBMS packages. The benchmark should be run in its "standard" form before modifications are made or tuning is performed. Then the benchmark can be run again after tuning is completed by the computer or DBMS vendor.

By comparing the original performance with the performance after tuning, it will be evident how much performance improvement resulted from the tuning. By comparing the original code with the modified code, it will be clear how much custom programming effort is required to get the performance improvement.

The benchmark should measure many different aspects of database performance at many different user levels and database sizes. The benchmark must report the results in detail so that both the strengths and weaknesses of the DBMS are uncovered.

The benchmark should be run in its standard form for multiple database products on a single computer platform to show relative performance of the DBMS packages. The benchmark should be run in its standard form with the same DBMS package on multiple platforms to show relative performance of the computer equipment.

Neal Nelson & Associates has developed a database benchmark to address these needs.

## 10.2   Description of the Benchmark Operation and Methodology

Since the benchmark is coded in industry standard SQL, it can run with almost any database product that supports SQL on many platforms, ranging from PC LANs to classical mainframes, including the wide variety of UNIX-based machines that are popular in the marketplace.

The benchmark is run by using Remote Terminal Emulation benchmarking techniques. With this methodology, two computers are connected "back to back" so that characters transmitted from ports on one machine (the Remote Terminal Emulator, or RTE) are sent into corresponding ports of a second machine (the System Under Test, or SUT).

Command files called scripts are executed on the RTE, which transmits keystroke sequences that emulate users performing various database activities.

The RTE test methodology allows the test suite to be run with one user, two users, three users, and so forth until a database/computer combination has been adequately stressed.

The RTE testing technique is the ideal method to test an application program such as a database. It recreates the exact loads caused by users running commands from terminals (including terminal input and output activity).

### 10.2.1   Running the Test

The first step is to create the database tables and their associated indexes. The database is then loaded to the first user level. (Each user level requires approximately 30 megabytes of disk space.)

With the database at the single user level, one user performs the various database functions that make up the database benchmark. Besides timing each function, the RTE validates the result of the function to ensure that it was processed correctly.

When the single user test is completed, the database is loaded to the two-user level, or approximately 60 megabytes. The number of active users performing each function is increased to two. When there is more than one active user, the execution of the various tasks is controlled so that each user runs his task at exactly the same time as all the other users.

The sequence of increasing the database size and adding an active user is repeated until the database reaches a particular size or the response times become excessively slow.

# 10.3 Description of the Database Design and Organization

The benchmark uses a test database that was patterned after a job-costing system, a common business application. The benchmark's test database has 13 tables, such as Customer Master, Employee Master, Department Master, a Transaction Table, and several cross-reference tables.

The benchmark suite includes a set of programs that generate fixed data for the various tables. These programs create known relationships between files (such as 100 jobs for each customer with 80 "open" jobs and 20 "closed" jobs). They load the data fields and key fields with values that allow automatic accuracy checks of the results returned by the database; for example, with a range of customer numbers that include ten customers, a select for "closed" jobs should return 200 rows, whereas a select for "open" jobs should return 800 rows. The database benchmark suite automatically logs error messages when there is an incorrect result.

The test database incorporates compound keys, large rows (one at least a kilobyte), and large tables (ranging from 20,000 to two million rows, depending on the number of emulated users). For example, the Customer Master table occupies approximately 540 kilobytes of disk space for a one-user test and 2.16 megabytes of disk space for a four-user test. The total storage requirement for the database is approximately 30 megabytes for each emulated user. The actual space required varies with each database product.

The known distribution of the database key fields allows different tests intentionally to create or prevent "hot spot" accesses. A "hot spot" occurs when many users access data elements that are located in a comparatively small portion of the database. Often, these areas are copied into the computer's disk cache buffers, which creates the false impression of superior database performance because no disk I/O is taking place.

The table below details some important aspects of the database tables.

**Table 10.1** Summary of Test Database Characteristics

| Table Name | Number of Columns | Number of Keys | Key Types[1] | Key Length | Row Size |
|---|---|---|---|---|---|
| Transaction Table | 108 | 3 | N | 11 | 440 |
| | | | N,C2 | 21 | |
| | | | A | 12 | |
| Job Master | 19 | 2 | N | 10 | 720 |
| | | | A,C2 | 22 | |
| Customer Master | 21 | 2 | A | 12 | 1,032 |
| | | | A | 40 | |
| Sales Rep Master | 13 | 1 | A | 12 | 236 |
| Employee Master | 13 | 2 | A | 12 | 248 |
| | | | A,C2 | 24 | |
| Department Master | 2 | 1 | A | 12 | 44 |
| Operations Master | 4 | 2 | N | 8 | 44 |
| | | | N,C2 | 16 | |
| Work Center Master | 3 | 1 | N | 8 | 40 |
| Qualification Master | 2 | 1 | N | 8 | 36 |
| Job Comments | 8 | 1 | A,C3 | 28 | 1,000 |
| Customer/Sales Rep Cross Reference | 4 | 2 | A,C2 | 24 | 32 |
| | | | A,C2 | 24 | |
| Department/Work Center Cross Reference | 2 | 1 | A,C2 | 16 | 16 |
| Employee/Qualification Cross Reference | 8 | 1 | A,C2 | 1 | 420 |

[1] N = Numeric, A = Alphanumeric, Cn = Compound Key, n = number of key parts.

# 10.4 Sample Queries

The database benchmark suite consists of over 30 measured functions. These functions are divided into the following six major groups:

1. Keyed queries: These queries are designed to test a database's ability to access rows and groups of rows through indexes.

2. Sequential queries: These queries are designed to measure access to the database when the requested information is not identified by an index.

3. Bulk functions: Bulk functions, such as import, export, batch insert, and batch delete, are included in the benchmark suite because they are frequently used and sometimes cause significant degradation.

4. Data manipulation: Locking of tables and records is a vital concern in a multi-user environment. The benchmark suite includes a variety of functions, such as insert, update, and delete, that require lock management services. The inherent multi-user design of the tests reveals the type and efficiency of the database's locking facility.

5. Transaction processing: This group performs a series of operations grouped together to form what is commonly called a transaction.

6. Aggregate queries: This group consists of SQL statements that contain one or more aggregate functions, such as "sum", "avg", or "count."

The tests are designed to answer many questions, such as "How dependent is the database product on specific programming techniques?" or "How will system performance degrade as the database becomes larger?" To answer the first question, queries are coded in different ways. For example, the two queries illustrated below are constructed using two formats where one query incorporates a nested format and the other a nonnested format.

### Nested version

```
select distinct emepno, dmdpno, omqlcd, qmdesc
from   empmst, dptmst, qlfmst, oprmst
where  omqlcd = qmqlcd and
       dmdpno = emdpno and
       emepno = '000100000000' and
       qmqlcd in ( select  eqqlcd
                   from    empqlf
                   where eqepno = '000100000000');
```

### Nonnested version

```
select distinct emepno, dmdpno, omqlcd, qmdesc
from   empmst, dptmst, qlfmst, empqlf, oprmst
where  omqlcd = qmqlcd and
       qmqlcd = eqqlcd and
       dmdpno = emdpno and
       emepno = eqepno and
       eqepno = '000100000000';
```

Although the end result is the same, the processing time may vary significantly.

Another aspect of the database benchmark is to gradually increase the complexity of a query. For example, a baseline measurement is taken where a query specifies one table. Five more tables are then added, and another measurement taken. Another five tables are added to the query (for a total of 11), and another measurement taken. Using the 11 table join query, another measurement is taken, this time reversing the order in which the tables are specified. Finally, the 11 table join is executed through a view to show the relative speed when accessing data through a view as compared with explicit SQL statements.

Even though queries make up an important part of any database benchmark test, common database functions such as import and export are also measured. Other tests are included that measure the overhead of the sort function and the effect of using secondary and compound keys.

Backup is also an important but seldom-discussed aspect of database management systems. Since most popular DBMSs encourage the use of "raw" disk devices and archiving of data to some external medium, the benchmark suite tests the speed and efficiency of the backup utilities.

# 10.5 Sample Test Results

This section contains two sets of tests that illustrate the type of information collected by the Neal Nelson Database Benchmark. We have intentionally omitted specific information such as brand, model, capacity, software version, access time, and operating system release. It is not our goal to draw any conclusion about whether a particular product is better or worse but rather to demonstrate that significant differences exist that can be measured and reported with the database benchmark.

The benchmark is designed to be configurable by customers at the time of a particular test. In particular, the typing speed and think delay can be set to reflect a customer's environment. The samples shown here were collected with think time set to zero to create maximum stress on the system being tested. In these tests, response times of several hundred seconds are resulting from only four active users.

The database and queries are designed to allow 1,000 emulated users. The number of actual users that a particular customer may choose to emulate will depend on the size and speed of the system being tested and choices for think delays and typing speed.

The first set of sample test results shows a comparison between two different database management system software products on the same computer. The sample shows ten different types of activity for one through four simultaneous users.

The results for DBMS 1 are plotted with dashed lines, and the results for DBMS 2 are plotted with solid lines in Figure 10.1.

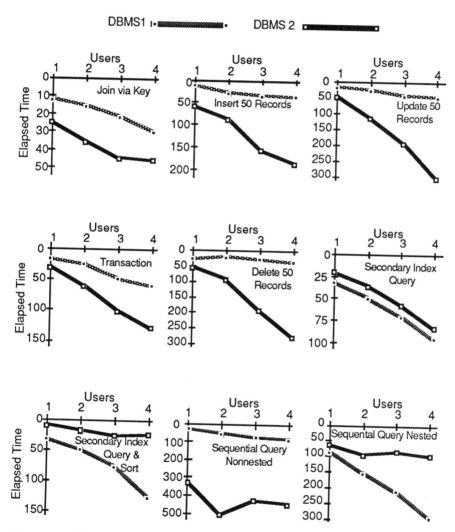

Figure 10.1 Comparison of two DBMS software products.

Both of these databases are major products. They are definitely in the top three or four in the market. They would be viewed by many people as being "comparable," and yet in seven of the ten tests shown, DBMS 1 is significantly (53 to 931 percent) faster than DBMS 2.

The sequential query nonnested versus sequential query nested test is interesting since identical functions are being performed, and yet by changing the syntax of the query, DBMS 1 went from being four to eight times faster to being up to two times slower.

The second set of sample test results in Figure 10.2 shows a comparison with the same DBMS product running on the same computer with two different disk drives installed for the two test runs.

When this test was conducted, the same ten measurements were taken that were shown in Figure 10.1. The first six sets of measurements in the second set of sample test results showed almost no difference between the ESDI and SCSI drives. These six graphs have been omitted to save space.

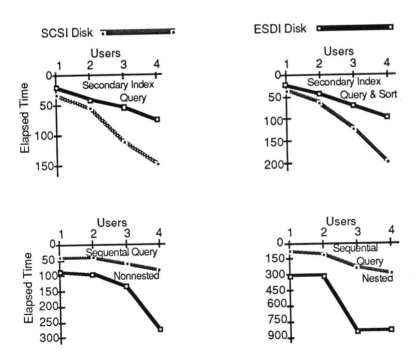

**Figure 10.2**
Comparison of a system using a SCSI disk and the same system using an ESDI disk

For the next two functions performed (keyed queries), the ESDI disk appeared to be significantly faster, and yet on the last two queries (which are both sequential scans of the entire database), the SCSI drive was two to three times faster than the ESDI drive.

Of course many factors affect the throughput of a disk subsystem (controller, driver, etc.), and the following data are presented only to illustrate that differences exist that can be measured and reported by a database benchmark.

# 10.6    Observations and Findings from Customer Uses of the Benchmark

The following examples show how the Neal Nelson Database Benchmark™ was used to solve specific business problems. The tests not only clocked how quickly each package executed a given problem; they also uncovered a number of quirks that could affect a user's evaluation of a given package.

## 10.6.1    Army Database

In June 1989, the U.S. Army used the Neal Nelson Database Benchmark™ to compare four database products on two different computers. The following describes some of the findings:

- In one test, the benchmark emulates multiple users concurrently inserting rows into an indexed file. Running this test showed that one popular database system locks the entire table when processing an insert and keeps the lock until the transaction commits. In some instances, this quirk raised the processing time for a single insert to as much as 25 seconds.

- The benchmark creates a table that, on most machines, exceeds the storage space of a single disk. The particular test was executed in four stages, with the size of the database doubled at each stage. By the third stage of the test, however, we discovered that two of the four products under consideration would not allow tables to span physical devices, and so we could not run the remainder of the test for those two products.

- SQL allows the user to structure queries in different formats to arrive at the same result. To address this issue, the benchmark compares nested queries with nonnested queries. This test provided unexpected results. When processing a nested query, some products actually reverted to searching the data sequentially, even when the key to the table was provided. In another instance, a product processed a query with sub-selects faster when keyed access was specified, but slower if the query searched the data sequentially.

- The benchmark also compares the speed and efficiency of the database product's backup facility. One product did not support a backup of raw device files.[1] In addition, although the size of the database did not vary, the number of tapes required to back up 400 megabytes varied from 3 to 17 for different DBMS products.

- The benchmark was apparently too rigorous for one database product. This product could not run the multi-user insert portion without core dumping, a discovery that initiated the first of what would ultimately be three product updates over the course of the test.

- At first, the test database included a 10,000-byte row; however, this test quickly uncovered the fact that one database product could not support a row larger than 2,048 bytes. To circumvent this problem, the row size was changed to 2,000 bytes.

- Because the test database includes tables with unique secondary indexes, it was discovered that one of the products would not support this feature.

- The test was planned with raw devices for all databases because there is a consensus that this would deliver the best performance. One of the products did not support raw devices, so it was run with UNIX file systems. The product using UNIX file systems ran twice as fast as some other products using raw file systems.

- No product tested included a utility to check the integrity of the indexes.

Overall, it was found that the fastest product ran approximately two times faster than the slowest product. We also found, however, that the fast-

---

[1]A "raw device" is sometimes preferred by DBMS vendors. With a raw device, I/O is sent straight from the DBMS program to the disk, bypassing any overhead provided by the operating system.

est product executed almost as quickly on a lower-priced machine as it did on a machine that was almost five times more expensive.

## 10.6.2 Retesting of an Existing Application

The Neal Nelson Database Benchmark™ was used in January 1990 to test a new release of a database product that was being recommended to a large military organization. This organization had already invested thousands of man-hours to test this product, yet the benchmark uncovered several problem areas with the new product, including the following:

- The multi-user insert test revealed that, during heavy use, the DBMS updated the wrong pointer in the index table, which then corrupted the database. This bug had been in existence for three years (from the time the product was introduced).

- When two or more users selected the SQL module within five seconds of one another, the application would hang.

- A select statement with no "order by" clause returned a different number of rows than the same select statement with an "order by."

- The SQL program required a temporary space equal in size to the database in order to perform more complex queries.

- When the same queries were run with different formats (nested versus nonnested, etc.), sometimes the execution time would double.

- The multi-user-insert test caused memory violation messages.

As these experiences show, an automated tool with a standard set of tests is a very sensible approach to validate new software and updates of existing software. For example, on the day of a software briefing, a representative of the database vendor appeared with a new version of their product. The person at the military organization responsible for validating this product tested the latest version that morning and by the afternoon presented the new findings to the briefing panel.

## 10.7 Checklist To Help Determine the Validity of Database Benchmark Results

There are several major reasons why database benchmark results can be deceptive or misleading. The following list of questions will help customers determine if a particular set of database-benchmark results provides significant information about the speed of the hardware or software product.

Each topic is organized into a major headline, explanatory text, and a question that might be asked of a vendor.

### Database Benchmark Source Code

The most fundamental concept of benchmarking (including database benchmarking) is comparison. The questions that are most frequently asked are "Which database is the fastest?" and "Which machine is the best choice for this database?"

A useful comparison cannot be made if different programs are used on different machines since any reported variance might be caused by the programming technique rather than by the machine or software product.

In some cases the computer or database vendor is allowed to write and/or extensively modify the benchmark program before a benchmark test. When this is done, it is difficult to sort out the effects of programming style from effects caused by the machine or software product.

*Question: Was the benchmark coded using essentially identical syntax, by the same individuals, for all appropriate hardware and software products?*

### Constant Test Platforms

The usefulness of a database benchmark is reduced if each different database product is tested on a different computer system. Reported variances between the results could be caused by either the software packages or the computer systems.

*Question: Are database benchmark tests for a variety of software packages run on a single computer system?*

## Cache — Cache Size and Test Database Size

Many computers will keep some of the recently accessed disk sectors in main memory in a series of buffers that constitute a cache. When an application program (such as a database package) requests data from the disk, the operating system first checks the buffer cache to see if the data is in memory. If so, the "read" is satisfied from cache, and the physical disk read is avoided. Cached disk I/O is dramatically faster than actual physical disk I/O (one or more orders of magnitude). If a test database is so small that it will fit substantially (or entirely) in disk buffer cache, the benchmark results will indicate that the configuration is very fast.

However, when the database size is large enough that it will no longer fit in buffer cache (which is normally the case), the actual performance will be quite slow compared with indications provided by the benchmark.

*Question: Is the size of the test database and/or the configuration of the test computer such that most (or all) of the disk I/O will take place in and out of cache?*

## Functions Measured and Reported

Database products must perform a large number of different tasks, such as:

1.  Import batches
2.  Export batches
3.  Interactive inserts
4.  Interactive deletes
5.  Lock, read, rewrite, unlock
6.  Change key fields (update indexes)
7.  Commit transactions
8.  Random keyed queries
9.  Queries by range
10. Sequential queries
11. Sorts
12. Aggregate functions such as count and sum
13. Backup

Database benchmarks that perform only a few of these activities and/or report only a few numbers will not provide an adequate report of the product's performance in different categories. A database product might have been tuned to provide excellent performance in random reads and inserts but deliver terrible performance in sequential queries and sorts.

If a particular benchmark performs only a few functions, or if a variety of different functions are used in combination and only a single result reported, it might be impossible to identify that some particular activity is quite slow.

*Question: Does the database benchmark measure, and report separately, a wide variety of different database activities?*

### Query Optimization

Most database management systems have built in query optimizers that are supposed to ensure that a query is performed in the fastest and most efficient manner. SQL allows a wide variety of "legal" ways to state a query, but when the query is actually performed there can be significant differences in speed, depending on the sequence of selects, sorts, and other functions.

The query optimizer is supposed to automatically identify the best way to perform a given query and automatically reformat the request into this most efficient structure.

If the query optimizer is inadequate, different users will experience dramatically different levels of performance, based on the syntax of their SQL queries. Users and programmers will be forced to learn what syntax delivers superior performance from a database package and to manually code their work to obtain efficient execution.

*Question: Does the database benchmark contain identical tasks coded with different SQL syntax to help determine how well the query optimizer works?*

### Increasing Test Database Size, Increasing Numbers of Users

Sometimes database products perform quite well up to a certain number of users or up to a certain database size, and then their performance degrades dramatically.

If a database benchmark reports its results at only one database size or with only one set of emulated users, it is impossible to know if the reported figures were before or after a possible fall off in performance.

*Question: Does the database benchmark report performance figures for a range of database sizes and/or a range of simulated users?*

### Emulate a Real-World Application

A database management system is the foundation of a wide variety of general business activities, such as order processing, accounts payable, and payroll. A database benchmark should emulate some common business activity to provide the most meaningful test results.

*Question: Does the database benchmark perform functions similar to the activities required for daily operation of your business?*

### Sufficiently Complex

If a database management system is going to break down, it will most likely happen during a time of high load or high stress. A benchmark should provide enough activity to cause significant stress during the test and to uncover problem areas before the product is installed.

*Question: Does the database benchmark generate enough stress to uncover problem areas?*

## 10.8 Conclusion

Vendors, scholars, and journalists have all focused on different parts of the performance puzzle and have developed different methodologies to try to solve the database benchmarking problem.

Neal Nelson & Associates has developed a database benchmark that supplements and extends other benchmarks by measuring performance factors that have not been previously reported.

The Neal Nelson Database Benchmark™:

1. Was written with standard SQL commands by a single group of programmers.

2. Can be run on a single platform with multiple DBMS packages to highlight software differences.

3. Can be run on multiple platforms with the same DBMS package to highlight hardware differences.

4. Can be run before and after tuning to show how much performance improvement results from what level of changes.

5. Can be run for the machines and software packages specified by the customer in a time frame defined by the customer.

6. Is sufficiently complex and scaleable to stress virtually any hardware/software combination.

7. Provides reports of degradation as the user load increases up to a configuration's breaking point.

8. Provides detail test results for scores of different functions to show both the strengths and weaknesses of a DBMS product.

Further information about the benchmark can be obtained by contacting:

Neal Nelson & Associates
35 East Wacker Drive
Chicago, Illinois 60601
(312) 332-3242

# 11

# Doing Your
# Own Benchmark

Tom Sawyer

*Performance Metrics Inc.*

## 11.1     Why Benchmark?

Vendors often use benchmarks for marketing purposes. These benchmarks are usually the public ones covered in this book, although IBM also runs its own set of proprietary benchmarks.

Occasionally, vendors run internal benchmarks to uncover software bottlenecks that might constrain the product regardless of hardware capacity. Examples of these constraints include a built-in limit on the number of concurrent users or the maximum size of a database. More often than not, these seemingly trivial limits prove difficult to remove.

Most customers use benchmarks to choose among vendors. Since transaction and batch response times are among the more obvious external measurements of a data processing system, speed is often emphasized in vendor selection. The selection committee may deem the public benchmarks to be inadequate and propose a benchmark tailored to the installation profile. While I would like to think that this chapter would be wildly interesting to programmers, analysts, and Pyrenean sheep herders, its primary audience is that group of masochists charged with managing or leading an in-house benchmark, and it will discuss some of the challenges they face.

## 11.2   Fundamental Questions

Embarking on a benchmark journey is similar to any learning endeavor. There are three major questions that must be addressed at the start and reexamined many times throughout the adventure. These questions are:

1.  What do you want to learn?

2.  How much are you prepared to invest?

3.  What are you prepared to give up?

Obviously they interact. The answer to the third question is really the *wish list* excised from Q1 by applying Q2. During the exercise, the quantity in the first question diminishes as quantities in the latter two increase. That is, you will always spend more and learn less than you desire.

There are several costs involved, including programmer time, machine resources, management time, and lost opportunity. These costs occur even if you attempt to unload the whole process on the vendors.

### 11.2.1   Programmer Time

There will be ample opportunity to spend this resource. The benchmark should have some basis in reality. This will mean generating the transaction workload, defining transaction logic, defining data access requirements, determining data distributions and generating the database, instrumenting and measuring the system, and more. For example, you may have to supply the database to all vendors to assure consistency.

### 11.2.2   Machine Resources

In addition to any machine resources used by the programmers, you may have to supply the hardware for the measurement. If you offer an enticing prize, the vendors may supply the hardware and testing environment. If not, they may insist on using your machine for the measurements and attempt to develop the benchmark on a smaller, nondedicated machine available in their branch. In the worst case, they may need to use your machine for benchmark development. This may affect your normal work-load more than somewhat.

### 11.2.3 Management Time

Management time is divided between reporting, administration, and adjudication:

- **Reporting:** The reporting requirement *comes with the territory.* Any effort exceeding a few person-months will require budgeting, progress reporting, and a final report.

- **Normal Administration:** The people assigned to the benchmark will require hand-holding, back-slapping, lower-back slapping, and all else that differentiates us from beast and machine. If vendor personnel are involved, assume two or three vendors equal one employee. The long days and normal problems that occur when products and people are pushed to limits will yield many opportunites for meaningful dialogues. Vendor personnel will participate in these activities.

- **Adjudication:** Adjudication consumes the most management time. The well-defined benchmarks (e.g., TPC-A, TPC-B) have areas that need interpretation. An installation-specified benchmark will present many opportunities for debate. Both managers and technicians will be involved in rulings that require fundamental tradeoffs between realism, fairness, and expense. An example could be the level of performance monitoring that should occur during a measurement. One vendor might have a very complete, albeit CPU-consuming, tool that is meant to run occasionally, whereas another might have efficient online reporting with little or no offline output available. A complex benchmark will leave managers with the feeling that Solomon had it easy.

### 11.2.4 Lost Opportunity

Economists call it opportunity cost; football linebackers call it the paralysis of analysis. Time spent choosing a system is time lost in implementing applications. In the extreme case, rapid deployment of an application albeit gracelessly implemented on the *wrong* DBMS may return enough profit in a year to rewrite the application ten times over.

The converse is the nightmare of a poorly performing implementation that is over budget and hated by the users.

# 11.3   What Can Be Learned

Most think of benchmarks as measures of speed (e.g., transactions per second). This is a narrow definition of performance. Performance encompasses function as well as speed. Indeed, a benchmark may be used to measure system functionality, ease of use, operability, ease of development, as well as other aspects of data processing. Most of the benchmarks discussed in this book are performance measurements, although the $AS^3AP$ benchmark begins to assess operational issues by including loading and recovery time (see Chapter 5). The State of California, Department of Motor Vehicles Operational Assessment is a good example of a measurement of both performance and operability [Department of Motor Vehicles, State of California, see references, Chapter 1].

Functional benchmarks are not highly publicized. Far too often, customers infer more capability in the vendor checklist of features than is actually present—e.g., the capabilities of DBMS stored procedures. Given the wide gaps between claimed function and usability, installations would be wise to specify a functional level of capability and test for compliance. Discussions on this aspect of benchmarking are beyond the scope of this chapter.

We shall focus on the decisions necessary when implementing a performance benchmark. Performance benchmarks are used to measure response time, batch throughput, and current hardware capacities. Fortunately, the implementation of a benchmark limited to performance aspects will also bring many development and operation issues to light.

## 11.3.1   What You Will Not Learn

- **Future Performance:** Performance benchmarks are reasonable measures of today's capabilities. They are not good measures of future capability. Measured performance is the result of the interplay of many hardware and software components. An improvement in one area may or may not affect your measured performance; improvements may interact, not necessarily to your benefit.

- **Vendor Support:** The support you receive during an acquisition benchmark has little bearing on the type of support you will receive after you buy the system.

# 11.4 Benchmark Specification— An Extended Example

A benchmark has two major components: the workload specification and the measurement specification. The workload specification requires some analysis of what we hope to implement. To the extent that the new system has roots in current systems, the specification will have some real numbers. If the system is completely new, some effort must go into database and application design before any work specification can be performed.

Imagine we are attempting to benchmark a new system containing both online and batch components. For simplicity, assume the online component consists of several online transactions and several ad-hoc queries. Assume the batch component has an update and a report job. Assume that the application system being benchmarked will be a complete rewrite and redesign of an existing system. Also assume that the system receives some input from other application systems that are not part of the rewrite and cannot be modified. The benchmark will be used to select a hardware and DBMS platform for the new application system.

These assumptions imply that we have some idea of reasonable response times for the new and rewritten transactions. Current data exist, although they will be much augmented when the new system is complete. Reasonable projections of the database and workload can be made.

A first step in the specification is to describe the database. To simplify even further, assume that the bidders will supply relational DBMSs (perhaps at our request) and that tables have been designed with some idea of what columns go with them.

## 11.4.1   The Online Transactions

The new system will support the current transactions (possibly enhanced) and will also contain new transactions. The first order of business is defining the transactions to be benchmarked.

We have both current transactions and some of the major projected transactions. This is the first of many opportunities to trade off realism for simplicity. Online transactions have the following components:

- data transmission (input and response)

- teleprocessing

- application logic

- database access

- operating system overhead

Every component we either eliminate or modify will remove some element of reality and hopefully simplify the benchmark. The decisions on how much to slice may also affect the fairness of the benchmark. You will get lots of vendor assistance on this topic. Let us examine them in easy-to-difficult order.

### Application Logic

Unless you have compute-intensive applications, application logic should be the first thing eliminated from a benchmark. Application logic rarely accounts for more than 10 to 15 percent of the CPU load. Specifying application logic, then verifying it across all bidders, is time consuming and error prone.

The rationale for retaining application logic is that a single transaction module may have several different paths from top to bottom, each with a different data-access type. Retaining data-access patterns is important, as we shall see in the next section.

One simplifying approach is to treat each path as a separate transaction type and weight it accordingly. For instance, transaction type X has separate paths for retrieval, update, insert, and delete, and if the percentage for each path and the overall rate for the transaction are known, then the transaction can be decomposed as follows:

| Path Name | Path Percentage | tps Rate | Path Rate |
|---|---|---|---|
| X-Retrieve | 70 | 10 | 7 |
| X-Update | 15 | 10 | 1.5 |
| X-Insert | 10 | 10 | 1 |
| X-Delete | 5 | 10 | .5 |

Do not round up the X-Update number; as we shall see in the next section, there will be ample opportunity to make adjustments.

## Database Access

Database access should not be omitted. Most online applications spend the majority of the time in DBMS code. The trick is to get coverage of most database access patterns with as few transactions and as little data as possible.

I recommend using a two-dimensional grid to record the tps rate (transactions per second) and the access patterns of the major applications. Once this is done, transactions may be combined. We can use the following table as an example:

| Transaction | tps | Table 1 | Table 2 | Table 3 | Table 4 | Total |
|---|---|---|---|---|---|---|
| Tran 1 | 6 | 2R 1U | 6F | - | 1R | 3R 1U 6F |
| Tran 2 | 12 | - | 3F | 1R | 1R | 2R 3F |
| Tran 3 | 4 | 2R | 3F | - | 1R | 3R 3F |
| Tran 4 | 1 | 1R | 1U | 9F | 1R | 2R 1U 9F |
| R = Random read | | | U = Update | | F = Sequential Fetch | |

Note that Transactions 2 and 3 are similar in pattern, although different tables get accessed. If the tables are large, there is little chance that any caching will occur. We could combine the transactions by dropping Tran 3 and raising Tran 2's rate to 16 tps.

Similarly, Tran 4 could either be dropped (1/23 = 4.35 percent loss) or combined with Tran 1 by raising Tran 1's tps rate to 7.

The combined matrix follows:

| Transaction | tps | Table 1 | Table 2 | Table 3 | Table 4 | Total |
|---|---|---|---|---|---|---|
| Tran 1-4 | 7 | 2R 1U | 6F | - | 1R | 3R 1U 6F |
| Tran 2-3 | 16 | - | 3F | 1R | 1R | 2R 3F |

Combining transactions may also allow elimination of tables. Table 3 is a candidate for elimination. If the Tran 2-3 Table 3 accesses are redirected to Table 1, the following matrix results:

| Transaction | tps | Table 1 | Table 2 | Table 3 | Table 4 | Total |
|---|---|---|---|---|---|---|
| Tran 1-4 | 7 | 2R 1U | 6F | - | 1R | 3R 1U 6F |
| Tran 2-3 | 16 | 1R | 3F | - | 1R | 2R 3F |

Retaining reality during these transformations is a challenge. If the affected tables are large, then little is lost in combining them. If each table has a single index, caching requirements will be slightly understated by eliminating the space needed to cache the index of the deleted table.

However, simplicity has been gained; there is one less table to deal with. This reduces the data-generation task. It also reduces the load on the vendors. They have one less table to load, build indexes on, back up, find physical disk space for, etc.

Such simplifications cost little and shorten the benchmark process.

## Teleprocessing

Teleprocessing includes the hardware terminal configuration, possibly with concentrators and the system software components. The benchmark should include a usable configuration. The trap to avoid is to benchmark a *high-performance* environment and discover later that making it operational involves added cost.

A example of this trap consists of emulating ASCII terminals via a LAN-based driver that submits complete messages in each packet. It later turns out that the terminals actually send packets of one character each, unless some intelligent, perhaps specially programmed concentrator is inserted between terminal and host. This character-at-a-time load multiplies the teleprocessing load on the host by a factor of 10 or 100, so the benchmarked system does not correspond to the real system.

Even more important, the actual number of users that will be simultaneously using the system should be simulated. A system that uses ten processes, each submitting one tps, may behave much differently than a system with one thousand users, each submitting at 0.01 tps. Yet the tps loads of the two systems are identical.

If transaction monitors (e.g., CICS, /T) are included in the configuration, the environment should be examined for operability as well as speed.

## Transaction Interarrival Rate

No discussion on transaction submission would be complete without addressing the issue of the timing of transaction submission. If one measures the time between transactions submitted by one terminal, that time is known as the interarrival time. If one counts the frequency that each of these times occurs and graph it, you have graphed the arrival distribution. The three favorite interarrival rates are constant, uniform, and negative exponential. If each simulated user submits each transaction exactly $x$ seconds after the previous transaction was submitted, the arrival rate is *constant*.

If transactions are submitted between the range of 80 seconds to 100 seconds with the count of transactions in any second of the range equalling the count in any other (e.g., 20 transactions were submitted every 84 seconds, and 20 transactions were submitted every 85 seconds ...), then the distribution is *uniform*.

The *negative exponential* interarrival rate is the most difficult to describe, the hardest to implement, and the closest approximation to the real world. The distribution has the property that most of the interarrival times are less than the mean, balanced by a few transactions that have very long times between them.

The rub is that, if you request this distribution, the odds are high that the vendor will not have the foggiest notion of how to implement it. A fairly straightforward C version has been provided by Jim Gray (see appendix for additional information) and is reproduced below. It returns a delay *tt* from a distribution with mean *m*.

$$tt = -m * log( rand());$$

You can convert this example to your favorite language, or you might consider generating a table of 1000 to 2000 entries and requesting the vendors to randomly sample your table for each think time.

## Operating System Overhead

If this were a DBMS only benchmark, then little consideration would need to be given to operating system overhead as long as all vendors ran with the same settings. In our example, the hardware and therefore the operating system are part of the procurement. The major decisions involve security, integrity, charge-back accounting, and system monitoring.

They all present interesting challenges. You need to decide some base level of function for each vendor. You will also need a mechanism to keep track of *goodies* each system supplies that are not measured but are of sufficient interest to be considered tie-breakers. In the event of a run-off, you may have to at least functionally test these features; when you do, measure performance effects on the benchmark also.

Integrity capabilities have large effects on performance. Panicked vendors may state that none of their customers uses *level-x* but uses *level-y* with no dire consequences. Vendor user groups are good sources of sanity.

These debates get particularly interesting when one of the systems is more thoroughly understood than the others. There is a tendency for the well-known system to get overly constrained while the others have their vendor claims accepted at face value.

## 11.4.2   Ad-Hoc Queries

In this hypothetical benchmark, the intent of the ad-hoc queries is to simulate some decision-support activity occurring in conjunction with operational transactions. Since the queries must be fair to all vendors, they must be defined in advance. This foreknowledge presents the vendors with some interesting tuning opportunities.

The art is specifying the rules surrounding the execution of these queries. These rules will have heavy bearing on the fairness of the tests. For example, one vendor's DBMS might use the order of the tables in the SQL FROM clause to determine internal order of query processing. This vendor will be most interested in being allowed to specify the table order. One argument in favor is that experienced query users will soon learn the proper order to list tables, or a view using the proper order could be provided to less experienced users. A competitor with an optimizer that makes its own assumptions about internal query processing might claim that *ad hoc* means exactly that, and users will often use the wrong table order. The second vendor's idea of fairness might encompass random order of tables or all orders averaged, etc.

There are other opportunities to exercise fairness.

The hypothetical benchmark assumes two queries, AH1 and AH2. Their makeup is not particularly important; we need them as examples for measurement purposes.

## 11.4.3 The Batch Jobs

Batch work should be included in the benchmark. Most shops that run online work during the day discover that the batch window is a critical resource. If no batch work is included in your measurements, the vendors may be tempted to use devices that have good online characteristics but have weak batch performance. For instance, disk drives connected using the SCSI interface perform well in online operations but do not have the sequential capabilities of IPI drives.

We shall assume that the goals of the proposed system include the ability to run batch jobs without degrading the performance of the online work.

You may also want to consider benchmarking a few key batch jobs that must be run frequently and can be run when the online environment need not be up.

The realism issue has several components, including the degree of preplanned access, the amount and nature of preprocessing allowed, and the amount and nature of processing allowed. Preplanned access issues include favorable table ordering and the content and number of secondary indexes.

The components have overlap. An example of overlap of the latter two occurred where a batch transaction job chosen for measurement was one of a string of jobs run daily in the department. The vendors were allowed some latitude in specifying the input sequence or other information needed to improve performance as long as it could be reasonably accommodated in the prior batch jobs.

All vendors elected to sequence the input on the same key as the major master file. The vendors also specified multiple input tapes, which were then run simultaneously as a group of batch jobs. This approach took advantage of the parallelism available from multiple processors in their configurations.

One vendor further specified an input file describing the number of records in each batch file and the deadline for the total job. This information was used by a *governor* process that scheduled the batch processes. This governor sampled the tps rate and available CPU capacity and scheduled batch transactions accordingly.

I have also seen cases where the batch input was provided by another department, and there was no control and little flexibility. Thus, no changes or additional information was allowed.

## 11.4.4 Error Checking

The batch jobs and online transactions should have minimal error checking. This checking is necessary to detect errors in the database and possible access pattern errors in the application. Without this checking, you may be measuring different patterns between the vendors.

One error-reporting approach is to insert a descriptive record into an error log table; this table may be checked at any time to monitor errors.

## 11.4.5 Omissions

Have we left anything out? Oh sure, astute readers may think of several areas that are ignored. For example, the effect on system performance of infrequent transactions. The small set of transactions to be measured make it easy to cache most programs needed by the measured transactions. However, most installations have some portion of the workload that is never resident.

For example, if 500 transaction types make up 20 percent of the workload, it would not be cost effective to dedicate resources (main memory) to each of the transaction types, thus the execution of this mix will place a larger burden on the system than a 20 percent increase in the resident workload. This missing workload could be simulated by creating one transaction that had a rough approximation to the access pattern of the 500 transaction types. This access pattern could then be mapped onto the existing table specifications. The code for this transaction would then be installed 500 times with the appropriate transaction names. The vendors would be required to generate 20 percent of the transaction rate with transaction names randomly spread over the 500 names. Such a process would be more realistic, but would also complicate the benchmark—it is a trade-off.

This augmentation successfully simulates the system portion of the transactions and to some degree simulates the database portion of the workload. However, by using the smaller benchmark set of tables, it does not simulate the system cost of managing the database portion of the workload —e.g., opening and closing OS files—another trade-off.

## 11.4.6 A Caution

Make certain you are measuring the hardware/software environment and not the implementation team's degree of cleverness. One team may come up with a processing scheme that would also work on the contenders' implementation. If this improvement is neither disallowed nor spread about, you have allowed a *confounding factor* to muddy any comparisons.

While cleverness should be rewarded, the clever people may disappear after you own the equipment.

# 11.5   The Measurement Environment

The second major hurdle in the benchmark specification is defining the measurement environment. Once again, the trade-off between reality and simplicity governs all. The major decision is, how much of the environment will be measured? In our case, we have both a batch and an online environment. Furthermore, our online environment has both production transactions and ad-hoc queries. We can resolve the batch environment fairly quickly.

## 11.5.1   The Batch Environment

We have two batch jobs, a report and an update. The key decision on these jobs is the extent of application process to be simulated. Again, the major effort should be spent capturing the database-access pattern.

The batch jobs should report some data that can be verified. This might include counts of records accessed, totals of columns known to have certain values, etc.

### DBMS Processing

Relational systems have more levels in their internal processing hierarchy than do file systems. File systems can be simplified to a single level of processing records—record selection. When a record passes the file system's selection criteria, it is passed in its entirety to the application.

Relational systems process data at several levels. Selection criteria may involve several tables (e.g., Join processing, Subselect using the Exists operator). Only after data pass these tests are they passed to the application. Even then, only the selected columns are returned.

This additional functionality adds complexity in two flavors: Are the vendor implementations functionally equivalent? Are they implementing your environment or a super/subset?

An example of this occurs when processing master-detail information using a *Join*. If there are master file records that must be examined even if no corresponding records exist in the detail file, the Join must be disallowed since it would not deliver any master records not matching a detail record.

Both vendors might have equivalent implementations, but they would not be implementing your environment. To do that, they must not use a Join but must return all master records to the application. It typically requires more CPU resources to pass the additional master records to the application than to reject them as part of Join processing.

## 11.5.2   The Report

There is little point in measuring printer time, hence we shall consider the report job complete when the report output file is closed.

The report job should be more extensive than the ad hoc queries; e.g., it should contain multiple SQL statements.

## 11.5.3   The Update

The challenge here is to push as much update activity into the SQL statements as makes sense. For instance, if the data to be updated do not need to be examined, the update may be performed directly in SQL. For example, an update that changes an account balance by some transaction amount could be coded:

```
Update charge_account
set balance = balance + :delta
whereaccount = :account_nbr
   and  (((balance - :delta) <= - account.credit_limit) or
          (:delta               >=  0))
```

This statement will accept charges (negative delta) that leave the balance positive or within the credit limit. It will accept payments (positive delta) in any case—i.e., as long as a negative balance gets less negative, we'll take the money.

Where data must be summarized and/or reported, ensure that the appropriate retrieval operations occur as well as the requisite updates.

We can consider this job complete when it writes a summary file. This file could contain totals and possibly a count of records updated by table. Often this latter information is available from SQL.

## 11.5.4    The Online Environment

There are three components of online transaction measurement: response time, transaction rate, and hardware configuration.

In the hypothetical example, the first two are specified; it is up to the vendor to minimize the third. We have already set the transaction rate by specifying by transaction type how many per second must be presented to the system. Now it remains to specify the response time. There are two components to a response time measurement: the response time and the percentile where measured.

### Transaction Response Time Percentile

Naive folks will use the average response time (which is close to but not equal to the 50th percentile); more sophisticated specifiers will opt for the 90th or 95th percentile. Figure 11.1 illustrates the danger of using the average.

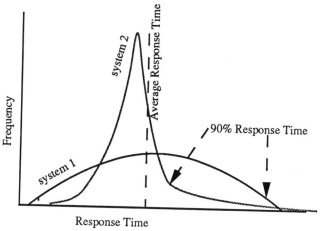

**Figure 11.1**
Two response time frequency curves with the same average response time but with very different 90 percent response times.

*There will be more smiley faces in the System-2 crowd.*

I recommend using the 90th percentile. The difference in effort required to maintain 95th percentile performance over the 90th is something most installations will not pay for.

You will have to decide on the appropriate response time. Your friendly vendors will help you keep it realistic. One rule of thumb is that each random disk access takes about 30 milliseconds; thus, the sum of a transaction's random disk accesses times .030 will yield a floor value. The amount of internal queueing/contesting for system resources will increase response times, as will processing of groups of records, e.g., all line items for a randomly chosen invoice.

The choice of response time value and percentile can have a large effect on the power of the processor needed to meet the benchmark requirements. A full discussion is beyond the scope of this chapter (and the author, for that matter); however, I shall pass on my simplified version.

Response time has two fundamental components: queueing and service time.

When a transaction is queued, it is waiting for something. This could be a disk arm in use by another transaction, a CPU working on a task of higher priority, etc.

Service time is the measured time it takes to do something, e.g., add two columns together, process an I/O interrupt, seek to a desired track, etc.

If the sum of all the service times approaches the response time constraint, very little queueing may be allowed. This means that most servers, disk arms, CPUs, etc., must run at low utilization. A busy server, like a busy doctor, has multiple transactions waiting for it. For example, if CPU processing is a significant part of the response time, it may be necessary to run the CPU at 30 percent utilization in order to meet the response time constraint. If the response time constraint were loosened, the CPU might be able to reach 80 percent utilization and produce a much higher tps rate. You could also achieve the higher tps rate by allowing the vendor(s) to use a more powerful CPU; however, you might not like the bill.

## Response Time Measurement Point

Before the response time can be fixed, we must decide where it is to be measured. Response time is the time difference between two complimentary points—e.g., from the time the user presses the Return key until the first character appears on the screen. There are several points at which response time could be taken, including:

- after the application commits the transaction
- after the teleprocessing code
- after transmission to the terminal
- after display on the terminal.

These points are illustrated in Figure 11.2.

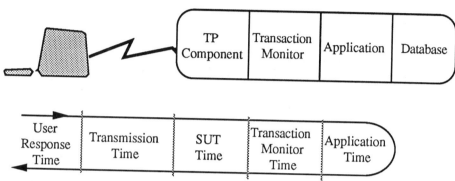

**Figure 11.2**
The various places response time can be measured.

The most difficult point to instrument is after the teleprocessing code and before the physical transmission component. The easiest response time calculation is to measure from receipt of transaction to commit of the transaction in the application.

The piece of realism lost will depend to some degree on whether the transactions are submitted through the teleprocessing component or read from disk. The latter implementation is easier to construct and does not require a separate machine to generate and time the transactions (often called a driver). This approach works well when the teleprocessing overhead is well known and the measured machine is not heavily loaded. If the measured machine is to be pushed to its limits, then the transactions must be submitted and timed from a driver machine (see next section).

If we assume block mode terminals or workstations as the submitting devices, we can simulate the environment with the configuration shown in Figure 11.3.

Some realism has been sacrificed. The submitting device is assumed to place no keying overhead on the SUT. Also, the transaction is submitted in the minimum number of LAN packets.

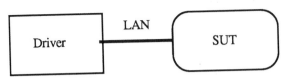

**Figure 11.3**
Test system consists of a driver and a system under test connected via a LAN.

Since the online portion will be submitted and timed externally, it would simplify our lives if we converted the batch jobs to single transactions and used their respective response times as the batch completion times. The one message needed to start or mark the end of a batch job will add little to the completion time and will allow us to collect all results in one place.

The ad hoc queries can be submitted by using very long interarrival (or think) times. Again we have simplified the reporting.

## Environment Calibration

One of the most important aspects of benchmarking is to be sure you are measuring the right bottleneck. All systems will have a bottleneck. The trick is to force the one you want to measure to be the constraining resource. Stated in converse, it does little good to measure different systems via the same LAN and later discover that the LAN was the bottleneck.

Sufficient headroom is needed in each ancillary component to allow the measured components to be saturated. A simple way to test this hypothesis is to replace the SUT transactions with ones that echo only and submit transactions with no think time. Since the echo transaction provides nearly instantaneous response time, either the network or the driver system will saturate at some tps rate; let's call this rate tps-network.

You must ensure that the benchmark does not come close to this rate, or the results will not be meaningful. If this rate is not sufficient to saturate your projected environment, you may be able to add drivers or additional networks to increase your headroom. If you suspect the network rather than the driver, and the driver scripts allow it, nullify the call to the network. The driver will saturate at some tps rate—called tps-driver. If this rate is close to tps-network, then the driver must be replicated. If not, you will want to consider multiple networks or perhaps a connection with more bandwidth—e.g., channel-to-channel or FDDI.

This saturation calibration is also necessary when the transactions are being timed on the measured machine. If the measured machine saturates, the response times will not be meaningful. This occurs because there is insufficient CPU capacity to process tasks that are on the ready queue. Thus they sit on the ready queue waiting to post their response times while the CPU is off fighting the Klingons.

## 11.6    Beware the War of Wizards

We shall also tell our vendors that this benchmark is a single trial; no excuses, no reruns. This prevents the escalating *war of wizards*. Let us assume vendor A wins the benchmark. Vendor B then says: "Well, we didn't realize vendor A was going to use one-star wizards, whereas we used our branch office folks. We would like to rerun the benchmark with the additional tuning and insight equivalent to that used by vendor A."

Vendor A will in turn want to rerun with two-star wizards, claiming that is who vendor B used, etc. This process can escalate past the four-star wizard ranking with lots of time lost.

A variant of this tactic is the new-and-improved release.

## 11.7    Summary

The late 1980s have shown that the *vaporware* announcements of PC days have been raised to new levels of professionalism. Some vendors have claimed that their competitors' products work only on one hardware platform—the foil projector. Sometimes they have been correct.

Often functional benchmarks may yield more meaningful results than performance comparisons. Unfortunately, functional benchmarks are more difficult to specify than performance ones, and harder to judge.

A benchmark should be treated in the same manner as a development project with a budget, goals, and time estimates. And as with any project, well-thought-out goals reviewed throughout the benchmark process will produce better results than a cavalry charge.

# Appendix A.
# Benchmark Software
# Distribution: Release 1.0

Michael J. Franklin

Much of the software described in the previous chapters has been gathered into a coherent collection in order to facilitate its distribution and use. The distribution provides the software necessary to execute several of the benchmark suites described in this book. The software provided includes:

- Data Generators

- Database Creation and Loading Programs

- SQL implementations of the benchmark queries

- Programs to execute and time the benchmark queries

In addition, instructions on how to use the software are provided with the distribution. The initial release of the distribution contains software for the following:

- TPC-A and TPC-B Sample Programs

- The Wisconsin Benchmark

- The Set Query Benchmark

- OO1 (Object Operations version 1)

The composition of the distribution will evolve as the existing benchmarks are modified and as new benchmarks are added. This appendix describes the contents of Release 1.0 of the distribution in more detail.

# A.1    Intended Use of the Distribution

The distribution is intended to serve as the reference implementations of the benchmarks provided. In addition, the distribution includes much of the supporting software required to execute the benchmarks. The software is written for a specific combination of operating system and database management system (DBMS). However, care has been taken to minimize the work required to port the software to other environments.

# A.2    System Environment and Language

The distribution software consists of ANSI C programs and C programs that contain embedded SQL. This format was chosen in order to reduce the dependency on any particular operating system or DBMS.

The first release of the distribution has been constructed using the INGRES Release 6.2 DBMS and the ULTRIX 4.0 operating system. Where possible, the SQL code has been made to comply with the ANSI standard. However, some changes may be required for use with other DBMS packages. Also, the C programs contain some operating system-dependent code in order to perform functions such as data generation and timing of queries. This code would need to be modified for use on non-UNIX-based systems or other variants of UNIX. The distribution includes information to help in porting the software.

# A.3    Distribution Contents

## A.3.1    TPC Sample Programs

The distribution includes the reference model implementations for both the TPC-A and TPC-B benchmarks. In addition, a terminal emulator is provided. This program is intended to show how to model the behavior of a teller at a terminal. It uses a think time determined by a negative exponential distribution with a specified mean. Also provided is a simple data generator that uses Embedded SQL to create data values and load them into the database.

## A.3.2  Wisconsin Benchmark

The Wisconsin Benchmark software includes the programs necessary to generate and load the database. The data values are generated in accordance with the distribution requirements specified by the benchmark.

A bulk load facility is used to load the database. SQL code for all of the queries described in Chapter 4 is provided.  The queries are implemented for the one million tuple database. Also included are programs to execute and time the queries in order to obtain the single-user benchmark results.

## A.3.3  Set Query Benchmark

The Set Query Benchmark software provides a complete implementation of the benchmark as described in Chapter 6. It includes programs for database generation, loading, indexing, and query execution.

## A.3.4  OO1 (Object Operations version 1 or Engineering Benchmark)

Support for the OO1 benchmark includes a C program which generates the Parts/Connections database according to the specifications in Chapter 7, An Engineering Benchmark. Embedded SQL versions of all of the benchmark queries are also provided.

# A.4    How to Obtain the Distribution

To obtain a copy of the distribution, contact the Sales & Marketing Department at Morgan Kaufmann Publishers, at the address and phone number below. They can provide information on the available media and current price, as well as information on any recent releases of this compilation. For more detailed information, a copy of the file directories and instructions appearing in the software are also available upon request.

Morgan Kaufmann Publishers
Sales & Marketing Department
2929 Campus Drive, Suite 260
San Mateo, CA 94403
phone: (415) 578-9911
fax: (415)578-0672

ULTRIX is a trademark of Digital Equipment Corporation.
UNIX is a registered trademark of AT&T.
INGRES is a trademark of Ingres, Inc.

# Appendix B.
# TPC-A, -B, -C Extended Results

## B.1 Summary of TPC Results (As of December 22, 1992)

The TPC is a non-profit corporation founded to define transaction processing and database benchmarks and to disseminate objective, verifiable TPC performance data to the industry. To that end, the TPC maintains and publishes the following list of all systems that have run the TPC benchmarks:

## B.2 Status of Benchmark Results

All TPC results that are accompanied by a full disclosure report are given the status of "submitted for review." These results remain in this status for 60 days while TPC members review the full disclosure reports, which document the benchmark test runs, the system configurations, and pricing of the systems (and maintenance over 5 years). If no objections are raised to a given report, or if these objections are resolved to the satisfaction of the TPC Council, the results and full disclosure report are given the status of "accepted."

# B.3    Description of TPC Benchmarks

### B.3.1    TPC Benchmark™ A (TPC-A™)

The TPC-A benchmark measures performance in update-intensive database environments typical in on-line transaction processing (OLTP) applications. Such environments are characterized by: multiple on-line terminal sessions, significant disk input/output, moderate system and application execution time, and transaction integrity. The benchmark uses a single, simple update-intensive transaction to load the system tested. Thus the workload is intended to reflect an OLTP application, but does not reflect the entire range of OLTP requirements typically characterized by multiple transaction types of varying complexities. TPC-A can be run in a wide area or local area network configuration. The metrics used in TPC-A are throughput as measured in transactions per second (tps), subject to a response time constraint; and the associated price-per-tps. The entire price of the system as configured during the test must be used, including all hardware, software, and hardware/software maintenance charges over a period of 5 years.

### B.3.2    TPC Benchmark™ B (TPC-B™)

TPC-B exercises the database components necessary to perform tasks associated with that class of transaction processing environments emphasizing update-intensive database services. Such environments are characterized by: significant disk input/output, moderate system and application execution time, and transaction integrity. TPC-B is not OLTP in that is does not require any terminals, networking, or think time. This benchmark can be looked at as a database stress test. The metrics used in TPC-B are throughput as measured in transactions per second (tps), subject to a response time constraint; and the associated price-per-tps. The entire price of the system as configured during the test must be used, including all hardware, software, and hardware/software maintenance charges over a period of 5 years.

### B.3.3    TPC Benchmark™ C (TPC-C™)

TPC-C is like TPC-A in that is an OLTP benchmark. However, TPC-C is more complex that TPC-A because of its multiple transaction types, more complex database and overall execution structure. TPC-C involves a mix of five concurrent transactions of different types and complexity either executed on-line or queued for deferred execution. The database is comprised of nine types of records with a wide range of record and population sizes. The metrics used in TPC-B are throughput as measured in transactions per second (tps), subject to a response time constraint; and the associated price-per-tps. The entire price of the system as configured during the test must be used, including all hardware, software, and hardware/software maintenance charges over a period of 5 years.

**Table B.1** TPC-A Local Results, As of Jan 4, 1993 (Page 1 of 4)

| Company | System | TPC Spec. Rev. | Total Sys. Cost | TPC-A local Through-put (tpsA) | Price perf. (system cost/tps) ($per tpsA) | Database Software | Operating System | Pricing Submitted |
|---|---|---|---|---|---|---|---|---|
| AT&T | StarServer E RI | 1.0 | $360,753 | 24.84 | $14,523 | INFORMIX-OnLine 4.00 | UNIX SVR4.0 V2.1 | Jul 10, 1991 |
| Bull | DPS6000 Model 621 | 1.0 | $305,024 | 9.07 | $33,630 | DM6/TP2.2, IDS II 2.2 | GCOS 6 HVS V2 | Jul 1, 1991 |
| Bull | DPS6000 Model 632 | 1.0 | $458,911 | 14.09 | $32,570 | DM6/TP2.2, IDS II 2.2 | GCOS 6 HVS V2 | Jul 1, 1991 |
| Bull | DPX/2 360 2 cpu | 1.0 | $430,259 | 26.91 | $15,989 | INFORMIX-OnLine 4.1 | B.O.S. 2.0 (UNIX) | Apr 15, 1992 |
| Bull | DPX/2 360 | 1.0 | $325,680 | 14.85 | $21,925 | ORACLE V6.0 | B.O.S. 2.0 (UNIX) | Apr 15, 1992 |
| Bull | DPX/2 360 | 1.0 | $299,742 | 17.97 | $16,680 | INFORMIX-OnLine 4.1 | B.O.S. 2.0 (UNIX) | Feb 8, 1993 |
| Bull | DPX/2 380 | 1.0 | $330,283 | 27.50 | $12,121 | INFORMIX-OnLine 4.1 | B.O.S. 2.0 (UNIX) | Feb 8, 1993 |
| Bull | DPX/2 380 2 cpu | 1.0 | $432,292 | 40.95 | $10,556 | INFORMIX-OnLine 4.1 | B.O.S. 2.0 (UNIX) | Feb 8, 1993 |
| Bull | DPX/2 384 | 1.0 | $632,280 | 63.85 | $9,902 | INFORMIX-OnLine 4.1 | B.O.S. 2.0 (UNIX) | Feb 8, 1993 |
| Bull | DPX/2 385 4 cpu | 1.1 | $569,070 | 69.91 | $8,140 | INFORMIX-OnLine 5.0 | B.O.S. 2.0 (UNIX) | Sep 22, 1992 |
| DG | AV 5225 c/s | 1.0 | $585,124 | 50.89 | $11,498 | INFORMIX-OnLine 4.1 | DG/UX 5.4.1 (UNIX) | Jan 22, 1992 |
| DG | AV 6280 c/s | 1.1 | $1,880,164 | 239.10 | $7,864 | ORACLE7 | DG/UX 5.4 V. 2.01 (UNIX) | Dec 15, 1992 |
| Digital | MicroVAX 3100 Model 30 c/s | 1.0,1.1 | $180,427 | 21.60 | $8,353 | VAX Rdb/VMS V4.1 | VMS V5.5 | Nov 9, 1992 |
| Digital | MicroVAX 3100 Model 40 c/s | 1.0,1.1 | $181,927 | 21.60 | $8,423 | VAX Rdb/VMS V4.1 | VMS V5.5 | Nov 9, 1992 |
| Digital | MicroVAX 3100 Model 80 | 1.0,1.1 | $220,209 | 27.90 | $7,893 | VAX Rdb/VMS V4.1 | VMS V5.5 | Nov 9, 1992 |
| Digital | MicroVAX 3100 Model 90 | 1.1 | $271,937 | 34.00 | $7,998 | VAX Rdb/VMS V4.1 | Open VMS V5.5-2 | Nov 9, 1992 |
| Digital | VAXserver 4000-100 | 1.1 | $396,866 | 51.95 | $7,639 | VAX Rdb/VMS V4.1 | Open VMS V5.5-2 | Nov 9, 1992 |
| Digital | VAXserver 4000-200 c/s | 1.0,1.1 | $223,472 | 17.80 | $12,555 | VAX Rdb/VMS V4.1 | VMS V5.5 | Nov 9, 1992 |
| Digital | VAXserver 4000-300 c/s | 1.0,1.1 | $309,807 | 31.90 | $9,712 | VAX Rdb/VMS V4.1 | VMS V5.5 | Nov 9, 1992 |
| Digital | VAXserver 4000-300 | 1.0,1.1 | $488,421 | 41.40 | $11,798 | VAX DSM V6.0 | VMS V5.4 | Nov 9, 1992 |
| Digital | VAXserver 4000-300 2 xDSSI c/s | 1.0,1.1 | $507,288 | 53.60 | $9,464 | VAX Rdb/VMS V4.1 | VMS V5.5 | Nov 9, 1992 |
| Digital | VAXserver 4000-300 3 xDSSI c/s | 1.0,1.1 | $705,785 | 75.80 | $9,311 | VAX Rdb/VMS V4.1 | VMS V5.5 | Nov 9, 1992 |
| Digital | VAXserver 4000-400 c/s | 1.1 | $471,344 | 51.28 | $9,192 | VAX Rdb/VMS V4.1 | Open VMS V5.5 | Nov 9, 1992 |
| Digital | VAXserver 4000-500 c/s | 1.1 | $608,818 | 70.32 | $8,658 | VAX Rdb/VMS V4.1 | Open VMS V5.5 | Nov 9, 1992 |
| Digital | VAXserver 4000-500 2x DSSI c/s | 1.0,1.1 | $951,350 | 103.10 | $9,227 | VAX Rdb/VMS V4.1 | VMS V5.5 | Nov 9, 1992 |
| Digital | VAXserver 4000-600 c/s | 1.1 | $810,481 | 103.87 | $7,803 | VAX Rdb/VMS V4.1 | Open VMS V5.5 | Nov 9, 1992 |
| Digital | DECsystem 5000 Model 240 c/s | 1.1 | $349,981 | 28.55 | $12,259 | Sybase SQL Server Rel 4.2 | ULTRIX 4.2A | Nov 9, 1992 |
| Digital | DECsystem 5100 | 1.1 | $243,137 | 10.60 | $22,937 | INFORMIX-OnLine 4.1 | ULTRIX 4.2A | May 29, 1992 |
| Digital | DECsystem 5500 | 1.1 | $379,026 | 21.10 | $17,963 | INFORMIX-OnLine 4.1 | ULTRIX 4.2A | May 29, 1992 |
| Digital | VAXserver 6000-610 c/s | 1.1 | $914,595 | 102.30 | $8,940 | VAX Rdb/VMS V4.1-0 | Open VMS V5.5 | Nov 9, 1992 |
| Digital | VAXserver 6000-640 c/s | 1.1 | $1,790,211 | 208.80 | $8,574 | VAX Rdb/VMS V4.1 | VMS V5.5 | Nov 9, 1992 |
| Digital | VAXserver 7000-610 c/s | 1.1 | $1,041,812 | 123.83 | $8,413 | VAX Rdb/VMS V4.1-0 | Open VMS V5.5-2 | Nov 9, 1992 |

**Table B.1** TPC-A Local Results, As of Jan 4, 1993 (Page 2 of 4)

| Company | System | TPC Spec. Rev. | Total Sys. Cost | TPC-A local Through-put (tpsA) | Price perf. (system cost/tps) ($per tpsA) | Database Software | Operating System | Pricing Submitted |
|---|---|---|---|---|---|---|---|---|
| HP | HP 3000 Series 957 | 1.1 | $703,433 | 84.93 | $8,282 | Allbase/SQL VF0.17 | MPE/iX V40.12 | Oct 23, 1992 |
| HP | HP 3000 Series 977 | 1.1 | $1,337,303 | 150.60 | $8,879 | Allbase/SQL VF0.25 | MPE/iX V40.12 | Oct 23, 1992 |
| HP | HP 9000 Series 800 Model F10 | 1.1 | $334,814 | 30.40 | $11,014 | INFORMIX ONLINE V4.0 | HP-UX 8.02 (UNIX) | Dec 8, 1992 |
| HP | HP 9000 Series 800 Model F20 | 1.1 | $446,990 | 51.27 | $8,718 | INFORMIX ONLINE V4.0 | HP-UX 8.02 (UNIX) | Dec 8, 1992 |
| HP | HP 9000 Series 800 Model F30 | 1.1 | $500,040 | 60.09 | $8,322 | INFORMIX ONLINE V4.0 | HP-UX 8.02 (UNIX) | Dec 8, 1992 |
| HP | HP 9000 Series 800 Model G30 | 1.1 | $499,232 | 60.15 | $8,300 | INFORMIX ONLINE V4.0 | HP-UX 8.02 (UNIX) | Dec 8, 1992 |
| HP | HP 9000 Series 800 Model G30 c/s | 1.1 | $727,621 | 88.10 | $8,259 | INFORMIX ONLINE V5.0 | HP-UX 9.0 (UNIX) | Dec 8, 1992 |
| HP | HP 9000 Series 800 Model G40 c/s | 1.1 | $892,501 | 110.53 | $8,075 | SYBASE SQLServer V4.9.1 | HP-UX 9.0 (UNIX) | Dec 8, 1992 |
| HP | HP 9000 Series 800 Model H20 | 1.1 | $523,971 | 51.85 | $10,106 | INFORMIX ONLINE V4.0 | HP-UX 8.02 (UNIX) | Dec 8, 1992 |
| HP | HP 9000 Series 800 Model H30 | 1.1 | $596,833 | 60.15 | $9,922 | INFORMIX ONLINE V4.0 | HP-UX 8.02 (UNIX) | Dec 8, 1992 |
| HP | HP 9000 Series 800 Model H40 | 1.1 | $975,781 | 88.10 | $8,259 | INFORMIX ONLINE V5.0 | HP-UX 9.0 (UNIX) | Dec 8, 1992 |
| HP | HP 9000 Series 800 Model H30 c/s | 1.1 | $814,207 | 88.10 | $9,242 | INFORMIX ONLINE V5.0 | HP-UX 9.0 (UNIX) | Dec 8, 1992 |
| HP | HP 9000 Series 800 Model H40 c/s | 1.1 | $1,063,239 | 130.46 | $8,150 | INFORMIX ONLINE V5.0 | HP-UX 9.0 (UNIX) | Feb 22, 1993 |
| HP | HP 9000 Series 800 Model H40 c/s | 1.1 | $937,227 | 110.53 | $8,479 | SYBASE SQLServer V4.9.1 | HP-UX 9.0 (UNIX) | Dec 8, 1992 |
| HP | HP 9000 Series S800 Model H50 | 1.1 | $1,398,787 | 153.13 | $9,135 | INFORMIX ONLINE V5.0 | HP-UX 9.0 (UNIX) | Dec 8, 1992 |
| HP | HP 9000 Series S800 Model H50 c/s | 1.1 | $1,732,388 | 184.55 | $9,387 | ORACLE7 V7.0.10 | HP-UX 9.0 (UNIX) | Dec 8, 1992 |
| HP | HP 9000 Series 800 Model I30 | 1.1 | $630,523 | 60.15 | $10,483 | INFORMIX ONLINE V4.0 | HP-UX 8.02 (UNIX) | Dec 8, 1992 |
| HP | HP 9000 Series 800 Model I40 | 1.1 | $1,144,154 | 120.69 | $9,480 | INFORMIX ONLINE V5.0 | HP-UX 9.0 (UNIX) | Feb 22, 1993 |
| HP | HP 9000 Series 800 Model I30 c/s | 1.1 | $862,823 | 88.10 | $9,794 | INFORMIX ONLINE V5.0 | HP-UX 9.0 (UNIX) | Dec 8, 1992 |
| HP | HP 9000 Series 800 Model I40 c/s | 1.1 | $1,213,512 | 130.46 | $9,302 | INFORMIX ONLINE V5.0 | HP-UX 9.0 (UNIX) | Feb 22, 1993 |
| HP | HP 9000 Series 800 Model I50 | 1.1 | $971,537 | 110.53 | $8,790 | SYBASE SQLServer V4.9.1 | HP-UX 9.0 (UNIX) | Dec 8, 1992 |
| HP | HP 9000 Series 800 Model I50 | 1.1 | $1,792,258 | 303.10 | $5,913 | Adabas V2.1 | HP-UX 9.0 (UNIX) | Mar 15, 1993 |
| HP | HP 9000 Series S800 Model I50 c/s | 1.1 | $1,445,462 | 153.13 | $9,439 | INFORMIX ONLINE V5.0 | HP-UX 9.0 (UNIX) | Dec 8, 1992 |
| HP | HP 9000 Series S800 Model I50 c/s | 1.1 | $1,835,581 | 184.55 | $9,946 | ORACLE7 V7.0.10 | HP-UX 9.0 (UNIX) | Dec 8, 1992 |
| HP | HP 9000 Series 807S | 1.0,1.1 | $328,272 | 30.40 | $10,798 | INFORMIX-OnLine 4.00 | HP-UX 8.02 (UNIX) | Sep 4, 1992 |
| HP | HP 9000 Series 817S | 1.0,1.1 | $439,032 | 51.27 | $8,563 | INFORMIX-OnLine 4.00 | HP-UX 8.02 (UNIX) | Sep 4, 1992 |
| HP | HP 9000 Series 827S | 1.0,1.1 | $492,368 | 51.85 | $9,496 | INFORMIX-OnLine 4.00 | HP-UX 8.02 (UNIX) | Sep 4, 1992 |
| HP | HP 9000 Series 837S | 1.0,1.1 | $572,416 | 60.09 | $9,526 | INFORMIX-OnLine 4.00 | HP-UX 8.02 (UNIX) | Sep 4, 1992 |
| HP | HP 9000 Series 847S | 1.0,1.1 | $592,592 | 60.15 | $9,852 | INFORMIX-OnLine 4.00 | HP-UX 8.02 (UNIX) | Sep 4, 1992 |
| HP | HP 9000 Series 847S c/s | 1.1 | $808,538 | 88.10 | $9,177 | INFORMIX-OnLine 5.00 | HP-UX 9.0 (UNIX) | Jun 26, 1992 |
| HP | HP 9000 Series 857S | 1.0,1.1 | $615,788 | 60.15 | $10,238 | INFORMIX-OnLine 4.00 | HP-UX 8.02 (UNIX) | Sep 4, 1992 |
| HP | HP 9000 Series 857S c/s | 1.1 | $831,734 | 88.10 | $9,440 | INFORMIX-OnLine 5.00 | HP-UX 9.0 (UNIX) | Jun 26, 1992 |
| HP | HP 9000 Series 867S | 1.0,1.1 | $893,928 | 74.93 | $11,903 | INFORMIX-OnLine 4.00 | HP-UX 8.02 (UNIX) | Sep 4, 1992 |
| HP | HP 9000 Series 867S c/s | 1.1 | $1,072,946 | 110.42 | $9,717 | INFORMIX-OnLine 5.00 | HP-UX 9.0 (UNIX) | Jun 26, 1992 |
| HP | HP 9000 Series 867S c/s | 1.1 | $919,995 | 110.53 | $8,323 | Sybase SQLserver V4.9.1 | HP-UX 9.0 (UNIX) | Jun 25, 1992 |
| HP | HP 9000 Series 877S c/s | 1.1 | $936,455 | 110.53 | $8,472 | Sybase SQLserver V4.9.1 | HP-UX 9.0 (UNIX) | Jun 25, 1992 |

**Table B.1** TPC-A Local Results, As of Jan 4, 1993 (Page 3 of 4)

| Company | System | TPC Spec. Rev. | Total Sys. Cost | TPC-A local Through-put (tpsA) | Price perf. (system cost/tps) ($per tpsA) | Database Software | Operating System | Pricing Submitted |
|---|---|---|---|---|---|---|---|---|
| HP | HP 9000 Series 877S | 1.0,1.1 | $908,428 | 74.93 | $12,124 | INFORMIX-OnLine 4.00 | HP-UX 8.02 (UNIX) | Sep 4, 1992 |
| HP | HP 9000 Series 877S c/s | 1.1 | $1,089,446 | 110.42 | $9,866 | INFORMIX-OnLine 5.00 | HP-UX 9.0 (UNIX) | Jun 26, 1992 |
| HP | HP 9000 Series 890 c/s | 1.1 | $5,866,533 | 710.43 | $8,258 | ORACLE7 V7.0.11 | HP-UX 9.0 (UNIX) | Feb 3, 1993 |
| HP | HP 9000 Series 897S c/s | 1.1 | $1,981,492 | 184.55 | $10,737 | ORACLE7 V7.0.10 | HP-UX 9.0 (UNIX) | Sep 15, 1992 |
| IBM | AS/400 9404 E10 | 1.0,1.1 | $98,697 | 9.92 | $9,949 | OS/400 int. rel. database | OS/400 Version 2 Rel. 1.1 | Mar 16, 1992 |
| IBM | AS/400 9406 E35 | 1.0,1.1 | $191,666 | 14.00 | $13,690 | OS/400 int. rel. database | OS/400 Version 2 Rel. 1.1 | Mar 16, 1992 |
| IBM | AS/400 9406 E70 | 1.0,1.1 | $987,792 | 54.90 | $17,993 | OS/400 int. rel. database | OS/400 Version 2 Rel. 1.1 | Apr 21, 1992 |
| IBM | RISC 6000/350 c/s | 1.1 | $558,210 | 58.98 | $9,464 | INFORMIX-OnLine 4.10.UE3 | AIX 3.2 (UNIX) | Jul 8, 1992 |
| IBM | RISC 6000/520H | 1.0,1.1 | $422,165 | 31.00 | $13,618 | INFORMIX-OnLine 4.00.UH1 | AIX 3.2 (UNIX) | Jul 16, 1992 |
| IBM | RISC 6000/530H | 1.0,1.1 | $600,531 | 42.00 | $14,298 | INFORMIX-OnLine 4.00.UH1 | AIX 3.2 (UNIX) | Jul 16, 1992 |
| IBM | RISC 6000/550 | 1.0,1.1 | $686,425 | 51.00 | $13,459 | INFORMIX-OnLine 4.00.UH1 | AIX 3.2 (UNIX) | Jul 16, 1992 |
| IBM | RISC 6000/560 | 1.0,1.1 | $837,803 | 61.00 | $13,734 | INFORMIX-OnLine 4.00.UH1 | AIX 3.2 (UNIX) | Jul 16, 1992 |
| IBM | RISC 6000/560 c/s | 1.0,1.1 | $886,927 | 72.00 | $12,318 | INFORMIX-OnLine 4.00.UH1 | AIX 3.2 (UNIX) | Oct 20, 1992 |
| IBM | RISC 6000/580 c/s | 1.1 | $972,823 | 120.97 | $8,042 | INFORMIX-OnLine 5.00.UC2 | AIX 3.2.3 (UNIX) | Apr 7, 1993 |
| IBM | RISC 6000/580 c/s | 1.1 | $1,483,461 | 157.20 | $9,437 | ORACLE7 | AIX 3.2.3 (UNIX) | Jul 16, 1992 |
| IBM | RISC 6000/950 | 1.1 | $883,041 | 65.00 | $13,585 | INFORMIX-OnLine 4.10.UE3 | AIX 3.2 (UNIX) | Jul 15, 1992 |
| IBM | RISC 6000/970 | 1.1 | $1,035,520 | 87.98 | $11,770 | INFORMIX-OnLine 4.10.UE3 | AIX 3.2.1 (UNIX) | Jul 16, 1992 |
| IBM | RISC 6000/970 c/s | 1.1 | $1,083,275 | 100.96 | $10,730 | INFORMIX-OnLine 4.10.UE3 | AIX 3.2 (UNIX) | Jul 16, 1992 |
| IBM | RISC 6000/980 c/s | 1.1 | $1,763,683 | 160.30 | $11,002 | ORACLE7 | AIX 3.2.3 (UNIX) | Sep 23, 1992 |
| ICL | DRS 6000 Level 450 | 1.1 | £424,960 | 55.66 | £7,635 | Informix-Online 4.10 | DRS/NX Version 6 L0 | Oct 5, 1992 |
| ICL | DRS 6000 Level 764 | 1.1 | £738,317 | 91.80 | £8,043 | Informix-Online 4.10 | DRS/NX Version 6 L1 | Dec 8, 1992 |
| NCR | NCR 3450 | 1.1 | $844,800 | 100.31 | $8,422 | INFORMIX-OnLine 5.00 | UNIX SVR4.0 MP-RAS | Jul 2, 1992 |
| NCR | NCR 3447 | 1.1 | $311,848 | 39.70 | $7,855 | INFORMIX-OnLine 5.00 | UNIX SVR4.0 MP-RAS | Oct 8, 1992 |
| NCR | NCR 3550 | 1.1 | $1,859,721 | 150.62 | $12,347 | INFORMIX-OnLine 5.00 | UNIX SVR4.0 MP-RAS | Dec 10, 1992 |
| NCR | NCR 3450 | 1.1 | $1,207,782 | 152.42 | $7,924 | ORACLE7 | UNIX SVR4.0 MP-RAS | Dec 10, 1992 |
| NCR | NCR 3550 c/s | 1.1 | $2,816,030 | 413.45 | $6,811 | ORACLE7 | UNIX SVR4.0 MP-RAS | Feb 25, 1993 |
| ORACLE | VAX 700 Model 640 c/s | 1.1 | $4,548,256 | 508.44 | $8,946 | ORACLE7 (7.0,10) | Open VMS V5.5-2 | Nov 18, 1992 |
| Pyramid | MIServer ES c/s | 1.1 | $6,945,809 | 645.19 | $10,765 | ORACLE7 V7.0.10 | DC/OSx 1.1 | Oct 5, 1992 |
| Sequent | Symmetry S2000/200 | 1.0 | $746,811 | 49.96 | $14,948 | INFORMIX-OnLine 4.00 | DYNIX/ptx 1.2 (UNIX) | May 15, 1991 |
| Sequent | Symmetry S2000/250 c/s | 1.1 | $1,592,602 | 183.34 | $8,686 | SYBASE SMP SQL Server 4.8.1.1 | DYNIX/ptx 1.4 (UNIX) | Sep 14, 1992 |
| Sequent | Symmetry S2000/700 | 1.0 | $2,867,501 | 129.19 | $22,196 | INFORMIX-OnLine 4.00 | DYNIX/ptx 1.2 (UNIX) | May 15, 1991 |

**Table B.1** TPC-A Local Results, As of Jan 4, 1993 (Page 4 of 4)

| Company | System | TPC Spec. Rev. | Total Sys. Cost | TPC-A local Through-put (tpsA) | Price perf. (system cost/tps) ($per tpsA) | Database Software | Operating System | Pricing Submitted |
|---|---|---|---|---|---|---|---|---|
| Sequent | Symmetry S2000/700 c/s | 1.0 | $2,476,493 | 168.91 | $14,662 | SYBASE SMP SQL Server 4.8.0.2 | DYNIX/ptx 1.3 (UNIX) | Dec 2, 1991 |
| Sequent | Symmetry S2000/750 | 1.0 | $3,921,184 | 214.53 | $18,278 | ORACLE V6.0.33.1.5 | DYNIX/ptx 1.3 (UNIX) | Jul 1, 1992 |
| Sequent | Symmetry S2000/750 c/s | 1.1 | $6,806,270 | 618.39 | $11,006 | ORACLE7 V7.0.10 | DYNIX/ptx 1.4 (UNIX) | Aug 14, 1992 |
| Sun | SPARCserver 690MP c/s | 1.0,1.1 | $855,926 | 95.41 | $8,972 | SYBASE SQLServer 4.8.1 | SunOS 4.1.2 | Apr 9, 1992 |
| Sun | SPARCserver 690MP c/s | 1.1 | $1,352,119 | 107.28 | $12,604 | ORACLE7 | SunOS 4.1.2 | Jun 11, 1992 |
| Unisys | U6000/35 | 1.1 | $385,508 | 35.81 | $10,765 | INFORMIX-OnLine 5.0 | Unisys SVR4-MP Rel. 1.1 | Dec 14, 1992 |
| Unisys | U6000/65 | 1.1 | $858,179 | 74.63 | $11,499 | INFORMIX-OnLine 5.0 | Unisys SVR4-MP Rel. 1.1 | Nov 9, 1992 |
| Unisys | U6000/85 | 1.0 | $3,151,087 | 129.09 | $24,410 | INFORMIX-OnLine 4.00 | Open/OLTP (UNIX) | Jun 3, 1991 |
| Unisys | U6000/85 c/s | 1.1 | $7,957,403 | 618.39 | $12,868 | ORACLE7 V7.0.10 | DYNIX/ptx V1.4 | Oct 21, 1992 |
| Unisys | A11-211 | 1.1 | $709,724 | 39.90 | $17,787 | Data Management System II | Master Control Program | Dec 14, 1992 |
| Unisys | A11-222 | 1.1 | $1,339,586 | 74.50 | $17,981 | Data Management System II | Master Control Program | Dec 14, 1992 |
| Unisys | A11-411 | 1.1 | $1,006,269 | 53.90 | $18,669 | Data Management System II | Master Control Program | Dec 14, 1992 |
| Unisys | A11-422 | 1.1 | $1,867,999 | 98.90 | $18,887 | Data Management System II | Master Control Program | Dec 14, 1992 |
| Unisys | A16-61E | 1.0, 1.1 | $9,323,313 | 272.50 | $34,214 | Data Management System II | Master Control Program | Dec 14, 1992 |
| Unisys | 2200/421 | 1.0 | $2,975,600 | 86.00 | $34,600 | TIP/FCSS | OS 1100 SBR 4R1 | Apr 23, 1991 |
| Unisys | 2200/421 | 1.0,1.1 | $2,289,649 | 57.57 | $39,772 | DMS | OS 1100 SBR 4R1 | Apr 15, 1992 |
| Unisys | 2200/421 | 1.0,1.1 | $2,851,750 | 90.40 | $31,546 | TIP/FCSS | OS 1100 SBR 4R2 | Apr 15, 1992 |
| Unisys | 2200/442 | 1.0,1.1 | $3,914,924 | 104.59 | $37,458 | DMS | OS 1100 SBR 4R1 | Apr 15, 1992 |
| Unisys | 2200/442 | 1.0,1.1 | $4,897,491 | 177.30 | $27,623 | TIP/FCSS | OS 1100 SBR 4R2 | Apr 15, 1992 |
| Unisys | 2200/462 | 1.0,1.1 | $5,023,566 | 133.16 | $37,726 | DMS | OS 1100 SBR 4R1 | Apr 15, 1992 |
| Unisys | 2200/462 | 1.0,1.1 | $6,410,096 | 228.50 | $28,053 | TIP/FCSS | OS 1100 SBR 4R2 | Apr 15, 1992 |
| Unisys | 2200/611ES | 1.0,1.1 | $6,938,572 | 159.40 | $43,529 | DMS | OS 1100 SBR 4R2 | Apr 1, 1992 |
| Unisys | 2200/622ES | 1.0,1.1 | $11,245,568 | 255.70 | $43,980 | DMS | OS 1100 SBR 4R2 | Apr 1, 1992 |

TPC-A uses terminology and metrics which are similar to other past or future benchmarks, originated by the TPC or others. Such similarity in terminology does not in any way imply that results are comparable to benchmarks other than TPC-A.

TPC-A can be run in a wide area or local area network configuation. The throughput metrics are "tpsA-Local" and "tpsA-Wide" respectively. The wide area and local area throughput and price-performance metrics are different and cannot be compared.

It is not fair (or permissable under TPC policy) to compare price or price/performance when the currencies used are not alike (e.g., dollars vs. pounds). Also, it is not fair (or permissable under TPC policy) to base a pricing comparison on a direct conversion of different currencies.

**Table B.2**   TPC-A Wide Results, As of Jan 4, 1993

| Company | System | TPC Spec. Rev. | Total Sys. Cost | TPC-A local Through-put (tpsA) | Price perf. (sys. cost/tps) ($per tpsA) | Database Software | Operating System | Pricing Submitted |
|---------|--------|----------------|-----------------|-------------------------------|------------------------------------------|-------------------|------------------|-------------------|
| Sequoia | Series 400 11:4:4 | 1.1 | $3,080,717 | 110.00 | $28,007 | ORACLE V6.2 | Topix 6.6 | Mar 23, 1992 |
| Tandem | CLX/R 1200 | 1.1 | $749,269 | 54.00 | $13,921 | NonStop SQL | Guardian C30.06 | Sep 14, 1992 |
| Tandem | 2xCLX/R 1200 | 1.1 | $1,491,713 | 108.00 | $13,870 | NonStop SQL | Guardian C30.06 | Sep 14, 1992 |
| Tandem | 4xCLX/R 1200 | 1.1 | $2,572,247 | 213.10 | $12,117 | NonStop SQL | Guardian C30.06 | Sep 14, 1992 |
| Tandem | 10xCLX/R 1200 | 1.1 | $5,737,506 | 501.50 | $11,533 | NonStop SQL | Guardian C30.06 | Sep 14, 1992 |

TPC-A uses terminology and metrics which are similar to other past or future benchmarks, originated by the TPC or others. Such similarity in terminology does not in any way imply that results are comparable to benchmarks other than TPC-A.

TPC-A can be run in a wide area or local area network confirguation. The throughput metrics are "tpsA-Local" and "tpsA-Wide" respectively. The wide area and local area throughput and price-performance metrics are different and cannot be compared.

It is not fair (or permissable under TPC policy) to compare price or price/performance when the currencies used are not alike (e.g., dollars vs. pounds). Also, it is not fair (or permissable under TPC policy) to base a pricing comparison on a direct conversion of different currencies.

**Table B.3** TPC-B Results, As of Jan 4, 1993 (Page 1 of 3)

| Company | System | TPC Spec. Rev. | Total Sys. Cost | TPC-B local Through-put (tpsB) | Price perf. (system cost/tps) ($per tpsB) | Database Software | Operating System | Pricing Submitted |
|---|---|---|---|---|---|---|---|---|
| AT&T | StarServer E RI | 1.0 | $128,650 | 45.05 | $2,855 | INFORMIX-OnLine 4.00 | UNIX SVR 4.0 V2.1 | Jul 10, 1991 |
| Compaq | DESKPRO 486/50L Model 510 | 1.0 | $112,199 | 43.32 | $2,590 | ORACLE V6.0.31 | Netware 3.11 | Aug 7, 1991 |
| Compaq | SYSTEMPRO 486 Model 840 | 1.0 | $92,503 | 30.63 | $3,020 | ORACLE V6.0.31 | Netware 3.11 | Aug 7, 1991 |
| Compaq | SYSTEMPRO/XL Model 2040 | 1.1 | $147,926 | 185.00 | $799 | ORACLE7 V7.0.10 | SCO 3.2v4 | Oct 5, 1992 |
| CDC | InfoServer 4330 | 1.1 | $85,187 | 48.93 | $1,741 | INFORMIX-OnLine 4.10 | EP/IX V1.4.3 | May 19, 1992 |
| CDC | InfoServer 4375 (2 cpu) | 1.0,1.1 | $368,034 | 52.26 | $7,042 | ORACLE V6.0.30.OM2 | EP/IX V1.4.2 | Mar 15, 1992 |
| CDC | InfoServer 4680-312 (1 cpu) | 1.1 | $412,904 | 118.00 | $3,499 | INFORMIX-OnLine 4.10 | EP/IX V1.4.3 | Jan 4, 1993 |
| CDC | InfoServer 4680 (2 cpu) | 1.0,1.1 | $681,018 | 112.61 | $6,048 | ORACLE V6.0.30.OM1 | EP/IX V1.4.2 | Mar 12, 1992 |
| CDC | InfoServer 4680 (4 cpu) | 1.1 | $677,018 | 160.51 | $4,218 | INFORMIX-OnLine 4.10 | EP/IX 1.4.2 | May 19, 1992 |
| DG | AViiON AV 4600 | 1.0 | $102,351 | 39.55 | $2,588 | INFORMIX-OnLine 4.00 | DG/UX 5.4 (UNIX) | Jul 31, 1991 |
| DG | AViiON AV 4620 | 1.0 | $140,318 | 58.21 | $2,411 | INFORMIX-OnLine 4.00 | DG/UX 5.4 (UNIX) | Jul 31, 1991 |
| DG | AViiON AV 5225 | 1.0 | $174,048 | 75.00 | $2,321 | INFORMIX-OnLine 4.00 | DG/UX 5.4 (UNIX) | Aug 1, 1991 |
| DG | AViiON AV 6240 | 1.0 | $428,927 | 102.94 | $4,167 | INFORMIX-OnLine 4.00 | DG/UX 5.4 (UNIX) | May 15, 1991 |
| DG | AViiON AV 6280 | 1.1 | $647,168 | 316.83 | $2,043 | ORACLE7 | DG/UX 5.4 Rev. 2.01 | Oct 9, 1992 |
| Digital | applicationDEC 400xP | 1.1 | $107,370 | 63.60 | $1,689 | INFORMIX-OnLine 4.10 | SCO/UNIX 3.2.4 | Aug 24, 1992 |
| Digital | applicationDEC 433MP | 1.0 | $156,480 | 60.10 | $2,603 | INFORMIX-OnLine 4.00 | SCO/UNIX 3.2.2, SCO/MPX 1.2.0 | Mar 18, 1992 |
| Digital | DECsystem 5000 model 25 | 1.1 | $61,800 | 23.80 | $2,597 | INFORMIX-OnLine 4.10 | ULTRIX 4.2A | Nov 9, 1992 |
| Digital | DECsystem 5000 model 240 | 1.1 | $100,551 | 42.49 | $2,366 | INFORMIX-OnLine 4.10 | ULTRIX 4.2A | Nov 9, 1992 |
| Digital | DECsystem 5100 | 1.0 | $66,130 | 28.20 | $2,345 | INFORMIX-OnLine 4.10 | ULTRIX 4.2 | Dec 3, 1992 |
| Digital | DECsystem 5500 | 1.0 | $160,113 | 40.60 | $3,944 | INFORMIX-OnLine 4.10 | ULTRIX 4.2 | Dec 3, 1992 |
| Digital | VAX 6000/560 | 1.0 | $1,148,731 | 193.76 | $5,929 | VAX Rdb/VMS V4.1 | VAX/VMS V5.4-2 | Feb 18, 1992 |
| Fujitsu | DS Server 7630 | 1.1 | ¥29,213,200 | 43.70 | ¥668,494 | INFORMIX-OnLine 4.10 | UXP/DS V10L20 | Jun 3, 1992 |
| Gupta | Compaq Systempro 486-840 | 1.0 | $127,857 | 67.00 | $1,908 | SQLBase for NetWare 5.0 | Compaq DOS 3.31 | Nov 27, 1991 |
| HP | HP 9000 Series 807S | 1.0,1.1 | $106,066 | 41.07 | $2,583 | INFORMIX-OnLine 4.00 | HP-UX 8.02 (UNIX) | Mar 16, 1992 |
| HP | HP 9000 Series 817S | 1.0,1.1 | $125,666 | 64.79 | $1,940 | INFORMIX-OnLine 4.00 | HP-UX 8.02 (UNIX) | Mar 16, 1992 |
| IBM | RISC System 6000/220 | 1.1 | $63,036 | 33.19 | $1,899 | INFORMIX-OnLine 4.10.UE3 | AIX 3.2 (UNIX) | Jul 16, 1992 |
| IBM | RISC System 6000/320 | 1.0,1.1 | $88,114 | 31.40 | $2,806 | INFORMIX-OnLine 4.00 | AIX 3.1.5 (UNIX) | Jul 16, 1992 |
| IBM | RISC System 6000/320H | 1.0,1.1 | $104,860 | 41.40 | $2,533 | INFORMIX-OnLine 4.00.UH1 | AIX 3.1.5 (UNIX) | Jul 16, 1992 |

**Table B.3** TPC-B Results, As of Jan 4, 1993 (Page 2 of 3)

| Company | System | TPC Spec. Rev. | Total Sys. Cost | TPC-B local Through-put (tpsB) | Price perf. (system cost/tps) ($per tpsB) | Database Software | Operating System | Pricing Submitted |
|---|---|---|---|---|---|---|---|---|
| IBM | RISC System 6000/340 | 1.0,1.1 | $134,489 | 56.47 | $2,382 | INFORMIX-OnLine 4.00.UH1 | AIX 3.2 (UNIX) | Jul 16, 1992 |
| IBM | RISC System 6000/350 | 1.0,1.1 | $148,640 | 66.98 | $2,219 | INFORMIX-OnLine 4.00.UH1 | AIX 3.2 (UNIX) | Jul 16, 1992 |
| IBM | RISC System 6000/520H | 1.0,1.1 | $106,309 | 44.76 | $2,375 | INFORMIX-OnLine 4.00.UH1 | AIX 3.2 (UNIX) | Jul 16, 1992 |
| IBM | RISC System 6000/530H | 1.0,1.1 | $142,387 | 52.68 | $2,703 | INFORMIX-OnLine 4.00.UH1 | AIX 3.1.5 (UNIX) | Jul 16, 1992 |
| IBM | RISC System 6000/550 | 1.0,1.1 | $198,148 | 69.20 | $2,863 | INFORMIX-OnLine 4.00.UH1 | AIX 3.1.5 (UNIX) | Jul 16, 1992 |
| IBM | RISC System 6000/560 | 1.0,1.1 | $216,995 | 80.09 | $2,709 | INFORMIX-OnLine 4.00.UH1 | AIX 3.2 (UNIX) | Jul 16, 1992 |
| IBM | RISC System 6000/950 | 1.0,1.1 | $337,381 | 74.20 | $4,547 | INFORMIX-OnLine 4.00.UH1 | AIX 3.1.5 (UNIX) | Jul 16, 1992 |
| IBM | RISC System 6000/970 | 1.1 | $307,639 | 110.32 | $2,789 | INFORMIX-OnLine 4.10.UE3 | AIX 3.2 (UNIX) | Jul 16, 1992 |
| ICL | DRS 6000 Level 442 | 1.0,1.1 | £135,558 | 65.20 | £2,079 | INFORMIX-OnLine 4.10 | DRS/NX V. 5L1 | Oct 5, 1992 |
| ICL | DRS 6000 Level 450 | 1.1 | £131,442 | 88.73 | £1,482 | INFORMIX-OnLine 4.10 | DRS/NX V. 6 L0 | Oct 5, 1992 |
| ICL | DRS 6000 Level 752 | 1.1 | £233,438 | 134.48 | £1,736 | INFORMIX-OnLine 4.10 | DRS/NX V. 6 L0 | Oct 5, 1992 |
| MIPS | RC3330 | 1.0 | $99,497 | 45.93 | $2,167 | INFORMIX-OnLine 4.10 | RISC/os 4.52 (UNIX) | Aug 31, 1991 |
| Motorola | Series 8000 Model 8640 | 1.1 | $132,117 | 70.30 | $1,879 | INFORMIX-OnLine 4.10 | UNIX V/88 Rel R32V3.1 | Jul 16, 1992 |
| NCR | NCR StarServer E R2 | 1.1 | $299,160 | 131.56 | $2,274 | INFORMIX-OnLine 5.00 | UNIX SVR 4.0 V3.0 | Apr 3, 1992 |
| NCR | NCR StarServer E R3 SMP 660 | 1.1 | $306,913 | 207.83 | $1,477 | INFORMIX-OnLine 5.00 | UNIX SVR 4.0 V3.0 | Aug 11, 1992 |
| Olivetti | LSX5015 | 1.1 | $53,034 | 42.50 | $1,248 | INFORMIX-OnLine 5.0 | SVR4.0 V2.1 (UNIX) | Dec 29, 1992 |
| Olivetti | LSX5020 | 1.0,1.1 | $100,244 | 40.49 | $2,475 | INFORMIX-OnLine 4.0 | SVR4.0 V1.3 (UNIX) | Mar 12, 1992 |
| Olivetti | LSX5025 | 1.1 | $64,033 | 66.00 | $970 | INFORMIX-OnLine 54.0 | SVR4.0 V2.1 (UNIX) | Dec 29, 1992 |
| Oracle | DG AViiON 4625 | 1.1 | $160,175 | 100.85 | $1,588 | ORACLE7 | DG/UX 5.4.1 (UNIX) | Jun 15, 1992 |
| Oracle | VAX 6000-540 | 1.0 | $1,752,905 | 57.04 | $30,731 | Rdb/VMS V4.0A | VAX/VMS 5.4-0A | Oct 21, 1991 |
| Oracle | VAX 6000-560 | 1.0 | $1,900,084 | 60.13 | $31,600 | Rdb/VMS V4.0A | VAX/VMS 5.4-0A | Oct 21, 1991 |
| Oracle | VAX 6000-560 | 1.0,1.1 | $2,366,289 | 153.93 | $15,375 | ORACLE V6.2 | VAX/VMS V5.4-0A | Mar 12, 1992 |
| Oracle | VAX 6000-560 | 1.1 | $1,488,522 | 315.00 | $4,725 | ORACLE7 | VAX/VMS A5.5 | Jun 15, 1992 |
| Oracle | VAX 6000-660 | 1.1 | $1,665,706 | 560.87 | $2,970 | ORACLE7 | VAX/VMS A5.5 | Jun 15, 1992 |
| Oracle | 3xVAX 6000-560 VAXcluster | 1.0,1.1 | $5,461,975 | 329.80 | $16,561 | ORACLE V6.2 | VAX/VMS V5.4-1 | Mar 12, 1992 |
| Oracle | 4xVAX 6000-560 VAXcluster | 1.0,1.1 | $6,949,784 | 425.70 | $16,326 | ORACLE V6.2 | VAX/VMS V5.4-1 | Mar 12, 1992 |
| Oracle | nCUBE 2, model nCDB-1000 | 1.0,1.1 | $2,662,779 | 1073.00 | $2,482 | ORACLE V6.2 | nCUBE Vertex V5.27 | Mar 12, 1992 |
| Pyramid | MIServer Model 12S/12 | 1.0,1.1 | $2,783,425 | 468.45 | $5,941 | UNIFY 2000 Rel. 2.1.2.1.0.0 | Data Center OSx 1.0 | Mar 4, 1992 |

**Table B.3** TPC-B Results, As of Jan 4, 1993 (Page 3 of 3)

| Company | System | TPC Spec. Rev. | Total Sys. Cost | TPC-B local Through-put (tpsB) | Price perf. (system cost/tps) ($per tpsB) | Database Software | Operating System | Pricing Submitted |
|---|---|---|---|---|---|---|---|---|
| Sequent | Symmetry 2000/250 | 1.1 | $479,483 | 173.11 | $2,770 | SYBASE SQL Server 4.8.1.1 | DYNIX/ptx 1.3 (UNIX) | Mar 30, 1992 |
| Sequent | Symmetry 2000/700 | 1.0 | $2,034,209 | 319.60 | $6,365 | ORACLE V6.0.33/2 | DYNIX/ptx 1.2 (UNIX) | Jan 20, 1992 |
| Siemens | RM600 Model 25 | 1.1 | $1,188,348 | 533.42 | $2,228 | ORACLE7 V7.0.10 | SINIX-P V5.41B (UNIX) | Dec 18, 1992 |
| Sun | SPARCserver 2 | 1.0,1.1 | $100,845 | 39.70 | $2,541 | INFORMIX-OnLine 4.00 | SunOS 4.1.1(UNIX) | Mar 9, 1992 |
| Sun | SPARCserver 2 c/s | 1.0,1.1 | $142,474 | 62.11 | $2,294 | SYBASE SQLServer 4.8.1 | SunOS 4.1.2(UNIX) | Feb 24, 1992 |
| Sun | SPARCserver 470 | 1.0,1.1 | $331,914 | 75.20 | $4,414 | INFORMIX-OnLine 4.00 | SunOS 4.1.1(UNIX) | Mar 9, 1992 |
| Sun | SPARCserver 630MP c/s | 1.0,1.1 | $272,637 | 121.49 | $2,245 | SYBASE SQL Server 4.8 | SunOS 4.1.2(UNIX) | Mar 9, 1992 |
| Sun | SPARCserver 670MP c/s | 1.0,1.1 | $289,774 | 121.49 | $2,386 | SYBASE SQL Server 4.8 | SunOS 4.1.2(UNIX) | Mar 9, 1992 |
| Sun | SPARCserver 690MP c/s | 1.0,1.1 | $372,832 | 134.90 | $2,764 | SYBASE SQL Server 4.8.1 | SunOS 4.1.2(UNIX) | Feb 24, 1992 |
| Sybase | VAX 6000/610 | 1.0 | $673,648 | 152.47 | $4,418 | SYBASE SQL Server 4.8 | VMS V5.5 | Oct 28, 1991 |
| Sybase | VAX 9000/420, DECstation 5000/200 | 1.0 | $3,458,250 | 261.00 | $13,250 | SYBASE SQL Server 4.8 | VMS V5.4 | Jul 8, 1991 |
| TI | TI 1500MP Model BB45 | 1.1 | $127,340 | 48.80 | $2,609 | INFORMIX-OnLine 4.0 | TI System V Rel. 3.3.1 | Apr 15, 1992 |
| TI | TI 1500 Model 1507 | 1.1 | $90,795 | 32.90 | $2,759 | INFORMIX-OnLine 4.1 | TI System V Rel. 3.3.1 | Aug 12, 1992 |
| TI | TI 1500 Model 1508 | 1.1 | $96,655 | 48.60 | $1,988 | INFORMIX-OnLine 4.1 | TI System V Rel. 3.3.1 | Aug 18, 1992 |

TPC-B uses terminology and metrics which are similar to other past or future benchmarks, origi-nated by the TPC or others. Such similarity in terminology does not in any way imply that results are comparable to benchmarks other than TPC-B.

It is not fair (or permissable under TPC policy) to compare price or price/performance when the currencies used are not alike (e.g., dollars vs. pounds). Also, it is not fair (or permissable under TPC policy) to base a pricing comparison on a direct conversion of different currencies.

**Table B.4**   TPC-C Results, As of Jan 4, 1993

| Company | System | TPC Spec. Rev. | Total Sys. Cost | TPC-C local Through-put (tpsC) | Price perf. (system cost/tps) ($per tpsC) | Database Software | Availability | Pricing Submitted |
|---------|--------|------|------|------|------|------|------|------|
| IBM | AS/400 9402 E04 | 1.0 | $52,801 | 22.75 | $2,321 | OS/400 Int. Rel. DB V2 Rel 2 | Sep 28, 1992 | Dec 4, 1992 |
| IBM | AS/400 9404 E10 | 1.0 | $83,253 | 33.81 | $2,462 | OS/400 Int. Rel. DB V2 Rel 2 | Sep 28, 1992 | Sep 1, 1992 |
| IBM | AS/400 9406 E35 | 1.0 | $188,562 | 54.14 | $3,483 | OS/400 Int. Rel. DB V2 Rel 2 | Sep 28, 1992 | Sep 1, 1992 |
| IBM | AS/400 9406 E70 | 1.0 | $1,052,830 | 268.76 | $3,918 | OS/400 Int. Rel. DB V2 Rel 2 | Sep 28, 1992 | Dec 4, 1992 |

TPC-C uses terminology and metrics which are similar to other past or future benchmarks, originated by the TPC or others. Such similarity in terminology does not in any way imply that results are comparable to benchmarks other than TPC-C.

It is not fair (or permissable under TPC policy) to compare price or price/performance when the currencies used are not alike (e.g., dollars vs. pounds). Also, it is not fair (or permissable under TPC policy) to base a pricing comparison on a direct conversion of different currencies.

**Table B.5**   Withdrawn Results, As of Jan 4, 1993

| Company | System | TPC Spec. Rev. | Total Sys. Cost | Through-put | Price perf. (sys. cost/tps) | Date Withdrawn | Withdrawn Category |
|---------|--------|------|------|------|------|------|------|
| Olivetti | LSX5015 | TPC-B 1.1 | $64,368 | 32.42 tpsB | $1,986 per tpsB | Dec 29, 1992 | # |
| Olivetti | LSX5025 | TPC-B 1.1 | $79,118 | 46.51 tpsB | $1,702 per tpsB | Dec 29, 1992 | #1 |

Results Withdrawn before December 15, 1992, are not included in this list. The results included in this list will remain on this list until March 15, 1992.

Category #1:  Results which have been withdrawn without prejudice.

Category #2:  Results which have been withdrawn by the test sponsor after compliance to the technical specification of the benchmark was challenged. This does not imply any admission of error by the test sponsor or judgement by the TPC Council.

Category #3:  Results which have been withdrawn by the test sponsor after the TPC Council has ruled the result was non-compliant with the technical specifications of the benchmark.

# References

*AIM Technology Procurement Guide.* (1989). Santa Clara, CA: AIM Technology.

Alexander, W., et al. (1988). Process and dataflow control in distributed data-intensive systems. *Proceedings of the ACM SIGMOD Conference.* Chicago, IL.

Anderson, T., Berre, A., Mallison, M., Porter, H., and Schneider, B. (1990). The HyperModel Benchmark. *Proceedings of Extended Database Technology '90* (Springer-Verlag Lecture Notes 416).

Anon et al. (1985). A measure of transaction processing power. *Datamation, 31*(7), 112–118.

Astrahan, M., et al. (1976). System R: Relational approach to database management. *ACM Transaction on Database Systems, 1*(1).

Auditor's report of IBM mid-range DebitCredit results announced October 11, 1988. *FT Systems, 75,* p. 14, and *FT Systems, 77,* p. 10.

Austin, T. M., & Sohi, G. (1992). Dynamic dependency analysis of ordinary programs. *ACM,* pp. 342–347.

Bailey, D. H., & Barton, J. T. (1985). The NAS Kernel benchmark program. NASA Tech. Memo. 86711, Aug. 1985.

Bancilhon, F., Delobel, C., & Kanellakis, P. (1992). *Building an Object-Oriented Database System: The Story of O2.* San Mateo, CA: Morgan Kaufmann.

Barrett, M. (1990). C++ test driver for object-oriented databases, personal communication.

Berry, M., Cybenko, G. & Larson, J. (1991). Scientific benchmark characterizations. *Parallel Computing,* 17:1173–1194 (December 1991).

Berry, M.D., Chen, D., Koss, P., & Kuck, D. (1988). *The perfect club benchmarks: Effective performance evaluation of supercomputers.* (CSRD Report No. 827). Urbana: University of Illinois, Center for Supercomputing Research and Development.

Betz, D. M. (1988). 1.6. Rev. 1.0, November 1988.

Blasgen, M. W., Gray, J., Mitoma, M., & Price, T. (1979). The convoy phenomenon. *Operating System Review, 13*(2).

Bitton, D., DeWitt, D. J., & Turbyfill, C. (1983). Benchmarking database systems: A systematic approach. *Proceedings of the 1983 Very Large Database Conference.*

Bitton, D., Hanrahan, M., & Turbyfill, C. (1987). Performance of complex queries in main memory database systems. *Proceedings of the International Conference on Third Data Engineering,* Los Angeles.

Bitton, D., Millman, J., & Orji, C. (1988). *Program documentation for DBGEN, a test database generator.* Chicago: University of Illinois.

579

Bitton, D., & Turbyfill, C. (1985). Design and analysis of multiuser benchmarks for database systems. *Proceedings of the HICSS-18 Conference.*

Bitton, D. & Turbyfill, C. (1985). Evaluation of a backend database machine. *Proceedings of HICSS-18.*

Bitton, D. & Turbyfill, C. (1986). Main memory database support for office systems: a performance study. *IFIP TC8 Conference on Methods and Tools for Office Systems*, Pisa, Italy.

Bitton, D., & Turbyfill, C. (1988). A retrospective on the Wisconsin benchmark. In M. Stonebraker (Ed.), *Readings in Database Systems*. San Mateo, CA: Morgan Kaufmann.

Boral, H., DeWitt, D.J., Friedland, D., Jarrell, N., & Wilkinson, W. K. (1982). Implementation of the database machine DIRECT. *IEEE Transactions on Software Engineering.*

Boral, H., & DeWitt, D.J. (1983). Database machines: An idea whose time has passed? A critique of the future of database machines. *Proceedings of the Third International Workshop on Database Machines*, Munich, Germany.

Boral, H. & DeWitt, D.J. (1984). A methodology for database system performance. *Proceedings of ACM Sigmod 1984.*

Business Applications Performance Corporation. 2801 Northwestern Parkway, MS NW1-20, Santa Clara, CA 95051. Telephone: (408) 988-7654, fax: (408) 765-4920.

Carey, M. J., DeWitt, D. J., & Naughton, J. (1992). *The OO7 Benchmark.* University of Wisconsin Computer Science Technical Report TR-92.99.

Carlton, A. (1992). CINT92 and CFP92 homogeneous capacity method offers fair measure of processing capacity. *SPEC Newsletter, 4* (2), June 1992.

Cattell, R.G.G. (1991). *Object Data Management.* Reading, MA: Addison-Wesley.

Cattell, R.G.G., and Skeen, J. (in press). Engineering database benchmark. *ACM Transactions on Databases Systems.*

Cheney, W., & Kincaid, D. (1980). *Numerical mathematics and computing.* Monterey, CA: Brooks/Cole Publishing Company.

Chou, H.T., DeWitt, D.J., Katz, R., & Klug, T. (1985). Design and implementation of the Wisconsin Storage System (WiSS). *Software Practices and Experience, 15*(10).

Copeland, G., Alexander, W., Boughter, E., & Keller, T. (1988). Data placement in Bubba. *Proceedings of the ACM-SIGMOD. International Conference on Management of Data.* Chicago.

DebitCredit: a standard? (1986). *FT Systems, 47,* pp. 2–8.

DeFazio, S., & Hull, J. (1991). Toward servicing textual database transactions on symmetric shared memory multiprocessors. *Proceedings, Fourth International Workshop on High Performance Transaction Processing Systems.* Asilomar Conference Center, September, 1991.

Department of Motor Vehicles, State of California. (1989). *Database Redevelopment Project: DBMS Operational Assessment Final Report, Volume 1: Project Summary, Volume 2: Test Specification, Volume 3: Vendor Results.* Sacramento, CA: Department of Motor Vehicles.

DeWitt, D.J. (1979). DIRECT—A multiprocessor organization for supporting relational database management systems. *IEEE Transactions on Computers.*

DeWitt, D.J., Katz, R., Olken, F., Shapiro, D., Stonebraker, M., & Wood, D. (1984). Implementation techniques for main memory database systems. *Proceedings of the 1984 SIGMOD Conference.* Boston, MA.

DeWitt, D., et al. (1986). GAMMA—A high performance dataflow database machine. *Proceedings of the 1986 VLDB Conference.* Japan.

DeWitt, D., Smith, M., & Boral, H. (1987). *A Single-User Performance Evaluation of the Teradata Database Machine.* (MCC Technical Report No. DB-081-87).

DeWitt, D., Ghandeharizadeh, S., & Schneider, D. (1988). A performance analysis of the gamma database machine. *Proceedings of the ACM-SIGMOD International Conference on Management of Data.* Chicago.

DeWitt, D., et al. (1990). The gamma database machine project. *IEEE Knowledge and Data Engineering, 2(1).*

Dixit, K. M. (1991a). Truth in SPECmarking. *SunWorld,* 4 (9), September 1991.

Dixit, K. M. (1991b). CINT92 and CFP92 benchmark descriptions. *SPEC Newsletter,* 3 (4), December 1991.

Dixit, K. M. (1991c). The SPEC benchmarks. *Parallel Computing,* 17 (December 1991): 1195–1205.

Dixit, K. M. (1991d). Interpreting SPEC Release 1 benchmark results. *SPEC Newsletter,* 3 (4), December 1991.

Dixit, K. M. (1992). New CPU benchmark suites from SPEC. *compcon92, Digest of papers,* pp. 305–310.

Dixit, K., & Novak, R. (1990). SPEC refines reporting format to ensure level playing field. *SPEC Benchmark Results,* 2 (1), Winter 1990.

Dixit, K. M., & Reilly, J. (1991). SPEC developing new component benchmark suites. *SPEC Newsletter,* 3 (4), December 1991.

Doduc, N. (1989). FORTRAN Execution Time Benchmark. *Framentec,* V29, March 1989.

Dronamraju, K., Naseem, A., & Chelluri, S. (Ram) (1990). System level benchmarking. *SPEC Newsletter,* 2 (4), Fall 1990.

Dronamraju, S. K., Bakab, S., & Morgan, T. (1991). System analysis and comparison using SPEC SDM 1. *SPEC Newsletter,* 3 (4), December 1991.

Editor's Notebook. (1986). *FT Systems, 47,* p. 1.

Elmagarmid, A. K. (1992). *Database Transaction Models for Advanced Applications*. San Mateo, CA: Morgan Kaufmann.

Englert, S., Gray, J., Kocher, T. & Shah, P. (1989). *A Benchmark of NonStop SQL Release 2 Demonstrating Near-Linear Speedup and Scaleup on Large Databases*. (Tandem Computers, Technical Report 89.4. Tandem Part No. 27469).

Englert, S. & Gray, J. (1989). Generating Dense-Unique Random Numbers for Synthetic Database Loading, Tandem Computers.

Epstein, R. (1987). Today's technology is producing high-performance relational database systems. *Sybase Newsletter*.

Faloutsos, C. (1985). Access methods for text. *ACM Computing Surveys*, 17, 1 (March, 1985), pp. 49–74.

Ferrari, D. (1978). *Computer Systems Performance Evaluation*. Englewood Cliffs, NJ: Prentice Hall.

Flemming, P. J., & Wallace, J. J. (1986). How not to lie with statistics: The correct way to summarize benchmark results. *Communications of the ACM* 29, 3 (Mar. 1986), 218–221.

*FT Systems*, a monthly newsletter published by ITOM International, PO 1450, Los Altos, CA 94023.

Gerber, R. & DeWitt, D. (1987). *The Impact of Hardware and Software Alternatives on the Performance of the Gamma Database Machine*. (Computer Sciences Technical Report #708). Madison: University of Wisconsin.

Good, B., Homan, P. W., Gawlick, D. E., & Sammer, H. (1985). One thousand transactions per second. *IEEE Compcon Proceedings*. San Francisco.

Graefe, G. (1990). Encapsulation of parallelism in the volcano query processing system. *Proceedings of the 1990 ACM-SIGMOD International Conference on Management of Data*.

Graefe, G., & Ward, K. (1989). Dynamic query evaluation plans. *Proceedings of the 1989 SIGMOD Conference*. Portland, OR.

Gray, J., & Putzolu, F. (1987). The five minute rule for trading memory for disk accesses and the 10 byte rule for trading memory for CPU time. *Proceedings of the 1987 ACM SIGMOD Conference*, pp. 395–398.

Gray, J.N., & Reuter, A. (1993). *Transaction Processing: Concepts and Techniques*. San Mateo, CA: Morgan Kaufmann.

Gray, J., Sammer, H., & Whitford, S. (1988). *Shortest Seek vs. Shortest Service Time Scheduling of Mirrored Disks*. Tandem Computers.

Greenfield, Mike, Raynoha, Paul, & Bhandarkar, Dileep (1990). SPEC adopts new methodology for measuring system throughput. *SPEC Newsletter*, 2, 2 (Spring 1990).

Gustafson, J., Rover, D., Elbert, S., & Carter, M. (1990). SLALOM, the first scaleable supercomputer benchmark. *Supercomputing Review*, 3(11), 56–61.

Harrington, W. J. (1984–85). A brief history of computer-assisted legal research. *Law Library Journal, 77*(453), 543–556.

Haskin, R. (1982). Hardware for searching very large databases. *Proceedings on Database Engineering.*

Hennessy, J. L., & Patterson, D. A. (1990). *Computer Architecture, A Quantitative Approach.* Morgan Kaufmann Publishers.

Highleyman, W.H. (1989). *Performance Analysis of Transaction Processing Systems.* Englewood Cliffs, NJ: Prentice Hall.

IBM, DEC disagree on DebitCredit results. (1988). *FT Systems, 75,* pp. 1-5.

International Data Corp. (1991). *Workgroup Application Systems, Full-Text Retrieval Systems Market Review and Forecast, 1989/90–1995.* Framingham, MA,

Jain, R. (1991). *The Art of Computer Systems Performance Analysis: Techniques for Experimental Design, Measurement, Simulation, and Modeling.* New York: John Wiley.

Keatts, B.l, Balan, S., & Bodo, P. (1991). matrix300 Performance Concerns. *SPEC Newsletter, 3* (4), December 1991.

Keith, B. (1992). LADDIS File Server Benchmark. *SPEC Newsletter, 4* (1), March 1992.

Khoshafian, S., Chan, A., Wong, A., & Wong, H. K. T. (1992). *A Guide to Developing Client/Server SQL Applications.* San Mateo, CA: Morgan Kaufmann.

Kitsuregawa, M., Tanaka, H., & Moto-Oka, T. (1983). Architecture and performance of database machine GRACE. *Proceedings of the International Conference on Parallel Processing.* St. Charles, IL.

Knuth, D.E. (1973). *The art of computer programming,* Vol. 3. Reading, MA: Addison-Wesley.

Livny, M., Khoshafian, S., & Boral, H. (1987). Multi-disk management algorithms. *Proceedings of the 1987 SIGMETRICS Conference.* Banff, Alberta, Canada.

Lorie, R., Daudenarde, J., Hallmark, G., Stamos, J., & Young, H. (1989). Adding intra-transaction parallelism to an existing DBMS: Early experience. *IEEE Data Engineering Newsletter, 12*(1).

Maier, D. (1987). *Making Database Systems Fast Enough for CAD Applications.* (Technical Report CS/E-87-016). Beaverton, OR: Oregon Graduate Center.

Mashey, J. (1990). SPEC results help normalize vendor Mips-ratings for sensible comparison. *SPEC Newsletter, 2* (3), Summer 1990.

Melton, J. & Simon, A. (1993). *Understanding the New SQL: A Complete Guide.* San Mateo, CA: Morgan Kaufmann.

Melton, J. (Ed.). (1990) Database language SQL 2 (ISO working draft. (ANSI X3H2-90-264). Washington, D.C.: American National Standards Institute.

Novak, R. E. (1991). SPEC defines two new measures of performance. *SPEC Newsletter,* 3 (1), Winter 1991.

ONEKAY: IBM's 1K tps transaction benchmark. (1987). *FT Systems, 63,* pp. 1-5.

O'Neil, P. E. (1989). Revisiting DBMS benchmarks. *Datamation, 35*(18), pp. 47–52.

O'Neil, P.E. (1991). The Set Query Benchmark. In J. Gray (Ed.), *Database and Transaction Processing Performance Handbook.* San Mateo, CA: Morgan Kaufmann.

Ozsu, T., & Valduriez, P. (1990). *Principles of Distributed Database Systems.* Englewood Cliffs, NJ: Prentice Hall.

Park, S., and Miller, K. (1988). Random number generators: Good ones are hard to find. *CACM 31*(10).

Patterson, D.A., & Hennessy, J.L. (1990). *Computer Architecture, a Quantitative Approach.* San Mateo, CA: Morgan Kaufmann.

*PC Week.* (1990). Database Shootout: 17 database vendors go head-to-head to build a real-world computing solution. Aug 27, pp. 70–78.

Phillip, M. J. (1992). Performance issues for the 88110 RISC Microprocessor. *compcon92, Digest of papers,* pp. 163–168.

Rubenstein, W.B., Kubicar, M.S., & Cattell, R.G. (1987). Benchmarking simple database operations. *Proceedings of ACM Sigmod 1987.*

Savedra-Barrera, R. H. (1990). The SPEC and Perfect Club benchmarks: Promises and limitations. Hot Chips-2 Symposium, August 20, 1990.

Schneider, D. & DeWitt, D. (1989). A performance evaluation of four parallel join algorithms in a shared-nothing multiprocessor environment. *Proceedings of the 1989 SIGMOD Conference.* Portland, OR.

Schneider, D. & DeWitt, D. (1990). Tradeoffs in processing complex join queries via hashing in multiprocessor database machines. *Proceedings of the Sixteenth International Conference on Very Large Data Bases.* Melbourne, Australia.

Schwartz, J., & Samco, R. (1990). Object-oriented DBMS evaluation, personal communication.

Serlin, O. (1989). Toward an equitable benchmark. *Datamation,* p. 47. Feb. 1, 1989: Vol. 35, No. 3.

Serlin, O. (1990). Measuring OLTP with a better yardstick. *Datamation,* p. 62. July 15, 1990: Vol. 36, No. 14.

Smith, J. E. (1988). Characterizing computer performance with a single number. *Communications of the ACM,* 10 Oct 1988, pp. 1202–1206.

Smith, M., et al. (1989). An experiment in response time scalability. *Proceedings of the Sixth International Workshop on Database Machines.*

SPEC. (1990, September). SPEC benchmark suite, release 1.0. *Supercomputing Review*, *3*(9), 48–57.

Stallman, R. M. (1989). GNU CC Compiler Version 1.35. Free Software Foundation, 675 Mass Ave., Cambridge, MA, April 1989.

Stephens, C., Cogswell, B., Heinlein, J., Palmer, G., & Shen, J. (1991). Instruction level profiling and evaluation of the IBM RS/6000. *Computer Architecture News, 19* (3): 180–189, May 1991.

Stonebraker, M. (1986). The case for shared nothing. *Database Engineering, 9*(1).

Stonebraker, M. (1986). *The Ingres papers*. Reading, MA:Addison-Wesley.

Stonebraker, M., and Rowe, L.A. (1984). PORTALS: A new application program interface. *Proceedings of VLDB Conference.*

*Supercomputing Review*, 8445 Camino Santa Fe, San Diego, CA 92121.

*Tandem NonStop SQL benchmark workbook*. (1987). (Tandem Publication No. 84160.)

Tandem Database Group. (1989). Nonstop SQL, A distributed, high-performance, high-reliability implementation of SQL. In *High Performance Transaction Systems*. (Springer-Verlag Lecture Notes in Computer Science, 359). New York: Springer-Verlag.

Tandem Performance Group. (1988). A benchmark of non-stop SQL on the Debit Credit Transaction. *Proceedings of the 1988 SIGMOD Conference*. Chicago, IL.

Tandem Performs Massive DebitCredit Benchmark. (1987). *FT Systems, 55*, pp. 4-8.

Teradata. (1983). *DBC/1012 data base computer concepts & facilities* (Teradata Corp., Document No. C02-0001-00).

Teradata. (1985). *DBC/1012 database computer system manual release 2.0* (Teradata Corp., Document No. C10-0001-02).

The TP1/ET1 fiasco. (1986). *FT Systems, 47*, pp. 5-6.

TP1 vs. DebitCredit: what's in a name? (1988). *FT Systems, 67*, pp. 1-7.

*TPC Quarterly Review*. Shanley Public Relations, 777 N. First Street, Suite 600, San Jose, CA 95112-6311. Telephone: (408) 295-8894, fax: (408) 295-9768.

Transaction Processing Performance Council (TPC). (1989). *TPC Benchmark, a Standard*. Los Altos, CA: ITOM International Co.

Turbyfill, C. (1987). *Comparative benchmarking of relational database systems*. Unpublished doctoral dissertation, Cornell University.

Turbyfill, C. (1988). Disk performance and access patterns for mixed database workloads. *Database Engineering, 11*(1).

Turbyfill, C., Orji, C., & Bitton, D. (1989). ASAP: A comparative relational database benchmark. *Proceedings Compcon 1989.*

Turbyfill, C., Orji, C., & Bitton, D. (1991). AS$^3$AP: an ANSI SQL standard scaleable and portable benchmark for relational database systems. In *The Performance Handbook for Database and Transaction Processing Systems*. San Mateo, CA: Morgan Kaufmann.

UC Berkeley, CAD/IC Group, EECS/ERL (1987). SPICE2G.6. Release Date March 1987.

UC Berkeley, EECS Department (1988). Espresso Version #2.3. Release Date 01/31/88.

UC Berkeley, Industrial Liaison Program (1985). Eqntott #V9. Released 1985.

Weicker, Reinhold P. (1991). A detailed look at some popular benchmarks. *Parallel Computing*,17 (December 1991): 1153–1172

Weicker, R., & Bays, W. (1992). Point: Why SPEC should burn (almost) all flags, counterpoint: Defending the flag. *SPEC Newsletter,* 4 (2), June 1992.

Yao, S.B., Hevner, A.R., & Myers, H.Y. (1987). Analysis of database system architectures using benchmarks. *IEEE Transactions on Software Engineering*, *13*(6) pp. 709–725.

Zipf, G. (1965). *The Psycho-biology of Language: An Introduction to Dynamic Philology.* Cambridge, Mass.: MIT Press; Boston (1935): Houghton Mifflin.

# Index

# TPC-B Price/Performance vs Performance as of 1 November 1991

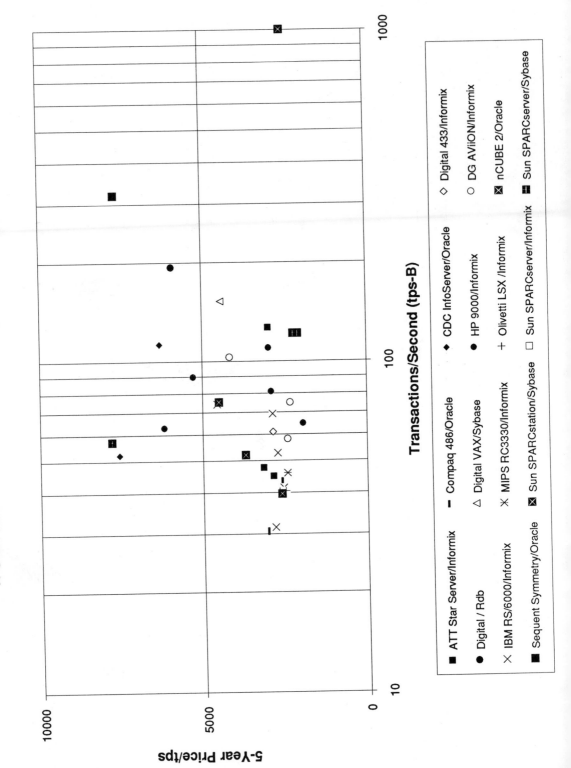

**Transactions/Second (tps-B)**

**5-Year Price/tps**

| | |
|---|---|
| ■ ATT Star Server/Informix | — Compaq 486/Oracle |
| ● Digital / Rdb | △ Digital VAX/Sybase |
| ✕ IBM RS/6000/Informix | ✕ MIPS RC3330/Informix |
| ■ Sequent Symmetry/Oracle | ◪ Sun SPARCstation/Sybase |
| ◇ Digital 433/Informix | ◆ CDC InfoServer/Oracle |
| ○ DG AViiON/Informix | ● HP 9000/Informix |
| ◪ nCUBE 2/Oracle | + Olivetti LSX /Informix |
| ▦ Sun SPARCserver/Sybase | □ Sun SPARCserver/Informix |